PARADISE
Family Guides
Maui

11th Edition

The Most Complete Guide to Family Fun and Adventure!

Candy Adair Aluli

Ulysses Press

Published by: Ulysses Press
P.O. Box 3440
Berkeley, CA 94703
www.ulyssespress.com

ISSN 1544-1377
ISBN 1-56975-499-3

Printed in Canada by Transcontinental Printing

10 9 8 7 6 5 4 3 2

Managing Editor: Claire Chun
Editor: Lily Chou
Copy Editor: Steven Zah Schwartz
Editorial and Production: Lisa Kester, Matt Orendorff, Tamara Kowalski, Barbara Schultz, Kathryn Brooks
Cartography: Pease Press
Cover Design: Leslie Henriques, Sarah Levin
Indexer: Sayre Van Young
Front Cover Photography: Gettyimages/Photodisc Green (large image); Photos.com (small images)
Contributing Editors: Dona Early, Jody Van Aalst, Mark Halvorson

Distributed by Publishers Group West

Maui No Ka Oi
(Maui Is the Best)

Dedicated to Nane, my companion in travel and in life.
With you, the journey is a joy.

Write to Us!

If in your travels you discover a spot that captures the spirit of Maui, or if you live in the region and have a favorite place to share, or if you just feel like expressing your views, write to us and we'll pass your note along to the author.

Ulysses Press
P.O. Box 3440
Berkeley, CA 94703
E-mail: readermail@ulyssespress.com

Table of Contents

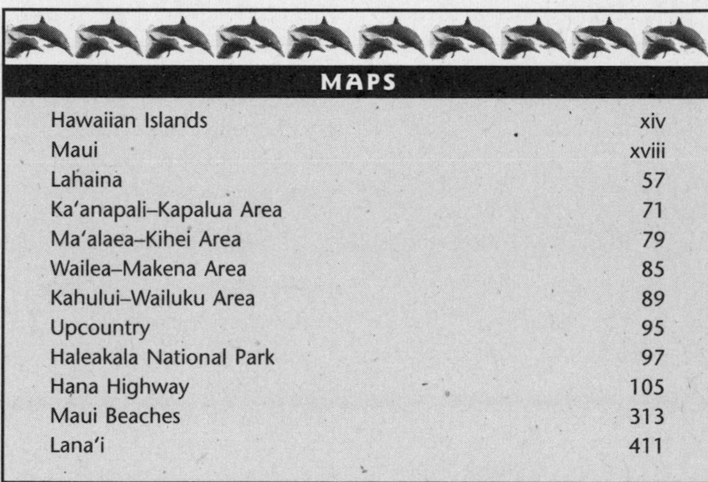

MAPS

★ indicates personal favorites and listings that are highly recommended

indicates child-friendly amusements, locations and businesses

indicates shops and malls

indicates bed-and-breakfast inns

Kawaipunahele

Nou e Kawaipunahele	For you Kawaipunahele
Ku'u leu aloha mae'ole	My never-fading lei
Pili hemo'ole, pili pa'a pono	Never separated, firmly united
E huli ho'i kaua	Come, let's go back
E Kawaipunahele	O Kawaipunahele
Ku 'oe me ke ki'eki'e	You stand majestically
I ka nani a'o Wailuku	In the splendor of Wailuku
Ku'u ipo henoheno,	My cherished sweetheart
Ku'u wehi o ka po	My adornment of the night
E huli ho'i kaua	Come, let's go back
E Kawaipunahele	O Kawaipunahele
Eia ho'i 'o Keali'i	Here is Keali'i
Kali'ana i ka mehameha	Waiting in loneliness
Mehameha ho'i au, 'eha'eha ho'i au	I am lonely, I hurt
E huli ho'i kaua	Come, let's go back
E Kawaipunahele	O Kawaipunahele
Puana 'ia ke aloha	Tell of the love
Ku'u lei aloha mae 'ole	Of my never-fading lei
Pili hemo'ole, pili pa'a pono	Never separated, firmly united
Ke pono ho'i kaua	When it's right, we'll go back
E Kawaipunahele	O Kawaipunahele

Music and lyrics by Keali'i Reichel, arrangement by Moon Kauakahi. Used with the permission of Punahele Productions, Wailuku, Maui. From Keali'i Reichel's CD recording, *Kawaipunahele.*

Although the islands have changed greatly during the century since Mark Twain visited the islands, there remains much to fall in love with. Despite the influences of what may seem to some like rampant commercialism, the physical beauty and seductiveness of the land remains ... and the true aloha spirit does survive. I am confident that as you explore these islands, you too will be charmed by their magic. Keep in mind the expressive words used by Twain over 100 years ago when he fell in love with the islands of Hawai'i.

"No alien land in all the world has any deep strong charm for me but that one, no other land could so longingly and so beseechingly haunt me, sleeping and waking, through half a lifetime, as that one has done. Other things leave me, but it abides; other things change, but it remains the same. For me its balmy airs are always blowing, its summer seas flashing in the sun; the pulsing of its surfbeat is in my ear; I can see its garlanded crags, its leaping cascades, its plumy palms drowsing by the shore, its remote summits floating like islands above the cloud wrack; I can feel the spirit of its woodland solitudes, I can hear the splash of its brooks; in my nostrils still lives the breath of flowers..."

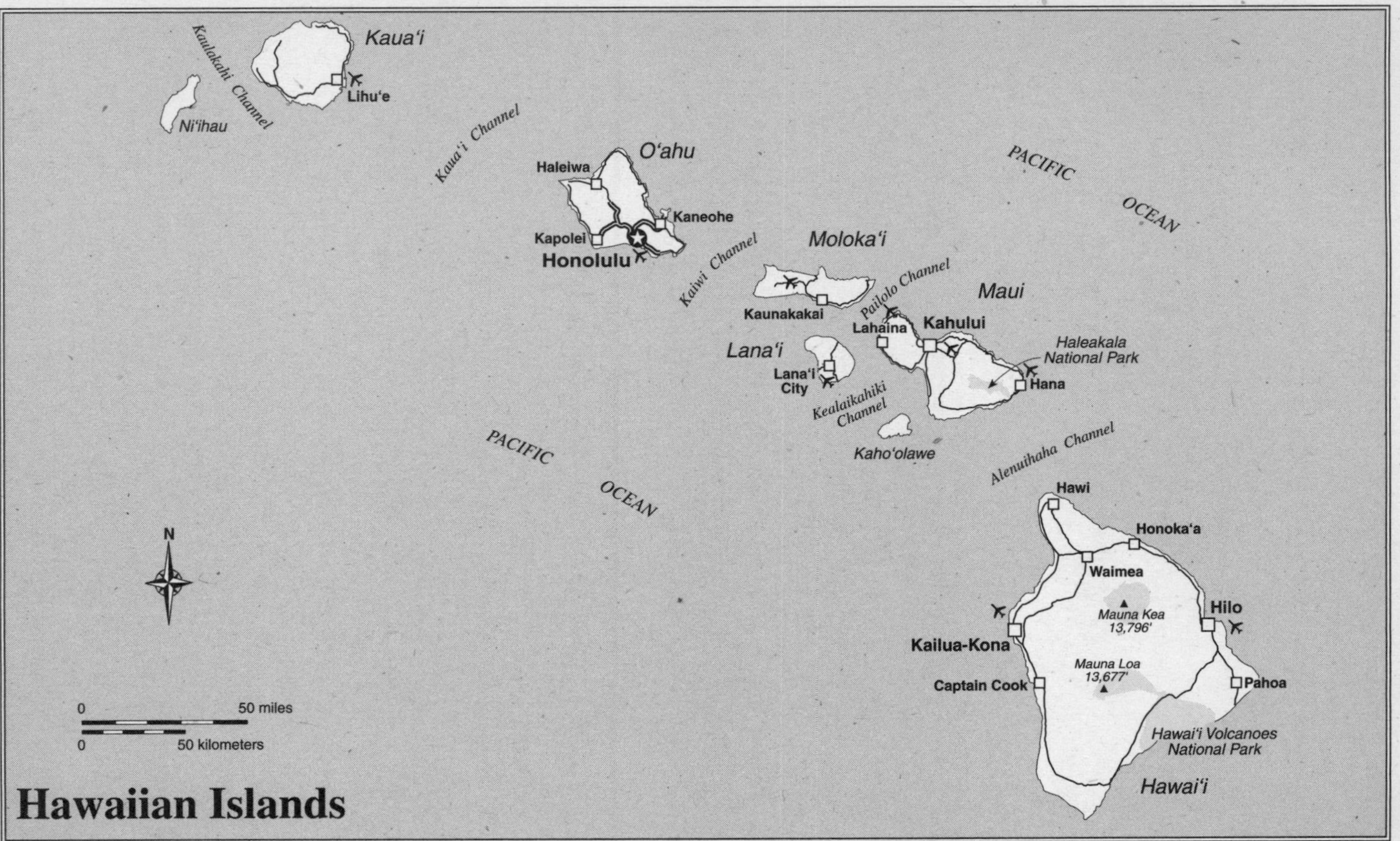
Hawaiian Islands
Kaua'i
Lihu'e
Ni'ihau
Kaulakahi Channel
Kaua'i Channel
O'ahu
Haleiwa
Kaneohe
Kapolei
Honolulu
Kaiwi Channel
Moloka'i
Kaunakakai
Pailolo Channel
Maui
Lahaina
Kahului
Haleakala National Park
Hana
Lana'i
Lana'i City
Kealaikahiki Channel
Kaho'olawe
Alenuihaha Channel
PACIFIC OCEAN
PACIFIC OCEAN
Hawi
Honoka'a
Waimea
Mauna Kea 13,796'
Hilo
Kailua-Kona
Mauna Loa 13,677'
Captain Cook
Pahoa
Hawai'i Volcanoes National Park
Hawai'i
N
0
50 miles
0
50 kilometers

Introduction

Aloha and congratulations on choosing the beautiful island of Maui as the site of your vacation. When you visit, you'll discover for yourself why Maui is referred to with the slogan, *Maui No Ka Oi* (Maui is the best). Those of us who live here are not the only ones who love this island. For the past decade, from 1994 through 2004, Maui has been chosen as the "Best Island in the World" by readers of *Conde Nast Traveler* magazine. The sun, the sand, the tropical sunsets combined with some of Hawai'i's finest dining, an incredible array of activities and spectacular lodgings blend sublimely to create a perfect holiday paradise.

Although this guidebook is dubbed a "family travel guide," any Maui traveler will find it useful. The comprehensive information provided here covers a wide range of topics from children's activities to romantic getaways and adventurous excursions. These days, there are many kinds of families traveling to Maui: single parents, grandparents traveling with the grandkids, couples planning to marry in Maui with family members accompanying them, adult sisters or brothers traveling together or with friends, and family reunions for travelers of all ages. "Family" can mean anything. *Ohana*, the Hawaiian word for "family," is also used to refer to extended families—there is an *ohana* of friends, neighbors, coworkers, you name it. When you visit a resort, they will tell you that you have become a part of their *ohana*. So rather than limit this book to the needs of just "traditional" families, we've taken the Hawai'i approach—there is something for everyone here. This guide is for you, the traveler, to help plan the best Maui or Lana'i vacation experience. (The island of Lana'i is part of Maui County, as is the island of Moloka'i.)

The chapters on sightseeing and shopping, accommodations, dining and beaches are conveniently divided into regional areas, and indexes are provided at the end of the book. This makes it easy for you to locate information relating to the area you are in—or the area you intend to visit. Except for Hana, which requires a full-day excursion, and perhaps Haleakala (depending on where you are driving from), other areas of Maui are all within an hour's drive of each other. I encourage you to get out and explore all the various regions and attractions of the island.

Maui can be extravagantly expensive or relatively inexpensive, depending on your preferences in lodging, activities and dining arrangements. I have tried to provide information to fit every budget—from those who are visiting Maui for an all-out splurge to those who are looking for ways to cut costs. The opinions expressed are based on my personal experiences or on those of others I know and trust (and in some cases, the experience of Christie Stilson, the author of previous editions of this book). These are our own personal opinions and you may have a completely different experience, good or bad. I welcome your feedback and would like to hear about your Maui experiences and recommendations. To contact me, see the "Write to Us" section in the first pages of this book.

To assist you further in your planning and decisions, I have included a "Best Bets" section at the beginning of each chapter except Chapter 2, as well as a star ★ on items throughout the book that are personal favorites or that I feel deserve a high recommendation.

A special acknowledgment and *mahalo* (thank you) to co-publisher Christie Stilson, who for the past 20 years authored this Maui book herself. With this edition, for the first time, she turned "her baby" over to another author, and I promised her she was placing it in good hands. Many of the personal opinions and recommendations in this book still reflect Christie's experiences, as well as those of Maui resident Dona Early who has collaborated with Christie in past years. It's impossible for me to personally visit and experience everything on Maui, so I have at times adopted Christie and Dona's experiences as my own. Thank you, ladies, for your extensive research over the years and for your support and guidance.

And *mahalo* to my husband, Nane, who was born and raised in the islands and has provided me with a valuable island education and a fabulous Native Hawaiian family. Thank you for your unending patience as I scribbled notes on restaurant menus by candlelight during romantic dinners, forced you to drive all over the island with me to explore every nook and cranny, and stayed up until the wee hours of the morning—night after night—working on this manuscript. You are a saint.

Aloha and happy travels to you!
Candy

This guide is as accurate as possible at the time of publication; however, for an island known to operate in its own easy-going "Maui time," changes occur rapidly and unexpectedly. Ownerships, managements, names, menus and prices all change frequently. For the most current and ongoing updates on the island, I recommend you subscribe to Paradise Publications' quarterly newsletter, *The Maui Update*. You can receive a complimentary introductory issue by sending a self-addressed stamped envelope to: Paradise Publications, 8110 SW Wareham, Portland, OR 97223. Or, if you'd prefer to receive your copy via the internet, email your request to paradyse@att.net. A yearly subscription is $10, well worth the investment to keep up on the latest Maui news for travelers.

If your itinerary includes visits to the other islands, the Paradise Family Guide Series offers guidebooks for Kaua'i and the Big Island as well. All books, as with this one, are written by residents of those particular islands, so you receive inside tips and advice from authors who know and love the island.

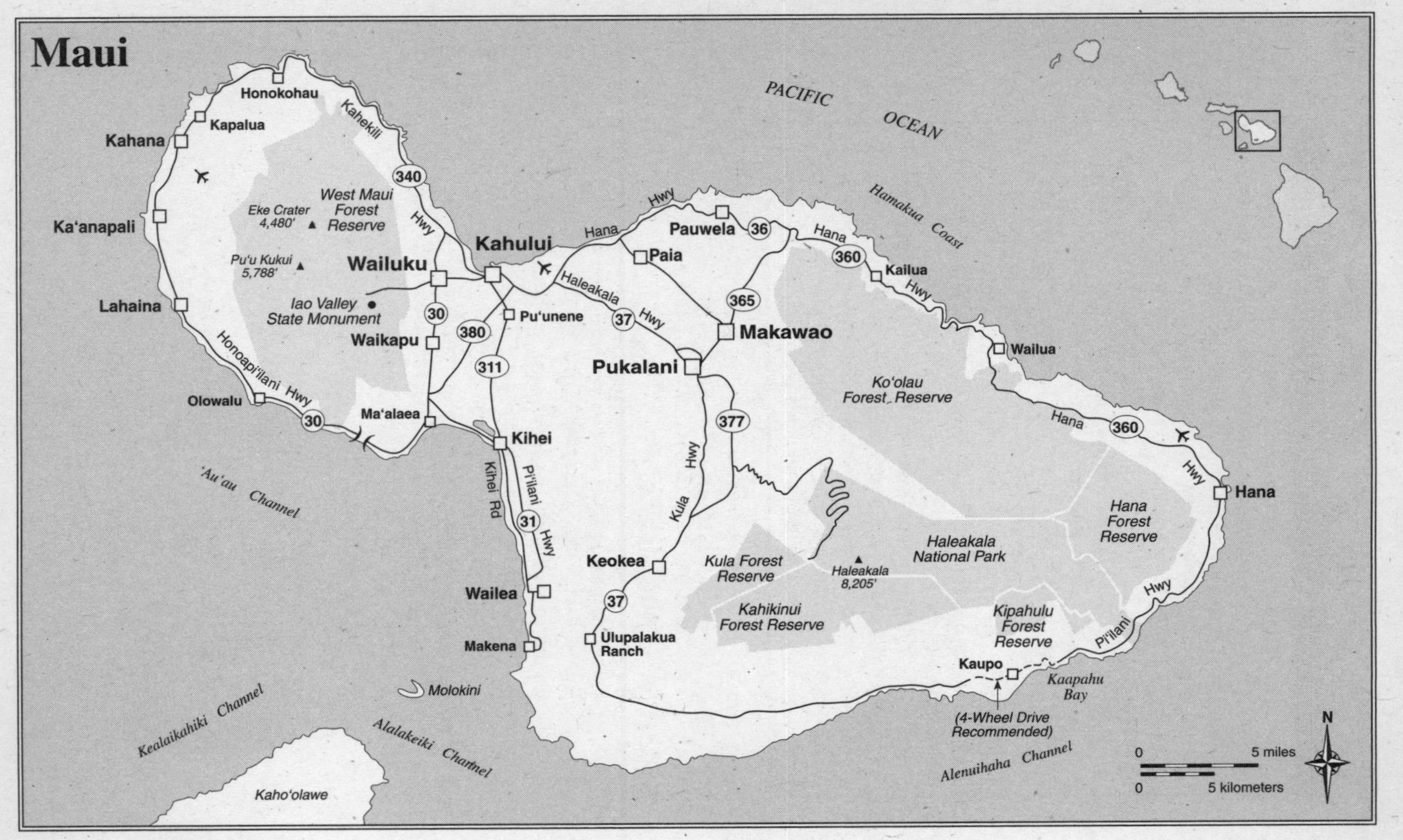
Maui
PACIFIC OCEAN
Hamakua Coast
Honokohau
Kapalua
Kahana
Kahekili
340
Hwy
Ka'anapali
Eke Crater 4,480'
West Maui Forest Reserve
Pu'u Kukui 5,788'
Wailuku
Kahului
Lahaina
Iao Valley State Monument
30
380
Pu'unene
Waikapu
311
Honoapi'ilani Hwy
Olowalu
Ma'alaea
Kihei
Kihei Rd
Pi'ilani
31
Wailea
Makena
Molokini
Hana
Pauwela
36
Paia
Haleakala
37
365
Makawao
Pukalani
377
Kula
360
Kailua
Wailua
Ko'olau Forest Reserve
Keokea
Kula Forest Reserve
Haleakala 8,205'
Haleakala National Park
Hana Forest Reserve
Kahikinui Forest Reserve
Ulupalakua Ranch
Kipahulu Forest Reserve
Kaupo
Kaapahu Bay
(4-Wheel Drive Recommended)
'Au'au Channel
Kealaikahiki Channel
Alalakeiki Channel
Alenuihaha Channel
Kaho'olawe
0
5 miles
5 kilometers
N

CHAPTER 1

General Information

This chapter highlights the basics for your Maui vacation: background on the islands, the language, weather conditions, what to pack, discounts for the seniors traveling in your family. There are lots of options to make your vacation a memorable one. Enjoy my "best bets" throughout the book—these are some of my family's favorite things to do, places to eat and locations to shop.

Maui's Best Bets

Aloha Wear Traditional tourist garb is available in greatest supply at the 17,000-square-foot Hilo Hattie factory in the Lahaina Center. They also have a location in Kihei at the Pi'ilani Shopping Center.

Cheap Aloha Wear While not for every traveler, the Salvation Army can be a great place to pick up some Hawaiian clothes to wear on your vacation. A muumuu for less than $5 is great for a beach cover-up or for wearing to a luau. Their thrift stores are located in Lahaina and Kihei. There are a number of other thrift stores on Maui, operated by churches and other nonprofit organizations. Take a look in the Maui phone book's Yellow Pages for a complete list.

Shopping • *Affordable and fun:* Kahului Swap Meet each Saturday, Kihei Kalama Village in Kihei and the International Open Marketplace on Honoapi'ilani Highway in Lahaina. • *Fun, but maybe not so affordable:* Lahaina's Front Street at any time. • *Practical:* Queen Ka'ahumanu Center in Kahului. • *Extravagant:* Whalers Village Shopping Center in Ka'anapali and the Shops at Wailea with many designer boutiques. • *Odds and ends:* Longs Drug Store (Kahului, Lahaina and Kihei) and Costco (near the airport) to stock up on vacation food, supplies and even snorkel gear. Wal-Mart and Big Kmart are also in Kahului.

Most Spectacular Resort Grounds The Hyatt Regency Maui at Ka'anapali and the Grand Wailea Resort Hotel & Spa in Wailea tie for first place.

Excursions • *Most spectacular*: a helicopter tour. • *Best adventure on foot*: a personalized hike with Hike Maui. • *Best sailing:* a day-long snorkel and picnic to Lana'i with the congenial crew of *Trilogy*.

New Sport Beyond windsurfing, beyond skiing, you can now kite surf. This craze meshes the best of a board and a kite for an aquatic thrill.

Aquatic Activity Snorkeling: Easy, inexpensive, fun for young and old alike and incredibly beautiful in Maui's waters.

Beaches • *Beautiful and safe*: Kapalua Bay and Ulua Beach. • *Unspoiled*: Oneloa (Makena) and Mokule'ia (Slaughterhouse) beaches. • *For young kids*: try Pu'unoa Beach near Lahaina.

Body Surfing Slaughterhouse in winter (only for experienced surfers and strong swimmers).

Surfing Honolua Bay in winter (for experienced surfers only).

Snorkeling • *North end:* Honolua Bay in summer. • *Kapalua area:* Kapalua Bay and Namalu Bay. • *Ka'anapali:* Black Rock at the Sheraton. Olowalu at mile-marker 14. • *Wailea:* Ulua Beach. • *Makena:* 'Ahihi-Kina'u Natural Reserve. • *Island of Lana'i:* Hulopo'e Beach Park and Molokini Crater.

Whale Watching From the shore, you can't beat the view from the Pali (around the mountain bend on the road to West Maui and Lahaina). In South Maui, Makena Beach is a good location and in West Maui, anywhere from Ka'anapali to Kapalua. While whale-watching boat excursions are great, you'll be in for a real thrill if you can view whales from a helicopter. Sign up for a helicopter excursion to Moloka'i that crosses the Pailolo Channel.

Windsurfing Ho'okipa Beach Park (for experienced windsurfers).

Postcard Home Write your personal greetings on a coconut, mail it and surprise someone back home. (That's right, no box, no envelope, no wrapping … just the coconut in all its glory.) They are available at various stores; the more expensive ones have been painted.

Unusual Gift Ideas • For the green thumb, be sure to try Dan's Green House in Lahaina for a Fuku-Bonsai planted on a lava rock. They are specially sprayed and sealed for either shipping or carrying home. • Big Kmart (and other stores) have mouse pads with Hawaiian designs—the perfect gift for all your internet friends. • Maui Crafts Guild in Paia has unusual handcrafted gifts. • Upcountry jeweler Neil Coshever makes one-of-a-kind jewelry and ornaments out of real Maui orchids cast in fine silver. They are absolutely exquisite and are not available anywhere else but Kula Marketplace. • If you'd like to share a little Hawai'i with friends back home, consider a CD of Hawaiian music. A great choice is *Holoholo Mai—Maui: A Musical Journey Around the Island*, a CD of songs written specifically about Maui places. • Head over to Del Sol at Whalers Village in Ka'anapali and have fun with all the items they offer that change color in the sun—great gifts for young people. • *The Maui Onion Cookbook* is a great little book, die-cut in the shape of an onion and filled with recipes from Maui chefs and residents. It's unusual, inexpensive and easy to pack. (Tip: Take home a few Kula onions to go with it.) • Hotel Hana-Maui has wonderful handcrafted soaps in their rooms, made specially for the hotel. If you're in Hana, check 'em out (at the hotel's gift shop).

T-shirts My favorite is Crazy Shirts (regular or "flavored"), more expensive than the run of the mill variety, but excellent quality and great designs. • Also the Red-Dirt Shirts (Front Street) colored with the infamous red dirt of the islands—pretty clever. • The swap meet in Kahului on Saturday has a huge selection of T-shirts and prices are usually half of what they are in the mall shops.

Unique Swimsuits for Little Ones Karen Welck, a West Maui resident, makes unusual swimsuits for toddlers. These are custom-made "floating swimsuits" that help very young children learn to swim by providing buoyancy. Check out Karen's website and order a suit before your trip, www.learn2swimsuits.com, or call 808-283-6004 when you're on Maui.

Take-home Food Products • Tropical fruit, macadamia nuts (they have delicious flavored nuts only available in Hawai'i: Kona coffee glazed, butter candy glazed, onion/garlic, etc.). Costco has great prices on macadamia nuts if you want to buy a large amount for gifts. • Maui chips and Maui onions.

Flowers For the best flower values visit the Maui Swap Meet in Kahului. Leis are sometimes available there also. Many grocery stores have flower sections with cut flowers and leis. Costco, Wal-Mart and Kmart all carry leis for a very reasonable price. For shipping flowers home, check the phone book for a number of florists that can airship to you or your family and friends. One is Maui Floral: 888-826-1444; e-mail: floral@maui.net; www.mauifloral.com.

Indulgence Select from a bath menu at The Ritz-Carlton, Kapalua and luxuriate in a butler-drawn bath. Your choice of oils or scents along with music, chocolate truffles, a chilled carafe of mai tais with "The Kapalua Bath," a split of champagne with "The Romance Bath," or a plate of sliced fruits and freshly squeezed juice for "The Travelers Relief Bath."

Gift for Friends Traveling to Maui A copy of *Paradise Family Guides: Maui* and, of course, a subscription to the quarterly *Maui Update* newsletter.

Free (or Almost Free) Stuff

Around the island:

- Free introductory scuba instruction offered poolside at many of the major resorts.
- A self-guided tour of the Grand Wailea or Hyatt Regency Maui.
- Public beaches with their free parking.
- Free snorkel guide from Maui Dive Shops.
- Free hikes with Sierra Club.
- A local church service. Churches in Hawai'i have less to do with "religion" than with fellowship, celebration, wonderful music and aloha.
- Community fairs and fundraisers. Sometimes free admission, sometimes not, but always fun with lots of *ono* food booths and great deals to be had on island activities at "silent auctions." Check the local papers to see what's happening when you're here. Visitors are always welcome at these events.

Lahaina: • Free "Maui Historical Walking Guide" can be picked up at displays around Lahaina town. • Arts-and-crafts fairs at Banyan Tree Park. • Friday night "art night" in Lahaina. You may have an opportunity to meet the artists and possibly get some free refreshment. • Front Street's Halloween Parade and Kamehameha Day Parade (June). • Visit Pioneer Inn, now an official U.S. Historic Landmark. • Canoe races held at Honoka'o'o Park. • The shuttle bus in West Maui is $1 and travels between Lahaina, Ka'anapali and The Ritz-Carlton. • $1 admission to Wo Hing Temple in Lahaina. • The Crazy Shirts shop located on the north end of Lahaina town has a display of whaling memorabilia and a big cannon sits out behind the shop. • Gift and Craft Fair, Sunday 9 a.m. to 4 p.m. at Lahaina Civic Center. $1 admission benefits non-profit organizations (808-879-7594). • Every Tuesday and Friday at 11:30 a.m. enjoy a free hula show at the Maui Theatre (808-661-9914) at Old Lahaina Center. • Hale Kahiko is a replica of a Hawaiian village located at Lahaina Center and open daily with free guided tours and weekly hula shows (see Chapter 2 for more information). • The Lahaina Cannery Mall presents free *keiki* hula shows Saturday and Sunday at 1 p.m. and a free Polynesian dance show at 7 p.m. on Tuesday and Thursday.

Ka'anapali–Kapalua Area: • Don't miss the traditional torch lighting and cliff diving ceremony that takes place each evening at sunset at the Sheraton Maui Resort. It's free, and you can watch it from the Ka'anapali beachwalk. But you'll be able to hear the narration if you sit in the hotel's outdoor lounge area and enjoy a drink during the presentation. • Check out the free tour of the artwork at the Westin Maui at Ka'anapali. • The Sheraton Maui also offers a free historical walking tour of their property • Enjoy the free hula show at the Ka'anapali Beach Hotel, held nightly at 6:30 p.m. with Hawaiian arts and crafts on display each Monday, Wednesday and Friday. • Pacific Whale Foundation's Coral Reef Information Station (808-249-8811) offers a free guided morning reef tour at Kahekili Park in Ka'anapali Friday through Sunday. • Craft fair at Napili Plaza every Wednesday and Saturday. • The Kapalua Shops hosts a number of free cultural activities and performances daily.

Ma'alaea–Kihei–Wailea–Makena Area: • Pacific Whale Foundation's Coral Reef Information Station (808-249-8811) offers a free guided morning reef tour at Ulua Beach in Wailea. • Hawaiian music in the Lobby Lounge of the Four Seasons Resort 5:30 to 7:30 p.m. Monday through Saturday. • Free hula show every Monday, Wednesday and Friday at 6 p.m. in the Molokini Lounge at the Maui Prince Resort. • The walk along the Wailea waterfront is wonderful. • The Shops at Wailea hosts WOW! Wailea on Wednesdays with gallery events, fashion shows and entertainment, 6:30 to 8:30 p.m.

Kahului–Wailuku Area: • Visit the Iao Needle located near Wailuku. • Watch windsurfing at Ho'okipa Beach on Maui's windward shore. • See the Maui Botanical Gardens in Wailuku. • The Maui Tropical Plantation has free admission to their marketplace. • Free behind-the-scenes tour of the Maui Arts & Cultural Center. Call for reservations (808-242-2787 ext. 228). • Free Hawaiian entertainment at Queen Ka'ahumanu Center (808-877-3369) every Saturday at 11 a.m. • Wailuku Public Library *keiki* storytime, 10 a.m. on Wednesday, stories, songs and crafts for preschool-age children (808-243-5766).

Upcountry: • Visit Hui No'eau Visual Arts Center in Makawao or take a guided tour. • Visit Hot Island Glass Studio in Makawao to see glass blowing and tour the nearby art galleries. • Makawao Parade held the Fourth of July weekend. • Free natural and cultural history programs and guided hikes at Haleakala (808-572-4400). • Free tour and sampling at Tedeschi Winery. (Stay and star gaze: the elevation at Kula makes the stars seem bigger and clearer.)

History of Maui

THE ISLAND Far beneath the warm waters of the Pacific Ocean is the Pacific Plate, which moves constantly in a northwesterly direction. Each Hawaiian island was formed as it passed over a hot vent in this plate. Kaua'i, the oldest of the major islands in the Hawai'i chain, was formed first and has since moved away from the plume (the source of the lava) and is no longer growing. Some of the older islands even farther to the northwest have been gradually reduced to sandbars and atolls. The Big Island is the youngest in the chain and is continuing to grow. A new island called Lo'ihi (which means "prolonged in time"), southeast of the Big Island, is growing and expected to emerge from the oceanic depths in about a million years.

It was explosions of hot lava from two volcanoes that created the island of Maui. Mauna Kahalawai is the oldest and created the westerly section with the highest point (elevation 5,788 feet) known as Pu'u Kukui. The great Haleakala, the world's largest dormant volcano, created the southeastern portion of the island. (The last eruption on Maui took place around 1789 and flowed over to the Makena area.) A valley connects these two volcanic peaks—the source of Maui's nickname, "The Valley Isle."

POLYNESIANS The first Hawaiians came from the Marquesa and Society Islands in the central Pacific. (Findings suggest that their ancestors came from the western Pacific, perhaps as far away as Madagascar.) The Polynesians left the Marquesas around the 8th century and were followed by natives from the Society Islands sometime between the 11th and 14th centuries. The Hawaiian population may well have been as high as 300,000 by the 1700s, spread throughout the chain of islands. Fish and poi were diet basics, supplemented by various fruits and occasionally meat from chickens, pigs and even dogs.

Four principal gods formed the basis of their religion until the missionaries arrived. The stone foundations of *heiau*, ancient religious temples, can still be visited on Maui.

The major islands had a history of independent rule with, at times, open warfare. On Maui, Kahului and Hana were both sites of combat between the Maui islanders and the warriors from neighboring islands.

Visit the **Maui Friends of the Library Used Bookstore** located behind Pu'unene School, open Monday through Saturday from 8 a.m. to 4 p.m. Forget to bring some paperbacks? Pick them up here for a dime! (If you're coming from Kahului, get on Pu'unene Avenue heading for Kihei. Where the road veers to the right, by the Pu'unene Sugar Mill, keep going straight and then follow the signs on the dirt roads that will take you left, then right and then right again.) 808-871-6563.

CAPTAIN COOK The islands were left undisturbed by Western influence until the 1778 arrival of Captain James Cook. He spotted and visited Kaua'i and O'ahu first and is believed to have arrived at Maui on November 25 or 26, 1778. He was later killed in a brawl on the Big Island of Hawai'i.

KAMEHAMEHA Kamehameha the First was born on the Big Island of Hawai'i around 1758. He was the nephew of Kalaiopi, who ruled the Big Island. Following the king's death, Kalaiopi's son came to power, only to be subsequently defeated by Kamehameha in 1794. The great chieftain Kahekili was Kamehameha's greatest rival. He ruled not only Maui, but Lana'i and Moloka'i, and also had kinship with the governing royalty of O'ahu and Kaua'i. King Kahekili died in 1794 and left control of the island to his son. A bloody battle (more like a massacre since Kamehameha used Western technology, strategy and two English advisors) in the Iao Valley resulted in the defeat of Kahekili's son, Kalanikupule, in 1795. Kamehameha united all the islands and made Lahaina the capital of Hawai'i in 1802. (It remained the capital until the 1840s, when Honolulu became the center for government affairs.) Lahaina was a popular resort for Hawaiian royalty who favored the beaches in the area. Ka'ahumanu, the favorite wife of Kamehameha was born in Hana, Maui, and spent much of her time there. (Quiet Hana was another popular spot for vacationing royalty.)

Liholiho, the heir of Kamehameha the Great, ruled as Kamehameha II from 1819 to 1824. Liholiho was not a strong ruler so Ka'ahumanu proclaimed herself prime minister during his reign. She ended many of the *kapu* of the old religion, thus creating a fortuitous vacuum that the soon-to-arrive missionaries would fill.

MISSIONARIES These New England missionaries and their families arrived in Lahaina in the spring of 1823 at the invitation of Queen Keopuolani. They brought drastic changes to the island with the education of the natives both spiritually and scholastically. The first high school and printing press west of the Rockies was established at Lahainaluna. Built just outside of Lahaina, it now houses a museum and is open to the public. Liholiho and his wife were the first Hawaiian royalty to visit the United States. When their travels continued to Europe, they succumbed to the measles while in London. Liholiho was succeeded by Kauikeaouli (the youngest son of Kamehameha the Great), who ruled under the title of Kamehameha the III from 1824 to 1854. The last monarch was Liliuokalani, who ruled from 1891 to 1893. Hawai'i became a territory of the United States in 1900 and achieved statehood in 1959.

WHALERS Beginning in 1819 and continuing for nearly 40 years, whaling ships became a frequent sight, anchored in the waters off Lahaina. The whalers hunted their prey north and south of the islands, off the Japanese coast and in the Arctic. Fifty ships were sometimes anchored off Lahaina, and during the peak year of whaling, over 400 ships visited Lahaina, with an additional 167 in Honolulu's harbor. Allowing 25 to 30 seamen per ship you can quickly see the enormous number of sailors who flooded the area. While missionaries brought their Christian beliefs, the whaling men lived under their own belief that there was "No God West of the Horn." This presented a tremendous conflict between the sailors and missionaries, with the islanders caught right in the middle. After months at sea, sailors arrived in Lahaina anxious for the grog shops and native women. It was the missionaries who set up guidelines that forbade the island girls to visit the ships in the harbor. Horrified by the bare-breasted Hawaiian women, the missionary wives quickly set about to more thoroughly clothe the native ladies. The missionary women realized that their dresses would not be appropriate for these more robust women and using their nightwear as a guideline, they fashioned garments by cutting the sleeves off and enlarging the armholes. The muumuu was the result, and translated means "to amputate or to cut short."

In 1832, a coral fort was erected near the Lahaina harbor following an incident with the unhappy crew of one vessel. The story goes that a captain, disgruntled when he was detained in Lahaina for enticing "base women," ordered his crew to fire shots at the homes of some Lahaina area missionaries. Although the fort was demolished in 1854, remnants of the coral were re-excavated and a corner of the old fort reconstructed. It is located harborside by the Banyan Tree.

The whaling era strengthened Hawai'i's ties with the United States economically, and the presence of the missionaries further strengthened this bond. A combination of events brought the downfall of the whaling industry: The onset of the Civil War depleted men and ships, (one Confederate warship reportedly set 24 whaling vessels ablaze), and the growth of the petroleum industry lessened the need for whale oil. Lastly, the Arctic freezes of 1871 and 1876 resulted in many ships being crushed by the ice. Lahaina, however, continues to maintain the charm and history of those bygone whaling days. (Ironically, Maui is now the headquarters for the Hawaiian Island Humpback Whale National Marine Sanctuary, the nation's twelfth, and the only one dedicated to this species. Encompassing waters from Kaua'i to the Big Island, the Sanctuary was designated in 1998.)

AGRICULTURE Sugar cane brought by the first Hawaiians was developed into a major industry on Maui. Two sons of missionaries, Henry P. Baldwin and Samuel T. Alexander, as well as Claus Spreckels played notable roles in the expansion of the industry with their construction of a water pipeline to irrigate the arid central isthmus of

Maui. This act secured the future of other agricultural development on the island.

Pineapple, another major agricultural industry, has played an important role in the history of Maui. Historians believe that pineapple may have originated in Brazil and was introduced to the modern world by Christopher Columbus on return from his second visit to the Americas. When it arrived in the islands is uncertain, but Don Francisco de Paula y Marin writes in his diary on January 21, 1813, that "This day I planted pineapples and an orange tree." The first successful report of pineapple agriculture in Hawai'i is attributed to Captain James Kidwell, an English horticulturist. He brought the smooth cayenne variety of pineapple from Jamaica and began successfully cultivating and harvesting the fruit on O'ahu in 1886.

Since the fresh fruits perished too quickly to reach the mainland, Captain Kidwell also began the first cannery, called Hawaiian Fruit and Packing Company, which operated until 1892 when it was sold to Pearl City Fruit Company. James Dole, a young Harvard graduate, arrived on O'ahu from Boston in 1899, and by 1901 had established what has today become known as the Dole Pineapple Company.

Grove Ranch and Haleakala Ranch Company both began pineapple cultivation on Maui in 1906. Baldwin Packers began as Honolua Ranch and was owned by Henry Baldwin who started it in 1912. The Grove Ranch hired David T. Fleming as company manager and began with several acres in Haiku that soon increased to 450 acres. W. A. Clark succeeded Fleming as Grove Ranch manager and while the acreage increased, for some unknown reason the pineapples failed. For ten years the fields were leased to Japanese growers who were successful.

During these early years Haleakala Ranch Company continued to expand their acreage and to successfully produce pineapples. J. Walter Cameron arrived from Honolulu to become manager of Haleakala Ranch Company around 1925. In 1929 the ranch division was separated from the pineapple division and the company became Haleakala Pineapple Company. In 1932 the Company and Grove Ranch merged, forming Maui Pineapple Company Limited; 30 years later in 1962, Baldwin Packers merged with Maui Pineapple Company to form what we know today as Maui Land and Pineapple. Maui Land and Pineapple continues to grow pineapples as well as develop land into the fine resort area known as Kapalua. The company owns 29,800 acres of land

An interesting fact is reported in the 1846 Lahaina census. The count included 3,445 Hawaiians, 112 foreigners, 600 seamen, 155 adobe houses, 822 grass houses, 59 stone and wooden houses, as well as 528 dogs!

and uses 8,400 acres for company operations while employing approximately 1,870 people on a year-round or seasonal basis. While competition from abroad (particularly Thailand) has been fierce, Maui Land and Pineapple has chosen to maintain its market by supplying a quality product. Maui Land and Pineapple Company is the only 100 percent Hawaiian producer of canned pineapple in the world.

It was about 100 years ago that the first macadamia nut trees arrived from Australia. They were intended to be an ornamental tree since they had nuts that were extremely difficult to crack. It was not until the 1950s that the development of the trees began to take a commercial course. Today, some sugar cane fields are being converted to macadamia. It is a slow process, taking seven years for the grafted root (they do not grow from seed) to become a producing tree. While delicious, beware of their hazards: a half-ounce of nuts contains 100 calories!

The Kula area of Maui has become the center for many delicious fruits and vegetables as well as the unusual Protea flower, a native of South Africa. Wineries have also made a comeback with the success of the Tedeschi Winery at Ulupalakua. Tedeschi started by producing an unusual pineapple wine followed by a champagne in 1984 and a red table wine in 1985. Be sure to also sample the very sweet Kula onions raised in this area (these are not the same as "Maui onions" that can be grown anywhere in Maui County) that are available to ship home.

Hawaiian Language

The Hawaiian language is an interesting one. Each vowel is pronounced, which can produce some tongue-tangling challenges. Older children might enjoy the *New Pocket Hawaiian Dictionary* by Mary Kawena Pukui and Samuel Elbert. They also co-authored *Pocket Place Names of Hawai'i.* We've listed some of the common place names and their meanings along with a number of fun Hawaiian words that kids will love using on Maui and back home.

The following are some of the more commonly used words that you may hear or see:

ali'i—(ah-LEE-ee)—chief
aloha—(ah-LOH-hah)—greetings
hale—(HAH-lay)—house
hana—(HA-nah)—work
hana hou—(ha-nah HO)—to do it again, encore
heiau—(HEY-ow)—temple
haole—(HOW-lee)—a caucasian
ipo—(EE-po)—sweetheart

kai—(kye)—ocean
kahuna—(kah-HOO-nah)—teacher, priest
kama'aina—(kah-mah-AYE-nuh)—native born
kane—(KAH-nay)—man
kapu—(kah-POO)—keep out, forbidden
keiki—(KAY-kee)—child
lanai—(lah-NAH-ee)—porch or patio
lomi lomi—(loh-mee LOH-mee)—to rub or massage
luau—(LOO-ow)—party with entertainment and imu-cooked food
mahalo—(mah-HA-low)—praise, thanks
makai—(mah-KYE)—toward the ocean
malihini—(mah-lee-HEE-nee)—a newcomer or visitor
mana—(MAH-nah)—supernatural or divine power
mauka—(MAU—*rhymes with cow*—kah)—toward the mountain
mauna—(MAU-nah)—mountain
mele—(MAY-leh)—Hawaiian song or chant
menehune—(may-nay-HOO-nee)—Hawaiian dwarf or elf
moana—(moh-AH-nah)—ocean
nani—(NAH-nee)—beautiful
ono—(OH-no)—delicious
pali—(PAH-lee)—cliff, precipice
paniolo—(pah-nee-O-low)—Hawaiian cowboy
pau—(pow)—finished
poi—(poy)—a paste made from the taro root
pua—(POO-ah)—flower
puka—(POO-ka)—a hole
pupus—(POO-poos)—appetizers
wahine—(wah-HEE-nay)—woman
wiki wiki—(wee-kee wee-kee)—hurry

MAUI'S NAMES AND PLACES

Haiku—abrupt break
Haleakala—house of the sun
Hali'imaile—maile vines spread
Hana—rainy land
Honoapi'ilani—bays of Pi'ilani
Honolua—double bay
Ho'okipa—welcome
Iao—cloud supreme, name of star
Ka'anapali—land divided by cliffs
Kahana—meaning unknown, of Tahitian origin
Kaho'olawe—taking away by currents
Kahului—winning
Kapalua—two borders

Kaupo—night landing
Ke'anae—the mullet
Keawakapu—sacred harbor
Kihei—shoulder cape
Kula—open country, school
Lahaina—unmerciful sun
Lana'i—meaning lost
Ma'alaea—area of red dirt
Makawao—forest beginning
Makena—abundance
Napili—pili grass
Olowalu—many hills
Paia—noisy
Pukalani—sky opening
Ulupalakua—ripe breadfruit
Wai'anapanapa—glistening water
Wailea—water Lea (Lea was the canoe maker's goddess)
Wailua—two waters
Wailuku—water of slaughter

Island Ecology

Flashlights can turn the balmy Hawaiian evenings into adventures. One of the most friendly island residents is the Bufo. In 1932 this frog was brought from Puerto Rico to assist with insect control in the cane fields. Today this large toad still emerges at night to feed or mate and seems to be easier to spot during the winter months, especially after rain showers. While they can be found around most condominiums, Kawiliki Park (the area behind the Luana Kai, Laule'a and several other condominium complexes with access from Waipulani Road off South Kihei Road) seems to be an especially popular gathering spot. I suggest you don't touch them, however—the secretions may cause skin irritation. You might also enjoy searching for beach crabs and the African snails that have shells that may grow to a hefty five inches. Find a beach with near-shore coral reef and no waves (e.g., Pu'unoa Beach in Lahaina), shine your flashlight into the water and see marine life—even eels—feeding.

The other Hawaiian creature that cannot go without mention is the gecko. They are finding their way into the suitcases of many an island visitor, in the form of T-shirts, sun visors and jewelry. This small lizard is a relative of the chameleon and grows to a length of three or four inches. They dine on roaches, termites, mosquitoes, ants, moths and other pesky insects, so island residents like having them around.

While there are nearly 800 species of geckos found in warm climates around the world, there are only about five varieties found in Hawai'i. The house gecko is the most commonly found, with tiny rows of spines that encircle its tail, while the mourning gecko has smooth, satiny skin and sports pale stripes and pairs of dark spots. The mourning gecko species is parthenogenic: there are only females that produce fertile eggs—no need for a mate! The stump-toed variety is distinguished by its thick flattened tail. The tree gecko enjoys the solitude of the forests, and the fox gecko, with a long snout and spines along its tail, prefers to hide around rocks or tree trunks. The first geckos may have reached Hawai'i with early voyagers from Polynesia, but the house gecko may have arrived as recently as the 1940s, along with military shipments to Hawai'i.

Geckos are most easily spotted at night, when they seem to enjoy the warm lights outside your door. I have heard they each establish little territories where they live and breed so you will no doubt see them around the same area each night. They are very shy and will scurry off quickly. Sometimes you may find one living in your hotel or condo. They are friendly and beneficial animals and are said to bring good luck, so make them welcome.

As for snakes, they are primarily only on display in the Honolulu Zoo. There are no snakes native to Hawai'i. Over the decades, a population of blind snakes (which you might mistake for large worms) and sea snakes (very rare) has developed, but the islanders wage a constant war to keep any other snakes out of Hawai'i. Snakes do occasionally get smuggled in, then released into the wild by irresponsible people. Or the creatures hitchhike in the cargo holds of planes from other snake-prone regions. However, Hawai'i is pretty much snake-free—and we hope to keep it that way.

Traveling with Children

Traveling with children can be an exhausting experience for parents and children alike, so the shorter the flight the better. There are a number of non-stop flights to Maui out of Portland, Seattle, San Francisco, Los Angeles, Chicago and Dallas, as well as from other major cities. These flights are very popular and fill up well in advance.

ON THE PLANE WITH KIDS

Many people don't realize that cabins are pressurized to approximately the 6,000-foot level during flight. Young children may have difficulty clearing their ears when the plane lands. To help relieve the pressure of descent, have infants nurse or drink from a bottle, and older children may benefit from chewing gum. If this is a concern of yours, consult with your pediatrician about the use of a decongestant prior to descent.

Packing a child's goody bag for the long flight is a must. A few new activity books or toys that can be pulled out en route can be sanity-saving. Snacks (boxes of juice or Capri Sun) can tide over the little ones at the airport or on the plane while awaiting your food/drink service. A thermos with a drinking spout works well and is handy for use during vacations. A change of clothes and a swimsuit for the kids can be tucked into your carry-on bag. (Suitcases have been known to be lost or delayed.) Another handy addition is a small nightlight since unfamiliar accommodations can be somewhat confusing for children during the bedtime hours. And don't forget a strong sunscreen.

TRAVELING IN THE ISLANDS WITH KIDS

CAR SEATS By law, children under 4 must travel in child safety seats in Hawai'i. While most rental agencies do have car seats for rent, you need to request them well in advance as they have a limited number. Prices run about $5 per day. You may wish to bring your own with you. Several styles are permitted by the airlines for use in flight, or it may be checked as a piece of baggage.

BABYSITTING Most hotels have some form of babysitting service that runs $12-$15 and up per hour. Check with your condo office as they sometimes have the numbers of local sitters. As you can easily figure from the rates, spending much time away from your children can be costly. Consider the feasibility of bringing your own sitter: it may actually be less expensive, and certainly much more convenient (and your sitter will love you forever).

With any of these agencies, or through your hotel, at least a 24-hour notice for a sitter is requested. I suggest phoning them *as soon* as you have set up your plans. At certain times of the year, with the limited number of sitters available, it can be nearly impossible to get one. If you can plan out your entire vacation babysitting needs, it might also be possible to schedule the same sitter for each occasion.

There are only a couple of independent childcare services on Maui. One reason might be the increased number of resorts and hotels that are now offering half-, full-day and evening childcare programs year round. Previously, many of the resorts had only offered programs during holidays and summer months. Beware, however, that most resort programs don't accept children younger than four or five years.

Our recommendation for your childcare needs is the **Nanny Connection.** They began serving Maui in 1991. Owner is Christine Taylor. I was told that all nannies have CPR and First Aid certification. Rates are $14 per hour for one child with a three-hour minimum. Extra child from the same family is an additional $2 per hour.

No travel fee, although there is a parking fee when applicable. Extra charge past midnight or holidays. Credit card is required to make and hold a reservation, but cash at the end of each service. P.O. Box 477, Pu'unene, Maui, HI 96784. 808-875-4777 (Kihei) or 808-667-5777 (Lahaina); www.thenannyconnection.com.

Happy Kids owner Sue Sargent has been providing childcare services on Maui for almost a decade. They are licensed, bonded and insured, and have their sitters undergo CPR certification. They can go to guest rooms and condos and have service early, late and even overnight with a three-hour minimum. Sitters can also travel on location with guests (such as on boat tours) to help out with the kids. They can also provide a day camp itinerary for children. All sitters are 25 to 55 years of age and can travel anywhere on the island. Contact them for rates. 808-667-5437, or from the mainland 888-669-1991; www.happykidsmaui.com.

Maui PlayCare is a new drop-in babysitting center located in Kihei, and with another just-opened location at Queen Ka'ahumanu Shopping Center in Kahului. You can drop off your child for as long as you wish—there is no minimum time requirement. Maui PlayCare is equipped with a climbing wall, dress-up clothes, art room, jumping cove and cartoon room. The facility also has extensive safety features, including closed-circuit video cameras. Maui PlayCare is state regulated, and staff members are experienced in early childhood development and care. Every person on staff is CPR/First Aid and First Response certified. The Kihei location is open Monday through Thursday, 8 a.m. to 7 p.m.; Friday 8 a.m. to 9 p.m.; Saturday 9 a.m. to 9 p.m. Closed Sunday. No appointment necessary,—this is a "drop-in" babysitting service. Located at Lipoa Center in Kihei. 808-891-2273; www.mauiplaycare.com.

CRIBS Most condos and hotels offer cribs for a rental fee that may vary from $5 to $10 per night. For an extended stay you might consider purchasing one of the wonderful folding cribs that pack up conveniently. There are several varieties that fold up into a large duffel bag. Depending on the length of your stay, they might be worth bringing along. You can also rent baby furniture and accessories from **Baby Furniture Rentals**. Check their website for information on what they offer. 808-879-4342; 877-299-2229; e-mail: info@pamelasaloharentals.com; www.babyfurniturerentals.com.

DINING You'll find *keiki* (children's) menus at most of Maui's restaurants. If any restaurant doesn't offer you a menu, ask if they have children's prices or smaller portions for their regular menu items. You can't go wrong at kid-friendly places like Ruby's Diner in Kahului. Look for the "child-friendly" icon in Chapter 4 for restaurants that are particularly good for families.

BEACHES—POOLS

Among the best beaches for fairly young children are the Lahaina and Pu'unoa beaches in Lahaina, where the water is shallow and calm. Kapalua Bay is also well protected and has fairly gentle wave action. Remember to have children well supervised and wearing flotation devices because even the calmest beaches can have a surprise wave. Several of the island's beaches offer lifeguards, among them the Kama'ole I, II and III beaches in Kihei. Kama'ole III Park also has large open areas and playground equipment. In the Ma'alaea area, follow the road down past the condominiums to the public access for the beach area. A short walk down the *kiawe*-lined beach—to the small rock jetty with the large pipe—is a seawater pool on either side that is well protected and ideal for the younger child. Look for the "child-friendly" icon in Chapter 5 for child-friendly beaches.

A number of resort complexes have small shallow pools designed with the young ones in mind. These include the Ka'anapali Ali'i, Hyatt Regency (with a sand pool), Sands of Kahana, Grand Wailea Resort and the Kahana Sunset. I recommend taking a life jacket or water wings (floaties). Packing a small inflatable pool for use on your lanai or courtyard may provide a cool and safe retreat for your little one. Typically, Maui resorts and hotels do not offer lifeguard services; never leave your child unattended near any body of water. Older children will be astounded by the labyrinth of pools and rivers at the Grand Wailea Resort. The Hyatt Regency and the Westin Maui both have great waterslides. The Wailea Marriott has a fun children's pool with slides and spray. To inquire about public pools (e.g., Lahaina's Aquatic Center and the Kihei community pool), or lifeguard status and information on county beaches, call 808-270-7383; www.co.maui.hi.us/departments/parks.

CHILDCARE PROGRAMS

During the summer, Christmas holidays and Easter, many of the resort hotels offer partial- or full-day activity programs for children. Rates range from free to $75 per day. Some of these children's programs are available to non-hotel or resort guests, and some are offered year-round (not just peak family travel seasons). Each resort generally has a theme and since these change very often, we'll summarize what might be offered: lei making, hula lessons and other Hawaiian arts and crafts, sandcastle building, nature walks, picnics, swimming, Hawaiian games and scavenger hunts. Some even provide tours to places such as the Whalers Museum at Ka'anapali or take the kids for a ride on the Sugar Cane Train. Most properties tend to center their operations outside, but a few, like the Grand Wailea, have very impressive indoor facilities. Many include lunch and a few give the kids a free T-shirt.

Following are some of the properties that offer children's programs on a regular basis. Please be sure to check with the resort for the current schedules, availability and prices for their children's programs. Check with your resort concierge for additional youth activities, as well. In Chapter 3, look for the "child-friendly" icon. It indicates a childcare program or a property that I feel is particularly good for families.

Embassy Vacation Resort's children's program, "Beach Buddies," operates year round from 8 a.m. to 2:30 p.m. This program is for resort guests only. Activities (hula, lei making, coconut weaving, movies, mini golf and crafts) are designed to keep children 5 to 12 years entertained as well as acquainting them with the Hawaiian way of life. Daily rate of $40 includes a T-shirt and lunch. 808-661-2000.

Fairmont Kea Lani Hotel offers "Keiki Lani" (Heavenly Kids) for kids 5 to 13 years. This program emphasizes Hawaiian culture and the island's ecosystems and is available year round from 9 a.m. to 3 p.m. to registered hotel guests only. Charge is $55 for first child, $40 for each additional child in the same family. 808-659-4100; www.fairmont.com/kealani.

Camp Grande–Grand Wailea Resort offers the most incredible 20,000-square-foot space devoted to youthful guests 5 to 12 years. The camp facility has a video room, arts-and-crafts center, special kiddie pool and movie theater. A huge area is designed with crafts in

ECO-FRIENDLY TOUR FOR KIDS

Camp Trilogy is a special kids' eco-enrichment program from Trilogy Excursions, offered as an add-on to their Discover Lana'i Adventure, an all-day trip to Lana'i. The program (available June through August and during major holidays) begins with a snorkel lesson from Camp Trilogy's counselors, who are certified Hawai'i wildlife marine naturalists. Then a guided reef tour lets kids learn about and view all kinds of marine wildlife. Organized beach games and activities teach team-building skills as well as respect for the environment. Camp Trilogy kids receive a special T-shirt and enjoy their own barbecue. Cost is $153 ($63 per person in addition to the regular child's fare of $90). Children must be 3 to 15 years old and able to swim. 808-874-5649; 888-628-4800; fax 808-667-7766; www.sailtrilogy.com.

KAPALUA KEIKI CLUB

The Kapalua Keiki Club is a seasonal family program of discounted special activities for parents and children to enjoy together. Offered during the summer months (and sometimes extended to other peak family travel periods), the program includes family golf and tennis activities, a pineapple plantation tour, snorkeling and a variety of activities at the Art School at Kapalua. The Kapalua Keiki Club is available to guests of Kapalua Resort, which includes the Kapalua Bay Hotel, Kapalua Villas and Ritz-Carlton, Kapalua. www.kapaluamaui.com.

mind. Adjacent is a 1950s-style soda fountain. Day camp from 9 a.m. to 4 p.m. includes lunch, $75. A half-day is 9 a.m. to 12:30 p.m. (including lunch) or 12:30 p.m. to 4 p.m. (snack included), $45. There is an evening camp from 5 p.m. to 10 p.m. including dinner for $55. Guests of the resort may join their children for lunch. Ask about one-hour daily workshops on authentic lei making, clay sculpting, tile painting and more for kids and adults (fee). Nanny services can be arranged as well. The Camp Video Arcade and Escapades are for all guests, not just kids. Candy, chips, juice and ice cream can be purchased. Parental supervision is required for children under 10 years of age. The arcade is complimentary to hotel guests. The whale wading pool, playground and kiddieland are complimentary to hotel guests, accompanied by their children. 808-875-1234; www.grandwailea.com.

The Four Seasons Resort Wailea features "Kids for all Seasons," a daily complimentary program for youths 5 to 12 with year-round supervised activities from 9 a.m. to 5 p.m. The program has great indoor and outdoor activities including swimming and beach games. "Ricky and Lucy," the parrot mascots, often stop by for a visit. The "Season's Club" is another program just for teens, offered seasonally. Reservations are required for events that might include a night at the movies, beach volleyball, an inline skate party, or a sail and snorkel. Some events are complimentary, others have a fee. During peak periods, the resort also offers evening children's programs for 3 hours (6 p.m. to 9 p.m.) at $45, which include a buffet dinner for kids. 808-874-8000; www.fourseasons.com/maui.

Hyatt Regency Maui operates Camp Hyatt for kids 5 to 12 years, featuring half-day, full-day and evening programs daily. Activities vary and may include Hawaiian arts and crafts, swimming, snorkeling, sandcastle building and visiting nearby attractions. Cost for the full day (9 a.m. to 3 p.m.) is $60 per child and includes lunch. Half-day (9 a.m.to noon or noon to 3 p.m.) is $35, including lunch. All kids receive a Camp Hyatt T-shirt. 808-661-1234; www.maui.hyatt.com.

Ka'anapali Beach Hotel has a creative unsupervised program called "Aloha Passport for Kids." Children 12 and under can participate to learn more about Hawaiian culture and receive a stamp on their "passport." They receive a free gift when they reach their destination. The program was implemented because they found that parents preferred spending time with their children while on vacation, rather than sending them off to a day camp. So all of the activities can be done with parents and older siblings. Destinations include flower lei making, hula lessons, cultural garden tour, *lau* (leaf) printing, pineapple cutting and ti leaf skirt making. For children ages 3 to 12. Infants through age 2 receive a passport card with their personalized Hawaiian name and a baby bucket full of goodies. 808-661-0011; www.kbhmaui.com.

Maui Prince Hotel offers a year-round program called the "Prince Keiki Club." Children 5 to 12 years can have hours of fun with activities such as bamboo pole fishing, sand castle building, pool swims, Hawaiian arts and crafts, and treasure hunts. Three sessions are offered to hotel guests throughout the day. 24-hour advanced notice is required. The morning session (9 a.m. to noon) and the afternoon session (noon to 3 p.m.) are each $25. Or combine the two sessions for a full day for $50. If there is only one child in the session, you can have a private session for double the cost. 808-874-1111; www.mauiprincehotel.com.

Napili Kai Beach Resort offers a Keiki Club for youth 6 to 12 years old during Easter/Spring break, mid-June through August and Thanksgiving and Christmas holidays. The fully supervised program is complimentary for resort guests and is offered two hours daily (except Sunday) from 10 a.m. to 12 noon. Activities include Hawaiian games, hula, lei making and nature walks. 808-669-6271; www.napili kai.com.

Renaissance Wailea Beach Resort provides Camp Wailea for in-house guests 5 to 12 years. Offered Tuesday, Thursday and Saturday from 9 a.m. to 1 p.m. Lots of fun activities with lunch included. $45 per child includes a Camp Wailea T-shirt. 800-992-4532; 808-879-4900; www.marriotthawaii.com.

The Ritz-Carlton, Kapalua's Ritz-Kids program is a half- or full-day program that explores the wonders of Maui. Theme programs focus on nature, culture, art, beach and Hawaiian games. Possible outings may include D.T. Fleming Beach for sandcastle building or the swimming pool for water games. Other activities that highlight the day are playing on the nine-hole putting green and the croquet lawn. The Ritz Kids program is for hotel guests. Full day program, 9 a.m. to 4 p.m., is $65 (includes lunch); half-day program, 9 a.m. to noon or 1 to 4 p.m., is $35. Siblings get a 20 percent discount. One night each week is Kids Night Out, from 5 to 9 p.m., with games, dinner, a movie and popcorn ($40 per child). 808-669-6200; www.ritzcarlton.com.

Sheraton Maui Resort offers a Keiki Kamp at its sister Starwood property, the Westin Maui Resort & Spa. (See Westin below for details.)

Wailea Marriott offers a supervised Activity Club for children 5 to 13 years. Cost is $50 per child per day and available only to registered guests. 808-874-7998.

Westin Maui Resort & Spa offers Keiki Kamp for kids 5 to 12 years who are guests of its hotel, or of the Sheraton Maui or Westin Ka'anapali Ocean Resort Villas. (A complimentary shuttle runs between the three hotels.) This program, a licensed childcare facility, is one of the very few resort-based children's programs that are open also to non-guests (although the fee is slightly higher). The program runs daily from 9 a.m. to 3 p.m. and includes lunch as well as a souvenir T-shirt on the first full day. A half-day program goes from 9 a.m. to 12:45 p.m., including lunch. An evening program is available as well, from 6:30 to 9:30 p.m. Cost for guests of the three resorts: full day $60, half-day $30, night program, $30. Cost for non-guests: full day $65, half-day $35, night program, $35. Discounted prices for siblings. Reservations recommended at least 24 hours in advance. 808-667-2525, ext. 2386; www.westinmaui.com.

SPORTS INSTRUCTION AND PROGRAMS FOR KIDS

A number of sports activity companies on Maui have special programs just for children. For instance, Wailea Resort and Kapalua Resort both offer junior tennis clinics and golf lessons for young people.

Using the "Discover" technique (so kids can learn on their own), **Ron Bass's Maui Sea Kayaking** offers special **kayaking classes** for children with appropriately smaller-sized equipment. He also coordinates special drug-free trips for youth to pick up litter and plant trees.

Kids (and their parents) will love learning to surf with **Goofy Foot Surf School**. An easy land lesson prepares you before you get wet. And **Maui Sports Unlimited** offers three-day Kid's Windsurfing Camps, June through August. For more information on these and other activities specifically for young people, see the listings in Chapter 6 "Where to Play."

ENTERTAINMENT FOR KIDS

In addition to the many free hula shows offered around the island at hotels and shopping centers, there are a variety of other entertainment options perfect for adults and kids. **Kupanaha: Maui Magic for All Ages** is an entertaining magic and dinner show at the Ka'anapali Beach Hotel that is designed for families to enjoy together. The Maui Theatre's **Ulalena** is a beautiful and fascinating show for adults and children, particularly older kids who won't mind sitting through a

LOVELY LOCAL LITTLE ONES

The Napili Kai Beach Resort hosts a one-hour Polynesian show every Tuesday at 5 p.m. in their Hale Aloha tent facility. What's so unusual about this particular Polynesian show? All the dancers are local children, ages 6 to 18—members of the Napili Kai Foundation, a non-profit organization that teaches Maui children the history, arts, crafts, language and dances of Polynesia. This charming presentation is open to the public. Admission is $10 adults, $5 children age 6 to 12; 5 and under free. For tickets call Napili Kai Beach Resort, 808-669-6271.

theater production. **Warren & Annabelle's** in Lahaina offers a family magic show seasonally, during peak family travel periods.

The **Napili Kai Beach Resort** offers a weekly hula show put on by local island children (see "Lovely Local Little Ones" sidebar). For more information on these and other entertainment options for families, see Chapter 6 "Where To Play."

MOVIES AND THEATERS FOR KIDS

Movie theaters are always a great option for family entertainment on the occasional rainy day. There is a six-plex movie theater at the Ka'ahumanu Center and a four-plex in Kihei's Kukui Mall. In Lahaina, there is a tri-cinema at The Wharf Cinema Shopping Center and another set of four theaters at the Lahaina Center off Front Street. The Maui Mall Megaplex in Kahului offers twelve theaters with stadium seating. Check the current *Maui News* for movie listings and times.

There are also a number of video stores around Maui that rent movies and equipment, and the major resorts have video rentals available for guests.

Maui has some great theater. **Maui On Stage** produces a full season of professional-quality plays and musicals performed almost every weekend from October through June. They are located in the Historic Iao Theatre on Market Street in Wailuku.

The **Maui Academy of Performing Arts** is an educational and performing arts organization for kids and adults, located in Wailuku. The **Maui Arts & Cultural Center** offers everything from local community events to concert performances by internationally known performers. For more information on these theater options for families, see Chapter 6 "Where to Play."

EXCURSIONS AND ADVENTURES WITH KIDS

As you explore the island of Maui, you'll discover many wonderful sights and attractions for families to enjoy. Following is a brief description of some of the most popular family excursions. They are discussed in more detail in Chapter 2 "What to See."

Upcountry Maui—Traveling up the slopes of Haleakala will bring you to Upcountry Maui. Upcountry Maui features astounding views of central Maui and self-guided, self-paced walking tours of the **Enchanting Floral Gardens** and the **Kula Botanical Gardens**. Shop in the rustic town of Makawao, Maui's cowboy town. Travel to Paia and visit Ho'okipa Park, one of the world's best windsurfing locations.

Central Maui (Kahului to Wailuku)—The **Maui Tropical Plantation** has become one of the top visitor attractions in the state. Admission to the market and restaurant are free, but there is a charge for the tram that takes you on a guided tour of the plantation. Visit the historic **Iao Valley**, and the **Bailey House Museum** for a view of Maui's ancient Hawaiian ancestry. The **Hawai'i Nature Center** at Iao Valley offers an interactive nature museum and gift shop. There are more than 30 exhibits focusing on Hawai'i's natural history. They also offer weekly guided hikes for children.

Enjoy a shopping excursion at Maui's largest mall, the **Queen Ka'ahumanu Shopping Center.**

In addition to baseball and mini-soccer fields, the 110-acre **Maui Central Park** (Keopualani Park) in Kahului offers playgrounds and picnic tables throughout, and a skateboard park. Adjoining are the **Maui Botanical Gardens** (formerly a zoo), a great stop-off to bring along a picnic lunch.

The **Paper Airplane Museum** in the Maui Mall features the unique juice-can creations of the Tin Can Man along with aviation model exhibits and pictures depicting the history of aviation in the Hawaiian Islands. They have 2,500 paper airplane kits that you can buy.

Check out this website for more information on family and children's activities at Maui resorts: www.hotelfun4kids.com/hotelandresort/ushotels/hawaii/maui.htm.

South Maui (Ma'alaea to Wailea)—Allow a minimum of two hours to visit the **Maui Ocean Center**, located in Ma'alaea, which offers a world-class aquarium (the only one of its kind in Hawai'i), reef, turtle and ray pools (plus an outdoor "touch pool"), a shark tank and a whale center. See Chapter 6 for more information. Keiki Ocean Discovery Time and a variety of children-friendly programs and exhibits can be found at the **Pacific Whale Foundation's Marine Resource Center** at The Harbor Shops at Ma'alaea. Maui Marine C.O.R.E. has monthly recreational outings designed to inspire youth about the natural environment. Most outings meet at the Pacific Whale Foundation's office at The Harbor Shops at Ma'alaea; ask the Pacific Whale Foundation for more information.

Heading toward Kihei from Ma'alaea, take a self-guided tour of the coastal wetlands and sand dunes of the **Kealia Pond National Wildlife Refuge**.

West Maui—The **Whaling Museum** at Whalers Village in Ka'anapali is a most interesting place to browse, and it's free. A stroll down Front Street is always fun for families—make sure you stop for a photo in front of **Bubba Gump's** restaurant. The **Sugar Cane Train** is an enjoyable outing, particularly for young children (see "All Aboard" sidebar).

At **Glow Putt Mini Golf**, a unique indoor miniature golf course in Lahaina Center, you play in the dark and everything glows. See details in Chapter 6.

Especially for Seniors

More and more businesses are now offering special savings to seniors. Whether for a boating activity, an airline ticket or a condominium, be sure to ask about special senior rates. And be sure to travel with identification showing your date of birth.

SENIOR DISCOUNTS Many properties and rental agents offer senior programs or senior discounts. Mention you are a senior (some as low as age 50) and receive incredible discounts or bonuses. For example, Pleasant Hawaiian Holidays features a "Makua Club" with special rates for seniors. Outrigger offers a "Fifty-Plus Program"; Aston calls theirs the "Senior Sun Club." RSVP booking agency offers special rates for seniors who book accommodations through them. They are listed in the Rental Agents section of Chapter 3.

A number of airlines have special discounts for seniors. Some have a wonderful feature that provides a discount for the traveling companion who is accompanying the senior. Coupon books for senior discounts are also available from some airline carriers.

Remember that AARP members get many travel discounts for rooms, cars and tours. Check the Yellow Pages when you arrive on Maui for the senior discount program logo. Look for a black circle with a white star in the ads.

All Maui movie theaters offer senior discounts (many for those over 62) anytime, and most also have assisted listening devices to pump up the volume—or turn it down if it's too loud.

MAUI SENIOR SERVICES Check out the Kaunoa Senior Services at 401 Ala Kapa Place, Paia, 808-270-7308, which offers volunteer opportunities and classes for folks 55 years and up, and a dining program for those 60 years and older.

Elderhostel Hawai'i arranges inexpensive housing in college dorms during summer months along with special interest classes and

ALL ABOARD

In the Lahaina–Ka'anapali area, the colorful **Sugar Cane Train**—a steam locomotive—runs a course several times a day along Honoapi'ilani Highway from Ka'anapali to Lahaina. After arrival in Lahaina, take some time for a stroll. Wander a few blocks down to Front Street, stop by the Baldwin Missionary Home, and have lunch at one of the oceanfront eateries before returning to the train for the trip home. The Sugar Cane Train also has an evening activity; the Paniolo Express Dinner Train is the first scheduled evening train in the history of the railway. The Dinner Train departs from the Pu'ukoli'i Station in Ka'anapali each Thursday at 5 p.m., then stops for a *paniolo*-style barbecue. The kids will love the hearty dinner of chicken, ribs, hot dogs, hamburgers and a salad bar. Top it off with smoothies to drink and mix with a little cowboy-hula entertainment. Reservations required for the Paniolo Express, $76 adult, $43 children 3 to 12. Daytime trains run 363 days a year (closed Thanksgiving and Christmas) from 10:15 a.m. to 4 p.m. from Pu'ukoli'i, Ka'anapali and Lahaina. For the Sugar Cane Train, prices are $12.95 round trip for children 3 to 12; for adults it's $18.95 round trip. 808-667-6851, 800-499-2307; e-mail: mail@sugarcanetrain.com; www.sugarcanetrain.com.

sports activities. Call 808-262-8942 on O'ahu for information on Maui accommodations. For kayaking and snorkeling, Ron Bass on Maui (808-572-6299) works with Elderhostel to provide senior excursions addressing their special needs.

Travel Tips for the Physically Impaired

Make your travel plans well in advance and inform hotels and airlines when making your reservations that you are a person with a disability. Bring along your medical records in the event of an emergency. It is recommended that you bring your own wheelchair and notify the airlines in advance that you will be transporting it. There are no battery rentals available on Maui.

Additional information can be obtained from the State Commission on Persons with Disabilities, c/o State Department of Health, 54 High Street, Wailuku, Maui, HI 96793 (808-984-8219; fax 808-984-8222). Or call the State Commission on Persons with Disabilities on O'ahu: 808-586-8121; fax 808-586-8129. They offer a book entitled *Aloha Guide to Accessibility*, which is divided into sections that provide services and information for persons with disabilities on the accessibility of hotels, beaches, parks, shopping centers, theaters and auditoriums, and visitor attractions. They will send specific sections or the entire guide for the cost of postage ($3 to $5 per section; $15 complete).

ARRIVAL AND DEPARTURE On arrival at the Kahului airport terminal, you will find the building easily accessible for mobility-impaired persons. Parking areas are located close to the main terminal for disabled persons. Restrooms with handicapped stalls (male and female) are also found in the main terminal.

TRANSPORTATION There is limited public transportation on Maui (although there is an airport shuttle) and taxi service can be expensive. For short hops, the Lahaina–Ka'anapali route of the "West Maui Shopping Express" has a wheelchair-accessible bus. See "Getting Around: Rental Cars and Trucks" section later in the chapter for phone numbers of rental agencies. They need some advance notice to install the equipment. Accessible Vans of Hawai'i offers wheelchair-accessible van rentals with hand controls, and delivery and pick up of island visitors. They can also assist you if you'd like to rent a specific car and require special needs such as hand controls. 800-303-3750; 808-871-7536; fax 808-871-7536. Also check Wheelchair Get-Aways, 800-638-1912.

ACCOMMODATIONS Each of the major island hotels offers one or more handicapped rooms including bathroom entries of at least 29" to allow for wheelchairs. Due to the limited number of rooms, reservations should be made well in advance. Information on condominium accessibility is available from the Commission on Persons with Disabilities (see above). Accessible Vans of Hawai'i also has condo listings as well as additional information on the availability of roll-in showers and wheelchair-accessible bathrooms.

ACTIVITIES Accessible Vans of Hawai'i and Hawai'i Care Van Shuttle and Tour offer wheelchair-accessible touring and can provide information on recreational activities for the traveler. Among the options are wheelchair tennis or basketball, bowling and swimming. Contact them in advance of your arrival. Wheelchair access to some of the tourist attractions may be limited. One of a few boats to offer access for the handicapped is *The Pride of Maui*.

Maui County continues to make the beaches more accessible for disabled travelers with handicapped designations at beach parking lots, sidewalks and curb cuts, comfort stations, picnic tables, showers and an accessible pathway onto the beach. Currently beaches that have been made accessible include Kama'ole I, II and III, Hanaka'o'o Beach and Kanaha Beach.

Ron Bass is an independent tour guide who specializes in kayaking and snorkeling for the disabled. His special equipment includes three-person kayaks, view boards and beach-access wheelchairs. Ron also operates "Wilderness Wish," a non-profit organization that assists disabled folks to experience new adventures by discovering and exploring out-of-the-way places. P.O. Box 106, Pu'unene, HI 96784. 808-572-6299; fax 808-572-6151; www.maui.net/~kayaking.

MEDICAL SERVICES AND EQUIPMENT **Maui Memorial Hospital** is located in Wailuku and there are also good clinics in all areas of the island. Check the local directory.

Several agencies can assist in providing personal care attendants, companions and nursing aides while on your visit. **Hale Mahaolu** at 808-872-4130, www.maui.net/~hmahaolu provides personal care attendants, as do **Aloha International Employment Service** 808-871-6373, and **Interim Health Care** 808-877-2676.

Lahaina Pharmacy (Old Lahaina Center) has wheelchairs, crutches, canes and walkers. 808-661-3119.

Gammie Home Care, Kahului Industrial Center, 292 Alamaha Place, Kahului, HI 96732, can provide medical equipment rentals, from walking aides to bathroom accessories or wheelchairs as well as oxygen services. 808-877-4032; fax 808-877-3359; www.gammie.com; e-mail: gammie@maui.net. Or go to www.thestateofhawaii.com/homehealth.html#maui for a listing of home health care specialists.

Accessible Vans of Hawai'i is the only travel, tour and activity agency on Maui that specializes in assisting the disabled traveler. "Imagination is your limit," they report when it comes to the activities they offer. They can assist in making reservations at a condominium or hotel to fit the needs of the traveler, make airport arrangements including ticketing and arranging for a wheelchair. They can make arrangements for personal care such as attendants, pharmacists or interpreters as well as arrange for rental cars or vans with hand controls. Accessible Vans of Hawai'i is a one-stop shopping connection for the disabled traveler and the Maui (and State of Hawaii) Representative for Accessible Vans of America. And as your personal Hawaiian concierge, travel consultant Carol Miller is happy to make recommendations (no charge). Inquire about island recreation such as snorkeling, scuba diving, helicopter tours, bowling, golf, horseback riding, boating, luaus, tennis (disabled opponent available), tours, jet skiing or ocean kayaking. Wedding and honeymoon arrangements, too. Accessible Vans of Hawai'i can also provide sand/beach wheelchairs with big inflatable rubber tires. Carol Miller: 296 Alamaha, Suite C, Kahului, HI 96732. 808-871-7785, 800-303-3750; fax 808-871-7536; www.accessiblevanshawaii.com; e-mail: carol@accessiblevanshawaii.com.

HEARING IMPAIRED Both the Wallace and Consolidated movie theater chains have assisted listening devices available at their Lahaina, Kihei and Kahului theaters. The headsets increase the volume (or decrease the noise) on an individual basis. The Maui Arts &

Cultural Center also provides headsets for plays and concerts and, as one of Maui's newer constructions, is completely ADA accessible.

VISION IMPAIRED Legislation allows seeing-eye dogs to travel to Hawai'i without quarantine, providing that current proof of vaccinations is provided.

What to Pack

When traveling to paradise, you won't need too much. Comfortable shoes are important for all the sightseeing and shopping. Sandals are the norm for footwear. Dress is casual for dining. Many restaurants require men to wear sport shirts with collars, but only one or two require a tie. Clothes should be lightweight and easy care. Cotton and cotton blends are more comfortable for the tropical climate than polyesters. Shorts and bathing suits are the dress code here. A lightweight jacket with a hood or sweater is advisable for evenings and occasional rain showers.

The only need for warmer clothes is if your plans should include a stay Upcountry, hiking/camping in Haleakala Crater or seeing the sunrise. While it may start out warm and sunny, the weather can change very quickly Upcountry. Even during the daytime, a sweater or light jacket is a good idea when touring the area. (The cooler weather here is evidenced on the roofs of the homes where chimneystacks can be spotted.) Tennis shoes or hiking shoes are a good idea for the rougher volcanic terrain of Haleakala or hiking elsewhere as well. Sunscreens are a must. A camera, of course, needs to be tucked in. Binoculars are an option and may be well used if you are traveling between December and April when the whales arrive for their winter vacation. Special needs for traveling with children are discussed above. Anything that you need can probably be purchased once you arrive. Don't forget to leave some extra space in those suitcases for goodies that you will want to take back home.

Weddings & Honeymoons

If a Hawaiian wedding (or a renewal of vows) is in your dreams, Maui can make them all come true. While the requirements are simple, here are a few tips, based on current requirements at time of publication, for making your wedding plans run more smoothly. I advise you to double check the requirements as things change.

REGULATIONS Both bride and groom must be over 18 years of age (16 years old with written consent from parents or legal guardians).

Birth certificates are not required, but you do need proof of age such as a driver's license or passport. You do not need proof of citizenship or residence. If either partner has been divorced, the date, county and state of finalization for each divorce must be verbally provided to the licensing agent. If a divorce was finalized within the last three months, then a decree must be provided to the licensing agent.

Your personal vows for a Catholic wedding require special arrangements between your home priest and the Maui priest. If both bride and groom are practicing Catholics, the Church requires that you marry within the church building, unless you are granted special permission from the Bishop in Honolulu.

A license must be purchased in person in the state of Hawai'i. Call the Department of Health in Maui (808-984-8210) for the name of a licensing agent in the area where you will be staying. Both bride and groom must appear in person before the agent. The fee is currently $60. There is no waiting period once you have the license, but the license is valid for only 30 days. Check with the Chamber of Commerce in Kahului (808-871-7711) for information regarding a pastor. Many island pastors are very flexible in meeting your needs, such as an outdoor location. (For $8 you can buy a package with a booklet and information on planning a wedding.)

For copies of current requirements and forms, write in advance to the State of Hawaii, Department of Health, Marriage License Section, P.O. Box 3378, Honolulu, HI 96801; 808-586-4545. You can also call the Maui Visitors Bureau (808-244-3530) for a copy of the requirements as well as information on free public wedding locations at Hawai'i state and national parks and how to book a marriage ceremony with a judge. (The Courthouse is at 2145 Main Street in Wailuku.) You can also go online to obtain Department of Health forms and information at www.state.hi.us/doh/records/vr_marri.html or e-mail them at vr-info@mail.health.state.hi.us.

There are several websites devoted to getting married, renewing vows and/or honeymooning on Maui. You can start by checking out www.mauiweddingnetwork.com, www.mauiweddingassociation.com, or www.visitmaui.com. See below for a list of wedding providers or visit www.mauichamber.com under "Weddings."

WEDDING BASICS

Formal Wear Rentals

Gilbert's Formal Wear. 104 North Market Street, Old Wailuku Town; 808-244-4017.

Lahaina Towne Tuxedos. Old Lahaina Center, 845 Wainee Street; 808-667-4040.

Limousines

Arthur's Limousine Service has locations in Kahului, South Maui and West Maui; 877-408-9559; 808-871-5555 (Kahului), 808-875-4955 (Kihei/Wailea), 808-662-9522 (Lahaina). Also try **Carey Limousine Hawaii**, aka Town & Country Limousine (808-572-3400) or **Star Maui Limousine** (808-875-6900).

Photography

John Pierre's Photographic Studio has been providing wedding photo packages since 1977. 143 Dickenson Street, Lahaina, Maui, HI 96761; 808-667-7988; e-mail: jpsm@maui.net; www.maui.net/~jpsm.

Video Tape Services

Hawai'i **Video Memories**, 230 Hana Highway, Suite 11. 808-871-5788; 888-255-7080; www.hawaiivideomemories.com.

Other Wedding Services

Royal Hawaiian Carriage Co. has two carriages (one white, one black) for four passengers each, with two Clydesdales, one Belgian and one Percheron horse. The company provides wedding transportation to and from the ceremony and/or reception. They are based at the Kapalua Resort. Rates for the Kapalua area are $300 for the first hour, $175 each additional hour. Extra charge for carriage rides out of the Kapalua area. They also provide restaurant transportation, horse-drawn picnics and other romantic excursions such as sunset tours. They can provide private locations such as a tropical valley or an oceanview gazebo for your wedding. 24-hour advance booking suggested. 808-669-1100; fax 808-669-4702; www.royalhawaiiancarriages.com.

Arrange for a private sunset dinner cruise for your reception. See "Cruises" in Chapter 6 regarding scheduled or private charters.

Tropical Gardens of Maui provides a garden area with waterfalls and a gazebo in the Iao Valley, $150 for up to 10 people and $200 for 11 to 20 people. 200 Iao Valley Road, Wailuku, HI 96793; 808-244-3085; fax 808-242-6152; e-mail: info@tropicalgardensofmaui.com; www.tropicalgardensofmaui.com.

Trilogy Excursions can make the most memorable day of your life an ocean adventure, too. Imagine crossing the channel to the island of Lana'i while exchanging vows. They offer one to three catamarans on Saturday and Sunday and can accommodate large or small groups ranging from 25 to 160 guests. Once on Lana'i, the bride and groom have exclusive use of the Hale O Manele pavilion for their Hawaiian-style luau celebration. The captain and crew will prepare dinner while you enjoy live entertainment before a starlit sail back to Lahaina. (Trilogy does not supply a minister or wedding cake.) 888-628-4800; e-mail: info@sailtrilogy.com; www.sailtrilogy.com.

Wedding Coordinators

There are many, many wedding coordinators and wedding support services on Maui. I recommend you start your research by visiting the Maui Wedding Network's website at www.mauiweddingnetwork.com.

Basic wedding packages run $200 to more than $3,000. Although each company varies the package slightly, it will probably include assistance in choosing a location and getting your marriage license, a minister and an assortment of optional extras such as champagne, photography, cake, leis and a bridal garter. Videotaping, witnesses and music are usually extra. Here are just a few of Maui's wedding coordinators:

A Dream Wedding Maui Style—One-on-one service, weddings and vow renewals. Tracy Flanagan, Consultant. 143 Dickenson Street #201, Lahaina, HI 96761; 808-661-1777; 800-743-2777; fax 808-661-0072; e-mail: dreamwed@maui.net; www.adreamwedding.net.

A White Orchid Wedding—Have your wedding "Aloha Ea Oi" (I Love You) at a "Historic Hawaiian Church," or where the "Lava Meets the Sea." They can also arrange travel, activities and vow renewals. They have packages and an a la carte shopping system. Contact Carolee Higashino. P.O. Box 2696, Wailuku, HI 9679; 808-242-8697; 800-240-9336; fax 808-242-6853; e-mail: awow@maui.net; www.whiteorchidwedding.net or www.whiteorchidwedding.com.

All Ways Maui'd Weddings & Ceremonies—They specialize in smaller, more intimate weddings, vow renewals, holy unions and blessings, and also offer digital and 35mm photography services. Ceremonies are usually held at Maui's public beaches or parks, but private tropical and oceanfront gardens or a Hawaiian wedding chapel are also options. Owned and operated by Rev. Kolleen O'Flaherty Wheeler, a non-denominational, state-licensed minister, and Bruce Wheeler, coordinator and photographer. "Short-notice" weddings are okay with them. P.O. Box 817, Pu'unene, HI 96784-0817; 808-244-1167; 877-906-2843; fax 808-242-8019; cell phone 808-385-1195; e-mail: weddings@maui-angels.com; www.maui-angels.com.

Dolphin Dream Weddings—This company has been organizing beach weddings for nearly 14 years. They can arrange for the minister only or for elaborate weddings with full receptions at a variety of locations. They also coordinate vow renewals and like to include the entire family in the vow renewal ceremony, with parents exchanging leis with their children. Contact: Vickie Jackson. P.O. Box 10546, Lahaina, HI 96761; 180 Dickenson Square, Suite #210, Lahaina; 808-661-8525; 800-793-2933; www.dolphindreamweddings.com.

Royal Hawaiian Weddings—Janet Renner can assist you with your most special occasion. Choose from dazzling beachside sunsets, private oceanfront settings, tropical gardens, a Hawaiian luau, and enchanted waterfall, or remote helicopter landings. Vow renewals, too. 808-875-

8569; 800-659-1866 U.S. & Canada; fax 808-875-0623; e-mail: info@royalhawaiianweddings.com; www.royalhawaiianweddings.com.

In addition to independent wedding coordinators, many of Maui's major resorts offer wedding coordination services and a range of wedding and honeymoon packages at their properties. These resorts offer spectacular sites for weddings and can arrange all your needs, from an intimate ceremony for two to a huge celebration for hundreds. Following is a list of just a few of the Maui resorts that provide on-property wedding services. Contact them directly for more information:

Diamond Resort—A wedding gazebo here has a view of the ocean and the mountains. Great for smaller, intimate weddings. 555 Kaukahi Street, Wailea, HI 96753; 808-874-0500; 800-800-0720; e-mail: info@diamondresort.com; www.diamondresort.com.

Four Seasons Resort Wailea—This luxury property features a variety of destination wedding packages. Amenities include musician(s), champagne and cake, floral decor, clergy, photography and use of a wedding location. Services include assistance by their wedding coordinator and a 20 percent discount on accommodations. The Ku'uipo Point Gazebo on the third level of the sculpture gardens with ocean and mountain vistas can accommodate 40 guests. The oceanfront lawn overlooking Wailea Beach is enhanced with floral archway and white aisle runner. It can accommodate up to 100 guests. The Seasons Lawn is a secluded garden for private ceremonies for 2 to 10. Seasons Point is set atop a gushing waterfall with bougainvillea and koi ponds and is a perfect spot for a Maui sunset as a backdrop. 3900 Wailea Alanui, Wailea, HI 96753. 808-874-8000; 800-334-6284; fax 808-874-2222; www.fourseasons.com/maui.

Grand Wailea Resort Hotel & Spa—The extraordinary Grand Wailea has constructed a New England wedding chapel on their grounds. The picturesque white chapel features stained-glass win-

TIME

You'll find that Hawai'i has not discovered daylight-saving time. They are also in a different time zone. During "standard time" in the continental U.S. (November through March) Hawai'i is two hours behind the Pacific time zone. Because they don't switch to daylight-saving time, from April through October they are three hours behind Pacific Time. You may hear references to "Hawaiian Time" or "Maui Time"—these local phrases often refer not to the hour, but to a lack of punctuality. Things on Maui happen in their own time, not necessarily on schedule. So "hang loose" and be flexible.

dows that depict a royal Hawaiian wedding. Woods of red oak, teak and cherry dominate the interior, which is accented by three handcrafted chandeliers from Murano, Italy. Outside the chapel is a flower-filled garden with brass-topped gazebos. A beautiful indoor location for your wedding. They also offer weddings in their chapel gardens or on Wailea Beach. Sunset weddings cost more than the daytime weddings. The Grand Wailea offers a 20 percent discount for rooms for the bride and groom only. 3850 Wailea Alanui, Wailea, HI 96753. 808-875-1234; 800-888-6100; fax 808-879-4077; e-mail info@grandwailea.com; www.grandwailea.com.

Hyatt Regency Maui Resort & Spa—A wedding and catering coordinator can assist with your wedding day plans. A wedding gazebo, designed from ohia wood from the Big Island, is set amid tropical Hawaiian gardens and waterways. Check out their wedding planning guide online. Very helpful. 200 Nohea Kai Drive, Lahaina, HI 96761; 808-661-1234; 800-554-9288; www.maui.hyatt.com.

Lana'i Weddings—The Manele Bay Resort and The Lodge at Koele on the island of Lana'i offer the assistance of a wedding coordinator. The ceremony site can be either the gazebo at The Lodge at Koele or the Hawaiian or Bromeliad garden at the Manele Bay Hotel. Honeymoon and Romance packages are also available and include amenities such as aromatic bath salts and oils, massage or an intimate breakfast in bed. P.O. Box 630310, Lana'i City, HI 96763; 800-321-4666; fax 808-565-3868; e-mail: reservations@lanai-resorts.com; www.lanairesorts.com.

Royal Lahaina Resort—Rows of pink and white hibiscus line the walkways leading to the cottage courtyard and wedding gazebo that features six open-air windows. The Royal Lahaina Resort has also introduced a unique wedding custom: they provide stepping stones engraved with the bride and groom's name and wedding date. Contact their wedding consultant, ext. 2211. 2780 Keka'a Drive, Lahaina, HI 96761; 808-661-3611. Managed by: Hawaiian Hotels & Resorts, 800-222-5642; www.hawaiianhotelsandresorts.com.

Westin Maui Resort & Spa—Located on Ka'anapali Beach, this resort has its own resident Director of Romance who will assist you with your wedding and honeymoon plans—even if you want to be married while parasailing or scuba diving. For more traditional romantics, they offer the release of 2 to 40 white wedding doves from white wicker baskets. Various packages are available. 2365 Ka'anapali Parkway, Lahaina, HI 96761. Hotel info 808-667-2525; reservations 808-921-4655; www.westinmaui.com.

Ritz-Carlton, Kapalua—Wedding packages can be arranged to include the use of the historic Kumulani Chapel. Construction on the 60-seat New England–style plantation church began in the late 1930s, but due to the war, it was not completed until 1951. Weddings can also be arranged at the gazebo on the lawn of the chapel, at Lava Point, or on the Beach House lawn. 1 Ritz Carlton Drive, Kapalua, HI 96761. 808-669-6200; 800-262-8440; fax 808-669-1566; www.ritz carlton.com.

Helpful Information

INFORMATION BOOTHS Visitor information booths located at the shopping areas can provide helpful details and lots of brochures. Look for the new wallet-size mini-brochures that are purse- and pocket-friendly.

For all kinds of information about Maui, contact the **Maui Visitors Bureau**: 1727 Wili Pa Loop, P.O. Box 580, Wailuku, HI 96793; 808-244-3530; 800-525-MAUI; fax 808-244-1337; www.visit maui.com.

BANKS Basic hours are 8:30 a.m. to 3 p.m., but some are open until 5 or 6 p.m. Most will cash U.S. traveler's checks with a picture ID.

CREDIT CARDS A few small condominiums still do not accept any form of credit card payment, but stores and hotels almost always do. Some smaller restaurants also do not accept credit cards.

SALES TAX A sales tax of 4.167% is added to all purchases made in Hawai'i. There is an additional room-use tax added to your hotel or condominium bill.

HOLIDAYS Holidays unique to the state of Hawai'i: March 26 is Prince Kuhio Day, June 11 is Kamehameha Day and August 21 is Admissions Day.

Communications

TELEVISION The Paradise Network, shown island-wide on Channel 7, is designed especially with visitors in mind. Information is provided on recreation, real estate, shopping, restaurants, history, culture and art.

RADIO KPOA 93.5FM/92.7FM plays great old and new Hawaiian music. KLHI ("The Point") at 101.1FM has adult alternative rock; KHPR (90.7FM) is Hawai'i Public Radio with classical music; and KDLX 94.3FM offers all country. KJMD 98.3FM is rhythmic/hip hop; KONI 104.7FM plays oldies; KAOI ("I") FM on either 95.1 or 96.7 (Upcountry) has soft rock. KNUI 99.9FM features adult contemporary; KNUQ ("Q") 103.7 offers contemporary island music and KPMW 105.5FM ("Wild 105") has top 40 and contemporary hits with ethnic programming on the weekends. Mana'o Radio at 91.5 KEAO-LPFM is a new listener-supported, non-profit station that offers an eclectic mix of music and information. On the AM dial, KMVI has sports talk at 550; KNUI 900AM plays traditional Hawaiian; and KAOI 1110AM has news, talk and sports.

PERIODICALS Some of Maui's free visitor publications have self-explanatory titles: *MENU*, *Maui Menus*, *Lahaina Historical Guide*, *101 Things To Do on Maui*, and many, many more. Peruse all the guides to find maps, shuttle schedules, entertainment calendars, shopping tips, activity directories, etc. They all have lots of advertising, and most offer coupons that will give you discounts on everything from meals to sporting activities to clothing. It may save you a bit to search through these before making your purchases. *Maui No Ka Oi* is Maui's only "real" magazine—a glossy quarterly ($3.95) with columns and features on people, politics, business, lifestyles, current events, environment, history and culture.

There are also a number of newspaper publications that offer helpful and interesting information. The *Maui Bulletin* is a free newsprint booklet with classified ads and television listings. The free *Maui Weekly* has more local stories. *Haleakala Times* is a free regional newspaper serving Upcountry Maui. *Maui Time* is a free bi-weekly on music, sports and art (surfing and live entertainment are highlighted, dude). *Lahaina News* is a small weekly newspaper containing local and West Maui news, columns and lots of advertisements. Fee is 25¢. *Maui News* is the primary Maui newspaper, published Monday through Saturday for 50¢; $1.50 for the larger Sunday edition. This is a great source of local information. The Thursday Scene supplement has entertainment and dining news. (Hint: You can pick up free copies of both the *Lahaina News* and *Scene* from the Lahaina Visitor Center.)

FOR YOUR PROTECTION

Do not leave valuables in your car, even in your trunk. Many rental car companies urge you to *not* lock your car as vandals cause extensive and expensive damage breaking the locks. Many companies also warn not to drive on certain roads (Ulupalakua to Hana and the unpaved portion of Highway 34) unless you are willing to accept liability for all damages.

WEBSITES FOR VISITORS As cyberspace continues to boom, this is an ever-growing category for guidebooks. I have intermingled some websites and e-mail addresses throughout the text as space allows. If there is no e-mail address, you can probably contact them through their websites. Following are some general websites that might be of interest to you. These will have links to assist you with other information. One that I know will be helpful is www.infomaui.com, a website directory with detailed descriptions and over 500 links to Maui web pages. It's kind of an online guidebook that includes Things To Do, Places to See, Shopping, and an interactive Q&A section.

Concierge Connection is an excellent resource and offers complimentary advice, information and recommendations on all aspects of your Maui vacation. 808-875-9366; 888-875-9366; e-mail: info@mauiconcierge.net; www.mauiconcierge.net.

The Maui Accommodations Guide is a free publication that lists over 130 Maui properties with photos, amenities, maps and rental rates. The guide is updated on a quarterly basis, so the information remains current. You then book directly with the accommodation you choose from the guide. To receive a free Maui Accommodations Guide, visit www.mauiaccommodationsguide.com or call 800-221-6118.

Here are some helpful Maui-related websites:
Maui Visitors Bureau: www.visitmaui.com
Maui On-Line: www.mauionline.com
Maui Net: www.maui.net
Tom Barefoot's Tours: www.tombarefoot.com
AskaboutMaui: www.askaboutmaui.com
Jon's Maui Info: www.Mauihawaii.org
Activity Owners Association of Hawai'i: www.maui.org

INTERNET ACCESS Looking to get connected while on Maui? There are many "internet cafes" on Maui, offering internet access. Rates vary, so check around. Here are a few locations. *West Side*: **Buns of Maui**, located at Old Lahaina Center (the Front Street side of the center), currently offers internet services at the rate of 8 cents a minute (the lowest rate I know of on the island). Open Monday thru Friday 7:30 a.m. to 5:30 p.m.; Saturday and Sunday 8 a.m. to 2 p.m.. **Maui Swiss Café**, located between Burger King and Wharf Center in Lahaina (10 to 15¢/minute). **Jungle Joose Internet Center** at the Wharf Center (10¢/minute). **Aloha Internet Center**, 900 Front Street, Lahaina Center (a complete internet center, including computer sales and service). *South Side*: **Cyberbean Internet Café** at 1881 South Kihei Road by Foodland (20¢/minute). **Hale Imua Internet** shop at 2463 South Kihei Road near Denny's Restaurant. *Central*: **Hale Imua** on Main Street in Wailuku. **Café Marc Aurel** on North Market Street in Wailuku. *Hana Highway:* **Livewire Cafe** in Paia (15¢/minute).

Most of the major hotels and resorts now offer in-room internet access (many with free high-speed service and Wi-Fi hot spots on property). Others have business centers that are available for guests, and some of these also allow non-guest use.

Rates can really run away with you, if you don't pay attention. Some places charge a minimum and a maximum per hour, but others charge as much as 25¢/minute . . . which adds up to $15 an hour!

Medical Information

EMERGENCIES There are several clinics around the island that take emergencies or walk-in patients. Your condominium or hotel desk can provide you with recommendations nearby, or check the phone book. **Kaiser Permanente Medical Care Facilities** are located in Wailuku (808-243-6000), Lahaina (808-669-6900) and Kihei (808-891-3000). On Maui's west side **Doctors on Call** (Hyatt, Westin or Ritz-Carlton: 808-667-7676) and **Dr. Ben Azman** (Whalers Village: 808-667-9721) all specialize in visitor care. See "Helpful Phone Numbers" at the end of the chapter for more numbers. Calling 911 will put you in contact with local fire, police and ambulances.

Hazards

SUN SAFETY The sun's rays are stronger in Hawai'i than on the mainland, so a few basic guidelines will ensure that you return home with a tan, not a burn. Use a good lotion with a sunscreen, reapply after swimming and don't forget your lips and your scalp where your hair parts. (That area is often overlooked and can produce a painful burn on the top of your head.) Be sure to moisturize after a day in the sun and wear a hat to protect your face. Exercise self-control and stay out a limited time the first few days, remembering that a gradual tan will last longer. It is best to avoid being out between the hours of noon and three when it is the hottest. Be cautious of overcast days when it is very easy to become burned unknowingly. Don't forget that the ocean acts as a reflector and time spent in it equals time spent on the beach.

NATURAL DISASTERS All of the Hawaiian islands are susceptible to hurricanes, tsunamis (tidal waves), flash floods and occasional earthquakes. Fortunately, with the exception of earthquakes—which can occur unexpectedly but so far have tended to be relatively minor in Hawai'i, we usually have some type of prior warning before an impending disaster. Flash floods can result from heavy rains, and often the news service will post "Flash Flood Warnings" for certain areas. If you are camping or traveling through wilderness areas, streams, valleys or flood-prone regions during heavy rainstorms, be very alert for possible flash flooding.

Hurricane season in Hawai'i is generally June through November, when hurricane storms are active in the Pacific. There are usually several days of warning prior to a hurricane drawing close to the islands, allowing visitors and residents to make the necessary preparations.

A tsunami is a "tidal wave" produced by an undersea earthquake, volcanic eruption or landslide. Tsunamis are usually generated along the coasts of South America, the Aleutian Islands, the Kamchatka Peninsula or Japan and travel through the ocean at 400 to 500 miles an hour. It takes at least four-and-a-half hours for a tsunami to reach the Hawaiian Islands, unless it is caused by an earthquake on the Big Island—in which case less than 30 minutes warning is likely. A 24-hour Tsunami Warning System was established in Hawai'i in 1946. When the possibility exists of a tsunami reaching Hawaiian waters, the public is informed by the sound of signal sirens. This particular signal is a steady one-minute siren, followed by one minute of silence, repeating as long as necessary.

What do you do if you hear the siren? Immediately turn on a TV or radio; all stations will carry CIV-Alert emergency information and instructions, including the arrival time of the first waves. Move quickly out of low-lying coastal areas that are subject to possible inundation.

The warning sirens are tested throughout the state on the first working Monday of every month at noon, so don't be alarmed when you hear the siren blare. The test lasts only a few minutes and CIV-Alert announces on all stations that the test is underway. Since 1813, there have been 112 tsunamis observed in Hawai'i, with only 16 causing significant damage.

Tsunamis may also be generated by local volcanic earthquakes. In the last 100 years there have been only six, with the last one, November 29, 1975, affecting the southeast coast of the Big Island. The Hawaiian Civil Defense has placed earthquake sensors on all the islands and, if a violent local earthquake occurs, an urgent tsunami warning will be broadcast and the tsunami sirens will sound. A locally generated tsunami will reach the other islands very quickly. Therefore, there may not be time for an attention alert signal to sound. Any violent earthquake that causes you to fall or hold onto something to prevent falling is an urgent warning, and you should immediately evacuate beaches and coastal low-lying areas.

Hawai'i's civil defense agencies have provided Disaster Preparedness Info in the front section of Maui's phone books for easy reference. In addition, your hotel or condo should be able to provide you with the latest information on any advisories or alerts posted by the Pacific Tsunami Warning Center, the National Weather Service or Civil Defense.

Getting There

Arrival and departure tips: During your flight to Hawai'i, the airline staff will provide you with a two-sided visitor information sheet. One side is used by the Hawai'i Visitors Bureau to track the number of visitors and their island destinations. The other side is where you must report any animals, fruits, vegetables or plants that will need to be inspected upon arrival in Honolulu. (Law requires filling out this portion of the form.)

AIRLINE INFORMATION

Good prices on major air carriers can generally be arranged through a reputable travel agent who can often secure air or air-with-car/hotel packages at good prices by volume purchasing. Prices can vary considerably so comparison-shopping is a wise idea. It is good to be an informed traveler, so do some research yourself by checking a variety of travel websites, even if you are dealing directly with a travel agent or an airline. There are a number of excellent websites offering travel arrangements and often discounted travel prices. A few of these are: www.orbitz.com; www.travelocity.com; www.expedia.com; www.priceline.com and www.cheaptickets.com. Keep in mind that these websites don't necessarily post all airline schedules. If you don't care what carrier you travel on and are flexible with your travel plans, check out www.hotwire.com. With Hotwire, you aren't advised of your air carrier or travel time until you have booked, so you have to like surprises.

TRAVEL WHOLESALERS

Sun Trips "Airfare Only" is available through Sun Trips (on their Sun Country Charters). These prices are incredibly good values, but on the downside you have to depart from their West Coast gateway, Oakland. Sun Trips has now been serving Hawai'i-bound vacationers for several years. Currently they are using Oakland, California, as their gateway to the Pacific. This means that if you live in California you might get a great deal, but the rest of you have to make your own travel arrangements to the Oakland airport. Fly/drive, air only and combination packages including rental cars are available for O'ahu, Maui, Kaua'i and the Big Island. Alamo Rent a Car handles the ground transportation. Aloha Airlines is the carrier for the interisland flights. Single- or multiple-island packages are available. For airfare only, rates are staggered based on the day of the week you depart and the time of the year. Call for free catalog or request one online. 800-SUN-TRIPS; www.suntrips.com.

Creative Leisure High-end accommodations with packages that include airfare and car if you choose. On Maui they currently have packages with nearly all of the top luxury resorts; they also have many condominium packages available. On Lana'i, they have packages for Manele Bay Hotel and The Lodge at Koele. They work in association with United Airlines. 800-413-1000; www.creativeleisure.com.

Pleasant Hawaiian Holidays Founded in 1959 as Pleasant Travel Service in Point Pleasant, New Jersey, Edward Hogan and his company have grown and expanded to provide a range of airfare, air only and land only options. Their non-stop scheduled "Air Cruise" is available from Los Angeles and San Francisco to Honolulu and Maui. They can also arrange for rental cars and they work with many properties on Maui and offer some of the best air/land packages to be found. Check their "Last Minute Desk" for those of you trying to find space on short notice. 800-242-9244; www.pleasantholidays.com.

Remember: Be sure to check all the air carriers, as well as their websites, which might have internet-only specials. Experience has taught me that a little legwork pays off. Sometimes the best deals are through one of these wholesale agencies, but if you have the time, it's worth a little investigation. I have discovered that United Airlines may offer promotional specials that far and away beat these packages and even the charters. Always make sure you let the airline know if

AGRICULTURAL INSPECTION

When you arrive at the airport to check in for your return flight to the mainland, your checked baggage must go through an agricultural inspection. If you are checking baggage at the Kahului airport, you need to complete the agricultural inspection at the main entrance of the airport before proceeding to your airline ticketing counter to check in. Once you've checked in your inspected bags and you proceed to the gates, you may (depending on what aircraft you are on and whether or not it goes via Honolulu) go through another agricultural screening for your carry-on bags.

If you are connecting through Honolulu from the interisland terminal, you'll pass through another agricultural inspection center for your carry-ons as you enter the main terminal of the Honolulu Airport. (In case this is your first trip, the screening areas look like regular airport baggage security screeners.) You'll be amazed to see the apples, oranges and other fruits stacked up at the agricultural inspection centers. Even though they may have originally come from the mainland U.S., the fruits will not pass inspection to get back there. Pre-inspected Maui onions, pineapples and protea, anthurium starts, ti plants and orchids are allowed. Fruit and flowers can be purchased in inspected and sealed cartons from reputable island retailers. Generally, you will not have trouble with most flowers and/or leis. But don't plan on tucking an apple into your purse for a snack on-board. It will end up in the pile at the screening area. If you are unsure of what is transportable, contact the U.S. Department of Agricultural at 808-877-8757 or 808-877-5261.

you are flexible on your arrival and departure days. You may be able to squeeze into some price-cut promotional window that offers an even better value for your flight dollar.

FLIGHTS TO THE ISLANDS

Most of the airlines have their own websites. These are especially handy for getting an idea of flight schedules and prices; you can even book your reservation and often obtain a discounted internet-only fare. The major American carriers that fly from the mainland to the Honolulu International Airport on O'ahu or to Kahului Airport on Maui are:

Aloha Airlines—800-367-5250; 808-484-1111; www.alohaairlines.com.

American Airlines—800-433-7300; 808-833-7600 in Honolulu; 808-244-5522 on Maui; www.aa.com.

Air Canada—From Vancouver, B.C. www.aircanada.com.

Continental Airlines—800-525-0280; 800-523-3273; www.continental.com.

Delta Air Lines—800-221-1212; flight information 800-325-1999; www.delta.com.

Hawaiian Airlines—800-367-5320; in Honolulu 808-838-1555; www.hawaiianair.com.

Northwest Airlines—800-225-2525; 808-955-2255; www.nwa.com.

United Airlines—United has more flights to Hawai'i from more U.S. cities than any other airline. Reservations 800-241-6522; flight information 800-824-6200; www.ual.com or www.united.com.

INTERISLAND FLIGHTS

Hawai'i is unique in that its intrastate roads are actually water or sky. For your travel by sky, there are a few interisland carriers that operate between Honolulu and Maui.

The flight time from O'ahu to Kahului on Maui is less than 30 minutes. If you are connecting in Honolulu, traveling to/from the main carrier and the interisland terminal can be rather exhausting and confusing. It's easiest to take the airport's Wiki Wiki shuttle bus to and from the interisland terminal.

If you are traveling light and have only brought carry-on luggage with you, be advised that what is carry-on for the major airlines may be too large to be carry-on for the interisland or commuter carriers. Knowing this in advance may help you in packing your check-in and carry-on bags accordingly.

Most visitors arrive at the **Kahului Airport** via non-stop or interisland flights. The Kahului Airport is convenient with accessible park-

AIRLINE TIPS

The direct flights available on United, Delta and American Airlines save time and energy by avoiding the otherwise necessary stopover on O'ahu. Travel agents schedule at least an hour and a half between arrival on O'ahu and departure for Maui to account for any delays, baggage transfers and the time required to reach the interisland terminal. If you do arrive early, check with the interisland carrier. Very often you can get an earlier flight that will arrive on Maui in time to get your car, and maybe some groceries, before returning to pick up your luggage when it arrives on your scheduled flight.

ing, an on-site rental car area and even a restaurant that offers runway views (although the walk from the United Airlines gate to the baggage claim area can be quite a distance). From the airport it is only a 20- to 30-minute drive to the Kihei–Wailea–Makena areas, but a 45- to 60-minute drive to the Ka'anapali/Kapalua areas. If your destination is West Maui from O'ahu, Kaua'i or Hawai'i, it might be more convenient to fly into the **Kapalua West Maui Airport**. This small, uncrowded airport is serviced by Island Air.

INTERISLAND CARRIERS

Aloha Airlines—Aloha offers daily non-stop service between Maui and Honolulu, with connecting flights through Honolulu to Kauai and the Big Island. They fly over 1,200 flights weekly with their fleet of 17 Boeing 737s. When making your reservations, you might inquire about any special promotions, AAA membership discounts, AARP discounts or passes. Current rates are $69 to $89 one-way to Honolulu, with an additional $10 fee to connect through to another island. 800-367-5250; in Honolulu 808-484-1111; on Maui 808-244-9071; www.alohaairlines.com.

Island Air—Island Air is a commuter airline that specializes in serving Hawai'i's smaller community and resort destinations. Their fleet consists of twin-engine De Havilland Dash 6 Twin Otters (turboprop) aircraft and 37 passenger DH Dash 8s. They are currently the only airline that goes in and out of the Kapalua West Maui Airport or to the islands of Lana'i and Moloka'i. From Maui, Island Air offers non-stop flights to Honolulu, Hilo, Kona and Moloka'i. Flights to Lana'i are available via Honolulu. If you don't mind the smaller aircraft, Island Air does offer some convenient benefits over Aloha and Hawaiian in that it flies in and out of the commuter terminals where there are fewer people, shorter lines and a much faster security process. In Hawai'i 800-652-6541; on the mainland 800-323-3345; in Honolulu 808-484-2222; www.islandair.com.

Hawaiian Airlines—Hawaiian flies Boeing/McDonnell Douglas DC9s between Honolulu and Maui, Kauai and the Big Island. Cost is currently $63 to $103 for a one-way coach class ticket. Mainland 800-882-8811; Maui 808-872-4400; www.hawaiianair.com.

Pacific Wings—Pacific Wings offers scheduled flights and charter service between Kahului and Hana (Maui), Honolulu (Oahu), Hilo, Kona and Kamuela (Big Island) in their eight-passenger, twin-engine Cessna 402C. 888-575-4546; 808-873-0877; e-mail: info@pacificwings.com; www.pacificwings.com.

Currently there is no regularly scheduled ocean transportation for passengers between the Hawaiian Islands other than a commuter ferry service that runs between Maui and Lana'i and Maui and Moloka'i. There is talk of a "super ferry" transportation system starting up between the islands, but the plans are not yet definite and may take years to implement. Meanwhile, we are dependent on our local air carriers.

Cruise Lines

Norwegian Cruise Lines (NCL) has two beautiful ships that offer luxury cruises in the Hawaiian islands, with a third ship—the *Pride of America*—that started sailing Hawaiian waters in June 2005. The cruise line began service in the islands in 2001.

Currently, a 7-day cruise of the islands is offered year-round on NCL's *Pride of Aloha*, which visits interesting island ports and makes a variety of port excursions. The *Norwegian Wind* offers longer 10- and 11-day cruises of Hawai'i and Fanning Island (which requires a passport). NCL's newest ship, *Pride of America*, will begin sailing 7-day roundtrip island cruises from Honolulu on July 23, 2005.

The majority of the NCL crewmembers are from Hawai'i, giving you a genuine taste of the "aloha spirit" while you cruise in luxury. This is a fabulous way to see Hawai'i, and the ships are planning longer days in port (with less time at sea) so passengers can do more exploration of the islands.

Pre- and post-cruise packages, air add-ons and Hawaiian shore excursions are available. For information on NCL's ships, itineraries and prices, contact your travel agent or go online to Norwegian Cruise Lines at www.ncl.com; 800-327-7030 from the U.S. and Canada.

Getting Around

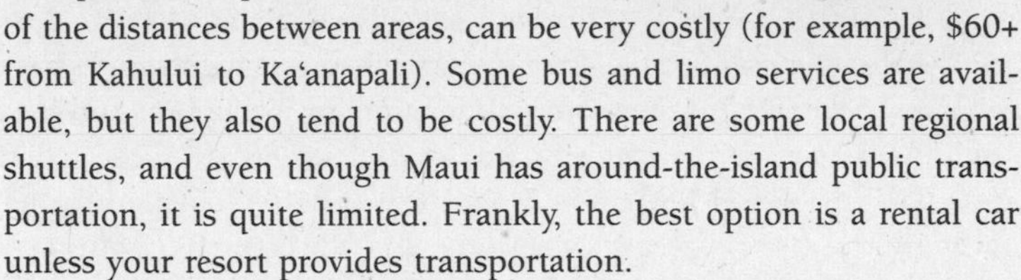

FROM THE AIRPORT After arriving at the Kahului Airport, there are a few transportation options. Taxicabs, because of the distances between areas, can be very costly (for example, $60+ from Kahului to Ka'anapali). Some bus and limo services are available, but they also tend to be costly. There are some local regional shuttles, and even though Maui has around-the-island public transportation, it is quite limited. Frankly, the best option is a rental car unless your resort provides transportation.

PUBLIC TRANSPORTATION For years, Maui offered no public transit system, but now I am happy to report some Maui Mass Transit options. MEO (Maui Economic Opportunity, Inc.) and Roberts Tours have teamed together to offer island transportation on both sides of the island.

MEO is more of a shuttle, a free county bus service (although donations are appreciated) that travels within the Kahului–Wailuku area, making stops at shopping areas, grocery stores, theaters, post offices and government buildings. **Roberts** is a privately owned service that is linked with MEO, but primarily travels between South and West Maui (from The Shops at Wailea to the Lahaina Wharf Cinema Center), stopping at the condominiums, hotels and shopping areas in between. It connects with the MEO system at Ma'alaea. (Akina Tours, another private company, operates a shuttle service between The Wharf Cinema Center and Ka'anapali.)

Point-to-point Roberts fares run from $1 to $3 one way, depending on distance. Weekly, monthly and senior passes are available. The service runs every day but Sunday. To find out more detailed information or get a bus schedule, contact www.co.maui.hi.us/bus. (As this is a relatively new service, the buses sometimes run on Maui time, so be sure to check connecting schedules and allow plenty of time. And they are still working on coordinating benches and signs at the bus stops, so in the meantime don't be shy about flagging down an approaching bus.)

LIMOUSINE SERVICES Travel in style with one of the limousine services. Rates are competitive: $79 and up per hour plus tax and gratuity, minimum two hours. (They also do tours and weddings.) **Arthur's Limousine Service** currently commutes to most resorts from the Kahului airport (877-408-9559, 808-871-5555, fax 808-877-3333). Also try **Carey Limousine Hawaii** (aka Town & Country Limousine) 808-572-3400, 888-563-2888, **Star Maui Limousine** 808-875-6900, **Wailea Limousine** 808-875-4114, **Kapalua Executive Limousine** 808-669-2300 or **ABC Rider/Coastline Limousine** 808-875-6389.

TAXIS/SHUTTLES For cab service, try **Alii Cab** 808-661-3688 or **Executive Cab** 808-667-7770. **Airport/SpeediShuttle** offers door-to-door airport service that fits your schedule. Individual fares—from $20 (Kihei) to $38 (Ka'anapali)—are far less expensive than a cab and an even better deal if there are two or more of you. (The more people in the shuttle, the less you pay.) Mainland 800-977-2605; 808-661-6667 or 808-875-8070 on Maui; or just press #65 from the airport courtesy phone board; www.speedishuttle.com. (In addition to airport service, they also offer transportation to or from anywhere on the island.)

FREE SHUTTLES The free Ka'anapali **Trolley** services Ka'anapali hotels, golf courses and Whalers Village shopping center. Pick up times are about every 20 minutes, except for lunch and dinner breaks for the driver. You can pick up a schedule at your Ka'anapali hotel. The Kapalua Resort has a shuttle running 6 a.m. to 11 p.m. between the condos, golf courses, restaurants and the Kapalua hotels. Call your hotel's front desk to request information.

There is a free shuttle in Wailea that offers transportation between hotels, restaurants and shops. Check with the front desk or concierge at the property where you stay.

RENTAL CARS AND TRUCKS It has been said that Maui has more rental cars per mile of road than anywhere else in the nation. This is not surprising when you realize that Maui has a population of well over 100,000, more than two million visitors per year and limited mass transit. So, given the status of public transportation on Maui, a rental car is still the best bet—sometimes the only way to get around the island and, for your dollar, a very good buy.

A choice of more than 20 car rental companies offers luxury or economy and new or used models. Some are local island operators, others are nation-wide chains, but all are very competitive. The rates vary, not only between high and low season, but also from week to weekend and even day to day. The best values are during price wars, or super summer discount specials. Prices vary as much within the same company as they do between companies and are approximated as follows: Vans, Jeeps and Convertibles are all in the high-end range from $50 to $90, Full-size $35 to $50, Mid-size $30 to $45, Compacts $25 to $40. The least expensive choice is a late-model compact or economy. Often these cars are only two to three years old and in very good condition. Also available from specialty car rental agencies are a variety of luxury cars. Vans are available from a number of agencies, but camping in them is not allowed.

Rental car discounts are few and far between. You might be able to use some airline award coupons, but they are often very restrictive. If you are a member of AAA you can receive a discount with some rental companies. Check with Aloha or Hawaiian Airlines for some interisland fly and drive packages.

Many of the rental companies have booths next to the baggage claim area at the Kahului Airport. There is a free phone for the rental agencies that don't have an airport booth or regular shuttle service so you can call for pick up. A few agencies will take your flight information when your car reservation is made and will meet you and your luggage at the airport with your car.

The policies of all the rental car agencies are basically the same. Most require the driver to be a minimum of 21 to 25 years of age. And those that do allow rentals to the under-25 group will make you pay extra. Nearly all require a major credit card. All feature unlimited mileage with you buying the gas (nearing $3 per gallon at press time) so check for "discount days" in Wailuku/Kahului. Be sure to fill up before you return your car; the rental companies charge a lot more to do it for you.

Insurance is an option you may wish to purchase and can run an additional $15 to $25 a day. A few agencies will require insurance for those under 25. Most of the car rental agencies strongly encourage you buy the optional collision damage waiver (CDW), which provides coverage for most cars in case of loss or damage. I suggest you check with your own insurance company before you leave to verify exactly what your policy covers. Some credit cards now provide CDW coverage for rental cars if you use that credit card to charge your rental fees. This does not include liability insurance, so you need to check to see if your own policy will cover you for liability in a rental car. Add to the rental price a 4 percent sales tax and a $2 per day highway road tax.

A few of Maui's roadways are rough and rugged. The rental agencies recommend that cars not traverse these areas (shown on the map they distribute) and that if these roads are attempted, you are responsible for any damage. Some don't allow driving to Haleakala because drivers often ride the brakes down the steep road. In addition to the rental agency's *Maui Drive Guide* magazine and maps, you can pick up a free *Maui Driving Map* at most brochure racks. The front section of the phone book also has some excellent detailed street maps.

See "Traveling with Children" earlier in this chapter for information on car seats for kids.

RENTAL CAR LISTINGS *Note:* Dollar is the only car rental company on the island of Lana'i. For more information, see Chapter 7.

Adventures Rent a Jeep has both new and used Jeep Wranglers and Cherokees. 800-701-5337; 808-877-6626; e-mail: mauijeeps@shaka.com; www.mauijeep.com

Alamo, 800-327-9633; Kahului 808-871-6235; Lahaina 808-661-7181; www.goalamo.com (usually offering some excellent on-line discounts)

Avis, 800-831-2847, Kahului 808-871-7575, Ka'anapali 808-661-4588, Kihei 808-874-4077, Wailea 808-879-7601; www.avis.com

Budget, 800-527-0700, Ka'anapali 808-661-8721, Wailea 808-874-2831, Kahului 808-871-8811; www.budget.com

Dollar, 800-800-4000, Kahului 808-877-2731, Ka'anapali 808-667-2651, Interisland 800-342-7398; www.dollar.com

Enterprise, 800-736-8222, Kahului 808-871-1511, Lahaina-Ka'anapali 808-661-8804; www.enterprise.com

Hertz, 800-654-3011, Kahului 808-877-5167, Westin 808-667-5381, Kapalua Villas 808-669-8088

Hummer Rentals, 808-873-8448; www.hummtours.com

Kihei Rent-a-car, 800-251-5288, Kihei 808-879-7257; www.kiheirentacar.com

National, 888-868-6207, Kahului 808-871-8851; www.national.com

Thrifty Car Rental, 800-847-4389, Kahului 808-871-2860; www.thrifty.com

Word of Mouth Rent a Used-Car, 800-533-5929, Kahului 808-877-2436; e-mail: word@maui.net; www.mauirentacar.com

EXOTIC CAR AND MOTORCYCLE RENTALS There is no helmet requirement for motorcycles, but you do need to show a valid motorcycle endorsement from your state of residence. (You must be 21 to rent a motorcycle or jeep; 25 to rent an exotic car. Scooter rentals: 18 with driver's license *and* experience)

Aloha Toy Store rents Harley-Davidsons, exotic cars, jeeps, mopeds and bicycles. 640 Front Street, 808-662-0888; Fairway Shops in Ka'anapali, 808-661-9000; www.alohatoystore.com.

Hawaiian Riders rents Harley-Davidsons as well as mopeds, bikes, jeeps and exotic cars. Lahaina/Ka'anapali 808-662-4386 or Kihei/Wailea 808-891-0889; www.hawaiianriders.com.

Hula Hogs Motorcycle Rentals offers Harley-Davidson and other motorcycles for daily or weekly rentals. Although there is no helmet law in the state of Hawaii, Hula Hogs offers helmets, raingear and accessories at no charge. Hotel and airport shuttle provided. Group rates available. Currently the only company that lets you bike to Hana. 1279 South Kihei Road; 808-875-7433; 877-464-7433 for reservations; www.hulahogs.com.

Island Riders has Harleys and exotic cars for rent. Kihei 808-874-0311, Lahaina 808-661-9966; 800-529-2925; www.islandriders.com.

Grocery Shopping

Grocery store prices may be one of the biggest surprises of your trip. While there are some locally grown foods and dairies, most of the products must be flown or shipped to the islands, so prices are generally higher than on the mainland. The local folks can shop the advertisements and use the coupons, but it isn't so easy when traveling.

Longs Drug Stores carry some food items as do **Big Kmart, Wal-Mart** and **Costco** (all in Kahului). Many tourists pull into Costco, conveniently located just outside the airport, and stock up on their supplies for the week. So be sure to pack your Costco card.

The three major grocery stores in Kahului are **Foodland**, **Safeway** and **Star Market**.

In Lahaina you can choose between the **Foodland** at Old Lahaina Center and the **Safeway** (open 24 hours) at Lahaina Cannery Mall. There is a **Star Market** in Honokowai, and Napili has a smallish grocery store, **Napili Market**.

In Kihei, there is a **Foodland** and a **Star Market**. On the Pi'ilani Highway in Kihei you'll find a 24-hour **Safeway**. It is currently the largest Safeway in the state. You'll find the same variety as your hometown store and the prices are better than at the small grocery outlets.

FARM FRESH

There are a number of small "farmer's markets" that take place on Maui throughout the week, offering fresh produce and flowers. Dates, locations and times tend to change, so check the local paper for current listings of farmer's markets in your area. Currently in *Kahului/Wailuku*, the **Aloha Maui Produce Market** takes place Tuesday and Friday mornings at Maui Mall. The **Ohana Farmer's and Crafter's Market** is from 6:30 a.m. to 1 p.m. Wednesday at the Kahului Shopping Center and 8 a.m. to 4 p.m. Friday at Queen Ka'ahumanu Shopping Center. The **Aloha Friday Farmer's Market** takes place every Friday from 7 a.m. to 1 p.m. at Maui Community College, outside the Paina Culinary Arts Building. In *Kihei*, the **Farmer's Market of Maui** takes place Monday, Wednesday and Friday, 1:30 to 5:30 p.m. at Suda's Store on South Kihei Road. In *West Maui*, the **Farmer's Market of Maui** is Monday, Wednesday and Friday, 7 to 11 a.m. across from Honokowai Park in the Hawaiian Moons parking lot. *Upcountry*, a farmer's market takes place every Saturday beginning at 6 a.m. at the Eddie Tam Gym in Makawao.

In Hana there is **Hasegawa's** and the **Hana Ranch Store**, both open limited hours.

The **Maui Swap Meet**, held Saturday mornings in Kahului, has some good food values, although not always a very diverse selection. Usually you can pick up papayas, pineapple and coconuts as well as some vegetable items. Lots of flowers here, too. Small admission fee charged for adults.

Local grocery shopping, away from the familiar Safeways of the world, can be a bit adventuresome. In addition to the regular food staples, they often have deli sections that feature local favorites and plate lunches. **Takamiya's** at 359 North Market Street in Wailuku has a huge deli section with perhaps more than 50 cooked foods and salads as well as very fresh meats. **Ooka** is a landmark local grocery in Wailuku, slated to close sometime in 2005 after a long, rich history. If you're lucky enough to experience it before it goes, you'll notice that the packed parking lot and crowded aisles are a testament to its popularity and low prices. Besides the usual sundry items, they have a fascinating and unusual array of foods. How about a tasty fresh pig ear, pig blood, tripe, calf hoof or tongue? In the seafood aisle check out the opihi, cuttlefish, *tobiko*, *lomi* salmon, a great variety of ahi *poke* (tuna), and whole or filets of fresh island fish like catfish or *onaga*. They even have some reef fish, such as parrot fish. Definitely an adventure.

For those looking for health foods there's **Hawaiian Moons** in Kihei and **Down to Earth** (with the largest selection) in Kahului. Each has a hot food buffet and salad bar, in addition to groceries.

How about no grocery shopping and no dining out? Here is an alternative: **Dish Simple**, located at 150 Hana Highway (next to 24 Hour Fitness) offers prepared meals. Designed for busy Maui residents who don't have time to cook, it's a great alternative for visitors in condos that have cooking facilities. Dish offers 12 meals for $250 or individual meals for $22 that will serve 4 to 6 people. The "half dish" program includes 12 meals for $145 or individual meals at $13 each, serving 2 to 3 people. Call ahead to order your meals, then stop by and pick 'em up. Keep them frozen, then just follow the simple cooking directions. Located near the Kahului Airport. 808-877-1414; www.dishsimple.com.

Calendar of Annual Events

The following list is by no means a complete calendar of events on Maui, but it's a sampling. For the exact dates of many of these events, visit the Maui Visitors Bureau website at www.visitmaui.com, or contact the MVB at P.O. Box 580, Wailuku, HI 96793. Check the local papers for dates of additional events. Another good Maui calendar resource is at www.calendarmaui.com.

January

Professional surfing—Honolua Bay

Hula Bowl—Wailuku War Memorial Complex

Mercedes Championships—PGA Tour—Kapalua

Maui Film Festival First Light Academy Screenings—www.mauifilmfestival.com

February

Chinese New Year celebrations—various locations

Whale Fest—Locations around the island

March

Ocean Arts Festival—Lahaina Town and West Maui

Whale Regatta/Whale Day celebrations—Kihei

Prince Kuhio Day (March 26)—State holiday

East Maui Taro Festival—Entertainment, exhibits and demonstrations in Hana

St. Patrick's Day celebrations

April

"Art Maui"—Free juried show with works by island artists at Hui No'eau Visual Arts Center

Earth Day festivities

Banyan Tree Birthday Party—Lahaina

"Celebration of the Arts"—Cultural festival at the Ritz-Carlton, Kapalua

Ulupalakua Thing—Agricultural trade show at Ulupalakua Ranch/Tedeschi Winery with Maui product booths, entertainment, cooking contests, chef's demonstrations and lots of free samples

Annual Maui Scholastic Surf Championships—Ho'okipa Beach

May

Lei Day—Celebrations across the island (check with hotels for their events)

Wailea Open Tennis Championships—Wailea

Pineapple Jam—Two-day festival on Lana'i with arts, crafts, entertainment, cooking contests and samplings

Seabury Hall annual craft fair—Held in Makawao the Saturday prior to Mother's Day

Hard Rock Cafe World Cup of Windsurfing—Ho'okipa Beach Park

Starbucks Molokai Challenge—One-person kayak and canoe race

International Festival of Canoes—Two-week cultural event in Lahaina and West Maui

June

Obon Season (late June through August)—Bon Odori festivals are held at the many Buddhist temples around the island. They are announced in the local newspapers and the public is invited

King Kamehameha Day Celebration—Front Street parade with *pa'u* riders and floral floats

Maui Upcountry Fair—Eddie Tam Center, Makawao

Maui Film Festival—Wailea

King's Trail Triathlon—Maui Prince, Makena

Ki Hoalu Slack Key Guitar Festival—Maui Arts & Cultural Center, Kahului

July

Fourth of July celebrations with **fireworks**—various locations

4th of July Rodeo & Parade—Makawao

Kapalua Wine and Food Festival—A weekend of wine seminars and tastings, including a couple of great food festivals: the Grand Tasting and the Seafood Festival

Pineapple Festival—Lana'i

Victoria, B.C. to Maui Yacht Race—Lahaina Yacht Club

August

"Maui Calls"—Celebration of Hawai'i's "boat days" at the Maui Arts & Cultural Center

Tahiti Fete—War Memorial gym, Wailuku

Maui Onion Festival—Whalers Village, Ka'anapali

August 21 is **Admissions Day**—State holiday

Maui Writers Conference—Wailea

September

Maui Marathon—From Kahului to Lahaina

Aloha Festivals—Events stretch into October

Garden Party—Maui Academy of Performing Arts, Wailuku

"Taste of Lahaina"—Food festival with over 30 participating restaurants

LifeFest Kapalua—Kapalua Resort

Maui Chefs Present—Gala food festival

October

Just Desserts—Fundraiser for Maui Humane Society

Maui County Fair—Wailuku War Memorial Complex

Molokai Hoe Canoe Race

Halloween—Major parade and Halloween festivities in Lahaina

Xterra World Championship—Makena Resort

Terry Fox Run/Walk—Four Seasons Resort, Wailea

November

EA SPORTS Maui Invitational Basketball Tournament—Lahaina Civic Center

Christmas House—Hui No'eau, near Makawao, Christmas craft fair featuring pottery, wreaths and other holiday artwork and gifts

Hula O Na Keiki—Children's hula festival

Friendly Isle Ultra Marathon—Moloka'i

December

Many **Christmas craft fairs** across the island
Christmas Treelighting Ceremony—The Ritz-Carlton, Kapalua
Treelighting—Historic Banyan Tree, Lahaina

Weather

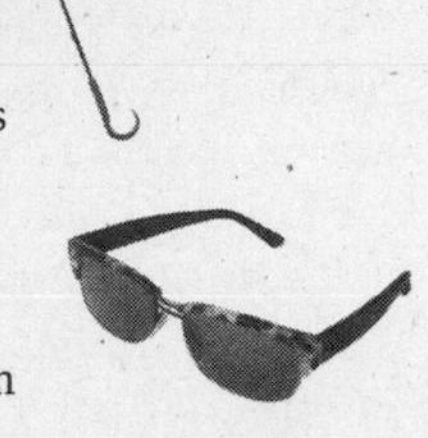

When thinking of Hawai'i, and especially Maui, one visualizes bright sunny days cooled by refreshing trade winds, and this is the weather at least 300 days a year. But what about the other 65 days? Most aren't really bad—just not perfect. Although there are only two seasons, summer and winter, temperatures remain quite constant.

Average Highs and Lows

January	80°F/64°F	July	86°F/70°F
February	79°F/64°F	August	87°F/71°F
March	80°F/64°F	September	87°F/70°F
April	82°F/66°F	October	86°F/69°F
May	84°F/67°F	November	83°F/68°F
June	86°F/69°F	December	80°F/66°F

Spring and winter: Mid-October through April, 75 to 80 degrees during the day, 60 to 70 degrees at night. Trade winds are erratic, ranging from calm to vigorous. Kona winds are more frequent, causing widespread cloudiness, rain showers, mugginess and even an occasional thunderstorm. Eleven hours of daylight.

Summer and fall: May to mid-October, 80 to 85 degrees during the day, 70 to 80 degrees at night. Trade winds are more consistent, keeping the temperatures tolerable. When the trades stop, however, the weather becomes hot and sticky. Kona winds are less frequent. Thirteen hours of daylight.

Summer-type wear is suitable year round. However, a warm sweater or lightweight jacket is a good idea for evenings and trips to cooler spots like Haleakala. If you are curious about the types of weather you may encounter, or are confused by some of the terms you hear, read on. For further reference consult *Weather in Hawaiian Waters*, by Paul Haraguchi, available at island bookstores.

Trade Winds Hawai'i's weather is greatly affected by the prevailing northeast trade winds, which are an almost constant wind from the northeast through the east and are caused by the Pacific anticyclone, a high-pressure area. This high-pressure area is well developed and remains semi-stationary in the summer, causing the trades to remain steady more than 90 percent of the time. Interruptions are much more frequent in the winter when they blow only 40 to 60 percent of the time.

Kona Winds The Kona wind is a stormy, rain-bearing wind blowing from the southwest, basically from the opposite direction of the trades. These conditions are caused by low-pressure areas northwest of the islands. Kona winds strong enough to cause property damage have occurred only twice since 1970. Lighter non-damaging Kona winds are much more common, occurring a few times every winter (November to April).

Kona Weather Windless, hot and humid weather is referred to as Kona weather. The interruption of the normal trade wind pattern brings this on. The trades are replaced by light and variable winds and, although this may occur any time of the year, it is most noticeable during summer when the temperature is generally hotter and more humid, with fewer localized breezes.

Kona Low A Kona low is a slow-moving, meandering, extensive low-pressure area that forms near the islands. This causes continuous rain, with thunderstorms over an extensive area, and lasts for several days. This usually occurs from November through May.

Rain Rainfall can be drastically different from one part of Maui to another. Kihei and Wailea are almost deserts, with minimal rain each year. Lahaina tends to receive fewer showers than Napili and Kapalua to the north. And, of course, Hana and the northern coastline lead off each month with the highest average rainfall. No wonder the Hana coast is so lush and green. January is the wettest month with Lahaina averaging 3.49 inches, Hana 9.45 and Kahului 4.14. December is not far behind. June typically has the lowest average amount of rainfall per year, with Lahaina getting less than one inch, Kahului only a quarter inch and Hana four inches. (Fortunately for Hana visitors, the rainfall is often at night!) For more weather-related information as well as daily forecasts check out www.hawaiiweather today.com.

Hurricanes Hurricanes (called typhoons when they are west of 180 degrees longitude) have damaged the Hawaiian islands on several occasions. The storms that affect Hawai'i usually originate off Central America or Mexico. Most of the threatening tropical storms weaken before reaching the islands, or pass harmlessly to the west. Their effects are usually minimal, causing only high surf on the eastern and southern shores of some of the islands. At least 21 hurricanes or tropical storms have passed within 300 miles of the islands in the last several years, but most did little or no damage. Hurricane season is considered to be June through November. Hurricanes are given Hawaiian names when they pass within 1,000 miles of the islands.

Hurricane Dot in 1959, Hurricane Iwa in 1982 and Hurricane Iniki in 1992 caused extensive damage. In each case, the island of Kaua'i was hit hardest, with lesser damage to southeast O'ahu and very little damage to Maui, except for the beaches.

Tides The average tidal range is about two feet or less. Tide tables are available daily in the *Maui News* or by calling the marine weather number; 808-877-3477.

Sunrise and Sunset In Hawai'i, day length and the altitude of the noon sun above the horizon do not vary much throughout the year. This is because the temperate regions of the island's low latitude lie within the sub-tropics. The longest day is 13 hours 26 minutes (sunrise 5:53 a.m., sunset 7:18 p.m.) at the end of June, and the shortest day is 10 hours 50 minutes (sunrise 7:09 a.m. and sunset 6:01 p.m.) at the end of December. Daylight for outdoor activities without artificial lighting lasts about 45 minutes past sunset.

Helpful Phone Numbers

The area code for the entire state is (808). Calls anywhere on Maui are considered local calls. If you are calling another island, you must do so by dialing 1-808-plus the phone number, and it is long distance. Note that most resorts charge between 75¢ and $1 for each local call you make and an additional surcharge for long distance.

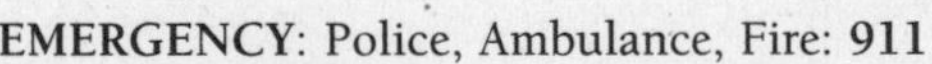

EMERGENCY: Police, Ambulance, Fire: **911**

Police Non-emergency:

Lahaina 808-661-4441
Hana 808-248-8311
Wailuku 808-244-6340
Kihei 808-875-8190

Civil Defense Agency: 808-270-7285
Poison Control (on O'ahu): 800-222-1222
Helpline (suicide & crisis center): 808-753-6879
Red Cross: 808-244-0051
Consumer Protection: 808-984-8244
Directory Assistance:

Local (1) 411
Interisland 808-555-1212
Mainland 1-(area code)-555-1212

Hospital (Maui Memorial):

Information 808-242-2036
Switchboard 808-244-9056

Camping Permits:

State Parks 808-984-8109

County Parks 808-270-7230

Maui Visitors Bureau: 808-244-3530

Time of Day: 808-242-0212

Information—County of Maui (Information & complaint office): 808-270-7866

Haleakala National Park information (recording): 808-572-4400

'Ohe'o Headquarters Ranger Station (10 a.m. to 4 p.m.): 808-248-7375

Weather:

Maui 808-877-5111

Marine (also tides, sunrises, sunsets) 808-877-3477

Recreational Area (Haleakala) 808-871-5054

Check the Aloha Pages in the front of the phone book for various hotline numbers to call for community events, entertainment, etc., on Maui. While the call is free, the companies pay to be included, so information is biased.

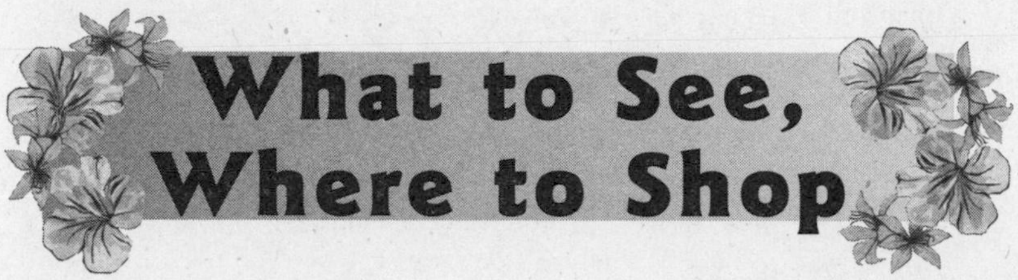

CHAPTER 2

What to See, Where to Shop

Lahaina

No matter where on the island you stay, you should pencil in at least part of a day to tour the historical and cultural aspects of this quaint town and spend some time strolling through shops or enjoying a fine meal.

Lahaina is the bustling tourist center of Maui. There is much to see and do in busy Lahaina Town, which has maintained the aura of more than a century ago when it was the whaling capital of the world. Located about a 30-minute drive from the Kahului Airport (depending on traffic), this coastal port is noted for its Front Street, which is a multiblock strip of shops and restaurants along the waterfront. Lahaina Harbor is filled with boats of varying shapes and sizes, eager to take the visitor aboard for a variety of sea excursions. The word *Lahaina* means "merciless sun," and it does tend to become quite warm, especially in the afternoon, with little relief from the tropical trade winds.

Historical memorabilia abounds in Lahaina. The Lahaina Restoration Foundation has done an admirable job restoring and maintaining many historical landmarks. These are all identified by numbered markers and can be located with the Lahaina Restoration Foundation's free walking tour map of Lahaina, entitled *Lahaina O Mo'olelo*. Look for free copies of this pocketsize guide on corner display racks in Lahaina Town or at the Lahaina Restoration Foundation office located in the historic Baldwin Home, 120 Dickenson Street (808-

661-3262). The Lahaina Town Action Committee (located upstairs in the Old Lahaina Courthouse, 808-667-9175) also offers a free brochure detailing a self-guided walking tour of the **Lahaina Historic Trail**, made up of 62 significant historic locations that have been identified and marked.

The famous **Banyan Tree**—the largest in the state of Hawai'i—is very easy to spot at the south end of Lahaina, adjacent to Pioneer Inn on Front Street. It was planted on April 24, 1873, by Sheriff William Owen Smith, to commemorate the 50th anniversary of Lahaina's first Protestant Christian mission. You may find art shows or other events happening under the cool, shady boughs of this spectacular tree. With its long, heavy limbs, supported by wood braces and 12 solid trunks that have re-rooted themselves over a 200-foot area, visitors find it hard to believe this is all one tree!

The stone ruins of the **Old Fort** can be found harborside near the Banyan Tree. The fort was constructed in the 1830s to protect the missionaries' homes from the whaling ships and the occasional cannonball that would be shot off when the sailors were too rowdy. The fort was later torn down and the coral blocks reused elsewhere. A few blocks were excavated and the corner of the fort was rebuilt as a landmark in 1964.

On the corner near the Pioneer Inn is a plaque marking the site of the **1987 Lahaina Reunion Time Capsule**, which contains newspapers, photos and other memorabilia.

Pioneer Inn is the distinguished green-and-white structure just north of the Banyan Tree. It was a haven for interisland travelers during the early days of the 20th century. Built back in 1901, it managed to survive the dry years of Prohibition, later adding a new wing, center garden and pool area in 1966. Two restaurants operate here and accommodations are available.

The history of Pioneer Inn is an interesting one. George Freeland, a robust 300-pound, 6-foot-5-inch Englishman, had relocated to Vancouver, Canada, and become a Royal Canadian Mountie. He was sent to Hawai'i in 1900 to capture a suspect, but failing to do so, chose to make Maui his home. He formed the Pioneer Hotel Co., Ltd., and sold $50 shares of stock. In October 1901 he constructed the hotel as accommodations for interisland travelers. Similar to the plantation house of the Maunalei Sugar Company on Lana'i, the total cost of constructing the hotel was $6,000. (Note: On Lana'i I heard a report that the Maunalei Plantation House was transported to Maui and became Pioneer Inn, but this was not accurate. Apparently, years ago, the *Honolulu Star-Bulletin* printed an article to this effect. George Alan Freeland, son of Pioneer Inn's founder George Freeland, spoke with Lawrence Gay, the owner of most of Lana'i at the turn of the

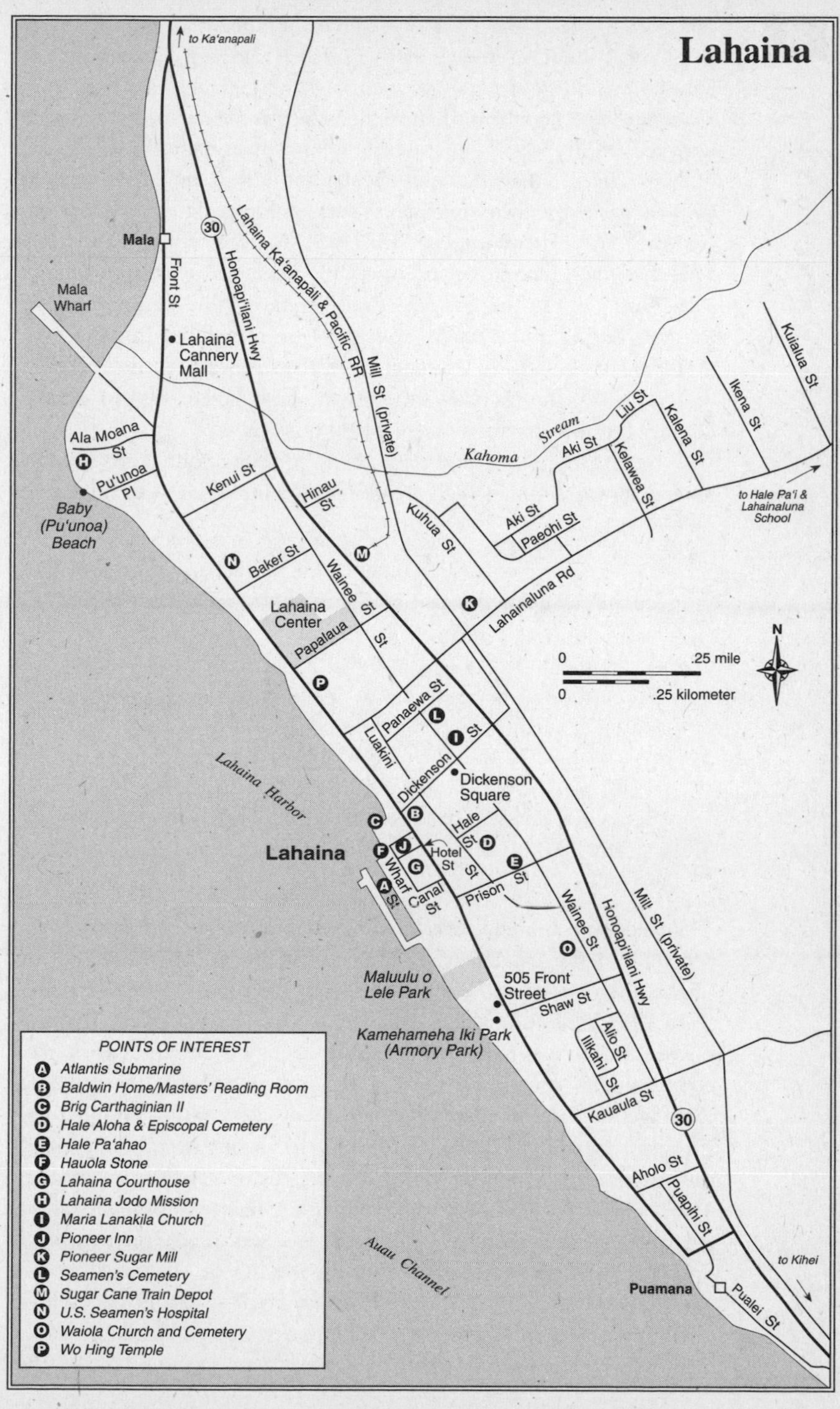
Lahaina
to Ka'anapali
Mala
Mala Wharf
Front St
30
Honoapi'ilani Hwy
Lahaina Ka'anapali & Pacific RR
Mill St (private)
Lahaina Cannery Mall
Ala Moana St
Pu'unoa Pl
Baby (Pu'unoa) Beach
Kenui St
Hinau St
Kahoma Stream
Liu St
Aki St
Kelawea St
Kalena St
Ikena St
Kuialua St
to Hale Pa'i & Lahainaluna School
Kuhua St
Aki St
Paeohi St
Lahainaluna Rd
Baker St
Wainee St
Lahaina Center
Papalaua
Panaewa St
Luakini
Dickenson St
Dickenson Square
Lahaina Harbor
Lahaina
Hale St
Hotel St
Wharf St
Canal St
Prison St
Wainee St
Honoapi'ilani Hwy
Mill St (private)
0 .25 mile
0 .25 kilometer
N
Maluulu o Lele Park
505 Front Street
Shaw St
Kamehameha Iki Park (Armory Park)
Alio St
Ilikahi St
Kauaula St
30
Aholo St
Puapihi St
Auau Channel
Puamana
Pualei St
to Kihei
POINTS OF INTEREST
A Atlantis Submarine
B Baldwin Home/Masters' Reading Room
C Brig Carthaginian II
D Hale Aloha & Episcopal Cemetery
E Hale Pa'ahao
F Hauola Stone
G Lahaina Courthouse
H Lahaina Jodo Mission
I Maria Lanakila Church
J Pioneer Inn
K Pioneer Sugar Mill
L Seamen's Cemetery
M Sugar Cane Train Depot
N U.S. Seamen's Hospital
O Waiola Church and Cemetery
P Wo Hing Temple

20th century, and was told that when the construction of Pioneer Hotel was completed, the similarly designed building on the island of Lana'i was still standing.)

Soon George Freeland opened the Pioneer Saloon, the Pioneer Grange, the Pioneer Wholesale Liquor Company and, in 1913, the Pioneer Theater. The Pioneer Theater ran silent movies to packed crowds and stage shows and plays were held in the theater as well. George Freeland died on July 25, 1925, survived by his wife, a Hawaiian woman, three sons and four daughters. His eldest son, George Alan Freeland, ran the business until the early 1960s. His grandson, George "Keoki" Freeland, is now the Director of the Lahaina Restoration Foundation. In the late 1960s the inn was expanded and at that time the theater was torn down. A complete history of the Pioneer Inn is available along with their brochure.

A guest in 1901 would have been required to adhere to the following "house rules," which are still posted in the lobby of the hotel:

> You must pay you rent in advance. You must not let you room go one day back. Women is not allow in you room. If you wet or burn you bed you going out. You are not allow to gamble in you room. You are not allow to give you bed to you freand. If you freand stay overnight you must see the mgr. You must leave you room at 11 am so the women can clean you room. Only on Sunday you can sleep all day. You are not allow in the down stears in the seating room or in the dinering room or in the kitchen when you are drunk. You are not allow to drink on the front porch. You must use a shirt when you come to the seating room. If you can't keep this rules please dont take the room.

You'll find **the Old Lahaina Courthouse** under the Banyan Tree, across from the Lahaina Harbor. It was built in 1859, at a cost of $7,000, from wood and stone taken from the palace of Kamehameha II. In 1925 the building was extensively remodeled to serve as courthouse, post office, police station and tax office. In 1999 work was completed on its second renovation. Tenants include the **Lahaina Heritage Museum**, operated by the Lahaina Restoration Foundation. It's open daily from 9 a.m. to 5 p.m. (free admission; $1 suggested donation), with a docent to explain the history of the courthouse. Two **art galleries**, one on the main floor and another in the basement (the old jail), are operated by the Lahaina Arts Society (9 a.m. to 5 p.m.). A visitor center is located on the *makai* side of the main floor and serviced by volunteers as a part of the Lahaina Town Action Committee. A meeting and video room is open to the public for community meetings and public ADA restrooms are located on the main floor and upstairs.

The **Lahaina Harbor** is in front of the Pioneer Inn and the Old Courthouse. You can stroll down and see the boats and visit stalls where a wide variety of water sports and tours can be arranged. (See Chapter 6.)

The **Brig Carthaginian II**, anchored in the harbor at the north end of Pioneer Inn, is a replica of a 19th-century square-rigger, typical of the ships that brought the first missionaries and whalers to these shores. The first *Carthaginian* sank on Easter Sunday, April 2, 1972. The 130-foot vessel had been built in 1921 in Denmark as a schooner and had sailed the world as a cargo ship. She was purchased by Tucker Thompson and sailed to Hawai'i in 1964. Her original name was *Wandia*, but was re-christened *Carthaginian* in Honolulu with a bottle of passion fruit juice. The ship was used in the South Pacific for a time and later restored to resemble a whaling vessel for the movie version of Michener's *Hawai'i*. The Lahaina Restoration Foundation worked to acquire the *Carthaginian* for $75,000. The ship found a home at the Lahaina wharf, becoming its definitive exhibit of the whaling era. On June 20, 1971, the ship's skipper, Don Bell, discovered that the vessel was sinking. The ship was pumped and a large hole was patched, the cause seeming to be dry rot. It was decided the following year to tow her to Honolulu for repairs in dry dock. However, 150 yards from dock she became lodged on the reef and valiant efforts to save her were not successful. An immediate search

PARKING IN PARADISE

Parking in Lahaina can be somewhat irksome. Several all-day lots are located near the corner of Wainee and Dickenson (only a couple of blocks off Front Street). The farther away you get, the cheaper the lots. The prices also change seasonally and can be anywhere from $4 to $10 per day. The inexpensive lots fill up early in the day with folks going out on the tour boats. The Old Lahaina Center has a lot that is free with validation. The Lahaina Center across the street has pay parking, validated with a movie ticket or purchase from one of the stores. If you don't mind a short walk, parking is available across the road from the 505 Front Street shops. Other paid parking lots are primarily on side streets off Front Street. On-street parking is limited and if you are fortunate enough to find a spot, many are only for one hour. *Beware:* The police here are quite prompt and efficient at towing.

began for a replacement and it was found in the Danish port of Soby. The ship was a 97-foot steel-hulled freighter that had originally been a schooner, but had been de-masted. The ship called *Komet* had been built in the shipyards in Germany in 1920 and was purchased for $20,500. An all-Lahaina crew sailed via the Panama Canal and arrived in Hawai'i in September 1973. Volunteers set to work transforming the ship into the vessel it is today and it was christened *Brig Carthaginian* on April 26, 1980. Unfortunately, even with the great care it has received over the years, the ship has experienced natural deterioration, and it was recently determined that the *Brig Carthaginian II* could no longer be maintained. Plans are in the works for the once-proud ship to begin a new life as a dive site off the shores of Lahaina. Atlantis Submarines Hawaii will undertake the project to sink the ship, creating an artificial reef that will alleviate pressures facing natural reefs and increase the reef and fish biomass in the region's waters.

Adjacent to the *Carthaginian* is the **Lahaina Lighthouse**—adopted by the Lahaina Restoration Foundation, which added new railings and a connecting ramp. The Lighthouse predates any others on the U.S. Pacific coast. It was on this site in 1840 that King Kamehameha III ordered a nine-foot wooden tower built as an aid to navigation for the whaling ships. It was equipped with whale oil lamps, kept burning at night by a Hawaiian caretaker who was paid $20 a year. In 1866 it increased to 26 feet in size and was rebuilt again in 1905. The present structure of concrete was dedicated in 1916. (Information is from an engraved plaque placed on the lighthouse by the Lahaina Restoration Foundation.)

The **Hauola Stone**, or Healing Rock, can be found in front of the Lahaina Library next to the harbor. Look for the cluster of rocks marked with a Visitors Bureau "warrior" sign. The rock, resembling a chair, was believed to have healing properties that could be obtained by merely sitting in it with feet dangling in the surf. Here you will also find remnants of the **Brick Palace** of Kamehameha the Great.

The **Baldwin Home** is across Front Street from Pioneer Inn (corner of Front and Dickenson Streets). Built from 1834 to 1835, it was the home of Reverend Dwight Baldwin and his family from 1838 to 1871. The residence of this medical missionary has been restored and contains many original pieces of furniture. Open daily 10 a.m. to 4 p.m., with tours available. Adults $3, seniors $2, family rate of $5. 695 Front Street. 808-661-3262. The empty lot adjacent was once the home of Reverend William Richards, and a target of attack by cannonballs from angry sailors during the heyday of whaling.

On the other side of the Baldwin Home is the **Masters' Reading Room**. Built in 1833, it is the oldest structure on Maui. Its original purpose was to provide a place of leisure for visiting sea captains.

Village Gifts & Fine Arts is now housed here, offering a wonderful selection of art, jewelry and unique island crafts (808-661-5199).

Hale Pa'ahao (Old Prison) on Prison Street just off Wainee is only a short trek from Front Street. Upon entry you'll notice the large gatehouse that the Lahaina Restoration Foundation reconstructed to its original state in 1988. Nearby is a 60-year-old Royal Palm and, in the courtyard, an enormous 150-year-old breadfruit tree. The cell-block was built in 1852 to house the unruly sailors from the whaling vessels and to replace the old fort; it was reconstructed in 1959. In 1854 coral walls (the blocks taken from the old fort) were constructed. The jail was used until the 1920s, when it was relocated to the basement of the Lahaina Courthouse next to the Harbor. While you're at Hale Pa'ahao be sure to say hello to the jail's only tenant, George. He is a wax replica of a sailor who is reported to have had a few too many brews at Uncle Henry's Front Street Beer House back in the 1850s, then missed his ship's curfew and was tossed into jail by Sheriff William O. Smith. George will briefly converse with you by means of a taped recording. The grounds are open to the public daily.

The construction of the **Waiola Church** began in 1828. The original church was called the Wainee Church, and was made of stone and was large enough to accommodate 3,000 people. **Hale Aloha** was built in 1858 as a branch of the church and was used as a school. Its name, "House of Love," was a way of giving thanks that the citizens of Lahaina did not suffer in a smallpox epidemic that ravaged the island of O'ahu in 1853. The Waiola Church is now a United Church of Christ with worship in Hawaiian and English. In 1951 a fierce wind, called a Kaua'ula wind, seriously damaged the church and Hale Aloha. (The wind is named for a narrow valley in the mountains above Lahaina, called Kaua'ula, through which it blows and gains force. Legend has it that the wind blows when the *ali'i* die.) Among the damage incurred during the wind of 1951 was the loss of the Hale Aloha belfry. Hale Aloha and the church were both sold to the county in the 1960s. In 1996 the belfry was restored as a result of efforts of the Lahaina Restoration Foundation. In the neighboring **cemetery** you will find tombs of several notable members of Hawaiian royalty, including Queen Keopuolani, wife of Kamehameha the Great and mother of Kamehameha II and III. The church is located on Wainee and Shaw streets.

The **Maria Lanakila Church** is on the corner of Wainee and Dickenson. The first Roman Catholic mass took place on Maui in 1841, and there has been a Catholic church on this site since 1846. Built in 1928, the present church is a concrete replica of an earlier wooden structure. Next door on Wainee Street is the **Seamen's Cemetery**. Herman Melville's cousin and one of his shipmates are buried here.

The **Wo Hing Temple** on Front Street opened following restoration in late 1984. Built in 1912, it now houses a museum that features the influence of the Chinese population on Maui. Hours are 10 a.m. to 4 p.m. Admission $1; children free. The adjacent cookhouse has become a theater that runs movies filmed by Thomas Edison during his trips to Hawai'i between 1898 and 1906. In 1993 a Koban information booth was added near the Wo Hing Temple.

Follow Front Street toward Ka'anapali to find the **U.S. Seamen's Hospital**. This classic two-story coral structure was originally built by King Kamehameha III as his personal hideaway and is well removed from town for a good reason. The king wanted to have some privacy away from the eyes of the missionaries who reproached him for his drinking and gambling ways. In 1844 it was leased to the U.S. State Department to provide care for sick and injured seamen. In 1973 the building was purchased by the Lahaina Restoration Foundation and renovations were completed by 1982. An interesting fact was the discovery of a human skeleton on the northwest side of the building. The LRF reports, "During the ancient times, when an *ali'i* had a building constructed that would house the royal family, a commoner was put to death with a blow of an adz to his head. The victim was then buried under the northwest support so that his spirit would be bound to the house and become the 'permanent guardian.' This finding underscores the cultural upheaval that was occurring at this time, for even though the king and his charges were raised as Christians, the old ways were still strong enough for this ritual to be carried out." The remains of this guardian were restored to his resting place in the northwest corner. Businesses now occupy space in this structure located on the Ka'anapali side of Front Street.

Hale Pa'i is a former printing press on the campus of **Lahainaluna School**. Founded in 1831, Lahainaluna is the oldest school west of the Rockies. You will find it located just outside of Lahaina at the top of Lahainaluna Road. An exact replica of an original Ramage Press in on display, along with facsimiles of old books, manuscripts and copies of Hawaiian newspapers. The hours fluctuate depending on volunteers, so call the Lahaina Restoration office at 808-661-3262 for current schedule. Their general hours are Monday through Friday 10 a.m. to 3 p.m.

The **Lahaina Jodo Mission** is located on the Ka'anapali side of Lahaina, on Ala Moana Street near the Mala Wharf. The great Buddha commemorated the 100th anniversary of the Japanese immigration to the islands at the mission in 1968. The grounds, but not the buildings, are open to the public. The public is welcome to attend their summer O'Bon festivals, usually in late June and early July. Check the papers for dates and times.

Walking south on Front Street past the Banyan Tree, you'll go by Kamehameha III School before you come to **Kamehameha Iki Park** (also known as Armory Park) on your right. Hui O Wa'a Kaulua (the assembly of the double-hulled canoe) is a nonprofit organization working with the County of Maui to develop and maintain the site as a Hawaiian cultural park that offers both exhibits and hands-on experiences. The focus will be the design, construction, sailing and maintenance of Hawaiian double-hulled sailing canoes constructed along traditional lines. Two *Hale Wa'a*, or canoe houses, will be constructed. They will be 37 feet tall, 41 feet wide and 100 feet long. The two *Hale Wa'a* will house three double-hulled canoes on the ground floor, with room in the ceiling for smaller or lighter canoes. A 62-foot double-hulled canoe of traditional design with a single sail has already been constructed. The canoe is named *Mo'okiha*, which means sacred lizard/dragon. They also have a 42.5-foot canoe called *Mo'olele*. Other plans include the construction of a kitchen as well as a covered picnic area with space for working, teaching and demonstrating Hawaiian crafts. Landscaping of the park will include vegetation that will serve Hawaiian activities such as ti, taro, bamboo, Hawaiian medicinal plants and bananas. Completion of these projects is anticipated within the next five years. If you would like more information or are interested in membership, contact Hui O Wa'a Kaulua, 505 Front Street, Suite 224B, Lahaina. 808-661-9290.

Across the street (at what is now an unassuming baseball field and parking lot) is **Moku'ula**, a sacred place for Hawaiian royalty and home to the Maui chiefs. It was placed on the National Register of Historic Places by the U.S. Department of the Interior in 1997. Beneath the flying dust of a baseball field was once a residence and a mausoleum for generations of rulers of Hawai'i. Legend says this moated island was also home to *Kihawahine*, a fearful lizard goddess who served as the guardian of the royal family. Once a *kapu* (forbidden) island in the center of an 11-acre fishpond (*Loko o Mokuhinia*),

LAHAINA HISTORY

Little known to most visitors, back in the early 19th century Lahaina had a series of canals that were used for crop irrigation. Lahaina was dubbed "Venice of the Pacific." For a fee you could travel the canal to reach the Government Market. Here, trade (not always fair—leading to the nickname "Rotten Row") was carried between visiting ships and the native people. This was one of Lahaina's earliest sites, but when the canals and the pond were filled in 1918 it became just a memory.

Moku'ula was part of the region known as *Kalua O Kiha*—the center of *ali'i* residence when Lahaina was capital of the kingdom. *Moku'ula* was a favored residence of King Kamehameha III—here he could enjoy a quiet retreat upon the island in the midst of a freshwater pond. Carbon dating and some preliminary archaeological excavation have revealed some of the oldest Hawaiian habitation in the islands. Many years ago the swampy area was filled in after complaints about mosquitoes, but fortunately no grading was done. Preliminary excavation shows that the remains of this once-important royal residence from the 16th to the 19th century might well remain intact beneath the earth. You can read more about it at www.mokuula.com, where you can also view a painting by Ed Kayton based on archaeological and historical documentation.

Maui Nei, a company devoted to cultural tourism in partnership with the Friends of *Moku'ula*, is a non-profit organization aimed at restoring the *Moku'ula* site. Maui Nei offers a walking tour through Lahaina's past. Tour side streets and local gardens with your *kumu* (teacher) to envision how the town known as "Lele" once looked. Local guides begin their discussion with the arrival of the early Polynesians and follow the history of the area through the times of the missionaries and up to the present. More than 20 sites are visited during the two-hour tour, including the oceanfront workshop of **Hui O Wa'a**, where you can see demonstrations of the legacy of the early Hawaiians and their sailing canoes. This is a not-to-be-missed tour for those who are fascinated by the rich history and culture of the islands and yearn to learn more. The tour begins at the Old Lahaina Courthouse, includes a short, shady respite with beverage midway, and ends on the beach near 505 Front Street. Tours are Monday through Saturday 9:30 to 11:30 a.m. Reservations are required 48 hours in advance. Cost is $39 adults, $25 kids 12 to 17. Maui Nei, 505 Front Street, Suite 234; 808-661-9494; e-mail: info@mauinei.com; www.mauinei.com.

Shopping is a prime activity in Lahaina and is such a major business that it breeds volatility. Shops change frequently, sometimes seemingly overnight, with a definite trendiness to their merchandise. It was several years back that visitors could view artisans creating scrimshaw in numerous stores. The next few years saw the transformation to T-shirt stores. (There still are plenty of clothing stores, and a little price comparison can be worthwhile.) The next theme was art, art and more art. Galleries sprang up on every corner. It was a wonderful opportunity to view the fine work of many local and international artists. Original oils, watercolors, acrylics, carvings and even pottery were all on display. There are still many galleries in Lahaina where you can enjoy fine artwork, and jewelry stores have multiplied (again, do some price comparisons before buying). Unfortunately, one development in the last few years is the emergence of numerous tour and activity booking agents. I find that they have infiltrated every nook and cranny, even a corner of one ice cream shop. While some are pleasant enough, others are obnoxious and extremely pushy in their attempts to sell you a visit to a timeshare in exchange for a discounted activity. So buyers beware.

Here are a few shops in Lahaina that I feel are worth a look:

Lahaina Center, on the Ka'anapali end of Lahaina, is composed of two parts, one older and one newer. At **Old Lahaina Center**, you'll find the Maui Theater production of *'Ulalena*, plus various eating establishments. This center is anchored by Foodland supermarket. **Buns of Maui** is located on the Front Street side of the center, offering homemade muffins, cookies and candies and known in particular for their great cinnamon buns. They also offer internet services at the rate of 8 cents a minute. Open Monday through Friday 7:30 a.m. to 5:30 p.m.; Saturday and Sunday 8 a.m. to 2 p.m.

The newer **Lahaina Center**, located across the street, is a low-level structure with pioneer-type architecture and a validated parking lot. A free exhibit housed here is the **Hale Kahiko** Hawaiian village, which depicts the living quarters of ancient Hawai'i with thatched *hale* (houses) on display. Open daily 9 a.m. to 6 p.m. There's a free Polynesian show Wednesday at 2:30 p.m. and a *keiki* hula show at 6 p.m. on Friday (808-667-9216). The 17,000-square-foot **Hilo Hattie** store is famous around the islands for its aloha wear. I would also recommend it for its good selection of souvenirs, ranging from key chains to jams and jellies, tropical candy and macadamia nuts. Hilo Hattie was known in past years for its splashy Hawaiian print clothes, but in recent years the company has expanded its offerings to include subtler, more stylish island fashions. I'll admit I have a few of them in my closet. The **Front Street Movie Theaters**, **Banana Republic**, **Gap** and **Glow Putt Mini Golf** are a few of the other businesses you'll find at this center.

Walking south along Front Street (heading toward the Banyan Tree), check out **Glass Mango Designs** (858 Front Street). This store features Maui-made, one-of-a-kind jewelry by local artist Janis Sweitzer. Her beautiful pieces are made from a variety of materials, including Venetian Murano glass beads, amber, opal, jade, Tahitian pearls, Keshi pearls and gemstones from around the world.

Across the street (ocean side) at 855 Front Street is **Elephant Walk Gift Gallery**, offering a great selection of gift items. A bit farther down is the **Lahaina Yacht Club Ship's Store** (837 Front Street).

The adjacent Lahaina Yacht Club restaurant/bar is a private membership club, but the Ship's Store offers a variety of yacht club logo wear to anyone interested in purchasing a T-shirt or cap that is uniquely Maui.

Stop by **One World Gallery**, 818 Front Street, for some out-of-the-ordinary artwork, jewelry, gifts and usable art (home furnishings). Say "aloha" to their wonderful life-like silicon residents. This store is always a delight for browsing, with its fun, creative art. It's a store with a sense of humor.

Art galleries abound on or around Front Street. **Lahaina Galleries**, a locally-based gallery founded in 1976, represents a variety of acclaimed artists. Their three Maui galleries are located at 828 Front Street, The Kapalua Shops, and The Shops at Wailea. Celebrity musicians such as Ron Wood, Miles Davis, John Lennon, Jerry Garcia and Bob Dylan are represented at **Celebritės Gallery of Fine Art** at 764 Front Street. **The Village Galleries** operates three gallery locations in Lahaina, each offering a different selection of art and handcrafted items. All three galleries are worth a visit: **Village Gift & Fine Art** at the corner of Front and Dickenson streets; **Village Gallery** at 120 Dickenson Street; and **Village Gallery–Contemporary** in Dickenson Square. **David Lee Galleries**, **Wyland Galleries**, **Galerie Lassen**, **Robert Lyn Nelson Studio** and **Kingwell Island Arts Collection** feature the works of their namesake artists. The **Curtis Wilson Cost Gallery** (710 Front Street) presents spectacular paintings of Maui scenes by upcountry artist Curtis Wilson Cost. The **Peter Lik Gallery** (712 Front Street) is a must-see, featuring stunning photos of the islands and nature at its most awesome.

> Enjoy a self-guided tour of the wonderful art galleries in Lahaina. **Friday Night Is Art Night** offers many free activities and a chance to meet some of the artists in person. Participating galleries feature a special event, usually between 6 and 9 p.m., that might include guest artists.

The **Lahaina Arts Society** is a nonprofit organization featuring work by more than 200 local Maui artists. Visit the open-air exhibition under the Banyan at their **Banyan Tree Arts Fair** from 8 a.m. to 5 p.m. most weekends. (Other weekends also feature Hawaiian arts and crafts.) Check the local paper for the current schedule or call The Lahaina Arts Society at 808-661-0111. Also visit the society's two galleries in the Old Lahaina Courthouse and Jail. (Open daily 9 a.m. to 5 p.m.)

The circa-1916 **Old Lahaina Store** is located in the middle of Lahaina Town (700 block of Front Street). You'll find **Billabong** (a surf and skateboard shop), **Vintage European Posters**, **Na Hoku** (jewelry store), and a blues, jazz and comedy club called **Paradice Bluz**. The **Lahaina Marketplace**, a small courtyard of shops and restaurants, is located at the end of the 700 block. Look there for **Maui Crystal**,

Maui's oldest glass gallery. Often you'll be able to watch a glass artist at work as you browse the store.

Environmental awareness has arrived at the **Endangered Species Store** across the street at 707 Front Street (oceanside). It's filled with T-shirts, collectibles, books and toys that all focus on endangered wildlife worldwide. Next door is **The Gecko Store**, a fun store with a novel idea that certainly makes this shop stand out from the many others that line Front Street. Step through the portal and take a look at what is under your feet.

Although built nearly a century later, **Dickenson Square**—a short walk up Dickenson Street off Front Street—bears a strong resemblance to the Pioneer Inn. The **Whalers General Store**, **Lahaina Coolers** restaurant and **Penne Pasta Café** are located here.

Island Sandals is tucked away in a niche of the **Wharf Cinema Center** (located on Front Street across from the Banyan Tree) at 658 Front Street, Space #125. Look for the "sandal maker" sign on Front Street. Michael Mahnensmith is the proprietor and creator of custom-made sandals. He learned his craft in Santa Monica from David Webb, who made sandals for the Greek and Roman movies of the late '50s and early '60s. Webb created his sandal design based on the sandals used 3,000 years ago by the desert warriors of Ethiopia. He developed the idea while living in Catalina in the 1960s and copyrighted it in 1978. The sandals are all leather (which is porous and keeps the feet cool and dry) with the exception of a non-skid synthetic heel. The sandals feature a single strap that laces around the big toe, then over and under the foot and around the heel, providing comfort and good arch support. As the sandal breaks in, the strap stretches and you simply adjust the entire strap to maintain proper fit (which makes them feel more like a shoe than a sandal). They are clever and functional. His sandals have been copied by others, but never duplicated. So beware of other sandals that appear the same but don't offer the fit, comfort or function of Michael's. The charge for ladies is $165 for the right shoe (the left shoe is free). Men's sizes are $185 (slightly higher for sizes over 13). Michael stresses the importance of good footwear, so stop in upon your arrival. His business is booming these days and sandal making takes time, so allow three to six months for delivery of your sandals. Sandals can also be ordered by sending a tracing of both feet and both big toes, including the spaces in between, along with the purchase price and shipping charge of $10 (U.S.) or $20 (international) to Island Sandals. Michael can also assist with leather repair of your shoes, purses, bags or suitcases. 808-661-5110; www.islandsandals.com.

Other noteworthy shops in the Wharf Cinema Center are the **Simon-Jon Gallery**, featuring beautiful handcrafted wood pieces, and

Hana Botanicals, which offers soaps and bath items. Most days you'll be able to watch a craftsman sitting in front of this shopping center, carving Hawaiian woods. Validated parking is located behind the center.

Continuing south on Front Street, make a stop at **Maui Hands** (610 Front Street) for another store offering a great selection of unique art and jewelry by local artists. **Dan's Green House** at 133 Prison Street (a short walk up from Front) has a variety of beautiful tropical birds for sale as well as an array of plants for shipping home. Their specialty is Fuku-Bonsai "Lava Rock" plants. These bonsai are well packaged to tolerate the trip home. 808-661-8412. Open daily 9 a.m. to 6 p.m.

505 Front Street, an oceanfront shopping center next to Lahaina Shores, has struggled a bit over the years as shops have come and gone. It is, however, home to two of Maui's best restaurants (**Pacific 'O and I'o**), so it's definitely worth a stop. The **Feast at Lele** luau takes place on the beach in front of the center. While you're there, wander through the shopping center and you'll find art, jewelry and clothing, as well as day spa services at **Lei Spa Maui** (808-661-1178). Stop by **The Needlework Shop**, where you can enjoy a free one-on-one lesson in Hawaiian quilting (808-662-8554).

An area located a few blocks up (toward the mountains) from Lahaina's Front Street is termed the industrial area. Follow Honoapi'ilani Highway and turn onto Hinau Street by the Pizza Hut to the main depot of the **Lahaina Ka'anapali & Pacific Railroad**, affectionately referred to as the **Sugar Cane Train**. In Lahaina in 1862, the harvesting of sugar cane was one of the island's biggest industries. More than 45,000 tons were produced from 5,000 acres. The Lahaina Ka'anapali & Pacific Railroad began in 1882, replacing the slower method (mules and steers) of hauling sugar cane between the harvest area and the Pioneer Sugar Mill. This allowed a greater area of cane to be planted as well. By the 1900s the railroad was also transporting an ever-increasing number of workers to their jobs. In 1970, the Sugar Cane Train was once again restored, but financial difficulties silenced the train whistle once more. In 1973, Mr. Willes B. Kyele purchased the railroad and brought life back to its engines. Currently two trains operate on a three-foot narrow-gauge railroad, pulled by two steam locomotives, *Anaka* and *Myrtle*. The locomotives were built in 1943 and were restored to resemble those that were used in Hawai'i at the beginning of the 20th century. For information on the daily excursions and Thursday night dinner train, see "Land Tours" in Chapter 6.

Also in the industrial area, **The Bakery** has some fine pastries and breads. You'll also find a variety of stores featuring collectibles, jewelry, art and other items, tucked away in this "warehouse" area.

ART & CRAFT FAIRS

Some of the most enjoyable shopping and unique finds on Maui take place at the various art and craft fairs held around the island. There is usually no admission for these fairs, and you'll find an array of souvenirs, gift items, jewelry, clothing, food products and everything else under the sun. Check the local papers for current details, as dates, times and locations do change. Here are some that are currently taking place on a regular basis: *West Maui*—**The International Open Marketplace**, corner of Lahainaluna Road and Honoapi'ilani Highway, Monday, Thursday and Friday, 10 a.m. to 5 p.m. (808-879-7594); **Napili Plaza**, Monday, Wednesday and Saturday 9 a.m. to 4 p.m.; **Ka'anapali Beach Hotel**, 9 a.m. to 1 p.m. every Friday; **Lahaina Arts Society**, alternate weekends, Saturday and Sunday 9 a.m. to 5 p.m. at Banyan Tree Park; **Gift & Craft Fair** at Lahaina Civic Center, 9 a.m. to 4 p.m. every Sunday, $1 admission (808-879-7594). *South Maui*—**Gift & Craft Fair** at Kukui Mall, Kihei, Tuesday and Wednesday 9 a.m. to 4 p.m.; **Renaissance Wailea Beach Resort Craft Fair**, Wednesday and Friday, 8 a.m. to 2 p.m. in the hotel lobby (808-879-4900, ext 6516); **Gateway Plaza Open Market**, Sunday, 9 a.m. to 4 p.m., Pi'ilani Highway at Ohukai in Kihei; **Wailea Marriott Resort Arts & Crafts Fair**, Friday, 9 a.m. to 2 p.m. in the south lobby. *Central Maui*—**Aloha Craft Fair** at Maui Mall, Friday, 10 a.m to 4 p.m.

On the Ka'anapali side of Lahaina (a drive of less than a mile) is the **Lahaina Cannery Mall**, which opened in 1987. The original structure, built in 1920, was used as a pineapple cannery until 1963. The current facility was built to resemble its predecessor and is easy to spot as you leave Lahaina heading for Ka'anapali. A large free parking area makes for convenient access. This enclosed air-conditioned mall is anchored by **Safeway** and **Longs Drug Store** and includes around 50 shops and eateries. There are several fast-food outlets in the Pineapple Court—excellent for a family with varied tastes. There is also sit-down dining at **Compadres** restaurant. This mall offers an interesting selection of stores, and both locals and visitors frequent it. Shops include **Sir Wilfred's** for gourmet coffee and cigars, **Totally Hawaiian Gift Gallery**, **Starbucks**, GNC and **Borders Express**, along with various jewelry, clothing and sundry stores. Kids might enjoy checking out **Maui Toy Works**. The Lahaina Cannery Mall presents free *keiki* hula shows Saturday and Sunday at 1 p.m. and a free Polynesian dance show at 7 p.m. on Tuesday and Thursday. Mall hours are 9:30 a.m. to 9 p.m. daily.

Across the road from Lahaina Cannery is another (smaller and newer) industrial area (turn off the highway onto Keawe Street). If you take a drive up there, you'll see a mix of commercial and warehouse sites, with a few retail locations mixed in. Look for the **Artist in Paradise** sign and you'll find the studio and shop of local artist Robert Bedard, featuring Maui-made pottery, paintings and T-shirts. Emerald Plaza, facing the street. 808-662-0600. This is a new, developing area and it changes often, so it might be worth a drive-through. You never know when you'll find that off-the-beaten-path gem.

Ka'anapali

The drive from Lahaina to Ka'anapali is just a few short minutes (unless it's rush hour—or "luau time"). As you head north from Lahaina, the vista opens up with views of the Hyatt Regency and the beginning of the Ka'anapali Beach Resort area running along the beachfront. The Ka'anapali area is beautifully framed by the West Maui Mountains on the right, the peaks of Moloka'i (appearing to be another part of Maui in the background), the island of Lana'i off to the left and, of course, the ocean. The name *Ka'anapali* means "rolling cliffs" or "land divided by cliffs" and refers to the wide, open ridges that stretch up behind the resort toward Pu'u Kukui, West Maui's highest peak. The beaches and plush resorts here are what many come to Hawai'i to find.

Ka'anapali began in the early 1960s as an Amfac Development, with the first hotels, the Royal Lahaina and the Sheraton Maui, opening in late 1962 and early 1963, respectively. The Ka'anapali Beach Resort, encompassing 1,200 acres along three miles of prime beachfront, is reputed to be the first large-scale planned resort in the world. There are six beachfront hotels and five condominiums that total more than 4,800 rooms and units, two golf courses, 35 tennis courts and a shopping center.

The **Hyatt Regency Maui Resort and Spa** should be on everyone's list of places to see. Few hotels can boast that they need their own wildlife manager, but upon entry you'll see why this one does. Without spoiling the surprises too much, just envision a hotel with palm trees growing through the lobby, flamingos strolling by, and parrots perched amid extraordinary pieces of Asian art. The lagoon and black swans are spectacular. And did I mention there are penguins, too? The spacious pool area occupies two acres and features two swim-through waterfalls and a cavern in the middle with a swim-up bar. A swinging bridge is suspended over one of the two pools and a water slide offers added thrills, particularly for the young traveler.

There are exotic birds afloat on the lagoons that greet you upon your arrival and glide gracefully by two of the hotel's restaurants.

Be sure to take advantage of the lovely beachfront walkway that travels from the Hyatt Regency all the way to the **Sheraton Maui**. A post-dinner stroll in the twilight is a perfect way to end a perfect day in Paradise. You can walk beyond to the other side of Black Rock but it requires a bit of maneuvering through the Sheraton Resort to connect with the walkway on the opposite side. **Black Rock** is, of course, the premier snorkeling spot on this stretch of beach. Enjoy an afternoon swimming with the brightly colored fish. (See "Snorkeling" in Chapter 6 for more information.)

Whalers Village Shopping Center is located in the heart of Ka'anapali. It offers more than 65 restaurants and eateries, art galleries, jewelry stores, high-end designer shops and little boutiques. Designer stores include **Tiffany**, **Louis Vuitton** and **Coach**. Other shops include the **Body Shop**, **Del Sol** (very cool products that change color in the

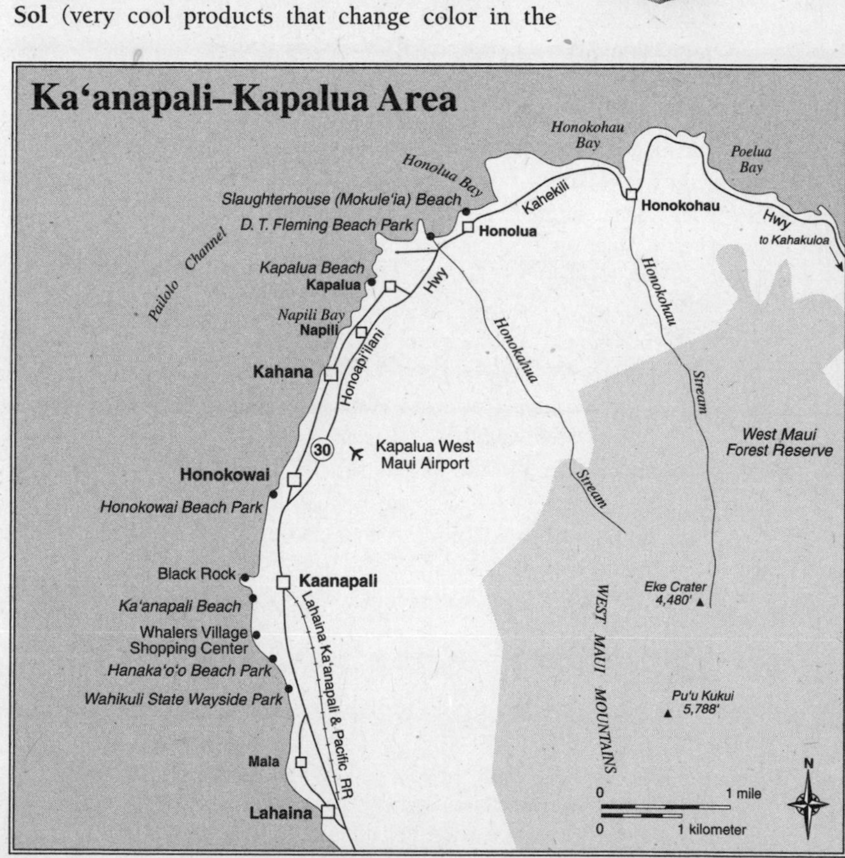

WHALERS VILLAGE MUSEUM AND THEATER

Whalers Village Museum and Theater is a free museum located on the upper level of Whalers Village Shopping Center in Ka'anapali. A self-guided audio tour is available in English, Spanish, German and Japanese. Short films on whales and whaling are also offered throughout the day in the small theater. The museum opened in 1984 under the directorship of curator and whale expert Lewis Eisenberg. It is dedicated to Lahaina's golden era of whaling (1825–1860), with hundreds of artifacts and graphics telling the story through the eyes of the ordinary whaleman. Included is a wonderful collection of 19th-century scrimshaw. Free guided tours by a marine naturalist are available on a pre-arranged basis. Open 9:30 a.m. to 10 p.m. daily. 808-661-5992.

sun), **Blue Ginger**, **Sand People**, **Cinnamon Girl** (one of my favorites for ladies' island fashions), **Lahaina Scrimshaw**, **Vintage European Posters** and **Lahaina Printsellers**. Restaurants include **The Rusty Harpoon**, **Leilani's** and **Hula Grill**. All are beachfront and good options for meals. The Food Court offers several additional dining options. The annual Whalers Village Maui Onion Festival is traditionally held the first weekend of August. Music and hula performances are presented several evenings a week at Whalers Village on the open-air main stage. Sunday evenings are currently featuring live jazz. All entertainment is free.

This is one of my favorite Maui shopping centers, offering a wonderful variety of stores. Whalers Village used to feature primarily high-end shops, but that's not the case any longer. There is a good mix of stores to suit every age and budget. The open-air, oceanfront mall is a pleasant place for an evening stroll and browsing before or after dinner, followed by a seaside walk back to your Ka'anapali accommodations on the paved beachfront sidewalk. A multilevel parking structure is adjacent to the mall. Parking is free for the first three hours with a $10 purchase validation from shops/restaurants; $2.50/hour thereafter. Open 9:30 a.m. to 10 p.m. every day of the year. www.whalersvillage.com.

Honokowai-Kapalua Area

Departing Ka'anapali, head north on the highway until you come to the intersection at Lower Honoapi'ilani Road. Turn left here, and you'll come across the **Honokowai Marketplace**, a Hawaiian-styled shopping center with green-tile roofing anchored by the 37,500-

square-foot **Star Market**. This shopping complex also offers **Leola's Family Funwear, Maui Dive Shop, Maui Art & Gifts**, a video store and Maui's first Martinizing dry cleaning outlet. **Subway, Java Jazz, Pizza Paradiso** and **Hula Scoops** are among the eateries here. Just up the road don't miss **Honokowai Okazuya** (see Chapter 4) for one of the best deals and best plate lunches in West Maui.

To the north of Honokowai—and about seven miles north of Lahaina—is a prominent cluster of high-rise condos with a handful of two-story complexes strung along the coast in its lee. This is **Kahana**. The beach adjacent to the high-rises is fairly wide, but tapers off quickly after this point. Several of the larger complexes offer very nice grounds and spacious living quarters with more resort type activities than in Honokowai. The prices are lower than Ka'anapali, but higher than Honokowai. I haven't found any great values in this area, and the beaches here simply aren't as fine as those to the north at Napili and Kapalua or south at Ka'anapali. There is a continuing algae problem in the Honokowai to Napili area. The algae bloom that clusters in the ocean offshore seems to come and go for reasons yet unknown. State officials continue their investigation but a cause or reason for this condition has not yet been determined. Of late, the problem seems to have improved. The algae doesn't appear to be any health risk, just an annoyance at times for swimming and snorkeling.

The Art School at Kapalua offers visual and performing arts classes and workshops throughout the year for residents as well as visitors. They also have a small art gallery featuring local artists. Summer programs for children are available. 808-665-0007; www.kapaluaart.com.

There isn't much to see here in Kahana. There are several shops on the lower level of the **Kahana Manor**. Nearby, **Kahana Gateway's** outlets include gift, clothing and dive shops, a gas station and **Whalers General Store**, art gallery, jewelry store, a laundry and eateries.

Napili's focal point is beautiful **Napili Bay** with good swimming, snorkeling and boogie boarding, and it even has tide pools for children to explore. Take time to stroll the beach or have a meal at the **Gazebo** or **Sea House** restaurants, both located oceanfront. The condominium units in Napili are low-rise, with prices mostly in the moderate range, and are clustered tightly around the bay. A number are located right on the beach, others a short walk away. The quality of the units varies considerably, but generally a better location on the bay and better facilities demand a higher price. The complexes are small, most fewer than 50 units, and all but one have pools.

At the nearby **Napili Plaza** shopping center you'll find a full-size grocery store and eateries, including **Mama's Ribs & Rotisserie, Maui**

Tacos and **Subway**. There is a boutique spa, a beauty salon, specialty coffee store and other services. An arts-and-crafts fair is held here every Wednesday and Saturday from 9 a.m. to 4 p.m.

Kapalua Bay is a small cove of pristine white sand nestled at the edge of a coconut palm grove. This area of Maui tends to be slightly cooler and rainier than in neighboring Lahaina, and the winds can pick up in the afternoon. The story of **Kapalua** begins in ancient times, for it is said that Mauna Kahalawai, the immense volcano that formed the West Maui Mountains, is the juncture between Heaven and Earth. Hawaiians settled in this region in abundance, they built their *lo'i*, or flooded fields, for growing their staple crop, taro. They harvested fish, *'ama'ama*, *moi*, *akule* and *opelo*, from the clear waters, never taking more than they needed, and always giving thanks. It was an area rich in blessing, much of it sacred. There was a temple of medicine and one for astronomy. The highest chiefs and their families gathered for sports and games in this place, which they deemed their special retreat and playground. They built *holua* sleds for sliding down the grassy slopes. They rolled lava balls in their game of *ulu maika*, lawn bowling. They wrestled, competed in spear hurling, swam and surfed the waves at Honolua on giant *koa* boards.

Ruins of ancient temples, fishing shrines and agricultural terraces can still be seen along the streams and shores, and people who sometimes find huge lava balls marvel at the prowess of the ancient bowlers. In earlier times, the Hawaiian lands were divided into *ahupua'a*. These pie-shaped land sections traverse forest to sea. They gave each person access to various elevations for different crops, and an outlet to the ocean for fishing. There were seven beautiful *ahupua'a*, called Honolua, Honokahua, Honokowai, Honokohau, Kahana, Mahinahina and Mailepai. They were joined to form Honolua Ranch, and parts later became Kapalua Resort.

The most important historic site at Kapalua is the **Honokahua Burial Grounds**, which were unearthed when excavation began for development of the Ritz-Carlton, Kapalua. As the significance of the discovery became apparent, the entire hotel was redesigned and moved inland. The mound, which contains over 900 ancient Hawaiian burials dating between 610 and 1800, has been recognized as a sacred site. The mound is now carpeted in lush grass and bordered by native *naupaka* bushes. Also at this site is a portion of the 16th-century *Alaloa*, or King's Trail, a footpath that once encircled the island.

The modern-day history of Kapalua dates back to 1836 when the Baldwin family of New England settled on the island of Maui as missionaries. The Baldwin family home is now a historical landmark in Lahaina. After 17 years of service, Doctor Baldwin was given 2,675

Kapalua is home to a number of outstanding annual events. In January, the Plantation Golf Course kicks off the PGA tour season by hosting the annual Mercedes Championships. In March, the Ritz-Carlton sponsors its annual cultural festival, "Celebration of the Arts." The Kapalua Tennis Jr. Vets/Sr. Championship is held each May. The acclaimed Kapalua Wine and Food Festival takes place annually in July, followed by the Kapalua Open Tennis Championships in September. LifeFest Kapalua, Hawai'i's premier health and wellness event, also takes place in September, featuring lectures and activities led by some of the country's leading wellness experts. And don't miss the Ritz-Carlton's annual Christmas tree lighting ceremony in early December.

acres, the lands of Mahinahina and Kahana *ahupua'a*, to use for farming and grazing. By 1902 the area known as Honolua Ranch had grown to 24,500 acres as a result of marriages, purchases and royal grants. The ranch crops included taro, mango, aloe and coffee beans. Fishing, along with cattle raising, also took place here. Kapalua became a bustling enclave on the island, with a working ranch that supplied pork and beef to the port of Lahaina. David Fleming arrived from Scotland and became the ranch manager. He experimented with a new fruit, *hala-kahiki*, or pineapple, and planted four acres. The ideal environment produced a very sweet pineapple. It was determined that the coffee operation should be moved upland to make room for a pineapple cannery, homes and bungalows for workers.

The area grew to include a railroad, store, churches and a new house for Fleming. Honolua Ranch became Baldwin Packers, the largest producer of private-label pineapple and pineapple juice in the nation. In the years that followed, Kapalua's acres of grassy slopes were transformed into geometric patterns of silver-blue pineapple fields and the first crop of this fruit was harvested in 1914. By 1946 the cattle operation had ceased. In the next two decades, Baldwin Packers merged with Maui Pineapple and in 1969 became Maui Land & Pineapple Company, Inc.

In the 1970s a new master plan for Kapalua began to take place when Colin Cameron (a fifth-generation descendent of the Baldwin family) chose 750 acres of his family's pineapple plantation for the development of this upscale resort. The result was the Kapalua Bay Hotel (which opened in 1979) and the surrounding resort area that now includes vacation rental villas and homes, a residential community, golf courses and The Ritz-Carlton Kapalua resort. Today the

Kapalua area encompasses 1,500 acres surrounded by 23,000 acres of pineapple plantation and open fields.

Perhaps the most unusual program that Maui Land & Pineapple Company, Inc. has undertaken is to develop a home for Koko, the gorilla. Dr. Francine "Penny" Patterson has been working with Koko for over 20 years, teaching her communication through sign language. Future plans call for Koko to relocate to 70 acres in West Maui. The compound will be called the Allan G. Sanford Gorilla Preserve in memory of the son of Mary Cameron Sanford, chair of Maui Land & Pineapple. Koko will be joined by two male companions, Michael and Ndume. Visitors will not be permitted at the compound, but there are plans for a visitor center that will have remote viewing via video cameras. For more information call the Gorilla Foundation (800-63-GO-APE).

The **Kapalua Heritage Trail** is a self-guided tour that follows a loop along the resort roadways, with stone monuments marking historical sites of interest and explaining the history of the area. The first marker is in front of the Honolua Store (one of the oldest buildings in the area), although you can begin at any point along the loop.

Big changes are in store for the Kapalua resort area. **The Kapalua Bay Hotel** and adjoining **Kapalua Shops** are to be demolished and redeveloped beginning in summer 2006, and plans are in the works for Honolua Village, a new development in the heart of the resort community that will include 50,000 square feet of new retail space. The first phase has broken ground and is scheduled to open in spring 2006. The second, larger phase is scheduled for completion in late 2007.

The **Maui Pineapple Plantation Tour** (reservations 808-669-8088) is offered Monday through Friday, 9:30 a.m. to noon and 12:30 p.m. to 3 p.m. Tours are approximately two-and-a-half hours with breathtaking views of the West Maui Mountains and a visit to the fields of the only pineapple canning operation in the United States. Must be 10 years or older. Cost is $29.

SERENADE BY SLACK KEY

The Masters of Hawaiian Slack Key Guitar Concert Series takes place weekly at the Ritz-Carlton Kapalua. Slack key is a traditional Hawaiian guitar style, and at these weekly concerts you will have the privilege of hearing Hawai'i's finest slack key artists in an intimate theater setting (120 seats). The concerts, featuring a different guest artist each week, take place Tuesday evenings at 6 p.m. and 8:30 p.m. Tickets are $40. 808-669-3858; 888-669-3858; www.slackkey.com.

The **Kapalua Shops** (located adjacent to the Kapalua Bay Hotel) offer a showcase of art, gifts, clothing and other treasures. Here you will find **The Kapalua Logo Shop** (808-669-4172), where everything—from men and women's resort wear to glassware—displays the Kapalua butterfly logo. **Kapalua Kids** (808-669-0033) features fashions for infant-sizes through boys and girls size 7.

A number of free cultural programs are offered throughout the week at the shops. Beginning hula lessons are available on Monday and Friday from 10:30 to 11:30 a.m. Learn the basic footsteps and the history behind this ancient dance. Ukulele lessons are provided on Tuesday from 1 to 3 p.m., with a limited supply of ukuleles available for class use. On Tuesday from 10:30 a.m. to noon, enjoy free Hawaiian music featuring slack key, steel guitar and hula. Thursday, 10 to 11 a.m., is a performance of ancient hula, and on Friday from 3 to 4 p.m. you can enjoy a presentation of Tahitian dance. Schedules and activities change occasionally, so check with the Kapalua Shops at 808-669-3754. The Kapalua Shops are open daily from 9 a.m. to 6 p.m.

The road beyond Kapalua (leading all the way to Wailuku) is paved and in excellent condition and offers some magnificent shoreline views. It is not as long and winding as the Hana Highway, but it is extremely narrow at some points, with one-way sections precariously perched at the edge of ocean cliffs. It is best negotiated in the daylight, as it does twist and turn, and this route can be nerve-wracking even under the best conditions. Most West Maui residents don't travel this road to Wailuku/Kahului, opting instead for the longer but faster southern route around the *pali* and through Ma'alaea. If you choose to experience this northern route, drive slowly and cautiously. Like the Hana Highway, there is just no way to "get there fast" on this road. Travel time from Napili to Wailuku on this route is about one-and-a-half hours. Some rental car companies may restrict your use of this road, so check your contract carefully.

Slaughterhouse (Mokule'ia) Beach is only a couple of miles beyond Kapalua and you may find it interesting to watch the body surfers challenge the winter waves. Just beyond is **Honolua Bay**, where winter swells make excellent board surfing conditions. A good viewing point is along the roadside on the cliffs beyond the bay.

Continuing on, you may notice small piles of rocks like granite snowmen. This is graffiti, Maui style. They began appearing several years ago and these mini-monuments have been sprouting up ever since. There are some wonderful hiking areas here as well. One terrain resembles a moonscape, while another is a windswept peninsula with a symbolic rock circle formation.

As you travel from Kapalua around the top of the island to Kahului there is plenty to see, including a delightful art gallery and gift shop that appears out of nowhere on this isolated road (you can't miss it). Some of the cliffs have incredible scenic viewpoints, so pull over (carefully) and enjoy the view. You will also pass the village of **Kahakuloa**. Some of the residents living here are descendants from the original settlement some 1,500 years ago. It was not many years ago that electricity finally arrived here, but much is still done in the way of old Hawai'i. Tours of the town are available. (See "Land Tours" in Chapter 6.)

Ma'alaea-Kihei Area

Ma'alaea, to many, is just a signpost en route to Ka'anapali, or a harbor for the departure of a tour boat. (Some even think that Buzz's Wharf, with its more visible and prominent sign, is the real name of the town!) However, Ma'alaea (which means "area of red dirt") is the most affordable and centrally located area of the island.

Ten minutes from Kahului, 25 minutes from Lahaina and 15 minutes from Wailea—it's easy to see the entire island while headquartered here. You can hop into the car for a beach trip in either direction. Even better is the mere six-mile jaunt to Kahului/Wailuku for some of Maui's best and most affordable eateries. This is a quiet and relaxing vacation retreat as well as a popular residential area. Seven of the ten condominium complexes are located on a sea wall on or near the harbor of Ma'alaea, while the other three are on one end of the three-mile-long Ma'alaea Bay beach.

The ocean and beach conditions are best just past the last condo, the Makani a Kai. There is less turbidity, providing fair snorkeling at times, good swimming and even two small swimming areas protected by a reef. (These are found on either side of the small rock jetty with the old pipe.) This length of beach is owned by the government and is undeveloped, providing an excellent opportunity for beach walkers, who can saunter all the way down to Kihei. The condominium complexes are small and low-rise with moderate prices and no resort activities. The vistas from many of the lanais are magnificent, with a view of the harbor activity and the entire eastern coastline from Kihei to Makena, including majestic Haleakala, as well as Molokini, Kaho'olawe and Lana'i. The view is especially pleasing at night and absolutely stunning during a full moon when its light shimmers across the bay and through the palm trees with the lights of Upcountry, Kihei and Wailea as a backdrop. No other part of the island offers quite such a tranquil and unique setting. Another plus are the almost constant trade winds (although sometimes a bit too windy) that provide non air-conditioned cooling as opposed to the sometimes scorching stillness of the Lahaina area.

The **Ma'alaea Harbor** area is a scenic port from which a number of boats depart for snorkeling, fishing and whale watching. **Buzz's Wharf** restaurant is one of the oldest on the island and still a prominent landmark. **The Harbor Shops** at Ma'alaea have been a welcome addition to the area. In the shopping center you'll find **Kaua'i Island Soap Factory** has opened their first outer-island store and makes products on location. Interesting to watch! **The Pacific Whale Foundation** is located here with information and an exhibit. Clothing, jewelry, art and a variety of eateries fill out the center.

In 1998 Coral World International opened their **Maui Ocean Center** as the first and most compelling feature of the Ma'alaea Harbor Village. The aquarium is the only one of its kind in Hawai'i. More information on the center is in Chapter 6 under "Aquariums." Allow a minimum of two hours to tour the Maui Ocean Center. It is a fascinating place for young and old alike.

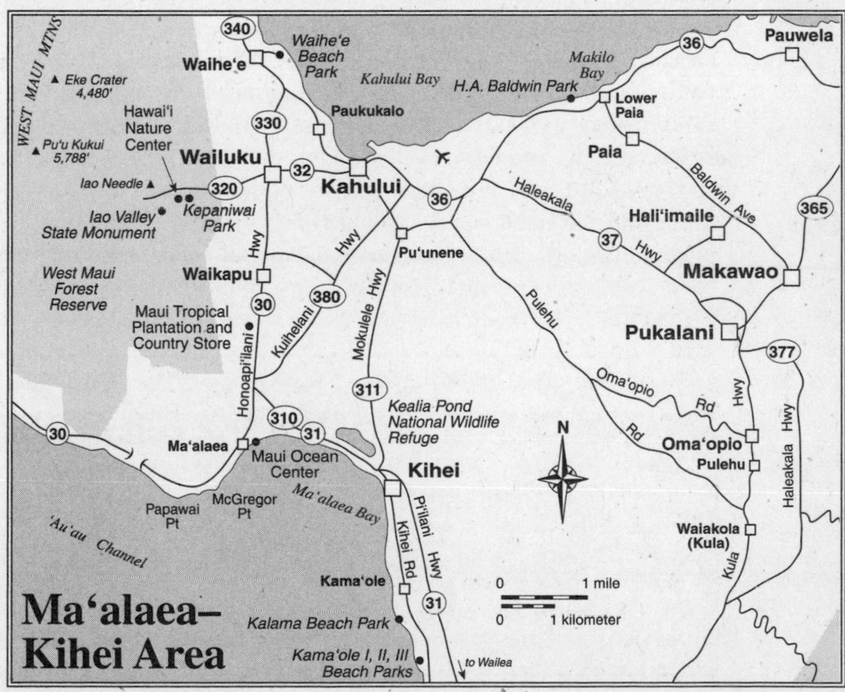

KIHEI

The Kihei area of South Maui has a much different feel from West Maui or Lahaina. There are no large resorts with exotically landscaped grounds, very few units on prime beachfront land and more competition among the properties, making this area a good value for your vacation dollar. (And a good location for extended stays.) Kihei always seemed to operate at a quieter and more leisurely pace than Ka'anapali and Lahaina, but recent years have seen a significant upsurge of development, not of condos but of shopping complexes.

There is no real distinct dividing line, but I have always sensed that the north end of Kihei and the south end of Kihei are two unique areas. North Kihei is 15 minutes from the Kahului Airport and the first area you come to in Kihei; the condominiums here stretch along a gently sloping white-sand beach. The pace is quieter here, and I feel that the beaches are better than at the southern end of Kihei.

Traveling south toward Kihei from Ma'alaea you'll pass large wetlands and **Kealia Pond National Wildlife Refuge** (note warnings to watch for sea turtles that sometimes make their way onshore here to nest and lay their eggs). Among the endangered species currently making their home in Kealia Pond are the Hawaiian coot and Hawaiian stilt. Kids and adults alike will enjoy a self-guided tour of the refuge's coastal wetlands and sand dunes. You'll see turtles (and whales) from the elevated vantage point, with the aid of interpretive signs along the elevated boardwalk (approximately .75 mile) on the tour trail. The family can learn about the cultural history of the area, bird identification, biology, ecology and watershed. The boardwalk is scheduled to be completed and officially opened in summer 2005. 808-875-1582.

The southern end of Kihei began its growth after that of West Maui, and the result is a sprawling six-mile stretch of coastline littered with more than 50 properties, nearly all condominiums, with some 2,400 units in rental programs. Few complexes are actually on a good beach. However, many are across Kihei Road from one of the

Summer in Ma'alaea is a time for surfing. Summer swells coming into the bay reportedly create the fastest right-breaking ridable waves in the world and are sometimes referred to as "the freight train." The local kids are out riding from dawn to dusk. Winter brings calmer seas with fair snorkeling over the offshore reef. The calm conditions, undisturbed by parasailing and jet skiing, also entice the humpback whales into the shallow waters close to shore.

Kama'ole Beach Parks. A variety of beautiful beaches are just a few minutes' drive away.

The only historical landmark in this area is a **totem pole** near the Maui Lu Resort that commemorates the site where Captain Vancouver landed.

The **Maui Research & Technology Park** is located up from the highway on Lipoa Street. Although generally not open to the public, it is worth a mention since their high-performance computing center is one of less than two dozen in the entire nation. It is also one of the largest configurations of IBM super-computing technology in the U.S.

A small shopping area is found at the Sugar Beach Condominiums, and several snack shops can be found along Kihei Road in this area. Down farther along South Kihei Road, you'll have plenty of shopping centers to choose from.

Every corner of Kihei seems to be sprouting a shopping mall. In general, the complexes all have a combination of restaurants, retail shops and commercial offices. Traveling east on South Kihei Road, the first shopping center is **Longs Drugs Kihei Center**, on the *mauka* (toward the mountains) side of the street. Here you'll find eateries that include **Big Wave Cafe**, **Antonio's** and **Sushi Paradise**, which offers karaoke after 9 p.m. (808-879-3751). Opposite this mall is McDonald's. Pi'ikea Street runs between this shopping center and the next one (Azeka Mauka), traveling up to the Pi'ilani Highway and the **Pi'ilani Village Shopping Center** with a huge Safeway. Be careful crossing! The cars whiz by down here.

Azeka Mauka (also called Azeka Place II) has a variety of shops, a bank, a Kaiser Permanente clinic, and several restaurants including **Hanafuda Saimin**, **Peggy Sue's**, **The Coffee Store**, **Stella Blues**, **Jawz Fish Tacos**, **Bocalino Bistro** and **Panda Express**. The little shop called **Who Cut the Cheese** (11 a.m. to 7 p.m.) features a selection of gourmet cheeses, wines and specialty meats to take out.

Directly across from Azeka Mauka, on the *makai* (toward the sea) side of South Kihei Road, is **Azeka Makai** (808-874-8400), also known as Azeka Place I, where Bill Azeka opened his first store in 1950. **Azeka's Ribs & Snack Shop** (7:30 a.m. to 3 p.m.), situated in front of Ace Hardware, continues to offer great deals on island-style plate lunches, and Azeka's ribs (available until 5 p.m.) are legendary on Maui. Buy them uncooked and take them back to your condo for a great barbecue ($8.99 pound). Other dining options include **Taco Bell**, **Baskin Robbins**, **Vietnamese Cuisine**, **Shabu Shabu Toji**, **Royal**

Thai Cuisine and **Home Made Cafe**. The post office is also located in this shopping center.

Continuing east on South Kihei Road, you'll come to East Lipoa Street (Star Market is on the right). Turn left on Lipoa and behind Kihei Plaza you'll find **Lipoa Center**, home to **Maui PlayCare**, a medical clinic and pharmacy, **Gold's Gym**, **Hapa's** nightclub, and two Mexican restaurants—**Horhito's** and **Fernando's**. When I stopped here recently, there were no retail shops at the center.

Further down South Kihei Road you'll find **Kukui Mall**, a large complex designed in Spanish-style architecture with movie theaters and an assortment of shops and restaurants: **Local Motion**, **The Blitz** fitness center, a hair salon, **Starbucks**, **Pizza Express**, **Thailand Cuisine**, **Subway**, **Tony Romas**, and **The Sweet Spot**, featuring fried ice cream, shave ice, smoothies and frozen yogurt.

Across the street from the Kukui Mall is the **Aloha Market**, featuring several small open-air shops with island clothing, shell art, Hawaiian print luggage, coral and shell jewelry, other souvenirs, gifts and handicrafts, fresh coconuts and shave ice. (9 a.m. to 7:30 p.m.) My recommendation: you'll find a larger selection of shops with more interesting items a bit farther down the road at Kihei Kalama Village.

The next shopping center, **Foodland/Kihei Town Center**, includes the Foodland grocery store, Kihei Police Station and a variety of shops and restaurants such as a Bali wood store, nail salon, **Fiber Bean Internet Cafe**, **Hirohachi**, **Aroma D'Italia** and **Sansei**.

On the same side of South Kihei Road look for **Kihei Kalama Village**, a delightful cluster of shops, restaurants and small eateries. Its original swap meet–type venue of open-air stalls has been transformed and renovated into a large open pavilion, sheltering the shops amid landscaped gardens and monkey pod trees. This is a great stop for browsing and shopping. Even as a local resident, I find this place fascinating. There are all kinds of creative products, from fine gifts to cheap souvenirs. Art, clothing, jewelry, handicrafts, knick-knacks. Hungry? Take your pick of **Pita Paradise**, **Alexander's Fish & Chips**, **South Shore Tiki Lounge**, **Sala Thai**, **Tastings Wine Bar & Grill**, **Kaiona Cafe**, **Neptune's Martini Lounge**, **Kihei Caffe**, or **Pupu Lounge Seafood Grill**. This is the must-stop shopping area in Kihei.

The next few shopping areas almost run together. The **Dolphin Plaza** at 2395 South Kihei Road is across from Kama'ole I Beach.

Between the Dolphin Plaza and Rainbow Mall is the tiny **Kama'ole Beach Center** at 2411 South Kihei Road. Here you'll find **Maui Tacos** and **Hawaiian Moons Natural Foods**, which features health foods, vitamins and organically grown produce and some cooked hot dishes.

The **Rainbow Mall** is a small center also on the *mauka* (toward the mountain) side of South Kihei Road. They offer jewelry, clothing and souvenir stores, and a stand that serves shave ice and espresso.

Kama'ole Shopping Center is one of the larger malls and has several restaurant selections, including **Denny's** and a **Lappert's Ice Cream** shop. **Haleakala Trading Co.** offers arts and crafts made by local Maui artists—everything from paintings to perfumes. There is also a **Maui Dive Shop, Whalers General Store** and several clothing shops.

The last shopping center in Kihei, across from Kama'ole III Beach, is the **Kai Nani Shopping Center** at 2511 South Kihei Road. Featured restaurants are **Greek Bistro, Annie's Deli, Kai Ku Ono** and **Harlow's.**

Now that you've covered Kihei Road, you can venture up to the **Pi'ilani Shopping Village**. To reach it from Kihei Road, turn *mauka* (toward the mountain) between the Longs Center and the Azeka Place II shopping center on Pi'ikea Road. You'll find the largest Safeway in the islands (open 24 hours). You'll also find the second Maui location for **Hilo Hattie**, as well as **Jamba Juice** and **Starbucks**, assorted gift and clothing stores, small eateries, plus **Roy's** and **Outback Steak House**.

Wailea-Makena Area

WAILEA

Wailea, developed by Alexander and Baldwin, is a well-planned and beautifully manicured resort on 1,500 acres just south of Kihei. There are outstanding luxury resorts and condominiums, as well as championship golf courses and a large tennis center.

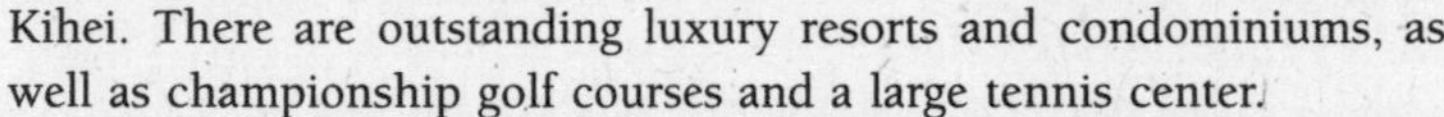

The spacious and uncluttered layout of Wailea is impressive, as is its series of lovely beaches. Spend some time sitting on a beach under a palm tree. There is a paved shoreline trail that travels between the Fairmont Kea Lani up to the Grand Wailea Resort, making it a wonderful option for a stroll, day or night.

The Wailea beaches are actually well-planned and nicely maintained public parks with excellent access, off-street parking and most have restrooms and rinse-off showers. Ulua Beach is a personal favorite.

Be sure you spend some time strolling through the imaginative grounds of the **Grand Wailea Resort Hotel**. The sea remains the theme throughout the resort. At the entry look closely for the Hawaiian sea spirits that are hidden amid this cascading waterfall. Each of the many Hawaiian sculptures has a legend or history—King Kamehameha stands out near the entry and was created by Herb Kane, a noted expert in Polynesian culture and history. He also created many of the mermaids, dancers and fisherman found by the resort's lagoons and streams. Inside the resort you'll find Hena, the mother of the demigod Maui. In the open-air walkway of the Haleakala Wing there are 18 bronzes around the grounds that were sculpted by world-famous artist Fernard Leger. Jan Fisher sculpted 10 life-size pieces for the resort including the maidens bathing and the two trios of hula dancers at the entry of the atrium. Take note of the beautiful relief painting on the walls of the Grand Dining Room. The murals were painted by Doug Riseborough and depict his version of the legend of the demigod Maui. In the center of the dining room is a sculpture done by Shige Yamada entitled "Maui Captures the Sun." Just outside the dining room is a small stage with a fabulous Hawaiian mosaic.

The central courtyard is called the Botero Gallery. These sculptures seem to be getting the most discussion—both good and bad. Fernando Botero is a contemporary artist from Colombia and his work is "oversized." The huge Hawaiian woman reclining on her stomach (smoking a cigarette in the buff) weighs 3,000 pounds and is appraised at $4 million. If you're on the upper levels, be sure to look down to see her from another interesting perspective. The resort offers a complimentary art tour twice weekly.

The Shops at Wailea is a 150,000-square-foot open-air shopping center with more than 65 shops, services and restaurants. There are many known names, including **Louis Vuitton**, **Tiffany**, **Tommy Bahamas**, **Endangered Species**, **Gap**, **Banana Republic** and **Coach**. Among the popular local tenants are **Serendipity**, **Martin & MacArthur**, **Lahaina Galleries**, **Reyn's**, **Noa Noa**, **Lappert's Ice Cream** and **Honolua Surf Company**. The two-story center features not one but two waterfalls, numerous fountains and escalators. Complimentary parking. Located at the intersection of Wailea Alanui Drive and Wailea Ike Drive. 808-891-6770; www.shopsatwailea.com.

MAKENA

Captain James Cook may have been the first Western explorer to visit and map the Hawaiian Islands, but he failed to even see Maui during his first voyage. On his second trip in 1779 he spotted the northeast coastline of Maui, but a rugged and rocky shore prevented him from landing. It was Admiral Jean-Francois de Galaup, Comte de La Perouse, who was the first Western explorer to set foot on Maui. Seven years after Cook had anchored offshore of Maui, Perouse departed from Easter Island and arrived in the Sandwich Isles in May 1786. His two frigates, the *Astrolabe* and the *Boussole*, sailed around the Hana coast searching for a location to land. Discovering Maui's south shore, he decided to land at Keone'o'io to conduct trading with the Hawaiians. He was greeted by local Hawaiians who were friendly and eager to trade. They exchanged gifts and La Perouse visited a total of four villages. This three-hour visit resulted in the Keone'o'io Bay being called La Perouse Bay.

Hiking beyond La Perouse affords some great ocean vistas. You'll see trails made by local residents in their four-wheel-drive vehicles and fishermen's trails leading to volcanic promontories overlooking the ocean. You may even spot the fishing pole holders that have been securely attached to the lava boulders. The **Hoapili Trail** begins just past La Perouse Bay and is referred to as the King's Highway. Another interesting hike is at the **Pu'u Ola'i cinder cone**, the red-earth hillock that juts out to the sea just beyond the cover fronting the Maui Prince Hotel. It is one of Haleakala's craters (under which is a large cave) and is said to be the sacred dwelling place of Mano, the ancestral shark deity. See "Hiking" in Chapter 6 for more information. Here in this area are the last really gorgeous and undeveloped recreational beaches on Maui.

The paved road (Makena Alanui) runs from Wailea past the Makena Surf and Maui Prince Hotel, exiting onto the Old Makena Road near the entrances to Oneuli (Black Sand) Beach and Oneloa (Big Makena)–Pu'u Ola'i (Little Makena) beaches. Past 'Ahihi-Kina'u Natural Reserve on Old Makena Road you will traverse the last major lava flow on Maui, which still looks pretty fresh after some 250 years, and the road continues to La Perouse Bay (see Chapter 5 for more beach information).

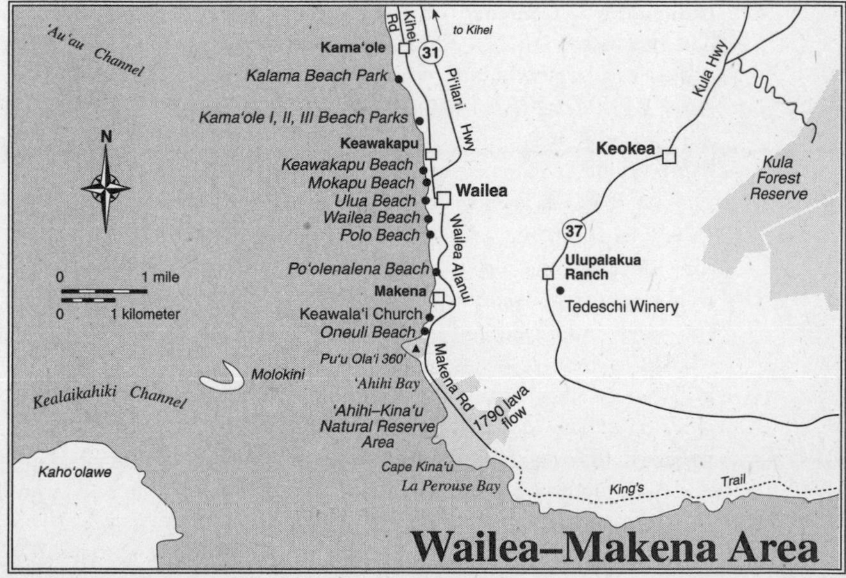

The **Keawala'i Church**, founded in 1832, was once the cultural and spiritual center of the community. The structure, completed in 1854, is three feet thick and made of melted coral gathered from the sea. It is surrounded by ti leaf that was planted because of the Hawaiian belief that it provides protection and healing. This charming historical church sits quietly along the ocean in Makena and is home to an active Protestant congregation. Services are in both English and Hawaiian.

Kahului-Wailuku Area

The twin towns of Wailuku and Kahului are located on the northern, windward side of the island. Wailuku is the county seat of Maui while Kahului houses not only the largest residential population on the island, but also the main airport terminal and deep-water harbor.

Kahului has a very colorful history beginning in the 1790s with the arrival of King Kamehameha I from the Big Island of Hawai'i. The meaning of Kahului is "winning" and may have had its origins in the battle that ensued between Kamehameha and the Maui chieftain. The shoreline of Kahului Bay began its development in 1863 with the construction of a warehouse by Thomas Hogan. By 1879, a landing at the bay was necessary to keep up with the growing sugar cane industry. Two years later, in 1881, the Kahului Railroad Company began. The city of Kahului grew rapidly until 1900, when it was purposely burned down to destroy the spreading of a bubonic plague outbreak. The reconstruction of Kahului created a full-scale commercial harbor, which was bombed along with Pearl Harbor on December 7, 1941. After World War II, a boom began with the development of reasonably priced homes to house the increasing number of people moving to the island. The expansion has continued ever since.

Wailuku has been the center of government since 1930. It is now, slowly, experiencing a rebirth. It is often overlooked by visitors, who miss out on some wonderful local restaurants and interesting shopping. Parking in Wailuku is easy and free along Market Street, or in the large municipal lot off Vineyard Street (entrances also from Market or Church streets).

You can begin your exploration of this region in Wailuku and work your way down to Kahului. Wailuku, in particular, offers a number of historical sites.

Ka'ahumanu Church, Maui's oldest remaining church, was built in 1837 at High and Main streets in Wailuku.

Hale Hoikeike houses the **Bailey House Museum**, circa 1834. To reach it, follow the signs to Iao Valley (heading north from Wailuku) and you will see the historical landmark sign on the left side of the road. Here you will find the Bailey Gallery (once a dining room for the female seminary that was located at this site) with the 19th-century paintings of Edward Bailey. His work depicts many aspects of Hawaiian life during earlier days. Also on display are early Hawaiian artifacts and memorabilia from the missionary days. The staff is extremely knowledgeable and friendly. They also have an array of Hawaiian history, arts, crafts and photographic books for sale. Originally, the Royal Historical Society was established in 1841, but it was not until 1956 that it was reactivated as the Maui Historical Society. The museum was dedicated on July 6, 1957. Of special interest are the impressive 20-inch-thick walls that are made of plaster using a special missionary recipe that included goat hair as one ingredient. The thick walls provided the inhabitants with a natural means of air conditioning. Open Monday to Saturday 10 a.m. to 4 p.m. Admission $5 adults; $4 seniors 60 and over; $1 kids 7 to 12; free 6 and under. 808-244-3326. www.mauimuseum.org.

The **Maui Jinsha Mission** is located at 472 Lipo Street in Wailuku. One of the few remaining old Shinto shrines in the state of Hawai'i, this mission was placed on the National Register of Historic Places in 1978.

The **Halekii** and **Pihana State Monuments** are among Maui's most interesting early Hawaiian historical sites. Both are of considerable size and situated atop a sand dune. These temples were very important structures for the island's early *ali'i*. Their exact age is unknown, although one source reported that they were used from 1765 to 1895. The Halekii monument is in better condition as a result of some reconstruction done on it in 1958. Follow Waiehu Beach Road across a bridge, then turn left onto Kuhio Place and again on Hea Place. Look for and follow the Hawai'i Visitors Bureau markers. Some say the Pihana *heiau* was built by the *menehune* (Hawai'i's legendary little people), while others believe the construction was done under the guidance of the Maui chieftain, Kahekili.

The **Iao Valley** is a short drive beyond Hale Hoikeike, just north of Wailuku. Within the valley is an awesome volcanic ridge that rises 2,250 feet and is known as the Iao Needle. A little known fact is that this interesting natural phenomenon is not a monolithic formation but rather the end of a large, thin ridge. (A helicopter view will give you an entirely different perspective.) Parking facilities are available and there are a number of hiking trails. The State Park is open 7 a.m. to 7 p.m. daily. No admission fee.

The **Tropical Gardens of Maui** is a four-acre botanical garden that features the largest selection of exotic orchids in the Hawaiian Islands. For a small fee you can stroll the grounds where they grow.

Picnic tables are available, and you are welcome to bring your lunch and enjoy a picnic in the gardens. (There is also a snack bar on the property.) Or just stop and visit the gift shop, which is filled with tropical flowers and Maui-made products. Plants can be shipped home. Open Monday through Saturday. Admission $3. 200 Iao Valley Road. 808-244-3085. www.tropicalgardensofmaui.com.

The County of Maui's **Heritage Garden—Kepaniwai Park** is an exhibit of pavilions and gardens that pays tribute to the culture of the Hawaiians, Portuguese, Filipinos, Koreans, Japanese and Chinese. Picnic tables and barbecues are available for public use. They are located on Iao Valley Road, just before the Hawaii Nature Center. Also a popular site for weddings and other functions, it is available for rent from the Maui Parks Department. The Heritage Garden and 7.6-acre park are open daily. 808-270-7232 or 808-270-7389.

Just outside Wailuku on Highway 30 between Wailuku and Ma'alaea is Waikapu, home of the **Maui Tropical Plantation and Country Store**. This visitor attraction has become one of the top ten most heavily visited in the state of Hawai'i. The 60 acres, which opened in 1984, have been planted with sugar cane, bananas, coconut, guava and many other island fruits and flowers. The visitor center includes exhibits, the Country Store (a marketplace featuring made-in-Maui and Maui grown products), and restaurant. There is no admission for entry into the store or the restaurant, but there is a charge ($9.50 adults, $3.50 children 3 to 12) for the 40-minute narrated tram ride around the fields. The tram ride departs every 45 minutes, starting at 10 a.m. It's a very interesting excursion, including several stops for exploring and photos, as well as a coconut-husking demonstration. Open daily 9 a.m. to 5 p.m. 808-244-7643; 800-451-6805; www.mauitropicalplantation.com.

In addition to baseball and mini-soccer fields, the $11 million, 110-acre **Maui Central Park** (Keopualani Park) offers four playground areas, walking and jogging paths and a skateboard park. There are 50 picnic tables scattered throughout. Go up Ka'ahumanu to Kanaloa Street and turn by the Wailuku War Memorial Park, now home of the Hula Bowl that is held there in January. Adjoining is the County's **Maui Botanical Gardens**. They no longer have a zoo, but it's still a nice place to stop. 150 Kanaloa Street.

Market Street, in the heart of Wailuku town, is alive with the atmosphere of plantation-days Hawai'i. The area, rich in history, was built on the site of ancient *heiau* and has witnessed decisive Hawaiian battles. Later, the area hosted the likes of celebrities from Mark Twain to Robert Redford.

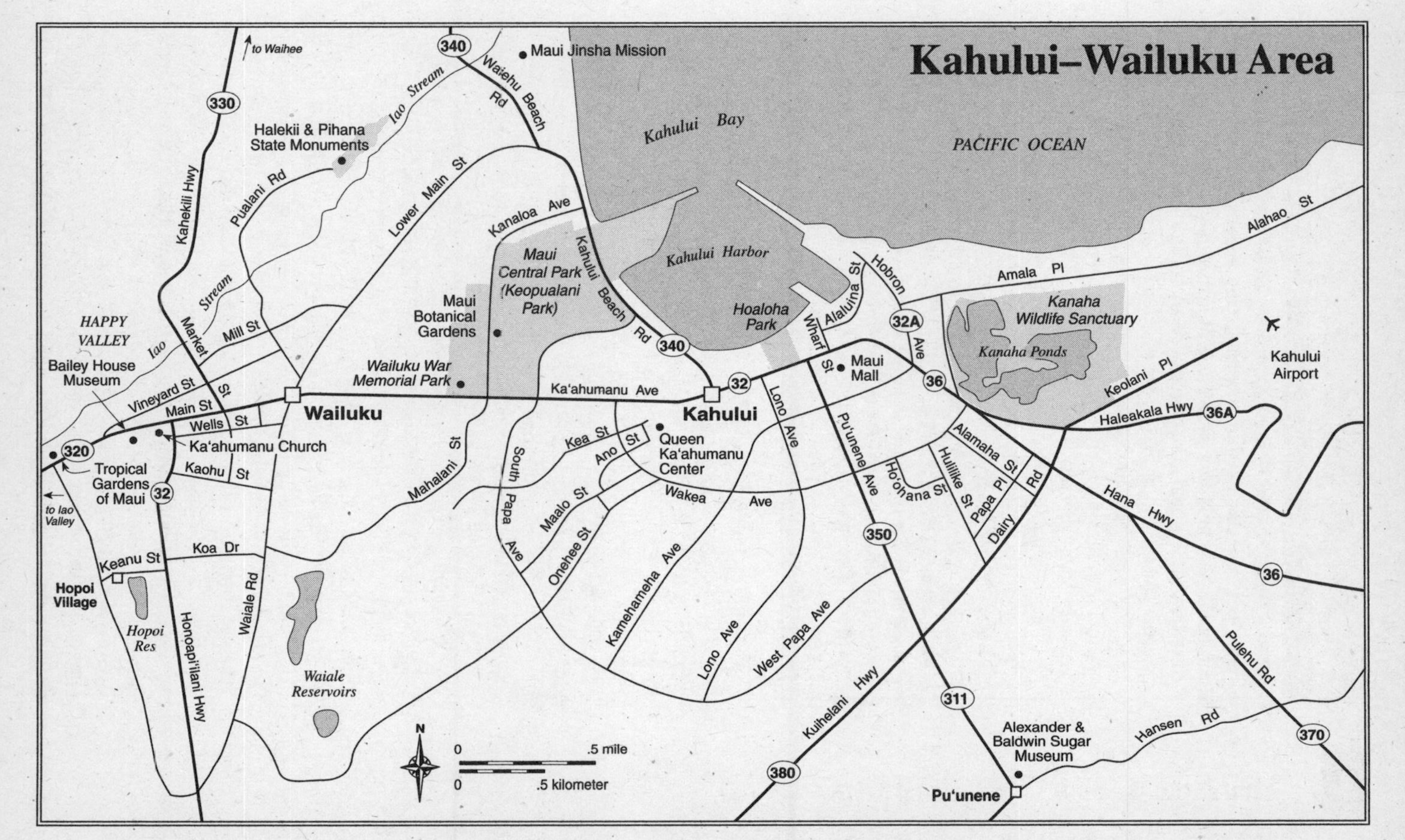
Kahului–Wailuku Area
PACIFIC OCEAN
Kahului Bay
Kahului Harbor
Hoaloha Park
Maui Jinsha Mission
to Waihee
Halekii & Pihana State Monuments
Iao Stream
Kahekili Hwy
Pualani Rd
Waiehu Beach Rd
Lower Main St
Kanaloa Ave
Maui Central Park (Keopualani Park)
Kahului Beach Rd
Maui Botanical Gardens
Wailuku War Memorial Park
HAPPY VALLEY
Bailey House Museum
Market St
Mill St
Vineyard St
Main St
Wells St
Wailuku
Ka'ahumanu Church
Tropical Gardens of Maui
to Iao Valley
Kaohu St
Koa Dr
Keanu St
Hopoi Village
Hopoi Res
Honoapi'ilani Hwy
Waiale Rd
Waiale Reservoirs
Mahalani St
South Papa Ave
Ka'ahumanu Ave
Kahului
Kea St
Ano St
Queen Ka'ahumanu Center
Maalo St
Onehee St
Wakea Ave
Kamehameha Ave
Lono Ave
West Papa Ave
Pu'unene Ave
Wharf St
Alaluina St
Hobron Ave
Maui Mall
Amala Pl
Alahao St
Kanaha Wildlife Sanctuary
Kanaha Ponds
Kahului Airport
Keolani Pl
Haleakala Hwy
Alamaha St
Hulilike St
Ho'oh'ana St
Papa Pl
Dairy Rd
Hana Hwy
Pulehu Rd
Hansen Rd
Kuihelani Hwy
Alexander & Baldwin Sugar Museum
Pu'unene
N
0 .5 mile
0 .5 kilometer
320
330
340
32
32A
36
36A
350
311
380
370

The Hawai'i Nature Center at Iao Valley offers a towering glass solarium and unique hands-on exhibits and activities focusing on Hawai'i's natural history. One excellent option requiring fairly light exertion is their guided rainforest walk through the Iao Valley. Follow ancient footpaths, explore rock terraces and settlement sites, and see forest birds, groves of kukui, guava and coffee trees. Led by naturalists, this walk is appropriate for adults and children over five years of age. Rainforest Walks take place at 11:30 a.m. or 1:30 p.m. Monday through Friday; 11 a.m. or 2 p.m. on Saturday and Sunday. Wear closed-toe shoes suitable for an uneven trail. Cost for the Rainforest Walk is $29.95 for adults and $19.95 for children (must be five or older). The fee includes a visit to the museum. The Museum and Gift Shop are open daily from 10 a.m. to 4 p.m. You can visit just the museum for $6 adults and $4 children age 4 to 11. Advance reservations for the Rainforest Walk are highly recommended. 875 Iao Valley Road; 808-244-6500; e-mail: hinature@maui.net; www.hawaiinaturecenter.org.

Now Wailuku emerges into a new century with a tip of the hat to the last. This rebirth is evident in Wailuku with the **Main Street Promenade**. The turn-of-the-20th-century architecture, old-style walkways, faux gaslight fixtures and a linear courtyard are all part of the ambitious revitalization plan for the town. An open-air food court was planned as a "draw" for both residents and visitors to eat, stroll and be merry. Iron-wrought benches and historic pictures of territorial Wailuku accent the one-acre, three-story building complex of offices, retail shops, additional parking and restaurants that comprise the 2000 block of Main Street.

You'll find a nice little cafe/bistro, **Cafe Marc Aurel**, on Market Street, offering Wi-Fi internet service along with coffee drinks and light meals. If you're interested in all that glitters be sure to stop by **Precision Goldsmiths**, next door at 16 North Market Street. The three proprietors of this little gem of a store produce world-class jewelry using high-tech equipment along with old-world craftsmanship. Darren, Brian and Gary invite you to stop in and visit their showroom Monday through Friday 9 a.m. to 5 p.m. You can also call to arrange after-hours appointments. 808-986-8282; www.precisiongoldsmith.com.

For snacks and sweets, stop by the **Island Hearts Chocolate & Candy Factory** at the corner of Market and Main, and the **Maui Popcorn Factory** just a little farther down Market Street. You should also take a look in the **Sig Zane** store. One of Hawai'i's top designers, Sig Zane's unique island clothing is prized among local residents. No well-dressed "local's" wardrobe is complete without at least one Sig Zane hanging in the closet. www.sigzane.com.

Set against the lush backdrop of the Iao Valley and the West Maui Mountains, the Wailuku area offers a quaint alternative to the hustle-bustle vacation centers of Lahaina and Kihei. Surrounding this area is a multitude of wonderful and inexpensive ethnic and local restaurants—refer to Chapter 4 "Where To Dine" for some Wailuku dining recommendations.

Many of Wailuku's shops are open only Monday through Friday during daytime hours, in order to capitalize on the business and government crowd, so if you want to explore as many of them as possible, make your Wailuku excursion midweek during the day.

Heading out of Wailuku toward Kahului, it's difficult to tell precisely where one town starts and the other leaves off. Wailuku subtly melts into Kahului, and before you know it the charm of old Wailuku is behind you and you are surrounded by fast-food restaurants, shopping centers and lots of traffic. This is Kahului.

The Kanaha Wildlife Sanctuary is off Route 32, near the Kahului Airport, and was once a royal fishpond. Now a lookout is located here for those interested in viewing the stilt and other birds that inhabit the area.

The **Alexander and Baldwin Sugar Museum** is located at 3957 Hansen Road in Pu'unene. Pu'unene is on Highway 35 between Kahului and Kihei. The tall stacks of the sugar mill (Hawai'i's largest working sugar factory) are easily spotted. The non-profit museum is housed in a historic 1902 home that was once occupied by the plantation's superintendent. The museum features six rooms of artifacts (some dating back to the 1800s), photomurals and interactive displays, as well as an actual working scale model of a sugar mill. Hours are Monday through Saturday 9:30 a.m. to 4:30 p.m. Open Sunday on a seasonal basis. Admission $5 adult; $2 children 6 to 17; free under age 6. 808-871-8058; www.sugarmuseum.com.

A historic tunnel of trees once lined Pu'unene Road between the mill and Kahului. The trees were taken down to make room for state and county road improvements. The monkeypods were more than 65 years old, but had suffered from time and were frankly rather pitiful. Thirty-five new monkeypod trees have been planted on both sides of the road to replace them.

There are four large shopping centers in Kahului, three of them on Ka'ahumanu Avenue. The **Maui Mall** is only a two-minute drive from the airport. Across the street from Safeway and the Ross Dress for Less store, this is where you'll find **Star Market** and a **Longs Drugs** that is great for picking up

A popular Saturday morning stop for local residents and visitors alike is the **Maui Swap Meet**, held at grounds around the Christ the King Church, next door to the post office off Pu'unene Highway 35. You'll find us referring to this event for various reasons throughout this guide. For a 50¢ admission (children free) you will find an assortment of vendors selling local fruits and vegetables, new and used clothing, household items, jewelry, hand-crafted items, art and many of the same souvenir-type items found at higher prices in resort gift shops. The swap meet is also a great place to pick up tropical flowers, and for only a few dollars you can lavishly decorate your condo during your stay. Protea are seasonally available here for a fraction of the cost elsewhere. This is also the only place to get true spoonmeat coconuts. These are fairly immature coconuts with deliciously mild and soft meat and filled with sweet coconut milk. I usually stock up on a week's supply at a time. These coconuts are the ones that are trimmed off the trees while still green and far different from the hard brown ones in the supermarkets. One booth I discovered had coconuts that could be inscribed with a message and mailed home as a postcard. Plain were around $10 including postage, painted were $15. Another must-purchase is a treat from Four Sisters Bakery (if they aren't here, check them out at their bakery location in Wailuku). Swap meet hours are 8 a.m. to noon. This is an outstanding family outing to central Maui. Combine it with breakfast or lunch at one of the local restaurants nearby. 808-877-3100.

sundry and souvenir items. Maui Mall offers the biggest (and, in my opinion, the best) movie theater on the island and a variety of small shops and restaurants, including a Maui institution: **Tasaka Guri Guri**, a kind of local creamy sherbet you can order with or without beans at the bottom of the cone. The **Paper Airplane Museum** (808-877-8916) features the unique juice-can creations of the Tin Can Man along with aviation model exhibits and pictures depicting the history of aviation in the Hawaiian islands. Tin can and paper airplane demonstrations, too. Open 9 a.m. to 5 p.m. Monday through Saturday, 11 a.m. to 5 p.m. Sunday. **Maui Creations** features handcrafted one-of-a-kind gift and jewelry items and **'Ano 'Ano Gallery and Gifts** (808-873-0233) features art, jewelry and sculpture by Maui artists. The newly instituted **Maui County Store** (808-984-3466) is also located in this mall. Operated by the Maui Community College Center for Entrepreneurship, the store features merchandise bearing logos from the County Firefighters, Maui Police Relief, Hawaii Lifeguard Association and University of Hawai'i. Open Monday through Friday 9 a.m. to 6 p.m.; Saturday 9 a.m. to 3 p.m.; closed Sunday.

The older, local-style **Kahului Shopping Center**, framed by monkeypod trees and filled with local residents playing cards, was devastated by a fire in March 2004. The destruction of **Ah Fook's** grocery, a landmark store beloved by local residents, was a blow to the community and the store's future is yet to be determined. The trees still stand, however, and many of the other stores survived the fire.

The largest shopping center—and the only genuine "shopping mall" on the island—is **Queen Ka'ahumanu Center**, with a second level that includes a food court. Two major department stores (**Sears** and **Macy's**) anchor this mall with the island's largest selection of clothing, jewelry and specialty shops in between. Here you'll find the **Fun Factory**, **Waldenbooks**, **Gap**, **Kids' Foot Locker** and a large food court, as well as **Ruby's Diner** and **Koho Grill and Bar**. A great place to spend a rainy day on Maui—shop, eat and see a movie at the **Ka'ahumanu Theatres**. **Maui PlayCare** offers day care services at this mall. Mall hours (retail stores) are 9:30 a.m. to 9 p.m. Monday through Saturday; 10 a.m. to 5 p.m. Sunday. 275 West Ka'ahumanu Avenue.

The fourth major shopping center is the **Maui Marketplace** (on Dairy Road), which includes a number of large, mainland-style stores (like **Sports Authority**, **Old Navy** and **Office Max**). This is where you'll also find **Borders Books**, **Music & Café**, **Jamba Juice** and **Starbucks** as well as a small food court.

There is a **Big Kmart** at the intersection of Dairy Road and the Hana Highway and next door is **Costco**, a wholesale warehouse. Membership is required, but it is good at any of their Hawai'i or mainland stores. Costco has some great deals; be sure to check out their Hawaiian CD music and books section—not a complete selection, but good prices on those items that they do stock. Big Kmart has convenient hours (7 a.m. to 10 p.m.) and some very good values on everyday items such as sandals. At the other end of Dairy Road there is a **Wal-Mart** and a **Home Depot**. All these stores make life easier for us here on Maui, but have definitely increased the traffic congestion on Dairy Road, which also is the route to the airport. Don't be surprised if you get slowed down in this area.

If you don't have accommodations with a kitchen or mini-refrigerator, you might want to pick up an inexpensive ice chest at one of these stores. Stock it with juices, fruit and snacks to enjoy in your hotel room and for use on beach trips or drives to Hana and Haleakala.

Upcountry

The western slopes of Haleakala are generally known as "Upcountry" and consist of several communities including Makawao, Pukalani and Kula. The higher altitude, cooler temperatures and increased rainfall make it an ideal location for produce farming. A few fireplace chimneys can be spotted in this region where the nights can get rather chilly. Upcountry, where the air is cool and clear, is an awesome location to spend at least part of your vacation holiday; if you love hiking and the outdoors the opportunities are in your backyard. If you have a two-week vacation, I suggest spending three or four of those nights Upcountry.

Haleakala means "house of the sun" and is claimed to be the largest dormant volcano in the world. While it rises 10,023 feet above sea level, the greater portion of this magnificent mountain lies below the ocean. If measured from the sea floor, Haleakala would rise to a height of nearly 30,000 feet. The volcano is truly awesome and it is easy to see why the old Hawaiians considered it sacred and the center of the earth's spiritual power.

Haleakala National Park was created in 1916, but the first ranger did not arrive until 1935. In July 1945 the park, concerned about the vandalism of endangered plants, began checking visitors' cars. The park encompasses two districts, the Summit District and the Kipahulu District. (The Kipahulu District, on the southeast shore near Hana, will be discussed later.) The charge for entry to the Summit District is $10 per car; U.S. residents 62 and older enter free. Free admission if you have a current card for the National Park System ($50 for a yearly pass to all parks). The most direct route is to follow Highway 37 from Kahului, left onto Highway 377 above Pukalani, and then left again onto Highway 378 for the last 10 miles. While only about 40 miles from Kahului, the last part of the trip is very slow. There are numerous switchbacks and many bicycle tours riding the 38-mile downhill coast. Two hours should be allowed to reach the summit.

Sunrise at the summit of Haleakala is a popular and memorable experience, but plan your arrival accordingly. Many visitors have missed this spectacular event by only minutes. The *Maui News*, the local daily, prints sunrise and sunset times. The park offers a recording of general weather information and viewing conditions that can be accessed by calling 808-577-5111. Be sure you have packed a jacket or blanket as the summit temperature can be 30 degrees cooler than the coast, and snow is a winter possibility. Early to mid-morning from May to October generally offers the clearest viewing. However, fog (or

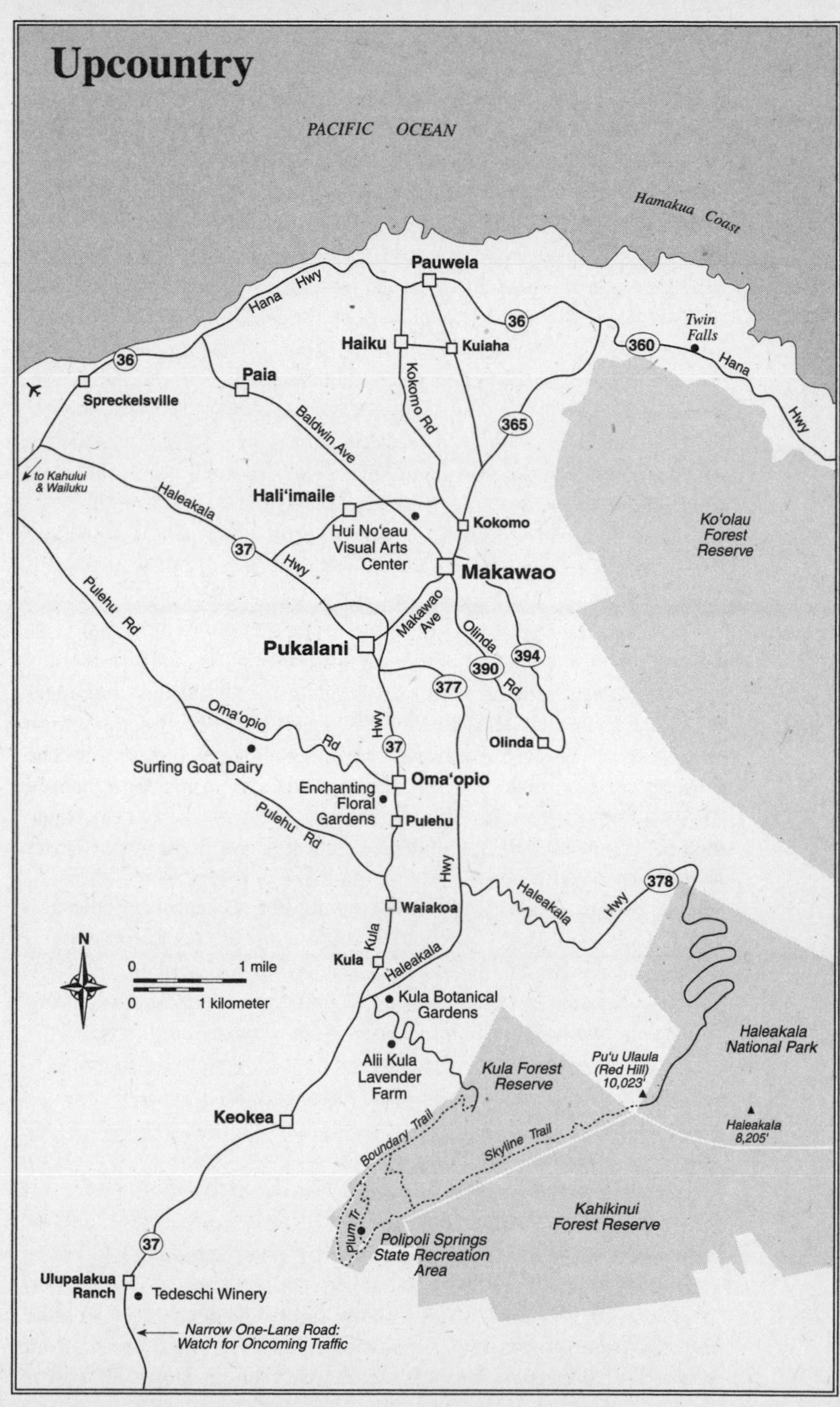
Upcountry
PACIFIC OCEAN
Hamakua Coast
Pauwela
Hana Hwy
36
Twin Falls
360
Hana Hwy
Haiku
Kuiaha
36
Paia
Spreckelsville
Kokomo Rd
Baldwin Ave
365
to Kahului & Wailuku
Haleakala
Hali'imaile
Kokomo
Hui No'eau Visual Arts Center
Ko'olau Forest Reserve
37
Hwy
Makawao
Pulehu Rd
Makawao Ave
Olinda Rd
Pukalani
390
394
377
Oma'opio Rd
Hwy
37
Olinda
Surfing Goat Dairy
Oma'opio
Enchanting Floral Gardens
Pulehu
Pulehu Rd
Hwy
378
Haleakala Hwy
Waiakoa
Kula
Kula
Haleakala
N
0 1 mile
0 1 kilometer
Kula Botanical Gardens
Alii Kula Lavender Farm
Kula Forest Reserve
Pu'u Ulaula (Red Hill) 10,023'
Haleakala National Park
Keokea
Boundary Trail
Skyline Trail
Haleakala 8,205'
Kahikinui Forest Reserve
Plum Tr.
Polipoli Springs State Recreation Area
37
Ulupalakua Ranch
Tedeschi Winery
Narrow One-Lane Road: Watch for Oncoming Traffic

vog—a volcanic haze from the Big Island) can cause very limited visibility. Thus, an advance call may save you a trip.

Safety Note: Don't combine scuba diving with any high altitude activity (like a trip to Haleakala or a helicopter ride) within 24 hours.

The first stop for visitors is **Park Headquarters** (808-572-4400). Hiking and camping information and permits are available here (see "Hiking" in Chapter 6 for information on trails). You can also see an example of the rare **silversword** that takes between 20 to 50 years to mature, then blooms in a profusion of small purplish blossoms in July or August. It then withers and dies in the fall. Some years many silverswords may flower, while in other years there may be none. The Hawaiian word for silversword is *'ahinahina* (Hina is the goddess of the moon). Once, the silverswords grew in abundance and were even used on floats for parades in the early part of the 1900s. By the 1930s, however, wild cattle, goats and sheep found them so appealing that there were only a few thousand silversword plants remaining.

Exhibits on Haleakala history and geology are in the **Haleakala Visitors Center**, located at an elevation of 9,745 feet. It is open daily from sunrise to 3 p.m.; hours may vary. A short distance by road will bring you to the **Summit Building**, located on the crater rim. This glassed-in vantage point (the Pu'u Ulaula outlook) is the best for sunrise. The rangers give morning talks here at 9:30, 10:30 and 11:30 a.m. The view, on a good day, is nothing short of awesome. The inside of the volcano is 7 miles long, 2 miles wide and 3,000 feet deep. A closer look is available by foot or horseback (see "Horseback Riding" in Chapter 6).

The park service maintains 30 miles of well-marked trails that access three cabins and two campgrounds. The three cabins are Holua, Kapalaoa and Paliku, all located within the Haleakala Wilderness Area. These cabins are for "real" hikers as they are accessible only by trail. (The closest cabins are 4 to 10 miles away from the trailheads.) These cabins are available through a lottery system. See "Camping: Haleakala National Park" in Chapter 6 for detailed information.

The **Haleakala Observatories** can be seen beyond the visitor center, but the buildings are not open to the public. They house a solar and lunar observatory operated by the University of Hawai'i, television relay stations and a Department of Defense satellite station. Eight telescopes (located on the top of Haleakala) perform work for the Department of Defense in space surveillance and optical research and development. www.ulua.mhpcc.af.mil/~det3.

There is more of Upcountry to be seen than just Haleakala. Plan to spend a leisurely day exploring this beautiful region, with or without a trip to the summit. The Maui Upcountry experience is completely different from the beach resort experience. Upcountry offers

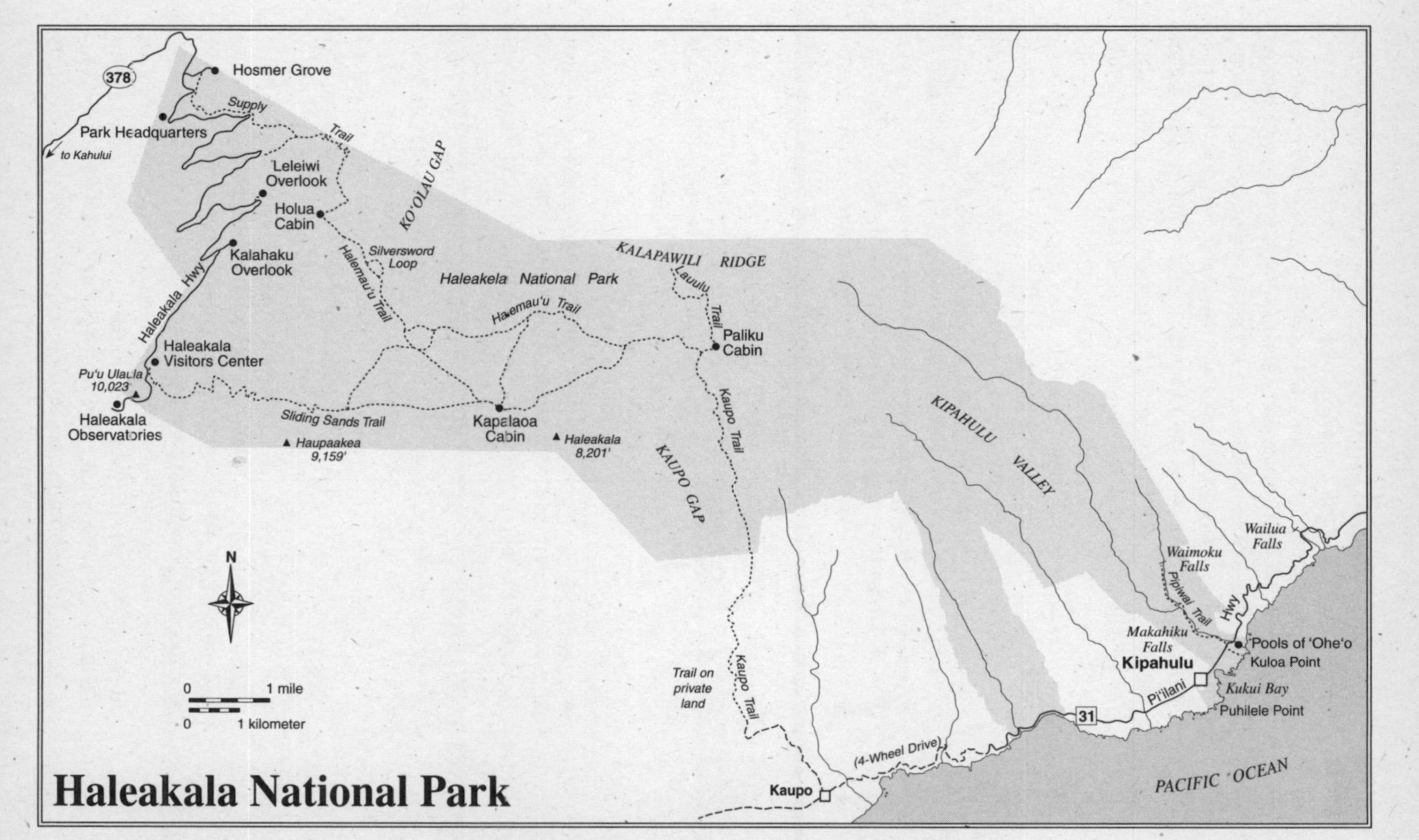

Haleakala National Park

panoramic vistas of the western half of Maui and the islands offshore; cool, fresh air scented with eucalyptus; acres of lush, rolling pasture lands with horses, cows and goats in abundance; and countless shades of green, dotted with the occasional vivid lavender of a blooming jacaranda tree. It makes for a truly lovely drive.

The **Kula** area offers rich volcanic soil, and commercial farmers harvest a variety of fruits and vegetables. Grapes, apples, pineapples, lettuce, artichokes, tomatoes and, of course, Maui onions are only a few examples. The magnificent protea, a floral immigrant from South Africa, has created a profitable upcountry business as well. You'll often see tiny roadside stands set up in front of homes or small farms, providing the opportunity to purchase a few protea stalks inexpensively. Kula can be reached by retracing Highway 378 down from Haleakala to the Upper Kula Road, where you turn left.

There are a number of interesting attractions in the Kula area:

The **Kula Botanical Gardens** offers six acres of gentle paths, a flowing stream, numerous beautiful collections of plant species, a koi pond, bird aviary (with love birds, doves, finches and one tiny "button quail"), and peaceful rest areas. The self-guided walking tour takes approximately 45 minutes at a leisurely pace. The garden, which was established in 1968, is privately developed and owned by Warren and Helen McCord. Admission is $5 adults, $1 children 6 to 12 years, free for children under 6. Open 9 a.m. to 4 p.m. daily. 808-878-1715.

HIKING HALEAKALA

A 2.5-hour hike down **Sliding Sands Trail** into the Haleakala Volcano is offered regularly by the park service. Check bulletin boards for schedules. They depart from the Haleakala Visitors Center. A hike featuring native Hawaiian birds and plants is also scheduled regularly. Keep your eye out for the many *nene* (Hawaiian geese) that inhabit the volcano. Check with the ranger headquarters (808-572-4400) to verify trips, dates and times.

The **Enchanting Floral Gardens**, on Highway 37 in Kula, is another beautiful place for a stroll. Owned by a local Japanese couple, the gardens are a labor of love—they admit the admission fees don't come close to covering the expenses to maintain the garden, but for them it is a pleasure to share such beauty with others. Each season you will experience something different at this garden, as new flowers bloom in colorful banks along the walkways. The garden encompasses eight acres and more than 2,000 species of plants and flowers from around the world. Lovely views, gazebos and quiet places to sit and enjoy the beauty of nature. The self-guided walking tour takes about 40 minutes. Admission is $5 adults, $1 children 6 to 11; under 6 free. Open 9 a.m. to 5 p.m. daily. 808-878-2531; www.flowersofmaui.com.

Alii Kula Lavender Farm is located in Kula on the slopes of Haleakala. Owned and operated by a local family, the garden offers tea and luncheon tours (lavender lemonade, anyone?), as well as self-guided tours and a delightful gift shop with every imaginable lavender product. Their products are being used by many of Maui's top restaurants, resorts and spas. Unfortunately, the tea and luncheon tours have become pretty pricey at $30 and $55 respectively, so I suggest you enjoy a self-guided tour of the garden and a lengthy stop at the wonderful gift shop. Many specialty tours and classes (such as holiday lavender wreath-making) are also offered. Check out their website for more information as well as a map to their farm—they are a bit difficult to find without explicit directions, but well worth the effort. Open 8:30 a.m. to 4:30 p.m. daily; gift shop open 9 a.m. to 4 p.m. daily. 1100 Waipoli Road, Kula; 808-878-3004; 808-878-8090 (tea/luncheon reservations); www.aliikulalavender.com.

Surfing Goat Dairy is a must-see, particularly if you have children traveling with you. Surfing Goat is a family business operated by Thomas and Eva-Maria Kafsack in Oma'opio (just below Kula). This area of Upcountry has a drier climate, which offers the goats mild weather, and there is plenty of room for grazing. The herd is made up of about 80 milking goats, and each year another 100 or so kids are added. A visit during "kid season" is absolutely delightful, with the baby goats frolicking about. The goats are three varieties, saanen (white), alpines (with upright ears) and Nubians (hanging ears). The guided tour gives you a close-up look at the process from milking the goats to the production of goat cheese (the farm's specialty). As for the cheeses, they are of the gourmet variety—winning awards and being snatched up by the top chefs on the island for their culinary creations. Take a look at the selection while you're there—a wide variety is available for purchase. The casual guided tour runs 20 to 30 minutes ($5 per person). Open Monday through Saturday 10 a.m. to 5 p.m. with the last tour at 4 p.m., and Sunday 10 a.m. to 2 p.m. with the last tour at 1 p.m. There are many special events and tours as well. Visit their website for details. 3651 Oma'opio Road (turn at the corner of Oma'opio and Ikena Kai Place); 808-878-2870; www.surfinggoatdairy.com.

Kula Marketplace is a great new addition to Upcountry shopping. The 2,800-square-foot shop, located next to Kula Lodge on Haleakala Highway, opened in 2005 and is full of unique island clothing, art, jewelry, crafts, furnishings, lotions, candles, soaps, music and foods, including a small gourmet market with organic fruits, beer, wine, snacks, sandwiches and international (including French) cheeses.

The store will create custom-made gourmet picnic baskets for you with your own selection of items, tucked neatly into a *lauhala* basket. (Call ahead to order, or choose your items while in the store.) They also have ready-made products that are easy to cook or prepare in your condo. I was told that 60 percent of the items in the Kula Marketplace are from Maui, 20 percent from across the state of Hawai'i, and 20 percent international. They have some unique items that I've seen nowhere else in Hawai'i. Don't miss the display case with local jeweler Neil Coshever's one-of-a-kind jewelry and ornaments made of real Maui orchids cast in fine silver. They are absolutely exquisite and are not available anywhere else. I highly recommend a stop at Kula Marketplace for a long, enjoyable browse. Open 8 a.m. to 7 p.m. daily. 15200 Haleakala Highway; 808-878-2135; e-mail: info@kulamarketplace.com.

Next to Kula Marketplace (before Kula Lodge) is a tiny shop called **Upcountry Harvest**, specializing in the flowers of Upcountry Maui: protea, heliconia, anthurium, orchids, ginger and more. Flowers are available fresh, dried or in wreaths, along with a selection of other gift items. You can also order gift boxes of flowers to be sent to the mainland. Open 8 a.m. to 5 p.m. daily. www.upcountryharvest.com.

Inside **Kula Lodge**, wander downstairs into the cozy **Curtis Wilson Cost** art gallery. If you have been enchanted with the beauty of Upcountry Maui, you'll see it captured in this artist's work. His gallery at Kula Lodge opened in 1973. (He has another gallery on Front Street, Lahaina.) Open 8:30 a.m. to 5 p.m. daily.

As you continue north from Kula (toward Tedeschi Winery at Ulupalakua), be sure and stop in Keokea at the landmark **Grandma's Coffee House**. This homey little restaurant is the place for some freshly made, Maui-grown coffee, hot-out-of-the-oven cinnamon rolls or a light lunch. Another great place to get picnic items, too. See Chapter 4 for more information.

Polipoli Springs State Recreation Area is a state park high on the slopes of Haleakala above Kula at an elevation of 6,200 feet. Continue on Highway 377 past Kula and turn left on Waipoli Road; if you end up on Highway 37, you've gone too far. The sign indicating Polipoli may be difficult to spot, so you could also look for the sign indicating someone's home that reads "Walker" (assuming the sign is still there when you visit). It's another 10 miles to the park. Fortunately, the road has been paved, making accessibility easy. The 10-acre park offers miles of trails, a picnic area, restrooms, running water, a small redwood forest and great views. This is an excellent trail for the non-athlete or family. Keep your eye out for earth that appears disturbed. This is an indication of one of the wild boars at work. While not likely, I still advise you to keep your ears alert—you don't want to encounter one.

Approximately nine miles past the Kula Botanical Gardens on Highway 37 is the **Ulupalakua Ranch**. The **Tedeschi Winery** (808-878-6058; www.mauiwine.com), part of the 30,000-acre ranch, made its debut in 1974 and is Maui's only commercial winery. The historic King's Cottage houses the Tasting Room (open 9 a.m. to 5 p.m.), which provides samples of their unique pineapple wines and grape table wines at a mango-wood bar (handcrafted from one of the many trees at the surrounding ranch). Their latest label is a raspberry dessert wine. Free daily guided tours are offered at 10:30 a.m. and 1:30 p.m. The tour begins at the Tasting Room, then continues on to view the presses used to separate the juice from the grapes, the large fermenting tanks, and finally the corking and the labeling rooms. It is an interesting behind-the-scenes tour. The winery grounds also provide a lovely picnic area, set under 100-year-old trees. If you haven't already picked up your picnic lunch from Kula Marketplace or Grandma's Coffee House, walk across the street to the **Ulupalakua Ranch Store & Deli**. Featuring an old-fashioned country store atmosphere, you'll find all kinds of gift and food items here. The store is open from 9:30 a.m. to 5 p.m. daily, but the grill hours are 11 a.m. to 1:30 p.m. After that, you'll have to be content with whatever prepared sandwiches and foods are available in the deli case. The grill features hormone-free Ulupalakua beef and elk (beef burger $6.95; elk burger $7.95) and other hot sandwiches.

If you continue on past the ranch and winery on Highway 37, it's another very long 35 miles to Hana with nothing but beautiful scenery. Don't let the relatively short distance fool you. It is a good two-hour trip (one way), over some fairly rough sections of road that are not approved for most rental cars. During recent years this road has been closed often to through traffic due to severe washouts. Check with the county to see if it is currently passable. I'd recommend doing just the first part of the road, driving as far as Kaupo. (See "Hana Highway" section for more information.)

If you are not continuing on, I suggest you turn around and head back—past Kula—to Pukalani and Makawao. You can take the route down via Makawao, the colorful "cowboy" town, and then on to Paia on the coastline, if you're still in the mood to explore.

Pukalani Terrace Center has a grocery store and a few small shops. There is a **Pizza Hut** for take-out only, **KFC**, **Subway** and local-style food at **Maui Mixed Plate**. I've heard very good things about **Pukalani Tamale** in Pukalani Square. Looks like a little hole-in-the-wall but I've heard the Mexican food is great. There's no real shopping of interest in Pukalani, so head on down to Makawao.

The town of Makawao offers a Western cowboy (*paniolo*) flavor with a scattering of shops down its main street. There are several good restaurants if you are feeling hungry. For a snack, I recommend the **Komoda Store & Bakery**, famed for its cream puffs. But get there early. If you arrive after 10 a.m. or so, the cream puffs will probably be sold out. Open Monday through Friday 7 a.m. to 5 p.m.; Saturday until 2 p.m.

There are many trendy boutiques, art galleries and other shops lining the two main streets of Makawao that can provide for an enjoyable afternoon shopping excursion. Most of the stores are open around 10 a.m. to 5 p.m. daily (11 a.m. on Sunday). And just a little ways up the street is the **Maui School of Therapeutic Massage**, where you can treat yourself to a relaxing massage for just $25. 1043 Makawao Avenue; 808-572-2277.

The Courtyard at 3620 Baldwin Avenue houses **Viewpoints Gallery** (808-572-5979), a fine cooperative gallery featuring local artists, and a cluster of interesting gift shops including **Hot Island Glass**. This glass-blowing studio and gallery is a Makawao must-see. Open 9 a.m. to 5 p.m. daily; glassblowing usually takes place from 10:30 a.m. to 4:30 p.m. Tuesday through Sunday. (Call to confirm, 808-572-4527). Also in the courtyard is **Designing Wahine**, a fun store for unique, island-style children's clothing and other gifts. 808-573-0990.

Fourth of July weekend is wild and wonderful in Makawao. Festivities include a morning parade through town and several days of rodeo events. Check the local paper for details.

The **David Warren Gallery** is a favorite of mine for its whimsical art. Take a look at the variety of items (napkin rings, flower vases, business card holders, mobiles, candle holders, etc.) made of recycled silverware. They are very clever. 3625 Baldwin Avenue; 808-572-1288.

Just past Makawao, the **Hui No'eau Visual Arts Center** may at first seem a little out of place (located at 2841 Baldwin Avenue). However, there could not be a more beautiful and tranquil setting than at this estate called *Kaluanui*, built in 1917 by famous Honolulu architect C.W. Dickey for Harry and Ethel Baldwin. The house was occupied until the mid-1950s, and in 1976 Colin Cameron (grandson of Ethel Baldwin) granted Hui No'eau the use of Kaluanui as a visual arts center. The small gift shop is open year-round with a selection of unique items made by local artists, and in early December they have a wonderful Christmas fair that draws shoppers from all across the island. Near the entrance to the nine-acre estate are the remains of one of Maui's earliest sugar mills. It utilized mule power and was the first Hawaiian sugar mill to use a centrifuge to separate sugar crystals. What were once stables and tack rooms are now ceramic studios. The Arts Center is open daily from 10 a.m. to 4 p.m. No admission, but donations are welcome. The center also welcomes visitors who might like to walk or picnic on the grounds. 808-572-6560; www.huinoeau.com.

Hana Highway

PAIA-HAIKU

A little beyond Kahului, along the highway that leads to Hana, is the small town of Paia. Paia means "noisy," but the origin of this name is unclear. This quaint town is reminiscent of the early sugar cane era when Henry Baldwin located his first sugar plantation in this area. The wooden buildings are now filled with antiques, art, boutiques, gift shops and cafes to attract the passing traveler. The advent of windsurfing, which takes place at nearby Ho'okipa Beach, has caused a rebirth in this small charming town.

The Maui Crafts Guild in Paia is a cooperative designed to give local Maui artisans a place to show their work. Established in 1982, coop-member artists take turns working in the store, so every day you have the opportunity to meet and chat with one of the artists. All work is made by hand and includes sculpture, tiles, baskets, framed art, hats, vases, clothing, jewelry and more. The store is located at 43 Hana Highway. Open 9 a.m. to 6 p.m. daily. 808-572-9697. Make sure you take a look upstairs in the Maui Crafts Guild building. The **Arthur Dennis Williams Gallery** is located there, featuring koa sculptures, furniture and paintings. 808-579-9331.

Maui Hands on Hana Highway is another interesting store that features the art and handicrafts of local artisans. On Baldwin Street, check out the **Hemp House** shop, featuring all things hemp, and the **Natural Impressions Gyotaku Gallery**, which showcases the ancient art of fish prints. For a sweet pick-me-up, drop into the **Cakewalk Paia Bakery** near the corner of Hana Highway and Baldwin. There are all kinds of sweet fresh-baked treats to tempt you.

Approximately two miles past Paia, if the winds are right, you will be able to spot what appear to be colorful giant butterflies darting along the ocean offshore. This is **Ho'okipa**, thought by some to offer the world's best windsurfing. There won't be much activity in the morning, but if you are heading past here in mid- to late afternoon when the winds pick up, you are sure to see numerous windsurfers daring both wind and wave. These waves are enough to challenge the most experienced surfers and are not for the novice except as a spectator sport. You'll note that on the left are the windsurfers, while surfers enjoy the waves on the right. A number of covered pavilions offer shaded viewing, and the beach, while not recommended for swimming, has some tide pools (of varying size depending on the tidal conditions) for children to enjoy a refreshing splash. This beach is also a popular fishing area for local residents and you may see some folks along the banks casting their lines.

At mile-marker 11 and mile-marker 14 are two well-marked turnoffs to Haiku and Makawao. Haiku is a couple of miles inland and noted for its two old canneries that have been converted into local, Hawaiian-style shopping areas. If you're traveling up Haiku Road from mile marker 11, the first is the **Haiku Marketplace** (located at the corner of Kokomo and Haiku Roads). If you're hankering for some of Maui's finest local grinds or a box lunch for the road, then definitely make a stop at **Hana Hou Café** located here. Farther along Haiku Road, turn left on West Kuiaha Road, and you'll come to the **Pauwela Cannery**, home to **Pauwela Café**, where you'll find excellent homemade breakfasts and lunches. In the same building, you'll see **Upcountry Sewing Center**, which offers a unique opportunity for visitors—particularly moms and daughters—who would like to learn to sew together and create a special memento from Maui that you can take home and wear. They will assist you in choosing island fabrics and a pattern, measuring, fitting, cutting and sewing until you have a one-of-a-kind finished product. 375 West Kuiaha Road; 808-575-9880.

The Hawaiian translation for *Haiku* is "abrupt break"; it is not unusual to experience some overcast, rainy weather here—and the weather conditions can change rapidly. Back on the Hana Highway, just past mile-marker 15 is **Maui Grown Market** (also with a location in Paia), offering a chance to pick up a picnic lunch and beverages before you continue on your way. Maui Grown Market has become very popular for their "loaner dogs." They have five adorable, friendly dogs that love to go for rides, and many visitors—missing their own canine pets—have enjoyed taking a dog with them for the day. Maui Grown Market says the dogs are free for the day—all you have to do is buy a picnic lunch—and return their dog at the end of the day, of course. 93 Hana Highway, Paia, 808-579-9345; or 4320 Hana Highway, Haiku, 808-572-1693.

Highway 36 ends just past mile-marker 16. At this point on Highway 365 there is an intersection with Kaupakulua Road. The Hana Highway continues from here, but it is now Highway 360 and the mile-markers begin again at zero. So begins the Hana Highway.

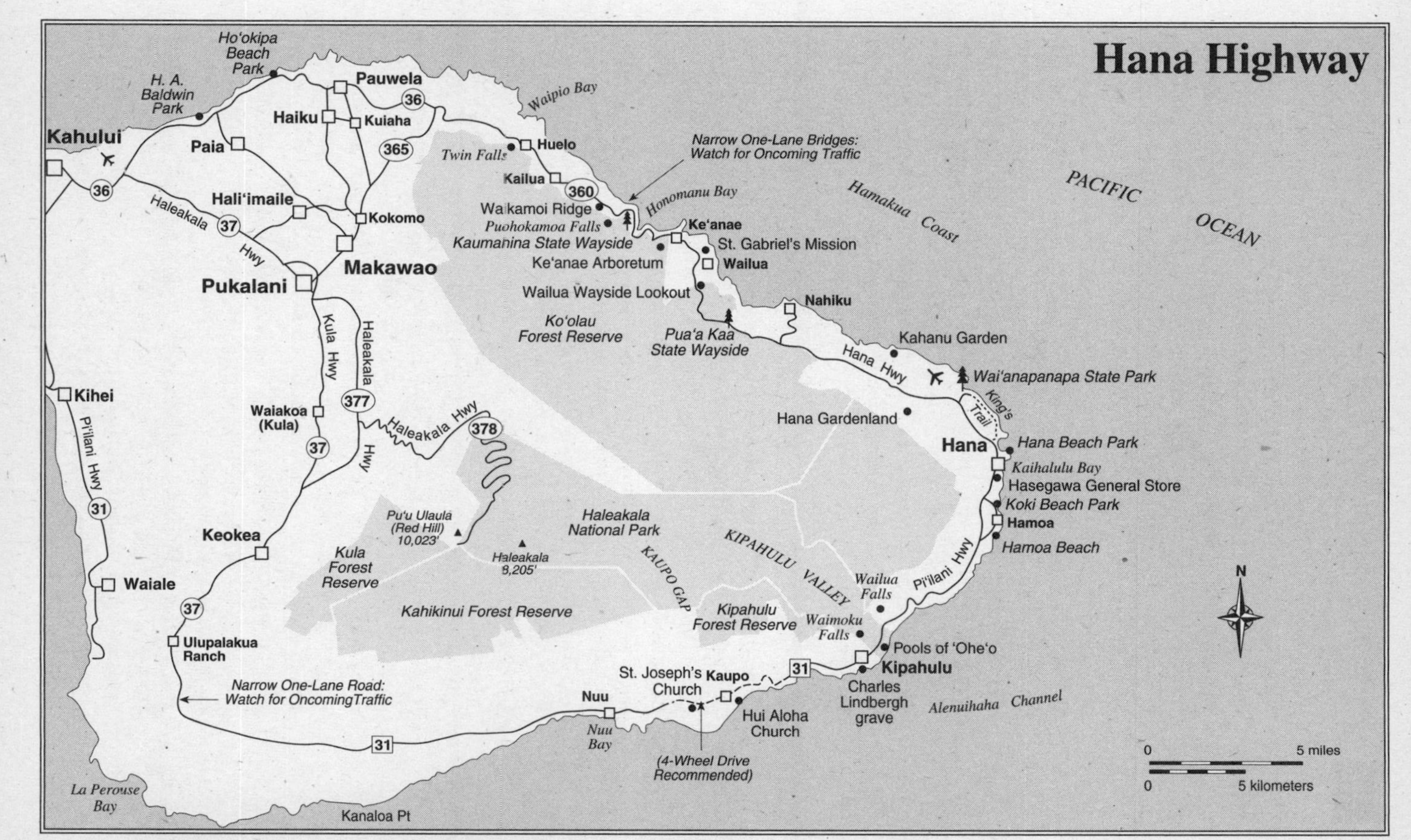
Hana Highway
Ho'okipa Beach Park
H. A. Baldwin Park
Kahului
Pauwela
Haiku
Kuiaha
Paia
Hali'imaile
Kokomo
Makawao
Pukalani
Haleakala Hwy
Kula Hwy
Waipio Bay
Twin Falls
Huelo
Kailua
Narrow One-Lane Bridges: Watch for Oncoming Traffic
Honomanu Bay
Waikamoi Ridge
Puohokamoa Falls
Kaumanina State Wayside
Ke'anae
St. Gabriel's Mission
Wailua
Ke'anae Arboretum
Wailua Wayside Lookout
Ko'olau Forest Reserve
Pua'a Kaa State Wayside
Nahiku
Hamakua Coast
PACIFIC OCEAN
Kahanu Garden
Hana Hwy
Wai'anapanapa State Park
King's Trail
Hana Gardenland
Hana
Hana Beach Park
Kaihalulu Bay
Hasegawa General Store
Koki Beach Park
Hamoa
Hamoa Beach
Kihei
Pi'ilani Hwy
Waiakoa (Kula)
Keokea
Waiale
Ulupalakua Ranch
Pu'u Ulaula (Red Hill) 10,023'
Haleakala 8,205'
Haleakala National Park
Kula Forest Reserve
Kahikinui Forest Reserve
KAUPO GAP
KIPAHULU VALLEY
Kipahulu Forest Reserve
Wailua Falls
Waimoku Falls
Pools of 'Ohe'o
Kipahulu
Charles Lindbergh grave
Alenuihaha Channel
St. Joseph's Church
Kaupo
Hui Aloha Church
(4-Wheel Drive Recommended)
Nuu
Nuu Bay
Narrow One-Lane Road: Watch for OncomingTraffic
La Perouse Bay
Kanaloa Pt
N
0
5 miles
0
5 kilometers

HANA

If you've heard any discussion at all about Maui, it has probably included a mention of the infamous **Hana Highway**. The twisted, narrow route starts on Maui's northern shore and follows the windward coast down to Hana, which is situated on the eastern side of the island. A tiny community that has changed little over the decades, Hana attracts the traveler who yearns to get a taste of real Hawai'i, as well as the celebrity attempting to find a little anonymity and seclusion. More native Hawaiians live in Hana than in any other part of Maui, and the area is relatively undeveloped. A substantial reason for the isolation of Hana is the Hana Highway. Unless you fly into the little Hana Airport, it takes a long time to get there.

You must approach your excursion on the Hana Highway with the understanding that the town of Hana is not the destination; the journey itself is the destination, and you need to relax and enjoy it as such. The road to Hana is an amazing experience, and you will miss that experience—and probably be disappointed—if you are in a rush to "get to Hana." As a destination, Hana town has very little to offer, aside from beautiful scenery and a charming look into Hawai'i's past. Some visitors arrive in Hana saying, "This is it??!" No fast food restaurants, shopping centers or high-rise condos here. Just incredible beauty, lush pastures dotted with white-faced cattle and a quiet Hawaiian community that has a rich history. There are sights to see in the Hana area, and I will cover those later in this section, but please be aware that the "Hana experience" is an all-day adventure that includes the journey to and from the actual town.

The trip to Hana by car from Kahului will take approximately two hours, one way, if you don't make any stops along the way. (Add another 45 to 60 minutes for travel from Lahaina/Kapalua areas.) However, you will certainly want to stop and enjoy the sites along this spectacular coastline, so plan on three hours or more one-way. While it may be true that it is easy to fall in love with Hana, getting there is quite a different story. Even with greatly improved road conditions as a result of repaving, the drive to Hana is not for everyone. It is not for people who don't like a lot of scenery, those who are in a hurry to get somewhere, or those who don't enjoy long drives. However, it is a trip filled with roadside waterfalls (particularly after a recent rain), lush tropical jungles, bamboo forests, wild guava and fragrant ginger growing along the roadside.

Maps are deceiving. It appears you could make the 54-mile journey from Kahului to Hana in much less than two hours, but there are 617 curves—many of them hairpin—and 54 one-lane bridges along this narrow road. (And believe it or not, each of these bridges has its own Hawaiian name.) You'll note in some places that the road is so narrow there isn't even room to paint a center line. With drivers visually exploring the many scenic wonders, you may find cars traveling in the middle of the road, thus making each turn a potentially thrilling experience.

If you're traveling to Hana, I highly recommend you spend at least one night there. Making all the stops to see the sights along the way will be much more pleasant (and less exhausting) if it can be done at a leisurely pace, and spending a night or two will give you the opportunity to explore other aspects of Hana. If you are in a rush to reach Hana and are not interested in traveling along the famed Hana Highway, there are commuter flights available from Kahului to the Hana Airport.

In addition to the slow pace of travel, for those (like myself) who are plagued with motion sickness, this road can be grueling. (I had never seen my iron-stomached husband experience motion sickness until we were on this road.) Prepare ahead of time by using your chosen motion sickness remedy—and take some extra along just in case, then drive the road slowly and enjoy the ride. I tend to have an extreme motion sickness problem, but have found that I can easily manage the road to Hana if we drive slowly (not swinging wildly around the curves!) and stop occasionally for a breath of fresh air at one of the many beautiful waterfalls, parks and scenic outlooks. There are many places to linger along the Hana Highway, and you should do just that.

There are a couple of good resources you might consider taking along on your drive. If you'd like a self-guided yet narrated tour, for less than $20 you can purchase a cassette tape "Best of Maui" that will guide you to the stops along the way. The tape allows you to drive at your own pace while listening to information on the legends and history of the islands. (That being said, I didn't find any information on the tape that wasn't already included in this guidebook.) General information about Hana can also be obtained at www.hanamaui.com, a website provided by the folks at Hana's Hasegawa General Store.

The drive to Hana can best be enjoyed before and after the throngs of daily visitors make their trips—they are all driving in during the morning and out in late afternoon—another argument for making your trip an overnight visit. The best travel days are Saturday and Sunday, since road crews are generally not at work and you won't encounter the many delivery trucks that keep Hana supplied with all its goods. The Hana road is particularly beautiful after a recent rain, as the waterfalls are larger and more numerous. However, stormy weather can also pose road hazards. Call 808-248-7800 for daily road conditions on the Hana Highway.

Along the Hana road you will discover a Maui different from the sunny, dry resort areas on the West and South shores. The coast here is turbulent with magnificent coastal views, rain forests and mountain waterfalls that create wonderful pools for swimming. (*Warning*: do not drink the water from these streams and falls—the water has a high bacteria count from the pigs that live in the forests above. Additionally, the beaches along the Hana Highway are generally unsafe for swimming.)

The Hana Highway was originally built in 1927 with pick and shovel (which accounts for its narrowness) to provide a link between Hana and Kahului. In days gone by when heavy rains caused washouts, it is said that people would literally climb the mud barricades and swap cars, then resume their journey. Today there can be delays on the road of up to two hours if the road is being worked on or a landslide has occurred. Despite all this, hundreds of people traverse this road daily, and it is the supply route for all deliveries to Hana and the small settlements along the way.

If I haven't convinced you to stay overnight and you want to experience this magnificent journey in a single day, be sure to leave as early in the morning as possible, so you won't be making a return trip on this road in the dark. Fill up the gas tank (the last stations before Hana are in Kahului or Paia) and pack some food and drink to take along. With the exception of an occasional fruit stand, there is no place to eat and only limited stops for drinking water along the way. There are a number of wonderful little cafes in Paia offering picnic items for your convenience before you start your Hana journey.

Whether you are planning a day or an extended visit in Hana, packing some rain gear and a warm sweater or sweatshirt is a precaution against the sometimes cooler weather and rain showers. Don't forget your camera, but remember not to leave it in your car unattended. I strongly recommend you take along some mosquito repellent as well.

If you drive, select a car with an automatic transmission, or be prepared for constant shifting. Another choice is to try one of the affordable van tours (or splurge with a company such as Temptation Tours) that go to Hana, and leave the driving to them. Good tour guides will be able to point out the sights of interest along the way that are easy to miss on your own.

If you are to be the driver, be aware that you will be so busy watching the winding road, you won't have much opportunity to enjoy the spectacular scenery along with your passengers. So, again, plan to stop often and enjoy the sights along the way.

On your return, if you don't wish to retrace your route along the windward shore's Hana Highway, check to see whether the tours are operating their vans around the other, leeward side of the island. (That will give you an indication as to the current road conditions.)

Just past the Ke'anae Arboretum is a dead-end that turns off *makai* (to the sea). Follow it down to the ocean and enjoy some beautiful pinnacle lava formations along this peninsula. With the azure Pacific pounding onto the volcanic coastline, it is truly spectacular. The small island offshore is Mokumana Island, a sanctuary for seabirds. This is a great stop to let the kids run around and stretch their legs. At Ke'anae Landing you'll find a little stand that serves up freshly made banana bread and delicious fruit smoothies. Located here is the small **Ke'anae Congregational Church**. The church was built in 1860 of lava and coral and invites visitors to come in and sign their guestbook.

This route follows the Pi'ilani Highway, and travel will depend on the road and weather conditions. You thought the Hana Highway was rugged? This alternate route can be traveled in your personal vehicle, but rental car disclaimers warn against or even prohibit travel along it. The exception is some companies that rent four-wheel-drive vehicles. Check with the rental companies for their guidelines and restrictions. The scenery along the Pi'ilani Highway, on this dry leeward side, is strikingly different from the windward coastal rain forests. Another alternative is to drive to Hana and then fly out of Hana's small airport back to Kahului.

So let's begin your journey. Just past mile-marker 2, you will reach the Hoolawa Bridge. You will probably spot a number of cars on the roadside as well as a fruit stand, the first of many you'll find along the road to Hana. Up the one-mile trail from here is a waterfall. This area, known as **Twin Falls**, offers a pleasant spot for swimming. The first pool has two waterfalls, but by hiking a little farther, two more pools of crystal-clear water created by waterfalls can be easily reached. This is a fairly easy hike, so a good one for the entire family. Remember, don't drink the stream water here or from any other freshwater stream or pool. Mosquitoes can be prolific, so pack bug spray.

There are no safe beaches along the Hana route for swimming, so for a cool dip, take advantage of one of the freshwater swimming holes. The many streams and waterfalls along the Hana Highway are too numerous to list, so enjoy discovering them as you go along and, when it is safe to do so, pull off the road for a closer look. Most have trails running up to the waterfalls, but please respect posted signs and private lands.

A bit past mile-marker 3 is **Huelo**. A short drive at the turnoff will take you down to a historic coral block church built in 1853.

About a half-mile past mile-marker 9 is the **Waikamoi Ridge Nature Trail**, well marked with signs. And near mile-marker 10 is the Waikamoi Bridge. A trail to the right of the bridge goes up from one pool to a beautiful, higher second pool. Also near mile-marker 10 is **Garden of Eden** arboretum. They have a picnic area, restrooms, viewpoints and a nature area. There are parrots that you can get a photo with, and the caretakers have done an excellent job of labeling the local flora. Open 8 a.m. to 3 p.m. Admission $7.50 per person.

Puohokamoa Falls is located near mile-marker 11. There is a pull-off area with parking for only a couple of cars. This area was, for many years, open to the public, with a small picnic area and a short trail leading to a spectacular swimming hole beneath the waterfall. Unfortunately, it is now closed to the public because of accidents and liability issues. Please respect the signs.

Kaumahina State Wayside is located just past mile-marker 12. Here you'll find a lovely park. This area overlooks the spectacular Honomanu Gulch, the rugged Maui coastline, and in the distance the Ke'anae Peninsula. This is a good opportunity to make use of the restroom facilities. (The state park is closed for improvements until late 2005.)

There is a dirt turnoff a half-mile past mile-marker 13. It travels down to **Honomanu Bay**. This is a pristine and peaceful black-lava bay. There is another entrance to the same bay by mile-marker 14, down a rougher piece of road. (At times these roads may be closed to traffic, but it is a short walk to the beach.)

Just past YMCA Camp Ke'anae is the **Ke'anae Arboretum** walking trail. This free six-acre botanical garden is managed by the Department of Land and Natural Resources and is home to myriad tropical plants. A number of the plants have been labeled. Traveling farther up the trail you can view taro patches and hike into the rainforest.

The **Ke'anae Peninsula** was formed by a massive outpouring centuries ago from the volcano Haleakala. The lava poured out of the volcano, flowed down the Ko'olau Gap and stopped in this valley. Today it is an agricultural area with taro, the principal crop. The taro root is cooked and mashed and the result is a bland, pinkish brown paste called poi. Poi was a staple in the diets of early Hawaiians and is still a popular local food product that can be sampled by visitors at lu'aus or purchased at local groceries. Alone, the taste has been described as resembling wallpaper paste (if you've ever tasted wallpaper paste), but poi is meant to be eaten with other foods, such as *kalua* pig. It is an acquired taste in most situations. My Native Hawaiian husband loves poi and eats it with many of his meals, as does his family; I, however, have never acquired the taste for it. So, the poi is all his! Poi is extremely healthy, full of minerals and well tolerated by young stomachs.

Around mile-marker 18, you'll be "Halfway to Hana" and will be greeted with a fruit stand where you can enjoy refreshments, as well as a porta-potty. Turn *makai* (left) here and you'll reach the main attraction in Wailua, **Our Lady of Fatima Shrine**, also known as the Miracle Church. This historical landmark has a fascinating history. In the mid-1800s the community lacked building materials for their church. The common practice was for men to dive into the ocean and bring up pieces of coral. Obviously, this was very laborious and time consuming. Quite suddenly a huge storm hit and, as if by some miracle, deposited a load of coral onto the beach. The story continues that following the construction of the church, another storm hit and returned the remaining coral back to the sea. Now painted over, the coral church walls are still standing today. It is set back from the road.

Another church on the road is the 100-year-old **St. Gabriel's Mission**. Coming up around a bend in the road near mile-marker 19 is the **Wailua Wayside Lookout**. Look carefully for the turnoff on the right. Park and follow the tunnel made by the *hau* plants up the steps to the lookout. The short trek up is worth the excellent view. Back up to the highway and head a few hundred yards to the next lookout. Here you can take a few photos of the incredible Ke'anae Peninsula. There are no signs, but it is easy to spot this gravel area on the left of the roadside.

The slice of this green wonderland seen from the winding Hana Highway is just a small piece of the rugged wilderness above. The **waterfalls** are spectacular along the road, but consider what they are like from the air! I had no idea of the vastness of this tropical forest until I experienced a bird's-eye view. Almost every waterfall and pool is preceded by another waterfall and pool above it, and above it there are yet others.

A half-mile past marker 22 is **Pua'a Kaa State Wayside**. This picture-perfect state park has two waterfalls that are only a short walk from the roadside. This is a favorite stop for a picnic lunch. The waterfalls and pools combine with this lush tropical locale to make you feel sure a *menehune* must be lurking nearby. Restrooms and drinking water are available here, too. Keep your eye out for mongoose (small furry creatures that look like a cross between a squirrel and a weasel). They have been "trained" by some of the van tour guides to make an appearance for a handout at some of these wayside stations. The best place to get a look at them is usually near the garbage cans—or racing across the highway in front of your car. If you don't spot a mongoose, you'll probably meet one of many stray cats in this area. They seem to subsist on the garbage that visitors leave here.

With a little effort a sharp observer can spot the open ditches and dams along the roadside. These are the **Spreckles Ditches**, built over

100 years ago to supply water for the young sugar cane industry. These ditches continue to provide the island with an important part of its supply of water.

At mile-marker 25, just past the bridge on the left is a road to Nahiku. This was once a rubber plantation that operated from 1905 to 1916. No real signs left. Between mile-markers 26 and 27 is **Nahiku Tropicals**, which has plenty of plants available to ship home to family, friends or yourself. If you're hungry there is a little roadside enclave on your left before mile-marker 29. **Nahiku Ti Gallery** offers some shopping options and the outdoor BBQ has smoked fish, hot dogs, *kalua* pork sandwiches, corn on the cob and even baked breadfruit. The small cafe has coffee drinks, pastries and other snacks. There's a fruit stand, too, with some rather unusual fruits, as well as fresh coconuts—they'll drill a hole and pop in a straw so you can drink the juice straight from the coconut.

Just before mile-marker 31, the road begins to straighten out. Look for the flagpoles to **Hana Gardenland**, which has gardens and trails to explore. When I last visited Hana, this garden was closed, but I understand it does still open on occasion.

The National Tropical Botanical Garden operates the 126-acre **Kahanu Garden**, reached by turning *makai* (toward the sea) on Ulaino Road, just past mile-marker 31. It is 1.5 miles to the entrance of the garden. The garden is located at Kalahu Point, which is also the location of one of Hawai'i's largest *heiau*, the **Pi'ilanihale Heiau**, dating back to the 16th century; it was constructed by the sons of Maui chief Pi'ilani in his honor. Restoration of the *heiau* is ongoing and two gardens have been added. Self-guided tours are available Monday through Friday, 10 a.m. to 2 p.m. (closed some holidays). Adults $10, children 12 and under free. 808-248-8912; e-mail: kahanu@ntbg.org; www.ntbg.org.

If you plan on arriving in Hana after 5 p.m., make sure you have made dinner plans at the Hotel Hana Maui or brought some food for your evening meal. The Hana Ranch Restaurant (also operated by the hotel) is open only three nights a week for full dinners. All other local restaurants close by 5 p.m.

The **Ka'eleku Caverns** are located in this area as well. Maui Cave Adventures offers fascinating tours of this ancient lava tube network. For more information, see Spelunking in Chapter 6.

Wai'anapanapa State Park is four miles before Hana at mile-marker 32. It covers an area of 120 acres. Translated, Wai'anapanapa means "glistening water." This area offers a number of historical sites, ancient *heiau* and early cemeteries. You can spot one of the many lava rock walls used by the early Hawaiians for property boundaries, animal enclosures and also as home foundations.

Wai'anapanapa is noted for its unusual black-sand beach made of small, smooth volcanic pebbles. From the rocky cliff protrudes a natural lava arch on the side of Pailoa Bay. This can be reached by following the short path down from the parking lot at the end of the road. The ocean here is not safe for swimming, but there is plenty to explore.

Splash on some mosquito repellent—tennis shoes are a good idea—and follow the well-marked trails to the **Wai'anapanapa Caves**. The trail is lined with thick vines, a signal left by the early Hawaiians that this area was *kapu* (off limits). The huge lava tubes have created spring-fed pools of cold, clear water. An ancient cave legend tells of a beautiful Hawaiian princess named Popoalaea who fled from Kakae, her cruel husband. She hid in the caves, but was discovered and killed. At certain times of the year the waters turn red. Some say it is a reminder of the beautiful slain princess, while others explain that it is the infestation of millions of tiny red shrimp.

In ancient times there was a trail that circumnavigated the entire island along a coastal route. Known as the King's Highway, it once traversed 138 miles. Maui is the only island to have had a trail that connected its entire coastline. Remnants of the **King's Highway** can be found from here to La Perouse Bay. Examining the King's Highway, you can almost imagine the Hawaiians of years gone by traveling over these smooth stones. The stones were placed on top of the sharp lava rock for obvious reasons. The effort it took to place this many stones must have been tremendous. You can follow this trail east toward Hana, passing a blowhole as well as *heiau* ruins and ending near Hana town at Kainalimu Bay. The trail also goes north toward the Hana Airport for a short distance.

Tent camping is allowed at Wai'anapanapa, and their rustic cabins are available for rent. (See Chapter 3 for more information.)

Now, back in the car for a drive into downtown **Hana**—but don't blink, or you might miss it. Hana offers a quiet retreat and an atmosphere of peace (seemingly undisturbed by the constant flow of tourist cars and vans) that has lured many a prominent personality to these quiet shores. Restaurant choices are extremely limited. The diversity between eating at Tutu's at Hana Bay and the fine dining of the Hotel Hana Maui is quite striking. Shopping is restricted to the Hasegawa General Store, the Hana Ranch Store or a few shops at the Hana Hotel.

Hana Cultural Center opened in 1983. It contains a collection of relics of Hana's past in the old courthouse building and a small museum, as well as an ethnobotanical garden. The museum houses thousands of photographs, along with hundreds of artifacts from early Hawaiian life. Tour the *Kauhale o Hana*, a complex of four authentic Hawaiian *hales*, as well as the restored Hana Courthouse and jail. Located on Uakea Street near Hana Bay—watch for signs.

Open daily 10 a.m. to 4 p.m. Donations appreciated. 808-248-8622; www.hookele.com.

Hana Bay has been the site of many historical events. It was a retreat for Hawaiian royalty as well as an important military point from which Maui warriors attacked the island of Hawai'i, and then were, in turn, attacked. This is also the birthplace of Ka'ahumanu (1768), Kamehameha's favorite wife.

The climate on this side of Maui is cooler and wetter, creating an ideal environment for agricultural development. The Ka'eleku Sugar Company established itself in Hana in 1860. Cattle ranching, also a prominent industry during the 20th century, continues today. You can still view the *paniolo* (Hawaiian cowboys) at work at nearby **Hana Ranch.** There are 3,200 head of cattle that graze on 3,300 acres of land. Every three days the cattle are moved to fresh pastures. Don't be surprised if a *paniolo* flags you to a stop on the road outside Hana while a herd of cattle surrounds your car en route to greener pastures.

Hana has little to offer in the way of shopping. However, the **Hasegawa General Store** offers a little bit of everything. It has operated since 1910, meeting the needs of visitors and local residents alike. Several years ago the original structure burned down, but they reopened in the old Hana Theatre location. This store has even been immortalized in song. You might just run into one of the celebrities who come to the area for vacation. Hours are Monday through Saturday 7 a.m. to 7 p.m., Sunday 8 a.m. to 6 p.m.

The town center (located across the street from Hasegawa General Store) offers a couple of cute gift shops for souvenirs, clothing and whatnot. The **Hotel Hana-Maui** features some lovely upscale gift and clothing shops, and houses the **Hana Coast Gallery**. Definitely worth a browse.

On **Lyon's Hill** stands a 30-foot-tall lava-rock cross in memory of Paul Fagan, a founding father of modern-day Hana. It was built by two Japanese brothers from Kahului in 1960. Although the access road is chained, the front desk of the Hotel Hana-Maui will provide a key. The short trip to the top will reward the visitor with a spectacular panoramic view of Hana Bay and the open pastureland of the Hana Ranch. About a quarter of a mile up toward the cross you'll find the beginning of a jogging/walking trail that follows the track of the old narrow-gauge railroad once used on the plantation. The path runs for about 2.5 miles.

A two-hour **Hana Ranch Eco-Safari** tour is offered daily aboard a 4x4 safari vehicle. The excursion explores the environment of Hana

Ranch, including ancient wetlands and the Koa Tree Reforestation Project to help perpetuate the East Maui Watershed, home to 300 endangered species. $89 per person; 808-248-7711 or 808-264-9566; www.hana-maui-ecoadventures.com.

For ocean activities in Hana, contact **Hana-Maui Sea Sports**. They offer a variety of ocean excursions including kayaking, snorkeling, free diving and surfing in the Hana area. 808-248-7711 or 808-264-9566; e-mail: hanaseasports@aol.com.

Kaihalulu Beach (Red Sand Beach) is located in a small cove on the other side of Kauiki Hill from Hana Bay and is accessible by a narrow, crumbly trail more suited to mountain goats than people. The trail descends into a cove bordered by high cliffs and is almost entirely enclosed by a natural lava barrier seaward. Far too many accidents have happened on this dangerous access so we can't recommend it. (See Chapter 5 for more details.)

Hamoa Beach is a lovely beach that has been very attractively landscaped and developed by the Hotel Hana-Maui in a manner that adds to the surrounding lushness. The long sandy beach is in a very tropical setting and surrounded by a low sea cliff. As you leave Hana toward the Pools of 'Ohe'o, look for the sign 1.5 miles past the Hasegawa store that says "Koki Park–Hamoa Beach–Hamoa Village." Follow the road, you can't miss it.

In ancient times, about 75,000 Hawaiians lived along this coastal region. Today, Hana is home to approximately 1,800 residents, the majority of whom are Hawaiian or part-Hawaiian.

As you head south out of Hana, you'll pass fields of grazing world-famous Maui beef cattle and re-enter the tropical jungle once more. Numerous waterfalls cascade along the roadside and after ten curvy, bumpy miles on a very narrow two-lane road (a 45- to 60-minute drive) you arrive at one of the reasons for this trip, the **Kipahulu Valley** and **Haleakala National Park**. The Kipahulu Ranger Station offers cultural demonstrations, talks and guided walks. $10 per vehicle or $5 per person for walk-ins, bikes or motorcycles. 808-248-7375.

Looking for the Seven Sacred Pools? They don't exist! The National Park Service notes that the term "Seven Sacred Pools" has been misused in this area for more than 50 years. Along the stream there are actually more than 24 large and small pools along the one-mile length of the gulch, so even the term "Seven Pools" is misleading and inaccurate. The term *'Ohe'o* refers to the name of the area where the Pipiwai Stream enters the ocean. When the Kipahulu District was acquired by Haleakala National Park in 1969, park rangers interviewed native Hawaiians born and raised in the area to document its history. Without exception all local residents claimed that none of the pools was ever considered sacred. In 1996 the Haleakala National Park finally settled on a name. So now when you head to Kipahulu you can visit the **Pools of ʻOheʻo**.

Beneath the narrow bridge, water cascades over the blue-gray lava to create the lovely lower pools. These are just a few of the more than 20 pools that have been formed as the water of this stream rushes to the ocean. When not in flood stage, the pools are safe for swimming, so pack your suit (*caution:* no diving allowed). Swimming off the black-sand beach is very dangerous and many drownings and near-drownings have occurred here. The best time to enjoy the park may be in late afternoon when the day visitors have returned to their cars for the drive home. (This is another good reason to make Hana an overnight trip.) The bluff above the beach offers a magnificent view of the ocean and cliffs, so have your camera ready.

This area is of historical significance and signs warn visitors not to remove any rocks. A pleasant hike will take you to the upper falls. The falls at **Makahiku** are 184 feet high and there is a fairly easy half-mile hike that passes through a forest. **Waimoku Falls** is another mile and a half. Three to four hours should be allowed for this hike that traverses the stream and winds through a bamboo forest. Heavy rains in the mountains far above can result in flash floods. Avoid swimming in these upper streams or crossing the stream in high water. Check with the park rangers who keep advised as to possible flooding conditions. Also check with the park service (808-248-7375) to see when the free ranger-guided hikes are available. Cultural demonstrations are given daily; check the bulletin boards for schedules.

Camping at Kipahulu is available at no charge. Be advised there is no drinking water. Bottled water may be available for a minimal cost at the ranger station, but I suggest you arrive with your own supply.

One interesting fact about Kipahulu is that many of the marine animals here have evolved from saltwater origins. Others continue to make the transition between the ocean's salty environment and the fresh water of the Palikea stream. One of the most unusual is the rare *oopu* that breeds in the upper stream, migrates to the ocean during its youth and then returns to the stream to mature. After a glimpse of the many waterfalls, this appears to be a most remarkable feat. The ingenious *oopu* actually climbs the falls by using its lower front fins as a suction cup to hold onto the steep rock walls. Using its tail to propel itself, the *oopu* then travels slowly upstream.

The upper Kipahulu Valley is a place visitors will never see. Under the jurisdiction of the park service, it is one of the last fragments of the native rain forests. The native plants in the islands have been destroyed by the more aggressive plants brought by the early Hawaiians and visitors in the centuries that followed. Some rare species, such as the green silversword, grow only in this restricted area.

HANA'S HOURS

St. Mary's Church (808-248-8030) Saturday Mass 5 p.m., Sunday 9 a.m.

Wananalua Protestant Church (808-248-8040) Established in 1838. Church services 10 a.m. Sunday

Hana Ranch Store (808-248-8261) 7 a.m. to 7:30 p.m. daily

Hasegawa General Store (808-248-8231) Monday through Saturday 7 a.m. to 7 p.m., Sunday 8 a.m. to 6 p.m.

Hana Community Health Center (808-248-8294) Emergencies 24 hours. Monday through Thursday 8 a.m. to 10 p.m., Friday 8 a.m. to 8 p.m., Saturday 8 a.m. to 5 p.m. Closed Sunday

Bank of Hawaii (808-248-8015) Monday through Thursday 3 to 4:30 p.m., Friday 3 to 6 p.m. (Hana must have been the place where they coined the term "Banker's Hours")

Library (808-248-7714) Monday 8 a.m. to 8 p.m., Tuesday through Friday 8 a.m. to 5 p.m. Closed Saturday and Sunday

Post Office (808-248-8258) Monday through Friday, 8 a.m. to 4:30 p.m.

Hana Gas Station, Monday through Sunday 7:30 a.m. to 6:30 p.m.

Hana Treasures Gift Shop, Monday through Friday 9 a.m. to 4 p.m., Saturday 9 a.m. to 3:30 p.m., Sunday 10 a.m. to 3 p.m.

Forever Hana's Choice (gift shop) Monday through Saturday 11 a.m. to 5 p.m., Thursday 10:30 a.m. to 4:30 p.m. Closed Sunday

Ohana Lei & Flowers, Monday through Saturday 10 a.m. to 5 p.m. Closed Sunday

Maui Stables is located in Kipahulu, approximately a mile past the National Park's parking lot. While you are visiting the Hana area, this is the ideal opportunity to experience a unique cultural horseback ride offered by the Hawaiian family that operates these stables (rather than driving three hours from your hotel in order to do it some other day!). For more information on Maui Stables, see the Horseback Riding section in Chapter 6.

Ono Organic Farms, located in the Kipahulu area, offers tours of their farm, including samples of many of their exotic fruits and organic coffee. The tour, about 90 minutes long, covers approximately one mile of easy walking. Tours depart Monday and Thursday at 2:30 p.m. Reservations are required. Adults $25; children 12 and under are free. 808-248-7779; www.onofarms.com.

Between mile-markers 41 and 40 (numbers are descending from this direction), you'll see **Laulima Farm**, a cute little roadside cafe offering coffee, fresh fruits, salads and other snacks. Kids love climbing on the bicycle-powered blender to make their own smoothie. Also in this area is the **Charles Lindbergh grave**, located in the small cemetery. Just past mile-marker 41 you'll see a sign for the Pala Pala Hoomanu Congregational Church. Turn *mauka* (toward the ocean) on this road called Ho'oma, at a sign indicating the 1850 **Kipahulu Hawaiian Church**. Lindbergh chose this site only a year prior to his death in 1974, after living in the area for a number of years. However, he never envisioned the huge numbers of visitors that would come to Hana to enjoy the scenery and visit his gravesite. There is a little-known point of interest relating to the graves near Sam Pryor and Pryor's wife, Mary, that bear only a single name and a hand-scribbled date on the worn cement marker. I was told these are the graves of six pet monkeys. Sam Pryor, the president of Pan American Airways, was instrumental in encouraging Lindbergh to relocate to Hana following the death of Lindbergh's young child. Pryor apparently had an affection for those primates, so buried his pets in this churchyard. Please respect the sanctity of this area.

As I mentioned earlier in this section, it is possible to travel the back road from Hana through Upcountry and back to Kahului. Sometimes the trip is more arduous than others, depending on the road and weather conditions. The trip from Hana to Ulupalakua is a very slow 37 miles. This is Maui's desert region and it is a vivid contrast to the lush windward environs. You will be following Highway 31 (Pi'ilani Highway) from Hana along the southern coast until you gradually move inland and begin the ascent up the slopes of Haleakala to the Upcountry area, joining Highway 37 or the Kula Highway.

While some consider this road an adventure, others term the drive foolhardy. They are both correct. Keep in mind that rental car companies have restrictions on travel along this route. Namely, if you get stuck or break down, it is your problem. These restrictions may not apply if you rent a four-wheel-drive vehicle, but check with the specific rental car company to be sure. It is very important to determine the current condition of the road and the current and future weather. Many of the ground tour vans now continue around this part of the island.

While usually parched, this route presents a hazard that can take visitors unaware. Flash floods in the mountains above, most likely between November and March, can send walls of water down the mountain, quickly washing out a bridge or overflowing the road. The road is sometimes closed for months due to serious washouts. Check with the county to see the current status of this route. Another good source of road information is the local folks in Hana. Although their viewpoints might differ, they generally seem well-informed about the road conditions. Recent rains can cause parts of this "road" (term used loosely) to become huge, oozing, muddy bogs. Currently the road is eroded in areas. Travel is reduced to about five miles an hour, or less, over these portions. The Drive Slowly signs that are posted are quite sincere (but hardly necessary).

The first section of the road past the ʻOheʻo area seems easily navigable. However, fairly quickly you may wonder if you made an incorrect turn and ended up on a hiking trail. This section of the unimproved road lasts 4.5 very long miles. You'll be challenged by steeply dropping cliffs to your left and the rocky walls on your right, chiseled just enough to let only a single car go by. However, if you have second thoughts at this point, you may be out of luck—there isn't room to turn around. The most harrowing portions, besides the huge muddy ruts, are the blind corners. If you have an open-top jeep, be sure you fight for the front seat or you'll be eating a lot of dust.

After mile-marker 38, a long stretch begins with intermittent paved and unpaved road. There are lots of potholes, and after rainy weather the unpaved areas can turn into pools of muddy water. This section of the route is very bumpy (as in teeth-jarring, mind-numbing) and lasts for approximately 12 miles. The Hana Highway is a breeze compared to this road.

There are several landmarks along this route, one of them the **Hui Aloha Church** built in 1859. There are small pullouts along the roadside that are worth a stop for a photo or two.

The next landmark of civilization is the **Kaupo Store**, after mile-marker 35. It has been operating since 1925. If the store is open, you can head to the back and choose from one of several refrigerators for a cool soda or the freezer for an ice cream. The walls are lined with an assortment of antiques, none of which are for sale. There are old bottles, an impressive collection of old cameras, radios and antique drugstore items.

The scenic attractions are pretty limited for the next few miles. There is **St. Joseph's Church**, built in 1862. Take note of the many lava rock walls along the roadside. This area supported a large native Hawaiian population and these walls served as boundaries as well as retaining walls for livestock, primarily pigs. The walls are centuries old and unfortunately have suffered from visitor vandalism and destruction by the range cattle. Cattle are now the principal residents. However, more people are gradually moving into this area.

You'll note the remnants of an old church on a bluff (*makai*) overlooking the ocean. This is the headquarters of **Kaʻohana O Kahikinui**. This self-help organization is attempting to put the Hawaiians back on Hawaiian land.

As you enter Upcountry and civilization once more, look for the Tedeschi Winery at the Ulupalakua Ranch. (See the "Upcountry" section earlier in the chapter for more information on sites in this area.)

CHAPTER 3

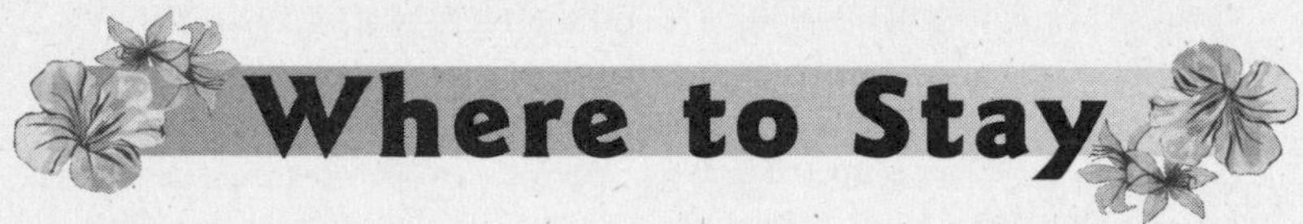

Where to Stay

Maui has more than 18,000 hotel rooms and condominium units in vacation rental programs, with the bulk of the accommodations located in two areas, West Maui and South Maui. This chapter contains a list of nearly all of the condominiums that are in rental programs, as well as the island's hotels and some bed-and-breakfast inns.

If you are physically impaired, see "Travel Tips for the Physically Impaired" in Chapter 1. While many accommodations do have facilities to accommodate the physically impaired, you may encounter difficulty with some of the tourist attractions. Access to many of them is limited.

If you are traveling with children, refer to Chapter 1 for information on children's programs at a host of resorts.

THINGS TO KNOW ABOUT USING THIS CHAPTER

As with the other chapters, we've divided Maui into geographic regions: Lahaina, Ka'anapali, Honokowai–Kapalua Area, Ma'alaea–Kihei Area, Wailea–Makena Area, Kahului–Wailuku Area, Upcountry and Hana Highway. Accommodations are listed alphabetically within these regions. For each of the properties you will find the local mailing address or P.O. Box as well as local, fax and toll-free numbers. I have also included e-mail addresses and websites. You can usually e-mail via the website as well. For ease in locating information, the properties are also indexed alphabetically in the Lodging Index at the end of the book.

Condos are abundant, and the prices and facilities they offer can be quite varied. Other options include hotels, private cottages and B&Bs; B&Bs are marked with a dresser icon. It is impossible for me to stay in or view all the units within a complex, and since condominiums are privately owned, each of those units can vary a great deal in its furnishings and condition. I have indicated my personal preferences for accommodations by the use of a star ★. Please see the "Best Bets" section for more highlights.

In many cases there are a variety of rental agents handling condo units in addition to the on-site management; an assortment of these have been listed under each condo's description. When you determine which condo interests you, call all of the agents. While one agent may have no vacancy, another may have several (in the same complex). The prices can also vary (sometimes greatly) from one to another. The quality of the furnishings and the care of the unit may also vary. The prices I have listed are generally the lowest available (although some agents may offer lower rates by reducing certain services such as daily maid service). Unfortunately, I've had at least one occasion where the cheaper rate was for a condo that needed not only a good cleaning, but complete renovation. However, a reputable rental agent will not let a unit fall into disrepair. At the end of this chapter is an alphabetical listing of rental agents. Due to space limitations, not all rental agents have been included in the individual property listings.

Travel agents will be able to book your stay in all Maui hotels and in most condominiums. If you prefer to make your own reservation, use the contact information I have provided. I have indicated toll-free numbers (prefixes 800, 866, 877 or 888) when available. Look for an 808 area code preceding the local Maui numbers. (It gets confusing with all those 8s.) You might also check the classified ads in your local newspaper for owners offering their units for rent, which may be a better bargain.

Prices are listed to aid in your selection and, while these were the most current available at press time, they are subject to change without notice. Although prices can jump, most go up no more than 5 to 10 percent per year. I felt it was important to include actual prices rather than just giving you broad categories such as "budget" or "expensive." After all, one person's "expensive" may be "budget" to someone else! The prices are listed with a slash dividing between low-season and high-season rates. (A few places offer a flat yearly rate, so there will only be a single price.) Prices listed do not include the Hawai'i state occupancy tax and sales tax, which together amount to 11.42 percent.

For the sake of saving space, I have made use of several abbreviations. Sizes of the condominiums are identified as one bedroom (1BR), two bedrooms (2BR) and three bedrooms (3BR). The numbers in parentheses following this refer to the number of people that can occupy the unit for the price listed, e.g., 2BR (4). The description will tell you how much it will cost for additional persons, e.g., extra person $10/night. (Additional persons generally run $8 to $15 per night per person with the exception of the high-class resorts and hotels, where the extra charge may run as much as $25 to $35.) Some facilities consider an infant as an extra person; others will allow children free up to a specified age. The abbreviations *o.f.*, *g.v.*, *o.v.* and *m.v.* refer to oceanfront, gardenview, oceanview and mountainview units.

Note: Many resorts now charge guests a daily parking fee or a resort fee. These are hidden charges that may surprise you once you check in, so ask ahead of time if there are any such fees.

WHERE TO STAY?

The *Lahaina* and *Ka'anapali* areas offer the visitor the hub of the island's activities, but accommodations are a little more costly. The beaches are especially good at Ka'anapali. The Ka'anapali Beach Resort area boasts the most convention space of any of the neighboring islands, with the Westin Maui and the Hyatt Regency being particularly popular convention sites. All the hotels are located beachfront, although some of the condos are situated above the beach in the golf course area. Nearly all are priced in the luxury range. The wide avenues and the spaciousness of the resort's lush green and manicured grounds are most impressive. Absence of on-street parking and careful planning have successfully given this resort a feeling of spaciousness. Nestled between a pristine white-sand beach and scenic golf courses with a mountain range beyond, this may be the ideal spot for your vacation.

The values and choice of condos are more extensive a little beyond Ka'anapali in *Honokowai*, *Kahana* (Lower Honoapi'ilani Road area), and further on at *Napili*. However, perhaps because of the shape of the sloping ridges of the West Maui Mountain, there can be slightly cooler temperatures here and oftentimes more rain. Some of the condominiums in this area, while very adequate, may be a little over-

LONG-TERM STAYS

Almost all condo complexes and rental agents offer the long-term visitor moderate to substantial discounts for stays of one month or more. Private homes can also be booked through the rental agents listed at the end of the chapter.

A Reminder: The accommodations are listed alphabetically within their regions. You will also find a Lodging Index at the back of this book to provide further assistance.

due for redecorating. While many complexes are on nice beaches, many are also on rocky shores. Many people return year after year to this quiet area, away from the bustle of Lahaina and Ka'anapali and where condo prices are in the moderate range.

Kapalua is a beautiful resort community that offers high-end condominium and hotel accommodations. Going the other direction, *Ma'alaea* is a half-hour drive from Lahaina, and beyond that is *Kihei*. Both of these areas offer some attractive condo units at excellent prices and, although few are located on a beach, there are plenty of easily accessible public beach parks. Many Maui vacationers feel that Kihei offers the best weather on the island in the winter months; annual rainfall is only about 3 inches on Maui's southern shore. There are plenty of restaurants in this area as well.

The *Wailea* and *Makena* areas are just beyond Kihei and are beautifully developed resorts. The beaches are excellent for a variety of water activities; however, this area is significantly more expensive than neighboring Kihei.

The twin towns of *Wailuku* and *Kahului* are located on the northwestern side of the island. There are motel-type accommodations around Kahului Harbor, and while the rates are economical and the location is somewhat central to all parts of the island, I cannot recommend staying in this area for other than a quick stopover that might require easy airport access. This side of the island is generally more windy, overcast and cooler, with few good beaches. Except for the avid windsurfer, I feel there is little reason to base your stay here. However, there are many good reasons to linger and explore the shopping and dining options.

Accommodations in *Upcountry* include a small lodge in Kula, a few cabins available from the park service for overnight use while hiking in the Haleakala Wilderness Area, and a number of interesting bed-and-breakfast inns. There are no large hotels or resorts in this area.

Along the *Hana Highway*, you'll find a scattering of B&Bs as well as a lovely resort in Hana, a few condos and some homes for rent.

HOW TO SAVE MONEY

Maui has two price seasons: high or "in" season and low or "off" season. Low season is generally considered to be mid-April to mid-December, although some accommodations also treat the summer months as a part of their high season. In general, the winter and summer months are the busiest on the island, with spring and fall being the slower seasons. Low-season rates are discounted at some places as much as 30 percent. Different resorts and condominiums may vary these dates by as much as two weeks and a few resorts offer a flat, year-round rate. Ironically, some of the best weather is during the fall when temperatures are cooler than summer and there is less rain than the winter and spring months. (See "Weather" in Chapter 1 for year-round temperatures). In addition to the low and high seasons, some accommodations charge a premium for the "Holiday Season" of Christmas through New Years. That is the busiest period of the year on Maui.

For a stay longer than one week, a condo unit with a kitchen can provide significant savings on your food bill. While this will give you more space than a hotel room at a lower price, the trade-off is that you may give up some resort amenities (shops, restaurants, maid service, etc.). It's easy to stock your condo kitchen, as there are several large grocery stores around the island with fairly competitive prices, although most groceries here will run slightly higher than on the mainland. (See "Grocery Shopping" in Chapter 1.)

The complimentary services of Concierge Connection can provide you with accommodations as well as package discounts, coupons and percentage-off cards for restaurants and activities. They even offer resort-guest prices for golf courses or places like the Grand Wailea Spa. They offer free advice, information and recommendations on all aspects of your Maui vacation—with discounts on those, too! 888-875-9366, 808-875-9366; e-mail: info@mauiconcierge.net; www.mauiconcierge.net.

Most condominiums offer maid service only upon checkout. A few might offer it twice a week or weekly. Additional maid service may be available for an extra charge. A few condos still do not provide in-room phones or color televisions, and some have no pool. Some units have washers and dryers in the rooms, while others do not. Many have coin-operated laundry facilities on the premises. Generally all units have microwaves in their kitchens.

In addition to traveling off-season or cutting back on dining bills by staying in a condo, you can also save money by carefully choosing the location of your accommodations—some regions of the island are much less expensive than others. There are some good deals in the Ma'alaea and Kihei areas, and the northern area above Lahaina (Honokowai to Napili) has some older complexes that are reasonably good values. The Wailea, Ka'anapali and Kapalua areas are the most expensive areas to stay in—but, of course, the resorts there are fabulous.

There are some pleasant condo units either across the road from the beach or on a rocky, less attractive beach. This can represent a tremendous savings, and there are always good beaches a short walk or drive away. Also, hotel rooms or condos with garden or mountain views are less costly than an oceanview or oceanfront room. In fact, many of the mountainview rooms, especially in Ka'anapali, are superior. The mountains are simply gorgeous and most people would rather be outside on the beach than inside looking at it, anyway!

GENERAL POLICIES Hotels and condominium complexes require a deposit, usually equivalent to one- or two-nights stay, to secure your reservation and guarantee your room rate. Some charge higher deposits during winter or over Christmas holidays. Often a 30-day notice of cancellation is needed to receive a full refund, so make sure you understand their cancellation policy in advance. Most condos require payment in full either 30 days prior to arrival or upon arrival, and many do not accept credit cards. The usual minimum condo stay is three nights, with some requiring one week in winter. Christmas holidays may have steeper restrictions with minimum stays as long as two weeks, payments 90 days in advance, and heavy cancellation penalties. It is not uncommon to book as much as two years in advance for the Christmas season.

Lodging Best Bets

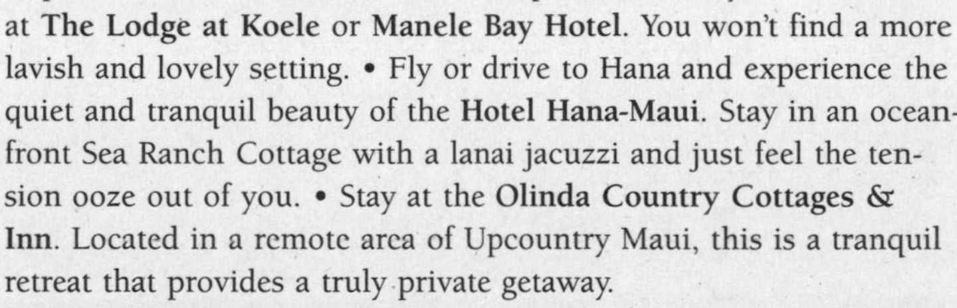

Get-Away-from-It-All Destinations There are several excellent options if you want to slow down and feel the true aloha of Hawai'i. • Hop on Island Air or take Expedition and head off to Lana'i to spend a few days at **The Lodge at Koele** or **Manele Bay Hotel**. You won't find a more lavish and lovely setting. • Fly or drive to Hana and experience the quiet and tranquil beauty of the **Hotel Hana-Maui**. Stay in an oceanfront Sea Ranch Cottage with a lanai jacuzzi and just feel the tension ooze out of you. • Stay at the **Olinda Country Cottages & Inn**. Located in a remote area of Upcountry Maui, this is a tranquil retreat that provides a truly private getaway.

Most Intimate Accommodations The Victorian-style **Lahaina Inn** is a step back in time. No ocean view here or televisions, but wonderfully romantic. A great couples destination. • **Plantation Inn** is equally charming, with a tropical feel and the added amenities of air conditioning, a pool and TV. This one would be a great location with or without children. • **Hotel Hana-Maui** is a very romantic choice, particularly the Sea Ranch Cottages.

Condos If You Can Splurge Makena Surf is a terrific luxury property. It's elegant, ideally located and the units are beautifully appointed. • The **Ka'anapali Alii** has long been a favorite of mine. • **Kapalua Villas** also has some wonderful luxury condos with great views.

TREEHOUSES

Nestled in the Nahiku rainforest, along the Hana Highway, you'll find Nahiku Tree House the perfect place to get away from it all. A lofted sleeping area with linens provided, full bathroom, a large lofty deck and time to catch up on that book you've been meaning to read. Nahiku is just past mile-marker 25 on the Hana Highway. A four-wheel-drive vehicle is recommended or you can walk the last 100 or so yards to the tree house. A little too primitive for my tastes, but it is a Boy Scout's dream come true. 808-248-4070; www.nahiku.com. Another option if a tree house is your ultimate dream accommodation: **Tree Houses of Hana**. 808-248-7241; e-mail: hanalani@maui.net; www.maui.net/~hanalani.

Discount Accommodations Check the internet for specials. One website, www.hotwire.com, offers great deals on "mystery" accommodations. Also check the websites for the accommodations listed in this chapter. Many of them offer internet-only specials to fill rooms during low booking periods.

LAHAINA **Puamana**—A nice residential-type community of two-plex and four-plex units, some oceanfront. Plenty of room for kids to run around. **Lahaina Shores**—A moderately priced colonial-style high-rise right on the beach and within walking distance of Lahaina shops. Fronting reef makes for calm waters for kids who enjoy the ocean. **Lahaina Inn**—A great couple getaway, not oriented to children. **Plantation Inn**—Tastefully done with all the elegance of bygone days and in the middle of town.

KA'ANAPALI **Hyatt Regency Maui Resort and Spa**—An elegant and exotic setting with a wonderful selection of great restaurants. **Westin Maui Resort & Spa**—A beautiful resort and a pool lover's paradise, with a brand new spa facility. **Ka'anapali Alii**—One of only three condominiums that are oceanfront. Luxurious and spacious. **Sheraton Maui Resort**—A lovely landmark property situated on the best spot on Ka'anapali Beach. **The Whaler**—Luxury condominiums on Ka'anapali Beach adjacent to the Whalers Village Shopping Center.

HONOKOWAI **Ka'anapali Shores**—A high-rise surrounded by lovely grounds on the best beach in the area. **Papakea**—A low-rise complex with attractive grounds and pool. **Embassy Vacation Resort**—A mix between a condo and a hotel with breakfast included. Spacious rooms and a good sandy beach.

KAHANA **Sands of Kahana**—Spacious units on a nice white-sand beach. **Kahana Sunset**—Low-rise condos surrounding a secluded cove and beach.

NAPILI Napili Sunset—Centered right on the edge of Napili Bay, rooms are well kept. **Napili Kai Beach Resort**—A quiet facility on the edge of Napili Bay. Large grounds and a restaurant on site. Resort activities are offered. **Honokeana Cove**—Great value and private location.

KAPALUA You can't go wrong with **The Kapalua Bay Hotel** or **The Ritz-Carlton, Kapalua.** Both are outstanding properties offering quiet elegance, top-notch service and great food with all the amenities. **Kapalua Villas** offers spacious living and complete kitchen facilities in condos throughout the Kapalua area. Any of the units would be excellent; however, not all are located within easy walking distance of the beach. A shuttle service is available for all resort guests.

MA'ALAEA **Kana'i a Nalu**—Attractive complex with all two-bedroom units on a sandy beachfront, affordably priced. **Lauloa**—Well-designed units oceanfront on the sea wall. **Makani A Kai**—Located on a sandy beachfront, two-bedroom units are townhouse style.

NORTH KIHEI **Kealia** and **Ma'alaea Surf.**

SOUTH KIHEI **Maui Hill**—Situated on a hillside across the road from the ocean, some units have excellent ocean views. The three-bedroom units here are roomy and a good value for large families. **Haleakala Shores**—Across from Kama'ole III Beach Park. **Mana Kai Maui**—One of Kihei's larger resorts, the units are fair but an extra plus is that they are located on good beaches.

WAILEA Affordable accommodations are not what the visitor will find here, but Wailea offers a variety of excellent condominiums and hotels from which to choose. Each is different, each is lovely and in fact there is not one property that I would not recommend. Many have wonderful kids programs. **Wailea Marriott**—A lovely resort featuring a tropical flavor with spacious grounds, excellent restaurants and two great beaches. **Renaissance Wailea Beach Resort**—This complex is smaller and more intimate as resorts go; it has lush, tropical grounds, and it is fronted by one of the island's finest beaches. The **Grand Wailea Resort Hotel & Spa**—This is an enormous resort, but also enormous fun. The pools are incredible, but if you prefer the ocean, Wailea Beach is right here. There is something for everyone at this resort. **Four Seasons Resort Wailea**—This resort is purely and simply elegant. From its white porte-cochere you enter a tranquil and serene environ. Simply sit by the pool or enjoy a day on the beach. No need to go further. The **Fairmont Kea Lani Hotel**—This is an all-suites resort, a blend of the best of resorts and the comforts of a condominium, all on Polo Beach. **The Palms at Wailea**—Very spacious units can comfortably accommodate a family. Tastefully appointed, the gardenview units are very affordable and only a short walk to the beach. **Polo Beach Club**—Luxury condominium units with easy access to two small but good beaches.

MAKENA The Maui Prince Hotel and Makena Surf—Both are first-class, luxury accommodations on beautiful beaches.

Lahaina

Pioneer Inn (Best Western)

658 Wharf Street, P.O. Box 243, Lahaina, HI 96764. 800-457-5457; fax 808-667-5708; 808-661-3636; e-mail: info@pioneerinnmaui.com; www.pioneerinnmaui.com.

With its colorful history, Pioneer Inn remains a nostalgic Lahaina landmark, as the oldest hotel on the island. It is located in the heart of Lahaina Town, adjacent to Banyan Tree Park and fronting the boat harbor. Best Western International took over management of this simple but charming oceanfront property in 1998 and renovated the rooms to include one queen bed or two twins, tiled modern bathrooms and air conditioning as well as ceiling fans, TV, radio and direct-dial telephones. The inn offers 34 rooms, all on the second floor, a courtyard swimming pool, and a restaurant fronting the marina. For an older property, the rooms are in pretty nice shape, but some are better than others (the condition of the carpeting, in particular, is inconsistent from room to room.) Daily maid service. Children under 12 stay free. Higher rates apply at Halloween and Christmas.

Rates: Standard $125-$145; deluxe $150-$170; deluxe suite $165-$185

Garden Gate Bed and Breakfast

67 Kaniau Road, Lahaina, HI 96761. 800-939-3217; 808-661-8800; fax 808-661-0209; e-mail: info@gardengatebb.com; www.gardengatebb.com.

Hosts Jaime and Bill Mosley offer suites with private bath, phones, refrigerators, TVs, VCRs, air conditioning, ceiling fans and ocean or garden views. Continental breakfast Monday through Friday in the garden area. Garden Gate is centrally located near Lahaina Town. Three-night minimum (but they can be flexible on this).

Rates: Standard suite $89-$99; deluxe suite $109-$139; oceanview suite $129-$179; extra person $15/night

House of Fountains

1579 Lokia Street, Lahaina, HI 96761. 800-789-6865; 808-667-2121; e-mail: private@alohahouse.com; www.alohahouse.com.

This B&B is located three blocks from the beach. Accommodations are in a 7,000-square-foot home. Air-conditioned rooms fur-

nished with queen bed and private bath. There's *koa* wood furniture and the rooms have a Hawaiiana style. Your host is Daniela Clement. House of Fountains received the Kahili award from the Hawai'i Visitors Bureau for the most Hawaiian accommodation in 2002.

Rates: $115/$125/$160

★ *Lahaina Inn*

127 Lahainaluna Road, Lahaina, HI 96761. 800-669-3444; 808-661-0577; fax 808-667-9480; e-mail: inntown@lahainainn.com; www.lahainainn.com.

Built in 1938 by Tomezo Masuda for his general store, Maui Trading Company, this property was a popular place for World War II Army men to "hang loose." Dickie, the Masudas' black German shepherd, became legendary for his mail run. He would make the trip to the Lahaina post office to fetch the store's mail. In 1949, the Tabata family purchased the business, but by the early 1960s the business failed and the building was placed at public auction. George Izaki bought the property and made the street-level store into four business spaces and transformed the second floor into a hotel. A fire destroyed the business in the mid-1960s. The interior was reconstructed and the Lahainaluna Hotel was developed in the second-story level. There were 19 rooms and three baths, but the hotel gradually deteriorated.

In 1986 Rick Ralston, who also owned Crazy Shirts, undertook renovations and the transformation was dramatic. Gone are the cheap "rustic" units. Lahaina Inn is now an elegant 12-room hotel in the heart of Lahaina Town. It provides an atmosphere of comfortable luxury with all the charm and romance of an intimate inn at the turn of the 20th century. Each room is individually decorated with authentic period furnishings, hand-quilted bed covers, antique lamps and oriental carpets. Relax in air-conditioned comfort or sit back in rocking chairs on your own balcony lanai. In-room phones offer free local calls. Considering you are in the center of town, the rooms are surprisingly quiet (with no TVs). A romantic, charming and intimate place to spend your Maui vacation. Adjacent is David Paul's Lahaina Grill. Parking $5 per day. Honeymoon packages. Children over age 15 are welcome.

Rates: m.v. $125; o.v. $145; Makai Room o.v. $175; Mauka Room o.v. and m.v. $175

Lahaina Roads

1403 Front Street, Lahaina, HI 96761. 808-661-3166. Agents: Chase 'N Rainbows.

These 42 700-square-foot, one-bedroom/one-bath oceanfront condominiums are decorated with tropical decor. They are equipped with full kitchen, telephone, bedroom air conditioning and ceiling fans. The large lanai overlooks the ocean and offers an incredible view of the warm Pacific. Covered parking and elevator to upper levels.

Chase 'N Rainbows rates: $115-$150

★ Lahaina Shores Beach Resort

475 Front Street, Lahaina, HI 96761. 808-661-4835 (hotel only, no reservations). Agents: Classic Resorts; Whalers Realty; Chase 'N Rainbows; Condominium Rentals Hawaii.

This seven-story plantation-style building offers 200 oceanfront units with air conditioning, lanais, full kitchens, daily maid service and laundry facilities on each floor. The beach here is fair and the water calm due to offshore reefs, but shallow with coral. With a family staying at Lahaina Shores you have the opportunity to enjoy the beach directly in front; there's also a pool and patio. Lahaina Town is only a short walk away, plus this complex neighbors the 505 Front Street Shopping Center, which offers several restaurants and a small grocery/convenience store.

Classic Resorts rates: Studio (2, max 3) m.v.-o.f. $185-$225; 1BR (2, max 4) m.v. $260, o.f. $290; penthouse (2, max 5) m.v. $290, o.f. $325

Maui Islander Hotel

660 Wainee Street, Lahaina, HI 96761. 808-667-9766. Maui Islander 800-367-5226. Managed by Outrigger Resorts under its Ohana Hotels brand: 800-462-6262; e-mail mih@ohanahotels.com; www.ohanahotels.com. Agents: RSVP.

The 276-unit property includes nine two-story buildings set on nearly 10 acres, featuring hotel rooms, studios, deluxe studios, and one- and two-bedroom suites. All include full kitchens, except for the hotel rooms, which have mini-refrigerators. Located in the heart of Lahaina Town, less than a 5-minute walk to the sea wall, yet far enough away to be peaceful. The back of the building borders the Honoapi'ilani Highway, so front units may be a bit quieter. Daily maid service, air conditioning, laundry facilities, tennis courts, pool. NOTE: This hotel will be converting to condominiums in early 2006 and will probably undergo a name change. Units may still be available for rental after that time, however, through individual owners or rental agents (yet to be determined).

Rates: Hotel room $159, 1BR $209, 2BR $299, family suite $179

★ Old Lahaina House Bed & Breakfast

P.O. Box 10355, Lahaina, HI 96761. 800-847-0761; 808-667-4663; fax 808-667-5615; e-mail: reservations@oldlahaina.com; www.oldlahaina.com.

Four rooms in a home in the historic Lahaina area. All rooms have air conditioning, private bath and access to refrigerator and microwave. Breakfast is included except on Sunday. Swimming pool. They are across the street from a neighborhood beach and four blocks from Lahaina Harbor.

Rates: Exclusive suite with queen bed, full kitchen and washer/dryer $150-$205, deluxe with king bed $115-$125, standard with queen bed and microwave $89-$99, budget with twin beds $69-$89

The Plantation Inn

174 Lahainaluna Road, Lahaina, HI 96761. 800-433-6815; 808-667-9225; fax 808-667-9293; e-mail: info@theplantationinn.com; www.theplantationinn.com.

This 19-room B&B has all the charm of a historic inn, while incorporating all the benefits of modernization. You'd never know you were just footsteps away from the bustle of Front Street Lahaina. Filled with antiques, beautiful Victorian decor, hardwood floors and stained glass, they also offer air conditioning, refrigerators and VCRs. Some units on the ground floor have lovely patios that extend out to the pool area. The second-floor units have balconies. Some units even have kitchens and jacuzzi tubs. Located just a block from the ocean in the heart of Lahaina, the inn has a 12-foot-deep tiled pool and a spa. (The spa is open 24 hours.) An added bonus is Gerard's restaurant, featuring fine French cuisine for your evening dining pleasure, and all guests of The Plantation Inn receive a $50 dining credit. For breakfast, fresh fruit, outstanding French toast and other specialties along with piping hot coffee are served in their lovely poolside pavilion or around the pool. Added value vacation packages are available at the inn's website.

Rates: Standard $160, superior $185, deluxe $215, suites $225-$255

★ *Puamana*

P.O. Box 11108, Lahaina, HI 96761. 800-628-6731; 808-667-2551. Agents: Maui & All Island; Maui Beachfront Rentals; Whalers Realty; Maui Vacation Properties.

A series of duplexes and fourplexes on a 30-acre oceanfront setting with 228 units. This large complex resembles a residential community much more than a vacation resort. The variation in price reflects location in the complex, oceanfront to gardenview. There's a beach suitable for swimming.

Whalers Realty rates: 1BR g.v. $115/$160, 1 BR o.f. $195/$245; 2 BR g.v. $175/$245; 2BR o.f. $275/$350; 3BR g.v. $255/$285; 3 BR o.f. $325/$395; 4 BR/3.5 bath o.f. $475/$495

Puunoa Beach Estates

45 Kai Pali Place, Lahaina, HI 96761. Agents: Classic Resorts; Whalers Realty Management; Maui Vacation Properties.

Amenities include full-size swimming pool, jacuzzi, his and hers sauna, and paddle tennis courts. Units include laundry rooms, lanais, master bath with jacuzzi, full bar and daily maid service. These luxury units are located on Pu'unoa Beach in a residential area just north of Lahaina. Beautiful and spacious air-conditioned units, convenient to restaurants and shops. The beachfront has a coral reef that makes for calm conditions for children, but swimming or snorkeling are poor due to the shallowness and coral.

Whalers Realty rates: 3 BR/3 bath o.f. $550/$650

Classic Resorts rates: 2 BR o.f. $700

★ Wai Ola

Contact: Wai Ola Vacation Paradise, 1565 Kuuipo Street, Lahaina, HI 96761; 800-492-4652; 808-661-7901; e-mail: contact@waiola.com; www.waiola.com.

This elegant 5,000-square-foot vacation rental home is conveniently located between Lahaina Town and Ka'anapali, two blocks from Wahikuli Beach. It offers 4 rooms and a private cottage, each with its own separate entrance and private bathroom. Guests can rent an individual unit or the entire property (max 12 people). This beautifully maintained property offers privacy along with panoramic ocean views and spectacular sunsets.

Rates: $99-$150; cottage $175; entire property $900 night

Ka'anapali

★ Hyatt Regency Maui Resort and Spa

200 Nohea Kai Drive, Lahaina, HI 96761. 800-554-9288; 808-661-1234; www.maui.hyatt.com.

This magnificent complex is located on 40 beachfront acres and offers 806 rooms and suites. The beach is beautiful, but has a steep drop-off. The adjoining Hanokao'o Beach Park offers a gentler slope into deeper water. The two-acre pool area is an impressive feature resembling a contemporary adventure that Robinson Crusoe could only have dreamed of. The pool is divided by a large cavern that can be reached on either side by swimming beneath a waterfall. The more adventurous can try out their waterslide. A large swinging rope bridge spans one side of the pool. The kids just love walking back and forth with the swaying motion. And the Hyatt has a children's fantasy pool. It's a 3,000-

square-foot sandy play pool with fountains, mist, a 24-foot slide and ocean features that resemble a tide pool. Penguins, jewel-toned *koi*, parrots, swans, cranes and flamingos around the grounds require full-time gamekeepers. The tropical birds are so at home here that some are reproducing, a rarity for some of these species in captivity. The lobby is a blend of beautiful pieces of oriental art and paths that lead to the grounds. Non-guests should definitely visit the Hyatt for a self-guided tour of the grounds, the art, the elegant shops, the fine restaurants or their lu'au show. There are children's day camps and evening programs. The beds in the guest rooms are so comfortable, the hotel is constantly being asked by guests where they can purchase one for their own homes. The Regency Club at the Hyatt consists of two floors that feature special services, including continental breakfast, evening cocktails and appetizers. No charge for children 18 and under sharing with parents.

Rates: Terrace $335; Golf/Mountain $385, partial o.v. $445, o.v. $555; Regency partial o.v. $530, o.f. $595, ocean suite $850; other suites $1,250-$4,000. Additional persons 19 and older $35 per night, $50 per night in Regency Club

★ *Ka'anapali Alii*

50 Nohea Kai Drive, Lahaina, HI 96761. 808-667-1400; www.kaanapalialii.com. Agents: Classic Resorts; Whalers Realty; Maui Beachfront Rentals.

All 264 units are very spacious and beautifully furnished, with air conditioning, microwaves, washer/dryer and daily maid service. Other amenities include security entrances and covered parking. The one-bedroom units have a den, which actually makes them equivalent to a two-bedroom. Three lighted tennis courts, pool (also a children's pool) and exercise room. No restaurants on the property, but shops and restaurants are within easy walking distance. A very elegant, high-class and quiet property with a cordial staff and concierge department.

Classic Resort rates: 1BRs g.v. $360, m.v. $390, partial o.v. $440, o.v. $490, o.f. $540; 2BR g.v. $490, m.v. $515, partial o.v. $550, o.v. $595, o.f. $685

★ *Ka'anapali Beach Hotel*

2525 Ka'anapali Parkway, Lahaina, HI 96761. 800-262-8450; 808-661-0011; fax 808-667-5616 (guests), fax 808-667-5978 (administration); e-mail: info@kbhmaui.com; www.kbhmaui.com.

Located on Ka'anapali Beach near Black Rock and Whalers Village Shops, this 430-room hotel has been welcoming guests since 1964. This hotel is the best value on Ka'anapali Beach. A great location, but not a "posh" resort, it is a special place where the staff is regularly instructed in Hawaiian culture. The hotel has earned its reputation as Maui's most Hawaiian hotel. There are four wings to this property that embrace a tropical courtyard featuring gardens, walkways, a whale-shaped swimming pool and an outdoor bar and grill. Each room is decorated with airy, island decor and offers a private balcony or lanai, air conditioning, mini-refrigerator, color cable TV, in-room safes and coffee maker. Nonsmoking rooms are available. Five rooms are equipped for the disabled traveler. The hotel offers two restaurants plus a poolside grill and bar. A variety of Hawaiian activities are scheduled daily. Among them are leaf printing, ti leaf skirt making, hula classes, lei making and *lauhala* weaving. Throughout the week there are craft fairs and special employee entertainment each morning at the complimentary 'Ohana Welcome Breakfast. Each night at sunset there's a free hula show in the Tiki Terrace Courtyard. Upon departure, guests receive a special farewell ceremony and souvenir *kukui* lei. Coin-operated laundry facilities are on the property. "Aloha Passport for Kids" is an amenity program, free for all children 12 and younger; see "Childcare Programs" in Chapter 1 for details. Cribs available at no charge. Rollaway bed $15 per night. Children under 18 free when sharing room with parents using existing bedding. Children 5 years and younger eat free at the hotel restaurants when accompanied by a paying adult. Special package rates available offering good value. "Fifty Plus" program offers special rates for seniors (I.D. card required at check-in). Higher rates for holiday period.

The off-Broadway show *Tony n' Tina's Wedding* debuted at the Hyatt Regency Maui Resort and Spa in late 2002. You'll be a part of the wedding and reception as two New York Italian families join in marriage with a splash of local aloha. For more information, see Lu'aus and Dinner Shows in Chapter 4.

Rates: g.v. $200, partial o.v. $235, o.v. $275, o.f. $295; suites $260-$600; extra person $25/night

Ka'anapali Plantation

150 Pu'ukolii Road (P.O. Box 845), Lahaina, HI 96761. Agent: Chase 'N Rainbows.

Sixty-two one-, two- and three-bedroom units in a garden setting overlooking golf course and ocean.

Rates: 2BR $160/$195, 3BR $200/$275

Ka'anapali Royal

2560 Keka'a Drive, Lahaina, HI 96761. 808-661-8687. Agents: Whalers Realty; Chase 'N Rainbows; RSVP; Maui Vacation Properties.

Situated on the 16th fairway of the Ka'anapali golf course overlooking the Ka'anapali Resort and Pacific Ocean, these very spacious condos (1,600 to 2,000 square feet) offer air conditioning, lanais, daily maid service and washer/dryers. Note that while all units have two bedrooms, they may be rented as a one bedroom based on space availability. Units are rented out by individual owners or rental agents. No on-property rental agent.

Whalers Realty rates: 2BR/2bath $190-$325

Maui Eldorado

Located on Ka'anapali North Golf Course. 2661 Keka'a Drive, Lahaina, HI 96761. 808-661-0021. Managed by Outrigger Resorts, 800-688-7444; e-mail: mer@outrigger.com; www.outrigger.com. Agents: Whalers Realty; Chase 'N Rainbows; Maui Vacation Properties; RSVP.

There are 204 newly renovated air-conditioned units with private lanais, full kitchens, washer/dryer and free HBO on cable TV. Daily maid service. Three pools. Free shuttle to private cabana for Maui Eldorado guests on nearby Ka'anapali beachfront.

Rates: Studio (1-2) g.v. $205/$225, partial o.v. $220/$240; 1BR (1-4) g.v. $255/$275, partial o.v. $275/$295; 2BR (1-6) g.v. $355/$440, partial o.v. $385/$480

Maui Ka'anapali Villas

45 Kai Ala Drive, Lahaina, HI 96761. 808-667-7791. Managed by Aston 877-997-6667. Agents: Chase 'N Rainbows; RSVP.

Located on Ka'anapali Beach, these units (except the hotel rooms) are all air-conditioned and have kitchen facilities. The upper floors of the tower unit have wonderful mountain or ocean views. All are privately owned and some units need updating. Three swimming pools, beach concessions, store nearby. Walking distance to Whalers Village shops and restaurants and adjacent to the Ka'anapali Golf Course. Aston's best rates are available as "E-pricebreakers" on-line.

Aston rates: Hotel room (2) $151/$220, studio w/kitchen (2) $177-$290/$218-$375, 1BR (4) g.v. $216/$385, o.v. $269/$460, oceanside $292/$475; 2BR 2bath $490/$600

Marriott's Maui Ocean Club

100 Nohea Kai Drive, Lahaina, HI 96761. 800-845-5279; 808-667-1200; fax 808-667-8300; www.marriottvillarentals.com.

After millions of dollars in major renovation this hotel resort is now a timeshare—the company has announced that it is ceasing hotel operations and will reopen by November 2005 as a timeshare property. You'll find a 3.5-acre "super pool" with waterslides, whirlpool spas, swim-through grottos and a children's beach. On-property restaurants include Va Bene Italian Beachside Grill and Nalu Sunset Bar & Sushi. Villas are available for nightly rental through Marriott under the timeshare operation.

Rates: One and two-bedroom villas starting at $349 per night

Royal Lahaina Resort

2780 Keka'a Drive, Lahaina, HI 96761. 808-661-3611. Managed by: Hawaiian Hotels & Resorts, 800-222-5642; www.hawaiianhotelsand resorts.com.

The 516-room hotel is located on Ka'anapali Beach just north of Black Rock. Situated on 27 tropical acres, the hotel is made up of the three-story Hale Ka'anapali wing, 12-story Lahaina Kai Tower rooms and suites and a number of cottages and cottage suites (which include kitchens). All rooms and suites include air conditioning, ceiling fans, color cable TV, refrigerator, safe, telephone with message alert, private lanai and daily maid service. As part of the Royal Lahaina's complimentary Hawaiiana program, guests have the opportunity to gain insight into Hawai'i's culture and arts.

Several shops are conveniently located on the property. The Royal Lahaina Tennis Ranch offers guests 11 courts and a tennis stadium. The hotel also has three swimming pools, with complimentary introductory scuba lessons held daily. Restaurants on the property are the Royal Ocean Terrace, Basil Tomatoes and Don the Beachcomber's. Tiki Grill is a poolside eatery and the Royal Scoop is an ice cream and sandwich shop. A lu'au is offered five nights a week in the lu'au gardens. Each child age 11 and under receives free breakfast, dinner and lu'au when accompanied by a paying adult. Room service is available for breakfast and dinner. Children under 17 sharing parents' room in existing beds are free. This hotel needs some sprucing up, but it has a lovely location and offers some good values. Check their website for substantial discounts and internet specials.

Rates: Hale Ka'anapali standard $280, o.v. $338, o.f. $378; Lahaina Kai Tower g.v. $360, p.o.v. $380, o.v. $450, o.f. $520; Cottages: g.v. room $390, o.f. room $550, 1BR g.v. cottage $640, 1BR o.f. cottage $750, 2BR g.v. cottage $750

★ Sheraton Maui Resort

2605 Ka'anapali Parkway, Lahaina, HI 96761. 808-661-0031; 888-488-3535; www.sheraton.com/maui.

One of the first resorts to be built along Ka'anapali, this beautiful landmark property opened in 1963. The 510-room resort stretches over 23 beachfront acres. The rooms include 14 luxury suites, 20 family suites, 12 junior suites, 15 handicapped accessible rooms and 10 rooms designated for hearing impaired. The buildings, each no taller than six stories, seem to emerge naturally from the surroundings. Each is named as a *hale* ("house"). The main structure of the original property remains, but the *makai* wing (nearer the ocean) is now Hale Nalu (House of the Surf), while the *mauka* portion is Hale Anuenue (House of the Rainbow). The Hale Moana (House of the Ocean) is on the point at black rock. The Hale Lahaina and Hale Ohana are at the south end of the property.

Standard guest rooms feature air conditioning, lanai, small refrigerator, iron and ironing board, coffee maker, TV and guest safe. The Sheraton can provide a room that fits the size of your *ohana* (family). They feature 20 family suites designed with three beds (two double beds and one pull-down double bed). Family suites also feature two connecting lanais with lounge chairs and tables. A nifty room divider can create two rooms for additional privacy. The bathroom is even family-sized, with two showers, one tub and a showerhead that is adjustable for those smaller family members. Children 17 and under staying in the same room and using existing bedding are free. Cribs are available at no charge and babysitting services are available in addition to their children's program, held within walking distance at their sister property, the Westin Maui Resort & Spa. Another family plus is the "Kids Eat Free" program where children 12 and under enjoy complimentary meals, one child per paying adult.

The lighting of the torches off Black Rock and Hawaiian music still welcome the sunset. Bridges, lagoons and lava rock landscape the extended grounds and there are two restaurants, Teppan Yaki Dan and the open-air Keka'a Terrace. Other options include the Lagoon and Sundowner Bars, and the Reef's Edge Lounge. A 142-yard freshwater swimming pool and kiddie pool are available for resort guests. Poolside bars offer cool, refreshing cocktails and hot barbecue snacks throughout the day.

Rates: g.v. $360/$385, m.v. $385/$425, partial o.v. $455/$495, o.v. $530/$560, o.f. $590/$610, deluxe o.v. $600/$630, deluxe o.f. $640/$680; Ohana Family Suites $800; other suites from $880; extra person $55/night; maximum four persons per room

Westin Ka'anapali Ocean Resort Villas

6 Ka'i Ala Drive, Lahaina, HI 96761. 888-488-3535; 808-667-3200; www.westin.com/kaanapalivillas.

This is the newest resort in Ka'anapali; the first phase is now open, with additional phases still under construction (at press time). Located on 14 oceanfront acres on the north side of Black Rock and Ka'anapali Beach, the resort is a timeshare property, but there is a vacation rental program available for visitors/non-owners. Currently the property has 184 studio, one and two-bedroom villas, with more units to come on board as construction continues. Each of the guest rooms/villas is very spacious and all offer Westin amenities, such as the Heavenly Beds and Heavenly Baths. All villas feature living room with queen-size sofa sleeper, separate dining area, fully equipped kitchens, private lanais, TV/DVD/stereo in the living room, washer/dryers and data ports. Daily maid service. There is a swimming pool with waterslide, as well as a children's pool. Fitness center, sauna and steam room; two lighted tennis courts; BBQ facilities. Children who are guests at the resort are welcome in the Keiki Kamp day program offered by the Westin Maui Resort & Spa nearby. The Ocean Pool Bar & Grill is a poolside bistro open daily from 6:30 a.m. to 11 p.m. In addition, the resort has the Pu'ukoli'i General Store, featuring baked goods, deli sandwiches, salads, carry-out pizzas and fresh meats and fish for grilling or in-room cooking—saves you a trip to the grocery store. All in all, this is shaping up to be a beautiful new addition to the Ka'anapali area. A great alternative for families or those who appreciate the comforts of a deluxe condo/villa more than a hotel room. Children under 18 are free when sharing same unit as adults. Max 5 persons to a room. NOTE: From summer 2005 through May 2007, the resort will be undergoing an expansion project, including the addition of two buildings with another 319 units and construction on the new Westin Ka'anapali Ocean Resort Villas North. As a result, the management is warning guests that they may encounter construction noise and dust during their stay.

Rates: Studio o.v. $575, deluxe o.v. $625, o.f. $725; 1BR o.v. $825, o.f. $975, deluxe o.f. $1,175; extra person/$50 night

★ *Westin Maui Resort & Spa*

2365 Ka'anapali Parkway, Lahaina, HI 96761. Hotel info 808-667-2525; reservations 808-921-4655; www.westinmaui.com.

This beautiful resort recently completed a major renovation (2004), adding a new $5 million, 14,000-square-foot luxury spa, salon and state-of-the-art workout facility, as well as multi-million dollar refurbishments to the lobby, restaurants, public areas and meeting rooms. The resort, located on 12 oceanfront acres on Ka'anapali Beach, offers 731 deluxe rooms and 27 suites (rooms underwent complete renovation in 2001). All rooms feature Westin's trademarked Heavenly Bath (featuring two shower heads and extra large plush towels), Heavenly Bed (with 10 layers of bedding) and its new Heavenly Crib (for the little ones), as well as private lanais to enjoy the view. Take a self-guided tour of the grounds and enjoy Westin's family of birds and their tropical surroundings. The property features lush gardens, streams, waterfalls and wildlife. At the heart of the property is the 87,000 square-foot aquatic playground with five pools, including an adult-only pool and jacuzzi, and a 128-foot waterslide. My three sisters and I, all of us middle-aged women, stayed together at the Westin a couple of years ago for a "sisters bonding weekend." We laughed ourselves silly going down that slide and swimming in and out of cave grottos. It's loads of fun for any age, so don't leave it all to the kids—jump in and have a ball! Parents can enjoy a brief respite while the kids have their own fun at the resort's Keiki Kamp for ages 5 to 12. (See "Childcare Programs" in Chapter 1 for details.) On-property restaurants include tropica (that's right, no capital) and 'OnO Bar & Grill. No extra charge for children 18 or under sharing the same room as parents, and kids under 12 eat free when accompanied by a paying adult.

Rates: Terrace $360-$390; g.v, golf, or m.v. $400-$440, o.v. $540-$570, deluxe o.v. $610-$650, premium deluxe ocean $670-$700, suites $1,000-$3,000; extra person $55 night

★ *The Whaler*

2481 Ka'anapali Parkway, Lahaina, HI 96761. 808-661-4861. Managed by Aston Resorts, 877-997-6667. Agents: Whalers Realty; RSVP; Maui & All Island; Chase 'N Rainbows; Maui Vacation Properties; Premier Resorts.

Lovely luxury condominium property with a choice location on an excellent beachfront site in the heart of Ka'anapali, next to the Whalers Village shopping center. A large pool area is beachfront and they provide a children's program during the summer. Underground parking. Aston's best rates are available as "E-pricebreakers" online.

Aston Rates: Studio 1 bath (2) g.v. $187/$245, o.v. $226/$290; 1BR (4) g.v. $244/$320, o.v. $291/$420, o.f. $383/$500; 2BR 2 bath g.v. (6) $331/$470, o.v. $431/$605, o.f. $522/$730

STAY AT ONE, PLAY AT ALL

Starwood's three Ka'anapali resorts—the Westin Maui Resort & Spa, Sheraton Maui Resort and Westin Ka'anapali Ocean Resort Villas—offer a dynamic amenity-sharing program called Stay at One, Play at All. The program allows guests staying at one property to enjoy many of the amenities and services at the other two resorts, including dining discounts at resort restaurants, use of the pools, and short-term parking privileges—access to three beautiful resort properties for the price of one. A complimentary shuttle runs between the three resorts every 15 minutes. A great program for guests of all ages, and the pool-hopping privileges are particularly nice for families.

Honokowai-Kapalua Area

HONOKOWAI

As you leave the Ka'anapali Resort area and head north, you will pass the new Ka'anapali Ocean Resort (a timeshare). Ahead, the intersection at Lower Honoapi'ilani Road signals the beginning of Honokowai.

Embassy Vacation Resort—Ka'anapali Beach

104 Ka'anapali Shores Place, Lahaina, HI 96761. 800-669-3155; 808-661-2000; www.mauiembassy.com.

On 7.5 acres, this pink pyramid structure with a three-story blue waterfall cascading down the side can't be missed. The all-suite accommodations blend the best of condo and resort living together. The pool (heated in the winter) area is large and tropical with plenty of room for lounge chairs. The lobby is open air and their glass-enclosed elevators will whisk you up with a view. On the lower roof, mezzanine level, families can enjoy the 18-hole miniature golf course. Each one-bedroom suite is a spacious 820 square feet; two-bedroom suites are 1,100 square feet. Each features lanai with ocean or scenic views. Master bedrooms are equipped with a remote-control 20-inch television and a large adjoining master bath with soaking tub. The living room contains a massive 35-inch television, stereo receiver, VCR player and cassette player. Living rooms have a sofa that pulls out into a double bed. A dining area with a small kitchenette is equipped with a microwave, small refrigerator and sink. Ironing equipment available upon request. On-site restaurants include North Beach Grille and a shop for sandwiches and sundries. Their children's program, Beach Buddies, is dedicated to perpetuating and preserving the heritage of the islands. (See "Childcare Programs" in Chapter 1.) Their health facility has state-of-the-art exercise equipment. They also offer salon and spa services. The resort has a gazebo for wedding ceremonies as well as a 13,000-square-foot meeting facility. Package plans also available.

Rates: 1BR scenic view (1-4) $390, o.v. $465, deluxe o.v. $565

Hale Kai

3691 Lower Honoapi'ilani Road, Lahaina, HI 96761. 800-446-7307; 808-669-6333; fax 808-669-7474; e-mail: halekai@halekai.com; www.halekai.com. Agent: Chase 'N Rainbows; Maui Lodging.

Forty units in a two-story building. The units have lanais, kitchens and a pool as well as VCRs and CDs. A simple and quiet oceanfront property. Laundry room next to office. Five-night minimum stay.

Maui Lodging Rates: 1BR (2) $120/$150; 1BR+loft (max 4) $175/$200

Hale Mahina Beach Resort

3875 Lower Honoapi'ilani Road, Lahaina, HI 96761. 800-367-8047 ext. 441; 808-669-8441; e-mail: halemahinabeachresort@msn.com. Agents: Chase 'N Rainbows; Maui Lodging.

Hale Mahina means "House of the Pale Moon." The resort offers 52 units in two four-story buildings and one two-story building. All feature lanais, ceiling fans, microwaves, washer/dryer, barbecue area, jacuzzi.

Chase 'N Rainbows rates: 1BR $130/$180, 2BR $190/$225

Hale Maui Apartment Hotel

P.O. Box 516, Lahaina, HI 96761. 808-669-6312; fax 808-669-1302; e-mail: halemaui@maui.net; www.maui.net/~halemaui.

All one-bedroom units sleep five. Lanais, kitchens, limited maid service, coin-operated washer/dryer, barbecue. Beachfront property. Weekly and monthly discounts. Three-night minimum.

Rates: 1BR (2, max 5) $95-$115; extra person $15/night

★ Hale Ono Loa

3823 Lower Honoapi'ilani Road, Lahaina, HI 96761. 808-669-6362. Agents: Maui Lodging; Chase 'N Rainbows.

Sixty-seven oceanfront and oceanview units. Beachfront is rocky. The units I toured were roomy and nicely furnished with spacious lanais. The grounds and pool area were pleasant and well groomed. A good choice for a quiet retreat. Grocery store nearby. Some rental agents may offer two-bedroom units.

Maui Lodging rates: 1BR $105-$140, 2BR $145-$175

Hoyochi Nikko

3901 Lower Honoapi'ilani Road, Lahaina, HI 96761. 800-487-6002; 808-669-8343; e-mail: hoyochi@aol.com. Agent: Maui Lodging.

All 18 units are one-bedroom (some with lofts), oceanview on a rocky beachfront with sandbar. Air conditioning. The two-story building bears an oriental motif. Underground parking, "Long Boy" twin beds, some with queens, stacking washer/dryer in units. Barbecue.

Maui Lodging rates: $115-$170

★ Ka'anapali Shores (Aston)

3445 Lower Honoapi'ilani Road, Lahaina, HI 96761. 808-667-2211. Managed by Aston, 877-997-6667. Agents: Maui & All Island; Chase 'N Rainbows; Whalers Realty; RSVP.

All 463 units offer telephones, free tennis, daily maid service and air conditioning. Nicely landscaped grounds and a wide beach with an area of coral reef cleared for swimming and snorkeling. This is the only resort on north Ka'anapali Beach that offers a good swimming area. Putting green, jacuzzi and the Beach Club restaurant located in the pool area. The resort features a year-round program for children ages 3 to 10 years. Activities are all held on property grounds and include hula and crafts. (Program for resort guests only.) Aston's best rates are available as "E-pricebreakers" online.

Aston rates: Hotel room w/refrigerator $155/$220; studio (1-2) partial o.v. $185/$325; 1BR (1-4) standard $207/$365, g.v. $229/$395, o.v. $263/$465; 2BR (1-6) g.v. $309/$570, o.v. $365/$630, o.f. $432/$730; suites $775-$1,000/$675-$900

Kaleialoha

3785 Lower Honoapi'ilani Road, Lahaina, HI 96761. Kaleialoha agent: 800-222-8688; 808-669-8197; e-mail: info@mauicondosoceanfront.com; www.mauicondosoceanfront.com.

Sixty-seven units in a four-story building. Oceanfront setting.

Rates: 1BR (2, max 4) superior $145, deluxe $135; extra persons 2 years and older $10/night

Kulakane

3741 Lower Honoapi'ilani Road (P.O. Box 5236), Lahaina, HI 96761. 800-367-6088; 808-669-6119; fax 808-669-9694; e-mail: info@kulakane.com; www.kulakane.com.

Forty-two oceanfront condominium suites. First and second floor suites are 1 BR/1 bath; third floor suites are 2 BR/2 bath. Free high-speed wireless internet for guests. Oceanfront pool. Thin stretch of sandy beach in front of the property, but it disappears during high tide or high surf. All units have private lanais, living room, dining area and full kitchens. Three to five-night minimum stay, depending on season. Off-season discounts for three nights or longer.

Rates: 1BR (4 max) $147, 2BR (6 max) $201

Kuleana

3959 Lower Honoapi'ilani Road, Lahaina, HI 96761. 800-367-5633; 808-669-8080. Agents: Maui Lodging.

All 118 one-bedroom units have queen-size sofa bed in living room. Large pool with plenty of lounge chair room. Tennis court. A short walk to sandy beaches.

Maui Lodging rates: 1BR o.f. $105-$145

Lokelani

3833 Lower Honoapi'ilani Road, Lahaina, HI 96761. 866-303-6284; 808-669-8110; fax: 808-669-1619; e-mail lokelanihi@aol.com; www.maui.net/~lokcondo. Agent: Chase 'N Rainbows; Maui Lodging.

Three three-story, 12-unit buildings with beachfront or ocean-view units. The one-bedroom units are on beach level with lanai, two-bedroom units are townhouses with bedrooms upstairs and lanais on both levels. Washer/dryers. Surcharge for stays less than seven nights.

Rates: 1BR (2) $145, 2BR townhouses (1-6) $185-$225

★ *Mahana*

110 Ka'anapali Shores Place, Lahaina, HI 96761. 808-661-8751. Managed by Aston, 877-997-6667. Agents: Maui & All Island; Whalers Realty; Maui Lodging; Chase 'N Rainbows; RSVP.

Mahana means "twins" as in two towers. All units oceanfront. Two 12-story towers with two tennis courts, heated pool, central air conditioning, saunas, elevators, small pool area. Located on narrow beachfront with offshore coral reef precluding swimming and snorkeling. A better swimming area is 100 yards up the beach. I haven't stayed here, but over the years have heard from many people that they wouldn't stay anywhere else. Higher rates from Aston may include added amenities, such as daily maid service, not offered by other agents. Aston's best rates are available as "E-pricebreakers" online.

Aston rates: Studio (1-2) o.f. $199/$345, 1BR 1 bath (1-4) o.f. $248/$465, 2BR 2 bath (1-6) o.f. $377/$675

Chase 'N Rainbows rates: Studio $150/$195, 1BR $160/$250, 2BR $300/$400

Mahina Surf

4057 Lower Honoapi'ilani Road, Lahaina, HI 96761. 800-367-6086; 808-669-6068; fax 808-669-4534; www.mahinasurf.com.

Fifty-six one-bedroom and two-bedroom units. Dishwashers. Located on rocky shore, the nearest sandy beach is a short drive to Kahana. A large lawn around the pool offers plenty of lounging room. Three-night minimum.

Rates: 1BR $130-$190/$150-$210, 2BR $160-$220/$180-$240; extra person including children $10/night

Makani Sands

3765 Lower Honoapi'ilani Road, Lahaina, HI 96761. 800-227-8223; 808-669-8223; fax 808-665-0756. Agents: Maui Lodging; Chase 'N Rainbows.

Thirty units in a three-story building. Dishwashers, washer/dryers, elevator. Oceanfront with small sandy beach. Some units with air conditioning. Onsite property managers.

Chase 'N Rainbows Rates: 1BR (2) $115-$140, 3BR (6) $195-$275

Maui Kai

106 Ka'anapali Shores Place, Lahaina, HI 96761. 800-367-5635; 808-667-3500; e-mail: reservation@mauikai.com; www.mauikai.com. Agents: Chase 'N Rainbows.

A single ten-story beachfront building with 79 units. Offering central air conditioning, private lanais, fully equipped kitchens and amenities including a swimming pool, jacuzzi, laundry facilities, plus free parking. Weekly/monthly discounts. Two-night minimum.

Hotel rates: Studio $155/$165, 1BR $191-$201/$202-$212; 2BR $303/$318

Maui Sands

3559 Lower Honoapi'ilani Road, Lahaina, HI 96761. Agents: Maui Resort Management; Whalers; Maui Lodging.

All 76 units have air conditioning and kitchens. Limited maid service. Microwaves, coin-op laundry facility, and rollaways and cribs available $9 night. A very friendly atmosphere where old friends have been gathering each year since it was built in the mid-1960s. They feature a large pool area with barbecues. Large boulders line the beach. A good family facility.

Maui Resort Management rates: 1BR (2, max 3) g.v. $105/$95, garden w/o.v. $125/$115; 2BR g.v. 150-$160/$130-$145, o.f. $180/$160

Noelani

4095 Lower Honoapi'ilani Road, Lahaina, HI 96761. 800-367-6030; 808-669-8374; fax 808-669-7904; e-mail: noelani@maui.net; www.noelani-condo-resort.com.

Deluxe oceanfront studios, one-, two-, and three-bedroom condos, all with complete kitchens. Washer/dryer and dishwasher in all but studio units. Complex has two oceanfront pools (heated), an oceanfront jacuzzi spa and maid service every other day. Oceanside barbecues with herb garden. Located on a rocky shoreline, but there's a small sandy cove at the north end of the property and it's just a short walk to Pohaku Beach Park. Under 18 free.

Rates: Studio (1-2, max 2) $107/$135, studio deluxe (1-2, max 3) $129/$150; 1BR 1 bath (1-3, max 4) $157/$180; 2BR 2 bath (1-4, max 6) $237/$257; 3BR 2 bath (1-6, max 8) $297/$317; extra person $10/night

Nohonani

3723 Lower Honoapi'ilani Road, Lahaina, HI 96761. 800-822-7368; 808-669-8208; fax 808-669-2388; e-mail: alohablu@maui.net; www.nohonanicondos.com. Agent: Maui Lodging.

Two four-story buildings contain 22 oceanfront two-bedroom units and five one-bedroom units with complete kitchens. Two-bedroom units have washer/dryer. Complex has large pool, telephones and is one block to grocery store. On-property management. Weekly and monthly discounts. Three-night minimum.

Rates: 1BR (1-2) $135/$140, 2BR (1-4) $158/$180; extra person $15/night

Paki Maui

3615 Lower Honoapi'ilani Road, Lahaina, HI 96761. 808-669-8235. Managed by Aston, 877-997-6667. Agents: Maui & All Island; Chase 'N Rainbows; RSVP.

This low-rise complex is surrounded by gardens, koi pond and waterfall. No air conditioning. Aston's best rates are available as "E-pricebreakers" online.

Aston Rates: Studio o.f. $180/$230; 1BR (1-4) g.v. $145-$230, o.f. $179/$300; 2BR (1-6) p.o.v. $227-$355, o.f. $251/$395

★ Papakea

3543 Lower Honoapi'ilani Road, Lahaina, HI 96761. 808-669-4848. Managed by Aston, 877-997-6667. Agents: Maui Resort Management; Maui & All Island; RSVP; Chase 'N Rainbows.

There are five four-story buildings with 364 units. Two pools, two jacuzzis, two saunas, tennis courts, putting green, washer/dryers and barbecue area. The shallow water is great for children because a protective reef is located 10-30 yards offshore, but poor for swimming or snorkeling. A better beach is down in front of the Ka'anapali Shores. One of the nicer grounds for a condominium complex, Papakea features lush landscaping and pool areas. A comfortable and quiet property that I recommend especially for families. Non-smoking units available.

Maui Resort Management rates: 1BR (4) $125-$210; 2BR/2 bath (6) $155-$220

Pikake

3701 Lower Honoapi'ilani Road, Lahaina, HI 96761. 800-446-3054; 808-669-6086. Agent: Maui Lodging; Chase 'N Rainbows.

A low-rise, two-story, Polynesian-style building with only 12 apartments completed in 1966. Private lanais open to the lawn or balconies. The beach is protected by a sea wall. Central laundry area. Ceiling fans, no air conditioning. All units are oceanfront.

Maui Lodging rates: 1BR (2, max 4) $115/$145, 2BR (4, max 6) $145/$185; extra person $10/night

Polynesian Shores

3975 Lower Honoapi'ilani Road, Lahaina, HI 96761. 800-433-6284, 800-488-2179 (from Canada); 808-669-6065; e-mail: polyshor@maui.net; www.maui.net/~polyshor. Agent: Chase 'N Rainbows.

Fifty-two units on a rocky shore with nice grounds featuring a deck overlooking the ocean. Heated swimming pool.

Rates: 1BR 1 bath (2) $145/$135; 2BR 2 bath (loft) (2) $185/$175, 2BR 2 bath end (4) $210/$200; 3BR 3 bath (4) $245/$225; additional person $10/night

KAHANA

Hololani

4401 Lower Honoapi'ilani Road, Lahaina, HI 96761. 800-367-5032; 808-669-8021; fax 808-669-7682. e-mail: hololani@hololani.com; www.hololani.com. Agent: Chase 'N Rainbows.

Twenty-seven two-bedroom, two-bath oceanfront units with full kitchens. Freshwater pool; sandy, reef-protected beach. Covered parking. Maximum six people per unit. Five-to-seven-day minimum stay.

Rates: 2BR 2 bath (4) o.f. $180/$220

Kahana Outrigger

4521 Lower Honoapi'ilani Road, Lahaina, HI 96761. 800-987-8494; 808-669-6550. Agents: Maui & All Island; Chase 'N Rainbows.

Sixteen spacious three-bedroom oceanview condo suites in a low-rise complex on a narrow sandy beachfront. Units have microwaves, washer/dryers and are appointed with Italian tile. These are rented as vacation "homes" with no on-property service provided.

Chase 'N Rainbows rates: 3BR $295-$400

★ *Kahana Reef*

4471 Lower Honoapi'ilani Road, Lahaina, HI 96761. 800-253-3773; 808-669-6491; fax 808-669-2192. Agents: Maui Condo & Home; Maui & All Island; Chase 'N Rainbows.

Eighty-eight well-kept units. Limited number of oceanfront studios available. Laundry facilities on premises. A good value. Amenities such as maid service may influence prices.

Maui Condo & Home rates: Studio o.f. $140-$160; 1BR o.f. $150-$170

★ *Kahana Sunset*

P.O. Box 10219, Lahaina, HI 96761. 800-669-1488; 808-669-8011; fax 808-669-9170. Agents: Premier Resorts; RSVP.

Ninety units in six two- and three-story buildings on a beautiful and secluded white-sand beach. Units have very large lanais, telephones and washer/dryers. Each unit has its own lanai, but they adjoin one another, adding to the friendly atmosphere of this complex. One of the very few resorts with a heated pool, heated children's pool and barbecue. You can drive up right to your door on most of the two-bedroom units, making unloading easy (and with a family heavy into suitcases that can be a real back saver). These are not luxurious units, but it is a location that is difficult to beat.

Premier Resorts rates: 1BR g.v. $140-$215/$170-$235, ocean/garden view $185/$265; 2BR ocean/garden view $200/$240, o.v. $220-$370/$255-$295, o.f. $300-$370/$355-$410

★ *Kahana Village*

4531 Lower Honoapi'ilani Road, Lahaina, HI 96761. 800-824-3065; 808-669-5111; e-mail: village@kahanavillage.com; www.kahanavillage.com. Other agents: Maui & All Island; RSVP; Chase 'N Rainbows.

Attractive townhouse units. Second-level units are 1,200 square feet; ground-level three-bedroom units have 1,700 square feet with a wet bar, sunken tub in master bath, Jenn-aire ranges, microwaves, lanais and washer/dryers. They offer a heated pool and attractively landscaped grounds. Nice but narrow beach offering good swimming. Five-night minimum.

Rates: 2BR o.v. $205/$280, o.f. $240/$320; 3BR o.v. $280/$370, o.f. $335/$435

Kahana Villas

4242 Lower Honoapi'ilani Road, Lahaina, HI 96761. 808-669-5613. Agents: Chase 'N Rainbows.

Across the road from the beach. Units have microwaves, washer/dryers, and telephones. Daily maid service. Property also has sauna, tennis courts and convenience store. Some studios and one-bedrooms are also available through agents.

Chase 'N Rainbows rates: 2BR 2 bath (1-6) $155-$195

Royal Kahana

4365 Lower Honoapi'ilani Road, Lahaina, HI 96761. 808-669-5911; fax 808-669-5950. Managed by Outrigger Resorts, 800-688-7444; e-mail rkr@outrigger.com; www.outrigger.com. Other agents: Chase 'N Rainbows; RSVP.

Built in 1975 with 236 oceanview condominium units on Kahana Beach, this 12-story high-rise complex is near grocery stores, restaurants and shops. Underground parking and air conditioning. Daily maid service. A nice pool area with sauna. Tennis courts. All units include full kitchens and washer/dryer. Daily maid service. Free parking. Extra person charge $20 per night includes rollaway. Cribs available. Two-night minimum stay.

Rates: Studio (1-3) g.v. $195/$225, o.v. $215-$235; 1BR (1-4) g.v $225/$255, o.v. $245/$275, o.f. $285/$325; 2BR (1-6) g.v. $315/$345, o.v. $335/$375, o.f. $415/$485

★ Sands of Kahana

4299 Lower Honoapi'ilani Road, Lahaina, HI 96761. 808-669-0423; fax 808-669-8409; Managed by Sullivan Properties: 800-580-8864; www.sands-of-kahana.com. Agent: Chase 'N Rainbows.

Ninety-six units on Kahana Beach. I stayed here some years back and enjoyed the spacious rooms and nicely appointed amenities. This property is among many in Kahana that have converted to timeshare, but they do still rent to the public for now. Pool, children's pool, jacuzzi and three tennis courts.

Rates (per night based on weekly rental): 1BR value view $190/$150, o.v. $225/$185, o.f. $265/$225; 2BR o.v. $295/$265, o.f. $335/$295; 3BR o.v. $375/$325, o.f. $410/$365; Penthouse $385-$410

Valley Isle Resort

4327 Lower Honoapi'ilani Road, Lahaina, HI 96761. 808-669-5511 (for brochure only, no reservations) Agents: Maui Lodging; Chase 'N Rainbows; Maui & All Island.

Partial air conditioning. Located on Kahana Beach. Chase 'N Rainbows has most of the private condo rentals at this property.

Chase 'N Rainbows rates: Studios $105-$150; 1BR $130-$190; 2BR $175-$240

Hale Napili

65 Hui Road, Lahaina, HI 96761. 800-245-2266; 808-669-6184; fax 808-665-0066; e-mail: halenapi@maui.net; www.maui.net/~halenapi.

Eighteen oceanfront units on Napili Bay. Daily maid service. Ceiling fans, full kitchens with microwaves, lanais and free laundry facilities on property. No pool. Children 12 and under free.

Rates: Studio (max 3) g.v./o.v. $129, o.f. $165; 1BR (max 4) o.f. $195; extra person $15/night

★ *Honokeana Cove*

5255 Lower Honoapi'ilani Road, Lahaina, HI 96761. 800-237-4948; 808-669-6441; www.honokeana-cove.com.

Thirty-eight oceanview units on Honokeana Cove near Napili Bay. Attractive grounds—and friendly sea turtles. Probably one of the best values in West Maui, and that is evidenced by the many returning guests. In calm weather you'll find lots of folks snorkeling in the cove. While each condo is privately owned and furnished with the owner's individual tastes, you'll find all units equipped with cable television, VCR, microwaves, blenders, etc. Private lanai with ocean views. Weekly and monthly discounts. Minimum stay 3/5 nights.

Rates: 1BR 1 bath (2) $156, 1BR 2 bath (2) $169, 2BR 1 bath $180; 2BR 2 bath (max 4) $216; 3BR 2 bath (max 6) $256; townhouse (max 4) $251; extra person $10-$15/night

Mauian

5441 Lower Honoapi'ilani Road, Lahaina, HI 96761. 800-367-5034; 808-669-6205; fax 808-669-0129; e-mail: info@mauian.com; www.mauian.com.

The Mauian hotel on Napili Beach is a small, charming hideaway on two acres of beachfront property. The hotel features 44 studio units with fully equipped kitchens and private lanais. They cannot guarantee any specific room number, but they will make every attempt to accommodate those guests requesting a particular building location. Rooms have one queen bed and one twin day bed. The Mauian has been providing Hawaiian hospitality on Napili Bay since 1959 and offers guests a relaxed island-style ambiance with no unwanted disturbances—the units do not have telephones or televisions. A courtesy phone is available in the lobby and a television is located in the hotel's Ohana Room. Complimentary continental breakfast is provided for guests each morning in the Ohana Room. Barbecue areas. Pool. This is a simple place—nothing fancy—but many families have returned to vacation at this quiet corner of Napili for years. Check website for special discounts.

Rates: Studio g.v. $165/$145, o.v. $185/$165, o.f. $195/$180

Napili Bay Resort

33 Hui Drive, Lahaina, HI 96761. 808-669-6044. Agent: Aloha Condos Maui, www.alohacondos.com.

This older complex on Napili Bay is neat, clean and affordably priced. Studio apartments offer one queen and two single beds, lanais, kitchens, daily maid service. Coin-op laundromat with public phones. Many of the individually owned studios are rented directly from the owners. Maximum two persons per unit.

Aloha Condos Maui rates: o.f. $155-$225, o.v. $120-$155

Napili Gardens

5432 Lower Honoapi'ilani Road, Lahaina, HI 96761. Agent: Maui Beach Front Rentals; 808-661-3500; 888-661-7200; www.napiligardens.com.

Lovely custom residential townhouses that offer double car garages, private rear yards, gourmet kitchens, lanais, plus washer/dryer. Located a short walk to the beach at Napili Bay. Units sleep up to eight.

Rates: 3BR 2.5 baths—rates vary depending on individual units available for rent; contact the rental agent.

★ *Napili Kai Beach Resort*

5900 Lower Honoapi'ilani Road, Lahaina, HI 96761. 800-367-5030; 808-669-6271; fax 808-669-0086; e-mail: stay@napilikai.com; www.napilikai.com.

A deluxe resort situated on 10 beachfront acres on Napili Bay. The resort offers 162 hotel rooms, studios and one- and two-bedroom suites (most with kitchen facilities) in 11 low-rise buildings. Nearly all (96 percent) of the units have ocean views. Some units have newly remodeled interiors (completed in late 2004). Two putting greens—one for adults, one for children. Exercise room; boutique spa. Complimentary beach equipment, putters and snorkel gear. Daily coffee and tea offered in the lobby and Beach Cabana. Sea House restaurant located on grounds. Four pools and a huge oceanview jacuzzi spa. The key here is location, location, location. The grounds are extensive and the area very quiet. A relaxed and friendly atmosphere, a great beach and a variety of activities may tempt you to spend most of your time enjoying this very personable and complete resort. A popular place for family reunions. Every Tuesday night a charming one-hour Polynesian show is presented at the resort (fee) by the children (ages 6 to 18) of the Napili Kai Foundation. A children's activity program is offered during the summer months for guests between the ages of 6 and 12. See "Childcare Programs" in Chapter 1. Complimentary parking and no resort fee. Two-night deposit, 14-day refund notice. Christmas rates slightly higher. Group rates available and packages, too.

Rates: Hotel room (2) g.v. $200, o.v. $240; family studio g.v. $250, o.v. $300; Studio o.v. $270, beachfront $290, o.f. $325; 1BR suite o.v. $385, beachfront $395, o.f. $405-$450; 2BR suite o.v. $555-$600, o.f. $700; 3BR suite o.v. $780-$900

Napili Point

5295 Lower Honoapi'ilani Road, Lahaina, HI 96761. Napili Point Resort Rental 808-669-9222; 800-669-6252; e-mail: napiliptresort@cs.com; www.napili.com. Agent: RSVP.

Located on rocky beach, next to beautiful Napili Bay. Units have washer/dryer, full kitchens with dishwashers and daily maid service. King- or queen-size beds in one-bedroom units. No air conditioning; most units have ceiling fans. Cribs available. Two pools. In some suites the second bedroom is loft-style.

Napili Point rates: 1BR o.v. $209/$239, o.f. $229/$259, Point o.f. $249/$279; 2BR o.v. $259/$329, o.f. $309/$379, Point o.f. $359/$429

Napili Shores

5315 Lower Honoapi'ilani Road, Lahaina, HI 96761. 808-669-8061; fax 808-669-5407. Managed by Outrigger Resorts, 800-688-7444; e-mail nsr@outrigger.com; www.outrigger.com. Agents: RSVP.

On lovely Napili Bay, 152 studio and one-bedroom units with private lanais, full kitchens. Laundry facilities on premises as well as two pools, adult hot tub, croquet and barbecue area. Restaurants, cocktail lounge and grocery store on property. Studios have one queen and one twin bed. Cribs and rollaways available.

Rates: Studio g.v. $175/$186, o.v. $206/$223, o.f. $235/$245; 1BR g.v. $212/$229, o.v. $248/$264

★ Napili Sunset

46 Hui Road, Lahaina, HI 96761. 800-447-9229 U.S.; 800-223-4611 Canada; 808-669-8083; fax 808-669-2730; e-mail: info@napilisunset.com; www.napilisunset.com.

Forty-one units located on Napili Bay. Full kitchens. Daily maid service. Ceiling fans, no air conditioning. These units have great ocean views and are well maintained. A very friendly atmosphere. The studio units are nicely kept, but I'd recommend the oceanfront one bedrooms. You can't get any closer to the beach than here. Three-night minimum.

Rates: Studio g.v. $120/$135 (2); 1BR 1 bath (2) beachfront $235/$255; 2BR (4) 2 bath o.f. $300/$350; extra person (over 2 years old) $15/night

Napili Surf

50 Napili Place, Lahaina, HI 96761. 888-627-4547; 808-669-8002; fax 808-669-8004; e-mail: relax@napilisurf.com; www.napilisurf.com.

These 53 units are on Napili Bay. Two pools, barbecue, shuffleboard, lanais, daily maid service and laundry facilities. Five-night minimum. No credit cards. Inquire about specials and monthly discounts.

Rates: Studio (2, max 3) g.v. $140, o.v. $185, o.f. $200; 1BR (2, max 4) partial o.v. $215, o.v. $235, o.f. $290; extra person $15/night

Napili Village

5425 Lower Honoapi'ilani Road, Lahaina, HI 96761. 800-336-2185; 808-669-6228; fax 808-669-6229; e-mail: napilivg@gte.net; www.napili village.com.

All vacation apartments are 500 square feet and feature king- or queen-size beds. Daily maid service. Laundry facilities on premises. Located a short walk from Napili Bay. Children 5 and under are free.

Rates: (2) g.v. $99/$129, o.v. $114/$134, g.v. premium $119/$139

One Napili Way

5355 Lower Honoapi'ilani Road #101, Lahaina, HI 96761. 808-669-2007; 800-841-6284; e-mail: onenapi@aloha.net; www.onenapiliway.com.

There are 14 condos available as one-, two- or three-bedroom units. Master baths feature jacuzzi tub, all units have washer/dryer. Four-night minimum. This is a time-share property, so be prepared to hear the sales pitch.

Rates: 1BR (1-4) $270, 2BR (1-6) $330, 3BR (1-8) $360

KAPALUA

Kapalua, meaning "arms embracing the sea," is the most northwestern development on Maui. The 1,650-acre master-planned Kapalua Resort community is surrounded by 23,000 acres of pineapple plantation and is home to three award-winning 18-hole golf courses and two highly ranked tennis complexes. Kapalua Bay has garnered top accolades from Dr. Beach and his "Best Beaches in America" awards. It is a perfect crescent of beach lined with palm trees. Kapalua is an upscale resort community—you won't find any budget properties here. Many of the Kapalua condominiums are nestled around the golf courses and you can take a shuttle down to the beach, drive (limited parking) or walk. The Kapalua Bay Hotel is just steps away from the bay. The Ritz-Carlton, Kapalua is situated above D.T. Fleming Beach, which is not as protected and safe as Kapalua Bay. Either resort offers outstanding amenities and every aspect of your stay will leave you feeling relaxed and pampered. More than 400 condominium units are available through Kapalua Villas. Spacious luxury homes and estates are also available as vacation rentals. The logo for Kapalua is the butterfly, and with a close look you can see that the body of the butterfly is a pineapple.

★ Kapalua Bay Hotel

One Bay Drive, Kapalua, HI 96761. 800-468-3571; 808-669-5656; fax 808-669-4694; www.kapaluabayhotel.com. Managed by Marriott/Renaissance.

The hotel offers 191 luxury hotel rooms and suites in an open-air terraced low-rise. Spacious rooms have service bars, mini-refrigerators, video cassette players and his-and-her vanities. Air conditioning and private lanais in all units. Their stunning lobby features floor-to-ceiling glass windows with that breathtaking view of Moloka'i and Lana'i showcased. The views continue in their fitness center located above the lobby. The Plumeria Terrace and the Gardenia Court are the hotel's two restaurants. The Lehua Lounge offers a great spot for sunset viewing in the evening. The hotel's signature oceanview pool is butterfly-shaped—the Kapalua logo. Lovely grounds, excellent beach and breathtaking views. The expanse of lawn gives way to lush tropical foliage, waterfalls, pools and gardens. This is elegance on a more sophisticated scale than the glitter and glitz of the Ka'anapali resorts. A very lovely property, secluded and intimate.

NOTE: Kapalua Bay LLC, the new owners of the Kapalua Bay Hotel, have announced they will demolish this hotel and redevelop the site beginning in the summer of 2006 as part of the overall redevelopment and revitalization of the Kapalua Resort community. So, this is your last chance to experience the landmark Kapalua Bay Hotel, the "grand lady" of Kapalua.

Rates: g.v. $390, partial o.v. $435, o.v. $480, deluxe o.v. $525, junior suite $935, o.v. suite $1,250; villas available in the adjacent Bay Villas community, $630-$820

★ *Kapalua Villas*

Kapalua Villas: 500 Office Road, Kapalua, HI 96761. 800-545-0018 U.S. & Canada; 808-669-8088; fax 808-669-5234; www.kapaluavillas.com.

The Kapalua Villas offer an excellent value for traveling families. There are more than 270 individually owned vacation rental units in three condominium communities, The Ridge, Golf Villas and Bay Villas, and each is spacious and beautifully appointed. Individually decorated and private, they feel much more like a home than a condominium and make wonderful accommodations for a large family or couples traveling together. Amenities include a 24-hour reception center, daily maid service, concierge, activity desk, preferred golf arrangements and complimentary tennis. The units include kitchens, washer/dryers and ceiling fans with two TVs, two telephones and a VCR. Recreational facilities include several pools, outdoor barbecues and tropical garden areas. Check with Kapalua Villas regarding special packages and offers throughout the year.

Rates: 1BR (max 4) fairway view $209, o.v. $259, o.f. $289; 2BR (4, max 6) fairway v. $309, o.v. $389, o.f. $479; 3BR (max 6) fairway $435, o.v. $510

★ *The Ritz-Carlton, Kapalua*

1 Ritz Carlton Drive, Kapalua, HI 96761. 800-262-8440; 808-669-6200; fax 808-669-1566; www.ritzcarlton.com.

This elegant oceanfront resort at D. T. Fleming Beach has a Hawaiian motif with a plantation feel that features native stonework throughout the hotel. The hotel offers 548 rooms, including 37 Club Level Rooms and 58 suites. The guest rooms are spacious and beautifully appointed. Amenities include twice-daily maid service, in-room terry robes, complimentary in-room safe, multilingual staff, babysitting and children's programs, boutique spa and full-service beauty salon. The Ritz-Kids program is a half- or full-day program for children ages 5 to 12; see "Childcare Programs" in Chapter 1. In addition, the Ritz-Carlton offers a complimentary V.I.K. (Very Important Keiki) program that makes kids feel welcome at the resort, from check-in—when families are presented with a scavenger hunt they can complete together—to turndown, when kids receive a special treat. While the kids are at play, spoil yourself with one of the many spa services at the fitness center; oceanside or in-room massage is available. Ten tennis courts plus a 10,000-square-foot, three-level swimming pool are among the amenities. Dining options include The Terrace restaurant, the poolside Banyan Tree, the Beach House, the Lobby Lounge, and the Pool Bar. (See Chapter 4 for more information.) The Ritz-Carlton is certainly a jewel for West Maui. I enjoyed a couple of days there and checked out the Club Floor. These special floors, available at many of the finer properties on Maui, have added security. A special key is required in the elevator to reach your floor. An exclusive club lounge area offered snacks almost continually. The continental breakfast was more than one would expect, with some wonderful cereals, pastries, freshly squeezed juices and fresh fruits. The midday snack included light sandwiches and fresh vegetables or fruits. The early-evening hours provided appetizers and wine or drinks. After dinner were chocolates and cordials. There were also cold drinks and hot coffee available all day. The lounge area was elegant yet homey, and the balconies provided entertaining views of golfers playing the course. Inquire about special packages and promotions.

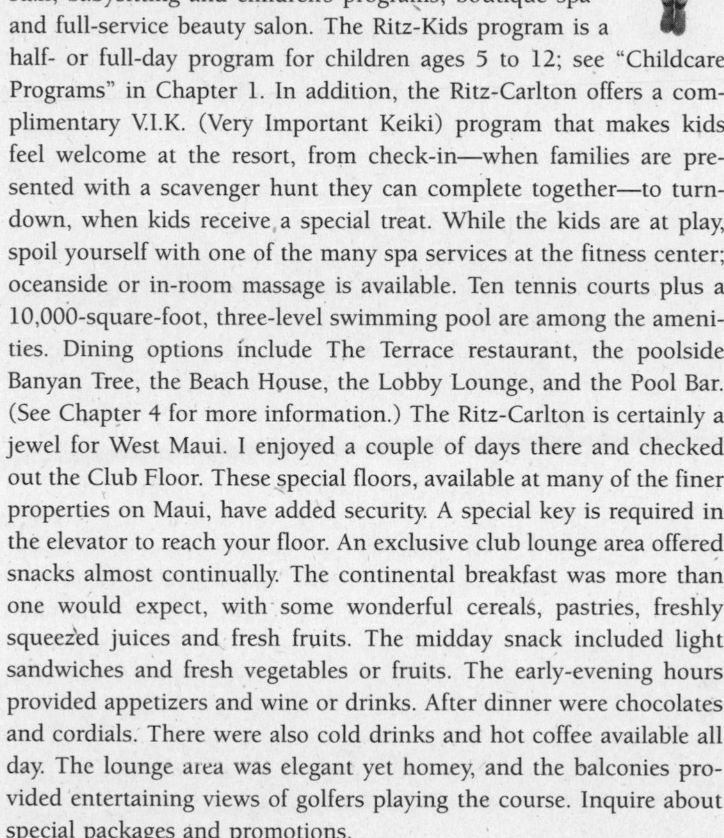

Rates: terrace view $365, g.v. $405, p.o.v. $475, o.v. $590; The Ritz-Carlton Club Level $675; 1BR Suites g.v. $675, o.v. $715; Club Suite $900; 1BR and 2BR Suites $1,150-$3,750

Ma'alaea-Kihei Area

MA'ALAEA

Hono Kai

280 Hauoli Street, Wailuku, HI 96793. 808-244-7012.
Agent: Ma'alaea Bay.

Forty-six units located on the beach. Choice of gardenview, oceanview or oceanfront. Laundry facilities, barbecue, pool. This complex is on the beach and gains the attention of the budget-conscious traveler, but don't expect any frills. Five-night minimum stay.

Rates: 1BR g.v. $115/$135, o.f. $135/$175; 2BR g.v. $130/$170, o.f. $160/$190; 3BR $200/$225

Island Sands

150 Hauoli Street, Wailuku, HI 96793. Island Sands Resort Rentals 800-826-7816; 808-244-0848; fax 808-244-5639. Agents: Ma'alaea Bay Rentals; Condominium Rentals Hawaii.

Eighty-four units in a six-story building. One of Ma'alaea's larger complexes located along the sea wall. Offers a Maui-shaped pool, a grassy lawn area, barbecue. Many of these units also have a lanai off the master bedroom; however, the lanais have a concrete piece in the middle of each railing that somewhat limits the view while sitting or lying in bed. Washer/dryers and air conditioning. Elevators. Weekly and monthly discounts. Four-night minimum. Children under three free; $200 deposit with 15-day refund notice.

Ma'alaea Bay Rentals rates: 1BR o.f. $135/$155, 2BR o.f. $150/$195; extra person $7.50/night

★ Kana'i a Nalu

250 Hauoli Street, Wailuku, HI 96793. Agent: Ma'alaea Bay Rentals.

Eighty units with washer/dryers in four buildings with elevators. No maid service. This is the first of three condominiums along a sandy beachfront. Its name means "parting of the sea, surf, or wave." The complex is V-shaped with a pool area in the middle. Nicely landscaped grounds, a decent beach and only a short walk along the beach to the best swimming and playing area along this section of coastline. While over the last couple of years the high-season prices have jumped a bit, the low-season rates have consistently remained an excellent value. Overall one of the best values in the Ma'alaea area. Five-night minimum, ten nights over Christmas. Weekly/monthly discounts.

Rates: 2BR (4) o.v. $155/$205, o.f. $185/$245

★ Lauloa

100 Hauoli Street, Wailuku, HI 96793. 808-242-6575. Agent: Ma'alaea Bay Rentals.

Forty-seven two-bedroom, two-bath units of 1,100 square feet. One of the Lauloa's best features is its floor plan. The living room and master bedroom are on the front of the building with a long connecting lanai and sliding glass patio doors that offer unobstructed ocean views. A sliding shoji screen separates the living room from the bedroom. Each morning from bed you have but to open your eyes to see the palm trees swaying in front of the panoramic ocean view. The second bedroom is in the back of the unit. These two-bedroom units are spacious and are in fair to good condition (depending on the owner).

Each has a washer/dryer in the unit. The pool area and grounds are along the sea wall. There are often local fishermen throwing nets and lines into the ocean. Five-night minimum. Maid service extra charge. Monthly discounts.

Ma'alaea Bay Rentals rates: 2BR 2 bath (4) o.f. reef $130/$175

Ma'alaea Banyans

190 Hauoli Street, Wailuku, HI 96793. 808-242-5668. Agent: Ma'alaea Bay Rentals.

Seventy-six oceanview units with lanai and washer/dryer. Weekly and monthly discounts. Oceanfront on rocky shore, short walk to beach. Pool area, jacuzzi, barbecues.

Ma'alaea Bay Rentals rates: 1BR (2) o.f. reef $125/$145; extra person $10/night

Ma'alaea Kai

70 Hauoli Street, Wailuku, HI 96793. 808-244-7012. Agent: Ma'alaea Bay Rentals.

Seventy oceanfront units. Laundry facilities, putting green, barbecue and elevators. Located on the harbor wall, the rooms are standard and quite satisfactory. Most have washer and dryer in the room. Pool area and large pleasant grounds in front along the harbor wall. A few blocks' walk down to a sandy beach. Weekly and monthly discounts.

Rates: 1BR (2) o.f. reef $115/$125, 2BR (4) o.f. reef $130/$175

Ma'alaea Yacht Marina

30 Hauoli Street, Wailuku, HI 96793. 808-244-7012. Agent: Ma'alaea Bay Rentals; RSVP.

All units are oceanfront; a beach is nearby. The units I viewed were pleasant with a wonderful view of the boats from most units and the added plus of having security elevators and stairways. Many of the units have no air conditioning; laundry facilities are located in a laundry room on each floor. A postage stamp–size grassy area in front and a small but adequate pool.

Ma'alaea Bay Rentals rates: 1BR (2) o.f. reef $115/$125, 2BR (4) o.f. reef $130/$175

★ Makani a Kai

300 Hauoli Street, Wailuku, HI 96793. Agent: Ma'alaea Bay Rentals.

These deluxe oceanfront and oceanview units are on the beach. Laundry room on property, pool, barbecue. This is the last property along the beach in Ma'alaea. Beyond this is a long stretch of sandy beach along undeveloped state land and about a four-mile jaunt down to Kihei—great for you beach walkers. The two-bedroom units are townhouse style. This is a very pleasant place to headquarter your Maui vacations. Five-night minimum, ten days over Christmas.

Rates: 1BR o.v. $115/$135; o.f. $145/$185; 2BR o.v. $135/$195; o.f. $175/$235

Milowai

50 Hauoli Street, Wailuku, HI 96793. Agents: Milowai Rentals 808-242-1580, fax 808-242-1634; Kihei Maui Vacations; Ma'alaea Bay Rentals; RSVP.

One of the larger complexes in Ma'alaea with a restaurant on location, The Waterfront. They offer a large pool area and a barbecue along the sea wall. The corner units are a very roomy 1,200 square feet with windows off the master bedrooms. Depending on condo location in the building, the views are of the Ma'alaea Harbor or the open ocean. The one-bedroom units have a lanai off the living room and a bedroom in the back. Washer/dryer. Weekly/monthly discounts.

Ma'alaea Bay Rentals rates: 1BR (2) o.f. reef $125/$145

KIHEI

Kihei is a popular place to stay due to its large selection of good, reasonably priced accommodations, a central but quiet location, nice beaches and certainly some of the island's best vacation buys.

Hale Alana

Located in Maui Meadows. P.O. Box 160, Kihei, HI 96753. 800-871-5032; 808-875-4840; fax 808-879-3998; e-mail: maui@alohajourneys.com; www.alohajourneys.com.

Your hosts are Karen and Ken Stover for this three-bedroom/three-bath home. There are two master bedrooms and a third bedroom with two double beds. Great ocean vistas from the private deck and beautifully appointed all around. One-week minimum. Add 20 percent to rates for high season, from December 15 to April 15.

Rates: house (for 4) $265; $30 each additional guest; $150 cleaning fee

Hale Hui Kai

2994 South Kihei Road, Kihei, HI 96753. 808-879-1219; fax 808-879-0600; 800-809-6284; www.beachbreeze.com.

Three-story condo oceanfront on Keawakapu Beach. Two bedroom two-bath apartments with kitchen. Each unit is unique and priced accordingly. Maximum occupancy six people. Coin-operated laundry. No air conditioning. Five-night minimum. No credit cards.

Rates: 2BR 2 bath o.f. $235-325/$290-$365; side o.v. $220-$250/$250-$290; g.v. $145-$190/$185-$250; extra person $15-$20/night

Hale Kai O' Kihei

1310 Uluniu Road (P.O. Box 809), Kihei, HI 96753. 808-879-2757; 800-457-7014; fax 808-875-8242. Agent: Condo Rentals Hawaii; Maui Vacation Properties; AA Oceanfront Condo Rentals.

Fifty-nine oceanfront units with lanais in three-story building. Sandy beachfront. Shuffleboard, putting green, barbecues, laundry, recreation area.

Condo Rentals Hawaii rates: 1BR (2) $130-$160, 2BR (4) $155-$205

Hale Kamaole

2737 South Kihei Road, Kihei, HI 96753. 800-367-2970; 808-879-2698. Agents: Maui & All Island; Condo Rentals Hawaii; Maui Vacation Properties.

There are 188 units in five buildings (two- and three-story, no elevator) across the road from Kama'ole III Beach. Laundry building, barbecues, two pools, tennis courts. Some units have washer and dryers. Cleaning fee charged for less than six nights.

Condo Rentals Hawaii rates: 1BR $125-$155, 2BR 2 bath $155-$200

Hale Pau Hana

2480 South Kihei Road, Kihei, HI 96753. 808-879-2715; 800-367-6036; fax 808-875-0238; www.hphresort.com. Agents: RSVP; Condominium Rentals Hawaii; Kihei Maui Vacations; Maui Vacation Properties; Kumulani.

Seventy-nine oceanview units in four buildings. Laundry facility, elevator, barbecue grills. Full kitchens. Located directly on Kama'ole II Beach. Lovely, well-kept grounds with a heated pool fronting the ocean. Minimum stay 4-7 nights.

Rates: Tower units, 1BR $184-$240/$215-$280, 2 BR $270-$335; lowrise units, 1 BR $173-$240/$205-$270; Anchor Cove suite, 2 BR/2 bath $380-$450

★ Haleakala Shores

2619 South Kihei Road, Kihei, HI 96753. 800-869-1097; 808-879-1218. Agents: Kihei Maui Vacations; Bello Realty.

Seventy-six two-bedroom units in two four story buildings. Located across the road from Kama'ole III Beach. Washer/dryer. Covered parking. A good value. Rentals through on-site manager are check only, no credit cards.

Bello Realty rates: 2BR 2 bath (1-4) $130/$100

Kamaole Beach Royale

2385 South Kihei Road, Kihei, HI 96753. 800-421-3661; 808-879-3131; fax 808-879-9163; e-mail: davi@aloha.net; www.mauikbr.com. Agent: Kumulani.

Sixty-four units with washer/dryers and single or double lanais in a single seven-story building across from Kama'ole I Beach. Recreation area, elevator, roof garden. No credit cards through on-site rental agent and a minimum stay of five nights required.

Rates: 1BR 1 bath (2) $90-$125; 2BR 2 bath (2) $115-$155; 3BR 2 bath (2) $145-$180; extra person $10/night

Kamaole Nalu

2450 South Kihei Road, Kihei, HI 96753. 808-879-1006; fax 808-879-8693; 800-767-1497; e-mail: relax@kamaolenalu.com; www.kamaolenalu.com. Agent: Maui & All Island.

Thirty-six two-bedroom, two-bath units with large lanai, dishwasher and washer/dryer in a six-story building. Located between Kama'ole I and II Beach Parks with all units offering ocean views. Weekly maid service. Five-night minimum.

Rates: 2BR 2 bath (2) g.v./o.v. $135/175, deluxe o.v. $175/$215, o.v. $155/$195, o.f. $195/$235; extra person $15/night

Kamaole Sands

2695 South Kihei Road, Kihei, HI 96753. 808-874-8700; fax 808-879-3273. Managed by Castle Resorts, 800-367-5004. Agents: Kumulani; Bello Realty; Maui Condo & Home; Kihei Maui Vacations; Maui & All Island; Condominium Rentals Hawaii; Maui Vacation Properties; RSVP; AA Oceanfront Condos.

Ten four-story buildings totaling 315 units all with full kitchens. Includes daily maid service, four tennis courts, pool and wading pool, babysitting services, two jacuzzis and barbecues. Located on 15 acres across the road from Kama'ole III Beach.

Castle Resorts rates: 1BR (1-4) standard $195/$225, deluxe partial o.v. $245/$275; 2BR (1-6) standard $275/$305; deluxe partial o.v. $345/$375

Kathy Scheper's Kihei Cottage

800-645-3753; 808-879-8744; fax 808-879-9100; e-mail: vacation@maui411.com; www.maui411.com.

Kathy offers a cottage in Kihei at very reasonable rates. It sleeps up to four people but is even more ideal for two and includes a private patio area, covered parking, washer and dryer, phone and all kitchen equipment. The beach is a short walk away. She also rents an oceanfront 2-BR/2-bath unit at Kamaole Nalu Resort and an oceanfront penthouse at Hale Mahina Beach Resort in West Maui.

Rates: Cottage $65/$125 day, $1,500-$1,800 month; condo at Kamaole Nalu $230/$275

Kauhale Makai (Village by the Sea)

930-938 South Kihei Road, Kihei, HI 96753. 808-879-8888. Agents: Maui & All Island; Maui Condo & Home; Kumulani; RSVP; Kihei Maui Vacations; AA Oceanfront Condo Rentals.

Two six-floor buildings offer 169 air-conditioned units with phones. Complex features putting green, gas barbecues, plus kids' pool, sauna and laundry center. The beach here is usually strewn with coral rubble and seaweed, but area condos have taken to "vacuuming" it daily.

Maui Condo & Home rates: Studio (2) $100/$120, 1BR (2) $110/$130, 2BR o.v. (4) $150/$180, 2BR o.f. $175/$205

★ Kealia

191 North Kihei Road, Kihei, HI 96753. 800-367-5222; 808-879-9159. Agent: Maui Condo & Home.

Fifty-one air-conditioned units with lanais, washer/dryers and dishwashers. Maid service upon request. The one-bedroom units are a little on the small side, but overall a good value. Well-maintained and quiet resort with a wonderful sandy beach. Shops nearby.

Maui Condo rates: Studio $95/$120; 1BR o.v. $125/$150, 1BR o.f. $150/$190; 2BR o.f. $175/$215

Kihei Akahi

2531 South Kihei Road, Kihei, HI 96753. 808-879-1881. Agents: Condo Rentals Hawaii; Maui Condo & Home; Kihei Maui Vacations; Maui & All Island; Maui Vacation Properties; AA Oceanfront Condos.

Across from Kama'ole II Beach Park, 240 units with washers and dryers. Two pools, tennis court, barbecues. Prices higher for units with air conditioning.

Condo Rentals Hawaii rates: Studio $100-$125; 1BR $115-$145, 1BR a.c. $125-$150; 2BR a.c. $155-$195

Kihei Alii Kai

2387 South Kihei Road, Kihei, HI 96753. 808-879-6770; 800-888-6284. Agents: Maui & All Island; RSVP; Bello Realty; Kihei Maui Vacations.

Four buildings with 127 units, all with washer/dryers. No maid service. Complex features pool, jacuzzi, sauna, two tennis courts, barbecue. Across the road and up the street from Kama'ole I Beach. Nearby restaurants and shops. Other rental agents offer two-bedroom units as well.

Bello Realty rates: 1 BD 1 bath w/loft $115/$95

Kihei Bay Surf

715 South Kihei Road (Manager Apt. 110), Kihei, HI 96753. 808-879-7650. Agents: Kihei Maui Vacations; Maui Vacation Properties; Maui & All Island; RSVP.

There are 118 studio units in seven two-story buildings. Pool-area jacuzzi, barbecue, laundry area, tennis. Across the road from Kama'ole I Beach.

RSVP rates: Studio $84/$104

Kihei Bay Vista

679 South Kihei Road, Kihei, HI 96753. 808-879-8866. Agents: Kihei Maui Vacations; Bello Realty; RSVP.

Complex offers pool, spa, jacuzzi, putting green, air conditioning, washer/dryer, lanais and full kitchens. A short walk across the road to Kama'ole I Beach. Overlooking Kalepolepo Beach. Four-day minimum or cleaning fee charged.

Kihei Maui Vacations rates: 1BR units $124/$144; discounts for long stays

★ Kihei Beach Resort Vacation Condominiums

36 South Kihei Road, Kihei, HI 96753. 800-367-6034; 808-879-2744; fax 808-875-0306; www.kbr.com. Agents: Kihei Maui Vacations; Maui Condo & Home; Maui & All Island; RSVP.

Beachfront units all with great ocean views, microwaves, phones. Kihei Beach Resort offers central air conditioning, recreation area, elevator, limited maid service. Conveniently located in North Kihei. The lobby has a pleasant guest lounge with coffee served each morning. Laundry facilities available (coin-op); however, some units have their own washer/dryer. Sparkling bathrooms with attractive taupe-hued tile. The units are cozy and well-maintained. Great whale watching, and the beach is truly just footsteps away.

Maui Condo & Home rates: 1BR 1 bath o.f. $160/$205

Kihei Garden Estates

1299 Uluniu Street, Kihei, HI 96753. 808-879-5785; 800-827-2786. Agents: Kihei Maui Vacations; RSVP.

Eighty-four units in eight two-story buildings. Jacuzzi, barbecues. Air conditioning. Across the road and a short walk to beaches. Four-day minimum or cleaning fee charged. No credit cards.

Kihei Maui Vacations rates: 1BR (2, max 4) $144-$174/$114-$134; discounts for long stays

Kihei Holiday

483 South Kihei Road, Kihei, HI 96753. 808-879-9228. Agents: Kihei Maui Vacations; RSVP.

Units are across the street from the beach and have lanais with garden views. Pool area, jacuzzi and barbecues.

RSVP rates: 1 BR $114/$134; 2BR $144/$174

Kihei Kai

61 North Kihei Road, Kihei, HI 96753. 888-778-7717; 808-891-0780; www.kiheirentals.com.

Twenty-four units in a two-story beachfront building. Recreation area, laundry room, units have air conditioning or ceiling fans. Barbecue. On a nice stretch of sandy beach.

Rates: 1BR (2, max 4) g.v. $105/$115, g.v./o.v. $110/$120, o.v. $120/$130, beachfront $130/$140; additional person $10/night

Kihei Kai Nani

2495 South Kihei Road, Kihei, HI 96753. 808-879-1430; 800-473-1493; e-mail: kkndiaz@maui.net. Agents: Bello Realty; Maui & All Island; Kihei Maui Vacations; RSVP; AA Oceanfront Condos.

This complex is one of the older ones along Kihei Road, composed of 180 one-bedroom units with lanai or balcony in a two- and three-story structure. Laundry room and recreation center. Across from Kama'ole II Beach. No credit cards through front-desk reservations.

AA Oceanfront Condos rates: 1 BR/1 bath $85/$100/$110

Kihei Resort

777 South Kihei Road, Kihei, HI 96753. Agents: Kihei Maui; RSVP.

Sixty-four units in a two-story building located across the street from the ocean; barbecues, pool-area jacuzzi. Two-bedroom units may be available from some rental agents. No credit cards.

Kihei Maui Vacations rates: 1BR $104/$124; 1 BR/2 bath $124/$144; discounts for long stays

Kihei Sands

115 North Kihei Road, Kihei, HI 96753. 808-879-2624; 800-882-6284; e-mail: kiheisands@msn.com; www.kiheisands.com.

Thirty air-conditioned oceanfront units, kitchens include microwaves. Shops and restaurant nearby. Coin laundry area. Four-night minimum summer, seven nights winter.

Rates: 1BR (2) g.v. $110/$125, o.v. $125/$145, o.f. $145/$165; 2BR (4) o.v. $145/$170, o.f. $165/$195; 3BR o.v. $165/$190; extra person $6/night

Kihei Surfside

2936 South Kihei Road, Kihei, HI 96753. 808-879-1488; 800-367-5240. Agents: Maui Condo & Home; Condo Rentals Hawaii; Maui & All Island; Maui Vacation Properties; AA Oceanfront Condos.

Eighty-three units on rocky shore with tide pools. Only a short walk to Keawakapu Beach. Large grassy area and good view. Coin-op laundry on premises.

Condo Rentals Hawaii rates: 1BR $150-$195

Koa Lagoon

800 South Kihei Road, Kihei, HI 96753. 800-367-8030; 808-879-3002; e-mail: barron@mauigateway.com; www.koalagoon.com.

These 42 oceanview units are in one six-story building. Full kitchens, air conditioning and washer/dryers in units. Pool-area pavilion and barbecues. Large manicured lawn area fronting the beach. Located on a small sandy beach that is often plagued by seaweed that washes ashore from the offshore coral reef. This stretch of Kihei is very popular with windsurfers. Cleaning fee of $45 for stays less than five days.

Rates: 1BR 1 bath (2, max 4) $110/$140, 2BR 2 bath (4, max 6) $140/ $170; additional person $10/night

Koa Resort

811 South Kihei Road, Kihei, HI 96753. 808-879-1161. Agents: Kihei Maui Vacations; Bello Realty; RSVP.

There are 54 units on spacious 5.5-acre grounds in two five-story buildings. Located across the road from the beach. Two tennis courts, spa, jacuzzi, putting green. Units have washer/dryers.

Bello Realty rates: 1BR 1 bath $110/$85; 2BR 1 bath $120/$100, 2BR 2 bath $130/$110; 3BR 2 bath $155/$135, 3BR 3 bath $180/$160

Leilani Kai

1226 Ulunium Road (P.O. Box 296), Kihei, HI 96753. 808-879-2606; fax 808-875-4735; e-mail: lkresort@msn.com; www.lkresort.com.

Eight oceanfront apartments with lanais in a serene garden setting. Full kitchens; saltwater swimming pool. On-site management. Monthly discounts. Four-night minimum may be required. Located behind Azeka Makai shopping center.

Rates: Studio (2) $85, 1BR (2) $100, 1BR deluxe (4) $115, 2BR (4) $125

Leinaala

998 South Kihei Road, Kihei, HI 96753. 808-879-2235; 800-334-3305 U.S. & Canada; fax 808-879-8366. Agent: Maui Condo & Home; Maui Vacation Properties.

Twenty-four one- and two-bedroom units in a four-story building. Tennis courts at adjoining park. Pool, cable TV. Oceanview. The property is fronted by a large park that stretches out to the ocean. Popular area for windsurfing, but lots of better sandy swimming beach parks a short drive away.

Maui Condo & Home rates: 1BR (2) $120/$145, 2BR (4) $160/$190

Luana Kai

940 South Kihei Road, Kihei, HI 96753. 808-879-1268; 800-669-1127; fax 808-879-1455; www.luanakai.com. Agents: Maui & All Island; Kihei Maui Vacations; Maui Vacation Properties; RSVP.

Located adjacent to a large oceanfront park with public tennis courts, 113 units with washer/dryers on eight acres. The grounds are nicely landscaped and include a putting green, barbecue area, pool area, sauna and jacuzzi. The beach, however, is almost always covered with coral rubble and seaweed.

Rates: 1BR (2) g.v. $99-$139/$119-$159, partial o.v. $109-$149/$129-$169, o.v. $119-$159/$139-$179; 2BR (6) g.v. $119-$159/$139-$179, partial o.v. $129-$169/$149-$189, o.v. $139-$179/$159-$199; 3BR partial o.v. deluxe $219/$269

★ Ma'alaea Surf

12 South Kihei Road, Kihei, HI 96753. 800-423-7953; 808-879-1267; fax 808-874-2884; e-mail: info@maalaeasurfresort.com; www.maalaeasurfresort.com.

Sixty units in eight two-story oceanfront buildings. These townhouse units have air conditioning and microwaves. Daily maid service, except Sunday and holidays. Two pools, two tennis courts, shuffleboard. Laundry facilities in each building. Very attractive and quiet low-rise complex on a great beach. In this price range, these spacious and attractive units, along with five acres of beautiful grounds, are hard to beat.

Rates: 1BR 1 bath (2, max 4) o.v. $250, o.f. $285; 2BR 2 bath (4, max 6) ground floor or townhouse o.v. $330-$350, o.f. $350-$390

★ ***Mana Kai***

2960 South Kihei Road, Kihei, HI 96753. 808-879-1561; 800-525-2025; fax 808-874-5042. Agents: Condo Rentals Hawaii; Kumulani; Maui & All Islands; Maui Vacation Properties; AA Oceanfront Condos.

Eight-story building with 132 rooms. The studio units have a room with an adjoining bath. The one-bedroom units have a kitchen and the two-bedroom units are actually the hotel unit and a one bedroom combined, each having separate entry doors. The Mana Kai offers hotel-like services, no minimum stay and daily maid service. This complex has laundry facilities on each floor, an oceanfront pool and a restaurant off the lobby. The Mana Kai is nestled at the end of Keawakapu Beach, and offers a great view of the ocean, the 10,000-foot-high Haleakala and Upcountry Maui. It is the only major accommodation in Kihei on a prime beachfront location. Keawakapu Beach is not only very nice, but generally very underused.

Condo Rentals Hawaii rates: Hotel room (2) $100-$135; 1BR 1 bath (2) o.v. $180-$220, 1BR deluxe $196-$240; 2BR o.v. $230-$280

Maui Banyan (Aston)

2575 South Kihei Road, Kihei, HI 96753. 808-875-0004. Managed by Aston Resorts 877-997-6667. Agents: Maui & All Island; Kihei Maui Vacations; Bello Realty; Kumulani; RSVP; AA Oceanfront Condos; Maui Condominiums.

Overlooking Kama'ole II Beach, these suites feature kitchens, washer/dryer, lanai, air conditioning, cable TV and telephone. Facilities include tennis court, pool and jacuzzi. Putting green and barbecue area. Hotel rooms have no kitchens. Aston rates include daily maid service. Aston's best rates are available as "E-pricebreakers" online.

Aston rates: Standard hotel room (1-2) $127/$200; 1BR (max 4) $155-$265/$168-$285; 2BR (max 6) $203-$345/$229-$385; 3BR/3 bath deluxe $303/$510

Maui Coast Hotel

2259 South Kihei Road, Kihei, HI 96753. 808-874-6284; 800-663-1144 or 800-895-6284; fax 808-875-4731; www.mauicoasthotel.com.

Owned and operated by Coast Hotels, they offer 265 rooms, 114 of them suites. The hotel offers a pool area plus children's wading pool, two outdoor whirlpools, Spices Restaurant in front, two night-lit tennis courts and complimentary laundry facilities. This is a great concept, a hotel with condominium conveniences, such as a small in-room refrigerator. Coffee makers with complimentary coffee, free cribs, jetted tubs in suites and room service. However, I found the standard room was too crowded with one king bed and the two kids on a sofa bed. Compared to the Wailea Resorts, this is a no-frills hotel option. Nicely appointed property located across the road from the Kama'ole Beach Parks.

Rates: Standard hotel room $195; alcove suite $225; 1BR suite $255

★ *Maui Hill*

2881 South Kihei Road, Kihei, HI 96753. 808-879-6321. Managed by Aston Hotels, 877-997-6667. Agent: RSVP.

Twelve buildings with a Spanish flair clustered on a hillside above the Keawakapu Beach area; 140 attractively furnished units with washer/dryers, air conditioning, microwaves, dishwashers and large lanais. Daily maid service. There is a moderate walk down and across the road to the beach. Upper units have better ocean views. The 3-bedroom units are very spacious. Large pool and tennis courts. Aston's best rates are available as "E-pricebreakers" online.

Aston rates: 1BR (1-4) g.v. $150/$285, o.v. $181/$315, 2BR (1-6) g.v. $200/$360, o.v. $233/$400; 3BR o.v. $332/$525

Maui Kamaole

2777 South Kihei Road, Kihei, HI 96743. 808-879-7668. Agents: Kihei Maui Vacations; Condo Rentals Hawaii; Maui & All Island; RSVP; Maui Vacation Properties; Maui Condo and Home; AA Oceanfront Condos.

Located on a bluff overlooking the ocean; across the street and a short walk down to Kama'ole III Beach Park or Keawakapu Beach. One-bedroom units are 1,000 to 1,300 square feet and two-bedroom units are 1,300 to 1,600 square feet This four-phase development is located on 23 oceanview acres. All are low-rise fourplex buildings grouped into 13 clusters, each named after Hawaiian flora. Weekly discounts available.

Condo Rentals Hawaii rates: 1BR 2 bath g.v. $145-$185, 1BR 2 bath o.v. $170-$210; 2BR 2 bath g.v. $200-$240, o.v. $220-$270

Maui Lu Resort

575 South Kihei Road, Kihei, HI 96753. 808-879-5881. Managed by Aston 877-997-6667. Agent: RSVP.

One of the first resorts in the Kihei area and unusual for its spacious grounds: 180 units on 28 acres. Pool is shaped like the island of Maui. Many of the hotel rooms are set back from South Kihei Road and the oceanfront units are not on a sandy beachfront. Aston's best rates are available as "E-pricebreakers" online.

Aston rates: Hotel room with refrigerator (1-2) standard g.v. $92-$139, superior g.v. $103-$158, deluxe o.v. $127-$188, o.f. $151-$225

Maui Oceanfront Inn (Best Western)

2980 South Kihei Road, Kihei, HI 96753. 800-263-3387; 808-879-7744; www.mauioceanfrontinn.com.

Located on Keaweakapu Beach. An 88-room boutique-style oceanfront inn, they feature classic Hawaiian art and furnishings in each room which augments the natural elegance and beauty of Hawaii. Mountain view and garden view guest rooms feature queen bed, entertainment center, built-in refrigerator, coffee maker and air conditioning. Front building has oceanfront units. Two rooms, connected by a door, can create a suite. Very cute and this beach is one of my favorites. A good value for an oceanfront location.

Rates: Hotel rooms, value rate $99, deluxe $109; two-room suites $129, o.f. $209

Maui Parkshore

2653 South Kihei Road, Kihei, HI 96753. 808-879-1600. Agents: Maui & All Island; Maui Condo & Home.

Sixty-four two-bedroom, two-bath oceanview condos with washer/dryers and lanais in a four-story building (elevator) across from Kama'ole III Beach. Pool-area sauna.

Maui Condo & Home rates: 2BR 2 bath (4) $145/$170

Maui Sunset

1032 South Kihei, Road, Kihei, HI 96753. 808-879-0674; 800-843-5880. Agents: Kihei Maui Vacations; RSVP; Maui & All Island; Kumulani; Maui Condo & Home; Maui Vacation Properties.

Two multistory buildings with 225 air-conditioned units. Tennis courts, pitch-and-putt golf green and sauna. Large pool, exercise facility, barbecues. Located on beach park with tennis courts. They resolve their longtime problem of seaweed and coral rubble on the beach with a daily beach "sweeping."

Maui Condo & Home rates: 1 BR $120/$140; 2BR $165/$190; 3 BR o.f. $275/$305

Maui Vista

2191 South Kihei Road, Kihei, HI 96753. 808-879-7966; Marc Resorts 800-535-0085. Other Agents: Maui & All Island; Kihei Maui Vacations; Maui Condo & Home; Bello Realty; AA Oceanfront Condos; Maui Vacation Properties; RSVP.

Three four-story buildings, across from the beach; 280 units. Some have air conditioning, some have washer/dryers. All have kitchens with dishwashers. The two-bedroom units are fourth-floor townhouses. Some oceanview units. Six tennis courts, three pools, barbecues. A great value if you don't mind a short walk to the beach, but I had a problem with sound from a neighboring unit.

Marc Resorts rates: 1BR g.v. (1-4 people) $190; 1 BR p.o.v. (1-4) $210; 2 BR p.o.v. (1-6) $260.

Menehune Shores

760 Kihei Road, Kihei, HI 96753. 808-879-0076. Agent: Menehune Reservations (no credit cards), P.O. Box 1327, Kihei, HI 96753, 800-558-9117 U.S. & Canada; 808-879-3428; fax 808-879-5218. Other agents: RSVP; Kihei Maui Vacations; Bello Realty.

Six-story building, 115 units with dishwashers, washer/dryers and lanais. A recreation room with roof garden, a whale-watching platform and shuffleboard. The ocean area in front of this condo property is the last remnant of one of Maui's early fishponds. These ponds, where fish were raised and harvested, were created by the early Hawaiians all around the islands.

RSVP rates: 1BR 1 bath (2) $124/$154; 2BR 2 bath (2) $154/$184; 3BR 2 bath (6) $174/$214

My Waii Beach Cottage

2128A Ili'ili Road, Kihei. Agent: Linda R. Owen, 877-802-6863; e-mail: info@mywaii.com; www.mywaii.com.

Linda offers a deluxe one-bedroom, two-bath oceanfront cottage. It is located 500 yards from Kama'ole Beach I and the front lawn area also adjoins a small beach. The cottage has a TV, VCR, stereo with CD, full kitchen, microwave, three telephones, ceiling fans. There is a dual king in the bedroom and a queen-size Murphy bed in the living room. Minimum stay of five nights or you'll be charged a cleaning fee.

Rates: $300; extra person (max 4) $10 each (5 percent discount if paid by check); 7th night free April 15-December 16

★ *Nani Kai Hale*

73 North Kihei Road, Kihei, HI 96753. 808-879-9120; 800-367-6032. Agents: Maui & All Island; Maui Condo & Home; Maui Lodging.

A six-story building holds 46 units. Under-building parking, laundry on each floor, elevator. Patio and barbecues by beach. Lanais have ocean and mountain views.

Maui Condo & Home rates: 1BR 2 bath (2) o.v. $125/$165, 2BR 2 bath o.v. $175/$215

Nona Lani

455 South Kihei Road (P.O. Box 655), Kihei, HI 96753. 800-733-2688; 808-879-2497; fax 808-891-0273; e-mail: nona@nonalanicottages.com; www.nonalanicottages.com.

Eight individual cottages with kitchens, TV, queen bed plus a rollaway and day bed, full bath with tub and shower, and lanais. Rooms have queen bed and bathroom, TV, ceiling fan and air conditioning. Large grounds, public phone, two barbecues and laundry facilities. Located across the road from sandy beach. No credit cards. Weekly discounts.

Rates: Rooms $85/$95, cottages $99/$105

Punahoa

2142 Ili'ili Road, Kihei, HI 96753. 800-564-2720; 808-879-2720.

Fifteen oceanview units with large lanais, telephones. No pool. Elevator, laundry facilities, beaches nearby. Some have air conditioning. No credit cards. Three seasons: May 1 to October 31 (low season); November 1 to December 14 and April 1 to April 30 (mid season); and December 15 to March 31 (high season).

Rates: Studio (2) $108/$122/$140; 1BR (2, max 4) $152/$170/$215; 2BR (2, max 6) $184/$214/$244; 1BR penthouse $175/$190/$240

Royal Mauian

2430 South Kihei Road, Kihei, HI 96753. 808-879-1263; 800-367-8009; fax 808-367-8009. Agents: Maui Condo & Home; Kihei Maui Vacations; AA Oceanfront Condos.

Complex has shuffleboard, carpeted roof garden and is next to the pleasant Kama'ole II Beach Park; 107 units with lanai and washer/dryer in a six-story building.

Maui Condo & Home rates: 1BR 1 bath o.f. (2) $165-$190; 2BR o.f. $220/$255; some 3BR may be available through rental agents

Shores of Maui

2075 South Kihei Road (P.O. Box 985), Kihei, HI 96753. Leisure Properties 808-879-6770; 800-888-6284; www.maui.net/condos.

This 50-unit two-level complex in garden setting offers barbecues, tennis courts and spa. Located across the street from a rocky shoreline and north of Kama'ole I Beach Park. Three-night minimum stay, one-week minimum over Christmas holidays. One of Kihei's good values.

Rates: 1BR $100/$135, 2BR $135-$150/$170-$190

Sugar Beach Resort

145 North Kihei Road, Kihei HI 96753. 808-879-7765. Agents: Maui & All Island; RSVP; Maui Condo & Home; Condo Rental HI; AA Oceanfront Condos; Maui Vacation Properties; Bello Realty.

Several six-story buildings with elevators, 215 units. Air conditioning. Jacuzzi, putting green, gas barbecue grills. Sandwich shop and quick shop market on location. A nice pool area and located on an excellent swimming beach. Popular with families, so expect lots of kids.

Condo Rental HI rates: 1BR g.v. $130-$175; p.o.v. $140-$185; o.f. $155-$220; 2BR/2 bath $245-$340

Wailana Kai

34 Wailana Place, Kihei, HI 96753. 800-541-3060; 808-879-3328; www.wailanakai.com. Agent: Bello Realty.

One-bedroom units have sofa sleepers in living area. Private phone lines, pool, laundry facilities.

Rates: 1BR 1 bath $85-$100, 2BR 2 bath $90-$125

Wailea-Makena Area

WAILEA

Diamond Resort

555 Kaukahi Street, Wailea, HI 96753. 800-800-0720; 808-874-0500; e-mail: info@diamondresort.com; www.diamondresort.com. Agent: Castle Resorts.

The 72-suite resort is made up of 18 two-story buildings on 15 immaculately landscaped acres. Each suite is 947 square feet and includes a master bedroom, dining area, kitchenette, sitting area, lanái and bath. Suites have ocean views, golf course views, or views of Haleakala. Two of their suites have been designed for physically challenged guests and four suites are nonsmoking. The spa facility, which includes a men and women's *daiyokujo* (traditional Japanese bath), a waterfall to gently massage your neck and shoulders, and a soothing Finlandia sauna, is one of the resort's highlights. The grounds are lovely with quiet waterfalls, magnificent koi ponds and bridges along the paths. A lovely and tranquil setting. This resort was once a private retreat for Japanese visitors, but now all can enjoy it. Restaurant Taiko and Le Gunji are both fine dining restaurants. Capische? is open evenings for casual dining or cocktails and live entertainment.

Rates: g.v. $270, partial o.v. $300, deluxe o.v. $370

★ Fairmont Kea Lani Hotel, Suites & Villas

4100 Wailea Alanui, Wailea, HI 96753. 808-875-4100; 800-441-1414; e-mail: info@kealani.com; www.fairmont.com/kealani.

There are 413 suites plus 37 one-, two- and three-bedroom oceanfront villas. Designed after Las Hadas in Manzanillo, the name means "White Heavens." Its Mediterranean style seems like a sultan's enormous villa dramatically set on 22 acres. You enter a drive lined with Norfolk pines and beyond the porte-cochere there is a large open lobby area with a fountain covered by nine domes. Decorations are in Hawaiian florals with mosaic tile ceilings and floors.

The spacious (840 square feet) one-bedroom suites each have a private balcony. (There are 45 pairs of connecting suites for those traveling with larger families.) Each is decorated in hues of cream and white and has a sunken marble tub, an enormous walk-in shower, king or two double beds, and two closets. A cotton kimono is provided for guests. The living room features a state-of-the-art compact and laser disc system, TV and VCR. Fresh-ground coffee and coffee maker are provided daily in the suite and a mini-kitchen offers a microwave, a small sink and mini-bar. An iron and ironing board are also available. In addition to the suites, there are also 37 townhouse-style villas that overlook Polo Beach—a little expensive, but it would be easy to feel at home here. Each has a private lanai, huge walk-in closets, full-size kitchen, washer and dryer, a generous living room and eating area. If you don't want to make that walk to the beach, you can just meander out onto the lanai and take a dip in your private swimming pool. That's right. Each villa has its own pool.

The exercise room is complimentary for guests. Massage, body treatments, facials and fitness programs are available in their luxury spa facility. (See "Spas/Fitness Centers/Health Retreats" in Chapter 6 for more information.) Restaurants include Caffe Ciao, Nick's Fishmarket Maui, and Polo Beach Grille and Bar. Complimentary daily golf clinics; for those who prefer to be beach bound they offer beach rental equipment, everything from a single kayak to a pool float. Beach butlers are on hand to ensure you have a great day at the beach. For a fee the resort offers "Keiki Lani" for children 5 to 11 years of age; see "Childcare Programs" in Chapter 1 for details. Honeymoon, wedding, family and golf packages are available.

Rates: 1BR moderate suite (4) $385, Fairmont suite. (4) $465, p.o.v. suite (4) $535; poolside suite $565; o.v. suite $595; deluxe o.v. suite $665; signature Kilohana suite $795. 2BR villa (1-6 persons) o.v. $1,600, o.f. $2,200; 3BR villa (1-8 persons) o.v. $2,200, o.f. $2,800

★ *Four Seasons Resort Wailea*

3900 Wailea Alanui, Wailea, HI 96753. 808-874-8000; 800-334-6284; fax 808-874-2222; www.fourseasons.com/maui.

This gorgeous property offers 380 oversized guest rooms (600 square feet) on eight floors encompassing 15 beachfront acres on Wailea Beach; the suites offer a large living room, one bedroom, full kitchen and a 439-square-foot lanai. This full-service resort features two pools (one large and one smaller lava pool) and a jacuzzi on each end of the main pool, one of which is set aside for children only. The layout of the grand pool provides shelter from the afternoon breezes. In addition there are two tennis courts, a croquet lawn, health spa, beauty salon, three restaurants and two lounges. The public areas are spacious, open and ocean oriented. (If I had a category for "Best Bathrooms" these would be the winners. They are elegantly decorated and each stall is like a mini-suite.) A very different mood from other Maui resorts, the blue-tiled roof and cream-colored building create a very classic atmosphere. Even the grounds, although a profusion of colors with many varied Hawaiian flora, vaguely resemble a Mediterranean villa. Throughout the resort's gardens and courtyards are an array of attractive formal and natural pools, ponds, waterfalls and fountains.

Their guest policy exhibits real aloha spirit, with no charge for use of the tennis courts or health spa and complimentary snorkel gear, smash or volleyball equipment. For the younger guests, strollers, car seats, high chairs, cribs and even complimentary baby baths and bottle warmers are available. Their year-round, complimentary "Kids for All Seasons" program is geared for children ages 5 through 12; see "Childcare Programs" in Chapter 1. Guest services, which distinguish the Four Seasons from other properties, include their early-arrival/late-departure program. Guests have their luggage checked and are escorted to The Health Centre, where a private locker is supplied for personal items. The resort makes available for these guests an array of casual clothing from workout gear and jogging suits to swimwear.

The Four Seasons Resort is peaceful and elegant. No glitz here, just what you come to Paradise for. A "children's only" hot tub allows the second adult hot tub to be a quiet respite. There are plenty of complimentary cabanas around the pool area and on the beach. Pool and beach staff members are on their toes providing prompt attention to guests in setting up their lounge chairs with towels and providing chilled towels or spritzers to cool the face. Ferraro's, the poolside restaurant and bar, makes it easy to spend the entire day without leaving your lounge chair. The snorkeling is best out to the left near the rocky shoreline, but go early in the day. Like clockwork, around noon the wind picks up and the water clarity rapidly deteriorates. Another plus for the Wailea area is the walkway that spans the shoreline between resorts. It is a pleasant walk over to the neighboring southern resort, the Fairmont Kea Lani; the Grand Wailea to the north is definitely worth a stroll (go during the day and again at night for a very different experience).

Numerous special package offers include a room and car, golf, romance and family packages. Restaurants are Ferraro's, Pacific Grill and Spago. Amenities for guests on the Club Floor include a private lounge, 24-hour concierge, complimentary breakfast, afternoon tea, evening cocktails and after-dinner liqueurs. Under age 18 free when sharing same room with parents, except on Club Floor add $60/night per child ages 5 to 17. Ask about special seasonal discounts, family rates (for a second room for children under 18) and packages. Prices shown are regular season and value season.

Rates: mountainside $365/$385, g.v. $465/$490, partial o.v. $545/$575, o.v. $625/$660, o.v. prime $705/$740. Club Floor: o.v. $815/$855. Executive suites $660-$1,050. Other 1BR and 2BR suites $775-$4,050

★ *Grand Wailea Resort Hotel & Spa*

3850 Wailea Alanui, Wailea, HI 96753. 808-875-1234; 800-888-6100; fax 808-879-4077; e-mail: info@grandwailea.com; www.grandwailea.com.

This beautifully appointed 780-room resort is a must-see, even if you aren't lucky enough to be staying here. In fact, make at least two trips—a second at night to enjoy dinner and tour the grounds when they are alight like a twinkling fairyland. Over $20 million was spent on the waterfalls, streams, rapids, slides, reflecting pools, swimming pools, river pool, scuba pool, saltwater lagoon and spa features. Strikingly beautiful, the formal reflecting pool leads you to the sweeping Wailea Beach. Beyond this pool is the hibiscus pool made of Mexican glass tile with gold leaf and lined with wide Mediterranean-style cabanas. The "activity pool" is a 770,000-gallon, 27,500-square-foot pool with nine large, free-form pools at various levels beginning at a height of 40 feet and dropping to sea level. Painted tiles depicting turtles and tropical fish in varying shades of green and blue line the bottom and sides, while huge rocks line the pools. At one end of the pool is an incredible waterslide, a 225-foot twisting ride that drops three stories. The "jungle pool," another part of the Wailea Canyon Activity Pool, offers a rope swing.

The pools are connected by a 2,000-foot river that carries swimmers at varying current speeds, ranging from whitewater rapids to a lazy cruise. Along the way are hidden grottos, three jacuzzis and saunas, seven slides, numerous waterfalls and bumpy rapids that have been created using special aquatic devices. At the bottom of the river is a one-of-a-kind water elevator that lifts the swimmers back up to the top again. Below the rocky waterfall is the scuba pool that gets prospective divers in the mood with an underwater mural featuring a coral reef and sea life made of tiles. It takes 50,000 gallons of water a minute to sustain this aquatic system. Streams and pools also meander through the elaborate Hawaiian and Japanese-themed gardens. The resort's spa, Spa Grande, is Hawai'i's largest spa facility, spanning 50,000 square feet in the atrium wing of the resort; see "Spas/Fitness Centers/Health Retreats" in Chapter 6. Six restaurants give guests plenty of choices: Kincha, Grand Dining Room, Café Kula, Humuhumunukunukua'pua'a, Bistro Molokini, and the Volcano Bar. There is also a swim-up bar.

I am fascinated by this resort's blend of enormity and grandeur combined with Hawaiian themes, tempered with outstanding craftsmanship. It seems to work. There is actually a great deal of fine detail (notice the twisted *ohia* wood rails that line the pathways) and I especially like the attention paid to the Hawaiiana aspects. The resort is visually very stimulating and each time you stroll around the resort you're sure to see something new. The chapel, set in the middle of the grounds, is a popular spot for weddings. The woodwork and stained glass windows are absolutely beautiful, and take note of the chandeliers above made of exquisite Murano glass. The 28,000-square-foot ballroom is a meeting planner's dream, with concealed projection screens, specialized audio equipment—the works. The ballroom also has three huge, beautiful and unique artworks in gold and silver leaf that depict the story of Pele, the fire goddess, and her two sisters. While you're there, look up at the 29,000-pound, Venetian-glass chandelier imported from Italy.

Now the rooms. There are 780 rooms, each 650 square feet, and 52 suites. The presidential suite (5,500 square feet) is a mere $12,000 per night and features what is lovingly referred to as the Imelda Marcos shoe closet, a private sauna, a room-sized shower with ocean view in one bathroom and a *koa* tub. A lot of marble was used throughout all the rooms and is accented by subtle beige wallpaper.

This may be the one resort that your kids will *insist* you come back to again and again. After you visit the kids' Camp Grande you will, at least momentarily, wish you could pass for a 10- or 11-year-old. See "Childcare Programs" in Chapter 1 for more information. All in all, if you're seeking an action-packed resort vacation, you'll find it all here. This resort has something for everyone.

Rates: Terrace $485, deluxe g.v. $640, o.v. $710, deluxe o.v. $775; suites $1,700-$3,000. Napua Tower rooms: Napua Club $875, 1BR and 2BR Napua suites $2,200-$12,000

★ *The Palms at Wailea*

3200 Wailea Alanui Drive, Wailea, HI 96753. 808-879-5800. More than half the units are managed by Outrigger Hotels, 800-688-7444; e-mail: palms.wailea@outrigger.com; www.outrigger.com. Agents: Maui Condo & Home; Bello Realty; Kumulani; Maui Vacation Properties; RSVP.

One- and two-bedroom condominiums on a bluff overlooking the Wailea area with views of the islands of Kaho'olawe and Lana'i. Two-story buildings with a total of 150 luxury units. Amenities include partial air conditioning (in bedrooms, not living rooms), VCR, in-room kitchens and washer/dryer, pool and spa. Each unit is privately owned, but all are kept up to a high standard. As part of the Wailea Resort Community, this property offers access to the two Wailea golf courses and tennis complex. Daily maid service offered through some rental agents. These condos are a great value and you're in beautiful Wailea. Even the one-bedroom units are incredibly spacious. Only a short walk to the beach. The upper units have lovely ocean vistas; the lower ones provide nice garden patio views. The kitchens are enormous and obviously designed to be adequate for long-term tenants. For value and location, The Palms at Wailea gets our star of approval. Outrigger rates include daily maid service.

Outrigger rates: 1BR g.v. villa (1-4) $245/$255, o.v. villa $260/$270; 2BR g.v. villa (1-6) $270/$295, g.v. villa deluxe $285/$310, o.v. villa $305/$330

★ *Polo Beach Club*

20 Makena Road, Wailea, HI 96753. 808-879-8847. On-site agent: Destination Resorts 800-367-5246. Other agents: RSVP; Maui Vacation Properties.

Seventy-one apartments in an 8-story building located on Polo Beach. The units are luxurious and spacious. Underground parking, pool area and jacuzzi. Located next to the Fairmont Kea Lani Resort on a crescent-shaped beach. Three-night minimum; 14-night minimum during Christmas holidays.

Destination Resorts rates, 7th night free 4/3-12/18: High Season: no 1BR available; 2BR o.v. $430, o.f. $485, prime o.f. $570. Low Season: 1BR o.v. $360, o.f. $385; 2BR o.v. $430, o.f. $485, prime o.f. $570

★ Renaissance Wailea Beach Resort

3550 Wailea Alanui, Wailea, HI 96753. 800-992-4532; 808-879-4900; fax 808-874-5370; www.marriotthawaii.com.

This luxury resort covers 15.5 acres above beautiful Mokapu Beach with 345 units, including 12 suites. Each guest room is 500 square feet and offers a refrigerator, individual air conditioner and private lanai. The rooms are decorated in soothing rose, ash and blue tones. An assortment of daily guest activities are available as well as a year-round children's program called Camp Wailea; see "Childcare Programs" in Chapter 1 for details. Guest services include complimentary in-room coffee, daily paper, complimentary video library, traditional Hawaiian craft classes and demonstrations, massage therapy and fitness center. Wailea offers complimentary shuttle service to shopping, golf and tennis within the Wailea Resort area. Fat City, a "multi-colored cat of undetermined lineage," has become the unofficial resort mascot. She has endeared herself to so many guests that she receives mail on a regular basis. Mokapu Beach Wing is a separate beachfront building with 26 units that feature open-beamed ceilings and rich *koa* wood furnishings, plus a small swimming pool. The resort's restaurants are the Maui Onion, Palm Court and Hana Gion. The Sunset Terrace has an excellent vantage point for a beautiful sunset. The beach offers excellent swimming. The best snorkeling is just a very short walk over to the adjoining Ulua Beach. The grounds are a beautiful tropical jungle with a very attractive pool area. Also inquire about their "roomful of packages," which includes romance options (chocolate-dipped strawberries included) or room and car as well as room and breakfast. They have some outstanding rates that definitely make this property a best bet for a fine, more intimate Wailea resort choice. They also offer discounted rates at the Wailea golf courses if you are a guest. Check with reservations for seasonal specials.

NOTE: Rumors are afloat that Starwood Capital, the new owner of this hotel, plans to make major changes in the future, possibly even demolishing the property and rebuilding a new hotel. As of press time, it has been difficult to track down any official word regarding future plans; however, I have been told that Marriott International has been contracted to manage the hotel (under its Renaissance brand) until mid-January 2006. After that, who knows? Be forewarned that changes are likely to take place at this resort over the next couple of years.

Rates: terrace view $430, garden view $500, ocean view $535, oceanfront Mokapu $705, beach suites $1,050-$4,000

★ Wailea Marriott

3700 Wailea Alanui, Wailea, HI 96753. 808-879-1922; fax 808-874-8331; 888-236-2427; www.waileamarriott.com.

When you arrive at the porte-cochere, the banyan trees are the focal point and a waterfall is the centerpiece. The lovely ocean view and the beautiful *koa* rockers tempt guests to sit, relax and enjoy. The lobby design is unpretentious, old Hawaiian and classic. The artwork is subtle with intricate chests from Japan, huge stone mochi bowls, New Guinea roof finials, and Big Island calabashes. The popular Hula Moons Restaurant is off the main lobby. Just beyond the main lobby, the stairway descends down and winds past a lily pond (a popular wedding site) to the central pool area. On the lower level you'll find the Kumu Bar & Grill. The guest rooms have a silversword theme with seafoam green accents in the fabrics, wallcovering and carpeting that matches the aloha wear worn by the staff. (Room interiors may change in the upcoming renovation.) Amenities in the rooms include a refrigerator, dataports, coffee maker with complimentary coffee and an in-room safe. Located on 22 acres, they have a half-mile of oceanfront property and access to two great beaches, Ulua and Wailea. There is a seven-story tower and six low-rise buildings. The wonderful layout of this resort allows 80 percent of all guest rooms to have an ocean view and the grounds are spacious and sprawling. No "packing them in" feeling here. The resort's third pool is adjacent to the lu'au pool. This miniature water park, called "Wailele," which means jumping waters, will delight the *keiki* with two water slides, climbing areas, lots of water spray and interactive possibilities. The main pool area is still spacious with lots of decking for a day in the sun with a good book. The resort offers the excellent *Hoolokahi* program, a series of Hawaiian classes available to guests and non-guests for a nominal fee, as well as a kids' program. Golf, tennis and honeymoon package plans are available. The Wailea Marriott underwent $25 million in major improvements during 2000, and another multi-million dollar renovation is now ongoing through June 2006. Plans include construction of a new oceanview restaurant, a 10,000 square-foot spa and a new adult pool featuring over-water cabana lounges. Children age 17 and under are free when staying with parents and occupying existing beds. Single/double occupancy is one rate all year.

Rates: g.v. $355, o.v. $425, o.f. $475, deluxe o.f. $525, suites $650-$3,000

Wailea Villas

3750 Wailea Alanui, Wailea, HI 96753. 808-879-1595; 800-367-5246. Agents: Destination Resorts; Maui Condo & Home (Grand Champion &

Ekolu); Kumulani (only Ekahi Condos); Maui Vacation Properties; Maui & All Island; Bello; AA Oceanfront Condos; RSVP; Kihei Maui Vacations (Grand Champion only).

Some agents may have a few units for slightly better prices than those quoted below. The price range reflects location in the complex. Children under 16 free in parents' room. Destination Resorts provides added amenities such as daily housekeeping service and concierge service, and they feature package specials. Destination Resorts guests also receive preferential golf and tennis rates at the Wailea and Makena resorts. The less-expensive properties on the hill are a better value, but if you're a beach lover, you might prefer the luxury of having it footsteps away.

Ekolu Village—Located near the tennis center and Wailea's Blue golf course.

Destination Resorts rates, three-night minimum stay, fifth night free 4/3-12/18: 1BR (2) g.v. $175/$205, o.v. $220/$250; 2BR (4) g.v. $210/$245, o.v. $255/$295

Ekahi Village—On the hillside above the south end of Keawakapu Beach; some units are right above the beach. I've stayed here a couple of times. Units are lovely and great for families.

Destination Resorts rates, three-night minimum stay, seventh night free 4/3-12/18: Upper Village garden view: studio (2) $200, 1BR (2) $260, 2BR (4) $355; Lower Village garden view: studio $215, 1BR $295, 2BR $400; Upper Village ocean view: studio $225, 1BR $295, 2BR $390; Lower Village ocean view: studio $245, 1BR $325, 2BR $450

Elua Village—Located on Ulua Beach, one of the best in the area. I would recommend these units, expensive though they are. Five-night minimum stay. Fourteen-day minimum during Christmas holidays. Seventh night free 4/3-12/18. An additional $60 check-in fee per reservation charged by Elua Village Owners Association.

Destination Resorts Rates: 1BR g.v. $260-$310, o.v. $325-$375, o.f. $490, prime o.f. $535; 2BR g.v. $370-$420, o.v. $470, o.f. $630, prime o.f. $680; 3BR g.v. $625, o.v. $680, o.f. $780, prime o.f. $880

Grand Champion Villas—*155 Wailea Iki Place, Wailea, HI 96753.*

Twelve lush acres comprising 188 luxury condominium units with garden view, golf view or oceanview units. The fourth and newest of the Wailea Villas, this is a sportsman's dream, located between Wailea's Blue Golf Course and the "Wimbledon West" Tennis Center. Bookings through Destination Resorts include daily maid service and concierge service. Golf, tennis and/or car packages available.

Destination Resorts rates offer fifth night free 4/3-12/18, three-night minimum stay, 14 days during Christmas holidays: 1BR (2) g.v. $185/$215, partial o.v. $235/$270, o.v. $245/$280; 2BR (4) g.v. $235/$270, partial o.v. $270/$305, o.v. $285/$320; 3BR (6) o.v. $310/$345, partial o.v. $350/$390, o.v. $370/$410

MAKENA

Just south of Wailea is Makena, which will probably be one of the last resort areas to be developed on Maui. This is an upscale and peaceful location, great for family vacationers who prefer to be away from the crowds.

★ *Makena Surf*

96 Makena Alanui Road, Makena, HI 96753; www.makenasurf.com. Agents: Destination Resorts; AA Oceanfront Condos; Maui Vacation Properties; RSVP; Jim Osgood privately rents his two-bedroom unit (e-mail: jim@makenasurf.com; 425-391-8900).

Located two miles past Wailea. All units are oceanfront and more or less surround Paipu (Chang's) Beach. These very spacious and attractive condos feature central air conditioning, fully equipped kitchens, washers and dryers, wet bar, whirlpool spa in the master bath, telephones and daily maid service. Two pools and four tennis courts are set in landscaped grounds. Three historic sites found on location have been preserved. When it was first built it seemed that the Makena Surf was very out of the way and removed from the rest of the Wailea area. That isn't the case anymore, but this property is still very private. The units are well maintained and luxuriously appointed. Looking out from the oceanfront units it is hard to imagine that this isn't your own private island. Pull up a lounge chair, open that bottle of wine and watch the whales frolic as the sun sets gloriously in the Pacific beyond them. It doesn't get any better than this! Destination Resorts handles most of the rental units. Five-night minimum stay. An additional $50 (plus tax) check-in fee charged by the Makena Surf Owners Association. Seventh night is free 4/3-12/18 in most room categories with Destination Resorts.

Destination Resort rates: high season: 1BR not available during high season; 2BR (4) o.f. $570-$615, prime o.f./beachfront $670-$730; 3BR (6) o.f. $785, prime o.f. $840; 4BR (8) o.f. $1,325; low season: 1BR o.f $455-$485, prime o.f./beachfront $625; 2BR o.f. $570-$615, prime o.f. $670, prime beachfront $730; 3BR o.f. $785, prime o.f. $840; 4BR o.f. $1,325; extra person $20

★ *Maui Prince Hotel*

5400 Makena Alanui, Makena, HI 96753. 866-774-6236; 808-874-1111; 800-321-6284; www.mauiprince.com.

In sharp contrast to the ostentatious atmosphere of some of the Ka'anapali and Wailea resorts, the Maui Prince radiates understated elegance. Its simplicity of color and design, with an oriental theme, provides a tranquil setting and allows the beauty of Maui to be reflected. The central courtyard is the focal point of the

resort, with a lovely traditional water garden complete with a cool cascading waterfall and ponds filled with gleaming *koi*. The 310 rooms are tastefully appointed. The units have two telephones and a small refrigerator. Terry robes are available for use during the guest's stay. A 24-hour full room-service menu adds to the conveniences. They offer the Prince Keiki Club program; see "Childcare Programs" in Chapter 1 for details. There is plenty of room for lounging around two circular swimming pools, or in a few steps you can be on Maluaka (Nau Paka) Beach with its luxuriously deep, fine white sand and good snorkeling, swimming and wave playing. The resort comprises 1,800 acres including two championship golf courses. Restaurants include Prince Court, Cafe Kiowai and Hakone. A variety of special packages are available for honeymooners, golfers and others, so be sure to check their website for the latest. My husband and I have selected this hotel more than once to be our getaway of choice in South Maui, preferring its simple elegance to the crowds and mega-resorts of Wailea.

Rates: Partial o.v. $335, o.v. $375, o.v. prime $420, o.f. $525; suites $700-$1,500; $40/night charge for third person; children under 17 free, using existing beds

Kahului-Wailuku Area

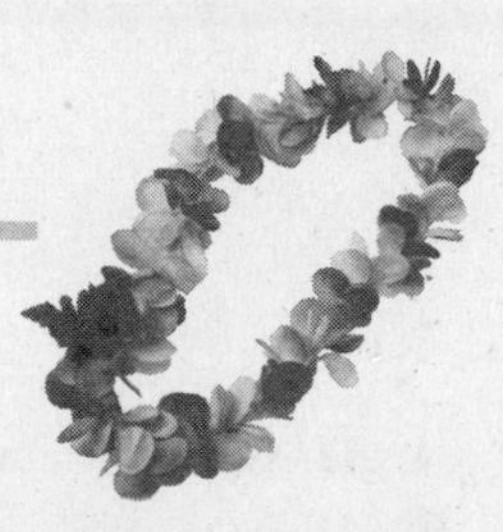

Banana Bungalow Maui—Hotel & International Hostel

310 North Market Street, Wailuku, HI 96793. 808-244-5090; 800-846-7835; e-mail: info@mauihostel.com; www.mauihostel.com.

Jim Heine reminds readers that his hostel is not a "youth" hostel, but accepts guests of all ages and can accommodate families of various ages and sizes; this is the only owner-operated hostel on Maui. His private rooms accommodate up to two people in beds, with a third on the floor with a futon mattress he provides. Young children sharing existing beds are free. Families of four to six can be accommodated in a dorm-style room where everyone can have their own bed. This historic plantation-style hostel has an indoor kitchen. The backyard boasts a tropical garden with hammocks and picnic tables. Jim also provides a free island tour: "Local tour companies charge as much as $125 for some of the tours we do for free and we visit all the secret places they do not!" Tours are aboard a 15-passenger van and guests can relax in the large jacuzzi when they return. He offers free high-speed and wireless internet access, free airport drop-off, free morning beach shuttle, free windsurf gear storage and discounts on windsurf equipment and car rentals. This international hotel and hostel, with clean and comfortable accommodations and a social atmosphere, attracts budget travelers, windsurfers and international backpackers. Rooms are equipped with closet, chair, mirror and nightstand. Bathrooms are shared. Passport or plane ticket off-island required for check-in. Check out is 10 a.m. and the office is closed 11 p.m. to 8 a.m. Laundry facilities on property. There are co-ed and women-only dorm rooms; private rooms have two twin beds or one queen bed.

Rates include taxes: Dorm rooms $22; private rooms $44.40 single, $55.50 double, $66.60 triple

Maui Beach Hotel

170 Ka'ahumanu Avenue, Kahului, HI 96732. 808-877-0051. Agent: RSVP.

This two-story, 152-room hotel is located oceanfront on Kahului Bay. All rooms have air conditioning and TV; some have balconies. Complimentary airport shuttle. Restaurant on property.

RSVP Rates: from $110

Maui Palms

170 Ka'ahumanu Avenue, Kahului, HI 96732. 808-877-0071.

This property is a 103-unit low-rise hotel with Polynesian decor. Built in 1953, the larger Maui Palms was constructed in 1968. In 1979 the Maui Beach purchased the Palms. I wouldn't recommend this property as a vacation stay, but it is convenient if you need a place for a night before an early morning flight from the Kahului Airport. Free airport pickup.

Rates: from $100

★ Old Wailuku Inn at Ulupono and Vagabond's House

2199 Kaho'okele Street, Wailuku, HI 96793. 808-244-5897; 800-305-4899; fax 808-242-9600; e-mail: mauibandb@aol.com; www.mauiinn.com.

Your hosts are Janice and Tom Fairbanks. Built in 1924 by a wealthy island banker as a wedding gift for his daughter-in-law, this historic Wailuku home has been lovingly restored. They were awarded the Kahili "Keep it Hawai'i" Award for Accommodations (from the Hawai'i Visitors & Convention Bureau) for "blending a nostalgic ambiance while at the same time providing all comforts and conveniences for the modern day traveler." In 2000 *Travel & Leisure* magazine named the inn number five in its list of top ten favorite B&Bs in the U.S. The rooms and overall theme of the inn are a tribute to Hawai'i's famed poet of the 1920s and '30s, Don Blanding. All rooms have high ceilings, wide crown molding, hardwood floors and all the comforts of home provided by cable television, VCR, ceiling fans, private baths and heirloom Hawaiian quilts. Three new rooms were added to the

inn in 2002 at the adjacent Vagabond's House. Full gourmet breakfast and daily maid service are included. Ten rooms. Two-night minimum. I have not stayed here myself, but I have friends on Oahu who love this place and wouldn't stay anywhere else. It's a charming choice.

Rates: Inn rates $120-$180 per night; Vagabond's House rates $140-$160; extra person $20/night

Upcountry

Banyan Tree House

3265 Baldwin Avenue, Makawao; 808-572-9021; fax 808-573-5072; e-mail: banyan@hawaii-mauirentals.com; www.hawaii-mauirentals.com.

Located on two acres in upcountry Maui, an area known in past decades as "Sunnyside" for its temperate climate. The historic three-bedroom three-bath home, hidden beneath exotic banyan and monkeypod trees, had a previous life as the home of a plantation manager. Adjacent to the home are four private cottages with full or half kitchens. Large swimming pool with jacuzzi. The main house has a restaurant-quality kitchen. Your host is Suzy Papanikolas. Weekly and monthly rates are available.

Rates: Main house: $115 (room), $375 (house); cottage apartments $85/$100/$110/$115

Haleakala National Park

Lottery: Haleakala National Park, Attention Cabins, P.O. Box 369, Makawao, HI 96768-0369; 808-572-4400; www.haleakala.national-park.com/camping.

Wilderness cabins at Holua, Paliku and Kapalaoa require a permit. Built by the Civilian Conservation Corps in the 1930s, each cabin has a wood-burning stove, cooking utensils and dishes, 12 padded bunks, pit toilets and limited water and firewood. There is no electricity. Water must be treated. In times of drought, all cookware will be removed and you will need to carry all your water in with you. Each cabin is allocated to one party as a unit, up to 12 people per night. You must enter the reservation lottery by writing to the address above at least 90 days before you get to Maui. Tell them the dates you want (the more flexible you are, the better your chances), which cabin, and how many people. Or call 808-572-4400 between the hours of 1 and 3 p.m.

Rates: $40 (1-6 people); $80 (7-12 people)

Kula Cottage

40 Puakea Place, Kula, HI 96790. 808-871-6230; 808-878-2043; e-mail: cecilia@gilbertadvertising.com; www.kulacottage.com.

Three thousand feet up on the slopes of Haleakala, in a lush half-acre mountain setting, is this one-bedroom hideaway. The cottage is equipped with a wood-burning fireplace, a full kitchen, laundry, private driveway, gas barbecue and a queen-size bed. Two-night minimum stay.

Rates: $95 per night

Kula Lodge

RR 1, Box 475, Kula, HI 96790. 15200 Haleakala Highway; 808-878-1535; 800-233-1535; fax 808-878-2125; e-mail: info@kulalodge.com; www.kulalodge.com.

Five-and-a-half miles past Pukalani, on Haleakala Highway, is the Kula Lodge, with a handful of rustic chalet-like cabins located at the 3,200-foot elevation. There's a lovely restaurant on the property. Vista View Chalets have queen bed, fireplace, lanai, and stairs to a loft with two twin beds. Mountain View Chalets have queen bed, private lanai and ladder to loft with two futon beds, suitable for children. The single-story Garden View Chalet is a studio with a queen bed and private lanai. Accommodations are log-cabin rustic, but clean and comfortable. We enjoyed our stay here and recommend the cabins that have fireplaces to ward off the night chill. Rates are for two people.

Rates: Vista view $175-$195; mountain view $145-$165; garden view $115-$135; ask about midweek special rates. Extra persons, including children, are $20 per night

★ Kula Lynn Farm

P.O. Box 847, Kula, HI 96789. 808-878-6176; 800-874-2666 ext. 211; e-mail: captcoon@verizon.net.

Your hosts are a part of the Coon family (Trilogy Excursions). The lower-level apartment is 1,600 square feet with a full kitchen and patio deck. The home is located in beautiful Upcountry on the slopes of Haleakala, in lower Kula. Maximum 6 people. Five-night minimum.

Rates: $119 per night (double occupancy); extra person $20/night

Maui Dream Cottages

265 West Kuiaha Road, Haiku, HI 96708. 808-575-9079; fax 808-575-9477; www.mauidreamcottage.com; e-mail: gblue@aloha.net.

Gregg Blue offers two cottages on a two-acre estate, which includes many fruit trees and over an acre of lawn for relaxing or for children to play. Both cottages are equipped with full kitchen, washer/dryer, phone, TV/VCR and sleep two to four people. There are ocean views from both cottages.

Rates: $623 (including tax) per week for two; each additional adult $10/night; additional nights $89 each

★ Olinda Country Cottages & Inn

2660 Olinda Road, Makawao, HI 96768; 800-932-3435; 808-572-1453; e-mail: olinda@mauibnbcottages.com; www.mauibnbcottages.com.

This delightful, tranquil getaway is located at the 4,000-foot level on the slopes of Haleakala, almost at the end of Olinda Road. A 5,000-square-foot Tudor-style country inn, with two secluded cottages, is set amidst an 8.6-acre protea flower farm. The new owners (since 2004), Susan and George Reul, also own the Hamoa Bay House & Bungalow in Hana. The inn has two beautifully decorated bedrooms with private bathrooms, as well as the "Pineapple Sweet"—a larger suite with private bath and kitchenette. The Hidden Cottage is a completely secluded cottage that is popular with honeymooners. The Country Cottage, where we stayed, is a spacious cottage with a full kitchen (equipped with everything including china tea cups), living room with fireplace, and bedroom. Outside is a private patio, screened by trellises of peach-colored roses and star jasmine. We arrived on a dark, rainy evening and were welcomed by the lights of the cottage (left on for our arrival) and logs on the hearth—ready for a fire. The inn's fat ginger-colored cat, Hari, greeted us at our front door, which was framed by climbing roses and wisteria. We loved our stay here—the large welcome basket full of fresh fruit, pastries, coffee and tea; the thick, fluffy bath towels; the manicured gardens and expansive lawns; the spicy, clean smell of the eucalyptus trees; the utter tranquility and peace. No traffic noise, no sirens, no crowds. No outside noise at all, except for the sound of the birds (and Hari's occasional meow). Satellite TV and a CD player stocked with Hawaiian CDs provided the comforts of home. This is what a country inn should be! A great place to de-stress when you first arrive on Maui or before you head home, and a very different Maui experience from the typical beach resort. No children under 14.

Rates: Inn rooms or Pineapple Sweet, $140 (2 night minimum); Country Cottage, $195 (3 night minimum); Hidden Cottage, $245 (3 night minimum), $220/night for 7 nights or more

Polipoli Springs State Recreation Area

Division of Parks, P.O. Box 537, Makawao, HI 96768.

A single cabin, which sleeps 10, has bunk beds, water, a cold shower and kitchenware. Sheets and towels can be picked up along with the key.

Rates: $45 (1 to 4 persons), extra person $5/night

Silver Cloud Upcountry Guest Ranch

1373 Thompson Road Kula, HI 96790.

The Silver Cloud ranch was originally part of the Thompson Ranch, which had its beginnings on Maui in 1902. The nine-acre ranch is located at the 2,800-foot elevation on the slopes of Haleakala. The guest ranch offers 12 rooms, suites and cottages, each with private bathrooms and most with private lanais and entrances. The ranch was recently purchased by Oprah Winfrey. At press time, her representatives were in the process of applying for the necessary permits to operate a vacation rental at this location. Meanwhile, the property is closed until further notice. Stay tuned.

Hana Highway

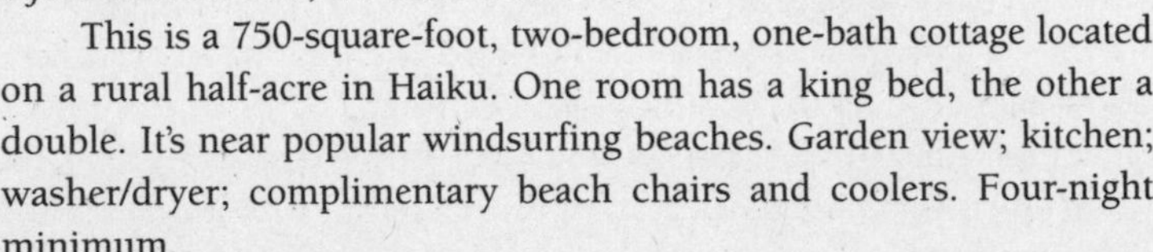

PAIA–HAIKU

Haiku Lani

808-575-9065; fax 808-575-9054; e-mail: info@haikulani.com; www.haikulani.com.

This is a 750-square-foot, two-bedroom, one-bath cottage located on a rural half-acre in Haiku. One room has a king bed, the other a double. It's near popular windsurfing beaches. Garden view; kitchen; washer/dryer; complimentary beach chairs and coolers. Four-night minimum.

Rates: $85 per night (1-2 people); $550/week; additional guest $10

Halfway to Hana House

P.O. Box 675, Haiku, HI 96708. 808-572-1176; fax 808-572-3609; e-mail: gailp@maui.net; www.halfwaytohana.com.

Located 20 minutes from Paia town along the scenic Hana Highway. The romantic guest studio is designed for two. It has a spectacular ocean view, hammock for two in the palms, private entrance and bath, mini-kitchen and covered patio. Complimentary Hawaiian coffees and herbal teas. Three-night minimum preferred. Breakfast is an additional $8 per person or $15 for two.

Rates: $85; 10 percent discount for 7 nights or longer

★ Huelo Point Lookout

P.O. Box 790117, Paia, HI 96779-0117. 800-871-8645; 808-573-0914; e-mail: dreamers@maui.net; www.mauivacationcottages.com.

Innkeepers Jeff and Sharyn Stone offer five unique lodging options on their two-acre garden estate. With an 8-year-old child themselves, they welcome families and family reunions that rent out the entire property. (Children must be "swim safe" as neither the pool nor hot tub is enclosed.) Sweeping ocean and mountain views, hot tubs, a 44-foot rock-walled swimming pool and an organic herb-and-vegetable garden provide a laidback North Shore vacation. The Haleakala Cottage has a full kitchen with a dishwasher, king bed, tropical flowers and mountain views. Situated on an acre of lush greenery, the Star Cottage has plenty of windows, ocean and mountain views, a king bed and a private hot tub. Perfect for honeymooners, the two-story Rainbow Cottage will spoil you with fantastic views, private lanais and hot tub. An elegant spiral staircase leads to the skylit master bedroom, which has a king bed. The 800-square-foot Sunrise Suite's glass-walled living room provides panoramic views, the bedroom suite has a king bed, and the bathroom comes with a view and tub for two. And the large two-story Lookout House, which accommodates up to eight people, has panoramic views, a private lanai with hot tub, wraparound porches, a kitchen, a dining room, and plenty of room for the kids. A massage, yoga classes or even gourmet meals can be arranged. It's a 30- to 40-minute drive from Kahului airport along the road to Hana. No credit cards. The accommodations generally require a one-week minimum, but shorter stays can be arranged.

Rates: Haleakala Cottage $1,225 week, Star Cottage $1,575 week, Rainbow Cottage $1,995 week, Sunrise Suite $325-$360 nightly, Lookout House $2,650-$2,850/week; extra person $30/night

Inn at Mama's Fish House

799 Poho Place, Paia, HI 96779. 800-860-4852; 808-579-9764; e-mail: info@mamasfishhouse.com; www.mamasfishhouse.com.

Fully equipped oceanfront cottages with private lanais. Laundry facilities and gas grills available. Daily maid service. Three-night minimum required.

Rates: 1BR cottage $175, 2BR beachfront cottages $475

Pilialoha Bed & Breakfast Cottage

2512 Kaupakalua Road, Haiku, HI 96708-6024. 808-572-1440; fax 808-572-4612; e-mail: cottage@pilialoha.com; www.pilialoha.com.

Your hosts are Bill and Machikio Heyde. Pilialoha, which means "friendship" in Hawaiian, is a split-level guest cottage on a private two-acre Haiku property. The cottage's master bedroom has a queen bed; an adjoining room has a twin bed. There's an open-air deck and full kitchen, which is stocked with an assortment of teas and coffees. Living room has satellite dish TV, VCR/DVD, CD player and telephone. Maximum capacity is three people (a child or baby is counted as one person). Suitable for a couple with one child (4 years or older). Three-night minimum. 10 percent discount for 7 nights or longer. Rates include breakfast, delivered daily to the cottage.

Rates: $110/night for one, $130 for two, $150 for three

HANA

Aloha Cottages

P.O. Box 205, Hana, HI 96713. 808-248-8420.

These simple but comfortable furnished two- to three-bedroom cottages are located in a residential area, just a short walk to Hana Bay. No in-room phones, but messages will be taken. There are pay phones nearby. Television optional. Daily maid service. No credit cards.

Rates: $60-$90; extra person $10-$20/night

Hamoa Bay Bungalow and Hamoa Bay House

P.O. Box 773, Hana, HI 96713. Contact Robin Gaffney at 808-248-7884; fax 808-248-7047; e-mail: hamoabay@maui.net; www.hamoabay.com.

The 600-square-foot studio cottage "bungalow" has a fully equipped kitchen, a king-size bamboo bed, a jacuzzi bath for two, a CD/tape player, a VCR and videos, a microwave and laundry facilities. The Balinese-inspired Hamoa Bay House offers mountain, jungle and sea views. You'll find king- and queen-size beds, a barbecue area, laundry facilities and an outdoor lava-rock shower. No smoking indoors. Three-night minimum. Children must be 14 or older.

Rates: Bungalow (2 people maximum) $195; house $250 for 2 people, $350 for 4 people

Hana Kai-Maui

P.O. Box 38, Hana, HI 96713. Located at 1533 Uakea Road in Hana. 800-346-2772; 808-248-8426, 808-248-7506; fax 808-248-7482; e-mail: hanakai@maui.net; www.hanakaimaui.com.

These 18 studio and one-bedroom condominiums are nestled on Hana Bay, with a wonderful location overlooking the black-sand beach. The units are clean, well-kept, and just a short walk to the bay. All units have fully equipped kitchens and private oceanview lanais. There is daily maid service. Amenities include a spring-fed lava-rock koi pond and beachside barbecue area.

Rates: Studio (2) $125-$145, 1BR (4) $145-$195; discounts available for longer stays

Heavenly Hana Inn

P.O. Box 790, Hana, HI 96713. Tel/fax 808-248-8442; e-mail: hanainn@maui.net; www.heavenlyhanainn.com.

This tranquil Japanese-style inn features two one-room suites and one two-room suite; each has a private bathroom, lanai, private entrance and a small sitting room with cable TV. The spacious bathrooms include a soaking tub. There are no in-room telephones or kitchen facilities. If you'd like to breakfast here, arrangements must be made at least one week in advance of arrival; breakfast is served at 8 a.m. and cost is $17 per person. No smoking. No children under age 15. Two-night minimum.

Rates: 1-room suites $210-$235, 2-room suite $300

Hana Gardenland

Hana Highway, about 3.5 miles before Hana town; 808-248-8610; e-mail: roberthe@sonic.net or devijuice@aol.com; www.hanapalmsretreat.com.

The Garden House and the Palms House are located within the private five-acre Hana Gardenland botanical estate. The Garden House

In the early 1940s, the end of Hana's sugar industry was close at hand; its 5,000 residents had dwindled down to only 500. Industrialist Paul Fagan consolidated five sugar plantations into a cattle ranch and built a small hotel in 1946, rejuvenating Hana. Originally known as the Kauiki Inn, Fagan's ten-room hotel was expanded over the years and eventually renamed the Hotel Hana-Maui. This Hana landmark, along with the ranch and flower nursery, now employs approximately a third of the town's residents.

has two separate and complete residences. They share an outdoor covered hot tub. The Garden Upper Residence has three bedrooms: a sun room with queen bed, a bedroom with two twin beds (or one king), and a bedroom with queen bed, bathroom, full kitchen, large living and dining area. Two-night minimum. The Garden Lower Residence has two bedrooms: a bedroom with two twin beds (or one king) and a bedroom with queen bed, bathroom, full kitchen, living and dining area. Two-night minimum. The Palms House has two bedrooms: upstairs large master bedroom with queen bed and half-bath; downstairs bedroom has queen bed, full kitchen, living room, sun porch dining area, bathroom, outdoor covered shower/bath on porch, outdoors covered hot tub. One-week minimum.

Rates: Garden upper $195, garden lower $140, Palms House $225/night

★ *Hotel Hana-Maui at Hana Ranch*

P.O. Box 8, Hana, HI 96713. 800-321-4262; 808-248-8211; fax 808-248-7202; e-mail: reservations@hotelhanamaui.com; www.hotelhanamaui.com.

This hotel is absolutely magical. If you are looking for a place to relax and de-stress in luxurious Hawaiian surroundings, look no further. The landmark Hotel Hana-Maui underwent extensive renovations in 2002 under its new ownership, Passport Resorts, and has been garnering national travel awards ever since. Maui's most secluded resort, the 66-room hotel resembles a small neighborhood with single-story buildings and cottages scattered about the grounds. The simple yet elegant rooms have wet bars, hardwood floors and large tiled bathrooms with deep tubs and walk-in showers. Wicker, bamboo and traditional *tapa* (bark cloth) patterns are also prominent. The resort prides itself on the fact that it has no televisions or radios in the rooms. This place is all about serenity. The Bay Cottages are large rooms and suites located in the U-shaped string of buildings close to the main lobby. The fabulous Sea Ranch Cottages, sprawled across a hillside sloping toward the sea, resemble early plantation-style houses; some of these spacious oceanview and oceanfront cottages also have private hot tubs on their lanai. Built in 1928, the resort's Plantation Guest House can be used as a guest home; it offers two bedrooms, two baths, a large living room with fireplace, dining room, library, bar and complete kitchen. The 4,000-square-foot building, set on four lush acres, was once the home of August Unna, Hana's first plantation owner.

Guest services include a complimentary shuttle to and from Hana Airport, Hamoa Beach or anywhere you want to go on the property; daily maid service, tennis courts, two heated pools, two outdoor jacuzzis, a fitness center, new full-service spa facility, three-hole par-3 practice golf course with complimentary clubs and balls, and Hawaiian arts and crafts. The hotel offers a buffet with a hula show on Friday evenings in the dining room. Many of the performers are hotel employees or their family members, which affords an authentic and very charming show. They also offer Hawaiian music in the bar Thursday through Sunday. Dining options include the upscale Main Dining Room and the informal Hana Ranch Restaurant; the bar serves *pupus* and lighter fare. They also provide poolside food service and in-room service.

A variety of activities are available during the day and evening. The hotel's shuttle goes to beautiful Hamoa Beach, which has private facilities and complimentary beach and snorkeling equipment for hotel guests. There are many hiking trails and horseback rides at Hana Ranch Stables. Guests can book tours to 'Ohe'o Gulch or the nearby underground caverns, or arrange for a variety of ocean activities (fee). Children's activities are offered during peak family travel periods, and babysitting services are also available.

The Paniolo Lounge is a bar with a large fireplace and an open deck with a quiet adjoining lounge. Enjoy some quiet reading in the library, which contains rare volumes of early Hawaiiana as well as popular novels. There are also a handful of small boutiques and gift shops, as well as an art gallery. The Club Room offers free internet access and a television for guests who just can't stay "unplugged."

The Hotel Hana-Maui offers an enchanting mix of elegance and sophistication combined with the simplicity and pure essence of Hawai'i. For example: adjacent to the beautiful lobby area with its lovely vases and tranquil pond you'll see a bunch of ripe bananas hanging by the Bell Desk . . . yours for the picking as you wander by. Elegant but intimate; sophisticated but not stiff or formal. This is a friendly place, as is the Hana community, and timeless—in more ways than one. There was no clock in my room.

May and September are adults-only months (18 years and older). Prices are based on single or double occupancy. Children under 18 stay free, using existing bedding. A variety of packages are available, so check with the hotel (or their website) for current offers.

Rates: Bay Cottages: garden jr. suite $395, deluxe jr. suite $425, o.v. hotel room $425, o.v. jr. suite $455; Sea Ranch Cottages: o.v. cottage $525, deluxe o.v. cottage $575, deluxe o.v. cottage with spa $625, o.f. cottage $625, superior o.f cottage $675, superior o.f. cottage with spa $725, o.f. suite with spa $895; Plantation Guest House: $2,500; extra person $140/night

Wai'anapanapa State Park

Contact: 54 South High Street, first floor, Wailuku, HI 96793. 808-243-5354.

The State Park Department offers 12 cabins that sleep up to six people. The units have electric lights, hot water, showers and toilet facilities (bring your own soap). There is a living room with two single beds and one bedroom with two bunks. Completely furnished with bedding, bath towels, dish cloth, and cooking and eating utensils. There's an electric range (no oven) and refrigerator. Mosquito repellent is strongly recommended, even for a short walk through the area. A five-day maximum stay is the rule and guests are required to clean their units before departure, leaving soiled linens. A 50 percent deposit is required for reservations and they are booked way ahead (six months to one year). Children are considered those ages 11 and under. No pets are allowed.

Rates: $45 for 1-4 persons; extra person $5/night

YMCA Camp Ke'anae

In Ke'anae. 808-248-8355. Reservations and information available through the Maui YMCA office at 250 Kanaloa Avenue, Kahului, HI 96732; 808-242-9007.

Located a half mile past mile-marker 16, the YMCA's Camp Ke'anae offers overnight dorm-style accommodations for men and women (housed separately) and two family cottages, accommodating up to four people. Arrival is requested between 4 p.m. and 6 p.m. Bring your own food and sleeping bag.

Rates: $17 dorm; o.v. cottage rental $125

Rental Agents

BED & BREAKFAST AGENCIES

An alternative to condominiums and hotels are the bed-and-breakfast organizations. They offer homes around the island at some very reasonable rates.

Affordable Accommodations Maui

2825 Kauhale Street, Kihei, HI 96753. 888-333-9747; 808-879-7865; fax 808-874-0831; e-mail: info@affordablemaui.com; www.affordablemaui.com.

Linda Little runs this agency, which offers bed and breakfasts, studios, cottages, condominiums and homes. Prices range from a $50/night budget accommodation to $5,000/night luxury home. Their objective is to find just the right place for you at your preferred price range. They can also arrange for outer island accommodations and rental cars.

Bed & Breakfast Hawai'i

P.O. Box 449, Kapa'a, HI 96746. 800-733-1632; 808-822-7771; fax 808-822-2723; e-mail: reservations@bandb-hawaii.com; ww.bandb-hawaii.com.

This agency is among the best known. To become a member and receive their directory (which includes the other islands) contact them.

CONDOMINIUM AND HOME RENTAL AGENCIES

★ AA Oceanfront Condo Rentals

P.O. Box 89, Kihei, HI 96753. (Office located at Azeka Mauka shopping center.) 800-488-6004; 808-879-7288; fax 808-879-7500; e-mail: info@aaoceanfront.com; www.aaoceanfront.com.

This company has been managing vacation rentals on Maui since 1983. They rent properties from Kihei to Makena in all price categories.

★ Aston Hotels & Resorts

2155 Kalakaua Avenue #500, Honolulu, HI 96815. 808-931-1400; 877-977-6667; e-mail info@aston-hotels.com; www.aston-hotels.com.

Large hotel and condo management company with many properties statewide.

Bello Realty-Maui Beach Homes

P.O. Box 1776, Kihei, HI 96753. 808-879-3328; 800-541-3060 U.S. & Canada; e-mail: vacations@bellomaui.com; www.bellomaui.com.

Specializing primarily in the Kihei–Wailea area, Bello rents condos and homes by the day, week or month.

Castle Resorts & Hotels

3 Waterfront Plaza, 500 Ala Moana Boulevard, Suite 555, Honolulu, HI 96813. 800-367-5004; www.castleresorts.com.

Chase 'N Rainbows

P.O. Box 11473, Lahaina, HI. 800-367-6092 U.S. & Canada; 808-667-7088; fax 808-661-8423; e-mail: info@chasenrainbows.com; www.chasenrainbows.com.

This company offers many condo rentals in West Maui.

Classic Resorts

180 Dickenson Street, #201, Lahaina, HI 96761. 800-642-6284; 808-661-3339; fax 808-667-1145; e-mail: info@classicresorts.com; www.classicresorts.com.

Condominium Rentals Hawaii

362 Huku Li'i Place #204, Kihei, HI 96753. 800-367-5242; 808-879-2778; e-mail: res@crhmaui.com; www.crhmaui.com.

★ Destination Resorts

800-367-5246; 808-891-6249; fax 808-874-3554; e-mail: info@drhmaui.net; www.destinationresortshi.com or www.drhmaui.com.

Offering condos in the Wailea/Makena area.

Elite Properties Unlimited

505 Front Street #224-2A, Lahaina, HI 96761. 800-448-9222 U.S. & Canada; 808-665-0561; fax 808-669-2417; e-mail: homes@eliteprop.com; www.eliteprop.com.

Rents family homes and luxury estates (3 to 7 bedrooms) on all four major islands. Weekly and monthly rentals. One-week minimum. Maid service, chefs and concierge services available.

★ Hana Maui Travel Company

P.O. Box 536, Hana, HI. 800-548-0478; 808-248-7742; e-mail: info@hanamauitravel.com; www.hanaalii.com.

They handle rental homes and cottages in Hana, with more than a dozen properties ranging from $80-$450+/night.

Hana Accommodations (a.k.a. Hana Plantation Houses)

P.O. Box 249, Hana, HI 96713. 800-228-4262; 808-248-7868; e-mail: info@hana-maui.com; www.hana-maui.com.

Offering a variety of excellent properties in the Hana area, from homes to studios and quaint cottages. Full payment is required in advance. Rates are $100/night and up.

Hawaiian Island Vacations

800-231-6958; 808-871-4981; fax 808-871-4624; e-mail: lastminute@hawaiianisland.com; www.hawaiianisland.com.

Home and condo rentals; vacation packages; car rentals.

Kathy Scheper's Maui Accommodations

800-645-3753; 808-879-8744; fax 808-879-9100; e-mail: vacation@maui411.com; www.maui411.com.

Condo and cottage in Kihei and penthouse at Hale Mahina in West Maui.

★ Kihei Maui Vacations

P.O. Box 1055, Kihei, HI 96753. 888-568-6284 U.S. & Canada; 808-879-7581; fax 808-879-2000; e-mail kmv@maui.net.

In addition to condos they offer homes and cottages in the Kihei, Wailea and Makena areas. No credit cards.

Kumulani Vacations & Realty
P.O. Box 1190, Kihei, HI 96753. 800-367-2954 U.S. & Canada; 808-879-9272; e-mail: info@kumulani.com; www.kumulani.com.

Specializes in South Maui vacation rentals, but can assist with almost any Maui property, as well as other islands. Car rentals, too.

★ ***Ma'alaea Bay Rentals***
280 Hauoli Street, Ma'alaea Village, HI 96793. 800-367-6084; 808-244-7012; fax 808-242-7476; e-mail: reservations@maalaeabay.com; www.maalaeabay.com.

Handling a variety of condominium rentals in Ma'alaea.

Marc Resorts
2155 Kalakaua Avenue, 3rd floor, Honolulu, HI 96815. 800-535-0085; 808-926-5900; fax 808-922-2421; e-mail: aloha@marcresorts.com; www.marcresorts.com.

Maui and All Island Condominiums and Cars
P.O. Box 1089, Aldergrove, BC, Canada V4W 2V1. U.S. Mailing address: P.O. Box 947, Lynden, WA 98264. 800-663-6962 U.S. & Canada; 604-856-4190; fax 604-856-4187.

Approximately 25,000 condos and homes rented weekly, bi-weekly and monthly.

Maui Beachfront Rentals
256 Papalaua Street, Lahaina, HI 96761. 888-661-7200; 808-661-3500; e-mail: beachfrt@maui.net; www.mauibeachfront.com.

Maui Condo and Home Realty
P.O. Box 1840, Kihei, HI 96753. 800-451-5008; 808-875-0028; fax 808-875-1769; www.mauicondo.com.

Homes and condos primarily in the Kihei–Wailea area.

Maui Lodging
3636 Lower Honoapiilani Road, Lahaina, HI 96761. 800-487-6002; 808-669-0089; fax 808-669-3937; e-mail: info@mauilodging.com; www.mauilodging.com.

Offers several West Maui homes and condos; all are non-smoking.

Maui Resort Management
3600 Lower Honoapi'ilani Road, Lahaina, HI 96761. 800-367-5037; 808-669-1902; e-mail: mrmreservations@maui.net; www.mauigetaway.com.

They handle West Maui condos.

Maui Vacation Properties
P.O. Box 1359, Haiku, HI 96708. 800-782-6105; 808-575-9228; fax 808-575-2826; e-mail: info@mauivacationproperties.com; www.mauivacationproperties.com.

Island-wide rental of condos, homes and cottages.

Maui Windsurfari

808-871-7766; 800-736-6284; e-mail: info@windsurfari.com; www.windsurfari.com.

Vacation rental agency offering private homes, cottages and condos from $50 up. Many of their vacation rentals are unusual with close proximity to windsurfing locations. Packages include accommodations, rental car, windsurfing equipment and excursions.

★ ***Outrigger Hotels and Resorts Hawaii***

2375 Kuhio Avenue, Honolulu, HI 96815-2992. 800-688-7444; toll-free fax 800-622-4852; 303-369-7777; e-mail: reservations@outrigger.com; www.outrigger.com.

★ ***Pacific Islands Reservations***

571 Pauku Street, Kailua, HI 96734; 808-262-8133; fax 808-262-5030; e-mail: pir@aloha.com; www.vacation-homes-hawaii.com.

Owner Ingrid Carvalho handles a variety of vacation rental homes and villas across the island.

Premier Resorts

3478 Buskirk Avenue, Suite 275, Pleasant Hill, CA 94523. 800-367-7052; e-mail: stay@premier-resorts.com; www.premier-resorts.com.

Handling rentals for The Whaler, Kahana Sunset and a Kahana-area beach house.

★ ***RSVP***

800-663-1118 U.S. & Canada; toll-free fax 888-294-7787; e-mail: reservations@rsvphawaii.com; www.rsvphawaii.com.

Ask about specials they may have for free rental cars, senior rates, military discounts, etc.

★ ***Whalers Realty Management Co.***

Fairway Shops, Suite 118, 2850 Keka'a Drive, Lahaina, HI 96761. 800-676-4112; 808-661-3484; fax 808-661-8338; e-mail: info@vacation-maui.com; www.vacation-maui.com

They offer high-quality condos and vacation homes at reasonable prices.

CHAPTER 4

Where to Dine

Whether it is a teriburger at a local café or a romantic evening spent dining next to a swan lagoon, Maui offers something for everyone. I'm confident that you will enjoy exploring Maui's diverse dining options as much as I have.

In an effort to avoid this book becoming a two-volume set, I have not included every restaurant on the island. I've omitted those restaurants that I find less interesting or not comfortable places for visitors, restaurants that are primarily local bars, and those so far off the beaten path that you would not likely venture to them (unless they are truly outstanding). In the case of new restaurants, I generally wait until they have survived their "shakedown" period of a few months to a year before I include them in the book. There are too many situations where a restaurant opens and then closes a few months later, and it would certainly be frustrating for you to read listing after listing of restaurants that no longer exist. I think it's more useful for me to provide you with information on restaurants that are open and somewhat stable—chances are they will still be here when you are making your visit. Meanwhile, you'll have fun discovering some of Maui's newest restaurants on your own.

Of course, I can't eat at every restaurant before the revision of each guidebook (although I would love to!), so I would appreciate hearing from you about your own dining experiences on Maui. It is quite a job to keep up on the restaurants that come and go. Some will become a permanent part of the Maui dining scene, while others will quickly disappear. And menus, prices, decor, concept, ownership—even restaurant names—can change at any time, so please accept the following restaurant descriptions as they are meant to be—current at the time this book went to press, but subject to change. Dining hours may change or be flexible as well. Many smaller restaurants post dinner hours but adjust their actual opening or closing times based on business each evening. Special events, holidays, weekends and particularly busy vacation seasons warrant later hours.

The restaurants are divided into the same geographical sections of the island as the "Where to Stay" chapter. The restaurant descriptions/listings are separated by price range, and listed alphabetically within those price ranges. This should simplify looking for that perfect place for breakfast, lunch or dinner based on your location. The price ranges are for one person: "*inexpensive*" items are mostly under $15; "*moderate*," most entrees $15 to $25; and "*expensive*," $25 and above. These estimates exclude tax, gratuity, alcoholic beverages and extras (like desserts). The prices listed were accurate at the time of publication, but could change at any time.

For quick reference, the type of food served at the restaurant is indicated next to the restaurant name. The restaurants are also indexed alphabetically, as well as by food type, in the back of the book. Sample menu offerings are also included in each restaurant description as a helpful guide. *Tip*: Check the local free papers or visitor publications for restaurant ads. You might find some seasonal specials or early-bird dinner offerings.

My recommendations for best family-dining restaurants are indicated with this "child-friendly" icon. I feel these particular restaurants have great food, good value (although some are fine-dining establishments and will not be inexpensive) and an atmosphere/ambience that is comfortable for families. Many restaurants (not just those I recommend as family-friendly) offer *keiki* menus. If there's no *keiki* menu, most restaurants are happy to downsize standard portions and reduce the cost for children.

In addition, my favorite restaurants are indicated by a star ★. These generally represent a real bargain for the price, serve a very high quality meal, or are outstanding or extraordinary in some way.

I have also indicated in the write-ups that some restaurants are recent ʻAipono Award winners. The ʻAipono Awards are the result of *Maui No Ka Oi* magazine's annual readers' survey to choose Maui's best dining spots. The awards are an excellent indication of which restaurants "the locals" consider to be the best on the island in a variety of categories, from best plate lunch to best dessert to best place to eat in a bathing suit. (You can visit *Maui No Ka Oi* magazine's website at www.mauimagazine.net.)

There are numerous fast-food/chain restaurants on Maui, but I have only included the larger, more "restaurant-like" ones in key locations. The fast-food chains all serve the same food you'd expect from their mainland counterparts, but most have slightly higher prices than the mainland. (Keep an eye out for special offers and promos, which tend to be the same price as the mainland.)

There are several food courts around the island. In Lahaina, the Food Court at the Lahaina Cannery Mall is an excellent stop for the traveling family; with so many selections, everyone will find exactly what they want and it won't pinch the pocketbook. You'll also find food courts at Whalers Village in Ka'anapali, and Queen Ka'ahumanu Center and Maui Marketplace in Kahului–Wailuku. Although not a food court, there are several small food outlets in Maui Mall as well.

Ethnic Foods

The cultural diversity of the Hawaiian Islands benefits visitors and residents alike. As immigrants arrived, they brought with them many varied foods from their native lands; some may be familiar to you while others are new and interesting. A little description of some of Hawai'i's ethnic dishes may tempt you to try a few new foods as a part of your dining adventure on Maui.

CHINESE FOODS

Bean threads: thin, clear noodles made from mung beans
Char siu: roasted pork with spices
Chow mein: thin noodles prepared with veggies and meat in various combinations, also cake-noodles style
Crack seed: preserved fruits and seeds—some are sweet, others are sour
Egg/Spring/Summer roll: deep-fried or fresh pastry roll with various veggie, meat or shrimp fillings
Kung pao chicken: deep-fried or sauteed spicy chicken pieces
Long rice: clear noodles cooked with chicken and vegetables
Mongolian beef: thinly sliced charbroiled beefsteak
Peking duck: charbroiled duck with *char siu* flavoring
Pot stickers: semi-soft pan-fried filled dumplings
Sweet-and-sour sauce: sugar-and-vinegar-based sauce with tomato sauce, salt and garlic flavorings
Szechuan sauce: hot chili–flavored sauce used extensively in beef, chicken, pork, and seafood dishes
Won ton: crispy deep-fried dumpling with meat or veggie fillings; also soft style cooked in soups or noodle dishes

FILIPINO FOODS

Adobo: chicken or pork cooked with vinegar and spices
Cascaron: a donut made with rice flour and rolled in sugar
Chicken papaya: chicken soup with green papaya and seasonings
Dinadaraan: blend of prepared pork blood and meats
Halo halo: a tropical fruit sundae that is a blend of milk, sugar, fruits and ice
Lumpia: fried pastry filled with vegetables and meats
Pancit: noodles with vegetables or meat
Pinacbet: stir-fry of bitter melon, okra, pork and various seasonings
Pork and peas: traditional entree of pork, peas, and flavorings in a tomato paste base
Sari sari: soup entree of pork, veggies and flavorings

HAWAIIAN FOODS

Haupia: a sweet custard made of coconut milk
Kalua pig: roast pig cooked in an underground *imu* oven, very flavorful
Kulolo: a steamed pudding using coconut milk and grated taro root
Laulau: pieces of pork or chicken, flavored with butterfish, topped with lu'au (taro) leaves, wrapped in ti leaves, then steamed
Lomi lomi salmon: diced and salted salmon with tomatoes and green onions
Long rice: clear noodles cooked with squid or chicken broth
Opihi: saltwater limpets eaten raw and considered a delicacy
Poi: pureed taro corms, best eaten fresh, although some Hawaiians prefer it aged and slightly fermented
Poke: raw fish that has been spiced. A variety of fish are used and are often mixed with seaweed; for example, *ahi poke* is raw tuna while *tako poke* is marinated octopus

JAPANESE FOODS

Chicken katsu: deep-fried, breaded chicken pieces served with *katsu* sauce
Donburi: chicken, pork or fish entree with veggies and special soy sauce served over steaming rice and topped with egg
Kamaboko: fish cake of white fish and starch steamed together
Miso soup: soup of fermented soybeans
Okazuya: this is a style of serving where you select dishes from a buffet line; the food represents a variety of ethnic cuisines
Sashimi: very fresh firm raw fish, usually yellowfin tuna (*ahi*), sliced thin and dipped in wasabi-*shoyu* sauce
Shabu shabu: thinly sliced beef with veggies, noodles and *ponzu* sauce

Soba/saimin: thin noodles served with/without broth; cold soba served as salad with vegetables

Sukiyaki: thinly sliced beef with veggies, noodles and tofu in a broth

Sushi: white rice rolls or cakes with various seafood, seaweed and veggie fillings

Tempura: deep-fried shrimp, fish, seafood and veggies dipped in a light flour batter

Teriyaki: flavorful, savory soy sauce and ginger marinade for beef, chicken, pork and seafood

Tonkatsu: pork cutlet grilled golden brown, served with *tonkatsu* sauce

Udon: noodles served with soup broth, green onions, fish cake slices, optional meat

Wasabi: very spicy green horseradish root used to dip sushi into

KOREAN FOODS

Kalbi ribs: flavored similarly to teriyaki, but with chili pepper, sesame oil and green onions

Kim chee: spicy pickled cabbage flavored with ginger and garlic

Mandoo: fried dumplings with meat and vegetable fillings

Mandoo kook, bi bim kook, yook kae jang: soups served with *mandoo* dumplings, noodles, vegetables, and a variety of meats

Meat or fish jun: fried or broiled beef or fish with teriyaki-type sauce

Spicy barbecue beef, chicken or pork: broiled soy sauce–flavored beef, chicken or pork laced with spicy hot chili

LOCAL FAVORITES

Bento: a box lunch might include tempura shrimp, veggies, scoop of noodles, sushi roll or rice

Loco moco: a combination of hamburger patty atop a bowl of rice with fried egg and gravy

Plate lunches: a traditional favorite might include teriyaki beef or chicken, hamburger with gravy, roast pork, fried fish or any of several other entrees; traditionally served with steamed white rice and often a scoop of macaroni salad

Saimin: noodles served in broth with fish cake, veggies

Shave ice: ground ice—mainlanders know it as snowcones, except the ice is more finely shaved—topped with flavored syrups such as strawberry, pineapple, guava, vanilla, mango, root beer, *lilikoi*

PUERTO RICAN FOODS

Pasteles: an exterior of grated green banana that is filled with pork and vegetables

THAI/VIETNAMESE FOOD

Fried noodles/fried rice: crispy/soft fried noodles with meat entree and soft rice with meat and vegetables

Green curry: choice of meat entree with peas, string beans, coconut milk and sweet basil

Mein noodles: egg noodle soup with shrimp, seafood or other entree

Musaman curry: curry with onion, peanuts, carrots and potatoes in coconut milk

Pad Thai: Thai-style pan-fried noodles with choice of meat entree or veggies garnished with sprouts

Pho noodle soup: noodle soup with beefsteak, meatball, chicken or combination with veggies

Red curry: choice of meat entree with bamboo shoots in coconut milk and sweet basil

Rice noodle soup: rice stick noodles with shrimp, pork, fish cake, squid or other seafood

Satay sticks: broiled chicken, pork or beef on skewer sticks, served as a side dish

Vermicelli cold noodles: thin, clear noodles combined with meat or seafood entree and veggies

Yellow curry: chicken with coconut milk and potatoes

A FEW WORDS ABOUT FISH

Whether cooking fish at your condominium or eating out, the names of the island fish can be confusing. While local shore fishermen catch shallow-water fish such as goatfish or *papio* for their dinner table, commercial fishermen angle for two types. Steakfish are caught by trolling in deep waters and include ahi, *ono* and mahimahi. The more delicate bottom fish include *opakapaka* and *onaga*, which are caught with lines dropped as deep as 1,500 feet to shelves off the island coastlines. Here is some background on what you might find on your dinner plate.

Ahi: yellowfin (Allison tuna) is caught in deep waters off Kaua'i and weighs 60 to 280 pounds; pinkish red meat is firm yet flaky and popular for sashimi

Aku: a bluefin tuna that has a stronger taste than ahi

Albacore: a smaller version of the ahi, averages 40 to 50 pounds and is lighter in both texture and color; also called *koshibi*

A'u: the broadbill swordfish, or marlin; a dense and sometimes dry fish

Ehu: orange snapper

Hapu: Hawaiian sea bass

Kamakamaka: Island catfish, very tasty but a little difficult to find

Lehi: a silver-mouth member of the snapper family, with a stronger flavor than *onaga* or *opakapaka* and a texture resembling mahimahi

Mahimahi: called the dolphin fish, but has no relation to Flipper or his friends; caught while trolling and weighs between 10 to 65 pounds; excellent white meat that is moist and light and very good sauteed; a seasonal fish that commands a high price when fresh. **Beware**: while excellent fresh, mahimahi is often served in restaurants having arrived from the Philippines frozen, making it far less pleasing. A clue as to whether it's fresh or frozen may be the price tag. If it runs less than $10 to $15 it is probably the frozen variety. Fresh mahimahi will cost more

Mu'u: I tried this mild white fish at the Makawao Steak House years ago and was told there is no common name for this fish. I've never seen it served elsewhere in restaurants

Onaga: caught in holes that are 1,000 feet or deeper, this red snapper has an attractive hot-pink exterior with tender, juicy white meat inside

Ono: also known as *wahoo*; a member of the barracuda family, its white meat is firm and more steak-like. *Ono* means "delicious" in Hawaiian

'Opae: shrimp

Opakapaka: pink snapper; meat is very light and flaky with a delicate flavor

Papio: a baby *ulua* caught in shallow waters

FOOD FESTIVALS

Grand Chefs at Kea Lani (Wailea) teams prominent chefs from the mainland and Hawai'i for a variety of events. The Lana'i Visiting Artists program at the Lodge at Koele frequently features guest chefs. April's "Ulupalakua Thing" (Upcountry) is an agricultural fair with food samplings. The Kapalua Wine & Food Festival in July is a chance to taste wines from all over the world and seafood from the island's best chefs. September's Taste of Lahaina offers both a dinner and food festival at which you can sample food from a variety of West Maui restaurants. For details on these and other upcoming culinary events call Interactive Events 800-961-9196 or e-mail: events@maui.net. (They can also help you create your own culinary event, whether it's meeting a favorite chef, adding to a cookbook collection, touring an agricultural farm or food manufacturing company, or attending a cooking class.)

Uku: grey snapper, light, firm and white meat with a texture that varies with size

Ulua: also known as pompano, this fish is firm and flaky with steak-like, textured white meat

Dining Best Bets

Top Restaurants My criteria for a top restaurant are excellence of food preparation and presentation, a pleasing atmosphere, and service that anticipates or responds promptly to one's needs. While the following exemplify these criteria, they are also all "deep pocket" restaurants, so expect to spend $100 or more for your meal, wine and gratuity for two. Generally, anything you order at these restaurants will be excellent. Remember, even the best restaurants may have an "off" night, but these are seldom. Also, chefs and management do change, rendering what you may have found to be excellent on one occasion to be quite different the next. However, the following have proven to be consistent through the years. Enjoy your meal, enjoy being a little bit spoiled, and remember that muumuus are great for covering up all those calories. *Lahaina:* Chez Paul; David Paul's; Pacific 'O; I'o. *Ka'anapali:* Swan Court. *Honokowai–Kapalua Area*: Plantation House; Roy's Kahana; Banyan Tree. *Wailea–Makena Area*: Hakone; Prince Court; Ferraro's; Spago.

Top Restaurants in a More Casual Atmosphere While some of these restaurants are slightly less expensive, it is still easy to spend $70 or more for dinner for two. They serve a superior meal in a less formal atmosphere. *Lahaina:* Canoes; Kimo's. *Ka'anapali:* Hula Grill; tropica; Va Bene. *Honokowai–Kapalua Area*: Sansei. *Ma'alaea–Kihei Area:* Five Palms Beach Grill; Sarento's; Waterfront Restaurant. *Wailea–Makena Area:* Le Gunji; Nick's Fishmarket; Sea Watch Restaurant; Taiko. *Upcountry:* Hali'imaile General Store.

Best Restaurants for a Great View *Lahaina:* Kimo's, Bubba Gump's, Pacific 'O; *Ka'anapali*: Castaway Café, tropica; *Napili*: Gazebo, Sea House; *Kapalua*: Plantation House; *Wailea*: Ferraro's, Sarento's, Sea Watch; *Kihei*: Five Palms Beach Grill; *Kula*: Kula Lodge.

"Local" Restaurants For years I have delighted in exploring the many small, family-owned "local" restaurants, especially in Kahului and Wailuku. The food in these establishments is not only plentiful and well-prepared, but also relatively inexpensive. The service is often better and friendlier than at many of the resort establishments. *Honokowai–Kapalua Area:* Honokowai Okazuya & Deli. *Kahului–Wailuku Area:* A Saigon Café; Fiesta Time; Mama

Ding's; Nazo's; Saeng's Thai Cuisine; Sam Sato's; Tasty Crust; Tokyo Tei. *Hana Highway:* Hana Hou.

Most Romantic Any of Maui's restaurants offering ocean and sunset views could be considered great spots for romance. Although it has no view, Chez Paul in Olowalu is a wonderfully intimate little French restaurant. Very romantic. Also, check out the Dinner Under the Stars program offered by the Sheraton Maui Resort on Ka'anapali Beach. They have three menus to choose from, or arrange your own customized selection of dining items. Several romantic and spectacular locations are on the property—by a waterfall, at the beach, on the ocean lawn, etc. You have your very own private server who sees to your every wish. For Valentine's Day, the Maui Ocean Center offers an incredibly romantic dining experience, with your own private table set alongside one of the spectacular indoor aquariums. Low lighting, soft music, private dining—offered only once a year, for valentines.

Best Ambiance Gerard's in Lahaina, The Waterfront in Ma'alaea, Swan Court at Hyatt Regency Maui, Ka'anapali, Hali'imaile General Store in Upcountry. *Oceanside Dining*: Hula Grill in Ka'anapali, Mama's Fish House in Paia.

The Place to See and Be Seen *West Maui:* David Paul's; *South Maui:* Spago.

Sushi Bar Sansei Restaurant in Kihei and Kapalua.

French Chez Paul in Olowalu.

Seafood Mama's Fish House in Paia, Waterfront Restaurant in Ma'alaea and Nick's Fishmarket at Fairmont Kea Lani in Wailea.

Seafood Buffet All of the top restaurants have wonderful seafood, but an all-you-can-eat buffet is a seafood-lover's dream come true. You'll find such buffets at Kapalua Bay Hotel's Gardenia Court Restaurant, Renaissance Wailea Beach Resort's Palm Court, Wailea Marriott's Hula Moons Restaurant and the Maui Prince Hotel's Prince Court.

Daily Breakfast Buffets Most of the large resort hotels offer a great breakfast buffet daily. Swan Court at Hyatt Regency Maui is one of the best. The least expensive and most casual is at the Ka'anapali Beach Hotel's Ka'anapali Mixed Plate.

Sunday Brunches There really are no "best" in Sunday brunches—they're all wonderful. (And you may not have to eat for the next two days.) However, the Sunday Brunch at the Prince Court (Maui Prince Hotel) and Gardenia Court (Kapalua Bay Hotel) both continue to be at the top of the list for locals and visitors year after year.

French Toast Castaway Cafe at Maui Ka'anapali Villas made with "Jeannie's bread."

Pizza BJ's Chicago Pizzeria in Lahaina.
Hamburger with a View Cheeseburger in Paradise, Lahaina.
Sandwiches The Peking Duck sandwich at Longhi's, Mr. Sub in Lahaina, Sub Paradise in Kahului, the *kalua* turkey sandwich at Pauwela Café in Haiku, the Vietnamese sandwiches at Ba-Le in Lahaina Cannery Mall and Kahului's Maui Marketplace.
Rotisserie Chicken Cilantro in Lahaina has the most delicious, moist rotisserie chicken. Eat in or take it back to your condo.
BBQ Ribs Azeka's Ribs & Snack Shop in Kihei; Mama's Ribs-n-Rotisserie in Napili.
Appetizers The lettuce wraps at Café O'Lei or Ma'alaea Grill; the Asian coconut milk soup at Spago; the rock shrimp cake at Sansei; the *carpaccio* or *frutta di mare* (a lavish array of seafood appetizers) at Sarento's; the fresh foie gras with scallops at Restaurant Taiko.
Dessert BJ's Chicago Pizzeria's own invention, the "pizookie," is a big winner. Roy's hot chocolate soufflé—à la mode, of course. And who couldn't love Kimo's hula pie?
Hawaiian Tiki Terrace or Ka'anapali Mixed Plate at the Ka'anapali Beach Hotel, Hana Hou in Haiku, Cary & Eddie's Hideaway in Kahului, Aloha Mixed Plate in Lahaina, Pukalani Country Club in Upcountry, and Da Kitchen in Kahului or Kihei.
Family Dining Experience Bubba Gump Shrimp Company, Lahaina; Ruby's Diner or Koho Grill and Bar, both at Queen Ka'ahumanu Center in Kahului.
Bakeries The Bakery in Lahaina (wonderful French pastries), central Maui's Home Maid Bakery (fantastic bread pudding), The Four Sisters Bakery in Wailuku (Filipino specialties), The Maui Bake Shop in Kahului (fine pastries and cakes). Stillwell's Bakery in Kahului—one of Maui's finest. Komoda Store and Bakery in Makawao is famous for its cream puffs. Arrive past 10 a.m. and you'll likely not get any!
Vegetarian Down to Earth is a "health food" store located in Kahului and Makawao; in addition to their grocery items they offer hot vegetarian dishes and a salad bar priced by the pound. Fresh Mint in Paia and Kahului offers excellent Vietnamese/Vegetarian/Vegan cuisine.
Lu'au The lu'au at Wailea Marriott; the Old Lahaina Lu'au.

EARLY-BIRD DINNERS

Hours vary, but early-bird dinners are offered during a small window of time usually beginning around 5 or 5:30 p.m. and ending by 6 p.m. Meals are often the same ones you would pay more for an hour later, but selections are limited. This used to be a huge marketing trend but now very few are available. Be sure to check in some of the local papers for seasonal dinner specials.

Lahaina

Inexpensive-priced Dining

A & J Kitchen Deli & Bakery *(Local)*

Lahaina Center, 900 Front Street; 808-667-0623.

Hours: 8 a.m.-3 p.m. Monday through Saturday; closed Sunday. *Sampling:* Big breakfasts are just the ticket for the hearty eater, with 3 eggs, rice, Spam or another breakfast meat; breakfast sandwich, pancakes and eggs ($6.59-$7.59). Breakfast specials ($5) offered 8-11 a.m. Kids' menus, too. Try local plates with two scoops rice, *kim chee* or macaroni salad and entrees like chicken *katsu*, *mochiko* chicken or chili and rice ($7-$8). Korean plates include *kalbi* ribs, meat *jun*, and even *mandoo* soup. Chef's favorites include egg foo yong, oyster-sauce chicken and *char-siu* fried rice ($7-$8.99). Also deli sandwiches and burgers ($5.50-$7.50). *Comments*: Two hours free validated parking at Lahaina Center.

Alexander's Fish, Chicken & Chips *(American)*

Lahaina Square, 840 Wainee Street, Lahaina; 808-667-9009; also a location in Kihei.

(See "Kihei Dining" for hours and menu description.) The Lahaina location has a large, open-air patio for dining.

★ ***Aloha Mixed Plate*** *(Local/Hawaiian)*

1285 Front Street, across from the Lahaina Cannery; 808-661-3322; www.alohamixedplate.com.

Hours: 10:30 a.m.-10 p.m.; happy hour specials 2-6 p.m. *Sampling:* Plate lunches, salads, *saimin* and other noodle dishes, "grilled stuff," burgers and sandwiches ($2.95-$9.95). Hawaiian plate lunches include *kalua* pig, *laulau*, and even *lomi lomi* salmon and *haupia* ($7.95-$12.95). *Comments:* Good food and reasonably priced. Pleasant outdoor patio dining with an ocean view. Very casual dining. Named "Best Plate Lunch" in the 2005 'Aipono Awards.

The Bakery *(Pastries)*

911 Limahana (turn off Honoapi'ilani Highway by Pizza Hut); 808-667-9062.

Hours: Monday through Friday 5:30 a.m.-3 p.m. Saturday 5:30 a.m.-2 p.m. Sunday 5:30 a.m.-noon. *Sampling:* Chocolate almond and whole-wheat cream cheese croissants, cinnamon rolls topped with pecans or honey or filled with raisins, and coconut macaroons. A daily selection of stuffed croissants usually sells out quickly. Also don't forget the great fresh breads and fruit tortes ($1.50-$5). *Comments:* A to-go eatery. Arrive early in the day for better selection. Everything is delicious and it's well worth the stop if you are a pastry lover.

★ ***BJ's Chicago Pizzeria*** *(Italian)*
730 Front Street; 808-661-0700.

Hours: 11 a.m.-11 p.m. Sunday through Thursday; until midnight Friday and Saturday. *Sampling:* Start with BJ's bruschetta, toasted ravioli or their own invention, the pizza-dilla: quesadilla-like triangles of pizza dough with a creamy topping of artichoke, spinach and cheese ($5.95-$9.95). Then order a basic cheese and tomato pizza and add your own toppings or try one of their innovative specialties like "BBQ Chicken" or "Shrimp Thermidor" ($8-$25). Calzones for one ($5.95) or two ($9.95), too. BJ's specialty salads include chopped Italian, sesame chicken or chopped barbecue chicken ($4.95-$9.70). Lots of pasta dishes ($8.50-$13.95), as well as homemade sandwiches on BJ's freshly baked rolls including meatball, Italian sub, and three varieties of chicken: barbecue, Caesar or Italian ($6.95-$7.45). *Comments:* This Front Street landmark is filled with woodwork, murals and historic photographs. Same menu all day. Their delicious deep-dish Chicago-style pizza has a crust that is thick while surprisingly light, and the toppings are fresh and innovative. Wash it down with a festive Tropitini, a spirited ice cream cooler, or BJ's original-recipe mai tai made with Grand Marnier. But leave room for dessert. You won't be able to resist the Pizookie n' Cream: a chocolate chip or white chocolate and macadamia cookie baked fresh in a mini-pizza pan and served warm with vanilla ice cream. Live contemporary island music nightly. Named "Best Pizza" in the 2005 'Aipono Awards.

Blue Lagoon Tropical Bar and Grill *(American)*
Wharf Cinema Center (lower level), 658 Front Street; 808-661-8141.

Hours: Breakfast 8:30 a.m.-11:30 a.m.; lunch/dinner continuous menu 10 a.m.-9 p.m. Happy hour 3-6 p.m. and 9-11:59 p.m. Tropical bar open until 2 a.m. *Sampling:* Breakfast offers *loco moco*, egg dishes, pancakes or French toast ($3.95-$8.95). Burgers and sandwiches include French fries or macaroni salad and range from tuna melt to BLT or burgers ($5.95-$9.95). House specialties include pineapple fried rice or beer-battered fish and chips. Pizzas, soups, pastas, steaks and salads round out the choices ($5.95-$15.95). *Comments:* Very attractive setting. Dine in the courtyard of the shopping center, surrounded by waterfalls and koi ponds.

Captain Dave's Fish & Chips/Pipeline Pizza *(Fish & Chips/Pizza)*
Lahaina Marketplace, 129 Lahainaluna Road off Front Street; 808-661-7888.

Hours: 8:30 a.m.-9:30 p.m. *Sampling: Ono* and chips, prawns and chips, clams and chips, calamari and chips, grilled *ono* or chicken strips; half orders also available. ($5-$10). Salads ($4-$7), sandwiches ($2-$6). Pizzas ($8-$10). *Comments:* All main-menu fish items can be ordered fried (in 100 percent canola oil) or broiled and come with French fries, Maui coleslaw (with pineapple) and homemade tartar or cocktail sauce.

Cheeseburger in Paradise *(American)*
811 Front Street; 808-661-4855. Sister location called Cheeseburger, Mai Tais & Rock 'N Roll at Shops at Wailea, 3750 Wailea Alanui; 808-661-4855.

Hours: Breakfast 8-11 a.m., lunch/dinner 11 a.m.-10 p.m. *Sampling:* This is the place to get a 100 percent natural Meyer Angus beef cheeseburger, or a variety of creative salads and sandwiches. The spicy island chicken sandwich is covered with Cajun spices; the Polynesian chicken salad sandwich has chunks of fresh grilled chicken blended with mango chutney, peppers, pineapple and other goodies. Gobble up a Portuguese turkey burger, garden burger or tofu burger. Calamari sandwich, tuna salad and other seafood sandwiches and a half-dozen salad selections. A basic cheeseburger is $7.95. Other sandwich selections $5.95-$9.95. Add seasoned fries for $3.75, *ono* onion rings for $4.75, chili cheese fries for $6. Finish off your cheeseburger your way with Ortega chilies, grilled Maui pineapple, bacon, guacamole or mushrooms $1-$2. Breakfast offers a varied menu of eggs, pancakes and other popular breakfast items ($5.95-$9.95). *Comments:* A casual and fun atmosphere with open-air dining and wonderful views of the Lahaina Harbor and Front Street from the upstairs loft. You can't go wrong with a cheeseburger and fries, and the other stuff is good, too. Try some of their tropical drinks like Trouble in Paradise (or if you want to stay out of trouble, try the thick and chunky non-alcoholic Oreo cookie smoothie). It can be crowded at meal times, but the lines move along pretty quickly.

★ ***Cilantro Fresh Mexican Grill*** *(Mexican)*
170 Papalaua Avenue, Lahaina (Old Lahaina Center); 808-667-5444; www.cilantrogrill.com.

Hours: Monday through Thursday 11 a.m.-9:30 p.m.; Friday and Saturday 11 a.m.-10 p.m.; Sunday 11 a.m.-8 p.m. *Sampling:* Try the guacamole "tom-tom" (a chunky mix of tomatoes and tomatillos with avocados and onions) served with homemade tortilla chips ($4.50). The tacos and burritos ($3.25-$7.95) have lots of interesting and unusual ingredients, are hearty and very fresh. Try a Muy Margarita burrito (with shrimp), a Taco Baja (beer battered *ono* topped with jicama slaw) or a *torta* (Mexican sandwich with grilled bread) of carne asada, *adobo* roasted pork, grilled *ono* or rotisserie chicken. Combo meals ($6.95-$8.95) and plenty of side dishes offer lots of diversity. Try the *horchata*, a Mexican beverage of rice milk with cinnamon. Save room for Tres Leches, a moist creamy vanilla cake served with peaches and cinnamon. There is a salsa bar offering a variety of chilies and condiments. *Comments:* Don't let the "Mexican" name discourage you—this is not your typical Mexican restaurant. The food here is great, and there's something for everyone. Fresh, fresh, fresh ingredients with great flavor combinations. A casual, colorful dining area. Eat in or take out. And their moist, delicious lemon-herb rotisserie chicken is hands-down the best rotisserie chicken on the island (buy a whole chicken and take it home—$13.75). Cilantro is a new addition to Lahaina, and it's a winner.

Cool Cat Café *(Diner)*

Wharf Cinema Center, 658 Front Street; 808-667-0908.

Hours: Lunch/dinner menu 11 a.m.-10 p.m. Take-out available. *Sampling:* Appetizers ($3.69-$10.99) include hula sticks (pineapple with sweet Maui onion marinated and charbroiled), onion rings, chili fries or ahi sticks. Burgers (all 1/3 lb. beef patty) include the Bogey Burger topped with bacon and cheese, the Marilyn Burger (because "some like it hot") with melted jack cheese and green ortega chile peppers, and The Duke, where you get your burger topped with bacon, cheese, onion rings and their special barbecue sauce ($7.49-$11.89). Other sandwiches include the Elvis melt (tuna), Betty Boop (BLT) or Chubby Chicken ($6.99-$11.99). Dinner selections are served with potato or rice and garlic bread and include ribeye steak, baby back ribs or fresh catch of the day ($14.95-$22.95). Kids' menu, too ($3.59-$4.99). *Comments:* Take a trip down memory lane with their black-and-white floor, mirrored walls and 1955 Seeburg 100 jukebox. Chrome chairs, Formica tables and a counter with barstools where you can sip on some real ice cream shakes and malts. A full bar with seating inside and outside. Live music.

Curry in a Hurry *(Vegetarian/Indian)*

Lahaina Square Shopping Center, 840 Wainee Street, Lahaina; 808-661-4370.

Hours: Monday through Friday noon-8 p.m. *Sampling and Comments:* Owners Hans and Lori Lee Mayne recently moved their Curry in a Hurry eatery from Kahului into a little kiosk in the parking lot of Lahaina Square Shopping Center. Don't let its rather unusual location dissuade you from giving this place a try. The food is good and very interesting. They specialize in Ayurveda cooking, which they describe as "matching your diet to your *dosha*, or mind-body type, to insure your health and well-being." All fresh food. No pre-fab, frozen, microwaved or deep fried. All items under $10.

Gaby's Pizzeria & Deli *(Italian)*
505 Front Street; 808-661-8112.

Hours: 11 a.m.-midnight. Happy hour noon-3 p.m. and 9-11 p.m. *Sampling:* Try one of their "original pizza rolls" ($7.95-$12.95) or house-special pizzas, Neapolitan or Sicilian ($18-$25). Half pizzas available as well, or by the slice. Their deli features assorted meats and Italian specialty items, or try their hot and cold sandwiches ($6.45-$8.95) as well as pasta dishes ($10.95-$14.95).

House of Saimin *(Local)*
Old Lahaina Center; 808-667-7572.

Hours: Tuesday through Thursday 5 p.m.-2 a.m. Friday and Saturday until 3 a.m. Closed Sunday and Monday. *Sampling:* Saimin, soups, sandwiches, burgers, stews ($3.50-$7). *Comments:* One big central counter and late-night hours. This little eatery was named "Best Mom-and-Pop Restaurant" in the 2005 'Aipono Awards.

Kahuna Kabobs *(Healthy/Local)*
Lahaina Marketplace; 808-661-9999.

Hours: 9 a.m.-9:30 p.m. (until 10 p.m. Friday and Saturday). *Sampling:* From the grill choose shrimp, chicken, tofu, steak or fish kabobs ($6.95-$9.50), all served with choice of sauce, rice and mac salad. Or try their chili and rice plate, Indian Blackened Ahi Steak Plate, "Island-Style" Curry, or meat or veggie wraps ($4.20-$11.95). A veggie burger, boca (soy based) burger or 1/3 lb. *kahuna* burger ($6.95). *Comments:* Dining available around the courtyard at shaded tables. Reasonably priced and a cool respite from your day in Lahaina Town.

Lahaina Cannery Mall *(Food Court)*
1221 Honoapi'ilani Highway, Lahaina; 808-667-0952; www.lahainacannerymall.com.

A great place for family dining (and shopping) where there is something for everyone. You'll find Edo Japan (teppanyaki, sushi, rice bowls), L&L Drive-Inn (local-style plate lunches), Athens Greek Restaurant (gyros, shish kebabs), Chopsticks Express (Chinese plate lunches), Pizza-Rama and Compadres (see individual listing). Also try Ba-Le Sandwiches for one of their *pho* soups or their delicious sandwiches served on their freshly baked French bread.

Maui Swiss Café *(Eclectic/Internet Café)*
640 Front Street; 808-661-6776; www.swisscafe.net.

Hours: 9 a.m.-8 p.m. *Sampling:* Hot and cold sandwiches include turkey broccoli melt, roast beef, ham or turkey and a number of vegetarian sandwiches and salads as well ($6.50-$8.95). Individual-size 8-inch pizzas ($7.95-$8.45). *Comments:* Sip a coffee drink, a smoothie or a milk shake while checking your e-mail at 15¢ per minute/$2 minimum (other rates available) for high-speed access. Or you can get a rate of 10¢ minute during internet "Happy Hour" 5:30-7:30 p.m. Located off Front Street between the Wharf Cinema Center and Burger King.

★ ***Maui Tacos*** *(Healthy/Mexican)*
Lahaina Square Shopping Center, 840 Wainee Street, 808-661-8883. Other locations at Napili Plaza, Napili, 808-665-0222; Kama'ole Beach Center, Kihei, 808-879-5005; Ka'ahumanu Center, Kahului, 808-871-7726.

Hours: 9 a.m.-9 p.m.; Sunday until 8 p.m. *Sampling:* Hard or soft tacos, quesadillas, nachos, and over a dozen varieties of huge burritos (14-16 ounces) with char-grilled steak, chicken and seafood marinated in pineapple, lime juices and spices from the islands. Vegetarian combinations with black beans. Nothing over $6.95. *Comments:* Guacamole and salsa made fresh everyday. No lard, no MSG—they use only vegetable oil, fresh beans and lean meats. The complimentary salsa bar offers several choices with jalapenos, onions, cilantro, hot sauce and more. This is not traditional Mexican food, nor is it traditional "fast food," but a healthier variation of both. Good, fresh food. Large servings.

Mr. Sub *(Sandwiches)*
129 Lahainaluna Road; 808-667-5683.

Hours: Monday through Friday 8 a.m.-5 p.m. Saturday until 4 p.m. Closed Sunday. *Sampling:* Sandwiches with one or two items like turkey, tuna, egg salad, roast beef, and Danish ham ($4.95-$6.95). Specialty sandwiches ($5.95-$8.95) or wraps ($6.25). Caesar, chef's, Chinese chicken, garden and fruit salads, or chicken or tuna in half a papaya ($2.95-$7.25). Great choice of breads, too. *Comments:* This place offers some of the best subs on the island and also features "wraps"—chicken Caesar, Salsa or Ranch rolled up burrito-style in a tasty spinach or jalapeno cheese tortilla. Pick up some for a picnic lunch. Free delivery in Lahaina Town Monday through Saturday 11 a.m.-2 p.m.

Moose McGillycuddy's *(American)*

844 Front Street, upper level of Mariner's Alley, a small shopping alley at the north end of town; 808-667-7758.

Hours: Breakfast 7:30 a.m.-11 a.m. Lunch 11 a.m.-4 p.m. Dinner 4-10 p.m. Happy hour 3-6 p.m. *Sampling:* Early birds can take advantage of the breakfast special for $1.99 (served 7:30-8:30 a.m.). Late risers can dine on "chicken feed" (3 eggs, meat, potatoes and toast), *loco moco*, moose cakes (buttermilk, macadamia or banana pancakes), breakfast quesadilla or other breakfast choices ($3.95-$11.95). For lunch sample a gourmet burger served with fries and your choice of toppings ($7.45-$11.95). Sandwiches such as fresh fish, meatballs or French dip and entrees such as chicken fajitas, lasagna, fish tacos or spaghetti ($6.95-$13.95). Dinner entrees include mahi macadamia, Moose's prime rib, chicken fried steak, garlic shrimp skewers, or Mexican and Italian entrees ($8.25-$21.95). There's chocolate "moose" pie for dessert ($5.95) and an extensive selection of fun, tropical drinks. *Comments:* A great stop for breakfast in Lahaina. Get a table with a balcony view. This place gets hopping at night with lots of young adults and live music. A good food value. Check for early-bird or nightly specials. Late-night entertainment and dancing.

★ ***No Ka Oi Deli*** *(Sandwiches & Salads/Local)*

Anchor Square, 222 Papalaua Street (facing Wainee Street); 808-667-2244.

Hours: Monday through Friday 10 a.m.-2 p.m.; closed Saturday and Sunday. *Sampling:* A good variety of subs (French dip, teri chicken or beef, pastrami, and seafood, tuna, egg or chicken salad) and salads (chef, Caesar, and Chinese chicken) plus daily plate-lunch specials. Nothing over $7. Side specialties, too, like spinach rolls. Fountain drinks, smoothies and shave ice. Homemade cookies or order a picnic to go. *Comments:* "Home of the Famous HOP WO Bread." The Hop Wo Store was a landmark on Front Street from 1917 to its closure in 1985 and now a younger generation of this family is carrying on the tradition.

Penne Pasta Café *(Italian)*

180 Dickenson Street; 808-661-6633.

Hours: Monday through Friday 11 a.m.-9:30 p.m. Saturday and Sunday 5-9:30 p.m. *Sampling:* This is another restaurant of Mark Ellman, known for his Maui Tacos chain. Pizzas and flatbreads ($2.25-$8.25). Sandwiches such as mozzarella, tomato, basil and greens, or roast chicken salad ($6.25-$7.95). Enjoy a variety of pastas from classic fettuccine alfredo to bolognese fettuccine to penne *puttanesca* and even whole wheat spaghetti with roasted eggplant and tomatoes ($6.75-$9.95). Add garlic ahi ($3.95) or chicken breast ($3.25) to any pasta. *Comments:* Good food; reasonable prices; casual dining. They deliver Monday through Friday 11 a.m.-2 p.m. in Lahaina Town.

Pho Saigon 808 *(Vietnamese/Vegetarian)*
658 Front Street, Lahaina (Wharf Cinema Center); 808-661-6628.

Hours: 10 a.m.-9:30 p.m. *Sampling:* Wide range of authentic Vietnamese soups, appetizers, salads, noodles, rice plate lunches, curry dishes, wok dishes, and clay pot specialties ($4.95-$15.95). Also a selection of vegetarian appetizers, burritos and entrees. *Comments:* Opened in 2004; owned and operated by husband and wife Phi Nguyen and Thanh Van Vo.

Ramon's Cantina *(Mexican)*
Wharf Cinema Center, 658 Front Street; 808-667-0845.

Hours: Breakfast 8-11 a.m. Monday through Friday, until 2 p.m. Saturday and Sunday; lunch/dinner daily 11 a.m.-10 p.m.; happy hours 2-6 p.m. and 10 p.m.-1 a.m. *Sampling:* Mexican- or American-style breakfasts such as omelets, pancakes and huevos rancheros ($2-$8.95). Lunch/dinner menu includes Mexican standards: burritos, tacos, enchiladas, chile relleno or taco salad ($5.95-$9.95). Full bar service.

Royal Seafood Chinese Restaurant *(Asian)*
Anchor Square, corner Papalaua and Wainee streets, across from McDonald's; 808-661-9955.

Hours: 10 a.m.-9:30 p.m. All-you-can-eat lunch buffet served until 2:30 p.m. *Sampling:* Seafood selections number almost three dozen, plus noodle dishes, soups, egg dishes, and vegetarian selections ($6.95-$18.00). Lunch buffet $7.55.

Sunrise Café *(Sandwiches/Light Meals)*
693A Front Street; 808-661-8558.

Hours: 6 a.m.-6 p.m. *Sampling:* Great patio dining just off the waterfront featuring quiche, pancakes, waffles and bagels ($4.95-$10.95). Lunch (until 6 p.m.) offers gourmet sandwiches and plate lunches such as mango barbecued beef or chicken, roast pork or tofu dishes ($5-$10). Homemade soups and plenty of salad options. *Comments:* This is a very small, quaint eatery with some nice outside tables or food available to go. It's all homemade and good, but the Hawaiian specialties stand out: *kalua* pork salad with Maui onions, pineapple, steamed cabbage and papaya; stuffed pasta shells with macadamia nut pesto; and mango barbecue chicken breast or *kalua* pork as a plate lunch or a sandwich.

Take Home Maui *(American)*
121 Dickenson Street; 808-667-7056. For mail order call 808-661-8067.

Hours: 7:30 a.m.-6:30 p.m. *Sampling:* You might pass by this place, but don't. Stop by for a yummy smoothie ($3.25) or sit on the porch and enjoy some quiche, empanadas, veggie lasagna, or sandwich ($2.50-$7). Bagels and breakfast pastries every morning ($2-$7). Ice cream and sodas in the freezer. *Comments:* Papayas, pineapples, onions and Hawaiian coffee are among the items to be shipped or taken home. They offer free airport or hotel delivery. The staff is helpful and friendly—lots of aloha here.

Thai Chef *(Thai)*
Old Lahaina Center, 880 Front Street; 808-667-2814.

Hours: Lunch Monday through Friday 11 a.m.-2 p.m. Dinner nightly 5-9 p.m. *Sampling:* Traditional Thai dishes such as Thai crispy noodles, Thai toast, green papaya salad, long rice chicken soup, Evil Prince, pad Thai, crab with yellow curry sauce, and more ($6.95-$15.95). Combination dinners for two to four ($36.95-$72.95). *Comments:* A very extensive menu ranging from noodle dishes to salads, seafoods, vegetarian fare, and curry dishes. Entrees available in mild, medium or hot. No bar, but you can bring your own bottle.

Zushi *(Japanese)*
Lahaina Square Shopping Center, 840 Wainee Street; 808-667-5142.

Hours: Lunch 11 a.m.-2 p.m. Dinner 5-8:30 p.m. Closed Sunday. *Comments:* Fried chicken teriyaki, tempura, *shoyu* chicken and udon are lunch entrees ($5-$7). Dinners include cooked fish, combination dinners and slightly higher prices and larger portions of the lunch items ($8-$13).

Moderate-priced Dining

★ ***Bubba Gump Shrimp Company Restaurant & Market*** *(Seafood)*
889 Front Street; 808-661-3111.

Hours: 11 a.m.-10:30 p.m. Bar open until midnight. *Sampling:* Start with Peel 'n Eat Shrimp, Bubba's Far Out Dip (spinach, artichokes, jack cheese and roasted red pepper), or Old Fashioned New England Clam Chowder ($4.29-$13.99). Shrimp entrees include Mama Blue's Southern Charmed Fried Shrimp, Shrimp New Orleans, Shrimp Shack Pasta, or Dumb Luck Coconut Shrimp—the best crispy, crunchy coconut shrimp I've ever tasted ($14.29-$18.99). If you're not a shrimp lover, there are plenty of other selections like Mama's Southern Fried Chicken, Bourbon Street Mahimahi, or Salmon and Veggie Skillet ($10.99-$18.99). Sandwiches include fishwich, barbecue pork, chicken or burgers ($7.99-$9.99). For dessert try a chocolate chip cookie sundae, Jenny's Strawberry Dream, Mama's Cinnamon Bread Pudding or sip on Forrest's Dr. Pepper Float ($4.29-$5.99). *Comments:* This is a great family restaurant, fun for kids as well as adults. Inspired by the award-winning movie Forrest Gump, this is a part of the chain that began in Monterey and San Francisco. "Gumpisms" prevail—from the "Run Forrest Run" sign that signals for service to the "box of chocolates" (as in "life is like") in the adjacent market. Like newspaper is to fish and chips, the funky boathouse decor and tin bucket table service is to Bubba Gump's. The friendly service, creative food presentations and general ambiance of silliness (the restaurant manager greeted our table with a shrimp bucket on his head) are more than enough to keep you interested, so it's impressive that they offer cut-above extras: tartar sauce with lime and orange rind, cocktail sauce with tequila, homemade coleslaw, and "real" Key lime pie. The all-day menu makes the entrees a bargain for dinner, but maybe a bit expensive for lunch unless you select a sandwich or salad. Portions are very generous, and they offer a child's menu ($4.59-$5.29). Overall good food and good value.

★ ***Café O'Lei*** *(Pacific Rim)*
839 Front Street; 808-661-9491.

Hours: Lunch 11 a.m.-3 p.m.; dinner 5-9 p.m. *Sampling:* Appetizers and salads include Manoa lettuce wraps (chicken, water chestnuts, shiitake mushrooms and ginger), and ahi-stuffed fried calamari. Or enjoy coconut ceviche with lobster and fresh island fish, feta potato cakes or *kalua* pork quesadilla, quinoa salad over baby greens, taro salad, or Caesar ($7.75-$14.95). Continuing with dinner entrees you can select from macadamia nut roast duckling, prime rib, grilled marinated jumbo shrimp or tempura mahi and chips as well as burgers, a crab club or an ahi sandwich ($7.95-$24.95). For dessert sample their pineapple upside-down cake (a specialty), *lilikoi* cheesecake, Kona coffee creme brulee or chocolate mousse cake ($5.95-$6.95). *Comments:* Great prices and oceanfront location; and great food, too. Rumor has it there will be new ownership and a new restaurant moving into this spot, but at press time Cafe O' Lei was still operating.

Café Sauvage *(Island Cuisine)*
844 Front Street; 808-661-7600.

Hours: Lunch 11:30 a.m.-3 p.m.; dinner 5:30-9:30 p.m. *Sampling:* Starters include sesame ahi poke, crisp calamari, or a salad of mixed greens, candied nuts, Asian pears and sesame ginger vinaigrette ($4.95-$12.95). Entrees range from peppered ahi steak and linguine with clam sauce to black sesame tempura prawns and grilled New York strip loin ($15.95-$26.95). *Comments:* A cozy little cafe tucked away in a courtyard off Front Street. Indoor or outdoor courtyard seating available.

★ ***Canoes*** *(American/Pacific Rim)*
1450 Front Street; 808-661-0937.

Hours: Lunch 11 a.m.–3 p.m.; dinner 5-9:30 p.m.; Sunday champagne brunch 9:30 a.m.-3 p.m. Lounge/bar open 4-10 p.m. *Sampling:* Lunch features a good selection of appetizers (crab and cheese won tons, Canoe Paddlers Crabcake), soup, salad, burgers and sandwiches ($6.95-$11.95). Lunch entrees such as chicken linguini, mango barbecue baby back ribs or crispy piña colada shrimp ($9.95-$16.95) Dinner appetizers include garlic steamed clams, *kalua* pork spring rolls or herb steamed artichoke ($5.95-$13.95). Dinners offer fresh catch, Asian tiger prawn pasta, Tahitian banana-mac chicken, pineapple braised beef shortribs, herb-crusted prime rib, and a variety of other steaks and seafood ($18.95-$34.95 including salad bar). *Comments:* This A-frame structure has been enhanced by polished wooden canoes hanging from the high ceiling and custom Hawaiian *ohia* wood railing around the open-air patio. An excellent salad bar is included with dinner entrees. The early bird special from 5-6 p.m. provides a three-course dinner for $22.95. A spectacular oceanfront view, lovely atmosphere, good quality and large portions for your vacation dollar.

Compadres *(Mexican)*
Lahaina Cannery Mall; 808-661-7189.

Hours: 8 a.m.-10 p.m., breakfast until noon. Lunch/dinner menu from 11 a.m. *Sampling:* Breakfast ($6-$10) features chorizo, enchilada, burrito egg dishes, huevos rancheros, and "grande" omelets. Gringo specialties include pineapple or macadamia pancakes, and sweet bread French toast. Their lunch/dinner menu starters include Mexican pizza, tortilla soup, *fajita* nachos, *chingalinga*, six-layer dip, *sopes* (Mexican bruschetta) and more ($5.95-$13.95). Then choose from a large selection of enchiladas, tacos, burritos, rellenos, chimichanga, salads, sandwiches and signature items such as *arroz con pollo, chile verde* and steak à la *tampiquena* ($7.50-$23.50). *Comments:* Compadres has an Oahu restaurant that I consider to be far better. I've found the food here to be inconsistent and the service sluggish. Not truly bad, but not really great, either. It's an "okay" place.

Front Street Grill and Bar *(Seafood/American)*
672 Front Street (upstairs), adjacent to the Wharf Cinema Center; 808-662-3003.

Hours: Lunch 11 a.m.–3:30 p.m.; dinner 5-9:30 p.m.; happy hour 3-5 p.m. *Sampling:* For lunch, salads, sandwiches, burgers and lunch plates ($5.50-$11.95). For dinner, fresh Hawaiian fish ($19.95-$24.95), seafood, pasta and entrees from the grill, such as ginger breast chicken, baby back pork ribs, prime rib or teriyaki sirloin ($14.95-$22.95). All entrees include fresh baked bread, rice and Caesar salad. *Keiki* menu ($5.25-$5.75). *Comments:* Upstairs open-air location overlooking Front Street. Nostalgic decor includes canoeing and surfing memorabilia, as well as other vintage items. Good food and generous servings; fast, friendly service.

★ ***Hard Rock Cafe*** *(American)*

Lahaina Center, 900 Front Street; 808-667-7400.

Hours: 11:30 a.m.-10 p.m. *Sampling:* Salads include grilled Chinese chicken, Cobb or Haystack chicken ($7.19-$9.39), burgers ($8.39-$9.29), or specialties such as grilled fajitas, Twisted Mac & Cheese, grilled sirloin steak or blackened chicken pasta ($10.99-$22.39). Smokehouse specialties such as barbecue ribs, chicken or pork, come with fries, barbecue beans and coleslaw ($9.39-$17.79). Their "Really Big Sandwiches" include Cajun chicken, grilled salmon or veggie ($8.99-$9.59). Full bar service. *Comments:* A lively atmosphere, if the music isn't too loud for you. Memorabilia on the restaurant walls and in the bathrooms include guitars owned by Eric Clapton, Slash of Guns 'N' Roses, the Grateful Dead, and Pearl Jam, plus Beatles photos and instruments. Homage is also paid to Hawai'i, surfing, and beach rock-and-roll. Great prices, good food and a trendy reputation make this a very popular eatery, so there may be a line waiting to get in during peak dining hours.

Hecocks *(American)*

505 Front Street; 808-661-8810.

Hours: Breakfast 8 a.m.-1:30 p.m. Lunch 11:30-2:30 p.m. Dinner 5-9 p.m. Bar open until 1:30 a.m. *Sampling:* Omelets, egg dishes, pancakes, French toast ($4.50-$8.75). Lunch offers salads and sandwiches such as French dip, teriyaki chicken, BLT or tuna ($3.25-$9.95). Dinner entrees feature seafood dishes like scallops, mahimahi or seafood picatta, Italian dishes such as sausage rigatoni and fettuccini alfredo, baby back ribs and steaks ($16.95-$26.95). *Comments:* My honest opinion? Don't bother. This restaurant is a waste of the ocean view, except maybe for breakfast. The meals I've had here were mediocre, and the last time I stopped in I was nearly choked by the cigarette smoke in the entry area and so put off by the attitude of the host I didn't stay. There are many better dining choices in Lahaina.

★ ***Kimo's*** *(American/Seafood)*
845 Front Street; 808-661-4811.

Hours: Lunch 11 a.m.-3 p.m. Dinner 5-10:30 p.m. Bar until 1 a.m. *Sampling:* For lunch, burgers, salads, sandwiches, *pupus* plus entrees like fish tacos and coconut-crusted fish ($4.95-$12.95) served on the oceanfront lanai. All dinner entrees include Kimo's Caesar salad, freshly baked carrot muffins and sourdough rolls, and steamed herb rice. Fresh fish of the day (prepared in one of five ways) is $21.95-$28.95. Steaks, prime rib, seafood or island favorites such as Polynesian chicken or Koloa pork ribs ($16.95-$29.95). *Keiki* menu. *Comments:* Great waterfront location and consistently good food. My experience has been very good service and well-prepared fresh fish. This is where you'll find the original hula pie (a huge piece of ice cream pie dripping with fudge topping)—it's still the biggest and the best, and heads turn every time one of these creations comes out of the kitchen. Dinners are served on the upstairs lanai—great for sunset-watching.

Kobe Japanese Steak House *(Teppanyaki/Sushi Bar)*
136 Dickenson Street; 808-667-5555.

Hours: 5:30-10 p.m.; sushi until 11:30 p.m. *Sampling:* Teriyaki chicken, sukiyaki steak, filet mignon, and plenty of combination dinners such as fish and chicken, scallops and steak, lobster and steak or shrimp and scallops ($9.95-$28.95). Dinners include soup, shrimp appetizer, vegetables, rice and tea. *Comments:* A sister of the Palm Springs and Honolulu restaurants, they offer teppan cooking (food is prepared on the grill in front of you) and the show is as good as the meal. Sunset specials served 5:30-6:30 p.m. ($11.95-$15.95). Sushi and sashimi items available individually or in chef-selected tray assortments. The sushi bar is popular with local residents and they're very accommodating to visitors. They'll make up your favorite sushi item if it is not on their menu. *Keiki* menu for children under 10 ($7-$11).

Lahaina Coolers *(American)*
Dickenson Square, 180 Dickenson Street; 808-661-7082. www.lahainacoolers.com.

Hours: 8 a.m.-2 a.m. Full dinner menu until midnight. *Sampling:* A variety of omelets, pancakes and specialty plates or make choices from a number of selections to create your own complete breakfast ($7.25-$10.95). For lunch they offer salads, sandwiches, burgers, pasta dishes, and other entrees, like fresh fish tacos ($8.50-$13.95). Dinners feature an interesting selection of salads along with pizzas and pastas ($12.95-$18.95). Entrees include their

Coolers Waimea pork chop, fresh catch, or seafood, chicken, steak variations ($13.95-$25.95). *Comments:* Quiet location off Front Street with patio, porch, or indoor open-air dining. Full bar service. We've had breakfast here a number of times and have always had a good experience.

Lahaina Fish Company *(Seafood/American)*
831 Front Street; 808-661-3472.

Hours: Lunch 11 a.m-5 p.m. Dinner 5-10 p.m. *Sampling:* Salads, sandwiches and burgers $7.95-$13.95 for lunch fare. The dinner menu features lots of seafood *pupus* from sashimi to oysters, steamer clams to peel-and-eat shrimp ($6.95-$13.95). Fish and shellfish entrees, homemade pasta dishes, steaks, local fare and poultry ($10.95-$28.95). Dinner also features several preparations of fresh fish ($21.95-$25.95). *Comments:* Pleasant setting on (in fact, right over) the ocean on Front Street. Children's menu (under age 10) $7.95.

Mala: An Ocean Tavern *(International)*
1307 Front Street, Lahaina. 808-667-9394.

Hours: Monday through Friday 11 a.m.-10 p.m.; Saturday 4:30-11 p.m.; Sunday 4:30-9:30 p.m. *Sampling: Tapas*-style dining with an international flair. The dishes have Latin, Indonesian and Middle Eastern leanings: shrimp à la plancha, spicy lamb pita, curry chicken wrap, *mulcajete* guacamole and salsa, and ahi croquette with *mojo verde*. Most items are in the $7-$15 range. Daily specials for lunch and dinner. *Comments:* This is the newest restaurant (opened 2004) by Mark and Judy Ellman, owners of Penne Pasta Cafe and Maui Tacos. The food items are fresh, unique, and often organic, with lovely presentations. Casual, open-air dining with seating inside or out. I found the dinner seating inside to be noisy and uncomfortably warm, so recommend you request a table outside looking over the water. Also found that the prices seem reasonable until you start ordering several of the *tapas* (servings are small and are meant to be shared), which can end up getting pretty expensive. Lunch for two was $33; dinner for four on another occasion was well over $100. The food is good and unusual, so Mala is worth a visit if you're looking for something different. But the food is probably a little too out-of-the-ordinary to suit children.

Pioneer Inn Bar & Grill *(American)*
Pioneer Inn; 808-661-3636.

Hours: Breakfast 6:30 a.m.-11:30 a.m. Lunch/dinner noon-10 p.m. *Sampling:* Breakfast includes papaya fresh fruit boat, and entrees such as macadamia nut pancakes, Hawaiian sweet bread French toast, omelets and frittata ($5-$9). The lunch/dinner menu offers an assortment of appetizers and sandwiches including turkey melt, fresh fish and grilled teriyaki chicken breast, as well as Portuguese bean soup and a variety of salads ($4-$15). Entrees include bread and choice of soup or salad and range from cioppino, chicken picatta or coconut shrimp to pork loin chop and New York strip ($11.95-$20.50). *Comments:* Charming restaurant with nice location overlooking Lahaina Harbor. I've heard breakfasts there are great, with their eggs Benedict especially good.

Smokehouse BBQ Bar & Grill *(Barbecue)*
930 Wainee Street; 808-667-7005.

Hours: Monday through Friday 11:30 a.m.-10 p.m.; Saturday and Saturday 3-10 p.m.; happy hour 3-6 p.m. *Sampling:* Lunch sandwiches served until 4 p.m. include grilled chicken breast, cheesesteak and veggie burger along with their *kiawe*-smoked meat sandwiches of pork, turkey and beef ($5.99-$7.99). Their dinner menu offers complete dinners with baked beans, corn bread, and choice of coleslaw, fries or white rice alongside chicken, fish and beef or pork ribs ($12.99-$19.99). Dinner sandwiches ($8.99-$9.99). *Comments:* Very good ribs. Full bar service.

Expensive-priced Dining

★ ***Chez Paul*** *(French)*
Five miles south of Lahaina, Olowalu; 808-661-3843.

Hours: Monday through Saturday 6-9 p.m. *Sampling & Comments:* Nestled in "you are now entering–you are now leaving" Olowalu (think of Chez Paul as the hyphen), the restaurant is operated by Chef Patrick Callarec (formerly of The Ritz-Carlton, Kapalua), who offers a menu as delightful and distinctive as its location. Sample chilled leak and potato soup, wild mushrooms and brie cheese in a flaky puff pastry with port wine sauce, foie gras, or lobster bisque with cognac ($9-$30). Entrees are served with freshly baked baguette, potatoes and two seasonal vegetables. Selections include crispy duck with seasonal fruits and raspberry vinegar sauce, coq au vin, rack of lamb with exotic chutney, lobster or fresh island fish poached in champagne and shallots ($32-$40). Save room for fabulous desserts. One of his classics is pineapple and vanilla crême brulée served in a pineapple shell. This small restaurant—in what could be a tiny village in France—opened in 1968 and has maintained its high popularity with excellent food and service. I've never been disappointed here. This place is simply fabulous. Named "Most Romantic Restaurant" in the 2005 'Aipono Awards.

★ ***David Paul's Lahaina Grill*** *(New American)*
127 Lahainaluna Road; 808-667-5117; www.lahainagrill.com.

Hours: Nightly from 6 p.m. *Sampling:* The menu is described as New American cuisine, which at this restaurant translates to all kinds of dishes, each one prepared and presented exquisitely. The appetizer menu ranges from Kona lobster crab cake to seared ahi and foie gras to crisp fried blue corn crusted chile relleno ($13-$19). The warm pecan-crusted goat cheese and baby arugula salad ($15) is heavenly. The signature tequila shrimp and firecracker rice and fall-off-the-bone tender *kalua* duck are just two of the entree selections, along with Kona coffee roasted rack of lamb, Maui onion and sesame seed crusted seared ahi, and four-cheese manicotti ($26-$58). The restaurant's signature dessert is triple berry pie (raspberries, blueberries and black currants), but I recommend the sampler for two or more to share—you get a half portion of the restaurant's four most popular desserts ($11-$19). *Comments:* David Paul's has won local and national awards for its innovative cuisine and artistic presentations, and deservedly so. Each time I've dined there, the experience has been perfection from start to finish. The menu is creative, the service is excellent, and the food is impeccably seasoned, garnished and presented. Fine dining just doesn't get much better than this. The seating area is attractively furnished with a crisp look to it. Black-and-white floors are contrasted with a beautifully detailed ceiling and colorful modern art. The bar in the main restaurant is wide and suitable for dining and socializing. The overall ambiance is a modern, casual elegance. This place is pricey, but it's a winner. Captured the "Best Service" category in the 2005 'Aipono Awards.

Gerard's *(French)*
Plantation Inn lobby, 174 Lahainaluna Road; 808-661-8939; www.gerardsmaui.com.

Hours: Nightly from 6 p.m. *Sampling:* The menu changes seasonally. Appetizer selections might include shiitake and oyster mushrooms in puff pastry, medallion of duck foie gras seared in spice crust or escargot with Burgundy butter and wild mushrooms in garlic cream ($10.50 up to $115 for Beluga caviar on ice). Soup and salads include chilled cucumber soup with goat cheese and dill, spinach salad with grilled scallops and fresh Kona lobster with avocado in an herb curry vinaigrette ($8.50-$24.50). Choose from fish and seafood or meat and poultry entrees such as ragout of Hawaiian lobster with garlic and tomato sauce, fisherman's ahi stew, Basque-style rack of lamb in mint crust, or confit of duck with garlic sausage, lamb and pork cassoulet ($32.50-$39.50). Desserts ($8.50) include their homemade island sorbets, gateau dacquoise (Gerard's hometown specialty cake made with macadamia nut and coconut, filled with Chiboust pistachio cream), or fabulous crème brulee. Also available is the local Ulupalakua raspberry dessert wine. Their wine list features a range of moderate to expensive selections from California, France and the Pacific Northwest. *Comments:* The intimate ambiance is equal to the fine cuisine, and although a Maui ocean view is wonderful to enjoy while dining, sitting beneath a mango tree on the veranda at Gerard's is hard to beat for a romantic setting.

★ ***I'o*** *(Pacific Rim)*

505 Front Street; 808-661-8422; www.iomaui.com.

Hours: 5:30-10:30 p.m. *Sampling:* Creative appetizers like Silken Purse (steamed wontons stuffed with roasted peppers, mushrooms, spinach and mac nuts), the I'o Crab Cake (*panko*-crusted crab and goat cheese cakes with Maui onion miso dressing), or Seafood Martini (seafood marinated in vodka and lime) ($8-$12) whet your appetite for equally creative entrees that include crispy ahi (rare ahi in a *nori* and *panko* crust, with green papaya salad), foie gras fish (fresh catch pan-roasted with foie gras) and Tiger by the Tail (wok-roasted giant tiger prawns with a *lilikoi* sauce) ($26-$32). Save room for the crème brulee served in a pineapple ring ($8.50). *Comments:* James McDonald is executive chef and co-owner of both I'o and the adjacent Pacific 'O restaurant. He is one of Maui's most acclaimed chefs and rightly so—his food is outstanding. There is a Euro-Asian influence to I'o's cuisine, and the dining area has a more modern, sleek decor than its sister restaurant. Indoor dining is available, but on the typically mild Maui evening the outdoor beachfront courtyard is the place to be. (You can hear the music from the Feast at Lele while you dine, but it's not obtrusive.) We enjoyed our dinner while watching the sun sink behind the island of Lana'i. I'o has won numerous awards for its food, as well as it wine menu. The flavor combinations are unique and the food is fabulous, from the pesto artichoke dip served with the fresh bread to the delicious macadamia brie salad to the final bite of dessert. And your meal here is a feast for the eyes as well—I don't believe I've ever seen such beautifully presented food. Every dish is a work of art. A children's menu is available.

Longhi's *(Continental)*

888 Front Street; 808-667-2288. Another location at Shops at Wailea, 3750 Wailea Alanui; www.longhis.com.

Hours: Breakfast 7:30-11:30 a.m. Lunch 11:30 a.m.-5 p.m. Dinner 5-10 p.m. *Sampling:* A landmark in Lahaina. For breakfast enjoy their signature eggs Benedict served over toasted French baguette and available traditional, Florentine or with crab cakes. French toast Longhi style has a touch of Grand Marnier. Other breakfast favorites, too ($5-$20). Lunch: great appetizers and salads to begin or enjoy seafood selections such as prawns Amaretto or Venice, or Shrimp or Scallops Longhi's ($18-$20). Sandwiches range from their fabulous Peking duck to their Italian hoagie with manikin peppers, classic New York Reuben or chicken saute ($9-$16). Lots of pasta and pizzas ($9-$15). Dinner offers some of the same lunch selections that they are famous for, as well as lamb chops, filet mignon with béarnaise, eggplant parmesan, and fresh island fish ($18-$31). Vegetables available on the side ($7-$10) and salads ($7-$14). The dessert tray is hard to resist, with ever-changing options like hot chocolate soufflé with *ganache*, lychee sorbet, fresh peach and cardamom pie, strawberry-carrot cake, chocolate zuppa, coconut *haupia* cream pie, or espresso torte. *Comments:* After more than 30 years on Maui, Longhi's has become a legend in Lahaina. The restaurant is known for its casual setting (yet fine food and service) with lots of windows open to view the bustling Lahaina streets; the accommodating breakfast hours that allow for both early risers and the laziest of late sleepers to enjoy the fresh-baked goods and tasty egg dishes; and of course, Bob Longhi himself, the "man who loves to eat" and hopes you do, too. Longhi's offers espresso and a good wine selection with valet parking nightly.

★ ***Pacific 'O*** *(Pacific Rim)*
505 Front Street; 808-667-4341; www.pacificomaui.com.

Hours: Lunch 11 a.m.-4 p.m.; dinner 5:30-10 p.m. Live jazz every Thursday to Saturday night. *Sampling:* Lunch offers starters and entrees such as *kalua* quesadilla, roasted Maui onion goat cheese salad, sesame-seared fish and homemade quiche ($8-$15.50). Award-winning dinner appetizers include a prawn and basil wonton ($12) and "Yuzu Divers" (crispy coconut rice rolls with seared diver scallops and a zesty *yuzu* lime sauce) ($11). Entrees include coconut macadamia nut–crusted catch, pink peppered beef (filet mignon topped with gorgonzola), sesame-crusted lamb and their Taste of Lahaina–winning dish: Hapa Hapa tempura with sashimi blocks wrapped in dry seaweed and fried to medium-rare ($24-$36). *Comments:* Executive Chef James McDonald has established a reputation for himself as one of the most creative and inventive chefs on the island, and Pacific 'O's menu and wine list have received numerous awards and accolades. The food is excellent for lunch or dinner, served in a great ocean-front setting that is casual enough for young children to feel comfortable. Indoor and outdoor lanai seating are available. A children's menu offers dishes priced from $10.95 to $13.95 and there is a creative "*Keiki*'s Cocktail Menu" offering such virgin classics as a Roy Rogers and a Shirley Temple.

Ruth's Chris Steak House *(Steakhouse)*
Lahaina Center, 900 Front Street; 808-661-8815. Another location at Shops at Wailea, 3750 Wailea Alanui; 808-874-8880.

Hours: 5-9 p.m. *Sampling:* Begin with shrimp *remoulade*, sizzlin' blue crab cakes or *carpaccio* tenderloin ($5.95-$16.95), or a salad of fresh asparagus and hearts of palm, Caesar or mixed greens ($5.95-$6.95). Entrees are à la carte (no side dishes on the plate) and include veal chop, center-cut pork chops, many steak selections, broiled chicken and catch of the day ($19.95-$38.95). Add potatoes, rice or vegetables, as desired ($2.95-$7.95). Their signature dessert is a New Orleans favorite—bread pudding with whiskey sauce; or sample their caramelized banana cream pie or chocolate sin cake ($6.95-$7.25). *Comments:* It was in 1965 that Ruth Fertel bought a restaurant named "Chris Steak House," and she acquired the right to use that name as long as the restaurant remained in the original location. But after a fire forced her to move, she needed a new name. Adding her name to the logo seemed a simple solution, so Ruth's Chris Steak House came to be. This is an upscale steak house restaurant chain. They use only premium cuts and the beef is fresh, never frozen. A good wine list as well. However, I've found the food and service here to be "acceptable," but not outstanding enough to warrant the high prices. Because the entrees are à la carte, by the time you've added a couple of side dishes to your dinner, the bill is really high. With so many excellent fine dining restaurants in West Maui, I usually opt to go elsewhere.

Ka'anapali

Inexpensive-priced Dining

C.J.'s Deli & Diner/The Comfort Zone *(Deli)*
Fairway Shops, Honoapi'ilani Highway in the strip mall near the Ka'anapali Resort's second entrance; 808-667-0968; www.cjsmaui.com.

Hours: 6:30 a.m.-7:30 p.m. *Sampling:* Breakfasts start with an early-bird special with eggs, breakfast meat and coffee ($4.95 before 7 a.m.). Other good morning offerings include plenty of omelets, pancakes, waffles and French toast ($3.75-$8.95). Lunches include an old-fashioned burger, deli-style sandwiches and some super salads, with side orders ranging from pineapple fried rice to sauteed mushrooms and garlic bread ($4.25-$9.95). Give "The Perfect Panini" a try ($7-$8). These Italian-style grilled sandwiches on focaccia are served with grilled chicken, portobello mushrooms or prosciutto and tomato. Try a plate lunch served with vegetables and rice or mashed potatoes, with chicken parmesan, sauteed mahimahi, or Mom's meatloaf as a few of the selections ($7.75-$9.95). And their kids' menu is dynamite: shark-bite cheeseburger, frankensteinfurter, mega cheese sandwich with fries, grilled chicken breast, mac and cheese with veggies, lizard toes and squid eyes soup. All items include soda, juice or milk ($3.95). A tasty selection of sweet treats: banana split, island cheesecake, fresh-baked pies or shakes, floats and smoothies. *Comments:* Pastries, even donuts, are made fresh on the premises. Popular place with locals and tourists. Good food.

Ka'anapali Mixed Plate *(American/Hawaiian)*
Ka'anapali Beach Hotel, 2525 Ka'anapali Parkway; 808-661-0011.

Hours: Breakfast buffet 6:15-10:30 a.m. ($11.25 adults/$7.75 kids). Lunch buffet 11 a.m.-1:30 p.m. ($11.25 adults/$7.75 kids). Dinner buffet 4-9 p.m. ($14.95 adults/$10.25 kids). Early-bird dinner buffet 4-6 p.m. ($12.95 adults/$9.50 kids). *Sampling:* "All Buffets, All the Time," with three all-you-can-eat buffets daily. Dinner features nightly prime rib buffet. *Comments: Keiki* prices for children 12 and under; children 5 and under eat free when accompanied by a paying adult. Pleasant coffee shop decorated with donated mementos that reflect the diverse ethnic and cultural background of the hotel employees. A description of the display items and explanation of the cultural foods is featured in a souvenir booklet given at each table. All buffets include salad bar, beverages and dessert. The best value in Ka'anapali, especially for those with a hearty appetite.

Nalu Sunset Bar & Sushi *(Asian)*
Marriott's Maui Ocean Club, 100 Nohea Kai Drive; 808-667-8292.

Hours: 5:30-10:30 p.m. *Samplings*: Nalu's features *pupus* of Asian hot wings, vegetable spring rolls, Thai chicken satay and others ($7-$14), as well as a few plate dinners such as citrus-seared ahi or teriyaki chicken ($14-$16). They also feature a sushi bar and sushi platters along with tropical libations. *Comments:* The popular Makai Bar capitalizes on the Pacific (both the view and the menu). It's a full-service bar and has a great sunset vista.

Moderate-priced Dining

Basil Tomatoes Italian Grille *(Italian)*
Adjacent to Royal Lahaina Resort, 2780 Kekaa Drive; 808-661-3611.

Hours: 5:30-10 p.m. *Sampling:* Classic Northern Italian fare with minestrone soup, fresh clams over linguine, seafood ravioli, rosemary lemon basil chicken, lamb shank *osso buco* and plenty of pasta dishes ($19.99-$34.99). Desserts range from Italian ices to banana crepes or tiramisu ($3.49-$5.99). *Comments:* Located at the entrance to the Royal Lahaina Resort; view of the Ka'anapali Golf Course. Basil Tomatoes' special basil tomato bread is served with all entrees. Children's menu.

★ ***Castaway Café*** *(American with a touch of the islands)*
Maui Ka'anapali Villas Resort, 45 Kai Ala Drive; 808-661-9091.

Hours: Breakfast 7:30 a.m.-2 p.m. Lunch 11 a.m.-2:30 p.m. Light fare 2:30-9 p.m. Dinner 5-9 p.m. *Sampling: Loco moco*, eggs Benedict, omelets or from the griddle (until 11 a.m.) enjoy macadamia nut, banana or pineapple pancakes, or the must-try Kula cinnamon raisin French toast ($4.50-$10.50). Lunches include Paradise chicken salad, burgers and dogs, sandwiches ($6.95-$10.50). Start your evening repast with coconut shrimp or an Asian sampler or perhaps soup or salad ($1.95-$9.95). Entrees include Panang seafood curry or fresh catch, prepared blackened, grilled with lemon butter, or macadamia crusted with tropical fruit salsa ($12.95-$19.95); served with rice or potato and fresh vegetables. Their dessert menu changes, but if you're lucky you can try a piece of their "real" New York cheesecake. *Comments:* Tuesday from 5-9 p.m. is pasta night with two-for-one pasta selections. Lovely location oceanside (next to the swimming pool at Ka'anapali Villas) and an excellent value compared to many other resort restaurants. The restaurant has compiled a remarkable selection of wines and has been recognized by *Wine Spectator Magazine* for the past three years. Full bar service.

Don the Beachcomber Restaurant *(Island)*
Royal Lahaina Resort, 2780 Kekaa Drive; 808-661-3611.

Hours: Breakfast 6:30-10 a.m. Dinner 6-9 p.m. *Sampling:* Breakfast offers omelets, pancakes and waffles as well as à la carte items and "Breakfast Special Deals" starting at $8.50. Their breakfast buffet is $14.95 adults, $7.50 children 6-11, 5 and under free, with fruits, pastries, cereals and yogurt. Hot items include corned beef hash and scrambled eggs along with daily special items such as waffles, banana pancakes or hash browns. Dinner features American and island-style soups, salads and à la carte entrees ($11.95-$24.95). *Comments:* Open-air setting overlooking the resort gardens and the ocean.

Giovani's Tomato Pie Ristorante *(Italian)*
Ka'anapali Resort where Ka'anapali Parkway meets Honoapi'ilani Highway by the Ka'anapali Golf Course; 808-661-3160.

Hours: 5-9:30 p.m. *Sampling:* Pick your pasta and combine it with your favorite sauce. Penne with alfredo, linguine with bolognese, and capellini with aioli are only a few of the options ($10.99-$15.99). Stuffed pasta, pizzas or parmigiana dishes with house dinner specials including calamari and seafood *pescatore* ($13.99-$19.99). Add antipasto or zuppa and saladas from $3.49. *Comments:* Kids' meals for age 10 and under $6-$10. Downstairs they have Jonny's Burger Joint open 11:30 a.m.-midnight, with the bar open until 2 a.m. (808-661-4500). There are better pizza and burgers elsewhere in the area.

★ ***Hula Grill*** *(Hawaiian Regional/Seafood)*

Whalers Village, 2435 Ka'anapali Parkway, on the beach; 808-667-6636.

Hours: Lunch 11 a.m.-10:30 p.m.; dinner 5-9:30 p.m.; Barefoot Bar all-day menu 11 a.m.-11 p.m.; cocktails until midnight. *Sampling:* The Barefoot Bar serves a continuous lunch/dinner menu featuring appetizers, meal-size salads, pizzas and sandwiches ($6-$14). Try the *gado gado* salad with Thai peanut dressing, focaccia chicken sandwich or Mauna Kea goat cheese pizza. For dinner try wood-grilled ahi steak, Kula vegetable and chicken stir fry or banana barbecued ribs ($16-$29). Lots of other delicious fresh fish dishes, chicken and steaks. *Kiawe* wood-burning oven pizzas available anytime (from $8-$9). *Comments:* The Hawaiian Regional cuisine is based on island fish and seafood. The casual oceanfront restaurant, reminiscent of a 1930s beach house, is surrounded by tropical gardens and ponds. The interior has a homey atmosphere with a cozy library room for a waiting area. Each room feels like part of a home and a collection of hula dolls and Hawaiian memorabilia are on display throughout. At the Barefoot Bar, you dine under thatched umbrellas, surrounded by "indoor" sand. There is an exhibition cooking line in front with a large *kiawe*-grill/barbecue, an *imu*-style oven for the pizzas, and a bar-counter to sit and eat and watch it all. Good kids' menu, too. Good food; great oceanfront location; fun, trendy beach atmosphere. The Barefoot Bar at Hula Grill was named "Best Place to Eat in a Bathing Suit" in the 2005 'Aipono Awards.

Keka'a Terrace *(American)*

Sheraton Maui Resort, 2605 Ka'anapali Parkway; 808-661-0031.

Hours: Breakfast 6:30-11 a.m.; lunch 11 a.m.-2 p.m.; dinner 5:30-9:30 p.m. *Sampling:* Choice of two breakfast buffets $22.95 (hot buffet) or $18.95 (continental buffet). A selection of à la carte entrees is available as well ($12-$18). Lunch includes salads such as Maui onion Caesar or Cobb as well as assorted sandwiches (Reuben, triple-decker club) and entrees such as Oriental-style chicken curry and fresh fish tacos ($10-$13). Begin your dinner with crispy calamari, Peking duck on bok choy or sauteed garlic shrimp "scampi-style" ($5.95-$10.50). Continue with fresh catch, seared Norwegian salmon, prime rib, Mediterranean chicken or lobster tail for dinner ($22-$39). *Comments:* Casual, all-day dining with views of the ocean and the resort's tropical lagoons.

★ ***Leilani's on the Beach*** *(American/Seafood)*
Whalers Village, 2435 Ka'anapali Parkway, on the beach; 808-661-4495.

Hours: Beachside Grill 11 a.m.-11 p.m.; upstairs dinner menu 5 p.m.-10 p.m. *Sampling:* Leilani's beachside grill, located on the lower-level oceanfront area of the restaurant, offers salads, sandwiches and appetizers including chicken quesadilla, a turkey wrap, and grilled ginger chicken salad ($4-$14). The upstairs dining room is open for dinner with fresh catch, shellfish, grilled steaks, and barbecue ribs all served with rice or potatoes ($15-$28). Save room for the hula pie, a huge piece of ice cream pie that can easily be shared ($6). *Comments:* The casual outdoor patio and terraced dining room are right on the beach, offering one of the best sunset-viewing spots in Ka'anapali. Kids' menu. Dinner reservations advised.

Mango Grill & Bar *(American)*
Located on Honoapi'ilani Highway at the entrance to Ka'anapali; Ka'anapali Golf Course clubhouse; 808-667-1929.

Hours: 7:30 a.m.-9:30 p.m. daily. Breakfast until noon; lunch 11 a.m.-3 p.m.; happy hour/*pupus* 3-6 p.m.; dinner 5:30-9:30 p.m. *Sampling:* Featuring a menu of "comfort foods," they pride themselves on keeping most of their dinner entrees under $20. Try meat loaf, roast turkey or roast pork, shrimp curry, mahimahi Polynesian, *kiawe* grilled pork chops, New York steak or filet mignon ($13-$24). Sandwiches are available on the dinner menu as well. For breakfast (under $10), pancakes, cheese blintzes, eggs Benedict, turkey hash and a selection of *mocos* (local mixed plates). Lunch salads and sandwiches, including a delicious chicken curry salad in a half papaya ($6-$13). *Comments:* Nice open-air setting overlooking the 18th hole and water feature of the Ka'anapali North Course.

'OnO Bar & Grill *(Island/Tapas)*
Westin Maui, 2365 Ka'anapali Parkway, located poolside on the ground floor; 808-667-2525.

Hours: Breakfast 6:30 a.m.-11 a.m. (breakfast buffet 6:30 a.m.-10:30 a.m.). Lunch 11 a.m.-5 p.m. Dinner 5-10 p.m. *Sampling:* Island breakfast buffet is served daily ($23.75 adults, $12 children age 4-12) and is a good value since it includes a variety of breakfast foods plus juices, coffees and fruits. À la carte entrees such as egg or pancake breakfasts fetch $7-$18. Lunches

include salads, burgers, sandwiches and wraps, with the *furakake*-crusted seared ahi sandwich being a particular favorite of mine ($7.50-$17). For dinner, the restaurant switches to a *tapas*-style menu. You can choose appetizer-size or larger portions of such dishes as *lomi* salmon, baked Surfing Goat Dairy cheese (from Upcountry), Haleakala Hokkaido sea scallops, baby back ribs, sauteed garlic shrimp and jumbo Thai chicken wings ($5-$19). Burgers and pizza are also available. *Comments:* Casual poolside bistro dining. And yes, it is actually spelled 'OnO.

Pavillion *(Pacific Rim)*

Hyatt Regency Maui Resort and Spa, 200 Nohea Kai Drive, lower level; 808-661-1234.

Hours: Lunch 11 a.m.-5 p.m.; bar 10 a.m.-7 p.m. *Sampling:* The Pavillion features casual dining with most selections under $10. Salads, burgers, sandwiches, paninis. The *keiki* menu includes a fountain drink and French fries. *Comments:* Fairly affordable for resort dining. Very casual indoor or outdoor seating. And yes, it is Pavillion with two Ls.

Rusty Harpoon *(American)*

Whalers Village, 2435 Ka'anapali Parkway; 808-661-3123.

Hours: Breakfast 8-11 a.m. Lunch 11 a.m.-5 p.m. Happy hour 2-6 p.m. and 10 p.m.-midnight. Dinner 5 p.m.-10 p.m.; late night bistro 10 p.m.-midnight; cocktails until 2 a.m. *Sampling:* The only full-service restaurant open at Whalers Village for breakfast. Belgian waffle bar (no pancakes on their breakfast menu), assorted egg dishes and other breakfast foods ($7.95-$12.95). Lunch features burgers and sandwiches ($7.95-$9.95). For dinner they offer some unusual specials such as Rusty's Mamasan seafood curry ($22.95) and a pineapple teriyaki chicken ($20.95). Seafood, beef, pasta and chicken entrees ($18.95-$29.95). *Comments:* A diverse menu and great ocean view make this a good dining choice for breakfast, but for lunch and dinner I've found the service to be sluggish and the food just okay. You'll do better at Leilani's or Hula Grill.

Tiki Terrace *(American/Hawaiian)*

Ka'anapali Beach Hotel, 2525 Ka'anapali Parkway; 808-661-0011.

Hours: Breakfast 7:30-11 a.m. Monday through Saturday; Sunday à la carte breakfast menu is served 7:30-8:45 a.m., followed by Sunday champagne brunch 9 a.m.-1 p.m. Dinner 6-9 p.m. *Sampling:* On Sunday they serve champagne brunch ($30.95 adults; $17 children age 6 to 12). For dinner, the Tiki Terrace has some interesting appetizers. Pig in a Pareo is

Hawaiian-style smoked pork with Maui onions wrapped in egg rolls, or try *opakapaka* pattycake, or their sweet Hapa Haole onion soup, Caesar or seared ahi salad ($3.95-$9.95). Entrees range from clam linguini to jumbo shrimp scampi, and for the land lover there is rack of lamb, barbecued pork ribs or teriyaki chicken ($17.95-$38.95). Dessert offers a Napili lime tart, pineapple cheesecake and Banana Caramel Eruption, which is warm, gooey and wonderful ($4.95). *Comments: Keiki* menu for children 12 and under; children 5 and under eat free from children's menu when accompanied by a paid adult. Live Hawaiian music nightly 6-9 p.m.; complimentary hula show 6:30-7:30 p.m. Before becoming Westernized, Hawaiians consumed less than 10 percent fat in their diet. If you'd like to sample a traditional native Hawaiian diet, they have a multicourse meal starting with a pohole fern salad and a choice of chicken or fish *lau lau* for your entree and culminating with a variety of fruits for dessert ($22.95).

Va Bene Italian Beachside Grill *(Italian)*
Marriott's Maui Ocean Club, 100 Nohea Kai Drive, Ka'anapali; 808-667-8290.

Hours: Breakfast 6:30-11 a.m. Dinner 5:30-9:30 p.m. *Sampling & Comments:* Two daily breakfast buffets with a "Healthy Start" featuring oatmeal, cold cereals, fresh fruits, yogurt, breakfast breads and juices ($13 adults, $7 kids 7-12 years), or a full buffet that adds eggs cooked to order and breakfast meals to the "Healthy Start" option ($18 adults, $9 kids 7-12 years). Lighter options include Danish, oatmeal or yogurt, or choose an egg entree (which includes coffee or juice) such as New York steak and eggs, Va Bene Benedicts, Va Bene frittata or the "All American Breakfast" ($5-$16). From the griddle enjoy waffles, pancakes and French toast ($6-$13). The dinner menu is a fun one. They have fish and seafood selections such as tiger prawns, seafood stew or seafood pasta ($15-$32). The pastas are available in *piccolo* and *grande* sizes and include gnocchi, risotto *alla* Monzese and hand-pulled pizzas in *piccolo* and *grande* sizes as well ($5-$13). But my recommendation is the chef's prix-fixe menu. It includes a starter, pasta, entree (three choices) and a *dolci* for $35 ($45 with wine). The wines are all red and a different 3 oz. glass is served with each course. The pasta course was made with grilled wild mushrooms and parmigiano reggiano cheese and I would have been delighted to have just this course for dinner. The smoked pork chop entree was huge and served with a sauce rich with roasted shallots and figs. The other entree was the beef tenderloin served with an herb and bread compound butter.

Expensive-priced Dining

★ ***Cascades Grille & Sushi Bar*** *(American/Sushi)*

Hyatt Regency Maui Resort and Spa, 200 Nohea Kai Drive; 808-667-4727

Hours: Dinner 5:45-10 p.m. Sushi bar 5-10 p.m. Lounge/bar 3 p.m.-midnight. *Sampling:* Dinner options start with appetizers, soups and salads ($4-$16), with entrees from the lava rock grill like rib-eye steak or filet mignon ($28-$36). Specialty entrees include seafood mixed grill, *hulihuli* chicken, baby back pork ribs ($25-$35) and island fish selections (market price). The sushi bar offers *maki* and *nigiri* sushi and sashimi ($7.50 and up) and sushi samplers ($18-$34). *Comments:* Perched above the pool and on the edge of one of the Hyatt's waterfalls, patio seating extends over the landscaped cliff, providing an ocean vista. Children can order most entrees on the menu at half price for half size. The dessert menu gets thumbs up for artistic presentation: coconut crème brulee is served in a partially edible fresh coconut shell; the chocolate mousse in a totally edible marbled white chocolate conch shell. The sushi bar is intimate yet spacious, with attractive wood, pleasant lighting, and Japanese artifacts.

Spats Trattoria *(Northern Italian)*

Hyatt Regency Maui Resort and Spa, 200 Nohea Kai Drive; 808-661-1234.

Hours: Dinner 6-10 p.m. Sunday, Monday, Wednesday and Friday. *Sampling:* A hearty assortment of Italian dishes. Antipasti selections include carpaccio, grilled prawns with polenta, or risotto crabcakes ($8-$14). *Zuppe e insalate* offers a Tuscan salad with warm goat cheese or a classic minestrone soup ($6.50-$10). Pesce and carne selections range from veal marsala or piccata to scampi con pancetta and pan-seared local snapper. Pasta selections offer linguine con *frutta di mare*, penne con funghi (roasted chicken with mushrooms and a marsala sauce) or fettuccine carbona ($18.50-$35). Tiramisu, amaretto cheesecake, ganache or chocolate silk torte may be among the evening selections for dessert ($6-$7). *Comments:* The atmosphere is comfortable and homey, yet very classy a la a parlor or drawing room of an old Italian mansion. Brass candelabras, sleek wood, beveled-glass partitions, and plush booths add to the distinctive ambiance. Focaccia, topped with cheese and herbs, arrives with a side of fresh pesto along with olive oil, balsamic vinegar, and herbs for dipping. Kids' menu available.

★ ***Swan Court*** *(Island Continental)*

Hyatt Regency Maui Resort and Spa, 200 Nohea Kai Drive; 808-667-4727.

Breakfast 6:30 a.m.-11:30 a.m. (until noon Sunday); Dinner Tuesday, Thursday and Saturday 6-9 p.m. *Sampling:* Breakfast buffet

($22.95; $10.95 children 5-12). Continental buffet includes fruits, pastries, cereal, plus juice, coffee or tea ($15.95 adults, $7.95 kids). Also breakfast à la carte. Their dinner menu changes every month, but here is a sample of what you might enjoy. Dinner appetizers include lobster, crab and shrimp spring roll, seared forest mushroom potsticker or guava-painted baby back ribs ($12-$16). Featured entrees are Maui sugar cane–skewered ahi with tempura sushi roll and Asian greens, lemongrass chicken with pancit noodles, hibachi pork tenderloin with Moloka'i sweet potato or a vegetarian sampler with exotic mushrooms, truffled asparagus and almond-crusted tofu ($32-$44). They have plenty of tempting desserts, including the signature Swan Court hot soufflé (allow 30 minutes), so save room. *Comments:* A pond of graceful swans, cascading waterfalls and a landscape of oriental gardens create the enchanting atmosphere. The ambiance alone is well worth the splurge for breakfast, a "best bet" for a daily breakfast buffet. The dinners are excellent and many unusual preparations are offered. Reservations are recommended.

★ ***Teppan Yaki Dan*** *(Japanese/Teppanyaki)*
Sheraton Maui, 2605 Ka'anapali Parkway; 808-661-0031.

Hours: 5:30-9 p.m. Closed Sunday and Monday. *Sampling & Comments:* Wonderful teppanyaki restaurant, with your meal skillfully prepared right before your eyes. Start with an appetizer of *sake* wasabi tobiko oyster shooter ($3) or miso soup with clams ($4). Then select your entree ingredients from a number of options such as filet mignon, lobster, shrimp, teriyaki chicken, jumbo scallops, hibachi salmon and many combinations. Entrees ($26-$48) include fresh vegetables, steamed white rice and two signature dipping sauces. Finish up with a choice of dessert specialties made by the restaurant's pastry chef. The food is great here, and the teppanyaki preparation is fun to watch.

tropica *(Pacific Rim)*
Westin Maui Resort & Spa, 2365 Ka'anapali Parkway, Ka'anapali; 808-667-2525.

Hours: Dinner daily 5:30 until 9 p.m. (hours may vary). *Sampling:* A fun and spicy menu. For starters you have firecracker spring roll, blue crab and rock shrimp cake, *kalua* pork quesadilla, Indonesian chicken satay and tangled coconut prawns ($10-$15) and a variety of table-top skewer appetizers (with an actual mini hibachi). Or try the oven-fired pizza ($14-$17). Their fresh island fish is served a number of ways including baked in a *ti* leaf with crabmeat stuffing. Chef's specialties include volcanic peppered prime rib, Colorado rack of lamb, grilled giant tiger prawns and a tantalizing selection of sizzling flame-grilled steaks ($21-$46). *Comments:* Great location, beachside right on the Ka'anapali walkway. Dine outside, just off the beach, under little oases of thatched-hut tables overlooking serene pools. Or dine inside beside the waterfalls. This restaurant and bar boasts a "hip island dining experience." Classy, romantic, fun.

Honokowai-Kapalua Area

Inexpensive-priced Dining

Beach Club *(American)*
Ka'anapali Shores, 3445 Lower Honoapi'ilani Road, Honokowai; 808-667-3720.

Hours: Breakfast 7-11 a.m. Lunch 11:30 a.m.-3 p.m. Café menu (light fare and happy hour) served 3-9:30 p.m. Dinner 5:30-9:30 p.m. *Sampling:* Large selection of omelets and other breakfast fare. Lunch primarily hot and cold sandwiches. Dinner features the usual array of chicken, beef, pasta and fish. Most meal items $9-$29.

China Boat *(Cantonese-Szechuan-Mandarin)*
4474 Lower Honoapi'ilani Road, Kahana; 808-669-5089.

Hours: Monday through Saturday lunch 11:30 a.m.-2 p.m.; dinner nightly 5-10 p.m. *Sampling:* Appetizers feature potstickers, jelly fish, spicy wonton ($3.75-$11.25). Entrees include mu shu chicken or pork, big clams with black bean sauce, seafood noodle soup or sesame beef ($7.95-$21.95). *Comments:* Take-out available. Free delivery in the Ka'anapali to Kapalua area.

(The) Coffee Store *(Coffee/Pastries)*
Napili Plaza; 808-669-4170. Other locations at 1279 South Kihei Road, 808-875-4244; Queen Ka'ahumanu Center, 275 Ka'ahumanu Avenue, Kahului, 808-871-6860.

Napili Hours: 6:30 a.m.-6 p.m. *Sampling:* Muffins, cinnamon rolls, sticky buns, quiche, desserts and assorted pastries. *Comments:* Freshly roasted coffee and really good coffee drinks (with some unusual selections like a banana mocha cooler or an Electric Brown Cow). Juices and flavored Italian sodas or smoothies. Good place to stop for a pick-me-up.

Dollies Pub & Cafe *(American/Italian)*
Kahana Manor, 4310 Lower Honoapi'ilani Road, Kahana; 808-669-0266; www.dolliespubandcafe.com.

Hours: 11 a.m.-midnight. *Sampling:* Large selection of sandwiches including Dollie's grinder, Reuben, turkey dip or Cajun chicken, and several salads ($5.50-$9.50). Hand-pressed pizza, cooked in a stone oven (from $14). Plenty of *pupus* ($3.25-$8.75) or try one of their pasta dishes ($12-$15.95). *Comments:* Dine in their casual cafe setting or order food to go. Good selection of beer, wine and coffee drinks. Full bar (Dollie's is also a sports bar). Popular spot with local residents. Looks like a little hole-in-the-wall, but we've found this to be a reasonably priced place when we're in the mood for nothing fancy. Sandwiches are good and servings are generous. Dollie's is particularly known for their pizzas, and they have great chili, too. The only bad experience we've had was with their spinach & artichoke dip, which was runny and unpalatable—stay away from that one.

★ ***Gazebo*** *(American)*

Napili Shores Resort, 5315 Lower Honoapi'ilani Road, Napili; 808-669-5621.

Hours: 7:30 a.m.-2 p.m. *Sampling:* Breakfast offers an assortment of omelets (from spinach to shrimp) and egg dishes, but they are most popular for their macadamia nut pancakes; pineapple and banana pancakes run a close second ($4.95-$9.75). The fried rice plate is delicious, too. Lunch selections include burgers and sandwiches (Monte Cristo, shrimp melt, chicken Monterey, patty melt) plus Caesar, shrimp, tuna and Southwestern chicken salads ($7.25-$9.75). *Comments:* This place is a favorite with local residents. Great food (and generous servings) at very reasonable prices, and you're located right on the ocean. Casual and comfortable, perfect for families. Be prepared for a wait, however. They don't take reservations and there is always a line to get in. Waiting time can be up to a half hour (with no shade), so wear sunscreen. Relax and enjoy the beautiful view. The wait is worth it. This place is a little jewel. It took second place for Best Breakfast in the 2005 'Aipono Awards.

★ ***Honokowai Okazuya & Deli*** *(Local/Eclectic)*

AAAAA Rent-A-Space Mall, 3600 Lower Honoapi'ilani Road, Honokowai; 808-665-0512.

Hours: Monday through Saturday 10 a.m.-2:30 p.m., 4:30-9 p.m. Closed Sunday. *Sampling:* Chicken *katsu*, Mongolian beef, *panko* fried mahi, teriyaki steak, veggie frittata, Szechuan eggplant, egg fu yung, Grandma's spicy tofu, pasta primavera, spaghetti with meatballs or sausage. Hot sandwiches (meatball, Italian sausage, turkey or tuna melt, broiled chicken, mahi) plus turkey, ham, club, BLT. Most menu items $6.75-$9.45. *Comments:* Former chefs from Ming Yuen and Buzz's Wharf offer what they call the "Best Take-out in Town"—an eclectic selection of local, Italian, Japanese, deli and vegetarian. Lunch and dinner plates come with rice and a choice of macaroni salad or stir-fried vegetables. Call ahead and order or you'll be watching all those folks who called ahead picking up their orders while your stomach growls.

Honolua General Store *(American)*
In the heart of Kapalua, between the Ritz-Carlton entrance and the Village Golf Course clubhouse. 808-669-6128.

Hours: General store open 6 a.m.-8 p.m. daily; grill and deli, breakfast 6 a.m.-10 a.m.; lunch 10 a.m.-3 p.m. *Sampling:* Breakfasts include pancakes, eggs and such. Lunches include plate lunch selections daily that might include stew or teri chicken or a smaller portion called a hobo, which is just a main dish and rice. Sandwiches and grilled items include tuna melt, burgers and hot pastrami served with fries. The Spam *musubi*, a local favorite, is usually sold out by noon. Prices are definitely the lowest in Kapalua ($2-$9). *Comments:* This is a general store that offers an assortment of Kapalua clothing, sundries, groceries and some locally made food products as well as gourmet teas and coffees.

★ ***Mama's Ribs 'N Rotisserie*** *(Barbecue)*
Napili Plaza; 808-665-6262.

Hours: 11 a.m.-7 p.m. Closed Sunday. *Sampling:* Home-cooked meals for dining in or takeout at this family-owned and -operated restaurant. Rotisserie chicken and barbecue ribs are their specialty. Chicken or rib plate lunch/dinners are offered with steamed rice, island-style macaroni salad or barbecue baked beans (from $5.75). Full rack of baby back pork ribs ($19.99) or whole roasted chicken ($11.50) in traditional or teriyaki citrus marinades along with à la carte side dishes such as coleslaw, chili, stew and pasta salads should feed the masses. They also have chili, beef stew and spinach lasagna plates ($4.75-$6.50). *Comments:* The ribs here are great. This place is a favorite of mine. Delicious food, great prices, good value. Cash only.

Nachos Grande *(Mexican)*
Honokowai Marketplace, 3350 Lower Honoapi'ilani Road, Honokowai; 808-662-0890.

Hours: 11 a.m.-10 p.m. Bar open until 2 a.m. *Sampling:* Burritos, nachos, enchiladas, tacos and quesadillas served with chicken, beef or vegetarian style ($3.99-$6.99). *Comments:* Check out their "wall of flame" with over 100 hot sauces from around the world. And after that, if you need to cool down, sample one of their mango margaritas. This place doesn't look like much, but what it lacks in ambiance it makes up in good food. The best Mexican food I've found on the West Side.

Ohana Grill and Bar *(American/Deli)*

Embassy Vacation Resort, 104 Ka'anapali Shores Place, Honokowai; 808-661-2000.

Hours: Lunch 11 a.m.-3:30 p.m.; dinner 5-10 p.m; appetizers all day. *Sampling:* For lunch, Oriental chicken salad, Caesar salad, pizza along with burgers and sandwiches such as *kalua* pork, Greek-style gyro and mahimahi ($7.25-$10.95). They offer pizza and burgers, as well as a dinner menu with entrees such as chipotle chicken fajitas, garlic butter baked baby shrimp and Hawaiian-style *kalua* pork and cabbage ($7.95-$13.95). *Comments:* Located poolside; casual dining. Live entertainment nightly. No reservations; walk-up dining only.

★ ***Pizza Paradiso*** *(Pizza/Italian)*

Honokowai Marketplace, 3350 Lower Honoapi'ilani Road, Honokowai; 808-667-2929; www.pizzaparadiso.com.

Hours: 11 a.m.-10 p.m. *Sampling:* Order a whole pizza ($12.95-$26.95) or by the slice. Salads include pastas or greens ($4.95-$6.95), and an affordable selection of pasta entrees ($7.95-$9.95) are available, such as spaghetti, fettuccine or penne; add chicken, shrimp, sausage or meatballs. Their Michelangelo sauce (creamy tomato with roasted garlic chips) was a winner at Taste of Lahaina. The adjoining Hula Scoops offers smoothies, gourmet ice cream, sundaes and desserts, including their tiramisu, which was voted the best in Maui ($2.79-$4.50). Warm up with a variety of hot café drinks or cool down with an espresso shake, a banana mocha cooler or an iced toddy. *Comments:* Pizza Paradiso has received many accolades for their homemade pies made with fresh herbs, mozzarella and secret sauce. Inexpensive gourmet cuisine in a casual setting, plus they have "Family Deal" meals that serve up to a family of four.

Moderate-priced Dining

(The) Beach House *(American)*

The Ritz-Carlton, 1 Ritz Carlton Drive, Kapalua; 808-669-6200.

Hours: 11:30 a.m.-4 p.m. *Sampling:* Lunch selections range from *kalua* pork sandwich or Beach House burger to a grilled ahi salad ($10-$18). *Comments:* Located adjacent to Fleming Beach, this open-air restaurant utilizes more than 40 fully grown coco palms to offer a natural roof. This is a really spectacular daytime location. On a sunny day, you couldn't enjoy a better outdoor dining experience, and if the whales are in town, an added bonus. Parking is available at D.T. Fleming Beach Park.

Fish and Game Brewing Company & Rotisserie *(Seafood/Rotisserie & Microbrewery)*
Kahana Gateway, 4405 Honoapi'ilani Highway #207; 808-669-3474; www.mauibrewingco.com.

Hours: Lunch 11 a.m.-3 p.m. Happy hour 3-4:30 p.m. Dinner 5-10 p.m. Bar menu available 11 a.m.-1 a.m. *Sampling:* Lunch offers appetizers, salads, sandwiches and other entrees like chicken caesar wrap, Philly cheesesteak and beer batter seafood and chips ($6.95-$12.95). Begin your dinner with crispy fried calamari, oysters on the half shell, flame broiled portobello mushroom or a cold seafood sampler ($8-$16). Entrees include pastas, rotisserie chicken, *kiawe*-smoked prime rib and eucalyptus-smoked rack of lamb ($18-$36). Their chowders (clam or oyster) as well as the Maui onion soup are homemade. Fresh island fish is available cooked in any one of four different preparations including seven-spiced, blackened Cajun or steamed oriental. The meats are prepared on their rotisserie and the *kiawe* grill. Burgers and a *keiki* menu also offered. *Comments:* The main dining room has an exhibition kitchen, oyster bar, and retail seafood market. A striking stone hearth rotisserie is surrounded by a marble dining counter and gleaming copper tanks of their glass-enclosed microbrewery. The sports bar side offers state-of-the-art equipment and satellite system. In the back is a separate dining room with elegant wood and brass designs reminiscent of a gentlemen's club. The atmosphere is cozy and intimate, but we've found this restaurant to be inconsistent. Our recent lunch there was dismal (service was awful and the fresh fish sandwich was dried out), but we've had some good experiences at dinner, including fresh ahi that was cooked to perfection.

Fish and Poi *(Steak/Seafood)*
Napili Shores, 5315 Lower Honoapi'ilani Road, Napili; 808-442-3700

Hours: Tuesday through Sunday 4:30-9 p.m. *Sampling:* Start your meal with an ahi *poke* martini, Pacific seafood chowder or brie and chicken quesadillas ($5.95-$8.95). Salads and light fare include taro salad, chicken curry salad or crab club ($7.95-$12.95). Dinner entrees such as grilled marinated jumbo shrimp, tempura mahi and chips, roast duckling or linguine with sage ($12.95-$20.95). *Comments:* The newest restaurant by Maui restaurateurs Mike and Dana Pastula (Cafe O' Lei/Ma'alaea Grill). Good food, reasonable prices.

Java Jazz & Soup Nutz *(Bistro)*
Honokowai Marketplace, 3350 Lower Honoapi'ilani Road, Honokowai; 808-667-0787; www.javajazz.net.

Hours: Monday through Saturday 6 a.m.-9 p.m. Sunday 6 a.m.-5 p.m. *Sampling:* Breakfast ($5.95-$10.95) features breakfast burrito, omelets, waffles, pancakes and egg dishes. Lunch includes soups made fresh daily, sandwiches and vegetarian burgers ($4.75-$11.95). Dinners (after 5 p.m.) offer fresh fish, chicken picatta, top-cut steaks ($10.95-$32.95) and homemade desserts ($6.95). Full bar. *Comments:* They call themselves "House of the Home Hearty Food." Cute little bistro-style café with a bohemian ambiance and a nice espresso bar.

North Beach Grille *(Pacific Rim)*

Embassy Vacation Resort, 104 Ka'anapali Shores Place, Honokowai; 808-661-2000.

Hours: 5:30-9 p.m. *Sampling:* Chili-glazed calamari, steamed Manila clams, and roasted spice Italian sausage are among the appetizers ($8.50-$14.95), and for your dinner entree enjoy grilled rare ahi over mashed potatoes, blackened snapper of the day, shredded chicken linguini or roasted vegetable pasta ($16-$28.95). *Comments:* Oceanfront dining; seafood with a Mediterranean flair. Nightly fresh fish specials.

★ ***Outback Steakhouse*** *(Steakhouse)*

Kahana Gateway, 4405 Honoapi'ilani Highway, Kahana; 808-665-1822. Another location at Pi'ilani Shopping Center, 281 Pi'ikea Avenue, Kihei (by Safeway), 808-879-8400; www.outback.com.

Hours: 4-10 p.m. weekdays; 3-10 p.m. weekends. *Sampling:* Start with "Aussie-tizers" such as Aussie cheese fries (a large plate of French fries topped with cheese and bacon, served with a ranch dressing dip), Kookaburra wings (buffalo chicken wings), grilled shrimp on the barbie, or their signature Bloomin' Onion—a huge fried onion like you've never seen before ($7.99-$9.49), or go for the Queensland Salad with seasoned chicken, egg, tomato, bacon and two cheeses or the Walkabout Soup O' The Day ($3.29-$11.79). Entrees include "Down Under Favorites" like Queensland Chicken 'N Shrimp, Jackeroo Chops (pork chops), or Alice Springs Chicken (a delicious dish of grilled chicken breast and bacon, smothered in mushrooms, melted cheeses and honey mustard sauce). Steaks, fish, and items "Grilled on the Barbie" round out the selection of entrees ($12.99-$29.49). Dessert-lovers will want to indulge in a Chocolate Thunder from Down Under (a pecan brownie with ice cream and chocolate sauce), Cinnamon Apple Oblivion (vanilla ice cream covered with chunks of cinnamon apples, pecans and caramel sauce) or other equally tempting options ($4.99-$7.49). Outback also offers a "Joey Menu" for kids under 10, with items priced "down under" ($4.29-$6.99).

Comments: Rustic ranch-house atmosphere with hardwood floors, wood-framed booths, and plenty of fun Aussie artifacts. Good food and very generous servings—you could make a meal on the Bloomin' Onion alone. A comfortable family restaurant.

Plumeria Terrace Restaurant and Bar *(International)*
Kapalua Bay Hotel, poolside; 808-669-5656.

Hours: 11 a.m.-4:30 p.m. Cocktails until 5 p.m. *Sampling:* Chicken quesadillas, buffalo wings and spinach-artichoke-crab dip with pita bread ($9-$15). Sample fisherman's soup (featuring the day's fresh fish) ($10) or a Kula vegetable or grilled chicken Caesar salad ($8-$16). They have pizza, a variety of sandwiches and fish and chips ($11-$16). *Comments:* The beautiful location of this casual poolside setting features an ocean view from every seat.

★ ***Sansei Seafood Restaurant and Sushi Bar*** *(Sushi/Pacific Rim)*
The Shops at Kapalua; 808-669-6286. Another location at Kihei Town Center, 1881 South Kihei Road, near Foodland; 808-879-0004.

Hours: Saturday through Wednesday 5:30-10 p.m., Thursday through Friday until 2 a.m. Karaoke and *pupus* Thursday through Friday 10 p.m.-1 a.m. *Sampling:* No matter what you select, it is going to be great. Sansei has won local, statewide and national awards too numerous to list for their creative sushi and seafood preparations. Award-winning signature items include the mango crab salad hand roll ($7.95), *panko*-crusted fresh ahi sashimi ($9.95), Asian rock shrimp cake ($6.95), Japanese calamari salad ($9.95), and Rock Shrimp Dynamite ($9.95). Or sample their Kapalua "Butterfry" Roll ($11.95) or Tea Duck Eggroll ($5.95). Their fresh Hawaiian ahi carpaccio ($10.95) is soaked with cilantro, peanuts, and Thai chili sauce. If you're not a seafood or sushi lover, try the roasted Asian duck breast, chili-porcini mushroom-crusted beef tenderloin filet or roasted Japanese jerk-spice chicken. Dinner entrees ($15.95-$28.95—lobster higher). Or just enjoy the diversity of flavors in the appetizers (Asian *tapas*) and rolls ($3.00-$16.95). Save room for their hot fresh Granny Smith apple tart, macadamia nut tempura fried ice cream, or homemade New York cheesecakes ($4.95-$6.95) and coffee served in a French press. *Comments:* Sushi and sashimi, as well as a selection of traditional Japanese and innovative Pacific Rim dishes, are made to share family-style with everyone at the table at this comfortable and inviting eatery. If you don't like sushi bars, you'll like this one. And if you *love* them, this will probably be your favorite. This is one of the best restaurants in the state, even without an ocean view. Reservations strongly suggested. Named Best Sushi and Best Late-Night Menu in the 2005 'Aipono Awards.

★ ***Sea House*** *(American)*
Napili Kai Beach Resort, 5900 Lower Honoapi'ilani Road, beachfront on Napili Bay; 808-669-1500.

Hours: Breakfast 8-10:30 a.m. Lunch 11:30 a.m.-2 p.m. Dinner 5:30-9 p.m. *Sampling:* Omelets, Hawaiian sweet bread French toast, banana macadamia pancakes, Belgian waffle, or poached eggs Napili Kai ($5.25-$11.95). Luncheon sandwiches include a tiger prawn club, turkey gyro, vegetarian sandwich or the focaccia filet mignon ($5-$14). Begin your evening meal with a *pupu* of fresh steamed clams, Taste of Lahaina award-winning crisp Pacific sushi, five onion soup, or papaya and goat cheese baby spinach salad ($7-$18). They have a *keiki* menu for those 12 and under with favorites such as fish and chips, hamburgers, chicken nuggets, pasta and three-cheese pizza ($5-$8). Dinner entrees include fresh island fish, seafood cioppino, vegetarian manicotti, veal piccata, and their signature Steak Gallagher ($18-$32). *Comments:* This is one of only a handful of island restaurants that sits right on the beach. You won't find a better ocean or sunset view than this. Lovely location; good food. Their Whale Watcher's bar serves cocktails, light lunches and *pupus*.

★ ***Vino Italian Tapas and Wine Bar (Italian/Pacific Rim)***
Located in the Village Golf Course clubhouse, 2000 Village Road, Kapalua; 808-661-8466

Hours: Full lunch menu 11:30 a.m.-2 p.m.; midday service 2-5:30 p.m.; dinner 6-9:30 p.m. *Sampling & Comments:* Lunch and midday service at Vino are designed for golfers and those seeking a fairly standard lunch menu of salads, sandwiches and snacks. But at dinner, Vino is transformed, and that's when this restaurant shines. Featuring Pacific Rim–inspired Italian *tapas* and pastas, the menu is varied and creative, and the mood is cozy and romantic. Signature items include asparagus Milanese ($5.95), jumbo lump crab cake ($10.95), Madeira-braised veal cheek open-face ravioli ($7.95) and pan-seared half-moon seafood ravioli ($8.95), a first place winner at the 2004 Taste of Lahaina food festival. The extensive selection of *tapas* (price range $4.95-$17.95) are generous in size and meant to be shared, but a few entree-size dishes are also available, such as *mudicca*-crusted pan-fried veal stuffed with prosciutto and sage, parmesan-crusted pork chop Milanese or tender braised center-cut *osso buco* for two ($19.95-$37.95). Owned by D.K. Kodama (who made his mark with the stellar Sansei Restaurant), Vino opened in 2003 and has already started to rack up the accolades, including a 2004 Award of Excellence from *Wine Spectator* magazine. The wine list is one of the best in the state, created by Hawai'i's only Master Sommelier, Chuck Furuya. Wine is served in Riedel glasses and the restaurant has a cruvinet with 24 spigots, making it possible to enjoy wines by the glass that would be unaffordable by the bottle. All in all, Vino is a good restaurant fast on the way to becoming a great restaurant. Dinner reservations are recommended. Named Best New Restaurant in the 2005 'Aipono Awards.

Expensive-priced Dining

★ ***Banyan Tree*** *(Asian/Hawaiian)*

The Ritz-Carlton, 1 Ritz Carlton Drive, Kapalua; 808-669-6200.

Hours: Dinner 5:30-9:30 p.m. Closed Sunday and Monday. *Sampling:* Starters of crispy salt and pepper oysters, quail and water chestnut sausage, Kobe beef carpaccio ($12-$18). Dinner entrees such as ahi tuna and seared foie gras, honey roasted duck breast, lamb and vegetable tajine, chicken and mushrooms ($30-$48). *Comments:* This place took top honors as the 2005 'Aipono Award winner for Best Overall Restaurant. A beautiful island restaurant with Ritz-worthy dining and a great ocean view. The signature soup of coconut, sweet corn and lemongrass, garnished with crab and cilantro salad is a favorite of mine.

★ ***Gardenia Court Restaurant*** *(Island Continental)*

Kapalua Bay Hotel; 808-669-5656.

Hours: Breakfast daily 6:30 a.m.-11 a.m.; Sunday brunch 9:30 a.m.-1 p.m. Dinner nightly 5-9 p.m. *Sampling:* Gardenia Court features a lovely daily breakfast buffet ($21/$26) but they enhance it for the fabulous Sunday brunch. À la carte is also offered for breakfast during the week. The daily breakfast buffet is a much better value than the à la carte menu if you choose to add orange juice or fruit and coffee to your breakfast fare. The Sunday brunch is $32 without champagne (half price for kids 6-12) and with champagne it's $37. The à la carte dinner menu offers a variety of appetizers and light fare, like sandwiches and burgers ($7-$16), as well as entrees such as lamb chops with a Hawaiian pepper mango glaze, natural organic chicken, penne pasta and vegetables, and fresh catch ($24-$38). The long-standing Friday night seafood buffet is a best bet on the island with a lavish array of your favorite foods from the sea ($38; half price for kids 6-12). Prime rib all-you-can-eat buffet is offered for $32 on Saturday evenings. *Comments:* Sunday through Thursday nights, from 5 to 7 p.m., a Sunset Dinner menu is offered, including a choice of entree, soup or salad, beverage and dessert. The menu changes daily but servings are generous and this is a great value at $16.95. The Sunday brunch and Friday-night seafood buffet are both very popular so reservations are highly recommended. This informal restaurant is open to gentle breezes and panoramic ocean views. Very pretty setting.

★ ***Plantation House*** *(Seafood/Continental)*
2000 Plantation Club Drive, Kapalua; 808-669-6299.

Hours: Breakfast/lunch 8 a.m.-3 p.m. Dinner from 5:30 p.m. *Sampling:* The breakfast/lunch menu is available until 3 p.m. Enjoy a Benedict of crab cakes, seared ahi or smoked salmon, various omelets, Molokai sweet bread French toast ($7-$12), or fresh field-picked pineapple (Kapalua is a working pineapple plantation) with a light cinnamon-sour cream sauce ($3.50). For lunch, fresh Hawaiian-catch sandwich, rosemary-garlic chicken breast sandwich on focaccia bread, Greek chicken salad with feta-lemon vinaigrette or *panko*-crusted goat cheese salad with passionfruit vinaigrette ($8-$17). Watch the sun set and start your dinner with crispy crab–stuffed ahi, sashimi or scallop skewers wrapped in apple-smoked bacon ($7-$10). Continue your dining pleasure with Diane's Linguini (tossed with Maui tomato, basil and garlic), Pacific prawns, oven-roasted Moloka'i pork tenderloin or Maui onion–crusted lamb rack. There are plenty of fresh fish selections prepared in your choice of creative ways such as Plantation Oscar—sauteed fish served with butter-braised local asparagus and Alaskan snow-crab meat, or A Taste of Maui—pistachio-crusted fish with sauteed Maui onions, Kula tomatoes and Upcountry spinach ($16-$30). If you have a sweet tooth, don't miss the bananas Foster for two ($10). *Comments:* Their location—in the clubhouse of the Plantation Golf Course—provides what is probably the best panoramic oceanview dining in West Maui. (Plan to arrive a half-hour or so before sunset for the full experience.) Just a short drive from Lahaina and Ka'anapali and worth it. Named Best Breakfast and Best Lunch on the Green in the 2005 'Aipono Awards.

Reilley's (Steaks/Seafood)
Kahana Gateway Shopping Center, 4405 Honoapi'ilani Highway; 808-665-1881.
Hours: Dinner 5:30-10 p.m. *Sampling:* Semolina fried scallops, rosemary skewered shrimp and sweet onion crab cakes are among the dinner starters ($7-$12), as well as Caesar salad and warm brie and baby spinach salad ($6-$8). Entree selections ($18-$45) include a variety of fish, meat and fowl, with preparations, seasonings and sauces changed seasonally to take advantage of the freshest ingredients available. When I dined there, entrees included pistachio-crusted seared rare ahi, hickory-roasted salmon, horseradish roasted rack

of lamb, maple guava duck breast, and a New York strip steak with garlic molasses glaze. Save room for the Leprechaun Pie (mint chocolate chip ice cream in an Oreo cookie crust), pumpkin honey crème brulee, or cherry cinnamon bread pudding ($6-$7). *Comments:* Spacious and intimate fine dining atmosphere, yet not too stiff or formal for kids. Nice wine menu. No view, but I experienced prompt and friendly service along with a very good meal. A more limited and less expensive bar menu is offered for dining at the bar or on the open-air lanai. Reilley's is a family-operated business that was founded in 1982 on Hilton Head Island, South Carolina. The restaurant offers a children's menu for ages 15 and under.

★ ***Roy's Kahana Bar & Grill*** *(Hawaiian Regional)*
Kahana Gateway, 4405 Honoapi'ilani Highway; 808-669-6999. Also Roy's Kihei Bar & Grill at Pi'ilani Shopping Village, Kihei; www.roys restaurant.com.

Hours: 5:30-10 p.m. *Sampling:* Roy's offers a menu that changes nightly, which means you'll have the freshest foods available. Appetizers ($8-$13) might include Roy's original blackened rare ahi, seared shrimp on a stick with spicy wasabi cocktail sauce, or shrimp and pork spring roll. With an ever-changing list of nightly specials in addition to Roy's Classics, which are always on the menu, Roy's offers you plenty to choose from—entrees ($18-$32) such as Hawaiian-style *misoyaki* butterfish, jade pesto–steamed Hawaiian white fish, "Yama Mama's" meatloaf served with crispy onion rings and natural mushroom gravy or honey-mustard beef short ribs served with scalloped potatoes, poi and *lomi lomi* tomatoes. *Comments:* The trend these days is toward comfort food and chef Roy Yamaguchi has certainly used his considerable talent to create comfort foods that are exciting and innovative. The food is as good as you've heard, and Roy's is deserving of its many rave reviews and dozens of national and local awards. Roy is one of the top chefs in the islands and was instrumental in the development of Hawaiian Regional cuisine and what he calls "Hawaiian fusion." The service at Roy's is always extraordinary and the food wonderful. They are child-friendly, too. On a recent visit with my 2-year-old grandchild, I was delighted to see a high chair miraculously appear, along with "toddler munchies" and small toys to keep little hands busy. The only down side at Roy's: the noise from the kitchen combined with the high ceilings makes it difficult to carry on a conversation. If you're looking for a serene, romantic dinner, this is not the place. But for consistently great food and service, you can't beat Roy's. (And keep an eye out for celebrity diners who might drop by.)

The Terrace *(Pacific Rim)*

The Ritz-Carlton, 1 Ritz-Carlton Drive, Kapalua; 808-669-6200.

Hours: Breakfast 6:30-11 a.m.; lunch noon-3:30 p.m.; dinner 5:30-9 p.m. *Sampling:* À la carte breakfast entrees ($8-$18). Lunch *pupus*, salads, burgers, sandwiches, pizzas ($10-$19). Dinner offers casual fare (similar to lunch offerings) for $14-$18. Regional specialty entrees include Hunan glazed pork tenderloin, lemon garlic roasted duck breast, Thai-style bouillabaisse or grilled *paniolo* rib eye ($24-$32). *Comments:* Overlooking the courtyard and pool area with great sunset views. The pleasant, informal atmosphere is enhanced by an extended patio with awning that makes it look like a conservatory or the garden room of an elegant stately home.

Ma'alaea-Kihei Area

Inexpensive-priced Dining

Alexander's Fish, Chicken & Chips *(American)*

1913 South Kihei Road, Kihei; 808-874-0788; also a location in Lahaina (see Lahaina Dining).

Hours: 11 a.m.-9 p.m. *Sampling:* Meals ($6.45-$10.95) include grilled or deep-fried shrimp, mahi, *ono*, ahi, clams, calamari, ribs and chicken. À la carte items include onion rings, hushpuppies, zucchini, rice or barbecue beans ($1.15-$4.95). Just want a snack? You can get chicken, fish, ribs and clams by the piece ($1.65-$6.95). Sandwiches of fish, chicken or shrimp ($7.25-$8.50). *Comments:* I feel the food is a bit inconsistent. Sometimes good, sometimes mediocre. They have limited seating at the counter or at a few patio tables. Very casual; beachwear is welcome.

★ ***Annie's Deli & Catering*** *(American)*

Nani Kai Village, 2511 South Kihei Road, Kihei; 808-875-8647.

Hours: 9 a.m.-4 p.m. Monday through Saturday; 10 a.m.-3 p.m. Sunday. *Sampling:* Breakfast featuring pancakes, French toast, lox and bagel, fresh fruit plate, breakfast croissant ($2.29-$6.49). Annie's Aloha Breakfast (2 eggs with toast, taters or rice, ham, sausage, bacon or cheese, and iced tea or coffee; $5.99). Sandwiches with choice of bread and cheese. Then select a side salad (potato, pasta, bean, or red slaw) to accompany your selection of turkey, ham, tuna, chicken salad, roast beef, French dip, Reuben, pastrami, corned beef, veggie or BLT with avocado, and pita melts ($4.95-$7.95). Daily specials (with entree, rice and salad). Smoothies and shakes, too.

Comments: Small café with indoor and outdoor seating. Across from Kama'ole Beach II.

★ **Aroma D'italia Ristorante** *(Italian)*

Kihei Town Center, 1881 South Kihei Road, Kihei, next to Foodland; 808-879-0133.

Hours: Dinner 5-9 p.m. Closed Sunday. *Sampling:* Antipasto and salads ($3.95-$9.95). Spaghetti with meat or meatless sauce, spinach lasagna with homemade Italian sausage, chicken parmigiana, grilled marinated shrimp, eggplant parmigiana, veal marsala, piccata or parmigiana ($8.95-$19.95). For dessert try a spumoni wedge, gelato truffle turtle, freshly made cannoli, or homemade tiramisu ($4.95). "Bambino" menu ($4.95-$7.95). Wine list, too. *Comments:* A casual, homey atmosphere (complete with red-checkered tablecloths) with some of the best food and most affordable prices to be found for Italian dining anywhere on the island. Dishes are made from scratch using family recipes. Ample portions, flavorful sauces. Save room for their wonderful spumoni wedge. Layers and layers of cake and ice cream. This is a charming, old-fashioned homestyle restaurant that has a lot of aloha—even if it is Italian.

Bada Bing *(Italian)*

1945 South Kihei Road, Kihei Kalama Village; 808-875-0188.

Hours: 11 a.m.-10 p.m. *Sampling:* All-day menu ranges from spinach-artichoke dip and fried ravioli marinara to shrimp scampi, seafood pasta and a variety of pizzas. Most items are well under $15. *Comments:* Bada Bing used to be a nightclub, but no longer. It is now an Italian restaurant featuring a fun, funky ambiance with walls loaded with memorabilia. A good family place.

Bocalino Bistro & Bar *(Mediterranean)*

Azeka Mauka, 1279 South Kihei Road, Kihei; 808-874-9299; www.bocalino.com.

Hours: Monday through Friday 5 p.m.-1:30 a.m.; Saturday and Sunday 7 p.m.-1:30 a.m.. *Sampling:* A simple menu (one page) of appetizers, salads, entrees and sides ($5-$25.95). Italian-style entrees include pasta alfredo, lasagna *al forno*, filet mignon *au* brie and chicken Diane. *Comments:* Attractive dining area. Entertainment 10 p.m.-1 a.m. No cover charge.

★ ***Da Kitchen Express*** *(Local)*

Rainbow Mall, 2439 South Kihei Road, Kihei; 808-875-7782. (There is another location in Kahului.)

Hours: 9 a.m.-9 p.m. *Sampling:* Breakfast served 9-11 a.m. (Kihei location only) includes *loco moco*, Maui-style French toast, or omelets ($5.75-$7.25). Plate lunches include two scoops of rice and potato-macaroni salad with entrees such as hamburger steak, teriyaki chicken, fish tempura, *laulau* or Hawaiian plate ($6.25-$9.25), and oodles of noodles ($5.25-$6.25). Sandwiches or salads, local style ($5.75-$6.50). *Comments:* Good value, very large portions, great local grinds. My husband, a "local boy," loves Da Kitchen, and I do, too. Apparently we are not alone. Da Kitchen (both locations) was named "Best Cheap Eats" in the 2005 'Aipono Awards.

Enrique's *(Mexican)*

2395 South Kihei Road, Dolphin Plaza (behind Pizza Hut); 808-875-2910.

Hours: 10 a.m.-9 p.m. Monday through Saturday; until 8 p.m. Sunday. *Sampling:* Flautas, tamales, hard-shell tacos, burritos or quesadillas ($2.50-$7.95). Entrees include beans and rice with main dishes such as chicken *barboca* or *mole* chocolate, shrimp chipotle, or fajitas with steak, chicken or fish ($8.95-$11.95). Bring your own wine or beer. *Comments:* Good Mexican fare from the chef's hometown of Veracruz, Mexico. The dining space is a bit limited, but you can always pick up your food to go and head for the beach across the street. Live music Friday and Saturday evenings.

Fernando's *(Mexican)*

Lipoa Shopping Center, 41 East Lipoa Street, Kihei; 808-879-9952.

Hours: 9 a.m.-9 p.m. *Sampling:* Traditional Mexican fare featuring combination plates ($5.75-$9.99) or à la carte hard and soft-shell tacos, enchiladas and quesadillas ($2.25-$4.99). The breakfast menu includes huevos rancheros, chorizo and eggs, and a breakfast burrito ($3.99-$5.99).

Hanafuda Saimin *(Local/Asian)*

Azeka Mauka, 1279 South Kihei Road, Kihei; 808-879-9033.

Hours: Monday through Thursday 7 a.m.-11 p.m.; Friday and Saturday 7 a.m. to 3 a.m.; Sunday 7 a.m.-9 p.m. *Sampling:* Features plate lunches such as fried saimin with teri beef, roast pork, chopsteak, curry or beef stew, chicken *katsu*, *kalbi* and *loco moco* ($6.25-$7.95). Sandwiches and burgers ($3.95-$4.75). Personalize your saimin ($4.95-$6.95) by adding your favorites from a variety of ingredients like *char siu* pork, teri beef strips, kim chee or won ton (add-ons $1-$2.50). Take-out saimin is available in medium size only ($4.95). *Comments:* In the tradition of saimin houses, they are open until 3 a.m. on the weekends, so you have someplace to go aftah da movie.

Hawaiian Moons Salad Bar & Deli *(Healthy/Vegetarian)*
2411 South Kihei Road, Kihei; 808-875-4356.

Hours: Store open 8 a.m.-9 p.m.; salad bar 8 a.m.-7:30 p.m. *Sampling:* Salad bar ($6.95/lb) offers organic greens and veggies plus rice and pasta salads all priced per pound. Hot entree selections include Third World macaroni and cheese, tofu enchiladas, African black-eyed peas, *ulu* stew, and curried potatoes, also per pound. Lasagna, homemade soup, and free-range turkey, turkey Reuben, and roasted veggie sandwiches are available. *Comments:* The Hawaiian Moons Natural Food Store offers vitamins, herbs, and natural grocery items like fresh organic produce. The juice bar also serves espresso, smoothies, soft serve, and fruit cups.

★ ***Hirohachi*** *(Japanese)*
Kihei Town Center, 1881 South Kihei Road, Kihei; 808-875-7474.

Hours: Lunch Wednesday through Friday 11:30 a.m.-2:30 p.m. Dinner Tuesday through Sunday 5-9:30 p.m. Closed Monday. *Sampling:* Lunches include chicken *katsu*, soba and udon noodles, or tempura *teishoku* ($8.50-$16.50). "Roll" into dinner with a Bamboo Roll, Banzai Roll, California Roll or Rock'n Roll sushi ($6-$15). Sushi dinner combination ($25-$30) or dinner dishes such as una don, ten don, tempura zen (seafood with vegetables) or chicken *katsu* zen ($16.50-$30), or noodle dishes ($10.50-$16.50). *Comments:* A large selection of sushi and sashimi. Cute little restaurant with five or six cozy tables, or dining at the sushi bar. Black and white tiled floor gives it a clean, crisp look.

Home Maid Bakery & Deli *(Bakery)*
Azeka Makai, 1280 South Kihei Road, Kihei; 808-874-6035.

Hours: Monday through Friday 6:30 a.m.-4 p.m.; Saturday 6:30 a.m.-2 p.m.; closed Sunday. *Sampling:* Sandwiches and local breakfast and lunch plates mostly under $6. *Comments:* Wonderful empanadas, *malasadas*, *manju* and bread pudding. (Original bakery is in Wailuku.)

Jawz Fish Tacos *(Mexican)*
Azeka Mauka, 1279 South Kihei Road, Kihei; 808-874-8226.

Hours: 11 a.m.-9 p.m. *Sampling:* The menu is basically $4-$10 and mahimahi or *ono* are the fish selections, shrimp, chicken and steak fill your taco, taco salad, burritos or kabobs. *Comments:* Opened in summer 2003, you'll recognize the menu and crew from the "Taco Van" that has been down at Makena Beach for years. *Keiki* menu, too.

Joy's Place *(Organic/Healthy)*
1993 South Kihei Road, Island Surf Building; 808-879-9258

Hours: 10 a.m.-5 p.m. Closed Sunday. *Sampling:* Specializing in homemade soups, sandwiches and salads featuring fresh organic ingredients (like free range turkey). Many vegan and vegetarian items offered. Fresh tuna salad sandwich (using fresh tuna caught locally, not canned), curried hummus wrap in collard green, falafel burger, Cobb salad ($4.95-$9.35). Smoothies and home-baked sweet treats such as coconut macaroons and chocolate brownies with oat crust (some are sugar free). *Comments:* Cute little eatery that just opened in 2004. Across from the Cove (a popular beach and surf spot), this is a great place to grab a healthy sandwich or bowl of soup.

Kaiona Café *(Gourmet Deli)*
Kihei Kalama Village, 1913-D South Kihei Road, Kihei; 808-891-2828.

Hours: 7 a.m.-5:30 p.m. Monday through Saturday; 7 a.m.-2 p.m. Sunday. *Sampling:* Breakfast items include French toast, omelets, *ratatouille*, crepes and a variety of eggs Benedict ($3.75-$6.75). For lunch, sandwiches and wraps, fresh salads, spaghetti and a variety of plate lunches ($5.95-8.95). Gourmet desserts range from crepes to crème brulee along with gourmet cakes and cream puffs. *Comments:* A casual little open-air cafe. Everything is baked fresh daily and is good to go or enjoy on the patio. Cream puffs are filled to order, and they make their own crepes. Picnics, coffee drinks and fresh pastries to go. They also sell their own blend of packaged gourmet coffee.

★ ***Kihei Caffe*** *(Continental)*
1945 South Kihei Road, Kihei; 808-879-2230.

Hours: 5:30 a.m.-2 p.m. daily; breakfast all day; lunch 11 a.m.-2 p.m. *Sampling:* Breakfast includes huevos rancheros, biscuits and gravy, veggie scramble, French toast, flavored pancakes, Mueslix and omelets ($4.95-6.95). Burgers, and sandwiches ranging from grilled Reubens and Rachels to pastrami, roast beef, turkey and tuna ($3.95-$6.95). Caesar, grilled chicken or fish, and honey cashew chicken salads ($6.95-$10.95). *Comments:* A popular local hangout that visitors have discovered as well. Coffee drinks plus fresh baked goods made daily. Really yummy breakfasts—not a steal, but a good value. Plan on a bit of a wait, as there seem to be plenty of early-to-rise locals and jet-lagged visitors who take advantage of the 5:30 a.m. opening. The French toast (made with Portuguese sweet bread) is light and fluffy. Huevos rancheros are wonderful, as are the omelets. *Keiki* breakfast and lunch menu with nothing over $3.95.

Life's a Beach *(American/Mexican)*

Kihei Kalama Village, 1913 South Kihei Road, Kihei; 808-891-8010.

Hours: 11 a.m.-10 p.m.; happy hour 4-7 p.m. daily; bar until 2 a.m. *Sampling:* Salads, burrito, soft tacos, burgers, hot dogs, nachos, quesadillas and sandwiches ($6.95-$11.95). *Comments:* There's real sand at the front entrance with tall tables and beach umbrellas for outdoor seating. Inside there's a wraparound bar with several TVs, lots of surfing and sports mementos, and bright yellow-and-white-striped tablecloths. Live entertainment most nights along with karaoke on Sunday. Mucho cheapo margaritas and mai tais ("home of the $1 mai tai"). More bar than restaurant.

Maui Thai Kitchen *(Thai)*

Rainbow Mall, 2439 South Kihei Road, Kihei; 808-874-5605.

Hours: Lunch Monday through Saturday 11 a.m.-2:30 p.m. Dinner nightly 5-10 p.m. *Sampling:* Thai crisp noodles, Thai toast, green papaya salad, long rice chicken soup, and chicken, beef, pork or shrimp served with Thai oyster sauce, Thai basil sauce, Thai ginger and more. Sample crab with yellow curry or sauteed mussels with chile sauce. Most items in the $8-$15 range. Combination dinners from $40 for two. *Comments:* A very lengthy menu ranging from noodle dishes to salads, seafood, vegetarian fare, and curry dishes. Chef's suggestions offer combinations for 2, 3 or 4 people. Entrees available in mild, medium or hot. Attractive eatery, spotlessly clean, with white tablecloths. Tucked in the back of the mall.

Panda Express *(Mandarin Chinese)*

Azeka Mauka, 1279 South Kihei Road, Kihei; 808-879-0883.

Hours: 10:30 a.m.-9 p.m. (until 8:30 p.m. on Sunday). *Sampling:* Combination plates with your choice of entrees. *Comments:* A restaurant chain started in California.

Peggy Sue's *(Diner)*

Azeka Mauka, 1279 South Kihei Road, Kihei; 808-875-8944.

Hours: 11 a.m.-10 p.m. Friday and Saturday, 11 a.m.-9 p.m. Sunday through Thursday. *Sampling:* The menu reflects the '50s diner/malt shop theme with a selection of creative sandwiches, burgers and hot dogs served with "the works" and a side of fries. Try a Good Golly Miss Molly (teriyaki burger with pineapple), Earth Angel (veggie burger) or Blue Moon (bacon and blue cheese burger), Sea Cruise (tuna salad sandwich), Splish

Splash (grilled mahi sandwich) or Funky Chicken (teriyaki chicken sandwich) ($4.95-$12.95). Entrees range from chili and rice to New York strip steak ($4.75-$14.95). *Comments:* They feature an original 1954 Seeburg jukebox that operates from the box or by remote from the dining table. The pink-and-blue decor gives the malt shop a "Peggy Sue" look and the waitstaff is dressed to match. There are plenty of cool, creamy old-fashioned fountain selections including malts, milkshakes, egg creams, sodas, sundaes and banana splits to keep the '50s tradition alive. I thought they did a better job with the chicken dishes and sandwiches than with the burgers, and the French "fries" were oven baked, which took away from their, well, "authenticity" (too healthy?). Cute place—the atmosphere is fun and friendly.

★ ***Pita Paradise*** *(Greek)*

Kihei Kalama Village, 1913 South Kihei Road, Kihei; 808-875-7679.

Hours: Lunch Monday through Saturday 11 a.m.-5 p.m.; dinner nightly 5-9:30 p.m. *Sampling:* The pita sandwiches (featuring handmade pita) include lamb, veggie, Mediterranean chicken, steak and Kula onions, teriyaki chicken, chicken Caesar or fresh catch (lunch $6.95-$11.95). Kabobs are served with sauteed veggies and herbed new potatoes ($12.95-$14.95). For dinner they have salads, pitas and pastas, ranging from Australian range lamb to ultimate veggie or seafood pasta. Dinner prices are slightly high but portions are bigger ($8.95-$18.95). Be sure to save room for the baklava ice cream cake ($5.95). *Comments:* Following in his father's footsteps, John Arabatzis (son of Ioannis "Yanni" Arabatzizs of the Greek Bistro) and Christine Graham started this small, casual eatery. I love the flavorful pita sandwiches. They serve wine and beer. Casual dining at patio tables on the deck or dine inside.

Royal Thai Cuisine *(Thai)*

Azeka Makai, 1280 South Kihei Road, Kihei; 808-874-0813.

Hours: Lunch Monday through Saturday 11 a.m.-3 p.m. Dinner nightly 4:45-9:30 p.m. *Sampling:* Traditional Thai appetizers, soups, salads plus entrees such as Evil Prince, lemon beef, Thai garlic or Thai ginger dishes ($6.95-$13.95). Complete dinners ($12.95-$13.95). *Comments:* The prices are pretty good, but the portions are a little small.

Seascape Ma'alaea Restaurant *(American)*

Maui Ocean Center, 192 Ma'alaea Road, Ma'alaea; 808-270-7043.

Hours: 11 a.m.-3:30 p.m. *Sampling: Pupus* include crisp onion rings or coconut shrimp with mango chutney ($3.95-$8.95). Several salad selections, or enjoy the "Local Boy Favorite," a sandwich filled with lobster salad and layers of shrimp with fresh dill aioli. sauteed mahimahi or grilled ahi as well as a Cajun chicken sandwich ($8.95-$15.95). Entrees include cashew chicken, fish and chips or teriyaki tofu ($13.95-$15.95). Tropical drinks and wine and beer available. *Comments:* Open to the public without admission to the ocean center. Separate entrance on Lahaina side or up from the harbor. Overlooks the Ma'alaea Harbor with large viewing windows into the "Edge of the Reef" tank to watch the tropical fish and reef sharks.

Shabu Shabu Toji (Japanese)

Azeka Makai, 1280 South Kihei Road, Kihei; 808-875-8366.

Hours: Tuesday through Saturday, lunch 11:30 a.m.-2:30 p.m.; Tuesday through Sunday, dinner 5:30-9:30 p.m.; closed Monday. *Sampling:* Shabu shabu is a Japanese-style fondue and translates to "swish." Order beef, pork, seafood or vegetables, "swish" them in a hot broth, then dip them into a variety of sauces. Shabu shabu meals (lunch $11.95-$14.75; dinner $18.75-$22.25) are served with steamed rice, vegetables and Japanese pickles. Japanese soups, salads, appetizers and plate lunches are also available.

★ ***Shaka Sandwich and Pizza*** *(Sandwiches/Pizza)*

1770 South Kihei Road, Kihei; 808-874-0331.

Hours: 10:30 a.m.-9 p.m. daily, Friday and Saturday until 10 p.m. *Sampling:* Hot sandwiches in 7" (small) or 14" (large) sizes include cheese steak, pizza steak, or cheese steak supreme, as well as grilled turkey and cheese, grilled veggie, or homemade meatball and cheese (small $5.10-$6.40; large $10.20-$12.80). Assorted cold hoagies (small $5.35-$5.75; large $10.70-$11.50). Authentic New York–style pizzas are made with Shaka's homemade sauce and are available in thin crust or Sicilian thick crust. Choose their combos or make up your own ($14.95-$26.95). Also calzone and stromboli ($13.50-$16.75). *Comments:* If you like New York subway-style pizza you're in for a real treat. Available for dine-in, take-out, or delivery.

Moderate-priced Dining

Antonio's *(Italian)*

Longs Center, 1215 South Kihei Road, Kihei; 808-875-8800.

Hours: Tuesday through Sunday 5-9 p.m. *Sampling:* Antipasti choices include homemade soup, sauteed calamari, and mozzarella, tomato and eggplant salad ($4.95-$8.95). Various pastas with seafood, meatballs, smoked salmon or vegetarian style ($8.95-$17.95), or entrees such as homemade Italian sausage ($14.95), risotto ($16.95-$17.95) and *osso buco* ($23.95). *Comments:* Charming little Italian cafe. You'll enter a little piece of Antonio's homeland when you walk through the door. Decor is simple, with cheery red-and-white checkered tablecloths and some amusing memorabilia along the walls. Antonio makes his own bread (baked on the premises) and a wonderful tiramisu. The food is excellent (the fourth-generation recipes are all made from scratch), and Antonio's enthusiasm for cooking and sharing his food really shines through.

Big Wave Cafe *(American)*
Longs Kihei Center, 1215 South Kihei Road, Kihei; 808-891-8688; www.bigwavecafe.com.

Hours: Breakfast and lunch 7:30 a.m.-2 p.m.; late lunch 2-5 p.m.; dinner 5-9 p.m. *Sampling:* For breakfast there's Hawaiian sweet bread french toast, breakfast burrito, eggs Benedict and many other breakfast favorites ($3-$13). Lunch offerings include burgers, sandwiches, plate lunches and entrees such as shrimp scampi and baby back ribs ($7.95-$14.95). Box lunches are available to go. Dinner entrees include blackened ahi, banana-crusted chicken, and spaghetti with meat sauce ($13.95-$20). *Comments:* Big Wave Cafe is operating in the location that used to house Stella Blues. Comfortable coffeeshop atmosphere, with indoor or outdoor patio dining.

Blue Marlin Harborfront Grill & Bar *(Seafood)*
Harbor Shops at Ma'alaea, (harborfront, lower level), Ma'alaea; 808-244-8844.

Hours: 11 a.m.-10 p.m. *Sampling*: À la carte items include crab and shrimp–stuffed mushrooms, summer rolls, pizza and ahi poke ($6-$13) and sandwiches including veggie foccacia and the shrimp burger ($7-$11). Entrees include plenty of fresh fish selections, and "real food" like pork ribs, roast chicken, and burgers ($15.95-$28.95). Super Specials include fish and chips or chopped steak meals for $12.95. *Comments:* This is a very comfortable harborfront eatery—it feels like you're outside when you're in! Or sit at one of the tables on the boardwalk and really be outside if you choose. I've eaten here several times, and the food has always been good.

★ ***Buzz's Wharf*** *(American/Seafood)*
Ma'alaea Harbor, 300 Ma'alaea Road, Ma'alaea; 808-244-5426.

Hours: Lunch 11 a.m.-3 p.m. Dinner 5-9 p.m. Sunday brunch 10 a.m.-3 p.m. *Sampling:* All-day *pupu* menu ($7.95-$12.95). Lunches offer fish and chips, burgers, a variety of sandwiches and other entrees ($6.95-$15.95). Dinners range from Buzz's specialty Prawns Tahitian to coconut milk shrimp curry, chicken marsala or prime rib ($16.95-$27.95). Entrees are served with salad, vegetables and fresh baked rolls. *Comments:* Offers a scenic view of the Ma'alaea

Harbor activities. Bar/lounge. Vegetarian entrees and a full-page *keiki* menu. I've dined here many times for dinner and have never been disappointed. Love the award-winning Prawns Tahitian.

Canton Chef *(Cantonese-Szechuan)*

Kama'ole Shopping Center, 2463 South Kihei Road, Kihei; 808-879-1988.

Hours: Lunch 11 a.m.-2 p.m. Dinner 5-9 p.m. *Sampling:* Same menu for lunch and dinner. Choose from sizzling platters, chicken and duck dishes, earthen pot courses, Szechuan selections, seafood, noodles or pre-set dinners. À la carte items from $6 for egg roll up to $50 for abalone with mushrooms. Most items $7-$13 range. Combination dinners for two or four people are available ($13.75-$34).

★ ***Greek Bistro*** *(Greek/Mediterranean/Italian)*

Kai Nani Shopping Center, 2511 South Kihei Road, Kihei; 808-879-9330.

Hours: 5-10 p.m. *Sampling:* From Greece sample moussaka, seafood souvlaki, sliced leg of lamb, or homemade spanakopita ($17-$24). Appetizers include traditional dolmathes, feta with kalamata olives, or bistro pita bread ($4-$10). *Comments:* Excellent Greek food—also try Pita Paradise at Kalama Village, run by another family member.

Isana *(Korean/Yakiniku/Sushi)*

Maui Beach Resort, 515 South Kihei Road, Kihei; 808-874-5700.

Hours: Monday, Tuesday and Sunday 11 a.m.-10 p.m.; Wednesday through Saturday until 1 a.m. Sushi bar 5-10 p.m. *Sampling:* Select from their Korean barbecue offerings ($13.95-$19.95) or *kalbi* ribs, beef loin, chicken or seafood. *Kalbi* tang, oxtail soup and bean paste stew are some of the more exotic selections ($9.50-$15.95). Full sushi bar. *Comments:* Cocktails upstairs at the Karaoke Lounge. Half-off sushi 10 p.m. to closing Wednesday through Saturday.

★ ***Kai Ku Ono Bar & Grill*** *(Sandwiches and Pupus)*

Kai Nani Shopping Center, 2511 South Kihei Road, Kihei; 808-879-1954.

Hours: 8 a.m.-midnight. *Sampling:* Breakfast menu is one of the best Kihei/Wailea values. Half eggs Benedict, two-egg omelets, egg white scramble with potato and bacon, French toast, and even Spam with eggs ($4.95-$9.95). Lunchtime sandwiches include their yummy barbecue *kalua* pig sandwich, French dip or KKO "killa" burger with Maui onions, mushrooms, bacon, barbecue sauce and cheddar ($7.95-$14.95). Evening selections served 5-10 p.m. offer macadamia nut chicken or fresh fish, mango barbecue ribs, giant Thai scallops and fish and chips ($12.95-$19.95). Kids' menu (under age 12) only $4.95 for cheese quesadilla, grilled cheese, chicken dinosaurs or pasta. *Comments:* Kai Ku Ono means the

"Good Bay" in Hawaiian, but they call it KKO for short. Get a table that is oceanfront and enjoy some people watching and even a sunset. All around good fare at good prices.

Lu Lu's *(Eclectic)*

Kihei Kalama Village, 1913 South Kihei Road, behind Bada Bing, Kihei; 808-879-9944.

Hours: 11 a.m.-11 p.m. full menu available; 11 p.m.-1 a.m. bar only, must be 21 or over. *Sampling:* Roast pork, meat loaf, steak, barbecue chicken, spare ribs or fresh catch ($13.95-$20.95). Burgers and sandwiches ($5.95-$10.95); spicy chicken wings, nachos, popcorn shrimp, quesadillas, island *poke*, crab cakes or steamers ($7.95-$10.95). *Comments:* An open, airy, upstairs "deck"' with a surprisingly great ocean view from this building in the rear of Kihei Kalama Village. Count up from 2 pool tables to 21 TVs, to 40 seats at the central bar. Bottle and draft beers. Fun, casual dining with live entertainment, and when the stage is not in use, it becomes a comfortable lounge area with leopard skin couches.

★ ***Ma'alaea Grill*** *(Hawaiian Regional)*

Harbor Shops at Ma'alaea, (Upstairs, harborfront), Ma'alaea; 808-243-2206; www.cafeoleirestaurants.com.

Hours: Lunch from 10:30 a.m. daily. Dinner 5-9 p.m. Tuesday through Sunday. *Sampling:* Lunch options include curry chicken, quinoa or taro salads and sandwiches such as crab club, seared ahi sandwich, or entrees such as creamy chicken fettuccini or tempura mahi and chips ($8-$11). Dinners offer appetizers such as Manoa lettuce wraps, tempura potato cakes or lemongrass chicken lumpia ($6.95-$12.95) and entrees range from rotisserie roast duckling to Pacific seafood fettuccine or *kiawe*-grilled New York steak ($14.95-$20.95). *Keiki* menu available ($2.95-$4.95). *Comments:* A great harborfront location. Owned and operated by chefs Dana and Michael Pastula, this is one of their three restaurants on Maui (and the largest). These folks give a great quality meal for a good price. Worth driving down for lunch or dinner from Wailea or Lahaina and a perfect stop after a trip to the aquarium or a boating excursion from the harbor.

Marco's Southside Grill *(Italian)*

1445 South Kihei Road, Kihei; 808-874-4041. (Also a location in Kahului.)

Hours: 7:30 a.m.-10 p.m. daily. *Sampling:* Breakfast (7:30 a.m.-2 p.m.) includes their special chocolate cinnamon French toast, create-your-own omelet, classic eggs Benedict, various pancakes and other selections ($5.95-$16.95). Sandwiches and more sandwiches for lunch or dinner, from deli style to hot-off-the-grill choices: Italian sausage, grilled veggie, chicken parmigiano, tuna melt with tomatoes, and more ($8.95-$14.95). Salads ($4.95-$14.95) include blue cheese, oriental chicken, Greek salad or stuffed tomato. For appetizers, enjoy mozzarella marinara, gnocchi, buffalo wings or spinach and artichoke dip ($5.95-$12.95); entrees include veal parmigiano, baked *opakapaka*, roasted chicken breast or clams and linguini, along with just about any other pasta dish you can imagine ($7.95-$28.95). For kids 12 and under they offer grilled cheese, pasta with marinara and chicken fingers ($7.95-$9.95). *Comments:* Good food and a nice atmosphere in a Mediterranean villa-type setting. Indoor seating or outdoor dining on the wraparound patio lanai that faces Kihei Road. Marco's has another restaurant in Kahului with the same menu but a more casual setting.

Pupu Lounge Seafood & Grill *(Seafood)*
Kihei Kalama Village, 1945 South Kihei Road, Kihei; 808-875-4111.

Hours: Lunch noon-5 p.m., dinner 5-10 p.m. *Sampling:* Selection of *pupus* (appetizers) and sandwiches for lunch ($7.99-$12.99). For dinner, start with a *pupu* of steamer clams, coconut shrimp or fried calamari, among others ($6.99-$15.99). Entrees include Mediterranean chicken orzo, blackened rare ahi, surf and turf and herb-roasted chicken ($16.99-$25.99). *Comments:* Attractive thatched hut, open-air decor. This is a relatively new addition to the Kihei dining scene.

★ Sansei Seafood Restaurant and Sushi Bar
(Sushi/Pacific Rim)
Kihei Town Center, 1881 South Kihei Road, Kihei; 808-879-0004; another location in Kapalua.

Hours: Dinner nightly from 5:30 to 10 p.m.; late night specials, Thursday through Saturday, 10 p.m.-1 a.m.

See "Kapalua Dining" for menu description.

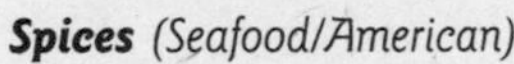

Spices *(Seafood/American)*
Maui Coast Hotel, 2259 South Kihei Road, Kihei; 808-891-8860; www.spicesmaui.com.

Hours: Breakfast 7-11:30 a.m.; lunch 11:30 a.m.-2 p.m.; dinner 5-10 p.m. *Sampling:* Breakfast omelets, crepes, island pancakes ($4.95-$12.95). Lunches include plenty of hearty soups and salads, burgers and sandwiches ($7.95-$12.95). Dinners include chef's daily roast specials, Big Island pork chops, Hawaiian-style cioppino, and prime rib ($16.95-$24.95). Fresh fish priced daily.

★ ***Stella Blues Cafe & Deli*** *(Eclectic)*

Azeka Mauka, 1279 South Kihei Road, Kihei; 808-874-3779.

Hours: Breakfast 7:30-11 a.m., Sunday until 2 p.m. Lunch daily 11 a.m. to 4 p.m. Dinner 5-10 p.m. *Sampling:* Breakfast offers egg dishes, French toast and flavored pancakes ($5.95-$12.95). Lunch salads include Asian chicken, Cobb, and several Caesars ($7.95-$12.95). Homemade soup, chicken chili and sandwiches such as chicken salad croissant, BLT, Mom's egg salad, French dip, and fresh fish and from Stella's grill there are burgers, pastrami or tuna melts, Reuben and quesadillas ($5.95-$10.95). For dinner, select from pasta, *kiawe*-oven pizza, fresh fish, jambalaya, miso shrimp, baby back ribs or tofu red curry ($12.95-$22.95). *Comments:* Attractive indoor dining space, as well as patio seating and a sleek, curved bar. The modern decor is tailored with open-beamed ceilings and wood accents.

★ ***Thailand Cuisine*** *(Thai)*

Kukui Mall, 1819 South Kihei Road, Kihei; 808-875-0839. Another location at Maui Mall in Kahului.

Hours: Lunch Monday through Saturday 11 a.m.-2:30 p.m. Dinner nightly 5-10 p.m. *Sampling:* Noodles, curries or salads Thai style. Menu is offered for lunch or dinner with the same prices. Pad Thai, green curry, ginger coconut soup, pineapple fried rice and other traditional Thai dishes ($5.95-$15.95). *Comments:* I tried the pad Thai and the pineapple fried rice for lunch. Both portions were very generous and the fried rice was attractively served in a scooped-out half-pineapple. Large dining facility and our hostess/waitress was garbed in authentic costume. Food was quickly prepared and came to the table steaming hot.

Vietnamese Cuisine Restaurant *(Vietnamese)*

Azeka Makai, 1280 South Kihei Road, Kihei; 808-875-2088.

Hours: 10 a.m.-9:30 p.m. (9 p.m. on Sunday). *Sampling:* Noodle specialties such as crispy egg noodle with seafood, rice plates, Vietnamese burritos (*banh hoi*), vermicelli noodles, and Chinese wok dishes filled with steamy vegetables and your choice of chicken, beef or seafood ($7.25-$21.95).

Expensive-priced Dining

Five Palms Beach Grill *(Pacific Rim)*

Mana Kai Resort, 2960 South Kihei Road, Kihei; 808-879-2607; www.fivepalmsrestaurant.com.

Hours: Breakfast/lunch 8 a.m.-2:30 p.m. Dinner 5-9:30 p.m.; *Pupu* menu and happy hour 2:45-6 p.m. *Sampling:* A nice breakfast menu including such unique items as short-ribs *moco*, *kalua* pork omelet and, my personal favorite, baked apple banana and cinnamon pancake with macadamia nut butter ($6.95-$16.95). Daily special features half-off on *pupus* from 2:45-6 p.m. in both the bar and open-air patio. *Pupu* menu includes baked artichoke, braised short ribs, lobster roll, calamari, spinach salad and seared ahi ($9-$16). For lunch enjoy a lobster BLT, prime rib French dip, grilled chicken sandwich, or a baby romaine salad ($7.95-$16.95). Sunset dinner specials are for 5 and 5:30 p.m. seatings only and are a prix-fixe three-course meal ($22.95). Dinner specialties include pineapple braised beef short ribs, Szechuan glazed rack of lamb, Hawaiian bouillabaisse, grilled Pacific salmon and fresh catch ($27.95-$42.95). *Keiki* menu offers French toast, buttered noodles, cheeseburger and fries or cheese pizza ($5.95-$8.95). *Comments:* Morning and afternoon meals are served out on the open-air patio, which is a lovely setting with views of Keawakapu Beach. Evenings dine inside, where you'll find rich wood and lovely chandeliers, with booths in brown and cream-colored brocades accented by Hawaiian paintings. It has a very warm Hawaiian feeling. This is one of Kihei's nicest beachfront dining locations and the food is consistently good.

★ ***Harlow's Kihei Prime Rib & Seafood House*** *(American)*

Kai Nani Shopping Center, 2511 South Kihei Road, Kihei; 808-879-1954.

Hours: 5-10 p.m. Early-bird 2 for 1 specials 5-6 p.m. *Sampling:* Appetizers include spicy garlic baked shrimp and lobster and crab cake ($9-$13). Entree "favorites" are served with vegetable, starch and rolls and include teriyaki grilled pork loin or cherry cola BBQ glazed beef ribs. From the *makai* (the sea) section of the menu choose an entree such as Hawaiian seafood casserole, giant Thai scallops or *opakapaka* mac nut; from the *mauka* (the land) enjoy their famous prime rib, filet mignon, grilled lamb chops or surf and turf (entrees $18-$37). *Keiki* menu, too. *Comments:* Second-floor location gives it a good ocean and sunset view. A long-time Kihei favorite.

★ ***Roy's Kihei Bar & Grill***

Pi'ilani Shopping Village, 303 Pi'ikea Avenue, Kihei; 808-891-1120; www.roysrestaurant.com. Another location in Kahana.

See "Honokowai-Kapalua Dining" for sampling and comments.

★ ***Sarento's on the Beach*** *(Italian)*

2980 South Kihei Road, Kihei; 808-875-7555.

Hours: Dinner nightly 5:30 p.m.-10 p.m.; lounge 5 p.m.-midnight. *Sampling:* Enjoy your evening meal with a first course of portobello Napoleon (a tower of prosciutto, eggplant, mozzarella and tomato with arugula pesto), smoked salmon Italiano, or calamari *fritta* ($9.95-$12.95). Entrees range from double pork chop with a Chianti dried-cherry sauce to *penne calabrese* (with homemade Italian sauce, eggplant with tomato, garlic and goat cheese) and lobster cannelloni with braised greens and grilled mushroom. ($25.95-$39.95). We tried the baked potato ravioli and it was a carbo lover's dream come true. We finished off our meal sharing profiteroles, a puff pastry filled with espresso gelato. Other dessert selections included tiramisu, citrus panne cotta and a chocolate crème brulee. *Comments:* This is one of the most outstanding dining vistas on Maui. You're right on the beach. Reminiscent of elegant dining in the 1940s, the ambiance is emphasized by the Frank Sinatra tunes playing in the background. As the sun goes down the overhead lights continue to light up the beach. Not only is the setting divine but the service is tops. The prices are no more than the fine resort hotels but the ambiance of being right on the beach makes this truly a fabulous evening of dining. Reservations highly recommended. They also have a small bar and a private vintners dining area.

★ ***The Waterfront Restaurant*** *(Seafood)*
Milowai Condo, Ma'alaea; 808-244-9028; www.waterfrontrestaurant.net.

Hours: Dinner nightly from 5 p.m. *Sampling:* For dinner you'll find a rotating menu with whatever freshest foods are available. They are renowned for their fresh island fish and you can choose nine preparations including baked *en papillote*, Hawaiian salsa, Southwestern, and Sicilian-style *provencale*. Or choose from other entrees such as veal scaloppine piccata, Chef Bob's wild game *du jour*, filet Diane or cioppino ($26-$38). *Comments:* A family operation, the Smiths have done a consistently excellent job ever since they opened, winning a number of well-deserved awards and accolades. Fish preparations are particularly innovative. Dinner entrees all start with a loaf of onion bread and beer cheese along with a garden salad with choice of four homemade dressings. They have the ideal location to get their fish right off the boat at the Ma'alaea Harbor. Can't get it much fresher.

Yorman's by the Sea *(Southern/Cajun)*
760 South Kihei Road, Kihei (at Menehune Shores); 808-874-8385; www.yormans.com.

Hours: Breakfast 8 a.m.-noon; dinner 5-10 p.m.; happy hour 4-6 p.m.; jazz Wednesday through Sunday from 7-10 p.m. *Sampling:* Yorman and Cherie Williams offer dishes as diverse as seafood jambalaya, gumbo, baby back ribs, okra, collard greens, steak, prime rib and coconut shrimp. Appetizers run $8-$14; soup/salad $7-$13;

entrees (with a choice of two side dishes) $20-$38. Try their pecan-encrusted chicken, "world-famous" Bennett pork chop or rib-eye steak with Cajun spices and melted blue cheese. *Comments:* Ocean views, jazz and gumbo all come together here. Dine while you enjoy Yorman playing the bass, accompanied by a pianist and drummer.

Wailea-Makena Area

Inexpensive-priced Dining

Café Kiowai *(Island)*
Maui Prince Hotel, 5400 Makena Alanui, Makena; 808-874-1111.

Hours: Breakfast only 6-11 a.m. *Sampling:* Extensive hot breakfast buffet ($23) or a continental buffet ($17) are available as well as à la carte breakfast entrees ($10-$18) such as corned beef hash with poached eggs, eggs Benedict on cornbread, vegetarian frittata or a Molokini omelet of bay shrimp, tomato, avocado and jack cheese. *Comments:* Kiowai means "fresh flowing water." A casual, open-air patio atmosphere bordered by a large koi pond. Lovely place for breakfast.

Café Kula *(Light Meals)*
Grand Wailea Resort Hotel & Spa, 3850 Wailea Alanui, Wailea; 808-875-1234.

Hours: Breakfast 6-11:30 a.m.; lunch 11:30 a.m.-2:30 p.m.; dinner (cold sandwiches and salads) 2:30-8 p.m. *Sampling:* Breakfast à la carte entrees include Portuguese sausage burrito, macadamia nut waffles or housemade granola with skim milk and dried fruit ($3.50-$10.95). Cold deli and hot sandwiches at lunch such as herb-marinated chicken breast or Kula hamburger ($6.50-$14.50). Salad selections range from Kula pasta salad or tomato and feta ($4.95-$12.95). Specialty pizzas and calzones ($10.95-$12.95). *Comments:* Open patio setting above flowering gardens with a panoramic view of the ocean. Fresh and healthy fast food. Kids' menu for breakfast and lunch. A good value for resort dining.

Makena Clubhouse *(American)*
5415 Makena Alanui, at the Makena golf course, beyond Wailea and just past the Maui Prince Hotel, Makena; 808-879-1154.

Hours: Lunch 11 a.m.-4 p.m.; *pupus* 4-5:30 p.m.; beverages 11 a.m.-sundown. *Sampling:* Garlic French fries smothered in cheddar and pepper Jack cheese and served with a ranch dipping sauce, Thai shrimp summer rolls or ahi sashimi ($4.75-$11.75). Salads include bay shrimp and chicken Cobb or grilled ginger beef salad ($10.75-

$12). Sandwiches run the board from hamburgers to pastrami Reuben or Maui cheesesteak ($6.75-$12.75). *Comments*: This open-air restaurant features an outstanding golf course view and one of the few ocean views where you can see Pu'u Ola'i (the rounded hill at the end of the island) up close.

Maui Onion *(American)*

Renaissance Wailea Beach Resort, 3550 Wailea Alanui, Wailea (poolside); 808-879-4900.

Hours: 11 a.m.-6 p.m. bar; 11:30 a.m.-5 p.m. lunch. *Sampling:* Start with their famous Maui onion rings ($7), Maui onion soup or other appetizers ($4.50-$12). Salads ($10-$14) include tropical fruit boat with banana nut bread, Chinese chicken or traditional Caesar. Sandwiches ($7.50-$14) range from island mahi to grilled Cajun-spiced chicken or their hearty half-pound Black Angus burger with cheese. Daily lunch specials. Ice cream treats, too! Smoothies, tropicals, beer and wine by the glass. *Comments:* Casual poolside restaurant surrounded by the resort's lovely gardens. The onion rings have long been a huge hit and some say these are Maui's best burgers.

Waterfront Deli *(Deli)*

Shops at Wailea, inside the Whalers General Store, Wailea; 808-891-2039.

Hours: 7 a.m.-9 p.m. *Sampling:* Classic New York deli sandwiches or try a combination sandwich like Benny's Heaven with smoked turkey Jack cheese and hot peppers or an Empire State Monster with hot steamed corned beef, or roasted turkey breast and cheddar. From the grill there is a Maui taro burger, cheese dog, garden or chicken burger ($3.95-$9.95). Pizza available by the slice or whole ($2.95-$11). Salads, too. *Comments:* This is a nice addition to the Shops at Wailea and the surrounding hotels. A very nice deli and hearty sandwiches all reasonably priced. Some patio seating.

Moderate-priced Dining

★ ***Caffe Ciao*** *(Italian)*

Fairmont Kea Lani Hotel, 4100 Wailea Alanui, Wailea; 808-875-4100.

Hours: Deli 6 a.m.-10 p.m. Restaurant 11 a.m.-10 p.m. *Sampling:* Full bakery and deli serves coffee drinks, salads, sandwiches, homemade sausages, antipasto items, Italian gelatos, breads, pastries and desserts. Salads, minestrone or gazpacho, homemade linguine or angelhair, panini, and fried calamari are on the lunch menu ($10-$20). All pizzas are baked in the outdoor brick oven, as are many of the lunch and dinner entrees. Pizzas are also available for dinner along with *bisteca* Toscana (grilled rib-eye with rosemary), lamb chops (with rosemary, mint and garlic) or *pollo all fiorentina* (roasted chicken breast with fresh artichoke, Maui onions, baby spinach and fontina cheese) ($21-$35). Accent your dinner with an assortment of "Gli Antipasti," "Le Zuppe" or "L'Insalate" ($9-$13). *Comments:* High ceilings, arches and stone inlays in this sleek black and gold deli that offers antipasti, focaccia sandwiches, gourmet condiments and food products—even fresh produce and an imported olive bar. While dining you can relax by reading one of a variety of complimentary international newspapers either indoors in the Art Deco ambiance or on the outside patio. They cure their own meats and produce their own private label of products to sell: macadamia blossom honey, Maui onion jelly, *poha* berry butter, pineapple mustard, and mango barbecue sauce. They also have full picnic and gift baskets and a variety of cheeses and other items imported from Italy. You can shop and eat at the same time—the best of both worlds.

★ ***Hula Moons Restaurant*** *(Contemporary Hawaiian-American)*
Wailea Marriott, 3700 Wailea Alanui, Wailea; 808-874-7831.

Hours: Breakfast 6-11 a.m. Dinner 5:30-10 p.m. *Sampling:* For breakfast try their Aloha Kakahiaka Buffet ($22.95 adults; $9.95 kids 9-12; $4.95 under age 9) or order off the menu with a selection including fruit plate, French toast, or Ulupalakua steak and eggs ($10.95-$19.95). Dinners highlight seafood with grilled ahi and jumbo tiger shrimp, Hula's "Moonfish" (opah) served with a *laulau* of mahimahi, a seafood duo with mahimahi and *opakapaka* or sauteed jumbo shrimp. From the land enjoy grilled guava-glazed chicken breast, *lilikoi* lamb chops or braised barbecue short ribs ($14.95-$36.95). They also offer a Friday-night seafood buffet ($39.95). *Comments:* A lofty open-air dining room with plenty of ocean breezes. The bright tropical colors of the decor do not outshine the incredible ocean view, which every table seems to have. Bob Puccini, restaurateur and designer out of San Francisco, was the creative genius behind the restaurant and lounge. Hula Moons Restaurant has a great trendy, upbeat and fun look; the adjoining Mele Mele Lounge also has a bright colorful motif and allows an opportunity for a beautiful sunset or late-night relaxation and a *pupu* menu.

Kumu Bar & Grill *(Pacific Rim)*
Wailea Marriott, 3700 Wailea Alanui, Wailea; 808-879-1922.

Hours: Lunch 11 a.m.-5 p.m. Happy Hour 3-5 p.m. Dinner 5-9 p.m. Cocktails 11 a.m.-9 p.m. *Sampling:* Appetizers are a nice selection of Maui onion soup, shrimp cocktail, smoked, seared or traditional ahi, or deep fried hot and spicy chicken wings ($5.95-$11.95). Dinners include combo specials with a house salad or Maui onion soup with fries and a burger, turkey BLT or grilled chicken sandwich for $14.95. Entree selections include miso garlic scampi, tofu stir-fry, barbecue baby back ribs or beer batter shrimp and fish ($13.95-$26.95). *Comments:* Hawaiian entertainment and hula from 6:30-9 p.m.

Mulligan's on the Blue *(American/Continental)*
100 Kaukahi Street, at the Wailea (Blue) Golf Course, Wailea; 808-874-1131; www.mulligansontheblue.com.

Hours: 8 a.m.-1 a.m.; breakfast 8 a.m.-3 p.m.; lunch 10 a.m.-3 p.m.; dinner from 5 p.m. *Sampling:* Breakfasts include corned beef hash with eggs, omelets, steak and eggs, and other dishes ($8-$11). The lunch menu offers steak and chips, Irish stew, traditional shepherd's pie, Irish bangers and mash, a turkey jalapeño melt, and barbecue chicken wrap ($9-$12). Dinner has many of the same lunch entrees but also a Guinness-marinated rack of lamb, corned beef and cabbage, Gaelic steak or roasted pork loin ($13-$30). Their *keiki* menu for wee lads and lasses age 12 and under is $7. Named Best Place to Wet Your Whistle in the 2005 'Aipono Awards.

Polo Beach Grille and Bar *(Island)*
Fairmont Kea Lani Hotel, 4100 Wailea Alanui, Wailea; 808-875-4100.

Hours: Grille 11 a.m.-5 p.m.; bar 10:30 a.m.-7 p.m. *Sampling:* Plenty of starters from crab cakes and potstickers to grilled and chilled shrimp cocktails ($8-$17). Salads offer island chicken, grilled Hawaiian fish and romaine or seared volcano spiced ahi ($13-$17). Taro burger, mango chicken breast sandwich or grilled fish wrap are available, along with other selections. *Comments:* A number of the items are highlighted as part of their lifestyle cuisine, which complements Fairmont's "Willow Stream" spas. The ingredients are unprocessed and naturally healthy and directed toward health and wellness. This café is situated amid the pools.

Expensive-priced Dining

★ ***Bistro Molokini*** *(California Island)*
Grand Wailea Resort Hotel & Spa, 3850 Wailea Alanui, Wailea; 808-875-1234.

Hours: 11 a.m.-9:30 p.m. *Sampling:* Enjoy bistro specialties, pastas and pizza from their *kiawe* wood-burning oven. Lunches include soups and salads as well as sandwiches and wraps such as fresh island fish panini, pizzas and bistro club ($10-$20). Evening entrees continue with pizza and salads with other entrees of penne pasta, braised chicken breast, oven-roasted filet mignon, or fresh catch ($14-$35). *Keiki* menu features penne pasta with tomato sauce, pizza, chicken fingers and burgers ($10). Smoothies, too. *Comments:* An open-air bistro overlooking the formal pool and the Pacific Ocean (pool service 11 a.m.-5 p.m.). Exhibition kitchen and wood-burning oven. Casual; shorts are acceptable. The menu is light and innovative. Extensive wine list, beer, coffee drinks, tropicals, smoothies and Italian sodas.

Capische? *(Italian)*
Diamond Resort, 555 Kaukahi Street, Wailea; 808-879-2224.

Hours: 5:30-9 p.m. *Sampling:* Appetizers include lobster ravioli, sauteed calamari, portobello mushroom, ahi carpaccio or quail *saltimbocca* ($13-$23), and soups and salads include roasted tomato soup or peppercress salad with pancetta, Asian pears and toasted almonds ($8-$14). Dinner selections include pasta and risotto dishes or entrees of savory sea bass and seared diver scallops, lamb *osso buco*, filet mignon or fresh catch ($29-$49). *Comments:* Capische? offers cozy dining on the hillside of Wailea with panoramic views. Won a 2004 *Wine Spectator* Award of Excellence. Live jazz Friday through Sunday, 7 to 9 p.m.

★ ***Ferraro's*** *(Italian)*
Four Seasons Resort, 3900 Wailea Alanui, Wailea; 808-874-8000.

Hours: Lunch 11:30 a.m.-4 p.m.; light lunch 4-6 p.m.; dinner 6-9 p.m. *Sampling:* For lunch enjoy a salmon and spinach burger, Maine lobster sandwich, chilled watercress vichyssoise soup or a turkey club sandwich along with an assortment of intriguing pizzas ($10-$21). Dinners might begin with an *insalata di campo* (mescalun greens with currant tomatoes), or fried calamari and jumbo shrimp in a spicy Calabrain chili sauce ($13-$18). For your first course there is a selection of delicious pasta dishes, gnocchi or lobster risotto ($28-$43). For a main course there is pan-seared ahi tuna, *cioppino di mare*, grilled rack of lamb or veal Milanese ($34-$46). And if you dare, there is lemon-lime sorbet or strawberries with mascarpone for dessert ($9). *Comments:* There is nothing to block the ocean view from this cliffside restaurant located right over the water. (Get there early and you'll be surrounded by the sunset.) Named Best Resort Restaurant in the 2005 'Aipono Awards.

★ ***Grand Dining Room*** *(Breakfast)*
Grand Wailea Resort Hotel & Spa, 3850 Wailea Alanui, Wailea; 808-875-1234.

Hours: Breakfast only 6:30-11 a.m. *Sampling:* Grand Breakfast Buffet ($25 adults/$12.50 children), continental buffet ($18). À la carte menu offers tropical fruits, a basket of pastries, omelets, eggs Benedict, banana mac-nut waffles, pancakes with berries, turkey or corned beef hash, homemade granola, Swiss Birchermuesli, sweet bread French toast, and a variety of breakfast meats ($5.50-$21). Grand Dining Room *keiki* breakfast menu includes French toast, eggs or pancakes ($7.95). *Comments:* Great buffet and a lovely terraced seating area.

★ ***Hakone*** *(Japanese)*

Maui Prince Hotel, 5400 Makena Alanui, Makena; 808-874-1111.

Hours: Dinner 6-9 p.m. Tuesday through Saturday; closed Sunday and Monday; subject to change; Japanese buffet on Saturday night. Other nights offer à la carte and sushi bar. *Sampling:* The Saturday night Japanese buffet features more than two dozen specially prepared Japanese delicacies ($45 adults, $25 children). The à la carte dinner menu, offered on other evenings, provides a wide selection of traditional Japanese appetizers, sushi, tempura and other starters ($4-$28). Complete dinner selections (*goyushoku zen*) include a small appetizer, miso soup, rice, pickled vegetables and ice cream along with a variety of entree choices such as lobster tail, broiled butterfish or breaded pork cutlet ($26-$45). Their *rakuen kaiseki* traditional course dinner is also available, with a choice of steak or seafood ($58). *Nabemono*, served and cooked tableside for a minimum of two, is $38 per person (reservation required). Their ice creams are freshly made and wonderful. Green tea or white chocolate ginger, azuki bean or Tahitian vanilla. Or sample their green tea cheesecake or macadamia nut mousse. Hot and cold *sake*, too. *Keiki* menu available. *Comments:* Authenticity is the key to this wonderful Japanese restaurant, from its construction (the wood, furnishings and even small nails were imported from Japan) to its food (the rice is flown in, as well). The food and atmosphere are both wonderful here and, of course, the presentation of the food is artistic. There is also a sushi bar, but with only 11 seats, it is definitely on a first-come basis.

★ ***Humuhumunukunukua'pua'a*** *(Island/Seafood)*

Grand Wailea Resort Hotel & Spa, 3850 Wailea Alanui, Wailea; 808-875-1234.

Hours: 5:30-9 p.m. *Sampling:* Starters include *kalua* pork and boursin cheese potstickers, macadamia nut prawns, or ahi lemongrass traps ($11-$21). Soup and salad choices ($8-$12) offer lobster tarragon soup or warm spinach salad. With a focus on foods from the sea you can enjoy blackened *onaga* snapper with tempura prawns, seared fresh ahi, sesame-seared *opah* (moon fish) and whole fried Hawaiian *moi*. For the land-lovers there is herb-roasted chicken breast, grilled New York sirloin or crispy duck breast (entrees $24-$38). Kona-raised Maine lobster and Pacific spiny lobster are available (fresh from their saltwater lagoon) for $36/lb or $56/lb respectively. Save room for your dining finale with warm chocolate lava cake, warm Hawaiian sweet bread pineapple cake or, if you can't decide, their Humu sampler ($9-$13). Plus a nice *keiki* menu with meals at $10. *Comments*: If you're curious about the restaurant's name, it is the Hawai'i state fish, the trigger fish. Since the Hawaiian name is rather a mouthful, the eatery is affectionately and briefly referred to as "Humu." Tucked in the front grounds of the resort, it is situated on top of a saltwater pond filled with aquatic life. The huge saltwater tank that divides the bar area is worth stopping by to just admire. The restaurant floats on the lagoon and the thatched roof and bamboo railings inspire exotic Robinson Crusoe fantasies. They have full-bar service and some wonderfully different tropical libations. (Skip the mai tai and try an exotic champagne cocktail.) Nightly entertainment 6-9 p.m.

Joe's *(Gourmet American)*

131 Wailea Ike Place, above the Wailea Tennis Club, Wailea; 808-875-7767; www.bevgannonrestaurants.com.

Hours: 5:30-9:30 p.m. *Sampling:* Dinners start with Bev's famous crab dip, barbecue chicken quesadilla, ahi carpaccio, or assorted salads ($8-$15) and continue with Joe's favorite meatloaf with garlic mashed potatoes, black market ribs (stolen from the Hali'imaile General Store—Bev's other restaurant), grilled rack of lamb with port wine sauce or pumpkin-seed crusted fresh catch ($24-$38). *Comments:* From the owners of the highly acclaimed Hali'imaile General Store, Joe and (Chef) Beverly Gannon. Bev's food is as good as it sounds, but nothing is overly trendy. Joe's background as a Hollywood producer-director and lighting designer sets the tone with the shiny hardwood floors, 43-foot copper bar and individual geometric designs on the tables. The theater lighting is soft, yet strong enough to highlight the wall of show-biz memorabilia from Joe's days working with film, TV and music celebrities. All this and an ocean view, too.

★ ***Kea Lani Restaurant*** *(Breakfast)*

Fairmont Kea Lani Hotel, 4100 Wailea Alanui, Wailea; 808-875-4100.

Hours: Breakfast buffet and à la carte 6:30-11 a.m. *Sampling:* Continental breakfast buffet includes juice, pastries, and coffee or tea ($22), or my recommendation is to enjoy the works with their fabulous breakfast buffet ($25 adults, $10 children age 6-12). There is a bagel and bread station plus plenty of fresh fruits and yogurts along with hot breakfast entrees. Fresh seasonal and organic tropical fruits, smoked Scottish salmon, Japanese station, eggs Benedict, omelets made-to-order, pancakes, potatoes and rice, bacon and sausage, assorted hot and cold cereals. Cereals including granola and oatmeal with a choice of toppings—from walnuts to wheat germ, pumpkin seeds to pecans and pastries, muffins and nut breads. À la carte items include classic omelet ($18.50), banana Foster waffles ($13.50) or mango cream cheese–filled French toast ($13.50). Comments: Excellent breakfast spot.

Kincha *(Japanese)*
Grand Wailea Resort Hotel & Spa, 3850 Wailea Alanui, Wailea; 808-875-1234.

Hours: Dinner only. Thursday through Monday 6-9 p.m. Closed Tuesday and Wednesday. *Sampling:* Traditional Japanese cuisine with an American-style menu. Appetizers and salads ($3-$18) are followed by traditional main courses including a sashimi dinner, tempura dinner sake (broiled salmon) or *wafu* steak (grilled filet mignon), $25-$39; or try their *wakadori* (boneless breast of chicken with a light teriyaki sauce), *hotategai* (broiled sea scallops), *yaki kani* (broiled Alaskan king crab legs), $28-$52; or the traditional dining experience of Japan *omakase* with multiple courses for $65. Desserts include an Asian pear crisp or try their tropical fruit sushi. Kincha's *keiki* menu offers the kids in your group teriyaki steak or chicken or tempura dinners ($12.50). Lots of fun *keiki* cocktails, too. They also have a sushi bar, which fills up fast, with sushi specialties along with the traditional sashimi and sushi selections. *Comments:* This tranquil Japanese restaurant was created from 350 tons of rock from Mount Fuji. The lush gardens and peaceful lagoons are an exquisite backdrop to contemporary Japanese cuisine.

★ ***Le Gunji*** *(Teppanyaki European-style)*
Diamond Resort, 555 Kaukahi Street, Wailea; 808-874-0500.

Hours: Dinner only with two seatings, 6 and 8 p.m. Closed Wednesday and Sunday. *Sampling:* A gourmet teppanyaki restaurant offering seven pre-set meals, including a children's course. The Diamond course is $75 and includes appetizer, soup, fresh catch, lobster, sorbet, steak, salad, rice, dessert and coffee; Mini-Diamond courses are the same except for the choice of either fish ($60) or lobster ($65). The Beef Steak course ($55) substitutes a sirloin or tenderloin steak in place of the lobster and fresh catch. There are also a Vegetable course ($40) and a Seafood course ($60). *Comments:* The prices may sound steep, but if you figure a dinner entree at most of the fine resorts is priced in the mid-thirties and add appetizer, soup and dessert it will easily match this price. The dining room is small and intimate with a beautiful garden courtyard located behind where the chef cooks. This teppanyaki is a bit different in that it is cooked with a French flair, a style that was introduced to the restaurant by the original chef, Gunji Ito (from Osaka), who had previously cooked French cuisine. After the 6 p.m. seating diners can retire to a dessert room to relax and chat. Reservations required. Shorts and sandals not permitted.

Longhi's *(Continental)*

Shops at Wailea, 3750 Wailea Alanui, 808-891-8883; Another location at Old Lahaina Center, 888 Front Street; www.longhis.com.

Hours: All day dining 8 a.m.-10 p.m. Monday through Friday; from 7:30 a.m. Saturday and Sunday.

See "Lahaina Dining" for sampling and comments.

★ ***Nick's Fishmarket Maui*** *(Seafood)*

Fairmont Kea Lani Hotel, 4100 Wailea Alanui, Wailea; 808-879-7224.

Hours: 5:30-10 p.m. *Sampling:* Begin your evening with a sampling of *kalua* pig pot stickers, escargot, iced fresh oysters, or firecracker salmon roll ($10.95-$20). Olowalu tomato salad or a Caesar of baby romaine leaves ($8.95-$11.95) can precede a selection from their interesting seafood menu. Potato "scaled" mahimahi with truffle potatoes, cabernet-pepper sauce and white truffle oil, seared Hawaiian swordfish with candied peanut crust or Hokkaido scallops with Molokai sweet potato gnocchi. Those preferring "Not Seafood" can select from Mongolian-style rack of lamb, herb-roasted chicken, and filet mignon ($27.95-$49.95). *Comments:* This fine-dining restaurant features 40-foot vaulted ceilings designed in a southern Mediterranean style and offers great ocean views. Shell-design lighting fixtures, fish-shaped chairs, wave-patterned mosaic tabletops, and an 800-gallon aquarium are all part of the blue and white aquatic theme. Private booths, indoor and outdoor seating, plus a glass mosaic bar for cocktails and *pupus. Keiki* menu features fresh island fish, barbecue beef, chicken or pasta along with dessert plus juice or milk for $13.95. Named Best Special Occasion Restaurant in the 2005 'Aipono Awards.

★ ***Pacific Grill*** *(American/Pacific Rim)*

Four Seasons Resort, 3900 Wailea Alanui, Wailea; 808-874-8000.

Hours: Breakfast 6-11:30 a.m. (buffet 6:30-11 a.m.; until noon on Sunday). Dinner 6-9 p.m.; closed for lunch. *Sampling:* The Wailea Buffet ($11) features fruits, cereals, assorted breads, and juices; the Full Island Buffet ($25) adds to that with French toast, pancakes, waffles, eggs and omelets along with breakfast meats and starches. À la carte breakfasts ($13-$19). Their egg-white omelet with baby spinach and grilled pita bread is one of their "alternative cuisine" selections and is so good you won't miss the fat or cholesterol. Dinners might begin with lobster carpaccio, tempura tiger prawns, crispy ahi poke tacos or a Peking duck wrap ($11-$27). Dinner entrees include wasabi-crusted ahi, Asian wok stir fry, curried rack of lamb or Hawaiian cassoulet ($29-$57). *Comments:* A pleasant dining environment with indoor or lanai seating overlooking the pool and the ocean. Great seafood and a *keiki* menu is available.

★ ***Palm Court*** *(International/Buffet)*
Renaissance Wailea Beach Resort, 3550 Wailea Alanui, Wailea; 808-879-4900.

Hours: Breakfast 6:30 a.m.-11 a.m. Dinner 5:30-9:30 p.m. *Sampling:* Two choices of breakfast buffets ($22 and $16) and a wide selection of traditional breakfast foods ($4-$20). Dinner offers starters, salads and sandwiches ($6-$15) such as ginger duck potstickers or mahimahi sandwich for those with a light appetite; or create your own pizza ($14-$16). Dinner entrees ($19-$33) include herb-braised chicken breast with cilantro pesto, linguine with clams and fresh basil cream and roasted rack of lamb with port wine sauce. The Palm Court dinner buffets ($35.50) are a great dinner option. Tuesday and Friday they feature a seafood buffet with a rotating menu that might include ahi Nicoise, sauteed mahi, grilled swordfish, and prime rib. Sunday takes you to the Mediterranean for pastas cooked to order, *osso buco*, eggplant parmigiano or risotto. Monday and Thursday feature the Pacific Rim with *gado gado* salad, minted couscous with shrimp salad, and the action station offering a featured item such as shrimp and vegetable tempura. Wednesday and Saturday nights offer the Oriental buffet. *Comments:* This open-air dining hall offers evening breezes and an ocean view.

★ ***Prince Court*** *(Contemporary Island)*
Maui Prince Hotel, 5400 Makena Alanui, Makena; 808-874-1111.

Hours: Dinner 6-9 p.m. (closed Tuesday); Sunday champagne brunch 9 a.m.-1 p.m. *Sampling:* Friday night they offer a prime rib and seafood buffet as well as the regular nightly dinner menu. The buffet is a feast for the eyes and palate ($40 adults, $25 children 6-12). Sample their seafood on ice, selecting from steamed Manila clams, snap-and-eat Dungeness crab legs, or fresh sashimi. Specialty salads range from baby artichoke salad with bay shrimp to ceviche of scallops with Maui onion. Plenty of salad selections and an impressive international cheese and bread display. The action and carving station features roasted herb-crusted prime rib or fresh fish served in a variety of styles. The chef's buffet selections might include herb-crusted chicken breast or seafood paella. The dessert table is a sumptuous spread that tastes as extravagant as it looks. The standard dinner menu begins with appetizers including rock shrimp potstickers, chilled seafood on ice, or crispy Dungeness crab cakes ($8-$16). Follow that up with an asparagus bisque, or a mango and avocado crab salad ($7-$9). Entrees include beef tenderloin and half-stuffed lobster, trio of fresh Hawaiian fish, mango duck breast, or Asian seafood house noodles ($24-$37). *Comments:* Prince Court is a lovely spot for dining. The cuisine is an incredible blend of flavors that highlights the best and freshest Hawaiian produce, meats and fish. Beautifully situated, the dining room offers a splendid view of both the ocean and landscaped hotel grounds. They have an excellent wine list with particularly good prices on champagne and wine selections. Their acclaimed Sunday champagne brunch is $43 adults, $25 children 6-12. Named Best Sunday Brunch in the 2005 'Aipono Awards.

Ruth's Chris Steak House *(Steakhouse)*

Shops at Wailea, 3750 Wailea Alanui; 808-874-8880. Another location at Lahaina Center, 900 Front Street.

Hours: 5-9 p.m. See "Lahaina Dining" for sampling and comments.

★ ***Sea Watch Restaurant*** *(Island)*

100 Wailea Golf Club Drive, Wailea; located in the Wailea Gold Golf Course clubhouse; 808-875-8080; www.seawatchrestaurant.com.

Hours: Breakfast and lunch menu served 8 a.m.-3 p.m. Grill menu 3-10 p.m. Dinner 6-10 p.m. *Sampling:* Breakfast specialties include Moki's Special (an omelet with *kalua* pork, Maui onion, potato and spinach) or try smoked salmon Benedict with caper hollandaise sauce ($9-$14). More conventional breakfast fare, as well. Plenty of salads and sandwiches ($8-$14) for those appetites worked up from a round of golf. Dinners can start with macadamia nut–crusted Brie, ahi sashimi, tiger prawns, crab cakes, or porcini-seared sea scallops ($6-$15). Entrees include miso-glazed tiger prawns, rack of lamb with garlic mashed potatoes, pork loin stuffed with sauteed mushrooms, or a selection of fresh island fish ($24-$29). *Comments:* Romantic dining. An elegant "grand hall" entrance with tall ceilings leads to the restaurant and several distinctive dining areas. The wide lanais offer the best views of Molokini, Kaho'olawe, Makena and Ma'alaea and the grill room is highlighted by giant glass doors and artwork from Arthur Johnson, a Big Island muralist. The lounge has a white baby grand piano as its centerpiece. Spacious seating; descriptive wine list. The breakfast/lunch menu is served from 8 a.m. to 3 p.m., so you can get lunch for breakfast or breakfast for lunch.

★ ***Spago*** *(Contemporary American-Hawaiian)*

Four Seasons Resort, 3900 Wailea Alanui, Wailea; 808-879-2999.

Hours: Dinner 6-9 p.m.; bar open 6-11 p.m. *Sampling:* Where to begin! Spago's menu changes nightly, so you might find a completely different set of dishes than I experienced. You absolutely have to try the Thai coconut-galangal soup. It has always been one of my favorite Thai dishes but I've never tasted one like this! The tempura Kaua'i prawns with island-grown vegetables had an amazingly light batter. Other starters include stir-fried *onaga* lettuce wraps or island seafood risotto ($11-$23). As an entree you might enjoy big-eye tuna grilled rare with wasabi butter, baked *opakapaka* with macadamia nut crust and Moloka'i yams or free-range chicken with Yukon gold potato puree. I tried the fabulous pan-seared *onaga* with Kula corn, asparagus succotash and lobster *nage*. The caramelized pork chop with *lomi lomi* tomatoes and creamy sage polenta was a huge portion—more like a pork roast. (Entrees $31-$48). *Comments:* One of the few truly fine-dining experiences to be enjoyed on Maui, this romantic indulgence offers tranquil elegance indoors or on the terrace—both with an ocean view. The service is, of course, exemplary and the waiter was extremely knowledgeable about their extensive wine selection. And there's a children's menu: chicken fingers, mac and cheese, spaghetti or cheese pizza; includes special kids' dessert for $15. Came in second place in the 2005 'Aipono Awards Best Overall Restaurant category and took top honors as Most Innovative Restaurant.

★ ***Taiko*** *(Japanese with a French flair)*
Diamond Resort, 555 Kaukahi Street, Wailea; 808-874-0500.

Hours: Breakfast 7-10 a.m.; Lunch 10 a.m.-12:45 p.m. Dinner 6-9 p.m. (no dinner on Tuesday). *Sampling:* Choose a traditional, *okayu* or Japanese breakfast, all priced at $14. Lunches feature sandwiches and burgers along with Japanese specialties including *tenazru* udon, *unatama don*, *zaru* soba or *wakadori* teriyaki don (an assortment of hot and cold noodle or rice dishes), $7-$17. For dinner (entrees $20-$37) you can choose sushi or sashimi, but I recommend that you jump to the appetizer menu and sample some extraordinary flavor combinations. The foie gras and scallops saute ($14) is simply fabulous. The entree of Boursin garlic and fine herb-stuffed duck cotelette ($36) won the '99 Boursin Chef of the year contest. There are several complete Japanese-style meals, as well, so sample black cod with orange miso sauce, fresh *onaga* salted and broiled, or *panko*-crusted chicken, seafood and vegetables fried until golden brown ($24-$29). The tempura is light and fluffy. You can sear your own meal on a cast-iron hibachi. The sukiyaki is a classic with beef, tofu, vegetables and udon in a huge pot. Dessert selection changes, but they are all great, with ice creams that are specially made in Japan. *Comments:* Diamond Resort is a gem. If you haven't discovered this fine restaurant, then it is time. Very simple, yet elegant in decor and almost cathedral in style. The menu is "innovatively French Japanese cuisine."

★ ***Tommy Bahamas Tropical Cafe*** *(Caribbean)*
Shops at Wailea, 3750 Wailea Alanui, Wailea; 808-875-9983.

Hours: 11 a.m.-10 p.m. *Sampling:* Select an appetizer for lunch or dinner such as warm macadamia nut–crusted Big Island goat cheese served with mango salsa or Crab Calloway (griddled crab cakes with a light coconut crust), $9-$17. Soups, side salads and sandwiches ($8-$17) include a shrimp BLT, St. Kitt's Kabana Salad or Cooper Island crab bisque. Entree-size salads include the Rum-Runners fruit salad, Saba steak salad with grilled marinated tenderloin tips or a Fandango Mango chicken salad with char-grilled chicken, mango, hearts of palm, pecans and baby greens ($13-$18). Dinner entrees range from hot Jamaican jerked spiced pork tenderloin to Tommy's Papa's Pasta with sauteed jumbo shrimp to Boca Chica Chicken with the chicken breast lightly breaded and sauteed in a tropical tequila lime sauce ($23-$36). *Comments:* This is a highly creative menu with some very fresh flavor combinations. Festive atmosphere and pleasant open-air dining, with indoor or outdoor

While not restaurants, two of my favorite haunts for "local-style" baked goods are worthy of mention. The **Home Maid Bakery**, open 5:30 a.m.-10 p.m. daily, is an island institution. It has more than just donuts: you'll find unusual specialties such as *empanadas, manju* and bread pudding. They began over 40 years ago on Maui and do not add any preservatives to their made-from-scratch formulas. They are the home of the original Maui Crispy Manju and noted for their Maui Crunch bread. Some items are available at island groceries. Hot *malasadas* daily from 5:30-9:30 a.m. and 4-10 p.m. 1005 Lower Main Street, Wailuku; 808-244-7015.

The **Four Sisters Bakery** in Wailuku town is open Monday through Friday 5 a.m.-6 p.m., Saturday until 4 p.m., and Sunday until 11 a.m. It is run by Melen, Mila, Beth and Bobbie, who arrived from the Philippines after helping their father run a Spanish bakery in Manila for 15 years. Not a large selection, but delicious and different items. They offer a sweet bread filled with a cinnamon pudding, a sponge cake "sandwich," as well as cinnamon rolls and butter rolls. The only place you can purchase these goodies is at the bakery or the Kahului Swap Meet. Corner of Vineyard and Hinano, Wailuku; 808-244-9333.

seating. The portions are large, and the food is excellent. I'll drive out of my way to eat here just for their fabulous crab bisque.

Kahului–Wailuku Area

In Wailuku, there are a number of local restaurants that are not often frequented by tourists and may well be some of the island's best-kept secrets. Don't expect to find polished silver or extravagant decor, but do expect to find reasonable prices for large portions of food in a comfortable atmosphere. Note that many of these local restaurants may not accept credit cards. In addition, Dairy Queen, Pizza Hut, McDonald's, Burger King and Jack-in-the-Box are a few of the fast-food restaurants in and around Kahului and the Maui Mall. These don't require elaboration.

Inexpensive-priced Dining

A.K.'s Cafe *(American)*

1237 Lower Main Street, Wailuku; 808-244-8774; www.akscafe.com.

Hours: Lunch 10:30 a.m.-2 p.m., dinner 4:45-8:30 p.m. Closed Saturday and Sunday. *Sampling:* For lunch, enjoy local favorites like stews, curries, burritos and burgers, as well as more gourmet options like chicken with Thai chili sauce or with lemon basil garlic, mahimahi with papaya pineapple salsa, and garlic crusted *ono* with cucumber ginger relish ($6.25-$6.75). Dinners include lemongrass duck breast with *ponzu* sauce, roasted macadamia nut chicken with sweet potato stuffing, honey-baked salmon with ginger fruit relish, linguine with roasted chicken and basil pesto cream sauce, and tofu Napoleon with ginger pesto ($11-$14). *Comments:* Chef-owner Elaine Rothermel (previously the chef at Simply Healthy) opened this little cafe for families to enjoy healthy, inexpensive food in a fun, casual atmosphere. Dine-in, take-out, or free delivery service for lunch in the Wailuku–Kahului area.

★ ***A Saigon Café*** *(Vietnamese)*

1792 Main Street, Wailuku; 808-243-9560.

Hours: 10 a.m.-9:30 p.m. Sunday until 8:30 p.m. *Sampling:* Spring or summer rolls, shrimp pops marinated and grilled on a sugar cane stick ($4.75-$9.50), rare lemon beef or shrimps, chicken and green papaya salads, saimin, chow fun, or hot-and-sour soup. Sample entrees include catfish or mahi in clay pot, wok "wonders" served with jasmine rice, sauteed dishes, sweet-and-sour meals, or their Saigon classic fondue where you cook your meal at your table. Most dishes $6-$10, with a few seafood selections that are slightly under $25. *Comments:* If you haven't tried Vietnamese food, now is the time and this is the place. It's all fresh, fresh, fresh—right out of owner Jennifer Nguyen's own garden. Lemongrass, cucumbers, sour garlic sauce, daikon pickles, fresh island basil, and mint leaves are among the many distinctive ingredients used for seasoning dishes such as *ga xao xa ot* (curried chicken with lemongrass) or *bo lui* (grilled beef sirloin rolls). The most fun—and one of their most popular items—is *banh hoi*: fill rice paper with a variety of meats or seafood (along with bean sprouts and vermicelli cake noodle) then dip in hot water and wrap. A little hard to find (easiest way is from the road behind Ooka's) but well worth it. They are so popular they don't even have a sign. Look for the big stars that are lit on the roof. Simple atmosphere, great food, ample portions, prompt and friendly service—they deserve all their accolades and awards. Considered by Maui residents to be the best Vietnamese restaurant on the island. This is the benchmark. Named Best Dinner Value in the 2005 'Aipono Awards.

Ale House *(Steaks/American/Sports Bar)*

355 East Kamehameha Avenue (just off Hana Highway), Kahului; 808-877-9001.

Hours: 11 a.m.-2 a.m. Lunch/dinner menu served until 10 p.m. *Sampling:* Same menu for lunch/dinner offers a basic burger you can top with onion, melted blue cheese or bacon, or garden burgers. Roll-up sandwiches are shrimp, ahi, chicken or steak in a soft tortilla. Specialty salads, gourmet pizza, calzones or sandwiches along with a large pupu appetizer selection ($7.95-$18.95). *Keiki* menu items $4.95. *Comments:* Pool tables, dartboards, video games and lots of TVs. Late-night entertainment.

Aloha Grill *(Diner)*

Maui Marketplace, 270 Dairy Road, Kahului; 808-893-0263.

Hours: Monday through Saturday 8 a.m.-9 p.m.; Sunday until 7 p.m. *Sampling:* Regular and large hot dogs (Moon Doggie, Hound Dog). Burgers with bacon, teriyaki, ham, chiles, chili and names like Buddy Holly and Gidget plus a good variety of vegetarian burgers. Surfer (sloppy) Joe and other sandwiches plus fountain treats like sundaes, shakes, malts, floats—even flavored colas and banana splits. Prices are very affordable ($3-$10). *Comments:* Small (one counter) '50s-style soda fountain with stools in the Kau Kau Food Court. Plenty of seating in the food court area.

Asian Star *(Vietnamese)*

Millyard Industrial Park, 1764 Wili Pa Loop, Wailuku; 808-244-1833.

Hours: 10 a.m.-10 p.m. Sunday until 9 p.m. *Sampling:* Fresh island fish (market price). Plenty of authentic Vietnamese fare including *pho* (beef noodle soup), *goi* (salads) and *con dia* (rice plates). Wok dishes are vegetarian or with beef, chicken, seafood or pork. Make your own Vietnamese burritos with boneless chicken breast, shrimp or beef sirloin rolls. Vietnamese fondue with beef, shrimp or calamari cooked at the table. A huge menu and we've heard some very good things about this restaurant. Most dishes are $6.95-$11.95.

★ ***Café Marc Aurel*** *(Coffee/Bistro/Wine Bar)*
28 North Market, Wailuku; 808-244-0852.

Hours: Monday through Saturday 7 a.m.-9 p.m. (or later); closed Sunday. *Sampling & Comments:* This opened a few years ago as a cute European-style coffee house with great espresso drinks and pastries. In 2004, owner Marc Aurel expanded and renovated. The result is a somewhat larger area, but still cozy and intimate—and still cute. A coffee and internet bar by day with pastries, sandwiches and quiches ($5-$7), it is transformed from 4 p.m. into a charming bistro and wine bar. Marc offers more than 80 wines by-the-glass (served in Riedel crystal), as well as a nice selection of ports, gourmet cheeses and other appetizers ($2-$12). Live music (blues/jazz) on Thursday nights; open mike on Saturdays for poetry, drama, music. Also Wi-Fi internet access ($3.95/day or $19.95/month).

Café O'Lei *(Healthy Salads & Sandwiches)*
Hawaii Nature Center, 875 Iao Valley Road.

Hours: 10:30 a.m.-3 p.m. *Sampling:* Changing menu with interesting taste treats ($5-$10). You might find creamy chicken fettuccine or blackened mahi or sandwich selections that include fresh Maui vegetables, crab club, Italian prosciutto with an Asian salad, hot chicken salad or curry chicken salad. *Comments:* Pick up a great lunch to take on your hike. One of a small chain of Maui restaurants popular with residents and tourists alike.

Cupie's *(American/Local)*
134 West Kamehameha Avenue, Kahului; 808-877-3055.

Hours: Monday 9 a.m.-4 p.m.; Tuesday through Saturday 9 a.m.-9 p.m. Closed Sunday and holidays. *Sampling:* Breakfast omelet plates ($4.65-$6.65). Plate lunches and *bentos* ($4.65-$7.65), burgers or a bacon deluxe cheeseburger ($2.75-$4.85). Soup, Caesar salad and Cupie's Fried Chicken by the piece ($1.49-$3.09) or by the bucket ($16.29-$31.59). *Comments:* This used to be one of those old-fashioned drive-ins where you sat in your car with the trays on your window. Now it's a drive up with orders to go or limited seating. The price is right, and it still has that old-fashioned feeling.

★ ***Da Kitchen Express*** *(Local)*

Triangle Square, 425 Koloa Street (off Hana Highway), Kahului; 808-871-7782. (There is another location in Kihei.)

Hours: 11 a.m.-8 p.m. Monday through Friday; 11 a.m.-3 p.m. Saturday; closed Sunday. *Sampling:* See "Kihei Dining" for sampling and comments.

Down to Earth Natural Foods & Café *(Vegetarian)*

305 Dairy Road, Kahului; 808-877-7548. Another location at 1169 Makawao Avenue, Makawao; 808-572-1488.

Hours: 8 a.m.-7:30 p.m. Store open 7 a.m.-9 p.m., Sunday 8 a.m.-8 p.m. *Sampling:* Soups and hot vegetarian entrees like bell pepper with couscous, "to fu young," enchilada pie, lasagna and mock chicken tofu plus freshly made sandwiches, burritos, spring rolls, quesadillas and wraps ($7). Salad bar $6.49 lb. Low-fat, whole-grain bakery items include streusel, carrot cake, toffee bars, muffins, baklava, almond walnut and tea cookies, and date bars; also tofu cheesecake and vegan carob chip cookies. *Comments:* The mock chicken is tasty by itself or with added stir-fry vegetables. Desserts and bakery goods are yummy (and healthier than most). Pleasant seating area upstairs. Retail store has fresh organic produce, bulk items, and packaged vegetarian food products. Named Best Vegetarian Fare in the 2005 'Aipono Awards.

★ ***Dragon Dragon*** *(Chinese)*

Maui Mall, 70 East Ka'ahumanu Avenue, Kahului; 808-893-1628.

Hours: Lunch 10:30 a.m.-2 p.m. (until 2:30 on Saturday and Sunday), Dinner 5-9 p.m. (until 9:30 on Friday and Saturday). *Sampling & Comments:* You can tell right away from the honey walnut stir-fried prawns or the drunken clams with Chinese wine offered as appetizers that this will be an innovative menu. Featuring familiar Chinese dishes (their lemon chicken is top-notch), as well as creative offerings: seasonal live lobster and crab are served with black bean, ginger and green onion, or supreme sauce, or try the fried peppery salt pork chops, five-flavored roast duck, stir-fried *ong choy* with bean curd sauce, or beef fried rice with lettuce. There are 83 dishes on the menu ($5-$15), plus daily and seasonal specials. They also serve dim sum for lunch daily, the only restaurant I know of that does. A classy, clean Chinese restaurant with consistently good food.

★ ***Fiesta Time*** *(Mexican)*

1132 Lower Main Street, Wailuku; 808-249-8463. Another location in the Harbor Shops at Ma'alaea.

Hours: 11 a.m.-8 p.m. *Sampling:* Great tostadas, burritos, enchiladas à la carte. Most items $5-$6, with steak or shrimp at $10.95. *Comments:* A hole-in-the-wall with very little counter seating. Food is excellent, fresh and inexpensive.

Fresh Mint *(Vietnamese/Vegan)*

199 Dairy Road, Kahului; 808-873-6468. Another location in Paia.

Hours: 11 a.m.-9 p.m. Monday through Saturday. See "Paia Dining" for sampling and comments.

International House of Pancakes *(American)*

Maui Mall, 70 East Ka'ahumanu Avenue, Kahului; 808-871-4000.

Hours: Sunday through Thursday 6 a.m.-midnight. Friday and Saturday until 2 a.m. Breakfasts begin in the $5 range, dinners from $12. *Comments:* A very large facility with a menu that is popular with all family members. Something for everyone at reasonable prices. This particular IHOP's claim to fame is Camille Velasco of *American Idol*—Camille's family operates this IHOP, and before she was "discovered" by *American Idol*, she waited tables here.

★ ***Koho Grill and Bar*** *(American)*

Queen Ka'ahumanu Center, 275 Ka'ahumanu Avenue, Kahului; 808-877-5588.

Hours: Breakfast 7-11 a.m. Lunch 11 a.m.-5 p.m. Dinner 5 p.m.-midnight. *Sampling:* Omelets, pancakes and other favorite breakfast foods ($4.45-$7.25). Plate lunches, burgers, sandwiches, fajitas and salads ($5.95-$10.45). Dinner entrees include your choice of soup or Kula greens salad. Rib plate, chicken stir fry, steaks, pastas or catch of the day prepared five different ways ($9-$15). *Comments:* Comfortable coffee shop atmosphere with a diverse menu and affordable prices, which boils down to good family dining and good value. They also have a great *keiki* menu. Sports bar and large-screen TV.

★ ***Las Piñatas of Maui*** *(Mexican)*

395 Dairy Road, Kahului; 808-877-8707.

Hours: Monday through Saturday 10:30 a.m.-8 p.m. Sunday 11 a.m.-8 p.m. *Sampling:* Nachos, tostadas, hard and soft-shell tacos, enchiladas, burritos, quesadillas, Mexican salads ($2.45-$8). Combination plates ($6.95-$8.50). Plus daily specials. *Comments:* A family operation with affordable prices. Everything is made from scratch, from the beans to the salsa, and they use only 100 percent cholesterol-free oils. Dine in or take out. A small, fast food–sized place; very convenient to the airport.

Main Street Bistro *(American)*
2051 Main Street, Wailuku; 808-244-6816.

Hours: 10:30 a.m.-2:30 p.m. Monday through Friday. *Sampling:* "Small Plates" might be soup of the day, crispy shrimp-and-crab ravioli or a mini burger ($2.95-$7.95). "Big Plates" include roasted Chinese chicken salad, blackened chicken and shrimp pasta salad or hot crab sandwich ($4.95-$12.95). "Bistro Favorites" include slow-cooked baby back ribs with *poha* honey–mustard glaze, seared aged sirloin with wild mushroom sauce, and center cut ahi with caramelized apple and pear butter ($6.95-$12.95). *Comments:* This is a very new addition (opened in 2005) to the Wailuku dining scene. Chef Tom Selman (previously with such stellar restaurants as David Paul's and Sansei) calls his cuisine "refined comfort food." The dishes are creative and Main Street Bistro definitely brings a welcome gourmet touch to the lunch options in Wailuku. Give it a try.

★ ***Mama Ding's Pasteles Restaurant*** *(Puerto Rican/Local)*
255 East Alamaha Street, Kahului; 808-877-5796.

Hours: Monday through Friday 7 a.m.-2 p.m. *Sampling:* Eggs Bermuda (2 eggs scrambled with cream cheese and onion) served with potatoes or rice and toast, French toast (choice of cinnamon or sweet bread), or Puerto Rican breakfast with eggs, meat, half *pastele*, and *gandule* rice ($4.95-$6.95). The Puerto Rican plate lunches come with pastele, *gandule* rice, *empanadilla*, choice of meat, *bacalao* salad, and dessert ($6.95-$7.50). Other lunches include teri beef or fried rice plate, saimin, sandwiches and a homemade chorizo burger ($3.00-$6.95). *Comments:* Ready for a different breakfast? Skip Denny's and try this cozy restaurant tucked away in the Kahului Industrial Area. Try a pastele, which has an exterior of grated green banana and a filling of pork, vegetables and spices that is then steamed. Delicious! I've tried several of their breakfasts, all were good. No credit cards. They also sell specialty breads in flavors like coconut-papaya-pineapple, strawberry guava, and Portuguese sweetbread as well as cinnamon, apple-cinnamon or potato bread.

★ ***Marco's Grill & Deli*** *(Italian & American)*
444 Hana Highway, Kahului; 808-877-4446. (Also a location in Kihei.)

See "Kihei Dining" for hours and menu description. *Comments:* The Kahului location has a more casual, coffee-shop feeling than the Kihei restaurant and is a comfortable place for families. This location also features a cocktail lounge with big-screen TV. Marco's in Kahului is a favorite dining choice for us when heading to or from the airport, which is just two minutes away.

★ ***Maui Bake Shop & Deli*** *(European Pastries/Deli)*
2092 Vineyard Street, Wailuku; 808-242-0064.

Hours: Monday through Friday 6 a.m.-4 p.m. Saturday 7 a.m.-1 p.m. *Sampling:* Everything is on a readerboard and updated daily. Sample one of their ready-made salads, homemade soups, and sandwiches ($4-$6.50); the breads are all freshly homemade. They have a full bakery with lots of delicious sweets and coffee or espresso drinks. *Comments:* An early-morning arrival assures a greater selection from the goodies like handmade puff pastry or fresh fruit tarts. This European-style bakery is the combined effort of French chef Jose and his wife, Claire Fujii Krall. The big stone oven is left over from the Yokouchi family that was in this location in the 1930s. A few tables inside or get your lunch and head to the beach.

Maui Coffee Roasters *(Light Meals)*
444 Hana Highway, Kahului; 808-877-CUPS.

Hours: Monday through Friday 7 a.m.-6 p.m. (kitchen closes 4:30 p.m.). Saturday 8 a.m.-5 p.m. (kitchen closes 4 p.m.). Sunday 8 a.m.-2:30 p.m. (kitchen closes 1:30 p.m.). *Sampling:* They specialize in the "ultimate veggie burger" made of low-fat grains and vegetables with green chile pesto, or try a veggie melt or veggie wrap. Also plenty for meat eaters with roast beef, ham and cheese, or tuna caper. Bagel sandwiches. ($4.95-$7.45). And pastries, of course, to accompany your coffee drinks. *Comments:* Brightly and whimsically decorated with counter and table seating. Hawaiian, imported and flavored coffees, freshly roasted for retail sale or to order off the menu. Specialty drinks include granitas, rice milk, Maui juices, flavored teas, espressos, lattes and cappuccinos. Named Best Coffee House in the 2005 'Aipono Awards.

Maui Mall
70 East Ka'ahumanu Avenue, Kahului; 808-872-4320; www.mauimall.com.

Not a food court, but there are several small food outlets here. Among them are *Siu's Chinese Kitchen*, *Maui Island Breeze Cafe*, *Maui's Mixed Plate* and *Tasaka Guri Guri* for a local type of creamy sherbet you can order with or without azuki beans. *IHOP*, *Thailand Cuisine* and *Dragon Dragon* are listed individually.

Maui Marketplace *(Food Court)*
270 Dairy Road, Kahului; 808-873-0400.

Food Court hours: Monday through Saturday 8 a.m.-9 p.m.; Sunday until 7 p.m. The Kau Kau Food Court offers some small food outlets including *Ba-Le Sandwiches* (tasty Vietnamese sandwiches), *Aloha Grill* (see individual listing), *L&L Drive-Inn* (generous plate lunches) *Fernando's* (Mexican) and *Chopsticks Express* (Chinese plate lunches).

Nazo's *(Local)*

Puuone Plaza, 1063 Lower Main Street, Wailuku; 808-244-0529.

Hours: Monday through Saturday lunch 10 a.m.-2 p.m. (breakfast until 11 a.m.); dinner 5-9 p.m. Closed Sunday. *Sampling:* Mini-plates include one scoop rice and one scoop mac salad with entrees of chicken cutlet, breaded teri beef, chop steak or oxtail soup ($4.50-$8.50). They offer more diverse selections such as salmon steak, shrimp tempura, and liver with bacon and onions. Noodle dishes (pigs feet on Thursdays and Saturdays), saimin, dry mein, and won ton ($4.25-$6.75); salads, too, with tuna-stuffed tomato, chicken Caesar, or Chinese chicken ($4.25-$4.95). A variety of burgers and sandwiches including ham, tuna, BLT, club and egg combos ($2.50-$4.95). *Comments:* A small, family-owned restaurant. Very affordable. Known for their oxtail soup.

Pizza in Paradise *(Pizza)*

60 Wakea Avenue, Kahului; 808-871-8188.

Hours: Sunday through Thursday 11 a.m.-9 p.m. Friday and Saturday until 10 p.m. *Sampling:* Pizza and more pizza ($8.49-$22.99) including local specials like *kalua*, Portuguese and ranch classic chicken. Traditional calzones and a selection of tossed salads. Two slices of pizza $2.87-$4.97. *Comments:* All their dough and sauces are made fresh with olive oil right in the store. They have a large dining area and chessboard tables. Thursday from 6:30-9 p.m. is Chess Night.

Queen Ka'ahumanu Center *(Food Court)*

275 Ka'ahumanu Avenue, Kahului; 808-877-3369; www.kaahumanu.net.

The Queen's Market Food Court features several upstairs restaurants near the main entrance. *Edo Japan* has teppanyaki plate dinners, rice bowls, saimin and sushi. *Yummy Korean BBQ* offers *kalbi* and barbecued meats, noodle and dumpling soups, plus curries. *Maui's Mixed Plate* has local food. *Panda Express* (Chinese), *Paradise Cafe* (deli), *Maui Tacos* and *McDonald's* round out the choices. Prices under $10. Adjacent to the Food Court, *Sushi Go!* serves sushi fast with a popular Japanese food service system called *kaiten*, which uses a conveyor belt that passes dishes around the counter in front of customers. About 20 different types of sushi ($1.50-$2.25) per plate; $22.99 for all-you-can-eat sushi Wednesday 4-8 p.m. *Koho Grill and Bar* and *Ruby's Diner* are listed individually.

★ *Ruby's Diner* *(Diner)*

Queen Ka'ahumanu Center, 275 Ka'ahumanu Avenue, Kahului; 808-248-7829.

Hours: Monday through Friday 7 a.m.-9:30 p.m.; Saturday and Sunday 7 a.m.-11 p.m. *Sampling:* Nothing on the menu over $10. Try Ruby's special cinnamon roll French toast for breakfast, an array of omelets or huevos rancheros. Try a Ruby Burger with an old-fashioned shake or a malt. Healthy food alternatives include vegetarian specialties, lots of salads and even "lite fries." Dinner specialties include meatloaf, turkey and stuffing, shrimp and chips or country fried steak. Plenty of burgers served with cheese, chiles, mushrooms, bleu cheese, bacon or guacamole. Salads include Cobb, chicken Caesar or Chinese chicken. Save room for a classic hot fudge sundae, banana split, or fresh-baked apple pie. A fun kids' menu with breakfast and lunch/dinner favorites like grilled cheese, chicken fingers and PB&J. *Comments:* Back in 1962, Ruby visited Hawai'i aboard the famous Lurline cruise ship. Discovering that Maui was *no ka oi*, she returned with her friends and family for many years. In 2002 her son Doug (who lives part-time in Hana) brought one of the Ruby restaurants to Maui. Ruby's Diner has a fun ambiance, featuring airplane models that were a part of Hawai'i's aviation history. Plenty of comfort food and a broad menu that will suit anyone. Great old-fashioned malts, too. Seniors will find Ruby's "Jitterbug Club" a swinging place. If you are 55 or older you'll receive 10 percent off your entire check. And yes—that is the check of your entire party, up to six people. Good food, good value, good fun at Ruby's. Named Most Family-Friendly Restaurant in the 2005 'Aipono Awards.

★ *Saeng's Thai* *(Thai)*

2119 Vineyard Street, Wailuku; 808-244-1567.

Hours: Lunch Monday through Friday 11 a.m.-2:30 p.m. Dinner 5-9:30 p.m. *Sampling:* Bean cake, stuffed chicken wings, broccoli satay, and other appetizers ($4.95-$7.50). Entrees of assorted curry dishes, barbecue dancing prawns, cornish game hen, seafood saute, and lots of vegetarian selections ($8.50-$12.95). *Comments:* A little Eden with lots of plants providing privacy between tables. This is one of the most attractive local restaurants in Wailuku and one of the best restaurants on Maui for Thai cuisine. Not only is the service attentive, but the portions are generous.

Sam Sato's *(Local)*

1750 Wili Pa Loop, Wailuku; 808-244-7124.

Hours: Breakfast and lunch 7 a.m.-2 p.m.; bakery open until 4 p.m. *Sampling:* Omelets, hot cakes, or set breakfast ($2.50-$5). Plate lunches include teriyaki beef, stew, chop steak, spare ribs ($5.50-$6.25). Sandwiches and burgers ($2.35-$2.65). But what you really come to Sam's for is the saimin. Dry noodles, saimin, chow fun, won ton ($3.75-$5) are available in small or large sizes. Take-out noodles available for $14-$26-$46 (to feed 10-15, 25 or 50 people). *Comments:* The homemade pastries are wonderful; peach, apple and coconut turnovers are fragrant and fresh and they also specialize in *manju*, a Japanese tea cake. These tasty morsels are filled with a mashed version of lima beans.

Simply Healthy *(Healthy)*
Cameron Center, 95 Mahalani Road (near the hospital), Wailuku; 808-249-8955.

Hours: Monday through Friday 11 a.m.-2 p.m. *Sampling:* Lunch plate ($4.50), veggie plate or sandwich ($3.50), chef salad ($4), soup or soup and half sandwich ($3-$4). *Comments:* Affordable, diabetic-friendly foods that are high fiber, low fat, low sodium and sugar-free. The menu changes daily, but there is always a choice of soup, salad, vegetarian and another entree. Take out or dine in. The seating area is not particularly inviting, but you can take your boxed meal out to the picnic tables or head for the beach.

★ ***Stillwells Bakery & Cafe*** *(Bakery/Deli)*
1740 Ka'ahumanu Avenue, Wailuku; 808-243-2243.

Hours: Monday through Saturday 6 a.m.-4 p.m.; closed Sunday; Lunch served 9:30 a.m.-3 p.m. (until 2 p.m. on Saturday). *Sampling:* Awesome sandwiches including pastrami with sauerkraut, ham and cheese, tofu burger, garden burger, vegetarian, or try a crab cake sandwich with or without soup. Once you've selected the filling, the bread is the hard part: wheat or white? Rye, croissant, focaccia? Salads include chicken Caesar, tofu, crab, Cobb and chef's or noodle dishes like chow fun, dry men, saimin and pasta. Menu items run under $10. Stillwells' signature pastries include cream horns, pecan butter balls, *lilikoi* cheesecake and big brownies. *Comments:* Stillwells is known as one of Maui's top bakeries. The bakery/cafe was shut down by a fire in August 2004, but has, thankfully, reopened and is continuing to serve its great sandwiches and baked goods in its newly remodeled "slightly retro" ambiance. Patio seating available under umbrellas.

Sub Paradise *(Sandwiches)*
395-E Dairy Road, Kahului; 808-877-8779.

Hours: Monday through Friday 7 a.m.-6 p.m.; until 5 p.m. Saturday; 7 a.m.-9 a.m. Sunday. *Sampling:* Caesar, Greek and chef's salads and over two dozen varieties of subs in 6" or 12" sizes: ham, turkey, pastrami, salami, roast beef, meatball, chicken, vegetarian, egg salad, cheese and combinations; if you're really hungry check out the Big Kahuna with eight meats and four cheeses. Most prices $5-$10.

Breakfast bagels until 11 a.m. *Comments:* Specials include turkey, bacon and avocado or Chinese chicken salad. Hana Picnic Lunch includes 6-inch sub, soda, chips, cookie, candy bar or orange for $7.40. Very good sandwiches—the bread is freshly baked and tastes it.

★ ***Tasty Crust Restaurant*** *(Local)*
1770 Mill Street, Wailuku; 808-244-0845.

Hours: 6 a.m.-10 p.m.; Friday and Saturday until 11 p.m. *Sampling:* Delicious crusty hotcakes are their specialty, two are a meal for $3. Waffles $2.75. Omelets and egg dishes ($3.60-$4.95). Lunch and dinner feature plate lunches of *loco moco*, *kalbi* ribs, teri meat, chop steak, chicken *katsu*, all with steamed rice and macaroni salad ($5.85-$6.75). Saimin, sandwiches and salads ($3.95 and up). *Comments:* Local atmosphere and no frills, just good food at great prices. Great pancakes and sweet/sour ribs. They've been here since 1943, so you know they're doing something right.

★ ***Tokyo Tei*** *(Japanese)*
1063 East Lower Main Street, Wailuku; 808-242-9630.

Hours: Monday through Saturday lunch 11 a.m.-1:30 p.m. and dinner 5-8:30 p.m.; Sunday 5-8 p.m. *Sampling:* Lunch specials include beef cutlet, sweet-and-sour pork, teriyaki meat, omelets and noodles ($6.75-$7). Saimin or fried noodles ($3.75-$4). *Teishoku* trays for lunch or dinner include shrimp tempura, sashimi, fried fish, teriyaki pork or steak ($10-$11). Dinner selections offer *hakata* chicken, seafood platter, calamari *katsu*, *yakitori*, tempura, teriyaki steak, broiled salmon, sukiyaki and *donburi* dishes that include rice, miso soup, *ko-ko* and hot tea ($8-$11.25). *Comments:* Tokyo Tei is a long-time restaurant (although it has changed its Wailuku location) and an institution on Maui. Small and cozy. Take-out also available. Cocktails. Popular with both visitors and residents and deservedly so. Great tempura and teriyaki steak. A winner for local dining at its best; don't miss this one.

Waikapu Grill *(Salads/Sandwiches)*
Maui Tropical Plantation, 1670 Honoapi'ilani Highway, Waikapu; 808-244-7643.

Hours: 11 a.m.-2 p.m. *Sampling:* Soups, appetizers, salads, sandwiches and burgers, as well as stuffed mahimahi, fish tacos and fish and chips ($3.50-$13.75). *Comments:* Pretty view of the grounds, lagoon and mountains; menu features papaya, apple bananas, mangoes and avocados grown on the plantation. Beer, wine and tropical drinks available.

Wow-Wee Maui's Kava Bar & Grill/Wayne's Sushi World
(Sandwiches/Sushi)
333 Dairy Road, Kahului; 808-871-1414. www.kavamaui.com.

Hours: 6 a.m.-9 p.m. *Sampling:* For breakfast, eggs & potatoes, *loco moco*, breakfast burrito, omelets, mango/mac nut pancakes, homemade cinnamon raisin French toast ($4.50-$8.25). Lunch/dinner offers sandwiches, burgers, cheese steak, hot Maui melts, green salads ($3.95-$9.95). Wine, beer and sake. The sushi bar offers a large variety of fresh sushi in a non-intimidating atmosphere. *Comments:* This little eatery is the only place I know of on Maui that features kava, a traditional ceremonial drink made of the 'awa root. They offer various kava drinks (kava kolada, kava latte, etc.) so take your pick and give this unusual beverage a try. They also have their own line of yummy handmade candy bars (some with fruits and nuts). Cute little place. Very casual.

Moderate-priced Dining

★ ***Brigit and Bernard's Garden Café*** *(German/European)*
335 Hoohana Street, Kahului; 808-877-6000.

Hours: Lunch Monday through Friday 10:30 a.m.-3 p.m.; dinner Wednesday through Saturday 5-9 p.m. *Sampling:* The extensive lunch menu offers grilled burgers (including a pork "schnitzelburger" and salmonburger), fresh sandwiches, pastas, salads and six gourmet meals for heartier appetites ($7-$16.95). Begin your dinner with starters like shrimp Dijon or seared ahi ($7-$8.50). Dinners ($13-$29) feature a selection of several entrees plus daily specials. Dine on specialties like wiener schnitzel, chicken marsala, rack of lamb, and *jaegershnitzel*. *Comments:* Hearty food and always delicious. Select indoor seating or the charming outdoor patio for dining. This is a tiny little place off the beaten path, but worth the search to find. Reservations highly recommended, as space is limited.

Cary & Eddie's Hideaway *(American/Seafood)*
500 North Pu'unene Avenue, Kahului; 808-873-6555.

Hours: 11 a.m.-9:30 p.m.; Sunday 8 a.m.-2 p.m.; closed Monday. *Sampling:* Sunday breakfast buffet includes pancakes, potatoes, breakfast meats and fruit and salad bar ($10.99) or other breakfast entrees ($5.99-$6.99). Daily lunch specials, Hawaiian buffet and plate lunches ($6.99-$12.99). A nightly Hawaiian dinner buffet includes barbecued pork ribs, *kalua* pig and cabbage, chicken long rice and the works for $20.99. (Early bird 5-6 p.m. $18.99.) Other "ribstickin'" dinner entrees include barbecued shrimp stir-fry, ribs and combination plates. Sample teriyaki New York strip, T-bone steak or fresh fish ($13.99-$25.99). Good family dining spot.

The Class Act *(International)*
Maui Community College Campus, Kahului; 808-984-3280; www.hawaii.edu (then search for "Class Act").

Hours: Wednesday and Friday 11 a.m.-12:30 p.m. *Comments:* This is one of Maui's best little finds. Insiders know they are in for a treat when they stop by for a fine-dining four-course gourmet lunch prepared by the Food Service students of Maui Community College's culinary academy. At $25 (plus tip) it's become a bit expensive, but not when you know you're supporting such a worthwhile student program. Students shop, serve, clean and wait on tables and a different menu is offered each week, ranging from filet mignon to crispy duck. The program is only offered during the school year, so call ahead. Reservations are required (no more than 7 days in advance). The Class Act experience takes place in the fine dining room at the new Pa'ina Culinary Arts Center on the college campus. Enjoy dining at The Class Act or visit the new cafeteria (open to the public, 11 a.m.-2:30 p.m.) that is set up as a food court.

★ ***Mañana Garage*** *(Latin American/Cuban)*
Lono Building, 33 Lono Avenue, Kahului; 808-873-0220; www.mananagarage.com.

Hours: Lunch 11 a.m.-2:30 p.m. Monday through Saturday; mid-day menu 2:30-5 p.m. Monday through Saturday; dinner nightly 5-9 p.m.; late-night menu Wednesday through Saturday 9-10:30 p.m. *Sampling:* Mañana Garage offers an opportunity to sample some authentic Latin American cuisine. For lunch, adobo barbecue duck with sweet potato quesadilla, or chicken tortilla epozote soup ($6.50-$15). For dinner begin with a fried green tomato salad, rock shrimp ceviche or smoked salmon pastrami ($5-$15). Entrees such as pepper cumin New York steak, pumpkin seed–crusted garlic shrimp, or roasted vegetable enchilada ($16-$27.50). Lunch or dinner desserts include coconut rum raisin rice pudding, sweet potato praline pound cake and ice cream sandwich ($4-$6). *Comments:* This place has some outstanding fare, different from the run-of-the-mill. Bar open from 11 a.m. Live Latin music, Wednesday through Saturday nights.

Mike's Restaurant *(Local/Chinese)*
1900 Main Street, Wailuku; 808-244-7888.

Hours: 10:30 a.m.-9:30 p.m. *Sampling:* From their local food counter, try their island breakfast combo ($3.25) with a choice of three items; omelets, too ($5.50). Plate lunches include rice and macaroni salad with options such as pork *katsu*, teri beef or house specialties such as sesame chicken, New York steak or grilled mahi.

Lots of burgers, noodle dishes and combination plates ($4.95-$9.50). In their Chinese restaurant, choose from a wide selection of traditional dishes like egg flower soup, sweet and sour shrimp, roast duck mein and Peking duck. Most items range from $7.95 to $19.95. *Comments:* Mike's has operated a local lunch counter business for years with inexpensive dishes you can eat there (limited seating) or take out. Recently, they added a full fine-dining Chinese restaurant. Between the two dining options, there appears to be something for everyone.

Upcountry

Inexpensive-priced Dining

Café Del Sol *(Deli)*

3620 Baldwin Avenue, Makawao; 808-572-4877.

Hours: 8 a.m.-4 p.m. Breakfast served until 10:45 a.m. Closed Sunday. *Sampling:* A variety of egg dishes including eggs Benedict as well as other breakfast favorites like Belgian waffles and homemade blueberry muffins ($2.50-$9.50). For lunch enjoy salads, hamburgers and sandwiches ($6-$11.25). Macaroni and cheese or peanut butter and jelly ($3.75) for the kids. *Comments:* Good, fresh food. Eat indoors or in the patio garden. Tucked back in the shops.

★ ***Grandma's Coffee House*** *(Local)*

Located in Keokea, just five miles before the Tedeschi Winery; 808-878-2140; www.grandmascoffee.com.

Hours: 7 a.m.-5 p.m. *Sampling & Comments:* This popular little coffee house is run by Alfred Franco, who is encouraging the return of the coffee industry in Upcountry Maui. Born and raised in Upcountry, his grandmother taught him how to roast the coffee beans to perfection. He does this several times a day in his century-plus-old coffee roasting machine that was brought from Philadelphia by his great-grandmother. The coffee is sold by the pound at the coffee shop. Some of the beans used are grown on Moloka'i, which is part of Maui County. A few tables invite visitors to sit down, enjoy a cup of coffee, espresso, cappuccino or fresh fruit juice along with cinnamon rolls (get there early), muffins and other homemade pastries and desserts, all fresh from the oven. A bit more of an appetite might require one of their fresh avocado sandwiches, deli salads, or a bowl of chili and rice ($5-$8). With the popularity of this place, it is tough for them to keep up with the demand for these goodies. There is seating indoors, as well as a deck for outdoor seating with a great view. It's a very "homey" and unpretentious little place ... the kind where the person who takes your order also prepares your meal, serves it and cleans up afterwards. Good place to pick up picnic foods for a drive farther Upcountry.

Kitada's Kau Kau Corner *(Local)*
3617 Baldwin Avenue, Makawao; 808-572-7241.

Hours: 6 a.m.-1:30 p.m. Closed Sunday. *Sampling:* French toast, eggs and omelets ($3.25-$7.50). Small or large portions of beef teriyaki, hamburger steak, beef or pork tofu, chopsteak, beef stew, pork chops, and spare ribs served with rice, macaroni salad, and salted cabbage ($5.50-$7.50). Sandwiches and burgers ($2.50-$4.25), saimin from $3.50. *Comments:* Owned and operated by the same family for over 50 years! It is a popular local eatery and, with these prices and the variety of plate lunches, you can see why.

★ ***Makawao Garden Cafe*** *(Healthy Salads & Sandwiches)*
Paniolo Courtyard, 3669 Baldwin Avenue, Makawao; 808-573-9065.

Hours: 11 a.m.-4 p.m. Monday through Saturday. Closed Sunday. *Sampling:* Gourmet sandwiches such as snow crab and avocado, warm brie and bacon, grilled eggplant or roast breast of chicken ($6.25-$7.95). Sample taro salad, curry chicken salad and quinoa salad ($5.95-$7.95). Soup of the day by the cup ($1.95) or bowl ($3.90) along with a selection of coffees and espresso. *Comments:* This was previously Café O' Lei but was recently bought by Jody and Kathi Sparks, who changed the name but continue to offer the same popular Café O' Lei menu. If it ain't broke, don't fix it. Good, healthy food with fresh, organic ingredients in a charming setting. The European-style courtyard is lined with flowers and foliage; tables along the brick pathway make this a "real" sidewalk café. The menu is simple, but extra touches make it special: fresh herbs from the garden, lots of garlic in the creamy Caesar dressing, pungent lemongrass in the Asian salad. Nice little place.

Mixed Plate *(Local)*
Pukalani Terrace Center, 55 Pukalani Street, Pukalani; 808-572-8258.

Hours: 6 a.m.-1 p.m. *Sampling:* Four breakfast specials; plate lunch of chopsteak, *loco moco*, saimin, chicken *hekka* or hamburger ($3-$7). Daily specials, too.

Pizza Fresh *(Italian)*
1043 Makawao Avenue, Makawao; 808-572-2000.

Hours: 10 a.m.-9 p.m.; Sunday 3-9 p.m. *Sampling:* Pizza varieties include eggplant gouda, portobello, scampi, Thai chicken, or alfredo vegetarian, or create your own. Start with the basic cheese $8 for 9" up to $20 for 18" and add toppings for $1-$2 each. You even have a selection of sauces from sun-dried tomato pesto to marinara, basil pesto or alfredo. Choose between traditional or wheat crust (all made fresh daily). Caesar, garden or Greek salads also available as well as calzones. *Comments:* Delivery is available in the area.

★ **Polli's** *(Mexican)*
1202 Makawao Avenue, Makawao; 808-572-7808.

Hours: 11 a.m.-10 p.m. *Sampling:* Mexican pizza, taquitos, jalapeno poppers, tacos, tostadas, nachos, chili, steak *pupu* ($6-$12). Chile relleno or tamale plate, stuffed quesadilla, seafood enchilada, chimichanga, sizzling fajitas, burritos supreme, vegetarian chile ($6.95-$18.25). Choose from burritos, Mexican chicken or fish dinners, or Mexican *especialidades* such as *carnitas* or baked *bajas*. Also offered are barbecue chicken, ribs, steak and burgers ($8.95-$17.95). *Comments:* Black beans and chile verde sauce are two alternative menu options, and vegetarians can request any menu item made with tofu or vegetarian taco mix. Children's plates available—children's night is Tuesday, with meals only $2.50 for kids under 12. An extra charge to refill your basket of chips seems a little chintzy, though.

Pukalani Country Club Restaurant *(American/Hawaiian)*
360 Pukalani Road (turn right just before the shopping center at Pukalani and continue until the road ends), Pukalani; 808-572-1325.

Hours: Breakfast 7:30-10:30 a.m. (from 7 a.m. on weekends); Lunch 10:30 a.m.-2 p.m.; Dinner 5-9 p.m. *Sampling:* Hearty breakfasts such as omelets, pancakes, French toast, Belgian waffles, egg dishes ($4.75-$8). Popular for their local foods. For lunch you might choose between *kalua* pig, tripe stew, or *laulau* offered as Hawaiian plates ($9-$10), or you can get them à la carte. More traditional fare includes a tuna melt, jumbo hot dog, burgers, club or egg salad sandwich ($5.60-$7.40). Similar offerings at dinner (but slightly higher in price) along with steaks, breaded mahi or shrimp, fried chicken, and teriyaki beef ($9.50-$16). *Comments:* Lunch reservations are a must as this is a popular place with the tour groups. Or eat lunch elsewhere and stop back on the way down from Upcountry for a drink, the tropical sunset, and a wonderful view. In addition to their authentic Hawaiian menu, they also have nightly specials and a salad bar at dinner. *Keiki* menu available.

Stopwatch Sports Bar *(Italian/American)*
1127 Makawao Avenue, Makawao; 808-572-1380.

Hours: 11 a.m.-2 a.m. *Sampling:* Soups, salads, sandwiches including burgers, roast beef, grilled mahi or chicken breast ($6-$8). Entrees include fish and chips, New York steak or fried shrimp ($8-$17).

Moderate-priced Dining

★ ***Casanova Italian Restaurant and Deli*** *(Italian)*

1188 Makawao Avenue, Makawao; 808-572-0220.

Hours: Lunch Monday through Saturday 11:30 a.m.-2 p.m. Dinner nightly 5:30-9:30 p.m. Deli Monday through Saturday 7:30 a.m.-6 p.m., Sunday 8:30 a.m.-6 p.m. *Sampling:* The deli offers sandwiches with interesting combinations of lemon chicken, smoked salmon, roast peppers, mozzarella, eggplant, smoked ham, brie and pastrami plus Caesar, Greek and pasta salads ($5-$9). Breakfast pastries (*lilikoi* poppyseed cake, corn bread, blueberry scones), waffles, French toast, and omelets are served until 11:30. Lunch includes soups, salads, sandwiches, pizza and plenty of great pasta selections ($5-$15). The dinner menu offers antipasti with an Italian flair including cioppino, *insalata di tofu* and deep-fried calamari. Salads include Mediterranean or Caesar ($5-$9). Pizzas baked in their authentic wood-fired oven are in the tradition of Napoli, "where pizza was born." All pizzas are 12" ($10 and up). The pasta selection nears almost a dozen, with every shape and size served with seafood and chicken breast, or stuffed with ricotta ($13-$17). Entrees include fresh fish of the day, filet of ahi, filet mignon, New York steak, or grilled lamb chops ($22-$27). *Comments:* One of a few places left to go for dining and dancing. Western decor, cozy dining. Good food and a variety of entertainment (including special celebrity concerts) have won them accolades. Each night you'll find something different.

Kula Lodge *(American-Hawaiian)*

Five miles past Pukalani on Haleakala Highway; 808-878-1535.

Hours: Breakfast daily 7-11 a.m.; lunch 11:30 a.m.-4 p.m.; Garden Terrace (pizzas) 11 a.m.-7 p.m.; dinner daily 5-8:30 p.m. *Sampling:* Warm up from your early-morning visit to Haleakala with a cappuccino, latte, mocha or perhaps a Bloody Mary or mimosa. You'll get a hearty country breakfast at this restaurant along with a beautiful view: vegetarian eggs Benedict (with sliced tomatoes, artichoke crowns and mushrooms), *ono* fish eggs Benedict, *loco moco*. Select a tofu stir-fry or create your own omelet. And from the grill there is apple cinnamon French toast, malted Belgian waffle, bananas Foster pancakes, or buttermilk griddle cakes ($8-$14). The lunch menu offers a nice selection of soups, salads and appetizers, a great option if you'd just like a break and don't have a big appetite. Papaya shrimp salad, "broke da mouth" potstickers, "crabby crab cake," or three-cheese quesadilla. Sandwiches and burgers, or a main course of brick oven–roasted free-range chicken or grilled eggplant and portobello mushroom on polenta cake ($7-$16). Pizzas baked in the *kiawe*-wood-fired oven are served in the lovely Garden Terrace ($15-$19). Dinner soups, salads and appetizers are the same as those offered for lunch; follow it up with dinner entree of mango barbecue ribs, chicken *saltimbocca*, roasted duck leg & breast or fresh catch ($22-$29). *Comments:* Breakfast, the most popular meal of the day here, has the added benefit of the fireplace (a warming delight after a cold trip to the mountain top) and a spectacular panoramic view. Very nice children's menu.

Makawao Steak House *(American)*
3612 Baldwin Avenue, Makawao; 808-572-8711.

Hours: 5:30-9 p.m. *Sampling:* Sample their popular chicken Zoie (stuffed breasts with creamed spinach filling), teriyaki pork tenderloin, Kalaheo shrimp or calamari steak. But if you're hankering for beef don't miss their prime rib. Served while supply lasts. They also have good steaks: pepper steak, teriyaki top sirloin, beef tenderloin ($17.95-$27.95). Dinners come with potato or rice and breads. They have a small all-you-can-eat salad bar for an additional $3.95. Good kids' menu ($2.50-$3.75), too. *Comments:* This family-owned Makawao landmark has attractive *paniolo* artwork, wood floors and paneling, and a cozy ambiance with a stately fireplace that glows on those chilly Upcountry evenings. The general feeling among those I know is this restaurant isn't as good as it used to be, but you'll still get a decent meal here. They recently added a tea room in the back courtyard area, where a full traditional tea (tea, scones, finger sandwiches) is served, Wednesday through Saturday, starting at 1 p.m. ($12.75).

Expensive-priced Dining

★ ***Hali'imaile General Store*** *(Hawaiian Regional/Continental)*
Hali'imaile Road, Hali'imaile; 4.5 miles up Haleakala Highway (Highway 37), left at Hali'imaile sign, continue 1.5 miles). 808-572-2666; www.bevgannonrestaurants.com.

Hours: Lunch Monday through Friday 11 a.m.-2:30 p.m. Dinner 5:30-9:30 p.m. *Sampling:* The menu changes seasonally, but always features an innovative selection of dishes. Lunch includes their popular Nicoise with a toss, Upcountry-style Caesar, or baby back ribs ($7-$15). For dinner, begin with Bev's Boboli (crab dip served on a 6" Boboli), sashimi Napoleon, Asian pear and duck taco, or Brie and grape quesadilla topped with sweet pea guacamole ($8-$17). Entrees ($20-$32) include *kalua* pork enchiladas, Hunan-style rack of lamb, Szechuan barbecued salmon and crispy lacquered half-duck. Desserts tempt you from the display case and it is definitely worth saving room. *Comments:* This restaurant (and Cordon Bleu-trained Chef Beverly Gannon) has put Hali'imaile on the map, collecting rave reviews and top ratings since it opened in 1988. The original structure dates back to the 1920s when it served as the general store and hub of this community. The 5,000-square-foot wooden building maintains its original high ceiling; the floors are refurbished hardwood. The intricately designed bar in the front dining room is surrounded by tall pine shelves and an exhibition kitchen. The admirable wine list includes some nice port, sherry and cognac. The food is exquisite and it's well worth the drive across the island. *Keiki* menu and cocktails, too. Look for Beverly Gannon's cookbook and take a little of the island home with you, and enjoy her food service if you fly on Hawaiian Airlines. Named Best Hawaii Regional Cuisine in the 2005 'Aipono Awards.

La Provence *(French)*
Next to Kula Ace Hardware, Kula Highway, Kula; 808-878-1313.

Hours: Wednesday through Sunday, open 7 a.m. for breakfast; 11:30 a.m.-3 p.m. for lunch; 5:30-9 p.m. for dinner. Closed Monday and Tuesday; closed for dinner when raining. *Sampling:* French pastries for breakfast or lunch; quiche and stuffed croissants, too. Dinner starters are soup du jour ($6.95), three salads ($7.95-$9.95) and four appetizers, including traditional escargot and *coquilles* Saint-Jacques ($8.95-$11.95). Dinner entrees vary, but generally there are six entrees offered, including fish, duck, pork loin, filet mignon and chicken ($23.95-$30.95). *Comments:* Tiny French restaurant with outdoor patio seating (which explains why the restaurant closes for dinner on rainy evenings). Bring your own wine. Casual, simple ambiance, but excellent food. Cash/checks only; no credit cards. Recommend you call ahead for dinner reservations to make sure the restaurant is open that evening. When the weather is nice, there is a lovely sunset view from the patio. Fabulous breakfast pastries—stop in and take some back to your hotel or B&B.

Hana Highway

PAIA-HAIKU

Inexpensive-priced Dining

Anthony's Coffee Co. *(Coffee House/Deli)*
90 Hana Highway, Paia; 808-579-8340.

Hours: 5:30 a.m.-6 p.m. *Sampling:* Belgian waffle, French toast plain or with "fruit and whip," eggs Benedict regular style or with lox or *kalua* pork, breakfast croissant with a choice of meat, bagels plain or with toppings, catch of the day with toast, rice or potatoes ($5-$8). Cold sandwiches include pastrami, salami, roast beef or veggie ($5.95) or try a hot one such as tuna melt or a burger ($6.95) served with chips and a pickle. They feature made-on-Maui ice cream in their cones, shakes, sundaes, floats and smoothies ($2-$3.50). *Comments:* Counter and table seating with plenty of newspapers and magazines to read while you enjoy a variety of hot coffee drinks. They roast their own coffees and sell more than 20 international varieties. The roaster is in the shop, so if you time it right you can watch and smell as they toast up their beans. Cozy place and good prices.

Café Des Amis *(Creperie)*
42 Baldwin Avenue, Paia; 808-579-6323.

Hours: 8:30 a.m.-8:30 p.m. *Sampling:* Assorted crepes include spinach with feta; brie with avocado, apple and black pepper; and chicken, avocado, mozzarella ($7.25-$9). In addition to crepes, they offer curry dishes such as shrimp and coconut curry wrap or beef and mushroom curry ($8.25-$14.95). For dessert enjoy a sweet crepe made with bananas and chocolate, strawberries and cream, peaches with raspberry sauce, or caramelized apples with rum ($2.50-$4.75). *Comments:* Owners Bill and Tina serve up more than a small traditional crepe—it's a large, hearty, stuffed rectangular meal. Breakfast crêpes are available all day. Daily specials.

Café Mambo *(American/Healthy)*
30 Baldwin Avenue, Paia; 808-579-8021.

Hours: 8 a.m.-9 p.m. *Sampling:* Hawaiian pancakes, breakfast burritos and quesadillas, or egg dishes ($4-$8). Lunch (served 11 to 4) offerings include hot and cold sandwiches and burgers or salads ($6-$9). Plate lunches with two scoops of rice, Haiku greens, tropical fruit, or potato salad with selections ranging from teri beef or chicken to half herb-roasted chicken or catch of the day ($7-$9). Boxed picnic lunches, available from 8 a.m. to 2 p.m., include sandwich, fresh fruit, homemade cookie and beverage ($8-$10). Plenty of espresso and cappuccino if you're in need of an eye opener. Dinner (4 to 9 p.m.) offers *tapas*, burgers, fajitas ($8-$19). *Comments:* Coffee drinks and fresh baked pastries plus soft-serve ice cream and sundaes. A popular place to pick up some lunch goodies for the road to Hana or Haleakala.

Charley's *(American/Italian)*
142 Hana Highway, Paia; 808-579-9453.

Hours: Breakfast 7 a.m.-1 p.m., Sunday until 2:30 p.m. Lunch 11:30 a.m.-2:30 p.m. *Pupus*/burgers 2:30-5 p.m. Dinner 5-10 p.m. *Sampling:* Buttermilk, Hawaiian macadamia, whole wheat, or blueberry pancakes, or enjoy Charley's steak and eggs, *huevos rancheros,* or a vegetarian breakfast taco ($4-$12). Lunches include their popular one-third pound burgers ($7-$10) or choose from grilled fish, turkey, avocado or Charley's chicken sandwich ($7-$11). Lunch entrees include *ono* pan fry, fish and chips, or cashew chicken ($7-$11). Dinners of chicken marsala, seafood fettuccine, scampi, lasagna, barbecue ribs, hand-tossed pizza, calzone, *kiawe*-smoked ribs or marlin, and nightly fish specials ($8-$23). Pizza available from 3 p.m. to midnight. *Comments:* This is a Paia landmark. Big-screen TV for satellite sporting events. Charley's was named for the owner's black-and-white Great Dane (named for the movie *Goodbye, Charley* in which Debbie Reynolds was reincarnated as a Great Dane), which roamed freely around Front Street when the restaurant began as a small fruit juice stand in Lahaina. Charley the dog and Charley's moved to Paia in 1971 and Charley P. Woofer Restaurant and Saloon was born. Today, the original dog has been "reincarnated" several times, and the most recent one is "C.W."

Fresh Mint *(Vietnamese/Vegan)*
115 Baldwin Avenue, Paia (across from Paia Post Office); 808-579-9144. (There is another location in Kahului.)

Hours: 11 a.m.-9 p.m. daily. *Sampling:* A large selection of Vietnamese and vegetarian/vegan dishes. The restaurant uses no animal products. Appetizers, salads, soups, entrees, noodles, burritos and chef's specials like hot pot (rice tofu with vegetables), soy fish in clay pot or pan-fried crispy vegetable rice noodle. The most

SUNSET-WATCHING SUGGESTIONS

If you want to catch the sun sinking into the ocean (rather than over the island of Lana'i), winter sunsets are better in South Maui, and summer sunsets are better in West Maui. Here are some suggestions for great sunset viewing:

- Dinner at The Plantation House in Kapalua
- *Pupus* or dinner at the Sea House Restaurant in Napili
- Torchlighting, cliff diving and music nightly at sunset at the Sheraton Maui's Lagoon Bar
- A lanai table at the Sea Watch Restaurant in Wailea
- Dinner on the lanai at Capische? at the Diamond Resort
- From anywhere on the sea wall on Front Street, Lahaina
- An Upcountry sunset from Kula Lodge
- On a sunset cruise as you sail back into Ma'alaea or Lahaina Harbor
- En route down from Haleakala, at the Pukalani Country Club

expensive item on the menu is $12.95. *Comments:* Owners Michael and Mai Ly Beck opened their first restaurant in Paia, followed by a new (and larger) location recently opened in Kahului.

Linda's Beach House *(American)*
771 Haiku Road (right before Haiku Marketplace, near corner of Haiku & Kokomo); 808-575-5404.

Hours: 8 a.m.-4 p.m.; breakfast/lunch menu served all day. *Sampling:* Country breakfasts of egg dishes, omelets, cheese blintzes, French toast or ratatouille ($7.95-$9.95). Lunch offers a variety of sandwiches ($6.95-$10.95). Coffee drinks. *Comments:* Clean, friendly little place owned and operated by Linda Simpson. Dine inside or outside at one of the covered tables.

Paia Fish Market Restaurant *(Seafood)*
110 Hana Highway, on the corner of Baldwin Avenue and Hana Highway, Paia; 808-579-8030.

Hours: 11 a.m.-4:30 p.m. lunch; 4:30-9:30 p.m. dinner. *Sampling:* Charbroiled burgers, fish and chips, and lunch- or dinner-size portions of quesadillas or teriyaki chicken. They offer a variety of seafood prepared Cajun-style, blackened, sauteed or charbroiled ($7-$15.95). A blackboard slate details the fresh fish offerings. Beer and wine. *Comments:* Place your order at the counter then pick up your meal and seat yourself at a half-dozen oversized picnic tables. Humorous artifacts lining the walls make for interesting topics of conversation.

★ ***Pauwela Café*** *(Healthy)*
Pauwela Cannery, 375 West Kuiaha Road, Haiku; 808-575-9242.

Hours: Monday through Friday 7 a.m.-2:30 p.m. Sunday 8 a.m.-2 p.m.; closed Saturday. *Sampling:* Breakfast is served throughout the day and includes hot-out-of-the-oven coffeecake, muffins, scones breakfast breads ($1.75-$2.25). *Pain perdu* (French bread baked in vanilla orange custard) is a must-try for breakfast or as dessert; get there early because it often sells out quickly. Belgian waffles or homemade English muffins topped with scrambled eggs, turkey ham, tomato and cheese ($4.25-$7). Lunch selections include green leaf, Greek and Caesar salads. A little bigger appetite will enjoy the *kalua* turkey sandwich, taro burger or veggie burrito ($5.25-$7.50). Daily specials. Coffees, fresh orange or carrot juice, fruit and yogurt and (non-dairy) smoothies. *Comments:* The lively artwork of Nancy Hoke dresses the walls of this cannery café, located on Highway 36 in the old Libby Pineapple Cannery, about 15 miles from Kahului. Built in 1918, it now houses many famous manufacturers of windsurf and surfing gear. *Keiki* menu and take out available. Everything is made fresh with unbleached flour and raw sugar in all the baked goods.

★ ***Vasi's Gourmet Take-out & Bakery*** *(Deli)*
Haiku Town Center. 810 Kokomo Road, Haiku; 808-575-9588.

Hours: 8 a.m.-8 p.m.; closed Sunday. *Sampling:* Caesar, Oriental or Greek salads along with ahi, French dip or gyro sandwiches ($5.95-$7.95). Other selections include such items as spanikopita, vegetable torte, moussaka or hand-tossed pizzas ($5.95-$10.95). *Comments:* Order items to go, or eat in their cozy dining area; variety of coffee drinks, too.

Moderate-priced Dining

Colleen's *(American)*
810 Haiku Road, Haiku Marketplace; 808-575-9211.

Hours: 6:30 a.m.-9:30 p.m. daily. *Sampling:* Egg-stuffed croissant sandwiches, breakfast burritos, tofu vegetable wrap, traditional French toast, omelets and other egg dishes ($3.75-$8.75). For lunch, baguette sandwiches, burgers, fish, wraps ($6.75-$13.95). Dinner offers a range of salads ($8-$10) and entrees like pepper-crusted *ono* burger, vodka penne pasta, ahi fettuccine and filet mignon with handcut fries ($11.50-$23). *Comments:* Variety of hot and iced coffee drinks, including organic chai tea lattes. Recently remodeled; a fun, funky place.

★ ***Hana Hou*** *(Local)*
Haiku Marketplace, 810 Haiku Road, Haiku; 808-575-2661.

Hours: 10 a.m.-10 p.m. *Sampling:* Saimin ($5.50), burgers and plate lunches ($5.95-$9.95), Hawaiian plates such as *kalua* pork and cabbage or chicken long rice, New York steak, *paniolo* ribs, shrimp curry or pastas such as wild mushroom or Kula garden pasta. Hana Hou dinners ($7.95-$15). *Comments:* A great local diner in the old plantation home next to Haiku Cannery. There is a take-out window, or sit inside and enjoy. Thursday through Saturday they have entertainment 7-9:30 p.m.

★ ***Jacques' North Shore Restaurant and Sushi Bar*** *(Seafood/Sushi)*
120 Hana Highway Paia; 808-579-8844.

Hours: 5-10 p.m. *Sampling:* Appetizers include chicken martini, coconut shrimp ravioli with spinach and shiitake mushrooms, mini pesto caper pancakes, soup Pauvert (Jacques' special pumpkin coconut soup) or sushi from the sushi bar ($4.25-$12.95). Salads include spinach and shrimp with a citrus vinaigrette, salad Nicoise, lobster brochette with salad greens or a fried tofu salad ($4.25-$19.95). Vegans can enjoy an entree of vegetable tofu curry or a tofu stir-fry ($12.95). Fish is a specialty here and the preparations are all fabulous. All are served with seasonal vegetables and rice. North Shore fish with pumpkin sauce is a meal of fish, bananas and oranges served with a ginger pumpkin sauce and miso butter. Pacific free-range salmon or try pickled salmon (broiled in a unique marinade then poached medium rare and seared before serving on angel hair pasta), macadamia nut–crusted fish, or fish dynamite (with a portobello mushroom, havarti cheese, and spicy mayo) ($16.95-$26.95). For pasta you can try pork spare rib pasta, seafood linguini, or smoked chicken pasta ($10.95-$16.95). The meat lover can be satisfied with an entree of chicken piccata, spicy peanut chicken, pork on a sugar cane, beef sauteed in a peppercorn brandy cream sauce, or roast duckling ($13.95-$26.95). *Comments:* Jacques' has been in a few different locations on Maui. In Paia, they continue to offer delicious and innovative preparations at very reasonable prices, compared to the high-priced resort restaurants. It's definitely worth the drive to Paia for some top-notch cuisine.

Milagros Food Co. *(Tex-Mex)*

3 Baldwin Avenue on the corner of Hana Highway, Paia; 808-579-8755.

Hours: Breakfast 8-11 a.m. (Sunday until 12); lunch 11 a.m.-5:30 p.m.; dinner 5:30-10 p.m. *Sampling & Comments:* Outside veranda; coffee drinks and a full bar with margaritas and micro beers. Santa Fe–style Mexican food. Huge chicken burritos, but mine was mostly filled with beans and rice. Sitting outside is good for people watching, but a bit too noisy with the busy road right in front. Breakfast prices $6-$9; lunch $5-$12; dinner $12-$20.

★ ***Moana Café & Bakery*** *(Bakery)*

71 Baldwin Avenue, Paia; 808-579-9999; www.moanacafe.com.

Hours: Breakfast 8 a.m.-11 a.m. Lunch 11 a.m.-3 p.m. Dinner 3-9 p.m. *Sampling:* For breakfast sample a surfer's omelet, malted Belgian waffles or tropical pancakes plus quiche, saimin, frittata or local-style breakfast wrap ($5-$8). For lunch try their Caesar with creamy roasted garlic (served in an edible bread basket) or the crispy Thai chicken salad with colorful Asian veggies. Sandwiches range from grilled mahi or roasted vegetable to breast of turkey or roast lamb. But don't expect the usual; everything seems to come with a little something extra and different. For dinner starters try their roasted vegetable Napoleon or Hana Bay crab cake, then enjoy chili-seared ahi with Moloka'i sweet potatoes, taro leaves and mango salsa, or Thai red curry with coconut milk. Dinner prices top out at just about $22 for the rack of lamb. *Comments:* Full-service bakery featuring fresh pastries. Evening entertainment (schedule varies), ranging from blues, flamenco and vintage Hawaiian.

Text continued on page 294.

NIGHTLIFE

With so many activity options during the day, by nightfall you're likely to be ready to unwind (if not head straight for bed). But if you still have energy left, here are a few suggestions for after the sun goes down. The following spots generally offer entertainment, but as with everything else, schedules and formats change often. Call to see what's on for which nights. Check the "Scene" section of the Thursday edition of the Maui News, which lists current late-night happenings.

LAHAINA **Paradice Bluz Nightclub/Lounge** (808-667-5299) is open from 10 p.m. until 1 a.m. nightly with jazz, blues and comedy ($5 cover). Lots of couches and a cross between the old Blue Max and a Starbucks internet café. **Moose McGillycuddy's** (808-667-7758) is always hopping for the young crowd. They offer dancing nightly from 9:30 p.m. to closing at 2 a.m. **Kobe Japanese Steakhouse** (808-667-5555) offers karaoke on Friday and Saturday from 9:30 p.m. **Kimo's** (808-661-4811) has live entertainment most nights of the week. **Longhi's** (808-667-2288) has live entertainment on Friday nights. **BJ's Chicago Pizzeria** (808-661-0700) has lots happening with varying musical entertainment nightly from 7:30-10 p.m. **Cheeseburger in Paradise** (808-661-4855) offers music almost every night, with an early (4:30-7:30 p.m.) and a late (8-11 p.m.) set. **Compadres** (808-661-7189) at Lahaina Cannery Mall features salsa dancing from 10 p.m. to closing on Saturday. Check **Pioneer Inn** (808-661-3636) for music a few nights each week 6-9 p.m. There's also weekend entertainment (usually live jazz) at **Pacific 'O** (808-667-4341) at 505 Front Street.

KA'ANAPALI–KAPALUA AREA Most of the resorts have live music in their lounges. At **Kapalua Bay Hotel** (808-669-5656) the **Lehua Lounge** features nightly hula performances from 5:30 to 7 p.m. followed by contemporary Hawaiian music until 8:30. Both **Hula Grill** (808-667-6636), nightly, and **Leilani's** (808-661-4495), Friday-Sunday late afternoon, offer live Hawaiian music at their Whalers Village locations. **Fish & Game Brewing Company** (808-669-3474) in Kahana offers live entertainment most nights 6:30-9:30 p.m. **Sea House Restaurant** (808-669-1500) in Napili has live Hawaiian music nightly from 7 to 9 p.m. **Sansei** (808-669-6286) at Kapalua has karaoke Thursday and Friday nights starting at 10 p.m.

MA'ALAEA–KIHEI–WAILEA–MAKENA AREA Most resorts have great soft jazz or Hawaiian music in their lobby lounges. The **Botero Bar** at the **Grand Wailea Resort Hotel & Spa** (808-875-1234) offers live musical entertainment nightly from 6:30-9:30 p.m. The resort's 10,000-square-foot **Tsunami Night Club** is the

only true nightclub on Maui and operates Fridays and Saturdays 9:30 p.m.-2 a.m. for dancing to R&B, hip-hop, Top-40 and house music; evening resort wear and proper footwear required, no beachwear; $10 cover. At the **Four Seasons Resort** (808-874-8000), the **Lobby Lounge** offers Hawaiian entertainment 5:30 to 7:30 p.m. nightly, followed by other entertainment from 8:30 to 11:30 p.m. The **Fairmont Kea Lani's Caffe Ciao** restaurant (808-875-4100) features contemporary and jazz entertainment from 5:30 to 9:30 p.m. Thursday through Saturday. Entertainment is frequently available in the **Molokini Lounge** at **Maui Prince Hotel** (808-874-1111).

Sansei (808-879-0004) in Kihei has karaoke Thursday through Saturday nights, starting at 10 p.m. **Bocalino Bistro** (808-874-9299) has nightly entertainment 10 p.m. to 1 a.m. **Capische?** (808-879-2224) at the Diamond Resort in Wailea has live jazz music Friday-Sunday. Live jazz nightly at **Yorman's By the Sea** (808-874-8385). **Lulu's** (808-879-9944) in Kihei has 22 televisions and a pool table room, as well as live entertainment most nights. **Hapa's Nightclub** (808-879-9001) has something happening most nights of the week. Check out the classical Thai dance at **Thailand Cuisine** (808-875-0839) Monday through Thursday, 6:30-8:30 p.m..

Other spots to check out are **Life's a Beach** (808-891-8010) for the young bar scene, **Ma'alaea Grill** (808-243-2206), **Marco's Southside Grill** (808-874-4041), **Mulligan's on the Blue** (808-874-1131) at the Wailea Blue Course, and **Tommy Bahama Tropical Cafe** (808-875-9983) at the Shops at Wailea.

KAHULUI-WAILUKU AREA **Jerome E. Metcalfe's Kahului Ale House Sports Bar & Restaurant** (808-877-9001) has live bands, music with deejays as well as karaoke. **Manana Garage** (808-873-0220) and **Café Marc Aurel** (808-244-0852), a cute little wine bistro in Wailuku, are other night spots to check out.

UPCOUNTRY **Casanova's** (808-572-0220) in Makawao has a dance floor and features blues, jazz, Western, disco and a bit of everything else, every night at 9:30 except Monday and Tuesday. **The Stopwatch Sports Bar & Grill** (808-572-1380) in Makawao has live music primarily on weekends.

HANA HIGHWAY **Hana Hou** (808-575-2661) in Haiku has live Hawaiian entertainment Thursday-Saturday. Down in Paia check out **Charley's** (808-579-8085), **Sandbar & Grill** (808-579-8742) and **Cafe Moana Bakery & Cafe** (808-579-9999).

Expensive-priced Dining

Mama's Fish House *(Continental/Seafood)*
On Highway 36 just 1.5 miles past Paia at Kuau, look for the ship's flagpole and the angel fish sign; 808-579-8488.

Hours: Lunch 11 a.m.-2:30 p.m. *Pupus* 2:30-5 p.m. Dinner 5-9:30 p.m. *Sampling:* Warning—You may mistake the prices on the lunch menus as dinner fare. People from far and wide come to enjoy this landmark restaurant. Lunch appetizers, soups and salads range from macadamia nut crab cake and fire and ice relish to Chef Martin's classic fish chowder. There are oysters fresh from Fanny Bay, Pacific Northwest butter clams, or Polynesian lobster soup with coconut, fresh spinach, and Hana breadfruit crisps ($10-$18). Both lunch and dinner offer a twist that really personalizes the menu. You might enjoy *ono*, for instance, caught by Matt Moser trolling offshore from Hana Bay, mahimahi caught by Mark Hobson along the North Shore of Maui or *shutome* caught in local waters aboard the *Kawika.* Any fish may be served grilled with pineapple salsa, sauteed Mama's style, or with a bit more Pacific-Rim flair you could have your ahi seared in *nori* and roasted *kukui* nut with wasabi *beurre blanc* and soba noodles. Lunch entrees $24 and up. Luncheon salads ($17-$25) available and sandwiches include fresh fish or perhaps *kalua* pig with Asian pear chutney ($15-$22). Since Mama has her own fishing fleet you can expect the best and freshest fish. There are numerous seafood selections, or choose from non-seafood dinner entrees like crispy *kalua* duck or filet mignon. (Dinner entrees $32-$49.) But you really shouldn't go to Mama's without a hankering for fish, because the land-lover selections definitely take a back seat to seafood. The menu changes daily. *Comments:* Mama's opened in 1973, making it one of the island's oldest restaurants.. It has become somewhat of a legend, and although the food is fresh and good (and the beachfront location is fabulous), its prices have skyrocketed in recent years, and I personally think there are better restaurants on the island for this kind of money. When my husband and I ate there, the food was good but not incredible—which is what I would expect for these prices. My suggestion if you MUST dine at Mama's is to go for lunch, when you can enjoy the beautiful ocean view and afterwards stroll along the beach to watch the windsurfers. You might as well get your money's worth with an ocean view in the daylight. Valet parking. Reservations, especially for dinner, strongly recommended. Full bar service. Named Best Waterfront Restaurant and Best Dessert in the 2005 'Aipono Awards.

Inexpensive-Priced Dining

Hana Ranch Store

Hana Highway (a short walk past Hana Ranch Restaurant); 808-248-8261.

Hours: 7 a.m. to 7:30 p.m. daily. *Sampling:* Ready-made sandwiches and hot dogs; groceries.

Hasegawa General Store

5165 Hana Highway, Hana; 808-248-8231.

Hours: Monday through Saturday 7 a.m. to 7 p.m., Sunday 8 a.m. to 6 p.m. *Sampling:* A little bit of everything.

Tutu's (Local/Sandwiches)

174 Hana Bay, Hana; 808-248-8224.

Hours: 8 a.m.-4 p.m. *Sampling:* Sandwiches, plate lunches, burgers ($3-$7). *Comments:* People have been known to drive for miles for their *haupia* ice cream.

Moderate-priced Dining

Hana Ranch Restaurant (American)

5031 Hana Highway, Hana; 808-248-8255.

Hours: Lunch Daily 11:30 a.m.-3 p.m. (3-5:30 p.m. limited menu); Take-out window Wednesday/Friday/Saturday 7 a.m.-4 p.m., Sunday/Monday/Tuesday/Thursday 7 a.m.-7 p.m. *Sampling:* Lunch offers a full menu of salads, sandwiches and burgers ($7-$15). The burgers are good, offered with a variety of toppings, and we found the grilled fish sandwich ($11.50) to be especially good, made with fresh fish. Save room for the warm chocolate chip cookie dough sundae ($6.50), definitely a dessert for two or more. Dinner offers family-style appetizers (large servings to be shared) like Hawaiian chili pepper–spiced chicken wings or *kalua* pig taquitos ($11-$14), a variety of salads and pastas ($7-$22), flame-grilled burgers ($13-$16) or full entree plates including grilled beef tri-tip steak or barbecued baby back ribs (entrees $14-$19). *Comments:* Casual dining; indoor or outside patio seating with ocean view. *Keiki* dinner menu for age 12 and under. Children 8 and under eat free from 6-7 p.m.—one free *keiki* for every paid adult entree. A take-out window is also available and serves hamburgers on evenings when the restaurant is closed.

Expensive-priced Dining

Hotel Hana-Maui Dining Room (Continental)

Hotel Hana-Maui, Hana; 808-248-8211.

Hours: Breakfast 7:30-10:30 a.m. Lunch 11:30 a.m.-2:30 p.m. Dinner Saturday through Thursday 6-9 p.m.; Friday night buffet and hula show 6-8:30 p.m. *Sampling:* Breakfasts ($5-$15) include daily omelet, eggs Benedict, buttermilk pancakes or Hana Ranch sweet potato hash. Lunches ($9-$17) offer light selections of salads and starters, as well as burgers and sandwiches such as *kalua* pig melt, grilled fresh catch or herb marinated chicken. For dinner, entrees change daily depending on what fish is caught or what fresh produce is in season. You might try a starter of Kipahulu corn chowder or salad of Upcountry baby lettuces (starters/salads $10-$18). The night we dined there recently, entree choices included fresh Hana cardamom–crusted ahi, Hana-style bouillabaisse, and Painted Hills filet of beef (entree prices $33-$35). Desserts such as warm brioche tart with mascarpone cream and mangoes or chocolate espresso terrine with candied macadamia nuts and Kona coffee ice cream ($9). *Comments:* Keiki menus available; lovely dining room with view of the hotel's gardens and Hana Bay in the distance. The dinner menu offers the option of a three- or four-course tasting menu ($55/$65 per person), which ends up being a good value—rather than ordering several courses à la carte. We found the salads to be very generous in size; the entrees were somewhat small but sufficient. The food was delicious and the service was friendly and efficient. The restaurant is currently under the direction of head chef John Cox, who came to Hana from the Sierra Mar restaurant at the hotel's highly-acclaimed sister property in Big Sur, California, Post Ranch Inn. Cox and Chef de Cuisine David Patterson make a dynamic team. Their dishes are innovative and ever-changing, as they utilize fresh fish and organic fruits and vegetables from the area.

Lu'aus and Dinner Shows

Most of Maui's lu'aus are large events, with an average of 400-600 guests. Most serve traditional Hawaiian foods. The entertainment ranges from splashy Broadway-style productions to more subtle offerings of authentic Hawaiian dance and song. In general there are a few standard things to be expected at traditional lu'aus: an *imu* ceremony (to uncover the cooked pig that will be served that night), poi, *haupia* (coconut pudding) and mai tais. Upon arrival there may or may not be some waiting in line before it's your turn to be greeted with a shell or flower lei; a snapshot of your group (available for purchase after the show) is a sure bet.

It is very difficult to judge these lu'aus. While one person raves about a particular show, another person will express disappointment with the same event. Read the information provided, carefully keeping in mind that performers do come and go. All lu'aus are family-friendly, as they are designed for people of all ages to enjoy together. Therefore, I have not used the "family-friendly" icon in this section.

★ *Feast at Lele*

505 Front Street, Lahaina; 866-244-5353; 808-667-5353; www.feastatlele.com.

Lu'au meets fine dining. This is not a lu'au in the traditional sense of the word, but rather a gourmet feast with a Polynesian show. The evening celebrates the cuisine and culture of Polynesia, featuring a five-course dinner in a lovely terraced oceanfront courtyard surrounded by palms. The menu was developed by Chef James McDonald of the acclaimed Pacific 'O and I'o restaurants, and the food is delicious and plentiful—certainly the best "lu'au food" I've ever experienced. Each course corresponds to a specific region of Polynesia, which is depicted in a segment of the show with song and dance. Come hungry. The meal begins with "munchies" of banana, sweet potato and taro chips served with tropical ginger salsa. This is followed by native Hawaiian dishes of *pohole* fern and hearts of palm salad, seared fresh fish, *kalua* pig and poi. From New Zealand there is sea bean duck salad with *poha* berry dressing, fishcake patties, and roasted mushrooms with squash. From Tahiti you'll be served *poisson cru* (marinated fish), scallops on the shell and *fafa* (steamed chicken and taro leaf in coconut milk). The Samoan course brings you grilled steak (*supasui*) and *palusami* (breadfruit with taro leaf and coconut milk) along with shrimp and avocado with *lilikoi*. Dessert includes caramel macadamia nut tart with *haupia*, tropical fruits and Hawaiian chocolate truffles. Tropical drinks, cocktails and wine are included in the price—an open bar is available all evening. Seating is by reserved tables—you sit only with your own companions, not a hundred other people. A table for two, table for five, you name it. It's your own private table, and you are served by a friendly staff (no buffet line here) and presented with a hot towel at the end. My teenage niece who accompanied me (and has experienced various other lu'aus), was astounded by the friendly service. At one point after our server left our table, she turned to me in surprise and said, "They're actually TALKING to us!" That says it all. We had a great experience, and I highly recommend this to anyone who would enjoy a gourmet Polynesian dinner show

LU'AU VALUE

Check the *Maui News* for advertisements listing local lu'aus that might be held by churches or other community organizations as fundraisers. The public is welcome and the prices are usually half that of the commercial ventures. A terrific value and you're sure to enjoy some great "local" food.

instead of or in addition to a traditional lu'au. Offered seven days a week; $99 adults, $69 child (age 12 and under).

★ Hotel Hana-Maui

Hana; 808-248-8211.

This hula show has long been one of my favorites and wins a star from me for its refreshing charm and authenticity. Although the Hotel Hana-Maui has changed ownership and management many times over the years, the hotel's hula show has thankfully remained. You won't see a slick production or sophisticated sets here, just a group of Hana residents (many of them hotel employees and their family members) doing what they love to do—singing and dancing the Hawaiian way. The hotel dining room offers an excellent dinner buffet on Fridays starting at 6 p.m. with the most unusual salad bar selections I've ever seen—*pohole* fern salad, gourmet cheeses, sushi, chilled shrimp and several fresh fruits, including exotic varieties I had never tried before. In addition, there are several selections of hot entrees served up by the chefs, as well as a variety of island desserts. The hula show starts at 7 p.m. and lasts for an hour, taking place right there in the dining room. It is just what you would expect from Hana—real people sharing their music with you. Dancers are male and female and range from *keiki* (one little one couldn't have been more than 5 years old) to *kupuna* (seniors). It is an hour of Hawaiian music—no Tahitian dance or other Polynesian performances. Simple and genuine, it's a delight to watch. And at the end, every performer gets introduced along with an explanation about who they are ("and this is my auntie Leilani and her daughter Malia, who is married to ..."). This show is pure Hana. The real thing. Friday nights only; $45 adults, $31 children.

Hyatt Regency Maui Resort and Spa ("Drums of the Pacific")

200 Nohea Kai Drive, Ka'anapali; 808-667-4420.

"Drums of the Pacific" is more a dinner show than a lu'au. The performance is on the grounds of the Hyatt (Lahaina side) but there is no ocean view. The show is from 5-8 p.m. nightly and there is usually a bit of a line. Pictures are taken while waiting prior to admission to the grounds, where you are greeted with a lei and taken to a table by your server. The dinner buffet I experienced featured mahimahi, *shoyu* chicken, *kalua* pork, and steaks cooked on the grill. Baked potatoes, roasted sweet potatoes with pineapple glaze, Upcountry vegetable stir-fry, and island-style fried rice complete the dinner offerings. The desserts were a cut above: the *haupia* had good texture and coconut flavor, and the hot bread pudding was baked with a meringue topping. They also had chocolate macadamia nut pie and pineapple upside-down cake. The show starts off with the blowing of the conch and the beating of the drums. The *kahiko* hula followed the chant and had a very effective smoke-like mist surrounding the dancers. The *imu* ceremony was short and nondescript, but did have the "Pig Procession," carrying his piggly majesty through the center aisle of the audience. A separate side stage for solo dances made things visually interesting. Perhaps the best number was the Maui Waltz, a pretty song with girls in high-collared white Victorian blouses and colored skirts. Chief Fa'a, the fire dancer, continues to be one of the best. A good, professional and fast-paced production. All in all, a show worth seeing. Adults $78.95 ($65 for Hyatt guests), teens $52, children $37.

Kupanaha: Maui Magic for All Ages

Ka'anapali Beach Hotel, 2525 Ka'anapali Parkway, Kanahele Room Theater; 808-667-0128; 800-262-8450. (For details, see "Magic Shows" under Chapter 6.)

Marriott Lu'au, at Marriott's Maui Ocean Club

100 Nohea Kai Drive, Ka'anapali; 800-745-6997; 808-661-5828; www.marriottluau.com.

Offered nightly (except Monday), the evening begins with a 4:30 p.m. arrival with greeting and optional photo. They have open seating, so an early arrival affords the best seats. At 5 p.m. there are demonstrations of coconut husking, lei making, basket weaving and other Hawaiian arts and crafts. Dinner is a traditional lu'au buffet featuring *kalua* pig, *hulihuli* chicken, fresh mahimahi, grilled teriyaki steak, poi and assorted vegetables and salads followed by chocolate cake, coconut cake, and *haupia* for dessert. The open bar includes piña coladas and strawberry daiquiris. The Hawaiian/Polynesian show begins at 7 p.m. and lasts approximately one hour. Seating is in two areas—front and rear sections. Prices for front section, adults $99.95, children 3-12 $59.95; rear section, adults $79.95, children $39.95. Marriott Lu'au is provided by Ka'anapali Production Co., Inc., and is not produced by Marriott's Maui Ocean Club.

COUNTING CALORIES

Lu'aus are definitely not low-calorie dining options. So eat and enjoy, but just in case you're interested: • *kalua* pig: 1/2 cup 150 calories; • *lomi lomi* salmon: 1/2 cup 87 calories; • poi: 1 cup 161 calories; • fried rice: 1 cup 200 calories; • fish (depending on type served): 150-250 calories; • chicken long rice: 283 calories; • *haupia*: 128 calories; • coconut cake: 200-350 calories; • mai tai: 302 calories; • piña colada: 252 calories; • fruit punch: 140 calories: • Blue Hawai'i: 260 calories; • *chi chi*: 190 calories.

★ *Old Lahaina Luau*

1251 Front Street, Lahaina; 808-667-1998; 800-248-5828.

Start your lu'au evening with reserved seating, which means no need to stand in line for an hour or more before they open! You can choose cushioned seating on the ground or table seating (I'd recommend the latter). You'll be greeted with a fresh flower lei and a tropical drink and then visit the bar or have your waiter supply you with refills. The stage is in the round with buffet dining. Before the meal you can enjoy walking along the oceanfront site and watching island crafters at work. The traditional *imu* ceremony takes place oceanside, then you're called by tables to the buffet line. With plenty of buffets, there are no long lines while you wait for your food. The food is very good, with traditional Hawaiian lu'au dishes such as *kalua* pork, *lau lau*, poi and *poke* (marinated raw fish), as well as chicken, fish, grilled top sirloin steak and lots of salads and taro rolls. An excellent selection of items. At the end of your meal, waiters bring an assortment of island desserts to each table. Table service for beverages continues throughout the show so you don't have to miss anything. This isn't the usual lu'au show. It actually has a story line, following the immigration of the Polynesians to Hawai'i from the days of the Kahiko (ancient hula) to the 'Auana (modern hula). The raised levels around the stage mean every seat has a good view, and the beautiful oceanfront setting adds to the authentic ambiance of this lu'au. Nightly 5:30-8:30 p.m. Adults $85, children age 12 and under $55. Advance reservations are a must for this one. Named Best Lu'au in the 2005 'Aipono Awards, and deservedly so.

Royal Lahaina Resort In Ka'anapali

2780 Keka'a Drive, Ka'anapali; 808-661-9119.

Get ready for mai tais, fruit punch, open bar, and shell leis as the first order of business, with the photo opportunities to follow (photos available for purchase when the lu'au ends). The lu'au grounds are near the ocean, but without an ocean view (unless you peek over the hedge). Seating is at padded picnic table benches. The *imu* ceremony was the shortest I've seen and some people hadn't even reached the pit before it was over! While people are settling in, the host/hostess welcomes guests. Dinner begins around 6:15 p.m., with four tables and eight lines allowing people to flow quickly through. Large wooden trays are offered in lieu of standard plates, so there is plenty of room to pile on the teri chicken, *kalua* pig and turkey, grilled steaks, mahimahi, Hawaiian sweet potatoes, corn on the cob, *lomi lomi* salmon, poi, fresh fruit, taro bread, and an interesting selections of salads. The desserts included *haupia*, chocolate cake and a coconut cream cake. They also feature a *keiki* buffet with chicken nuggets, hot dogs, potato chips, macaroni and cheese, and more. Following the meal, the Polynesian revue features songs and dance that retell the story of Hawai'i, Tahiti and Samoa. The fire-knife dance highlights the close of the show. Drawbacks at this lu'au included the gravel-covered dirt ground that made annoying crunching sounds as people got up throughout the show to pick up a drink at the bar, which remained open during the show. This is a good but not great lu'au. A nice touch is the original music and choreography along with some of the old familiar favorites. Five nights a week (closed Monday and Saturday) at 5:30 p.m. $77 adults, $38 children.

Tony 'N Tina's Wedding

Hyatt Regency Resort and Spa, Ka'anapali; 808-667-4727; www.tonyandtinamaui.com.

This off-Broadway hit takes place every Tuesday, Thursday and Saturday night, starting with the wedding ceremony at the Hyatt's Weeping Banyan lounge and continuing with the dinner reception at Spats Trattoria Italian restaurant. The wedding has been celebrated in more than 40 American cities, and the Hawaiian production has some aloha twists. Guests are warmly greeted at the ceremony by the bride and groom's families and members of the wedding party. The minister, the nun and the party planner are among the characters, and you'll be selected to be a member of the Vitale family (bride Valentina's relatives) or the Nunzio family (groom's). Following the ceremony you and the other guests are ushered to dinner. The buffet includes hors d'oeuvres, vegetarian pasta primavera, meat lasagna, Italian penne pasta with roast chicken, Caesar salad and great focaccia. The play continues in an interactive format with a member of the wedding party (a.k.a. cast) coming to chat at your table. Play along and introduce yourself as the long lost rich aunt as you converse with the pregnant bridesmaid. And enjoy the champagne toast to the happy couple and the wedding cake for dessert. There are different plot lines if you sit on the bride's or groom's side of the dinner theater. Bar service available. Play and dinner 6:30-8:30 p.m. Adults $76.50. This is an adult-oriented show. Call for weekly schedule, as it is subject to change.

★ Wailea Marriott

3700 Wailea Alanui, Wailea; 808-874-7831.

The Wailea Marriott refers to their lu'au as "Wailea's Finest Lu'au" and I'd have to agree. The fabulous outdoor setting in their lu'au garden is both beautiful and spacious with a sublime ocean view. The stage is set up to offer the ocean and sunset as backdrop. An open bar is available. Dinner moves swiftly through several buffet lines serving sauteed fish with lemon macadamia nut butter, teriyaki steak and *kalua* pig (which was a notch above what I've tasted at some other lu'aus). *Laulau*, Hawaiian sweet potatoes, chicken long rice, taro rolls, and a variety of salads are just a few of the other offerings. The dessert table has a huge selection of cream pies and cakes, tropical fruit cobbler, macadamia nut cake, and coconut macaroons. The show begins just as the sun is setting with the music of Ka Poe o Hawai'i and Paradyse. First is a *kahiko hula*, which is followed by a *paniolo* number, traditional love songs, Tahitian number and finally the fire-knife dancer, Ifi So'o, who proved to be the best out of all the lu'aus. He did stunts, somersaults across the stage, and even seemed to twirl much faster than the others. After almost a dozen lu'aus, it is pretty hard to be impressed, but this guy was impressive. (And, by the way, he has won the World Championship Fire-Knife Dancer competition an unprecedented three times and remains the first and only one in the world to do so!) The show features a good range and quality of entertainment with one of the best outdoor settings. For overall food, entertainment and setting, this is a great lu'au. And at $72.86 adults ($33.33 children 6-12), it is also one of the least expensive. 5-8 p.m. Monday, Thursday and Friday.

Wailea Sunset Luau

Renaissance Wailea Beach Resort, Wailea; 800-992-4532; 808-891-7811.

This lu'au is held on Tuesday, Thursday and Saturday in the Lu'au Gardens and the adjoining Makena Lawn, both of which offer an ocean view and lovely sunset. The lu'au showcases the unique traditions and stories of Maui's ancient past. It begins with the blowing of the conch and the lighting of the resort's 37 torches. After feasting on the Hawaiian buffet, complete with favorites such as *kalua* pork, grilled fish, *lomi lomi* salmon and *hulihuli* chicken, guests enjoy a Polynesian revue produced by Tihati Productions. The show includes dances that focus on the legends of old Hawai'i and popular favorites such as a unique version of the Hawaiian Wedding song. Rounding out the evening is a performance by master fire dancer, Kikipi. $65 adults, $30 children 5-12, free children under 5.

CHAPTER 5

Beaches

If you are looking for a variety of beautiful, uncrowded tropical beaches, nearly perfect weather year-round and sparkling clear waters at enjoyable temperatures, Maui will not disappoint you.

Maui's beaches are special for good reason. If you check out a map of the Hawaiian Islands you'll quickly notice that Maui is situated with its south shore flanked by Lana'i, Moloka'i and Kaho'olawe. Millions of years ago, during the Ice Age, the seas were much lower than they are now. The water between these islands was obviously much shallower than it is today. This area became almost an inland sea and today remains more protected than the shores of the other islands. Hence, its beaches are actually safer (with regard to rip currents and shorebreaks) than those on other islands.

The beaches range from small to long, and sand can be white, black, rock or more exotic shades like green or salt-and-pepper. Many are well developed; a few (at least for a little longer) remain remote and unspoiled. There is something for everyone, from the lie-on-the-beach-under-a-palm-tree type to the explorer-adventurer. The Maui Visitors Bureau reports that there are 81 accessible beaches, 30 with public facilities, around an island with 120 miles of coastline.

Maui's beaches are publicly owned and most have public access. However, the access is sometimes tricky to find and parking may be a problem. Parking areas are provided at most developed beaches, but are generally limited to 30 cars or less, making an early arrival at the more popular beaches a good idea. In the undeveloped areas you will have to wedge along the roadside.

You can check with the Office of Economic Development, County of Maui, 200 South High Street, Wailuku, HI 96793, to see if they have any current shoreline-access maps. They don't seem to have them in stock regularly, but if they do, the maps nicely outline the facilities and accesses for each beach.

Pick up a copy of a free snorkel guide from Maui Dive Shop in Lahaina or Kihei. Any of the dive shops can assist you in choosing a beach that is the best and safest for your snorkeling ability.

At the larger developed beaches, a variety of facilities are provided. Many have convenient rinse-off showers, drinking water, restrooms and picnic areas. A few have children's play or swim areas. The beaches near the major resorts often have rental equipment available for snorkeling, sailing and boogie boarding, and even have underwater cameras. These beaches are generally clean and well maintained. Above Kapalua and below Wailea, where the beaches are undeveloped, expect to find limited signage to mark the location, no facilities and sometimes less cleanliness.

Since virtually all of Maui's good beaches are located on the leeward side of East and West Maui, you can expect sunny weather most of the time. This is because the mountains trap the moisture in the almost-constant trade winds. Truly cloudy or bad weather in these areas is rare but when the weather is poor in one area, a short drive may put you back into the sun again. Swells from all directions reach Maui's shores. The three basic swell sources are the east and northeast trade winds, the North Pacific lows and the South Pacific lows. The trades cause easterly swells of relatively low heights (2 to 6 feet) throughout most of the year. A stormy, persistent trade wind episode may cause swells of 8 to 12 feet and occasionally 10 to 15 feet on exposed eastern shores. Since the main resort areas are on leeward West and East Maui, they are protected.

North Maui and Hana are exposed to these conditions, however, along with strong ocean currents. Therefore very few beaches in these areas are considered safe for casual swimming.

Winter North Pacific storms generate high surf along the northwestern and northern shores of Maui. This is the source of the winter surf in Mokule'ia Bay

THEFT DOES HAPPEN

It is vital that you leave nothing of importance in your car because theft, especially at some of the more remote locations on Maui, is high. And be careful of watchful eyes if you stow your valuables in your trunk. There are some unscrupulous folks who may be looking for visitors to do just that. Car rental companies often advise customers to leave nothing in the car and keep the vehicle unlocked to minimize damage in a break-in.

(Slaughterhouse), renowned for body surfing, and in Honolua Bay, which is internationally known for surfing.

Land and sea breezes are local winds blowing from opposite directions at different times, depending on the temperature difference between land and sea. The interaction of daytime sea breezes and trade winds, in the Wailea–Makena area particularly, produces almost-daily light cloudiness in the afternoon and may bring showers. This is also somewhat true of the Honokowai-to-Kapalua region.

Oceanic tidal and trade wind currents are not a problem for the swimmer or snorkeler in the main resort areas from Makena to Kapalua except under unusual conditions such as Kona storms. Beaches outside of the resort areas should be treated with due caution since there are very few considered safe for casual swimming and snorkeling except by knowledgeable, experienced persons.

Maui's ocean playgrounds are probably the most benign in the world. There is no fire coral, jellyfish are rare and sharks are well fed by the abundant marine life so encounters are rare. However, you should always exercise good judgment and reasonable caution when at the beach.

Especially with little ones, be sure to pack plenty of water on your trip to the beach. With all the sun and surf it is easy to get dehydrated. Same for you parents, too. And don't forget the sunscreen. Maui's tropical sun can burn you fast, even on a cloudy day.

Beach Precautions

WATER SAFETY

Maui's beaches are far safer than those on, say, Kaua'i. The islands of Lana'i, Moloka'i and Kaho'olawe form an inland sea that makes for calmer shores. The southern shore of Maui has an extensive reef system that affords additional protection.

Most of the north shore beaches of Maui do not have the coral reefs or other barriers that are found on the south and west shores. I cannot recommend any water activities at north shore beaches. These wide expansive beaches pose greater risks for swimmers, with their strong currents and dangerous shorebreaks. You may see surfers at some of the beaches where we recommend that you enjoy the view and stay out of the water. Keep in mind that just because there is someone else in the water, it doesn't mean it's safe. Do not take undue risks. Others might be visitors just like you, but not as well informed. Common sense needs to be employed at all beaches.

We don't want to be alarmists, but we'd prefer to report the beaches conservatively. Always, always use good judgment. Here are some basic water safety tips and terms.

A **shorebreak** is when the waves break directly on the beach. Small shorebreaks may not be a problem, but waves that are more than a foot or two high may create undertows and hazardous conditions. Conditions are generally worse in the winter months. Even venturing too close to a shorebreak could be hazardous, as standing on the beachfront you may encounter a stronger, higher wave that could catch you off guard and sweep you into the water.

A **rip current** can often be seen from the shore. They are fast-moving river-like currents that sometimes can be seen carrying sand or sediment. A rip current can pull an unsuspecting swimmer quickly out to sea, and swimming against a strong rip current may be impossible. They are common in reef areas that have open channels to the sea.

LIFEGUARDS ON DUTY

For families concerned about water safety, the following beaches feature lifeguard stations, although they are not always attended: Hanaka'o'o Beach in Ka'anapali; Kanaha Beach in Kahului; D. T. Fleming Beach in Kapalua; H.A. Baldwin Park in Paia and Kama'ole Beaches I, II and III in Kihei. The Ocean Safety phone line is 808-270-6136.

Undertows happen when a rip current runs into incoming surf. This accounts for the feeling that you are being pulled down. They are more common on beaches that have steep slopes.

Kona winds generated by southern-hemisphere storms cause southerly swells that affect leeward Maui. This usually happens in the summer and lasts several days. Surf heights over 8 feet are not common, but many of the resort areas have beaches with fairly steep drop-offs that cause rather sharp shore breaks. Although it may appear fun to play in these waves, many minor to moderate injuries are recorded at these times. Resorts will post red warning flags along the beach during times of unsafe surf conditions. Most beaches are affected during this time with water turbidity and poor snorkeling conditions. At a few places, such as Lahaina, Olowalu and Ma'alaea, these conditions create good surfing.

Northerly swells caused by winter storms northeast of the island are not common but can cause large surf, particularly on the northern beaches, such as Baldwin, Kanaha and Ho'okipa beach parks.

All beaches located along the north shore road to Hana are dangerous so please stay onshore. The beaches beyond Kapalua (D. T. Fleming, Mokule'ia, Honolua) can be dangerous at anytime, so leave them to the experienced surfers when high winter surf arrives. These beaches share such cautionary features as a lack of a protective reef,

A good place and a "secret find" for small children is the park at the end of Hauoli Street in Ma'alaea, just past the Makani A Kai condos. There are two small, sandy-bottomed pools protected by reefs on either side of the small rock jetty.

Another great place for very young kids to learn to snorkel is at "Baby Beach," or Pu'unoa, located north of Lahaina. There is limited parking and no facilities but the offshore reef affords a chance to enjoy the water without currents or surf conditions. Wearing water shoes here is a great idea as there is coral rubble in the water and on the shore.

Quiet waters for young beginning snorkelers are available in front of the Lahaina Shores Resort as well.

a large channel in a reef where a strong current forms during high surf, and a river emptying into the sea. Most of them are also fairly remote and response times are prolonged.

Please, treat Maui's wild beaches with respect. Since many have no restroom facilities, try to use the bathroom before you head to the beach. If you must relieve yourself, go well away from the waterline and bury your deposit and any tissue you used. Also, remove your trash and bring out a little bit that someone else left, too.

TIPS

Here are some additional beach safety and etiquette tips:

- "Never turn your back to the sea" is an old Hawaiian saying. Don't be caught off-guard; waves come in sets, with spells of calm in between.
- Use the buddy system, never swim or snorkel alone.
- If you are unsure of your abilities, use flotation devices attached to your body, such as a life vest or inflatable vest. Never rely on an air mattress or similar device from which you may become separated.
- Study the ocean before you enter; look for rocks, shorebreak and rip currents.
- Duck or dive beneath breaking waves before they reach you.
- Never swim against a strong current, swim across it.
- Know your limits.
- Small children should be allowed to play near or in the surf *only* with close supervision and should wear flotation devices. And even then, only under extremely calm conditions. Pu'unoa in Lahaina is a quiet saltwater area ideal for kids, especially beginner snorkelers.

OCEAN MENACES

Maui's ocean playgrounds are among the most benign in the world. There are, however, a few ocean creatures that you should be aware of. I have provided some basic first-aid tips should you need them. However, to prevent a possible allergic reaction or infection, I suggest you contact a local physician or medical center if you have a close encounter with one of these creatures.

Portuguese Man-of-War is a sea animal seen only rarely, but caution is in order. It's one of those ocean critters to be avoided. These very small creatures are related to the jellyfish and are adrift in the ocean via the currents and the wind. The unique animals are sometimes blown on shore by unusual winds and can cover the beach with their glistening crystal orbs filled with deep blue filament. If they are on the beach, treat them as if they were still in the water—stay away. On rare occasions they will be seen drifting in the ocean during a snorkeling cruise or sea excursion and the cruise boat staff may change snorkeling destinations if this is the case. The animal has long filaments that can cause painful stings. If you are stung, rinse the affected area with seawater or fresh water to remove any tentacles. If you need to pick out the tentacles, do not use your bare fingers; use gloves, a towel or whatever is available to protect yourself. Vinegar, isopropyl alcohol and human urine, once considered effective remedies, are no longer recommended treatments.

In the water, avoid touching **sea urchins**: the pricking by one of the spines can be painful. And if you do encounter one, be sure the entire spine has been removed. Soaking the wound in vinegar helps to dissolve the spine; for pain, soak the puncture in hot water for 30 to 90 minutes.

Coral is made up of many tiny living organisms. Coral cuts require thorough disinfecting and can take a long time to heal. If an inflamed wound's redness begins to spread, it suggests an infection and requires medical attention. So stay off the coral—and don't touch it!

Cone shells look harmless enough, are conical and come in colors of brown or black. The snails that inhabit these shells have

- When exploring tidepools or reefs, always wear protective footwear and keep an eye on the ocean. Also, protect your hands.
- When swimming around coral, be careful where you put your hands and feet. Urchin stings can be painful and coral cuts can be dangerous. You can also damage or injure the coral. Yes! Coral is living and it grows very slowly so don't knock into it or stand on it while snorkeling.

a defense mechanism that they use to protect themselves—and to kill their prey. Their stinger does have venom so it is suggested that you just enjoy looking at them. Cleaning the wound and soaking it in hot water for 30 to 90 minutes will provide relief if you're stung.

Eels live among the coral and are generally not aggressive. You may have heard of divers who have "trained" an eel to come out, greet them and then take some food from their hands. We don't recommend you try to make an eel your pal. While usually non-aggressive, their jaws are extremely powerful and their teeth are sharp. And as divers know, sea animals could mistake any approach or movement as an aggressive or provoking act. Just keep a comfortable distance—for you and the eel. Also, should you poke around with your hands in the coral, they might inadvertently think your finger is food. This is another reason you shouldn't handle the coral. Eels are generally not out of their homes during the day, but a close examination of the coral might reveal a head of one of these fellows sticking out and watching you! At night during low tide at beaches with a protective reef, you might try taking a flashlight and scanning the water. A chance look at one of these enormous creatures out searching for its dinner is most impressive.

Sharks? Yes, there are many varied types of sharks in Hawai'i's waters. However, there are more shark attacks off the Oregon coastline than in Hawai'i. In the many years of snorkeling and diving, we have only seen one small reef shark, and it was happy to get out of our way. If you should see one, don't move quickly, but rather swim slowly away while you keep an eye on it. Avoid swimming in murky waters near river mouths after it rains. Also, stay out of the water if you have open cuts and remember, urine might attract sharks, so don't urinate in the water. Some Maui beaches are year-round shark breeding grounds; please heed the posted signs and stay out of the water.

- Respect the yellow and red flag warnings when placed on the developed beaches. They are there to advise you of unsafe conditions.
- After heavy rains, stay out of the ocean until the water clears.
- Avoid swimming in the mouths of rivers or streams or in any areas of murky water.
- Always use fins when boogie boarding.

- Don't feed the fish.
- Keep your distance from pole and net fishermen.
- Remember, it's illegal to approach or do *anything* that causes a dolphin, monk seal, turtle or whale to change its behavior, so stay away from them.

Surface **water temperature** varies little with a mean temperature of 73 degrees Fahrenheit in January and 80.2 degrees in August. Minimum and maximum range from 68 to 84 degrees. This is an almost ideal temperature (refreshing, but not cold) for swimming and you'll find most resort pools cooler than the ocean. Of course, if it's windy, it may feel chilly when you get out of the water.

Note: Ulysses Press, Paradise Publications and the authors of this guide have endeavored to provide current and accurate information on Maui's beautiful beaches. However, remember that nature is unpredictable and weather, beach and current conditions can change. Enjoy your day at the beach, but utilize good judgment. Ulysses Press, Paradise Publications and the authors of this guide cannot be held responsible for accidents or injuries incurred.

Best Bets

Lahaina: Olowalu has easy access and excellent snorkeling. Hanaka'o'o Beach, next to the Hyatt, has a gentle offshore slope and a park with lots of parking, good facilities and numerous activities.

Honokowai–Kapalua Area: Kapalua offers a well-protected bay with very good swimming and snorkeling.

Ma'alaea–Kihei Area: Keawakapu and Kama'ole II have gentler offshore slopes and excellent swimming.

Wailea–Makena Area: On South Maui, our favorite beaches are Makena for its unspoiled beauty, Malu'aka for its deep fine sand and beautiful coral, Wailea and Ulua–Mokapu for their great beaches, good snorkeling and beautiful resorts.

Using This Chapter

The following listings refer to a variety of beaches and beach parks. However, you'll find that some are not true beaches. For example, Spouting Horn is a beautiful beach location, but only for viewing and not good for aquatic activities.

The child icon indicates beaches that are recommended for family activities. They are more protected and most likely have lifeguards on duty.

Lahaina

These beaches are described in order from Ma'alaea through Lahaina and are easy to spot from Honoapi'ilani Highway. They are all narrow and usually lined with *kiawe* trees. However, they have gentle slopes to deeper water and the ocean is generally calmer and warmer than in other areas. The offshore coral reefs offer excellent snorkeling in calm weather, which is most of the time. These beaches are popular because of their convenient access and facilities as well as good swimming and snorkeling conditions.

Papalaua State Wayside Park

As you descend from the sea cliffs on your way from Ma'alaea you will see an undeveloped tropical shoreline stretch before you. At the foot of the cliffs, between mile-markers 10 and 11, Papalaua State Wayside Park is marked by an easily seen sign. There are portable restrooms. The beach is long (about .5 mile), narrow and lined with *kiawe* trees that almost reach the water's edge in places. The trees

If you are on a Maui beach and happen across what appears to be a large, fat furry lump on the sand, consider yourself fortunate, for you have just seen a rare Hawaiian monk seal. An adult Hawaiian monk seal measures about seven feet in length and weighs 400 to 600 pounds. These adorable-looking seals (they appear to be smiling) occasionally come on shore to rest, sun and sleep—and they may look like they're dead. Well-meaning spectators have been known to poke them or throw stones, to see if they are alive. Do not approach or harass the seal in any way. Hawaiian monk seals are endemic (meaning they are found nowhere else and are believed to have evolved here) to Hawai'i. They are an endangered species and are protected by Federal law. It is illegal to approach them, disrupt their behavior or harass them. Monk seals may approach swimmers or divers while in the water, but at no time should you approach them—this may be considered a form of harassment. When it is necessary to pass near a monk seal that has hauled itself onto the beach in front of you, remain at least 100 feet away. If it is a female monk seal with a pup, be even more cautious and never come between them. Report sightings of sick or injured seals or any cases of harassment to the National Marine Fisheries Service in Honolulu, 808-955-8831. Please respect these precious creatures. We thank you and the seals thank you.

provide plenty of shady areas for this beautiful beach. Good swimming and fair snorkeling; popular picnicking area. Also popular for surfing and bodyboarding.

Ukumehame Beach Park

The entrance to the park is between mile-markers 11 and 12, but there is no identifying sign. There is plenty of paved and roadside parking. Twelve concrete picnic tables. Barbecue facilities. Two portable restrooms. This is also a narrow .5-mile-long sand beach with lots of *kiawe* trees providing shade. Good swimming, surfing, fishing, fair snorkeling.

★ Olowalu Beach

About two-tenth's of a mile before and after mile-marker 14 you will see a large but narrow stand of *kiawe* trees between the road and the beach, followed by a few palm trees, then a few more scattered *kiawe* trees. Parking is alongside the road. No facilities. This narrow sand beach slopes gently out to water four or five feet deep, making it good for swimming and beach playing. There are extensive coral formations starting right offshore and continuing out a quarter mile or more, and a fair amount of fish expecting handouts. The ocean is generally warmer and calmer than elsewhere, making it a popular snorkeling spot. In 2002 they posted shark-warning signs for this beach, but it does not seem to be deterring snorkelers. At this or any beach there may, of course, be sharks.

Awalua Beach

The beach at mile-marker 16 may be cobblestone or sand depending on the time of year and the prevailing conditions. No facilities. At times when Kona storms create a good southern swell, this becomes a very popular surfing spot for locals until the swells subside.

Launiupoko State Wayside Park

This well-marked beach park near mile-marker 18 (at the traffic signal) offers a large paved parking area, restrooms, many picnic tables, barbecue grills, rinse-off showers, drinking water, a pay phone and a large grassy area with trees, all of which make for a good picnic spot. There is a large man-made wading pool constructed of large boulders centered in the park; this is child-friendly. (Sand has accumulated to the extent that even at high tide there is no water in the pool.) To the right is a rocky beach and to the left is a 200-yard dark-sand beach with a fairly gentle slope. It looks nice, but posted signs warn "Sharks have been seen in the

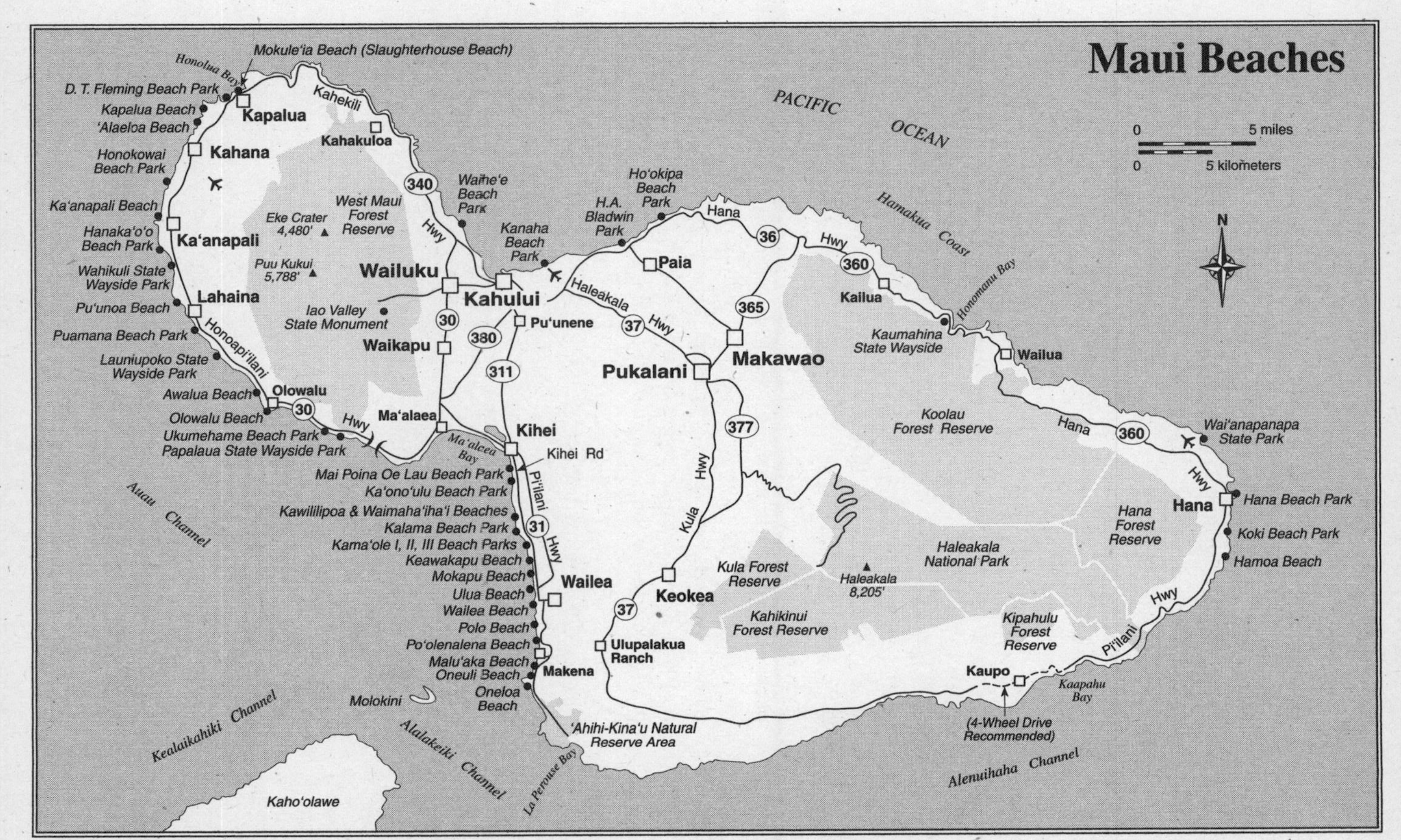
Maui Beaches
PACIFIC OCEAN
0 5 miles
0 5 kilometers
N
Mokule'ia Beach (Slaughterhouse Beach)
Honolua Bay
D. T. Fleming Beach Park
Kapalua Beach
'Alaeloa Beach
Honokowai Beach Park
Ka'anapali Beach
Hanaka'o'o Beach Park
Wahikuli State Wayside Park
Pu'unoa Beach
Puamana Beach Park
Launiupoko State Wayside Park
Awalua Beach
Olowalu Beach
Ukumehame Beach Park
Papalaua State Wayside Park
Kapalua
Kahekili
Kahakuloa
Kahana
Ka'anapali
Lahaina
Honoapi'ilani
Olowalu
Hwy
Eke Crater 4,480'
Puu Kukui 5,788'
West Maui Forest Reserve
Iao Valley State Monument
Wailuku
Waikapu
Ma'alaea
Ma'alaea Bay
Waihe'e Beach Park
Kanaha Beach Park
Kahului
Pu'unene
Kihei
Kihei Rd
Pi'ilani
H.A. Bladwin Park
Ho'okipa Beach Park
Paia
Hana
Haleakala
Pukalani
Makawao
Kula
Keokea
Ulupalakua Ranch
Mai Poina Oe Lau Beach Park
Ka'ono'ulu Beach Park
Kawililipoa & Waimaha'iha'i Beaches
Kalama Beach Park
Kama'ole I, II, III Beach Parks
Keawakapu Beach
Mokapu Beach
Ulua Beach
Wailea Beach
Polo Beach
Po'olenalena Beach
Malu'aka Beach
Oneuli Beach
Oneloa Beach
Wailea
Makena
Molokini
'Ahihi-Kina'u Natural Reserve Area
La Perouse Bay
Auau Channel
Kealaikahiki Channel
Alalakeiki Channel
Kaho'olawe
Hamakua Coast
Honomanu Bay
Kailua
Kaumahina State Wayside
Wailua
Koolau Forest Reserve
Kula Forest Reserve
Kahikinui Forest Reserve
Haleakala 8,205'
Haleakala National Park
Kipahulu Forest Reserve
Hana Forest Reserve
Wai'anapanapa State Park
Hana Beach Park
Koki Beach Park
Hamoa Beach
Kaupo
Kaapahu Bay
(4-Wheel Drive Recommended)
Alenuihaha Channel
340
30
380
311
37
36
365
377
360
31

shallow water off this beach. Entry into the water is discouraged." This area is rumored to be a shark breeding ground with shark fishing done here in the past. There is also a "No alcohol" sign posted. No camping. This beach does not seem to be used for much besides picnicking and some surfing and bodyboarding. However, a couple hundred yards offshore is good snorkeling and you may see snorkel excursions visit this shoreline when the weather prohibits a trip to Molokini or Lana'i.

Puamana Beach Park

This beach park is near mile-marker 19, just south of the Puamana Resort complex. Parking for 20 cars in paved parking area, with additional parking along the highway. Nice grassy park with ten picnic tables and plenty of shade trees. Barbecue facilities; two portable restrooms. At the park itself there is no sandy beach, only a large pebble beach. The only beach is a narrow 200-yard-long white-sand beach just north of the park and fronting Puamana Resort. Fairly gentle slope to shallow water.

Lahaina Beach

This narrow sand beach fronts the Lahaina Shores and 505 Front Street and is protected by a reef 30 to 50 yards out. The beach is generally sandy offshore with a gentle slope. The water stays fairly shallow out to the reef and contains some interesting coral formations. The area offers fair snorkeling in clear water on calm days. A good place for beginning surfers, snorkelers and children, but not good for swimming due to shallow water and abundant coral. There is a large paid public parking lot across from the 505 Front Street shopping center with easy access to the beach through the mall. Parking is also available at Kamehameha Iki Park nearby, as well as on-street near the Lahaina Shores with public right-of-way to the beach by the south end of the complex. Public restrooms and showers at 505.

Pu'unoa Beach

The beach, at the north end of Lahaina between Kai Pali Road and the old Mala Wharf, can be seen as you leave Lahaina on Front Street. This narrow, dense, dark-sand beach is about 300 yards long and well protected by a reef approximately 100 to 150 yards offshore. The beach slopes gently to water only 3 to 4 feet deep. Unfortunately, rock and coral near the surface make swimming unadvised. There are areas of the beach clear of coral 10 to 15 feet out where children can play safely in the calm, shallow water. At high tide there are more fish to see while snorkeling. Southern access: Take Kai Pali Road off Front Street. Parking for about 20 cars along the road, which is the entrance for the Pu'unoa Beach Estates. Public Beach access sign with concrete sidewalk to the beach. Mid-beach access: Take Pu'unoa Place off Front Street at the Public Beach access sign. Parking for about four cars at the end of the road that ends at the beach. A rinse-off hose here is the only facility for the beach. North access: Take Mala Wharf off Front Street. Parking for approximately 20 cars along the road just before the entrance to the Mala boat-launching parking area. Sadly, this has become an unsafe beach due to a recent trend in car break-ins and thefts of personal items. Even the locals here keep one eye on their things. So be cautious.

Wahikuli State Wayside Park
There are three paved off-street parking areas between Lahaina and Ka'anapali. Many covered picnic tables, restrooms, showers and barbecue grills are provided. The first and third parking areas are marked but have no beach. The second unmarked area has an excellent dark-sand beach with a gentle slope to deeper water. There is some shelf rock in places but it's rounded and smooth and not a problem. With handy facilities, trees for shade and the nice beach, this is a good (and popular) spot for sunning, swimming and picnicking.

★ ***Hanaka'o'o Beach Park (Canoe Beach)*** South of the Hyatt Regency, there is a large, well-marked, off-street parking area. The park has rinse-off showers, restrooms and picnic tables. Wide, dark-sand beach with gentle slope to deeper water, although the shore break can be dangerous. This is a popular area because of the easy parking, facilities, good beach, shallow water and good swimming, and proximity to the Hyatt Regency. There is a lifeguard tower here, but it is not always attended.

Ka'anapali

★ ***Ka'anapali Beach***
This beach fronts the Hyatt Regency, Maui Marriott, Ka'anapali Alii, Westin Maui, Whalers Village shopping center, The Whaler, Ka'anapali Beach Hotel and Sheraton Maui. Access is through the Ka'anapali Resort area. Turn off Honoapi'ilani Highway at either of the first two entrances. Parking is definitely a problem.

- The Hyatt end of the beach is only a short walk from the large parking area of Hanaka'o'o Beach Park.
- Public right-of-way with parking for 10 cars at the left of the Hyatt's lower parking lot.
- Public right-of-way between the Hyatt and Marriott, no parking.
- Public right-of-way between Marriott and Ka'anapali Alii with parking for 11 cars only.
- Public right-of-way between Ka'anapali Alii and Westin, no parking.
- Public right-of-way between Ka'anapali Beach Hotel and the Sheraton with parking for 11 cars only.
- Whalers Village shopping center has a three-story pay parking lot, but with beach access only through the shopping complex.
- There is no on-street parking anywhere in the Ka'anapali Resort complex.

The Hyatt Regency, Maui Marriott, Westin Maui and Sheraton Maui all have restrooms, beach showers, bars and beach rental equipment.

Ka'anapali is a beautiful, long, white-sand beach with an abrupt drop-off to deep water. There are small areas of offshore coral from the Hyatt to the Westin Maui at times, but no true offshore reef. Great swimming and good wave-playing with the exception of two or three points along the beach where the waves consistently break fairly hard. In the winter, snorkeling can be fair off the Westin when the coral is exposed underwater. The best snorkeling is at Black Rock, fronting the Sheraton. The water is almost always clear and fairly calm, with many types of nearly tame fish due to the popularity of hand-feeding by snorkelers. (Bread, frozen peas and packaged dry noodles seem popular.) Not much colorful coral. The best entrance to the water is from the beach alongside Black Rock.

★ *Alii Kahekili Nui 'Ahumahi Beach Park*

This beach, known as "Airport Beach" by local residents because it was formerly the site of the Ka'anapali Airport, begins at the north side of Black Rock and runs for over a mile to the north, fronting the Royal Lahaina Resort and the Maui Ka'anapali Villas. A lovely beach park has been developed here. Turn off Honoapi'ilani Road at the last Ka'anapali exit, a stoplight fronting the Maui Ka'anapali Villas and the new Westin timeshare development. The beach park is open 6 a.m. to 6:30 p.m. with plenty of paved parking spaces. There is a gate that is locked nightly 30 minutes after sunset. (For security, call 808-661-8986.) There are pavilions with dining tables and a very pleasant grassy lawn area dotted with barbecues and more tables. A rinse-off shower is available. This wide, (usually) white-sand beach has a steep drop-off to deep water and is usually calm—a good place to swim. Snorkeling around Black Rock is almost always good. Kahekili was the last ruler of Maui, and this park pays tribute to him. The park's name, which is quite a mouthful, translates to "Feather Cloaked Nightly Thunderer." Kahekili ruled 1766–1793.

Honokowai-Kapalua Area

Ka'anapali Beach (North End)

This section of beach fronts the Mahana Resort, Maui Kai, Embassy Vacation Resort, Ka'anapali Shores, Papakea, Maui Sands and Paki Maui from south to north, and ends at the Honokowai Beach Park. Access is generally only through the resorts. Most of the resorts have rinse-off showers convenient to the beach; however, no other facilities are available. This is a long, narrow, white-sand beach that is fronted by a reef. All the resorts except the Ka'anapali Shores and Embassy Vacation Resort have retaining walls along the beach. The Ka'anapali Shores has, over the last few years, suffered considerable erosion of its once-wide beach and has built an expensive under-the-sand retaining wall in an effort to stabilize and restore it. There is also a cleared area through the coral in front of the resort. This is the only good swimming area on the north section of the beach and is the only good access through the reef for snorkeling. The reef comes into shore at the south end of Papakea and again at the Honokowai Beach Park. At low tide the reef fronting Papakea can be walked on like a wide sidewalk. (See "Traveling with Children" in Chapter 1 for night walking on the reef.) The reef is generally only 10 to 20 yards offshore and the area between is very shallow, with much coral and rock making it undesirable for swimming and snorkeling.

Honokowai Beach Park

Turn off the Honoapi'ilani Highway (at the Honokowai sign) and get onto Lower Honoapi'ilani Road, which parallels the ocean. The park is across the street from the Lahuiokalanai Chapel. There is paved off-street parking for 30 cars. There are 11 picnic tables, five barbecue pits, restrooms, showers and a grassy park with shade trees. The white-sand beach is lined by a wide shelf of beach rock. Between the shelf rock and reef there is a narrow, shallow pool with a sandy bottom that is a good swimming area for small children. There is a break in the reef at the north end of the beach where you can get snorkeling access to the outside reef.

Kahana Beach

Kahana Beach is in front of the Kahana Beach Resort, Sands of Kahana, Royal Kahana, Valley Isle Resort and Hololani from south to north on Lower Honoapi'ilani Road. There is limited off-road parking at the south end of the beach. Another access is through the condos. The only facilities available are at the condos, usually rinse-off showers. Kahana Manor Grocery is across the street from Valley Isle Resort and a Whalers General Store is at the nearby Kahana Gateway shopping center. This white-sand beach varies from narrow to wide and its offshore area is shallow with rock and sand, semi-protected by reef. Good swimming, fair snorkeling. The beach may be cool and windy in the afternoons. Since 1989, this area has been particularly plagued by an unexplained green algae bloom that tends to concentrate here due to the wind, current and shoreline conditions. The beach is frequently unappealing for swimming and beach use due to the amount of slimy green algae on the beach and in the water.

★ *Keonenui Beach*

The beach is in front of and surrounded by the Kahana Sunset with no convenient public access. A lovely wide crescent of white sand slopes gently to the water's edge, then more steeply to deeper water. The beach is set in a small shallow cove about 150 yards wide, which affords some protection. At times, especially in winter, rough seas come into the beach. When calm (most of the time), this is an excellent swimming and play area with fair snorkeling.

'Alaeloa Beach ("The Cove")

This miniature jewel-like cove is surrounded by low sea cliffs. The small (approximately 25 to 30 yards long) white-sand beach has a gentle slope with scattered rocks leading into sparkling clear waters. Pavilion and lounge chair area for use by 'Alaeloa guests. Good swimming and snorkeling with very clear and calm waters except when storm-generated waves come in. Fortunately, or unfortunately, depending on your point of view, this small cove is surrounded by the 'Alaeloa residential area, which has no on- or off-street public parking. Thus, public access to this beach is very difficult.

★ *Napili Bay*

There are two public accesses to this beautiful beach. There is a small, easily missed public right-of-way and Napili Beach sign just past the Napili Shores at Napili Place Street. On-street parking at sign for Napili Surf Beach Resort. The public beach right-of-way sign shows the entrance to the beach. Public phone in parking lot of Napili Surf. The second entrance is at the public beach right-of-way sign on Hui Road. On-street parking and pay phone at entrance to beach walk. Napili Bay is a long, wide crescent of white sand between two rocky points. The offshore slope is moderately steep. Usually very safe for swimming and snorkeling except during winter storms when large waves occasionally come into the bay. At the south end of the beach are a series of shallow, sandy tidepools that are excellent for children, but only under close supervision. Coral formations 30 to 40 yards offshore can provide good snorkeling on calm days, especially at the northern end of the beach, and decent boogie boarding with mild swells. No lifeguard and no public facilities along the beach. A small grocery store is past the second entrance at the Napili Village Hotel.

★ *Kapalua Beach*

Just past the Napili Kai Beach Resort you will see a public beach right-of-way sign. Off-street parking area for about 30 to 40 cars. Showers and restrooms. A beautiful cove of white sand between two rocky points. The beach has a gentle slope to deeper water. From the left point, a reef arcs toward the long right point, creating a very sheltered bay, probably the nicest and safest swimming beach on Maui. Shade is provided by numerous palm trees lining the back shore area. Above the beach are the lovely grounds of the Kapalua Bay Hotel and the Coconut Grove residential condos. Swimming is almost always excellent with plenty of play area for children. Snorkeling is usually good with many different kinds of fish and interesting coral. It is no surprise that this beach has been selected as one of America's top ten beaches. Remember: Parking is limited, so arrive early.

★ *Namalu Bay*

Park at Kapalua Beach and take the concrete path along the beach, up through the Kapalua Bay Hotel's grassy grounds and out to the point of land separating Kapalua Bay from Namalu Bay. This small bay has a shoreline of large lava boulders, no beaches. On calm days snorkeling is very good and entry and exit over the rocks is easy. This little-known spot is definitely worth the short walk down the trail.

Oneloa Beach

Enter at the public right-of-way sign just past the Kapalua Bay Resort. Paved off-street parking for 12 to 15 cars only, no other facilities. Long, straight, white-sand beach with a shallow sand bar that extends to the surf line. The beach is posted with a sign warning "No swimming at time of high surf due to dangerous currents." This area tends to get windy and cloudy in the afternoons, especially in the winter months. I have usually found this beach deserted.

D. T. Fleming Beach Park

The County maintains a lifeguard on this beach. The Ritz-Carlton operates The Beach House restaurant. Off-street parking for 70 cars. Public showers. Private restrooms by The Beach House. The long white-sand beach is steep with an offshore sand bar that may cause dangerous water conditions when swells hit the beach. This beach was named for David Thomas Fleming (1881–1955), who became manager of the Honolua Ranch in 1912. Under his guidance, the Baldwin cattle ranch was converted into a pineapple plantation. This was once called "Stables Beach" because the Fleming family kept their horses at this site into the 1950s.

Mokule'ia Beach (Slaughterhouse Beach)

On Highway 30, past D. T. Fleming Beach Park, look for cars parked along the roadside and the Mokule'ia–Honolua Marine Reserve sign. Park your car and walk down the long, steep stairway. There are no facilities. The wide white-sand beach has a gentle slope to deep water and is bordered by two rocky points. The left middle part of the beach is usually clear of coral and rocks even in winter, when the beach is subject to erosion. During the winter this is a body-surfing spot, especially when the surf is heavy; however, very dangerous water conditions also exist here. In winter, this area is only for the strongest, most experienced swimmers. The summer is generally much better for swimming and snorkeling at this very popular beach. Snorkeling is fair to good, especially around the left rocky point where there is a reef. Okay in winter when the ocean is calm and visibility good.

Note: The beach is known as Slaughterhouse because of the once-existing slaughterhouse on the cliffs above the beach, not because of what the ocean can do to body surfers in the winter when the big ones are coming in. Remember: This is part of the Mokule'ia–Honolua Bay Marine Life Conservation District—look, but don't disturb or take anything from the bay or beach.

★ Honolua Bay

The next bay past Mokule'ia is Honolua Bay. Watch for a dirt side road on the left. Park here and walk in along the road. There is no beach, just cobblestone with irregular patches of sand and an old concrete boat ramp in the middle. Excellent snorkeling in summer, spring and fall, especially in the morning, but in winter only on the calmest days. In summer, on calm days the bay resembles a large glassy pond and in my opinion, this is the best snorkeling on Maui.

Note: After a heavy rainfall, the water may be turbid for several days before it returns to its sparkling clear condition again. You can enter at the boat ramp or over the rocks and follow the reefs either left or right. Remember, this is a Marine Life Conservation area, so look but don't disturb. There is an interesting phenomenon affecting the bay. As freshwater runoff percolates into the bay, a shimmering boundary layer (usually about three feet below the surface) is created between the fresh and salt waters. Depending on the amount of runoff it may be very apparent or not. It is less prevalent on the right side of the bay. Honolua Bay is also an internationally known winter surfing spot. Storm-generated waves come thundering in around the right point, creating perfect waves and tubes. A good vantage point to watch the action is the cliffs at the right point of the bay, accessible by car via a short dirt road off the main highway.

Ma'alaea-Kihei Area

The Kihei beaches aren't quite as beautiful as Wailea's. They don't have the nicely landscaped parking areas or the large, beautiful resort complexes (this is condo country). They do, however, offer better facilities such as barbecues, picnic tables, drinking water and grassy play areas. The Kama'ole I, II and III beaches even have lifeguards. The beaches are listed in order from Ma'alaea Bay to Wailea.

Ma'alaea Bay Beach

This gently curving white-sand beach stretches three miles from the Ma'alaea boat harbor to Kihei. For the most part, the beach is backed by low sand dunes and large, generally wet, sand flats. Public access is from many areas along South Kihei Road. There are no facilities. Casual beach activities are best early in the morning before the strong, prevailing, mid-morning winds begin to sweep across the isthmus. Due to the length of the beach and the hard-packed sand near the water, this has become a popular place to jog. Windsurfing is popular in the afternoons.

The beach begins in front of the last three condominiums in Ma'alaea, the Kana'i A Nalu, Hono Kai and the Makani A Kai. Just past the Makani A Kai on Hauoli Street is a public park and beach access. There is a good section of beach here with a fairly gentle drop-off. Also there are two small, sandy-bottomed pools, protected by the reef on either side of the small man-made rock jetty. These are good play areas for kids. The waves remain fairly calm, except at high tide or high surf conditions. The best snorkeling is out from the beach here, but the conditions are extremely variable, from fairly clear to pretty murky, depending on the time of year and prevailing conditions. Snorkeling is usually better in the winter months. The beach from this point to North Kihei is generally fronted by shelf rock or reef and is not good for swimming but excellent for a lengthy beach walk! The beach becomes excellent for swimming and other beach activities in front of the North Kihei condos. Snorkeling is fair. A beach activity center is located on the beach at the Kealia Beach Center.

Mai Poina Oe Lau Beach Park

On South Kihei Road, fronting Maui Lu Resort. Paved parking for eight cars at the Pavilion (numerous other areas to park are along the road). Five picnic tables, restrooms, showers, barbecue facilities. This is actually part of the previous beach. Shore bottom is generally sandy with patches of rock, fronted by shallow reef. Swimming and snorkeling are best in the morning before the early afternoon winds come up. Popular windsurfing area in the afternoon.

Ka'ono'ulu Beach Park

Located across the street from the Kihei Bay Surf. Off-road parking for 20 cars, restrooms, drinking water, rinse-off showers, picnic tables and four barbecue grills. Very small beach, well protected by close-in reef.

Kawiliki Pou Park

Located at the end of Waipulani Street. Paved off-street parking for 30 cars, restrooms, large grassy area and public tennis courts. Fronts Laule'a, Luana Kai and the Maui Sunset Hotel. Tall, graceful palms line the shoreline. Narrow sandy beach generally strewn with seaweed and coral rubble. (See "Traveling with Children" in Chapter 1 for frog hunting information.)

Kawililipoa and Waimaha'iha'i Areas

Any of the cross streets off South Kihei Road will take you down toward the beach where public right-of-ways are marked. Limited parking, usually on the street. No facilities. The whole shoreline from Kalama Park to Waipulani Street (3 to 4 miles) is an area of uninterrupted beaches lined by residential housing and small condo complexes. Narrow sandy beaches with lots of coral rubble from the fronting reefs.

Kalama Beach Park

Well-marked, 36-acre park with 12 pavilions, three restrooms, showers, picnic tables, barbecue grills, playground apparatus, in-line skating/skateboard park, soccer field, baseball field, tennis courts and volleyball and basketball courts. Lots of grassy areas. There is no beach in winter, only a large boulder breakwater. Good view of the cinder cone in Makena as well as Molokini, Kaho'olawe, Lana'i and West Maui.

Kama'ole I

Well-marked beach across from the Kama'ole Beach Club. Off-street parking for 30 cars. Facilities include picnic tables, restrooms, rinse-

off showers, rental equipment, children's swimming area and lifeguard. Long, white, sandy beach offering good swimming, poor to fair snorkeling. The small pocket of sand between rock outcroppings at the right end of the beach is known as Young's Beach. It is also accessible from Kaiau Street with parking for about 20 cars. Public right-of-way sign at end of Kaiau Street.

★ *Kama'ole II*

Located across from the Kai Nani shopping and restaurant complex. On-street parking, restrooms, rinse-off showers, rental equipment and lifeguard. White-sand beach between two rocky points with sharp drop-off to overhead depths. Good swimming, poor to fair snorkeling.

★ *Kama'ole III*

Well-marked beach across from the Kama'ole Sands Condominiums. Off-street parking, picnic tables, barbecues, restrooms, rinse-off showers, drinking water, playground equipment, a grassy play area and a lifeguard. This 200-yard-long, narrow (in winter) white-sand beach has some rocky areas along the beach and a few submerged rocks. Good swimming, fair snorkeling around rocks at south end of the beach. Kama'ole II and III are very popular beaches with locals and tourists because of the nice beaches and easy access.

Wailea-Makena Area

The Wailea area generally has small, lovely, white-sand beaches that have marked public access. Parking is off-street in well-maintained parking areas, and restrooms as well as rinse-off showers are provided. Several major resorts have transformed this area into a world-class resort destination rivaling Ka'anapali, and even surpassing it in some ways.

★ *Keawakapu Beach*

There are two convenient public accesses to this very nice and generally under-used beach, situated in Wailea between the Kihei Boat Ramp and Mokapu Beach. There is paved parking for 50 cars across the street from the beach, about .2 mile south of Mana Kai Resort, at the corner of South Kihei and Kilohana roads. Look for the beach access sign on the left as you travel south. There are two small crescent-shaped, white-sand beaches separated by a small rocky point. Good swimming, offshore sandy bottom, fair snorkeling around rocks at far north end. There are rinse-off showers and a restaurant at the Mana Kai, which is right on the beach. Access to southern end of beach: go straight at left turnoff to Wailea, road says "Dead End." Parking for about 30 cars. Rinse-off showers. Beautiful, very gently sloping white-sand beach with good swimming. Snorkeling off rocks on left. Popular scuba-diving spot. Four hundred yards offshore in 80 to 85 feet of water there is supposedly an artificial reef of 150 car bodies.

★ Mokapu Beach

A public access sign for these twin beaches (Ulua/Mokapu Beaches) is near the Renaissance Wailea Beach Resort, which is situated on Mokapu Beach. Small parking area, restrooms and showers. Rental equipment at nearby Wailea Resort Activities Center at Renaissance. Beautiful white-sand beach. Excellent swimming. Good snorkeling in mornings around the rocks that divide the two beaches. The best snorkeling is on the Ulua beach side.

★ Ulua Beach

A public access sign is located near the Renaissance Wailea Beach Resort. Small paved parking area with a short walk to beach. Showers and restrooms. Rental equipment is only a short walk away at the Wailea Resort Activities Center. Beautiful white-sand beach fronting the Ulua Resort complex. Ulua and Mokapu beaches are separated by a narrow point of rocks. The area around the beaches is beautifully landscaped because of the resorts. The beach is semi-protected and has a sandy offshore bottom. Good swimming, usually very good snorkeling in the mornings around the lava flow between the beaches. Parking is limited.

★ Wailea Beach

One half-mile south of the Wailea Marriott, there is a public beach access sign and a paved road down to a landscaped parking area for about 40 cars. Restrooms and rinse-off showers. Rental sailboats and windsurfing boards are available. Beautiful wide crescent of gently sloping white sand. Gentle offshore slope. Good swimming. Snorkeling is only fair to the left (south) around the rocks (moderate currents and not much coral or many fish). The Grand Wailea and Four Seasons are situated on this beachfront.

Polo Beach

Just past the Kea Lani Resort, turn right at the lava-rock wall sign (Wailea Golf Club—Blue Course—Restaurant) toward the Polo Beach Resort condominiums. The public access sign is easy to spot. Paved parking area for 40 cars. Showers and restrooms. The beaches are a short walk away on a paved sidewalk and down a short flight of stairs. There are actually two beaches, 400-foot-long north beach and 200-foot-long south beach, separated by 150 feet of large rocks. The beaches' slope begins gently, then continues more steeply offshore. It is not well protected. This combination can cause swift beach backwash that is particularly concentrated at two or three points with a rough shorebreak, especially in the afternoons. The beach is dotted with large rocks. Fair swimming, generally poor snorkeling.

The Makena area includes the beaches south of Polo Beach, out to La Perouse Bay (past this point, you either hike or need to have a four-wheel drive). The Makena beaches are relatively undeveloped and unspoiled, and not always easy to find. There are few signs and confusing roads, and some beaches are not visible from the road. Generally, no facilities, and parking where you can find it. I hope our directions will help you find these sometimes hard-to-find, but very lovely, nearly pristine beaches.

Palauea Beach

Palauea Beach is situated along Makena Alanui road, which is reached via Old Makena Road, but is not visible through the trees. There is a break in the fence .35 mile from Polo Beach with a well-worn path to the beach. Although this is all private and posted land, the path and the number of cars parked alongside the road seem to indicate that this beautiful white-sand beach is getting much more public use than in the past. Good swimming. No facilities. Both Palauea and Po'olenalena beaches have the same conditions as Polo Beach, with shallow offshore slope then a steep drop-off that causes fairly strong backwash in places and tends to cause a strong shorebreak in the afternoon.

Po'olenalena Beach

As you leave Wailea, there is a four-corner intersection with a sign on the left for the Wailea Golf Club and one on the right for the Polo Beach condos. About .8 mile past here turn onto the second right turnoff at the small "Paipu Beach" sign. At road's end (about .1 mile), park under the trees. Po'olenalena Beach lies in front of you. Walk several hundred feet back towards Polo Beach over a small hill (Haloa Point) and you will see Palauea Beach stretching out before you. A beautiful beach, largely unknown to tourists. The area above the beach at the south end has been developed with pricey residential homes. This is a lovely wide, white-sand beach with a gentle slope offering good swimming. This used to be a popular local camping spot; however "No Camping" signs are now posted. There is another section of this beach sometimes referred to as **Paipu Beach**, but it is a continuation of Po'olenalena. Continue another .2 to .3 miles on Makena Alanui, past Po'olenalena and you will come to Makena Surf (about 1.2 miles from the Wailea Golf Club sign). This development surrounds **Chang's Beach**; there is a public beach access sign and paved parking for about 20 cars. It's a short walk down a concrete path to the beach. A rinse-off shower and a portable restroom are provided. There is a small sandy beach used mostly by guests of the Makena Surf, but there is another public beach access there as well.

Ulupikunui Beach

Turn right just past the Makena Surf and immediately park off the road. Walk down to the beach at the left end of the complex. The beach is 75 to 100 feet of rock-strewn sand and not too attractive, but is well protected.

Five Graves

From the Makena Surf, continue down Old Makena Road another two-tenths of a mile to the entrance of Five Graves. Limited parking. The 19th-century graves are visible from Makena Road just a few hundred feet past the entrance. There is no beach, but this is a good scuba and snorkeling site. Follow the trail down to the shore where you'll see a rocky entrance to the water.

★ *Makena Landing—Papipi Beach*

This beach is about 75 to 100 feet long with a gentle slope, sometimes rock strewn. Not very attractive and used mostly for fishing, but snorkeling can be good if you enter at the beach and follow the shore to the right. Restrooms and showers available. Instead of turning right onto Old Makena Road at the Makena Surf, continue straight and follow the signs to the Makena Golf Course. About .9 mile past the Makena Surf there is another turnoff onto Old Makena Road. At the stop sign at the bottom of the hill, you can turn right and end up back at Makena Landing or turn left and head for Malu'aka Beach. About .2 mile past the stop sign you will see the old Keawalai Church U.C.C. (Sunday services continue to be held here) and cemetery. Along the road is a pay phone.

★ *Malu'aka Beach*

Past the Maui Prince Resort you'll turn right at the first paved dead-end road and find a beach park development created by the resort.

This public access has plenty of paved parking. The 200-yard beach is set between a couple of rock promontories. The very fine white-sand beach is wide with a gentle slope to deeper water. Snorkeling can be good in the morning until about noon when the wind picks up. There are interesting coral formations at the south end with unusual abstract shapes, and large coral heads of different sizes. Coral in shades of pink, blue, green, purple and lavender can be spotted. There are enough fish to make it interesting, but not an abundance. In the afternoon when the wind comes up, so do the swells, providing good boogie boarding and wave-playing.

Oneuli Beach

The entrance is a non-paved dirt road. The beach is composed of black lava, white cinder and coral combining to form a grayish-colored sandy beach. Just past the Maui Prince Resort is a dirt-road turnoff. A four-wheel-drive or high-ground-clearance vehicle is a good idea because the road can be a rutted, non-paved .3 miles to the beach. The beach is lined by an exposed reef. No facilities.

★ Oneloa Beach (Makena Beach, "Big Beach")

The entrance for Oneloa is the next paved dead-end road. On weekends, particularly Sundays, parking may be almost impossible. There is a second parking area a little farther along. Makena's very lovely white-sand beach is long (.75 mile) and wide and is the last major undeveloped beach on the leeward side of the island. Community effort is continuing in its attempt to prevent further development of this beach. The 360-foot cinder cone (Pu'u Ola'i) at the north end of the beach separates Oneloa from Pu'u Ola'i Beach. The beach has a quick, sharp drop-off and rough shorebreak particularly in the afternoon. Body surfing is sometimes good. Snorkeling around the rocky point at the cinder cone is only poor to fair with not much to see, and not for beginners due to the usually strong north-to-south current. Following years of car break-ins, there is now a citizens' patrol. Be sure you thank these people for their time and efforts. But still, don't leave any valuables in your car at any beach.

Pu'u Ola'i Beach (Little Makena)

Park at Oneloa Beach. From the beach (Big Beach) to your right you will see a cinder cone. You can hike uphill over the very sharp, steep and craggy cinder cone and down the other side to reach a flat, white-sand beach with a shallow sandy bottom that is semi-protected by a shallow cove. The shorebreak is usually gentle and swimming is good. Bodysurfing sometimes. Snorkeling is only poor to fair around the point on the left. Watch for strong currents. Although illegal, beach activities here tend to be *au naturel*.

★ 'Ahihi-Kina'u Natural Reserve Area

Past Makena Beach, a sign indicates the reserve, and a short distance past the sign there is a small, six-foot-wide, rocky and sandy beach alongside the remnants of an old concrete boat ramp in the water. Although the beach and cove are well protected, the water is shallow and the shoreline is rocky. Not good for swimming, mostly used for snorkeling and scuba. There is also very limited parking here. Up around the curve in the road is a large parking area. It's a short walk to the shore on a crushed lava-rock trail that leads to a large "pebble" beach. At the end of this beach you'll find a better entrance than over the slippery rocks. Remember, this is a marine reserve—look, but don't disturb. No facilities.

La Perouse Bay

Past 'Ahihi-Kina'u, over a road carved through Maui's most recent lava flow, is the end of the road unless you have a four-wheel drive. It is about 1.5 miles to the La Perouse Memorial Plaque. From here, if you choose, you can hike. Wear good hiking shoes, as you'll be walking over stretches of sharp lava rock. There are a series of small beaches, actually only pockets of sand of various compositions, with fairly deep offshore waters and strong currents.

Kahului–Wailuku Area

Beaches along this whole side of the island are usually poor for swimming and snorkeling. The weather is generally windy or cloudy in winter and very hot in summer. Due to the weather, type of beach, and distance from the major tourist areas on the other side of the island, these beaches don't attract many tourists (except Ho'okipa, which is internationally known for windsurfing).

Waihe'e Beach Park

From Wailuku take Kahekili Highway about three miles to Waihe'e and turn right onto Halewaiu Road, then proceed about .5 mile to the Waihe'e Municipal Golf Course. From there, a park access road takes you into the park. Paved off-street parking, restrooms, showers and picnic tables. This is a long, narrow, brown-sand beach strewn with coral rubble from Waihe'e Reef. This is one of the longest and widest reefs on Maui and is about 1000 feet wide. The area between the beach and reef is moderately shallow with good areas for swimming and snorkeling when the ocean is calm. Winter surf or storm conditions can produce strong alongshore currents. Do not swim or snorkel at the left end of the beach because there is a large channel through the reef that usually produces a very strong rip current. This area is generally windy.

Kanaha Beach Park

Just before reaching the Kahului Airport, turn left, then right onto Ahahao Street. The far south area of the park has been landscaped and includes barbecues, picnic tables, restrooms and showers. Paved off-street parking is provided. The beach is long (about one mile) and wide with a shallow offshore bottom composed of sand and rock. Plenty of thorny *kiawe* trees in the area make footwear essential. The main attraction of the park is its peaceful setting and view, so picnicking and sunbathing are the primary activities. Swimming would appeal mainly to children. Windsurfing and surfing can be good here. Weekend camping with county permit.

Hana Highway

H. A. Baldwin Park

The park is located about 1.5 miles past Spreckelsville on the Hana Highway. There is a large off-street parking area, a large pavilion with kitchen facilities, picnic tables, barbecues and a tent camping area. There are also restrooms, showers and a baseball and a soccer field. The beach is long and wide with a steep slope to overhead depths. This is a very popular park because of the facilities. The very consistent, although usually small, shorebreak is good for bodysurfing. Swimming is poor. There are two areas where exposed beach rock provides a relatively calm place for children to play.

Ho'okipa Beach Park

Located about two miles past Lower Paia on the Hana Highway. Restrooms, showers, four pavilions with barbecues and picnic tables, paved off-street parking and a tent camping area. Small, white-sand beach fronted by a wide shelf of beach rock. The offshore bottom is a mixture of reef and patches of sand. Swimming is not advised. The area is popular for the generally good and, at times (during winter), very good surfing. Ho'okipa is internationally known for its excellent windsurfing conditions. This is also a good place to come and watch both of these water sports.

Wai'anapanapa State Park

About four miles before you reach Hana on the Hana Highway is Wai'anapanapa State Park. There is a trail from the parking lot down to the ocean. The black beach is not made of sand but of millions of small, smooth, black volcanic stones. Ocean activities are generally unsafe. There is a lava tunnel at the end of the beach that runs about 50 feet and opens into the ocean. Other well-marked paths in the park lead to more caves and freshwater pools. An abundance of mosquitoes breed in the grotto area so bug repellent is strongly advised. Lodging, camping, fishing, hiking on an old trail that leads to Hana.

Hana Beach Park

If you make it to Hana, you will have no difficulty finding this beach on the shoreline of Hana Bay. Facilities include a pavilion with picnic tables, restrooms and showers, and also Tutu's snack bar. A 200-yard black sand beach lies between old concrete pilings on the left and the wharf on the right. Gentle offshore slope and gentle shorebreak even during heavy outer surf. This is the safest swimming beach on this end of the island. Snorkeling is fair to good on calm days between the pier and the lighthouse. Staying inshore is a must because beyond the lighthouse the currents are very strong and flow seaward.

Kaihalulu Beach (Red Sand Beach)

This reddish-sand beach is in a small cove on the other side of Kauiki Hill from Hana Bay and is accessible by trail. At the Hana Bay intersection follow the road up to the school. A dirt path leads past the school and disappears into the jungle, almost vanishes as it goes through an old cemetery, then continues out onto a scenic promontory. The ground here is covered with marble-sized pinecones that make for slippery footing. As the trail leads to the left and over the edge of the cliff, it changes to a very crumbly rock/dirt mixture that is unstable at best. This trail becomes two feet wide and slopes to the edge of a 60-foot cliff in one place. The trail down to the beach can be quite hazardous. Visitors and Hana residents alike have been injured seriously and fatally. *Hence, we cannot recommend this beach because of the dangerous access.* This cove is bordered by high cliffs and almost enclosed by a natural lava barrier seaward. The beach is formed primarily from red volcanic cinder, hence its name. There is also danger here of rip currents. And although illegal, beach activities here may be *au naturel* at times.

Koki Beach Park

This beach is reached by traveling 1.5 miles past the Hasegawa Store toward ʻOheʻo Gulch. Look for Haneoʻo Road, where the sign will read "Koki Park—Hamoa Beach—Hamoa Village." This beach is unsafe for swimming and the signs posted warn "Dangerous Current." Camping; picnic area with barbecue facilities.

★ *Hamoa Beach*

This gorgeous beach has been very attractively landscaped and developed by the Hotel Hana-Maui in a way that adds to the surrounding lushness. The long white-sand beach is in a very tropical setting and is hugged by a low sea cliff. To reach it, travel toward ‘Ohe‘o Gulch after passing through Hana. Look for the sign 1.5 miles past the Hasegawa Store that says “Koki Park—Hamoa Beach—Hamoa Village.” There are two entrances down steps from the road. Parking is limited to along the roadside. The left side of the beach is calmer, and offers the best snorkeling. Because it is unprotected from the open ocean, there is good surfing and bodysurfing, but also strong currents alongshore and rip currents are created at times of heavy seas. The Hotel Hana-Maui maintains the grounds and offers restrooms, a changing area and beach paraphernalia for their guests. There is an outdoor rinse-off shower for non-hotel guests.

CHAPTER 6

Where to Play

Maui's ideal climate, diverse land environments and benign leeward ocean have led to an astounding range of land, sea and air activities. With such a variety of things to do during your limited vacation time, I suggest browsing through this chapter and choosing those activities that sound most enjoyable. The following suggestions should get you started.

Remember: If you are making your vacation recreation plans from the mainland or another island you'll need to use the 808 area code. Toll-free numbers begin with 800, 866, 877 or 888. If you are a person with a disability, see "Travel Tips for the Physically Impaired" in Chapter 1 for more information.

Maui is abloom with street corner activity booths selling any and every form of recreational activity. You should be aware that there are several kinds of activity vendors. Some are what they appear to be. They explain the various activities and can book you on your choice. They may try to sway you toward their favorites. This is fine—recommendations are helpful—but if this is based on how much commission they receive from a certain tour operator, then they may not be giving you the full picture. Concierge desks at the major hotels and resorts can also book your activities. Most of these (in fact, probably all of them) also receive commissions. Those affiliated with the resort will no doubt give you the best service since they are a reflection of the resort. However, some activity desks at hotels, condos and the like are merely a concession. They rent the space, just like the activity booths on Front Street do; hence, the educated and informed visitor is ahead of the game in any case. The prices will be about the same, although there are those like Tom Barefoot's Cashback Tours who offer a 10 percent discount on every tour. (Barefoot's not only offers some great deals, they are also one of the few activity outlets I know of that *does not* sell timeshare. Read on.)

The other kind of tour activity broker is the one that *appears* to have the best deal: half price on a helicopter trip; $50 off on a lu'au; free meals. These are the folks that are using the activity as "bait." The "catch" is that you must attend some sort of breakfast meeting or tour of a property. Their aim is to sell you a timeshare unit on Maui. A timeshare (or the newest politically correct term of "vacation ownership") is an interval (usually one week) of time that you purchase once each year at a specific property. In a sense, you own 1/52 of a condominium. The cost is in the (many, many) thousands of dollars. You can put your week into a pool by joining one of several organizations and trade with someone else; this way you could get a week at some other location around the world. In addition to the purchase price you pay a yearly or monthly maintenance fee. It appears to us that this is a great deal for the condo owner/developer. For example, they charge you $15,000 a week for your one-bedroom oceanview condo. Then they find another 51 folks to do the same and *voila*, they have just made $780,000 for a condo that would sell for perhaps $300,000.

I am not against timeshares. On the contrary, I have friends and family members who own timeshares, use them and love them. It is important, however, that you be aware of these activity-booth approach tactics so you don't get taken by surprise if you're really *not* interested in purchasing a timeshare. You may be interested in learning more about them, in which case you could take advantage of one of these opportunities and have a free meal or save on an activity. If you have plenty of time and more patience than I do, then attending one of these sessions (even if you aren't interested in a timeshare) may be worth your while just to save money on an excursion. However, the timeshare programs I have attended were full of very high pressure sales tactics. Some are worse than others. The Activity Owners Association of Hawai'i regulates these activity booths. For information contact them at 800-398-9698 or check out www.maui.org.

The final option is to book the tour yourself by calling one of the numbers listed in this chapter. Ask your questions and inquire if they have any specials or discounts. (Many offer discounts for bookings you make online.) Since there is not a middleman to take a commission, you might be pleasantly surprised at the prices. In any case, it certainly won't hurt to ask. Enough of our editorial comments, now on to the rest of this chapter. (P.S. I do not get commissions on these activities, nor do I sell timeshares!)

Best Bets

- Experience the real Maui by taking a hike with guide Ken Schmitt and crew. (See more information under "Hiking.")
- Enjoy a guided walk through a lava cave in Hana with Maui Cave Adventures. (See "Spelunking.")
- Make the drive up to Makawao and enjoy a massage at the Maui School of Therapeutic Massage.
- For great snorkeling try Honolua Bay, Namalu Bay, 'Ahihi-Kina'u or Olowalu.
- Enjoy a romantic sunset sail.
- Plan to take in the magic show at Warren & Annabelle's in Lahaina—a very entertaining evening that you'll be talking about for days afterwards.
- Take a helicopter tour and get a super-spectacular view of Maui.
- Spend a few hours wandering through the Maui Ocean Center in Ma'alaea.
- Golf one of Maui's excellent courses.
- Sail to Lana'i and snorkel Hulopo'e Beach on a Trilogy cruise.
- Experience outrigger canoeing with the Kihei Canoe Club.
- If the whales are in residence (December through April), take advantage of a whale-watching excursion to view these magnificent creatures a bit more closely. An estimated 1,500 whales winter each year in the waters surrounding Maui.
- For an underwater thrill consider an introductory scuba adventure, no experience necessary.
- For those who like to stay dry in the water, take a submarine trip to view the underwater sights off Lahaina.
- For a wet and wild water tour—plus snorkeling—try an ocean raft trip.
- If you're really adventurous, consider parasailing (during the summer when the whales have gone back north) or sea kayaking, or try scuba kayaking at Kapalua.
- For great scenery at a great price, drive yourself to Hana and visit the Pools of 'Ohe'o at Haleakala National Park, or drive through Upcountry to Haleakala.
- Check out kiteboarding.

- Enjoy a *paniolo* horseback riding experience at Piiholo Ranch or a fascinating cultural tour on horseback into the mountains of Kipahulu with Maui Stables.
- Experience the most serene spa setting on Maui at the Hotel Hana-Maui's lovely new Honua Spa.
- Swing across a canyon on the "zipline."
- See the Ulalena show at the Maui Theater in Lahaina. Outstanding!

Adventures and Tours

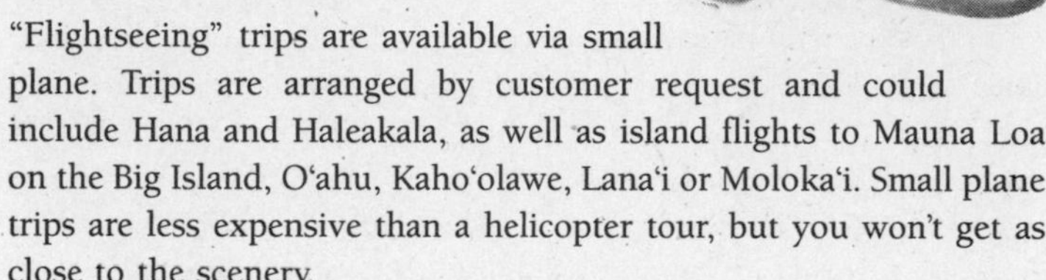

AIRPLANE TOURS

"Flightseeing" trips are available via small plane. Trips are arranged by customer request and could include Hana and Haleakala, as well as island flights to Mauna Loa on the Big Island, O'ahu, Kaho'olawe, Lana'i or Moloka'i. Small plane trips are less expensive than a helicopter tour, but you won't get as close to the scenery.

Paragon Air Paragon has 24-hour charter service to all islands in five- and nine-passenger planes. Excursions are quite different than helicopter tours. Their Kilauea volcano trip is a 2.5-hour narrated flight that travels to Hana along the picturesque coastline before traveling the 33 miles across the Alenuihāhā Channel to the Big Island of Hawai'i. Departs from Kahului, Kapalua and Hana. Combine this with a helicopter tour over Kilauea before returning by charter flight to Maui. Or plan a trip to Moloka'i with a tour of the Kalaupapa Peninsula or fly to Lana'i for a round of golf. *P.O. Box 575 Kahului, HI 96732. 800-428-1231; 808-244-3356; e-mail: wings@maui.net; www.paragon-air.com.*

Volcano Air Tours To date, Volcano Air Tours has a perfect safety record. Log on to their website to read about the unique ways to see the "fire in the sky" of a Maui sunset and the "fire down below" created by miles and miles of lava flow from the active volcano areas of the Big Island. There is no other way to see the lava so close or to see land actually forming and being created as you watch. The Big Island Volcano Tour ($315) takes you over the Parker Ranch and Mauna Kea before flying over the active volcano area of Kilauea and the cooling waterfalls of Kohala, before viewing Hana and the north shore back on Maui. Departures are from the West Maui Kapalua airport. The Sunset Volcano Tour ($290) departs two hours prior to sunset and also explores the active volcano areas and the sites above Maui and the Big Island. This tour departs from the

Kahului Airport. *808-877-5500; e-mail: info@volcanoairtours.com; www.volcanoairtours.com.*

ALL-TERRAIN VEHICLES

Haleakala ATV Tours Their tour starts you off at the 4,000-foot elevation and you'll travel 14 miles over upcountry terrain. The 3.5-hour tours include a picnic lunch in 'Ukulele Forest. The two-hour tour is available with no lunch stop. Kids 5 to 15 years old can ride along in a Jeep or Hummer with the guide. They are located 2.5 miles up Crater Road. Bring lots of clothing layers to accommodate the changing weather conditions; closed-toe shoes and long pants are recommended. They provide helmets and rain gear, as well as warm clothing if necessary. I have a friend who has experienced ATV tours by both companies listed here, and she liked this one better. The terrain was beautiful and the guides were very informative about local plants and the surrounding area. 877-661-0288, *808-661-0288; www.atvmaui.com.*

Maui ATV Tours Kick up some Maui dirt with Maui ATV Tours, which operates next to the Tedeschi Winery Tasting Room. The 4 hour ATV tour is $125 per adult, $105 for children ages 7 to 15. A 2-hour excursion is $90 per adult, $75 for children. Riders must be 16 years or older to ride alone on an ATV. Customers 7 years old and older may ride along as a passenger in the 3-passenger ATV. Kids (and adults) age 5 and older may participate in the 3.5-hour Pinzgauer trip. Adults $110; children (5 to 15) $90. The tour routes depend on the weather conditions. A variety of tours that climb up to 5,200 or down to the coastal King's Highway are available. Helmets and eye protection provided; long pants and closed-toed shoes are required. *808-878-2889; www.mauiatvtours.com.*

AQUARIUMS

★ ***Maui Ocean Center*** This is a wonderful attraction, and I highly recommend it for people of all ages. In 1998 Coral World International opened Maui Ocean Center. The aquarium is the only one of its kind in Hawai'i, but it is the sixth project developed worldwide by Coral World International. Their aim is to inspire appreciation for the ocean's environment and ecology and to provide education regarding the need for reef conservation. Part of the center has been set aside as an educational and research center. This non-profit arm presents tours, films and classes for groups, schools and the public.

The Maui Ocean Center features over 60 interactive exhibits, two restaurants and a gift shop. Upon entry to the Reef Building you will view a reef pool with seawater surge that replicates the coastal surf off Maui. The walkway descends and exhibits, including more than 40 aquariums from tiny to massive, can be viewed from different levels as you wander along. There are fascinating turtle and ray pools as well as an outdoor Discover Pool—a touch pool that delights children.

The Whale Discovery Center features life-sized humpback models and displays focusing on their feeding, migrating and mating habits. A 600,000-gallon tank in the Pelagic Building is home to tiger sharks, mahimahi and tuna. An acrylic tunnel allows visitors to walk through the tank with a 240-degree view of marine life. One portion of the floor is transparent, affording a very realistic in-the-ocean experience.

Plan on spending at least two hours to enjoy all the exhibits. Audio headset recorded tours are available in several languages. Open 9 a.m. to 5 p.m. every day of the year. Hours extend to 6 p.m. in July and August. Tickets are $21 adults; $18 seniors (65 and older); and $14 children 3 to 12. Harbor Shops at Ma'alaea. *808-270-7000. www.mauioceancenter.com.*

ARCHERY (See "Lana'i Pine Sporting Clays" in Chapter 7)

ASTRONOMY

Tour of the Stars The rooftop of the Hyatt Regency is home to Big Blue, the 16-inch recreational telescope. Three times each evening, a maximum of ten people head to the hotel's rooftop for a guided "Tour of the Stars" with the Hyatt's own Director of Astronomy. The program takes place at 8 p.m., 9 p.m. and 10 p.m. nightly. For Hyatt guests the cost is $20 adults, $10 children 12 and under. Non-resort guests pay $25 adults, $15 children. *808-667-4727.*

Star Gazers Maui They provide down coats and hot chocolate for an evening trip to the top of Haleakala. Watch the sun go down and then use a computer-guided telescope to see the stars in the clear Haleakala skies. The trip includes a picnic dinner, volcano crater viewing, snacks, beverages and geology lecture. *808-281-9158; e-mail: stargazersmaui@hotmail.com.*

BIKING

The Hawaiian Islands offer an endless array of spectacular air, sea and land tours, but only on Maui is there an experience quite like the bicycle ride down from the 10,000-foot summit of the world's largest dormant volcano. Bob Kiger, better known as Cruiser Bob, was the originator of the Haleakala downhill ride.

Cruiser Bob is reported to have made 96 individual bike runs himself to thoroughly test all aspects of the route before the first

BICYCLE SAFETY

If you are interested in doing some self-exploration on bikes, please use caution on the roadways. There are far too many accidents involving bicyclists and motorists. Remember that a good percentage of those behind the wheel of a car are island visitors who aren't familiar with the area, which perhaps is a contributing factor in these roadway accidents. There is a Maui County Bicycle Map that might assist you in your pursuits. It highlights all the major roads and rates them according to their suitability or unsuitability. It describes terrain features, elevation and even trade wind directions, and contains a distance guide. The map is available from Maui bike shops or from the **Maui Visitors Bureau**, 1727 Wili Pa Loop, Wailuku, HI 96793. 808-244-3530.

Note: Hawai'i State Law requires that children age 15 and under wear a helmet while riding a bicycle.

paying customers attempted the trip. Cruiser Bob's operations are now *pau* (ended), but there are a number of bike companies still operating Haleakala downhill and Upcountry trips.

Each downhill bike tour company differs slightly in its adaptation of the trip, but the principal is the same: to provide the ultimate in biking experiences. For the very early riser (2-3 a.m.) you can see the sunrise from the crater before biking down. Later-morning expeditions are available as well. In most cases, your day will begin with a van pickup at your hotel for a narrated trip to the Haleakala summit along with safety information for the trip down. The temperature at the summit can be as much as 30 degrees cooler than sea level, so appropriate clothing would include a jacket or sweatshirt. Dress in layers, as the temperature change can be dramatic.

General requirements are for riders to wear closed-toe rubber-soled shoes and sunglasses or prescription lenses (not all helmets have visors). A height requirement of about 5 feet is requested by some and no pregnant women are allowed on the trip. Bikers must also sign an acknowledgment of risk and safety consideration form. For the descent, riders are equipped with windbreaker jackets, gloves, helmets and specially designed bicycles with heavy-duty brakes.

A leader will escort you down the mountain curves with the van providing a rear escort. Somewhere along the way will be a meal break. Some tours provide picnics, others include a sit-down meal at the lodge in Kula or elsewhere. Actual biking time will run about 3 hours for the 38-mile downhill trip. The additional time (about 5 hours for the entire trip) is spent commuting to the summit, meals and the trip from the volcano's base back to your hotel. Prices for the various tours are competitive and reservations should be made in advance.

A few years ago I biked down with Maui Downhill and opted for the "late" 7 a.m. trip. I found them to be very careful, courteous and professional. Unfortunately they don't have control over the weather, and the day I chose was clear on the drive up, fogged in and misty at the summit, and there was a torrential downpour for more than half of the 38 miles down. Due to the weather, I couldn't enjoy much of the scenery going down. The leader set a fairly slow pace, not much of a thrill for the biking speedster, but safe and comfortable for most. Riders were invited to hop in the van at any time, but ours was a hearty group and after a stop to gear up in rain slickers, we all continued on. Our leader also advised that if the weather posed any kind of risk, he would load us on the van. The weather broke just long enough for us to enjoy sandwiches or salads at the Sunrise Market and to bask in the sun's momentary warmth. In radio contact with the group just ahead of us we were advised that the rain promised to await us just a little farther down the volcanic slope. As predicted, the drizzle continued as we biked down through the town of Makawao. We arrived in Paia only a little wetter for the experience.

Aloha Bicycle Tours This volcano bike adventure begins at Rice Park in Kula with a continental breakfast before boarding the tour van to the starting area at Haleakala National Park's entrance. Outfitted with safety gear you begin your descent with a stop at the Sunrise Market and Protea Flower Farm. Other stops at Kokea and the final descent to Tedeschi Winery for a deli-style lunch and time to tour the winery and tasting room. The distance is 33 to 40 miles. Minimum age is 14 years, height is 4'10". Cost is $120 per person (check their website for online discounts) with a 7 a.m. departure and return by 1:30 p.m. Groups are small and they promise that what sets this tour apart is their relaxed pace, stunningly beautiful route and personal service. *800-749-1564; 808-249-0911; e-mail: marc@mauibike.com; www.mauibike.com.*

Bike It Maui What makes this company unique is that they offer a two-way radio communication system for each rider. Safety and fun are their main concerns. They also offer Helly-Hansen cold-weather gear. There's a sunrise tour and a midday tour. Sunrise includes a continental breakfast and a sit-down breakfast at the finish of the ride. All tours are $109. Must be 12 years of age and 5 feet tall. *866-766-2453; 808-878-3364; e-mail: bikeit@maui.net; www.bikeitmaui.com.*

BIKE AND MOPED RENTALS

Bikes and mopeds are an ambitious and fun way to get around the resort areas, although you can rent a car for less than a moped. Available by the hour, day or week, they can be rented at several convenient locations.

A & B Moped Rentals—They have bicycles and mopeds in addition to beach equipment, surf and boogie boards, snorkel gear, fishing poles and underwater cameras. 3481 Lower Honoapi'ilani Road (at the ABC store) in Honokowai. 808-669-0027.

Island Biker—415 Dairy Road, Kahului. 808-877-7744. www.islandbikermaui.com.

Island Riders (moped rentals)—1975 South Kihei Road, Kihei (808-874-0311) and 126 Hinau Street, Lahaina (808-661-9966). www.islandriders.com.

West Maui Cycles—1087 Limahana Place, Lahaina. 808-661-9005. www.westmauicycles.com.

South Maui Bicycles—1993 South Kihei Road, Kihei. 808-874-0068.

Cruiser Phil's Chances are if you call it'll be Phil answering the phone at this owner-operated company. His sons and girlfriend are also on staff. They offer two tours daily: sunrise (pickup about 2 a.m.; $125) or morning (pickup at 7:30 a.m.; $100). Discounts are available for online bookings. They do a nice sit-down meal in Paia. Riders must be at least 12 years of age. Unable to ride? You can come along and enjoy the scenic van ride at a special price. *877-764-2453; 808-893-2332; e-mail: mauibikeman@aol.com; www.cruiserphil.com.*

Haleakala Bike Co. They have a sunrise special ($84.99) and Summit Deluxe ($74.99); both include a tour of the park. The Express trip is $54.99 but does not include a tour of Haleakala Park. These are unguided tours; a van takes you up and you bike down at your own pace. *1043 Makawao Avenue, Makawao, HI 96768. 888-922-2453; 808-575-9575; www.bikemaui.com.*

Maui Downhill Their 22- and 38-mile trips include sunrise, midday and sunset tours. Visit their website for current tours, prices and online discounts. The day and sunrise trips include a meal. All trips begin with a stop at their base-yard before your departure up the mountain. Must be over 12 years. Transportation from your hotel/condo. *800-535-2453; 808-871-2155; www.mauidownhill.com.*

Maui Eco-Adventures They have the only off-road Haleakala mountain biking trip as well as helicopter/biking combination tours. This trip is for experienced mountain bikers only and travels 4 to 6 miles depending on the group. Plan on a total of six hours for the trip to Upcountry, the biking and return to your hotel. Transportation, continental breakfast and a full lunch are provided. The trek is mostly downhill through private pastureland. Contact Maui Eco-Adventures for pricing information. *808-661-7720; www.ecomaui.com.*

Maui Mountain Cruisers Pickup provided from Kapalua, Ka'anapali, Lahaina, Kahului, Kihei and Wailea. Minimum age is 12 years; minimum height is 4'10". Closed-toe shoes and protective eyewear (sunglasses or prescription glasses) are required. Sunrise tour ($130) includes a continental breakfast prior to the tour and a sit-down stop for breakfast after the tour. Hotel pickup is 2:15 a.m. to 2:45 a.m. with a return about noon. The midday tour ($125) includes a continental breakfast and a lunch stop. Pickup time is 7 a.m. to 7:15 a.m., returning at 2:30 p.m. to 3:30 p.m. Online advance-booking discounts are available. *800-232-6284; 808-871-6014; fax 808-871-5791; www.mauimountaincruisers.com.*

Mountain Riders They offer a guided sunrise Haleakala tour ($115) that includes a breakfast stop and a day tour ($110) with lunch included. Also a 21-mile bike tour of Haleakala National Park, ending in Kula ($49.95). Hotel pickup available. *800-706-7700; 808-242-9739; e-mail: mtriders@maui.net; www.mountainriders.com.*

BODY SURFING

A number of beaches have good body surfing, depending on the season and daily weather conditions. One of the most popular is **Moku-le'ia (Slaughterhouse) Beach**. This is not a place for inexperienced or weak swimmers. When the surf is up, it can be downright dangerous. The high surf after a Kona storm brings fair body surfing conditions (better boogie boarding) to some beaches on leeward Maui. Inquire at local surfing shops as to where the safest conditions are during your visit.

BOWLING

Maui Bowling Center This is Maui's only bowling alley; ten lanes. Open Monday to Thursday from 10 a.m. to 10 p.m., Friday and Saturday until midnight, and Sunday from 9 a.m. to 10 p.m. Call for fees. *1976 Vineyard, Wailuku. 808-244-4596.*

CAMPING

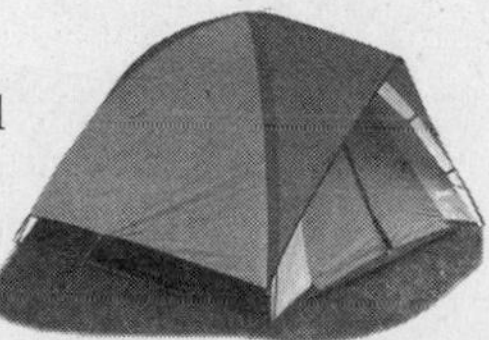

Safe and healthy camping is what it's all about. The State Department of Health office in Wailuku (54 High Street) has a wonderful free booklet called *Healthy*

Camping in Hawai'i that outlines some safety tips you should know while enjoying the island's outdoors: surf and currents, flash floods, heat stroke, fungal and bacterial infections, pesky critters, as well as diseases such as leptospirosis and giardiasis.

Camp Pecusa Located six miles southeast of Lahaina, it's halfway between the 14 and 15 mile-markers (behind the sugar cane fields). On the beach tent sites, $7 per person per night. No reservations. Maximum stay 7 nights per month. Toilets, showers, picnic tables, campfire pits, shade trees. No electricity. Managers-in-residence Norman and Linda Nelson advise us that the area is very safe and secure. Camp Pecusa also has cabins for groups. *808-661-4303; e-mail: norm@maui.net, linda@maui.net; www.maui.net/~norm/pecusa.html.*

Maui County Parks

County camping permits are available for H.A. Baldwin and Kanaha beach parks. The fee is $3 per night (children 50 cents) and camping is allowed seven days a week with a maximum of three nights. Camping is limited to weekends only at Kanaha Beach Park. Permits can be obtained by writing the Department of Parks and Recreation, County of Maui, 1580 Ka'ahumanu Avenue, Wailuku, HI 96793. *808-270-7230, 808-270-7389 (county-wide permits), 808-661-4685 (West Maui permits); www.co.maui.hi.us/departments/parks.*

H. A. Baldwin Park This county park is a grassy fenced area near the roadside. It is located near Lower Paia on the Hana Highway and has tent camping space, restrooms and outdoor showers.

Kanaha Beach Park Located near the Kahului airport, this park has picnic tables, restrooms, barbecues, showers. Open seven days a week, but closed the last Tuesday, Wednesday and Thursday of each month.

State Parks

There are several state parks on Maui where camping is allowed. There is a small fee for overnight camping at all state campgrounds including Polipoli Springs and Wai'anapanapa. The cost is $5 per family campsite (up to 10 people) per night. The revenues fund park maintenance and interpretive programs. For staying in the cabins at Polipoli and Wai'anapanapa, see "Upcountry" section in Chapter 3. For information on day-use of state beach parks, see Chapter 5. For permits and additional information, contact Department of Land and Natural Resources, Division of State Parks: *P.O. Box 621, Honolulu, HI 96809. 808-587-0300; www.hawaii.gov/dlnr/dsp/dsp.html.*

Polipoli Springs State Recreation Area Located in Upcountry, this park has one cabin (see "Upcountry" in Chapter 3) and offers tent camping. This is a wooded, two-acre area at the 6,200-foot elevation on Haleakala's west slope. The road has been improved, but check to see if a four-wheel-drive vehicle may be required to reach the park. Extensive hiking trails offer sweeping views of Maui and the other islands in clear weather. Seasonal bird and pig hunting. Nights are cold and can be near freezing in winter. Toilets, picnic tables. No showers.

Wai'anapanapa State Park Located near Hana, the park covers 120 acres. Tent camping and cabins (see "Upcountry" in Chapter 3). Restrooms, picnic tables, outdoor showers. This is a remote volcanic coastline. Shore fishing, hiking, marine study, forests, caves, blow holes, black-sand beach and a *heiau*. Bring mosquito repellent.

Haleakala National Park

A permit is currently not required to camp at either Hosmer Grove or 'Ohe'o (called "drive-in" campgrounds). A maximum stay of three nights is allowed; first-come, first-served. Wilderness campgrounds at Paliku and Holua require a permit. Permit camping is allowed on a first-come, first-served basis in designated areas only. There is no fee. Permits must be obtained the day of the trip at Park Headquarters between 8 a.m. and 3 p.m. 'Ohe'o Headquarters Ranger Station, open 10 a.m. to 4 p.m., has information for 'Ohe'o campgrounds. For Haleakala Crater camping information write to the park or call the recorded information line. For information on use of one of the three cabins located in the Haleakala Crater, please refer to the "Upcountry" section in Chapter 3. *P.O. Box 369, Makawao, HI 96768; 808-572-4400 (recorded information); 808-248-7375 ('Ohe'o station); 808-871-5054 (weather); www.haleakalanationalpark.com/camping.html#camp.*

Hosmer Grove Located at the 7,000-foot elevation on the slope of Haleakala in Haleakala National Park. Tent camping in this wooded area. Cooking area with grill, pit toilets, potable water, picnic tables. Hosmer Grove Campground is often cool, windy or rainy. Maximum 50 people.

'Ohe'o Located in Haleakala National Park, Kipahulu District, just outside of Hana. Tent camping. Chemical toilets, picnic tables, barbecue grills; bring your own water. No open fires allowed. Maximum 25 people.

Holua Located near the Holua cabin on the northwest side of the crater, about 4 miles down Halemau'u Trail (from the 8,000-foot level). It is the most accessible site and sits in a shrubland at the top of Ko'olau Gap. It has pit toilets, and a limited non-potable water supply. Water must be treated before drinking. You will have to carry your water in times of drought. No open fires are permitted. Maximum occupancy is 25 people in each campground.

Paliku Located on the southeast side, 6 miles down the Sliding Sands Trail (from the 9,740-foot level) at the base of a rainforest cliff.

Paliku is reached via a strenuous 10-mile hike from Sliding Sands trailhead. It has pit toilets and limited non-potable water.

Kapalaoa Kapalaoa is isolated in the cinder desert, six miles down Sliding Sands Trail. Pit toilets only.

CANOEING (OUTRIGGER)

Kihei Canoe Club They welcome visitors who would like to enjoy recreational (as opposed to competitive) paddling. The 30-day visitor fee is $25 and allows you to canoe twice a week (Tuesdays and Thursdays) at 8 a.m. If you fall in love with the sport and want to become a full member, you pay $150 a year. They also have some competitive events and social activities such as potlucks. They paddle from across the street from the Suda Store up in North Kihei with a small sign that appropriately enough reads, "Kihei Canoe Club." There is something very special about the stillness of the ocean and the camaraderie of paddling with five other folks, responding to commands called out in Hawaiian. You don't have to be incredibly athletic to enjoy paddling. You use your leg and stomach muscles as much as your upper body. The steersperson will explain things as you head out into the ocean toward a buoy where there are plenty of green sea turtles. You can jump overboard for a swim if you choose. You are then given additional instruction and some are asked to swim to different positions in different canoes. Ladies' attire should be swimsuits with shorts worn over the suit to prevent chafing from the seats. *P.O. Box 1131, Kihei, HI 96753. 808-879-5505; www.kiheicanoeclub.com.*

Fairmont Kea Lani This resort in sunny Wailea welcomes resort guests and non-resort guests for complimentary outrigger canoeing. They go out Tuesdays and Thursdays at 7 a.m., 7:45 a.m., 8:30 a.m. and 9:15 a.m. with four people plus two instructors. And yes, you *do* get to paddle. Call to confirm times and to reserve your paddle. *808-875-4100.*

CRUISES (See also "Sea Excursions")

Sunset and dinner cruises are quite popular on Maui with their free-flowing mai tais, congenial passengers, tropical nights and Hawaiian music that entertains while the boat cruises along the coastline. They are especially rewarding during whale season when you are likely to see some of these magnificent mammals frolicking during your trip. The sunset cruises are far more numerous than dinner cruises and are a pleasant way to enjoy a Maui evening on the water at less cost than the dinner cruises. Be aware that dinner aboard the smaller catamarans is most definitely not *haute cuisine*. The food is generally prepared ahead of time and often tepid by the time it is served. Balancing a plate on your lap with the wind in your face is anything but leisurely dining. Several dinner cruises serve a sit-down meal on a larger vessel, which would seem to be a better approach. Private charters are a more elegant way to enjoy a dinner cruise. I have not personally experienced all the sunset or dinner cruises so your appraisal (as always) is appreciated.

Dinner Cruises

Island Star Custom charter this 57-foot Columbia sailboat and you can enjoy a sit-down dinner for 8 on the aft deck or up to 28 if you arrange for *pupus* and buffet-style dining. They can work with any resort chef (as well as Chez Paul) so dine on steak and lobster or hamburgers. It's your call. They can arrange to depart from either Lahaina or Ma'alaea. 888-677-7238; *808-669-7827; www.islandstarsailing.com.*

Maui Princess Dine and cruise aboard the 118-foot *Maui Princess*. A daily tour of the West Maui coastline departs at 5:15 p.m. and returns at 7:45 p.m. The dinner menu features roasted chicken or prime rib, salads, vegetable, breads, desserts and beverage of your choice. Open bar and live music complement the dance floor. This is an attractive, upscale yacht with a good menu. Adults $79, children 12 and under $59. *800-275-6969; 808-667-6165; e-mail: ismarine@maui.net; www.maui.net/~ismarine.*

Shangri-La Aboard the 65-foot *Shangri-La* catamaran you can accommodate 2 to 49 guests for your dinner party. The *koa* dining table seats 10 passengers or buffet service is also available. They work with a number of chefs, and for groups of 12 or under they can arrange for an onboard chef to customize your dinner. Entertainment can be arranged. *Departure off Ka'anapali Beach. 888-855-9977; 808-665-0077; www.sailingmaui.com.*

Spirit of Lahaina The 65-foot *Spirit of Lahaina* is Maui's newest and largest catamaran. They feature a buffet dinner menu that offers a selection of shrimp, island fish and filet steak along with potatoes, rice, salad and desserts plus open bar. Cost is $69 for adults, $39 for kids. *808-662-4477; www.spiritoflahaina.com.*

Teralani They offer a sunset dinner and seasonal sunset/whale-watching excursion aboard their two catamarans, *Teralani I* and *Teralani II*. The dinner sunset whale-watching cruise is $75 adults, $65 teens and $55 children. The meal has an Italian flair with antipasto, Caesar salad and Giovanni's mahimahi or chicken marsala. *Passengers picked up from the beaches of the Sheraton and Royal Lahaina as well as Dig Me Beach in Ka'anapali. 808-661-0365; fax 808-661-0448; www.teralani.net.*

Sunset Cruises

Gemini This 64-foot glass-bottom catamaran is used by the Westin and departs from Ka'anapali Beach. They offer a champagne sunset sail nightly from 5 to 7 p.m. that includes *pupus*, champagne, mai tais, beer and wine, and non-alcoholic beverages; $55 adults, $45 teens (13 to 19) and $35 kids (2 to 12). This catamaran has long tables and padded seats inside. A wide passage area, accessible steps and ample headroom make it a comfortable boat. There are view ports on each side and big side windows. No music or entertainment, just a good chance to wind down on a pleasant sail. The *Gemini* also does snorkel sails. 800-820-7245; *808-669-0508; www.geminicharters.com.*

Paragon Their sunset sail departs at 5 p.m. from Lahaina, Monday, Wednesday and Friday, and is a two-hour trip with an open bar and appetizers. The vessel is licensed for 49 passengers but they only take 24 max. $51 adults, $34 for children 12 and under. Book online and save 15 percent. *808-244-2087; e-mail: paragon@maui.net; www.sailmaui.com.*

Scotch Mist Champagne and chocolate sunset sail, 2 hours, $40 adults, children 5 to 12 $20; no children under five permitted. 23 passenger max. Private charter available. *Departs Lahaina Harbor. 808-661-0386; www.scotchmistsailingcharters.com.*

Teralani They offer a sunset and seasonal sunset/whale-watching excursion aboard their two catamarans, *Teralani I* and *Teralani II*. Cost for the sunset sail is $59 adults, $49 teens and $39 kids. They also have a sunset dinner cruise. *Passengers depart from the beaches of the Sheraton and Royal Lahaina as well as Dig Me Beach in Ka'anapali. 808-661-0365; fax 808-661-0448; www.teralani.net.*

★ ***Trilogy*** Trilogy offers the Ka'anapali Sunset Sail three times each week. Departs along the beach, in front of the Ka'anapali Beach Hotel, for the two-hour trip. Departures change seasonally but plan on about 4 p.m. Enjoy an assortment of hot and cold appetizers that are heartier than average. The captain throws a flank steak on the grill and there is an impressive cheese tray. Staff moves around the deck delivering beverages, sushi rolls and other goodies. This is a lovely sail with an amazing Maui sunset as a backdrop (weather permitting) and a fabulous way to spend an evening. If you want to spread out the sunset experience head out of Lahaina Harbor for a popular 10 a.m.-to-7 p.m. sail to Lana'i plus a sunset sail home. All-day sunset sail is $179 adults; half-price children 3 to 15. Book online for discount. *888-628-4800; e-mail: info@sailtrilogy.com; www.sailtrilogy.com.*

DANCE

The **Hawaiian Ballroom Dance Association** lists some contacts for dancing on their website. *www.maui.net/~mpda/hbda.html.*

Paniolo Dance Association offers free line-dancing lessons as well as weekly line-dance opportunities. *Call Miki, 808-669-8343; e-mail: dance@mauipaniolodance.com; www.mauipaniolodance.com.*

Everyone is welcome to the **MCC (Maui Community College)** ballroom dance practice parties. Held at the MCC Student Lounge the music ranges from Latin to rock-and-roll, country, swing and ballroom. Bring your dance shoes. *808-579-9755; www.maui.net/~mpda/mcc.html.*

The **Maui Dance Council** has more options. *808-575-5227.*

Also see "Nightlife" in Chapter 4 for more ideas.

FISHING

Deep-sea fishing off Maui is among the finest in the world and no licenses are required for either trolling or bottom fishing. Fish that might be lured to your bait include the Pacific blue, black or striped marlin (*a'u*) weighing up to 2,000 pounds, yellowfin tuna (ahi) up to 300 pounds, Jack Crevalle (*ulua*) to 100 pounds, bonita-skipjack (*aku*) to 40 pounds, dolphin fish (mahimahi) to 90 pounds, wahoo (*ono*) to 90 pounds, mackerel (*opelu*), amberjack (*kahala*), grey snapper (*uku*), red snapper (*onaga*) and pink snapper (*opakapaka*). Boats generally offer half- or full-day fishing trips on a shared or private basis. Some are willing to take non-fishing passengers along at half-price. Most boats take 4 to 6 on a shared basis, but several can handle larger groups. All gear is provided.

Finding a charter: Your local activity center can direct you to a particular boat that they favor, or you could go down to the docks at the Lahaina or Ma'alaea harbors in the afternoon and browse around. There are also a number of activity booths at both harbors that can be consulted. When reserving a spot, be aware that some boats will give full refunds only if a 48-hour notice is given for cancellation. If you want to take children fishing, many have restrictions for those under age 12. If you are a serious fisherman, you might consider entering one of the numerous tournaments. Some charters offer tournament packages. Following is a list of just some of the charter fishing boats.

A word of advice: The young man had a grin that reached from ear to ear as he stood on the pier in Ma'alaea, holding up his small ahi for a snapshot of his catch. The surprise came when the deck hand returned the fish to the ice chest and continued on with his work. The family all stood on the dock, unsure of what to do. It appeared that the fish was to remain on board, though the family had envisioned a nice fresh fish dinner. One family member spoke up and a very unhappy crew member sliced a small filet, tossed it into a sack and handed it to the young man. Unlike sport fishing charters in some parts of the country, the fish caught on board generally remain the property of the boat. The pay to captain and crew is minimal and it is the selling of the boat's catch that subsidizes their income. Many vacationers booking a fishing excursion are unaware of this fact. There seems to be no written law for how fishing charters in Hawai'i handle this—at least everyone I talked to had different answers. Many of the brochures lead one to believe that you keep your fish, but they neglect to mention that it may be only a filet of fish. Occasionally you may find a boat that operates under a different sort of guideline. In this situation, you pay for your bait, gear and boat time and then keep the fish. In any case, be sure you check when you book your trip about just how much fish will be yours to keep. If the person at the activity desk assures you that you keep your catch, don't leave it there. Also check with the captain when you board. (I checked with Carol Ann of Carol Ann Charters and was told on board her vessel, you *do* get to keep your fish.) Communication is the key word—and have an *ono* day!

Aerial Sportfishing *No Problem* (37' Merritt) and *Aerial 111* (36' Chris Craft). Private Charters: 8-hour $750-$850 full-day, $650-$750 6 hours, and $550-$650 for 4 hours. Shared boat is $165 full day, $140 6-hour and $110 four-hour. Maximum of 6 passengers. *Departs from Lahaina Harbor. 808-667-9089; www.aerialsportfishingcharters.com.*

Carol Ann Charters 33' Bertram, max. 6. Private charters only. *Departs from Ma'alaea Harbor. 808-877-2181.*

Extreme Sport Fishing 39' custom force; 8-hour trip $180, $160 for six-hour excursion. The newest fishing option at Lahaina Harbor. *808-661-1118.*

Finest Kind Sportfishing *Exact*, 31' Bertram; *Finest Kind*, 37' Merritt; *Reel Hooker*, 35' Bertram; *Ikaika Kai*, 31' Bertram. Shared charters: 8-hour $175, 6-hour $160. Maximum 6 people. Private charters available. One of the top fishing charter companies on Maui. *P.O. Box 10481, Lahaina, HI 96761. 808-661-0338; 877-661-0338; www.finestkindsportfishing.com.*

Hinatea Sportfishing *Hinatea*, 41' Hatteras equipped with GPS. Shared rates: Full-day $160, 6-hour $145, 4-hour $130. *Slip #27, Lahaina Harbor. 808-667-7548.*

Ka'anapali Sportfishing *Desperado*, 31' Bertram. 8-hour $150, 6-hour $135. Shared-boat and private charters available. *Departs Ka'anapali. P.O. Box 11208, Lahaina, HI 96761. 808-667-5792; e-mail: info@kaanapalisportfishing.com; www.kaanapalisportfishing.com.*

Lahaina Charters *Judy Ann II*, 43' Delta (max 20). The *Alohilani*, 28' Topaz (max 6). 8 hours $125, 6 hours $100, 4 hours $75. Private charters available. *P.O. Box 12, Lahaina, HI 96761. 808-667-6672.*

Luckey Strike Charters *Kanoa*, 31' Uniflite, max. 6; *Luckey Strike II*, 50' Delta. Four-, six- or eight-hour trips. Shared-boat rates $115, $150, $175. Private charters available. *P.O. Box 1502, Lahaina, HI 96767. 808-661-4606; www.luckeystrike.com.*

Rascal Sportfishing Charters 40' Hataras *Rascal*. $155 for 6-hour shared, $170 for 8-hour shared charter. Private charters $650 for 4 hours, $750 for 6 hours and $850 for 8 hours. *Departs slip #13 at Ma'alaea. 808-874-8633.*

Start Me Up 42 ft. Bertram sportfisher is just one of several boats they offer. It is air-conditioned, and has TV/VCR, microwave, live bait and lures. Family-owned and -operated. 6 passengers maximum. *Departs from Lahaina Harbor. 800-590-0133; 808-667-2774; www.startmeupsportfishing.com.*

Unreel Sport Fishing 42' Ditmar & Donaldson. $125 for 4 hours; $150 for 6 hours; $175 8 hours. Private charters available. *Departs Ka'anapali. 808-244-2123.*

GOLF

Maui's golf courses have set a high standard of excellence for themselves. Many are consistently ranked among the top in the United States and the world by prominent golf magazines. Not only do they provide some very challenging play, but they also offer distractingly beautiful scenery.

If you are a real golf enthusiast, consider subscribing to *Hawaii Golf News & Travel*. It details lots of upcoming golf events throughout the islands. P.O. Box 4840, Mililani, HI 96789. There is also a very good and free magazine, *Maui Golf Review*, available around the island at various brochure racks.

The Dunes at Maui Lani The newest course on Maui, this 18-hole, links-style golf course, designed by Robin Nelson (who also designed Maui's Sandalwood course and the Mauna Lani course on the Big Island), winds its way from Wailuku through Kahului. The par-72 course measures 6,841 yards. There are four sets of tees to choose from. Green fee is $100 and twilight (after 2 p.m.) is $60. Club ($30) and shoe ($10) rentals are also available. Look for the sign on Kuihelani Highway (the main highway going into Kahului from West and South Maui). The course is located on the left, just before you reach Kahului. *808-873-0422; www.mauilani.com.*

Elleair Golf Course This non-resort course in Kihei offers a par-71, 6,404-yard, 18-hole course located off Pi'ilani Highway near

GOLF VALUES

Maui offers a tremendous variety in golf courses, including some of the most highly-ranked courses in the nation. Green fees can be high, in some cases exceeding $200 a round. Most courses, however, offer a range of discounted rates—and sometimes golf packages—that can save you a bundle if you know what to ask for. Ask about twilight fees (discounted rates for tee times starting in the afternoon, rather than the prime morning hours), second-round/same day discounts, junior discounts for young golfers, multiple-round discounts (playing the course more than once in a week) and any other special offers they might have during the time of your visit. Also ask your hotel or condo in advance if they offer any room-and-golf packages or golf discounts on nearby courses.

Lipoa Street. The course, which opened in 1986, was designed by Canadian Bill Newis. Green fees $100 for morning play. Ask about seasonal golf specials, twilight play ($80 after 1 p.m.) and discounts for a second round on the same day. Rental clubs $40. Driving range ($4) is open from 7 a.m. to 9 p.m. daily (Wednesday from 10 a.m.). 1345 Pi'ilani Highway, Kihei; *808-874-0777; www.elleairmaui.com.*

Ka'anapali Golf Courses There are two championship courses here in the heart of the Ka'anapali Resort area, with a lot of upgrades and renovations planned over the next couple of years. For renovation purposes, the South Course will be closed for six months in 2005, and the North Course will be closed for six months in 2006. By the end of 2006 both courses and the pro shop (which was renovated in summer 2005) should be in top condition, so plan to play a round or two here to experience the "new" Ka'anapali courses. Discounts are available for junior players (ages 7 to 17). A variety of special discounts and programs are offered throughout the year. Contact the pro shop for more information. The Ka'anapali driving range is located adjacent to the clubhouse. 866-454-4653; *808-661-3691; www.kaanapali-golf.com.* You can set up your tee time online.

Ka'anapali North Course—Designed by Robert Trent Jones, Sr., this 6,693-yard par-71 course places heavy emphasis on putting skills. It has been attracting celebrities since its inauguration when Bing Crosby played in the opening of the first nine holes. The first six holes run fairly level through the center of the Ka'anapali resort area, but with the seventh hole you begin climbing up the mountain side, providing more sloping play and scenic ocean vistas. Carts are equipped with a color satellite GPS system. Green fees are $160, resort guests $130. Twilight rate (2 to 6 p.m.) $77. *Note*: The North

Course will be closed for renovation for approximately six months beginning April 2006. Dates are tentative; please contact the golf course for current closure dates.

Ka'anapali South Course—This course first opened in 1970 as an executive course and was reopened in 1977 as a championship course after revisions by golf architect Arthur Jack Snyder. At 6,555 yards and par 71 it requires accuracy as opposed to distance, with narrower fairways and smaller, more undulating greens than the North Course. Green fees are $130; $105 for resort guests. Twilight rate (2 to 6 p.m.) $65. *Note*: The South Course will be closed for renovation through mid-November 2005.

Kapalua Golf Academy Located adjacent to the Village Course clubhouse, this state-of-the-art golf academy offers individual lessons, including junior instruction, on-course playing lessons or half-day, 2-day and 3-day schools. Indoor instruction utilizes digital video for swing and short game analysis. *808-669-6500; e-mail: info@kapaluagolfacademy.com; www.kapaluagolfacademy.com.*

Kapalua Resort In addition to offering some of the finest golf in the state (and the nation), Kapalua has demonstrated its dedication to the land. All three of its golf courses are Certified Audubon Cooperative Sanctuaries. Kapalua's courses received this Sanctuary designation by meeting the stringent environmental standards set forth by Audubon International for water conservation, habitat enhancement, public involvement, integrated pest management and more. Kapalua's courses are challenging as well as beautiful and should definitely be on the "must-play" list of any visiting golfer. Discounts for registered guests of Kapalua Bay Hotel, The Kapalua Villas and The Ritz-Carlton, Kapalua; twilight play (2 p.m. to 6 p.m.) is $85 to $100. Replay on any of the courses the same day is available for $55 to $60, as are club and shoe rentals. Special golf events held at various times throughout the year. *808-669-8044; www.kapalumaui.com.*

Bay Course—This beautiful and scenic 6,600-yard, par-72 course has a distinctly Hawaiian flavor. A design of Arnold Palmer, it opened in 1975 and sprawls from sea level to the mountain's edge. With its picturesque signature hole extending onto an ocean-framed black lava peninsula, the Bay Course is an excellent example of a premier resort golf course. It has plenty of hilly terrain, and you'll be challenged by eight water hazards as it meanders through the West Maui Mountains and down to the surf. The fourth hole is a par 4 and play is along the water, but it is the signature fifth hole that is impressive as it shoots out over the Pacific. The Bay Course has been host to a number of PGA tours and other national championships. Green fees $200 including cart; $140 resort guests.

Village Course—At par 70 and 6,378 yards, designer Arnold Palmer and course architect Ed Seay are reported to have given this course a European flavor. It opened in 1981 and sweeps inland along the pineapple fields and statuesque pine trees. Resembling the mountainous countryside of Scotland, it rises from sea level to over 800 feet—and this is over just the first six holes. By the last hole you've returned back down to sea level. With narrow fairways a player can battle 57 bunkers and the wind can play a factor on this course. The Village Course has a clubhouse adjacent to the Kapalua Golf Academy; Green fees $185 including cart; $130 resort guests.

Plantation Course—This spectacular 18-hole championship course is home to the Mercedes Championships every January. It opened in 1991 and was designed by Coore and Crenshaw of Austin, Texas. The Plantation Course, situated on 240 acres, presents Kapalua's ultimate golf challenge. The 7,263-yard course has a par 73 and features expansive fairways, deep valleys, island canyons, rolling natural terrain and large putting surfaces. You'll use every club in your bag on this course. The Plantation Course is golf on a grand scale. Green fees $250; $160 resort guests.

Lana'i Two 18-hole courses are available on Lana'i, **The Challenge at Manele** (808-565-2222) and **The Experience at Koele** (808-565-4653). Reservations can be made from the mainland by calling 800-321-4666. A day package that includes round-trip transportation via the Expeditions ferryboat out of Lahaina, green fees and Lana'i island transfers is available. See "Recreation and Tours: Golf" in Chapter 7 for more details.

Makena This area offers two beautiful courses designed by Robert Trent Jones, Jr. The original 18-hole course opened at the same time as the Maui Prince resort in the early 1990s. In 1993, the course was divided in half, and each half was combined with nine new holes to create the North and South Courses. *808-879-3344; www.mauiprince.com.*

South Course—This classic open-style course leads to the ocean. The large cacti that abound in this area were imported to feed the cattle that were once ranched here. This course is 7,014 yards from the resort tee with a par 72. Makena guest rate $105, non-guest rate $180, twilight play (after 2 p.m.) $105.

North Course—This narrower course travels along the slopes of Haleakala, offering some spectacular panoramic views. It's a par 72 and is 6,914 yards from the resort tee. Makena guest rate $95, non-guest rate $170, twilight play (after 2 p.m.) $95.

Maui Country Club This private course in Spreckelsville, originally opened in 1925, invites visitors to play on Mondays only. The course is fairly flat, especially when compared to many of the other island courses. The narrow fairways are lined with *kiawe* and banyan trees. Call Sunday after 9 a.m. to schedule Monday tee times. If you choose to play 18 holes, you'll be playing the 9-hole course twice for a total of 6,546 yards and a par 74. Green fees are $45 for 9 holes, $65 includes cart. *808-877-0616.*

Pukalani Country Club This semiprivate course nestled along the Upcountry slopes of Haleakala affords a tremendous panoramic view of Central Maui and the ocean from every hole. The course, designed by Bob Baldock, covers 160 acres. The first nine holes opened in 1978, with nine additional holes added, making the course 6,962 yards (par 72). Green fees are $60 until 11 a.m., $55 11 a.m. to 1:30 p.m.; twilight play (after 1:30 p.m.) is $45. *360 Pukalani Street, Pukalani; 808-572-1314; www.pukalanigolf.com.*

King Kamehameha Golf Club The Sandalwood Golf Course, located in a beautiful area called Waikapu set against the mountains of Wailuku, is under new ownership. The course is being redeveloped and reintroduced as the Kahili Course, part of the King Kamehameha Golf Club. (The adjoining Grand Waikapu course, which has been closed for years, is also being redeveloped under the new ownership.) The par-72 course was originally designed by Robin Nelson and Rodney Wright and constructed in 1992. While the course is under renovation, there may be only nine holes open at a time, but you can repeat the nine for an 18-hole round. Contact the course for current status of renovation and green fees. There will probably be some good deals offered here while the course is being redeveloped. *808-442-3361.*

Waiehu Municipal Course Located north of Wailuku on the windward side of the island, this course opened with nine holes in 1929; an additional nine holes were added in 1966. The course was constructed by Maui civil engineers. The 18 holes measure 6,330 yards with a par of 37-35-72. The front nine are at sea level along the beach with *kiawe* and ironwood trees framing this section of the course. The back nine are on an old sand dune above the shoreline. Green fees are $25 weekdays and slightly higher fees may prevail on weekends and holidays. A cart is optional at $15. Inexpensive food and drink at the Waiehu Inn located on the course. *808-244-5934.*

Wailea Resort Wailea Resort offers three highly acclaimed courses that are some of the best on Maui: the challenging Emerald, Blue and Gold. There are junior rates for children up to 17 years of age, ranging from $50 to $60. There are sometimes seasonal specials and other discount offers, so check with Wailea Resort for the most current details. *888-328-6284 (tee-time reservations); 800-332-1614* *(general information); 808-875-7450; e-mail: info@waileagolf.com; www.waileagolf.com.*

Emerald Course—*Golf Digest* and *Golf Magazine* have both ranked the Emerald in their top courses. This par-72, 6,825-yard course was designed by Robert Trent Jones, Jr., to provide a tropical garden experience. It also boasts spectacular scenery with an outstanding ocean view on the fourth hole. Definitely worth packing a camera along with your clubs. Green fees $185; $145 for guests of Wailea Resort.

Blue Course—A creation of Arthur Jack Snyder, this par-72, 6,765-yard course opened in 1972. Four lakes and 74 bunkers provide hazards along with the exceptional scenery. The 16th hole is particularly lovely with numerous people stopping to snap a picture from this magnificent vantage point. Green fees $175; $135 for resort guests. This is also the only Wailea course to offer a twilight discount (for play after 2 p.m., year-round $80 to $90).

Gold Course—Designed by golf course architect Robert Trent Jones, Jr., it opened January 1, 1994. Jones' design concept was to create a classical, rugged style of golf that takes advantage of the natural sloping terrain. The course is par 72 and stretches 7,078 yards across the lower slopes of Haleakala, affording exquisite views of the Pacific Ocean. Green fees $185; $145 for Wailea resort guests.

GOLF—MINIATURE

★ ***Glow Putt Mini Golf*** At this unique indoor miniature golf course, you play in the dark and everything glows, from the golf balls to the clubs to the colorful jungle-theme course to the complimentary bracelets. This new activity, which opened in 2004 at Lahaina Center, caters to young and old, singles and families. The music includes everything from oldies to local Hawaiian music, to suit everyone's tastes, and they provide short clubs for little ones so children as young as three can play. Air-conditioned and completely enclosed, it's a great place to enjoy a couple of hours on a rainy day or a hot afternoon. 18-hole course: $7 per person; $5 for children 5 and under. Play the course again on the same day for $5. Two-hour parking is validated with play. 11 a.m. to 11 p.m. Monday through Saturday; until 10 p.m. on Sunday. *900 Front Street (Lahaina Center); 808-667-2010.*

Maui Golf and Sports Park Located at the Ma'alaea Triangle, open 10 a.m. to 10 p.m. seven days a week. Featuring two 18-hole miniature golf courses, a bumper-boat lagoon with waterfalls, a trampoline and rock climbing. It's not the most creative miniature

golf course I've ever seen and it tends to get very windy, but it might be fun for young children. In my opinion, the Maui Ocean Center nearby is a much better option for the time and money. Fees apply for each activity. For mini golf: $13 adults; $10 children 12 and under; additional $5 each to play the second course. *808-242-7818.*

HANG GLIDING

Hang Gliding Maui Motorized flights out of Hana over the coastline and pristine waterfalls. Not offered everyday, so call ahead for reservations. Cost is $115 for half hour and $190 for full hour. Weight maximum is 240 pounds. *808-572-6557; fax 808-873-8960; e-mail: info@hangglidingmaui.com; www.hangglidingmaui.com.*

Proflyght No experience? That's okay. Tandem flights or solo flights fly mornings over Upcountry in the Polipoli area. Groups up to 6. $175 for 15-minute 3,000-foot jump. $75 for lower flights. $125-$275 for higher-elevation flights. *808-874-5433; e-mail: gliding@maui.net; www.paraglidehawaii.com.*

HELICOPTER TOURS

The price of an hour-long helicopter excursion may make you think twice. After all, it could be a week's worth of groceries at home. However, for many visitors it proves to be the ultimate island excursion. When choosing a special activity for your Maui holiday, I'd suggest putting a helicopter flight at the top of the list. Adjectives cannot describe the thrill of a helicopter flight above majestic Maui. A tour of the islands from the air is truly an unforgettable experience. Among the most popular tours is the Haleakala Crater/Hana trip, which contrasts the desolate volcanic crater with the lush vegetation of the Hana area. Maui's innermost secrets unfold as your camera's shutter works frantically to capture the memories (one roll is simply not enough) and pilots narrate as you pass by waterfalls cascading into secluded mountain pools. Virtually all the tour companies provide headsets for two-way communications between the pilot and passengers during the flight. Another option is the West Maui to Moloka'i tour, which affords an incredible opportunity to see the whales from a bird's-eye view between November and April.

Keeping up with the prices of helicopter tours is impossible. Listed are standard fares, and I hope you'll be delighted to find special discount rates if you call the helicopter company directly for reservations or check their website. Currently all helicopters depart from the Kahului heliport. Most companies include a video of your trip, though some are now charging an additional fee for this service. In choosing a helicopter tour, you should know that there are several different types of helicopters with different seating configurations. The four-passenger Bell Jet Ranger seats one passenger in front next to the pilot and three in the back seat. The AStar has two passengers in the front and four passengers in the rear seat. The ECO-Star is perhaps the most quiet and advanced avionic helicopter, offering unparalleled passenger comfort and cockpit design for fantastic sweeping views.

Safety Note: Don't combine scuba diving with any high altitude activity (like a helicopter ride) within 24 hours.

Interested in helicopter flight training while on Maui? Contact **D&H Hawaii, Inc.**, 808-875-8998. Or if you just want to go along for the ride, there are plenty of companies to accommodate you:

Air Maui Owner Steven Egger offers flights aboard a six-passenger AStar aircraft. Steve has been flying for 30 years and Air Maui is a family operation. The office staff and crew range from brothers and mothers to best friends. The 45-minute tour of Haleakala and Hana is $189; Circle the Island, one-hour, is $245. The one-hour West Maui and Moloka'i tour is $240; West Maui/Molokai Special, 45 minutes, $184. Online discounts are available. *877-238-4942; 808-877-7005; e-mail: info@airmaui.com; www.airmaui.com.*

Alexair They feature a four-passenger Hughes 500 and a six-passenger AStar helicopter. West Maui specials (20-minute tour) begin at $79. A variety of trips are available and include the Deluxe West Maui tour (30 minutes) $125, East Maui (45 minutes) $185, Circle the Island (55 minutes) $210. Deluxe Circle Island (65 minutes) is $245 and includes flight video. *888-418-8458; 808-871-0792; e-mail: info@helitour.com; www.helitour.com.*

★ ***Blue Hawaiian*** Dave and Patti Chevalier began their operation on Maui in 1985 and offer a variety of aerial and air/ground tour combinations in either the ECO-Star or AStar aircraft. The West Maui tour, 30 minutes, is $150 (this is ECO-Star price; AStar slightly less); Hana/Haleakala is 45 minutes, $215. A complete island tour, 60 minutes, is $275. Moloka'i/West Maui, 60 minutes, is $275. The Sky Trek is a six-hour event with a 36-minute flight and a landing and tour in Hana, $280. The Maui Spectacular is a West Maui/Haleakala flight with a 20-minute landing at the Ulupalakua Ranch, on the slope of the Haleakala volcano, $325. Their multi-million-dollar terminal encompasses 9,600 square feet and includes a customer lounge area with an atrium, waterfalls and a 1,000-gallon reef aquarium. Blue Hawaiian was chosen to help shoot the aerial photography on such Hawai'i-based films as Jurassic Park, The Lost World, George of the Jungle, Honeymoon in Las Vegas, Crimson Tide, Flight of the Intruder and Six Days Seven Nights. My niece and nephew experienced a Blue Hawaiian flight recently and gave it four thumbs up. They raved about the friendly, professional staff and said it was apparent their pilot really wanted the passengers to have the best possible experience. "Awesome," they said. That's good enough for me. *800-745-2583; 808-871-8844; fax 808-871-6971; e-mail: info@bluehawaiian.com; www.bluehawaiian.com.*

★ ***Sunshine Helicopters Inc.*** Fly in the comfort of their "Black Beauties." Sunshine offers AStar helicopters featuring state-of-the-art audio and video systems. Three external cameras and one cockpit camera capture live video of your actual flight including passenger reactions. Air-conditioned comfort and recordable CD players on board. The Hana/Haleakala 45-minute tour is $189. The Circle Island Explorer tour starts at $209. The Circle Island Special tour with a stop at Kaupo is $275. West Maui and Moloka'i flight tours also offered. I've flown with Sunshine on a number of occasions and can recommend their courteous ground crew along with their engaging and informative pilots. *800-469-3000; 808-871-5600; e-mail: sales@sunshinehelicopters.com; www.sunshinehelicopters.com.*

HIKING

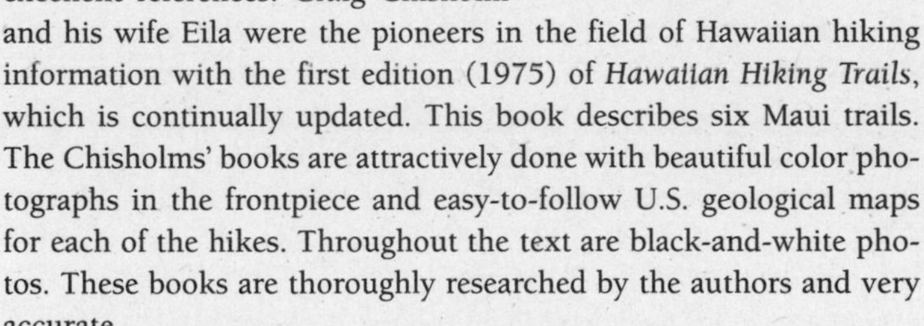

Maui offers many excellent hiking opportunities for the experienced hiker or for a family outing. Comprehensive hiking information is available from several excellent references. Craig Chisholm and his wife Eila were the pioneers in the field of Hawaiian hiking information with the first edition (1975) of *Hawaiian Hiking Trails*, which is continually updated. This book describes six Maui trails. The Chisholms' books are attractively done with beautiful color photographs in the frontpiece and easy-to-follow U.S. geological maps for each of the hikes. Throughout the text are black-and-white photos. These books are thoroughly researched by the authors and very accurate.

Robert Smith's *Hiking Maui* was first published in 1977. He continues to update his book every couple of years, the latest in 2003. The book is compact in size with a color cover and a scattering of black-and-white photographs and maps. The Maui edition covers 27 trails. Kathy Morey writes *Maui Trails*, which is published by Wilderness Press. There are over 50 trails listed in the hiking table of contents; however, some are really more walks than hikes. It has plenty of easy-to-use maps.

Hiking Trails

There are many interesting and diverse hiking opportunities on Maui. They vary from hiking in a volcanic crater, strolling among a grove of eucalyptus, exploring a rocky shoreline, or walking through a tropical rainforest. I'm not going to even attempt to cover the many hiking trails available on Maui, but would like to share with you several guided and non-guided hiking experiences that are available.

Haleakala National Park At Park Headquarters (open 7:30 a.m. to 4 p.m.; 808-572-4400), you can obtain hiking information and permits. Day-hike permits are not required. Keep in mind that the increased elevation may affect your endurance. Short walks include the .5-mile loop trail to **Hosmer Grove Nature Trail Lookout**, the .25-mile trek to the **Leleiwi Overlook**, the .5-mile hike to **White Hill** and a .67-mile hike to the first switchback on the Sliding Sands Trail. Day hikes include the 2.2-mile hike from **Halemau'u to the valley rim** and **Sliding Sands to Ka Lu'u o ka 'o'o**, a distance of 5 miles with a 1,400-foot change in elevation each way. For the hiker with more stamina, there is the 10-mile **Halemau'u to Silversword Loop** and the **Sliding Sands to Halemau'u Trailhead** that traverses 11 miles. *Caution:* The thin air and steep inclines may be especially tiring.

Hoapili Trail Referred to as the King's Highway, this trail starts just beyond La Perouse Bay. It is believed that at one time the early Hawaiians made use of a trail that circled the entire island and this is a remnant of that ancient route. The State Forestry and Wildlife Division and volunteers worked together putting in place stone barricades to keep the four-wheel-drive vehicles and motorcycles from destroying any more of the trail.

Lahaina Pali Trail This trail was originally built as a foot trail and later used as a horse trail. (While horses were introduced to the islands in 1803, their use was restricted to chiefs or *ali'i* until the middle of the century.) It traverses from sea level to an elevation of 1,600 feet on the Kealaloloa Ridge. Portions of the old trail were well preserved. Today, access to the trailhead is possible through the courtesy of the Wailuku Agribusiness Company. An interesting and informative guide for the trail and the area is provided by the Na Ala Hele Statewide Trail and Access Program, a Division of Forestry and Wildlife. It corresponds to markers along the trail and provides some fascinating historical narratives. For example, in bygone days robbers would wait along the trail, ready to pounce on unsuspecting travelers. If you'd like information on the trail call 808-871-2521.

Polipoli Springs State Recreation Area This park is ideally situated on the leeward slopes of Haleakala. Cool crisp mountain air provides a temperate climate for hiking and the trails are suitable for

FINDING MAUI ON FOOT

Among the most incredible adventures to be experienced on Maui is one or more of the hikes your personal guide **Ken Schmitt** and his staff at *Hike Maui* offer. (Ken has expanded from a one-man operation to a number of experienced guides, with specialties including archaeology, anthropology, botany, marine biology and Hawaiian history.) These hikes (for 4 to 8 people only) can encompass waterfalls and pools, ridges with panoramic views, rock formations, spectacular redwood forests, the incomparable Haleakala Crater or ancient structures found in East Maui. Arriving on Maui in 1979, Ken has spent much of that time living, exploring and subsisting out-of-doors, experiencing the natural energy of this island. This soft-spoken man offers a wealth of detailed knowledge on the legends, flora, fauna and geography of Maui's many diverse areas. Ken has traversed the island nearly 400 times and established his eight day-hikes after considerable exploration. His favorites are the 4- and 8-mile crater hikes that, he says, offer unique, incredible beauty and magic unlike anywhere else in the world. The early Hawaiians considered Haleakala to be the vortex of one of the strongest natural power points on earth.

A Haleakala hike with Ken or his crew is a thrill for all the senses. Not only does he pack a great lunch and yummy snacks, the hike provides beauty for the eyes; cool, fresh air for the lungs; tantalizing scents for the nose; peace and serenity for the ears; and an opportunity to touch and get in touch with Maui's natural beauty. The four-mile Crater Hike is a hike partway down both the switchback trail at 8,000 feet and the summit trail at 10,000 feet. They don't reach the crater floor, but you will get an opportunity to experience the volcano's power and its silence, plus those magnificent vistas from the vantage point up high. This is an excellent hike because it provides a true feeling of the crater without being overly strenuous. (Keep in mind the elevation adds tremendously to the level of exertion you will feel.) This moderate hike takes about seven hours. Cost is $120 for adults, children are approximately 20 percent less. The more adventurous and strenuous 11-hour, eight-mile hike will take you to the crater floor and is $145. (Online discounts are available.)

Hikes are tailored to the desires and capabilities of the individual or group (5 to 12 hours, $65 to $145, children less). Hikers are supplied with waterproof daypacks, picnic lunch, specially designed Japanese fishing shoes, wild fruit and, of course, the incredible knowledge of Ken and crew. Tours include transportation to the trails from the meeting spots in air-conditioned tour vans. Contact Hike Maui, P.O. Box 330969, Kahului, HI 96733; 866-324-6284, 808-879-5270, fax 808-893-2515; e-mail: hikemaui@hikemaui.com; www.hikemaui.com.

the entire family. Since the weather can be cool, warm attire and rain apparel should be included in your day or night pack. The clouds often clear, however, and treat visitors to a sunny and very mild afternoon. To get to the turnoff, go just past the Kula Botanical Gardens and turn on Waipoli Road, or go .3 mile past the junction of Highways 37 and 277. Follow the steep and windy paved road approximately eight miles. The last portion is graded, but rain quickly makes the roads impassable for all but 4-wheel-drive vehicles. *Warning*: Rental car agencies are not responsible for damage done to cars that travel this road. I have found it passable in a car with high clearance only if the road has been recently graded and is dry. Once you reach the park there is a gravel parking area and a grassy camping area. There are two barbecues and a flush toilet in a small outhouse. Drinking water is available. Trail options include a .8-mile trek to the Redwood Forest, a 6-mile Haleakala Trail, 4.8-mile loop trail, 1 mile to the cave shelter and 1.5 miles to Plum Trail.

The 4.8-mile loop is a very easy trail and, with frequent snack stops, even a young child can make it the entire distance. There is an array of lush foliage, and plums may be ripe if you arrive during June and July. The clouds can roll in quickly, causing it to be pleasant and warm one minute and cool the next. The cave shelter, however, is a bit of a disappointment. It is a shallow cavern and reaching it means a descent down a steep incline of loose gravel that can be difficult to navigate. The eucalyptus is especially fragrant as the fallen leaves crunch underneath your tennis shoes and you may see areas along the trail that have been freshly rutted by wild boars, demonstrating the incredible power of these animals. While you definitely want to avoid the wild boars, they are accustomed to being hunted and will also most likely choose to avoid you.

Pu'u Ola'i cinder cone This red-earth hillock juts out to the sea just beyond the cover fronting Wailea's Maui Prince Hotel. It is one of Haleakala's craters (under which is a large cave), and is said to be the sacred dwelling place of Mano, the ancestral shark deity. To reach the top of the cinder cone, turn right on the first dirt path after the hotel, then pass giant cacti and dry brush to reach the hiking trail. The short 15-minute hike uphill offers a rewarding sight of the coast—a black-sand beach just below the hill, and broad white beaches and black lava contrasting with the lush greens of the Makena Golf Course.

Hiking Groups and Tours

Haleakala National Park Haleakala National Park offers guided hikes and tours. The hikes are free of charge, but admission to the park is $10. *808-572-4400; weather and viewing information 808-871-5054.*

A reminder: Hiking off established trails without a knowledgeable guide is definitely not advised.

Hawai'i Nature Center See Wailuku sightseeing section in Chapter 2 for information on hikes sponsored by the Hawaii Nature Center in Iao Valley. Or contact them at 808-244-6500 for information or reservations. *875 Iao Valley Road; e-mail: hinature@maui.net; www.hawaiinaturecenter.org.*

Maui Cave Adventures Interested in hiking in a cave? See "Spelunking" later in this chapter.

Maui Eco-Adventures Maui Eco-Adventures tells us they are an "ecologically minded company dedicated to the education, exercise and entertainment of our visitors." I can tell you they have an excellent reputation on the island and offer some unique hiking excursions (with exclusive access to some of the destinations), as well as kayak and bicycle tours. The Maunalei Arboretum hike is a 4-hour trip to the arboretum established more than 70 years ago by D.T. Fleming. Cost is $80 for 4 to 12 guests. Their Waterfall Experience travels into the West Maui Mountains, Honolua Bay, the Nakalele Blowhole and Kahakuloa Village. $75 per person. The Hike/Kayak trip is a six-hour adventure through tropical rainforests with time for ocean kayaking in West Maui. $160 per person for 4 to 12 guests. The Rainforest Waterfall Hike is a six-hour tour in the West Maui Mountains that includes a continental breakfast and a deli-style lunch. $115 for 4 to 12 guests. The Hana Rainforest Waterfall Hike takes place in East Maui, $140 per person. Haleakala Crater Cloud Forest Hike is on private property on the slopes of Haleakala. $125 per person, with a helicopter option available. *180 Dickenson Street #102, Lahaina. 877-661-7720; 808-661-7720; www.ecomaui.com.*

Nature Conservancy of Hawaii The Nature Conservancy of Hawaii is an international nonprofit organization dedicated to protecting Hawai'i's native forests and wildlife. Nature Conservancy preserves on Maui include Kapunakea and Waikamoi, and, on the island of Lana'i, Kanepu'u. The Waikamoi Preserve is 5,230 acres and takes its name from a stream that runs through it; elevation ranges from 4,400 to 8,000 feet with annual rainfall between 50 and 200 inches and temperatures ranging from 35-70 degrees. This is a sanctuary for hundreds of native Hawaiian species, many of them endangered or rare. You might catch sight of the rare *'akohehekohe,* or Maui parrotbill, which exists nowhere else on earth. Much of the original forest on Maui has been lost or damaged but what remains is a vital watershed. Haleakala Ranch Company owned the lands since 1888 and conveyed it to the Conservancy for management in 1983. The ranch and the Conservancy work together to preserve the area. To reach Waikamoi Preserve travel to Haleakala National Park via Highways 377 and 378. Public hikes usually begin outside the Hosmer Grove campground. Access to the preserve is limited. The National Park Service conducts hikes at Waikamoi Preserve on the Bird Loop Trail Monday and Thursday at 9 a.m. and on the Boardwalk Trail the third Sunday of the month at noon (call for details and schedule; 808-572-4400). Access to Waikamoi Preserve is by permit only and guests can enjoy the preserve by joining a guided hike or a volunteer project. Permits for other access must be made through the preserve manager. *Honolulu office: 923 Nuuanu Avenue, Honolulu, HI 96817; 808-537-4508; e-mail: hawaii@tnc.nature.org.*

Sierra Club Maui Group of the Hawaii Chapter The Sierra Club invites the public to join their guided hikes. This is a wonderful and affordable way to enjoy Maui with a knowledgeable group of people. There are several weekend outings every month. They offer a variety of hikes: introductory, youth and educational. Donations are accepted. *808-573-4147; www.hi.sierraclub.org.*

HORSEBACK RIDING

Historically, the first six horses arrived on the islands in 1803 from Baja California. These wild mustangs were named *lio* by the Hawaiians, which means "open eyes wide in terror." They roamed and multiplied along the volcanic slopes of Maui and the Big Island until they numbered 11,000. They adjusted quickly to the rough terrain and had a reputation for terrific stamina. Today these ponies, also known as Kanaka ponies or Mauna Loa ponies, are all but extinct, with fewer than a dozen purebreds still in existence.

Lush waterfalls, pineapple fields stretching up the mountain's flanks, cane fields, *kukui* nut forests, and Haleakala's huge crater are all scenic environs that can be enjoyed on horseback. Beginner, intermediate or experienced rides can last from 1 or 2 hours up to three days. Most stables have age and weight restrictions, so check with them in advance.

Hotel Hana-Maui Hana Ranch Riding Stables offers guided trail rides around the 3,000-acre working cattle ranch on open range, shoreline, rainforest and mountains. One-hour Hana Coast ride $50. One-hour Ranch Trail Ride for intermediate riders, $50. Two-hour combination of the above rides, $90. Minimum age 12 years old (7 if they've taken riding lessons). *808-248-8211.*

Ironwood Ranch Located in the West Maui foothills. Follow Honoapi'ilani Highway 11 miles north of Lahaina to Napili, where the entry to the stables is located. Trips are available for beginning, intermediate or advanced riders. All rides are guided (no unescorted rides) in small groups, no more than seven guests per guide. Western-style rides tour lush tropical valleys through the Honolua pineapple plantation. They also offer a 2-hour sunset ride. $55 for one hour, $80 for 1.5 hours, $110 for two hours. Advanced ride $150. *877-699-4529; 808-669-4991; fax 808-669-4702; www.ironwoodranch.com.*

Makena Stables Operating since 1983, Patrick and Helaine Borge match each person to their horse by ability and offer help and lessons as needed. Their horses were personally raised and trained. All of their rides are on Ulupalakua Ranch, a 20,000-acre open-range ranch that overlooks the 'Ahihi-Kina'u Reserve, La Perouse Bay and the lava flows. A 2.5-hour ride, at $135 per person, goes out in the morning. This ride climbs to Kalua O Lapa, the vent that was the last eruption of Haleakala. It offers panoramic views of the south slopes of Haleakala, La Perouse Bay and the islands of Kaho'olawe, Molokini, Lana'i and Moloka'i. The sunset ride is 2.5 to 3 hours for $160. Private rides are available as well. All rides are guided and done Western style. They are all physically strenuous and it is recommended that all riders be in good physical condition. Weight limit is 205 pounds. Maximum of six riders. Children 13 and over are welcome when accompanied by an adult. Reservations required for all rides. *8299 South Makena Road, located at La Perouse Bay. 808-879-0244; www.makenastables.com.*

★ ***Maui Stables*** I hesitate to call this a trail ride, because it is so much more. Maui Stables in Kipahulu (on Maui's eastern shore) is operated by a Hawaiian family that has lived for generations in this beautiful area. During the ride, your guide—one of the family members—shares cultural and historical information with you, including pointing out plants along the way that were used in traditional Hawaiian healing. I knew this was going to be a unique experience when I was told the horses are each named after a Hawaiian wind or rain common to the Kipahulu area, and our "wrangler" guide, Keoni, started the tour with a Hawaiian chant. What transpired then was a wonderful, leisurely three-hour ride into the mountains of Kipahulu, with Keoni providing fascinating cultural and historical tidbits along the way, mingled with legends. When we left the road and began climbing into the hills, Keoni stopped to listen for the birds—a sign, he explained, that all is well ahead—then presented another chant before entering the mountains. As we climbed, we stopped for photos on a hill with the ocean in the background, and Keoni picked wild guavas from a nearby tree, tossing them to us as we sat astride our horses. When we reached our destination, a bluff overlooking Ohe'o Gulch—a magnificent valley of waterfalls—Keoni again offered a Hawaiian chant, this time a mahalo (thank you) for the safe passage. I had goosebumps running from head to toe. The horses are in beautiful shape—young, healthy and well-groomed. Not your typical haggard-looking trail horse. We were greeted before the morning ride with a platter of granola bars and fresh fruit (apple bananas) picked off the local trees, and at the end of the ride we enjoyed a deli lunch on the stables' picnic tables. Rides are offered at 9:30 a.m. and 1 p.m. daily, and groups are no larger than seven people to a guide (my group had only four). This is the only stable on Maui that has horses capable of handling weight up to 300 pounds. It's a long drive to Kipahulu and Maui Stables from the resort areas in South and West Maui, but this experience is worth it. Plan a full day to make the drive and to experience this cultural tour on horseback. Better still, incorporate this excursion into your Hana visit—it's less than 30 minutes drive from Hana. $150 for the morning or afternoon ride; children age 12 or older (as young as 7, if they've had riding lessons). *808-248-7799; fax 808-878-3914; e-mail: tours@mauistables.com; www.mauistables.com.*

Mendes Ranch Journey onto an actual working cattle ranch in the heart of West Maui. After a Western-style open-pit barbecue lunch, take off with Sunshine Helicopters for a full tour of West Maui. $130 for the Paniolo Horseback Adventure, which includes lunch but no helicopter tour ($85 without lunch). With helicopter tour $250. Call Sunshine Helicopters to book the helicopter/horseback experience. 808-871-0722. Weight limit 250 pounds, minimum age 7 years, Western saddle. *808-871-5222. www.maui.net/~mendes.*

★ ***Piiholo Ranch*** True *paniolo*-style hospitality from Maui's Baldwin family. Located on the slopes of Haleakala, bordering the paniolo-town of Makawao, the ranch is named for the cinder cone hill that is a predominant feature in Upcountry Maui. Henry Perrine Baldwin and some Honolulu businessmen began Haleakala Ranch back in 1888. Five generations of the Baldwin family have continued ranching operations, and today Peter Baldwin owns and operates Piiholo Ranch. I haven't experienced this ride, but I've heard rave reviews from those who have, and it sounds like it is far more than your standard horseback trail ride. Wranglers share the history of the paniolo along with stories and legends making this a very interesting choice for those of us who love Hawaiian history. Morning picnic ride (3.5 hours) $160; two-hour Country Ride $120; private rides and private lessons available. *866-572-5544; 808-357-5544; e-mail: info@piiholoranch.com; www.piiholo.com.*

Pony Express Tours Trips across Haleakala Ranch and into Haleakala Crater. Haleakala Ranch treks: one-hour introductory ride $65; two-hour intermediate $95; 3-hour picnic ride $115. Trips available Monday through Saturday. Haleakala Crater trips include lunch: 4-hour, 7.6-mile junction ride $169; 5-hour, 12-mile crater rides $195. *808-667-2200; www.ponyexpresstours.com.*

Thompson Riding Stables Located between 4,000 and 6,500 feet on the slopes of Haleakala, Thompson Ranch was established in 1902. They offer morning, picnic and sunset rides with snacks and beverages, and they welcome families. *Thompson Road in Kula. 808-878-1910; www.thompsonranchridingstables.com.*

Royal Hawaiian Carriages If you prefer a little something between you and the horse, Royal Hawaiian Carriages offers romantic excursions and sunset tours as well as wedding transportation by horse-drawn carriage. The carriage (and driver) rent for $300 per hour for a tour of Kapalua. (Additional time at $175 per hour). Ka'anapali and Wailea/Makena tours are available by special request at substantially higher rates. The narrated tour goes from the Kapalua Bay area to D. T. Fleming Beach Park, from the ocean to the top of Pineapple Hill, and through historic Cook Pine Drive. Pickup at The Ritz-Carlton or in the Kapalua Resort area. Hayrides are offered seasonally for large groups, parties, Christmas caroling and other functions. No alcoholic beverages allowed. 24-hour advance booking suggested. *808-669-1100; fax 808-669-4702; www.royalhawaiiancarriages.com.*

HUNTING/SPORTING CLAYS

Hunting Adventures of Maui, Inc. Owner/guide Bob Caires offers year-round hunting options. Game includes Spanish goat (*kao*) and wild boar (*pua'a*). Hunting on 100,000 acres of privately owned ranches with all equipment provided. Call for rates. Three-person maximum. Includes sunrise-sunset hunt, food, beverages, four-wheel-drive transportation, clothing, boots, packs, meat storage and packing for home shipment and Kahului airport pickup. Rifle rentals and taxidermy available. Sightseeing safaris also available. A non-resident hunting license is required ($100) and you must provide your hunter safety card to purchase the license. Trips scheduled weekdays only. *1745 Kapakalua Road, Haiku, HI 96708. 808-572-8214.*

Papaka Sporting Clays The 12.5-acre range is inside a small volcanic crater on the slopes of Haleakala, at Ulupalakua at a private ranch operated by Dave Barnes. Shotguns available at Papaka are 12-gauge, 20- and 28-gauge and 410s. They are open daily 8:30 a.m. to dusk. Since they are at a 1,000-foot elevation there should be no scuba diving at least 12 hours before coming up to the ranch. There are no live birds or rabbits, just clay targets used to mimic the flights of different game birds. Their program is designed for any ability ages 12 and up. Their "Birdbrain" computerized 5-stand course has five levels of difficulty and consists of 25 randomly selected targets to challenge the best marksman. Customers can be met at the Maui Prince Hotel in Makena for a shorter trip up the private road to upcountry. Two trips per day, one at 8:30 a.m. and the other at 1 p.m. Pickups available from the west side for an extra fee. Cost is $125 for 100 targets, $88 for 75 targets and $69 for 50 targets. *808-879-5649.*

JET SKIING

Thrillcraft activities, which include parasailing and jet skiing, are banned during whale season. The "open season" for jet-skiing recreation is May 16 to December 14.

Pacific Jet Sports/Jet Ski Maui Located at the south end of Ka'anapali Beach at Hanaka'o'o Beach Park. Their Waverunners are for 1 to 3 people. Rental prices are for one person, per jet ski, with an additional charge of $15 per person for more than one. (Three people max.) Half hour $55, 1 hour $85. Early-bird and online discounts available. Hawaiian law requires a person be 18 years old to operate a machine alone. Younger persons can ride as a passenger on the Waverunner with someone who is at least 18 years of age. All renters are fitted with a life vest. Daily 9 a.m. to 4 p.m. (weather permitting). 866-667-2001; *808-667-2001; www.mauiwatersports.com.*

KAYAKING

Big Kahuna Adventures Maui Kayak rentals (from $30 a day) and tours with certified kayak guides including Makena, La Perouse and Lana'i. They also offer surfing lessons and surf and boogie board rentals. *808-875-6395; www.bigkahunaadventures.com.*

Hawaiian Ultimate Adventures Eco-kayak and snorkel treks $79 for 3 hours; whale watching in season $49 for 2 hours. Design your own trek. Snacks or lunch and beverage included. They also offer hiking tours and surfing lessons. *877-247-3198; 808-669-3720; www.hawaiiultimate.net.*

Kelii's Kayak Tours Environmentally friendly tours with experienced guides. Small groups. Makena or Olowalu (West Maui) tours $59/2.5 hours; $89/4.5 hours. Honolua or La Perouse Bay $74/3 hours; $99/4 hours. Departures at 7:30 and 11 a.m. Lunch and/or refreshments included. Maui sunset tour at 4 p.m. $59/2 hours. *888-874-7652; 808-874-7652; e-mail: info@keliiskayak.com; www.keliiskayak.com.*

Makena Kayak Tours The only Hawaiian-owned and operated kayak company on Maui, they enjoy sharing their knowledge of the island and its history. They offer family-style tours, limited to small groups, departing twice a day. 2.5-hour tour ($55) or 4-hour

($85) tours that depart from Makena Landing, La Perouse Bay or 'Ahihi-Kina'u Natural Marine Reserve. *808-879-8426; www.makenakayak.com.*

Maui Eco-Adventures Hiking/kayaking combination tours twice daily at 8 a.m. and 2 p.m. Coastal kayaking through the caves of West Maui with exclusive access to the Maunalei Arboretum and a private tropical rainforest. Tours from $65 to $165. *808-661-7720; www.ecomaui.com.*

Maui Kayaks Kayak/snorkel with state-of-the-art equipment. Small groups with personalized service and attention to detail. Snacks and refreshments included on all tours. They offer several tour choices with some unique destinations, including an "extreme" Molokini tour. Visit their website for the latest information on tours and prices. *866-771-6284; 808-874-4000; www.mauikayaks.com.*

Ron Bass's Maui Sea Kayaking This independent guide has been leading kayak tours since 1988. He offers a variety of tours (half-day prices $75) and specializes in kayaking and snorkeling for the disabled. His special equipment includes three-person kayaks, view boards and beach-access wheelchairs. Ron also operates "Wilderness Wish," a non-profit organization that assists disabled folks in experiencing new adventures by discovering and exploring out-of-the-way places. *P.O. Box 106, Pu'unene, HI 96784. 808-572-6299; fax 808-572-6151; www.maui.net/~kayaking.*

South Pacific Kayaks & Outfitters They offer introductory paddle and snorkel excursions in south and west Maui. Short paddling distances combined with offshore snorkeling: 2.5 to 3 hours from $65. Some excursions are open to children age 5 and up. South Maui Explorer trip searches for turtles, dolphins and whales as it travels along the southern coast, with time for snorkeling and a deli lunch, $89 for 5 hours (ages 8 and up). Also available are single and double kayaks as well as car racks, life vests, snorkel gear and more. *Located in Kihei; 808-875-4848; www.southpacifickayaks.com.*

KITEBOARDING

This sport might appeal mostly to windsurfers who are looking for another challenge. Although the sport has been around for about 20 years in Europe and parts of the U.S., it didn't reach Maui until 1999 with the opening of the **Kiteboarding School of Maui**. The basic premise is that you take a board, not unlike a snowboard, and add a kite and wind. Check it out at "Kite Beach" at the lower end of Kanaha Beach Park and then call for lessons.

Kiteboarding School of Maui This was one of the first kiteboarding schools in the U.S. and the first permitted school on Maui. It is the only kiteboarding school on the island with its own retail shop. Lessons, on a one-on-one basis, include a 4-hour beginner course ($290), two-, three-, four- and five-day courses ($490-$975), as well as intermediate ($70/hour) and advanced ($80/hour) lessons. *22 Hana Highway, Kahului; 808-873-0015; e-mail: martin@ksmaui.com; www.ksmaui.com.*

Aqua Sports Offering group kiteboarding lessons, beginning through advanced, as well as private lessons. Kiteboarding Basics (3 hours) $198; Intro to Kiteboarding (full-day course) $325; and other more advanced classes. *808-242-8015.*

LAND TOURS

Land excursions on Maui are usually centered upon two major attractions, Hana/'Ohe'o Valley and Haleakala Crater. Lesser attractions are trips to the Iao Valley or around West Maui. You can do all of this in your rental car. However, with a tour and tour guide you can sit back and enjoy the scenery while a professional guide discourses on the history, flora, fauna and geography of the area. The single most important item on any tour is a good guide/driver and, unfortunately, the luck of the draw prevails here. Another somewhat expensive but interesting option is a personalized custom tour. A local resident will join you, in your car, for a tour of whatever or wherever you choose. You can choose to do the driving, or you can sign on a guide as an additional driver with your rental car company and let him/her do the driving. This may allow you the opportunity to linger at those places you enjoy the most, without following the pace of a group. Your personal guide may also be able to take you to locations the tour vans don't include.

Driving to Hana and back requires a full day and can be very grueling, so this is one trip I recommend you consider taking a tour. A Haleakala Crater tour spans 5 to 6 hours and can be enjoyed at sunrise (2 a.m. departure), midday or sunset. The West Maui and Iao Valley trips are half-day ventures. Only vans travel the road to Hana, although large buses as well as vans are available for other trips. Prices are competitive and those listed here are correct at the time of publication. Some trips include the cost of meals, others do not. Also available are one-day tours to the outer islands. The day begins with an early-morning departure to the Big Island, Lana'i,

O'ahu or Kaua'i. Some excursions provide a guided ground tour; others offer a rental car to explore the island on your own.

Carey Hawaii/Town & Country Limousine Enjoy a private Hana tour in a comfortable Lincoln Navigator. Daily tours include hotel pickup, a continental breakfast and lunch at the Hotel Hana-Maui, returning at around 5 p.m. Price is $239 per person for 2 people/$199 for 3/$179 for 4. Also airport limousine service. *888-563-2888; 808-572-3400; www.hawaiilimo.com.*

Ekahi Tours A small family-owned company specializing in van tours of Maui's most remote and "Hawaiian" areas: Hana, Haleakala and Kahakuloa. The Hana Tour includes hotel pickup, continental breakfast, deli-style box lunch, national park fees and a circular route that includes the Hana Highway and Upcountry Maui. $88.50 adult, $62.50 child (0-11 years). Watch the new day dawn from Haleakala on the Sunrise Haleakala Tour. $67.70 adult, $52.08 children (0-11). Includes hotel pickup, national park fees, and full breakfast at Pukalani Country Club. Some restrictions to guests with heart or breathing problems. Hidden Valley Tour to Kahakuloa $67.70 adults, $52.08 children, includes hotel pickup, light snacks and refreshments; since this is a hiking tour, no wheelchair guests. The Kahakuloa Valley tour is an opportunity to enjoy a cultural experience at a Hawaiian *kuleana* (parcel of land) that is part of an *ahupua'a* (land division extending from the uplands to the oceans) located along the northwest coast of Maui. This is an area where Hawaiians lived up to 1,500 years ago. Guides provide guests with background on the plants, taro farming and Hawaiian lifestyle. Charter tours to other areas may be arranged. *532 Keolani Place, Kahului, HI 96732. 888-292-2422; 808-877-9775; fax 808-877-9776; e-mail: tour@ekahi.com; www.ekahi.com.*

Hapa Papa's is a small company that will supply a knowledgeable island guide for private tours in a 6-passenger van. The Hapa Papa's guide will share with you their *mana'o* (knowledge) and aloha (love) for the *aina* (land) they call home. 808-242-8500; e-mail: hapa@lava.net.

Guides of Maui Discover Maui in your own car with an island resident as your guide. Explore the destinations of your choice. $249 per car for up to four people, 8 hours (plus your own gas in your own car). Discounts available online. *808-298-9434; e-mail: info@guidesofmaui.com; www.guidesofmaui.com.*

Polynesian Adventure Tours Haleakala Crater & Iao Valley $62 adult/$35 child; Haleakala Sunrise $65 adult/$45 child; Hana $81 adult/$50 child. They also offer one-day trips to O'ahu to see the

Arizona or the Polynesian Cultural Center ($256). Online 10 percent discounts. *800-622-3011; 808-877-4242; www.polyad.com.*

Robert's Hawaii Tours Offers land tours in their big air-conditioned buses or vans. They depart to all scenic areas from Kahului, Kihei, Wailea and the West Maui hotels. Tours include Haleakala/Iao Valley/Lahaina ($59 adults/$42 child, ages 4-11); Heavenly Hana ($85 adult/$53.50 child); Haleakala Crater ($43 adult/$30 child); Historical Tour ($43 adult/$30 child). *800-831-5541; 808-539-9400 (dispatch); www.robertshawaii.com.*

★ ***Temptation Tours*** With a maximum of 8 passengers, this is a very comfortable way to explore Maui—and what a treat to get to travel the Hana Highway and not drive it. If you'd really like to pamper yourself, then enjoy the luxury of a tour by these folks. The Hana picnic ($149/9 to 10 hours) is a round trip in their limo van that includes a continental breakfast and a beachside picnic lunch. Working in conjunction with a local helicopter company, they provide a

SUGAR CANE TRAIN

The Lahaina Ka'anapali and Pacific Railroad is affectionately referred to as the **Sugar Cane Train**. Currently two trains operate on a three-foot narrow-gauge railroad with eight departures daily between 10:15 a.m. and 4 p.m. The trains are pulled by two steam locomotives, "Anaka" and "Myrtle." The singing conductor will guide you through history as you wind through the 6-mile route. The main depot is located just outside of Lahaina (turn at the Pizza Hut sign onto Hinau street). The Ka'anapali Station is located across the highway from the resort area. The Pu'ukoli'i boarding platform and parking lot are located on the Kapalua side of Ka'anapali. Round-trip $18.95 adults; children 3 to 12 $12.95. Reservations are necessary for groups of 12 or more. The train ride itself is not particularly exciting, but it is a unique experience and certainly is fun for young children. I suggest you make a day of it by combining the train ride with an afternoon of browsing through Lahaina, then head back to Ka'anapali on a return train. The heart of Front Street is just a few short blocks away. I also recommend the weekly Dinner Train—a fun way to combine the train ride with a *paniolo* dinner. Board the Paniolo Express Dinner Train on Thursdays at 5 p.m. for a train ride to Lahaina just in time for sunset and then back to the Ka'anapali Station in time for the dinner bell. You'll enjoy a hearty Western dinner of chicken, ribs, hot dogs, hamburgers and a salad bar, along with a little cowboy-hula entertainment. Reservations required for the Paniolo Express $76 adult, $43 children 3-12. 808-667-6851; 800-499-2307; www.sugarcanetrain.com.

unique option to Hana with the Hana Sky-Trek ($259), available mornings or afternoons with guests checking in at the Kahului Airport. You travel either to or from Hana by helicopter and do the opposite direction on a 3.5-hour limo van tour. The Summit Safari ($249/9 to 10 hours) begins with a continental breakfast in Paia and then an ascent up Haleakala in their luxury limo van to the eucalyptus forests and pastureland of the Thompson Ranch. An hour and a half to enjoy the view on horseback is followed by an elegant picnic lunch. Or choose the Haleakala Rain Forest excursion ($179/9 to 10 hours) that includes a continental breakfast in Paia and then a scenic drive to the top of Haleakala volcano. You'll descend through Hosmer's Grove, a conifer forest and then stop at a protea farm. Have lunch Upcountry before heading east to Haiku to visit rainforests and waterfalls. A drive out to Ke'anae will give you a piece of what the Hana Highway is like. The Ke'anae Peninsula is still a traditional Hawaiian farming community with a rugged shoreline and some spectacular scenery. They also offer a Haleakala Sunrise Tour ($159/7 to 8 hours) that begins with a 3 to 4 a.m. pickup. A breakfast at Kula Lodge follows your sunrise experience at the Haleakala visitor center.

Interested in spelunking? Here's what you can expect when you combine a Temptation Tours luxury motorcoach trip with one of Maui's most interesting activities. This Cave Quest tour is $184/9 to 10 hours. After an early-morning pickup, a van transports up to eight guests to Paia Plantation for a continental breakfast. Then you are off. The comfy vans have nice views and our driver was both funny and informative and easy to hear with his microphone headset. There are many opportunities to take scenic photos. One of the stops includes a flower farm where a tour is given; a small bouquet of flowers is a pleasant tour souvenir. Once in the lava cave in the Hana area, you are outfitted with a hardhat, gloves and flashlight. You'll spend a couple of hours at Ka'eleku Caverns, with a full 1.25 to 1.5 hours underground. The leisurely walk through the winding trails of the cave is safe and easy. Trails consist mostly of cinder with flat lava rocks constructing stairs over any obstructions. After the hike the group loads up again in the luxury van and drives to Hana, stopping at Wai'anapanapa Beach for a delicious picnic lunch. There is time to explore this beach and take a swim before driving through Hana town to see all the sights. Check out the Hana Cave or other luxury trips available from Temptation Tours. *800-817-1234; 808-877-8888; fax 808-876-0155; e-mail: tmptour@aloha.net; www.temptationtours.com.*

Valley Isle Excursions Tour Hana in a 12-passenger motorcoach van. The Hana picnic trip includes continental breakfast and a picnic lunch with barbecue chicken, macaroni and green salads with dinner rolls. These trips go around the island. Special surround-sound makes it accessible for the hearing impaired. Call for rates; discounts offered for seniors (over 60) and children. *877-871-5224; 808-661-8687; www.tourmaui.com.*

MAGIC SHOWS

Kupanaha: Maui Magic for All Ages Kupanaha is the Hawaiian word for "amazing" and "marvelous" and Kupanaha: Maui Magic for All Ages is just that—an evening of cutting-edge large-scale illusions and sleight-of-hand magic tricks along with legends of Hawaiian demigods illustrated through hula and chant. The sit-down, three-course meal includes a choice of appetizers: Pig in a Pareo or roasted vegetable bruschetta; choice of entree—island fish, roasted stuffed chicken breast, steak and shrimp, or vegetarian. Finish with a dessert of Piña Colada Pineapple Cheesecake or Tropical Fruit Plate. Children can choose from hamburger and cheesy fries, breaded chicken nuggets, or spaghetti with meat sauce. Enjoy complimentary beer and wine or indulge in an exotic tropical drink like a Magic Tiki Tai (a mai tai in a souvenir tiki mug) or a Flashing Mojito, a fresh blend of lime and mint with rum and club soda served with a flashing ice cube that you take home. There are also Harry Potter smoothies for the kids. When I attended this program, the food was very good and service was friendly and efficient. The show is presented by a family—magician Jody Baran, assisted by his wife Kathleen and two daughters. Jody's illusions are mind-boggling and he is a polished performer. He was a pleasure to watch. My only disappointment was with his family—his wife's skimpy, Vegas-style outfits seemed inappropriate for a family show, and his two daughters who assisted him on stage appeared to be rather bored by the whole thing. All in all, however, this is a very entertaining evening for family members of all ages. Adults $75-$85, teens (ages 13-20) $49, children (ages 6-12) $35, under age 6 complimentary. Tuesday through Saturday from 5 p.m. to 8 p.m. (check-in 4:30 p.m.). Reservations required; complimentary validated self-parking. *Ka'anapali Beach Hotel, 2525 Ka'anapali Parkway, Kanahele Room Theater; 808-661-0011, 800-262-8450.*

★ ***Warren & Annabelle's*** This is a must-see show on Maui, and I highly recommend it to all my visiting friends and family members. I took my father, who is a magician, to see the show and even he loved it. High praise, indeed. Warren (the magician) and Annabelle (the ghost) invite you into their enchanted parlor, serving up a fun, entertaining—and at times, astounding—show along with a menu of pupus and desserts. Annabelle plays the piano as if by magic, and Warren's expert sleight-of-hand baffles the audience with card, coin and telepathy tricks that you can't "see" no matter how hard you look. Annabelle's parlor is elegant and sophisticated, a perfect spot to enjoy a menu of "spirits" and gourmet appetizers like stuffed mushrooms, chicken satay, crab cakes and coconut shrimp. For the sweet tooth there is crème brulee, chocolate truffle cake, rum cake, apple pie and cheesecake. The entire experience lasts about 3.5 hours, beginning at 5 p.m. Admission is $45, with food and beverage additional; food/drink/show packages are available at $72.95-$79.95 per person. The show is offered Monday through Saturday, and you must be 21 years old or over. There is a seasonal family show during major school vacations and holidays, performed by a guest magician. Children must be at least 6 years old, and teens must be accompanied by an adult. No food or alcohol is served. Seasonal Family Show: $36 adults; $26 teens (13 to 17); $20 children 6 to 12. Reservations at Warren & Annabelle's are required, and make them well in advance as this show sells out. 900 Front Street, Lahaina; 808-667-6244; www.warrenandannabelles.com.

PARASAILING

The parasail "season" on Maui is May 16 to December 14 due to the restrictions during whale season. For those that aren't familiar with this aquatic experience, parasailing is a skyward adventure in which you are hooked to a parachute and attached to a towline behind a boat. Before you know it you are floating high in the air with a bird's-eye view of Maui. The flight lasts 8 to 10 minutes, which may be either too long or too short for some. Prices $40 and up. Some allow an "observer" (friend) to go along on the boat for an extra fee.

CAPTURE YOUR TRIP WITH A PHOTO

Many visitors to Maui enjoy having a professional photo done while they're on the island, and there are a number of photographers who specialize in photo shoots for visiting couples, families, family reunions or other groups. I have such a photo from a few years back when my three sisters visited me on Maui, and I treasure it. Here are some recommended photographers who enjoy working with visitors to capture their Maui vacation:

Shooting Stars Photography Stephen Holding, 808-875-1388, www.shootingstarsphotography.com

Seventh Wave PhotoGraphics Bruce Wheeler, 877-906-2843, 808-244-1167, www.maui-angels.com/photographics

Vacation Portraits Greg Hoxsie, 877-891-8811, 808-276-8285 or 808-891-8811, www.tropicalimage.com

UFO Parasail They use a new wrinkle, a self-contained "winch" boat. You get started standing on the boat and as your parachute fills, you are reeled out 400, 800 or 1,200 feet. When it comes time to descend, you're simply reeled back in. Standard ride is 400 feet for 7 minutes, $52 ($47 for early bird at 8 a.m.); deluxe ride is 800 feet for 10 minutes, $62 ($57 for early bird at 8 a.m.); 1,200-foot ride for 10 minutes is $72. Observers can go for $25. *Departs Whalers Village. 800-359-4836; 808-661-7836; fax 808-667-0373; e-mail: flymaui@ufoparasail.net; www.ufoparasailing.com.*

West Maui Para-sail Uses "Skyrider" harness flights. Dry take-off and landing. Boat departs every 30 minutes with six passengers. Flights generally go up 500 to 600 feet, lasting 8 to 10 minutes. The crew is helpful and patient and gives plenty of instructions. They take a roll of pictures for you that you can purchase and develop yourself. Contact them for current rates. *Depart from Lahaina Harbor, Slip #15. 808-661-4060; parasail@maui.net.*

POLO

Maui Polo dates back to the late 1890s. More than 100 years of island tradition can still be enjoyed today. The polo arena season on Maui is April, May and June and field polo season begins August 31 with games on Sunday until the first part of November. Events take place in Makawao at the polo field on Haleakala Highway #377 near the junction with Kula Highway #37. Gates open at noon, games start at 1:30 p.m. Tickets (including a BBQ and live entertainment) are $5. Weekly activities may include practice, a club game or events such as the Oski Rice Memorial Polo Cup or the Annual Rocking Kapalaia Ranch Cup. *808-877-5544 or 808-877-7744; www.mauipolo.com.*

RUNNING

Maui is a scenic delight for runners. **Valley Isle Road Runners** can provide up-to-date information on island running events. *808-871-6441.*

SCUBA DIVING

Diving the waters of Maui and Lana'i is truly exciting and spellbinding for both the experienced diver as well as for those who have always desired to explore the mysteries and wonders of a whole new world below the surface. Virtually all dive operators offer boat excursions, beach dives, instruction and certification, and rental equipment. Your scuba endeavors can be arranged through many of the resorts and hotels or directly through the many dive operators on the island.

Approximately 21 percent of all Hawaiian marine life is unique to the islands, such as the bandit angelfish, belted wrasse and the burnt murex. Humpback whales make Hawai'i their summer home from late November through April. And if you are fortunate, you may have a once-in-a-lifetime encounter with the largest fish on the planet, the whale shark. Spinner dolphins are also plentiful (and playful). An encounter with a manta ray is always thrilling, and you will most probably see the enchanting green sea turtles. In any case, Hawaiian waters showcase a spectacular variety of marine life.

Water temperatures average around 82 degrees during the summer and 72 degrees in the winter. A wetsuit is always recommended. It is much better to be warm and comfortable during your dive experience than be distracted by a chill. Average depth for most dive sites is 30 to 60 feet, while the backside of Molokini provides diving to a depth of 130 feet, which is the limit for recreational purposes. Visibility is generally very good at all sites and especially at Molokini, where the visibility can be 100 feet or greater.

Introductory dives provide the first-time diver a chance to savor the wonders of scuba. If the bug should bite or already has bitten and your time on the island is sufficient, you can take your first step and become open-water certified. Open-water courses are widely available and usually require four days. If you already are open-water certified and wish to improve you scuba skills and knowledge, an advanced open-water certification will require three days. Since your vacation time is always too limited, the most popular option to become open-water certified is through the referral program. Basically, you complete your open-water course work and pool work at home. You then arrange with a dive operator on Maui who participates in the referral program and you present your PADI paperwork upon arrival. And in two days you can be open-water certified and maximize your vacation time. Pricing for open water, advanced open water and referrals vary significantly. If cost is of concern to you, you would be well-advised to consult several dive operators and compare prices. Pricing information is generally posted on each operator's website or call directly.

Although many dive operators are listed here, this is by no means a complete list of diving services on Maui. If you so desire, you may visit the following websites for additional sources of fun and adventure: www.maui.net, www.mauigateway.com, www.padi.com.

Safety Note: Don't combine scuba diving with any high-altitude activity (like a trip to Haleakala or a helicopter ride) within 24 hours.

B & B Scuba This family-owned operation offers introductory dives for the beginning diver as well as shore and 12-passenger boat dives to sites off South Maui and Molokini. Extensive PADI instruction is available through Dive Master and specialty courses. Retail store is available for accessories and equipment rentals. *1280 South Kihei Road, Shop #129, Kihei. 808-875-2861; e-mail: bvarney333@aol.com; www.bbscuba.com.*

Boss Frog's Dive and Surf Shop Since they cater to snorkeling and other beach and surf activities, scuba is not their primary focus. However, Boss Frog's does offer charters and will accommodate snorkel, Snuba and scuba divers as a group. All scuba divers must be certified. The primary destination is Molokini with several other alternate sites on the schedule. Scuba gear is included in the price. Boss Frog's has six locations throughout Maui: *150 Lahainaluna Road, Lahaina, 808-661-3333; Napili Plaza, 808-669-4949; Kahana Manor Shops, 808-669-6700; Kihei at Dolphin Plaza, 808-875-4477; Kihei at Long's Plaza, 808-891-0077; Honokowai, 808-665-1200; www.bossfrog.com* or *www.maui.net.*

Dive & Sea Maui For those folks looking for the intimate and relaxed dive experience, the *Sundance II* is a 26-foot boat for six passengers. Viewing sea life is the prime objective at dive sites off South Maui and Molokini. Open-water and advanced open-water certifications are offered. Complete your open-water book and pool work at home and become certified with Dive & Sea Maui. *1975 South Kihei Road, Kihei. 800-526-9915; 808-874-1952; e-mail: captron@maui.net; www.diveandseamaui.com.*

Dive Maui, Inc. Offers a variety of dive sites around Maui including Molokini, Lana'i and occasionally Moloka'i. Dive instruction available for introductory dives, open water and advanced open water. Divers can chose between shore and boat excursions, and those who prefer to snorkel can join in as well. *900 Front Street, Suite J6, Lahaina. 866-821-7450; 808-667-2080; fax 808-667-2351; e-mail: info@divemauiscuba.com; www.divemauiscuba.com.*

Ed Robinson's Diving Adventures Caters to certified divers although introductory shore dives are available for beginners. More experienced divers will enjoy the diverse array of dive sites including wreck dives off Maui, Lana'i and Molokini. Open-water and advanced open-water instruction is offered. Ed deploys two dive boats, each with a capacity for 12 divers. Underwater photographers are welcome. Enjoy a night dive as well. *800-635-1273; 808-879-3584; e-mail: robinson@maui.net; www.mauiscuba.com.*

Extended Horizons Caters mainly to certified and advanced divers. Introductory dives for the beginning diver are also available either from shore or boat. Open-water certification is also available. Extended Horizons offers a large variety of dive sites around Maui and particularly off the shores of Lana'i as well as Moloka'i, weather permitting. Equipment rentals and night dives, too. The 36-foot dive boat accommodates 13 divers in two groups (6 divers per guide). *94 Kupuohi #A-1, Lahaina. 888-348-3628; 808-667-0611; e-mail: info@scubadivemaui.com; www.scubadivemaui.com.*

Happy Maui Diving & Tours Dives mostly limited to the shores of Maui; however, boat dives are available to Molokini and Lana'i. Caters to beginning divers as well as introductory dives. Night dives and rental gear, too. *840 Wainee Street, Suite 106, Lahaina. 808-669-0123; fax 808-669-7800; e-mail: mmiller@maui.net.*

Island Scuba & Surf School Perfect for both certified and novice divers to share the experience with introductory dives for the beginner. Advanced instruction is also offered. Beach dives possible at Black Rock or Turtle Reef as well as charters. Boat destinations include extensive sites off Lana'i and Molokini. Go night diving or rent a scooter. *Based in Lahaina. 888-606-4608; 808-667-4608; e-mail: islscuba@maui.net; www.scubadivingmaui.com.*

Lahaina Divers PADI 5-star dive center. Addresses the needs of experienced or advanced divers and can provide a full range of services to all levels of divers including introductory dives for the beginner and PADI open-water certification. Advanced instruction offered for Dive Master, Nitrox, Rescue Diver and Rebreather. Charter boats include the 43-foot Reliant to accommodate 22 divers and the 50-foot Endeavor to accommodate 24 divers. Dive sites include Lana'i, Molokini and locations off Maui. Underwater photographers welcome. Check website for dive packages. *143 Dickenson Street, Lahaina. 800-998-3483; 808-667-7496; e-mail: lahdiver@maui.net; www.lahainadivers.com.*

Makena Coast Dive Charters Offers adventures for the certified diver as well as introductory dives for the beginner. Dive sites are located off South Maui and Molokini. Private chartered excursions to Lana'i are also an option. Underwater photographers and cinematographers are welcome. *800-833-6483; 808-874-1273; e-mail: diving@maui.net; www.mauiunderwater.com.*

Maui Diamond II Environmentally conscious divers will be happy to learn the *Maui Diamond II* is powered by recycled vegetable oil. This 40-foot vessel will accommodate up to 15 passengers. Caters to certified divers; however, introductory dives are available for the beginner with open-water and advance open-water instruction and certification offered. Dive sites include South Maui and Molokini. Private scuba and snorkel charters to Molokini are also an option. *Departs daily from Slip #23, Ma'alaea Harbor. 866-879-9119; 808-879-9119; e-mail: mauidiamond@maui.net; www.mauiscubatours.com.*

★ **Maui Dive Shop** Two dive boat charters depart from Ma'alaea Harbor. The 45-foot Maka Koa accommodates up to 18 divers while the Ala Kai II will take up to 12 divers. Dive destinations include Molokini and Lana'i, with night dives off South Maui. Caters to certified divers; however, introductory dives are available for the beginner. My scuba diving nephews use Maui Dive Shop when they visit me on Maui, and they've been very satisfied with the staff and services. Various shop locations around the island. *800-542-3483; e-mail: info@mauidiveshop.com; www.mauidiveshop.com.*

Maui Diving Scuba Center Caters to beginning divers and is a full-service scuba center. Shore and boat dives are available. Strong emphasis on safety and personal attention. Introductory dives $49.95. Scuba certification $125. Visit their website for other dive package information. *222 Papalaua Street, Suite 112, Lahaina. 800-959-7319; 808-667-0633; e-mail: info@mauidiving.com; www.mauidiving.com.*

Maui Scuba Diving A PADI International Resort Center. Caters to beginning and novice divers. Open-water and advanced open-water certifications are offered. Dive boats depart daily from Lahaina Harbor, Ma'alaea Harbor and Kihei to sites off West Maui, Lana'i and Molokini. Visit their website for a variety of scuba packages. *877-873-4837; e-mail: info@mauiscubadiving.cc; www.mauiscubadiving.cc.*

Maui Sun Divers Caters exclusively to beginning divers and referral programs as well as those who are in need of a refresher course. *877-879-3337; 808-879-3337; e-mail: sundiver@maui.net; www.mauisundivers.com or www.maui.net.*

Mike Severns Diving Provides a unique experience for certified divers. The 38-foot dive boat *Pilikai* accommodates up to 12 divers split into two groups, with excursions to dive sites off Maui and Molokini. Caters to underwater photographers and offers a relaxed approach to the dive experience. For those folks who embrace a keen interest in marine life, you will find yourselves in good company with Mike Severns. My experienced dive friends have had very good things to say about Mike and his crew. *808-879-6596; e-mail: severns@mauigateway.com; www.mikesevernsdiving.com.*

Pacific Dive Maui PADI 5-star dive center. Full-service facility for all levels of divers and offers experienced and advanced divers many options to satisfy their needs and desires. Instruction offered for all levels. Shore and boat charters are available for access to a variety of dive sites. *150 Dickenson Street, Lahaina. 877-667-7331; 808-667-5331; e-mail: pacificdive@tiki.net; www.pacificdive.com.*

Prodiver Maui Based out of the Kihei Boat Ramp, Prodiver Maui operates a 34' Delta custom fiberglass dive boat. The boat is Coast Guard-certified for 16 passengers, but they limit excursions to only 6 divers. Bring your own gear, or they can provide what you need. For certified divers only. Boat departs at 6 a.m. and, after two dives, the boat returns to the ramp by 10:30 a.m. $129 per diver, includes diving, gear, snacks and beverages. *808-875-4004; www.pro divermaui.com.*

Scuba Gods Offers services to both certified and non-certified divers. Shore dives available off South Maui as well as boat dives to Molokini aboard a 40-foot vessel, which will accommodate 12 divers split into two groups. Introductory dives available for the beginning diver as well as beginning (PADI) and advanced instruction up to Dive Master and specialty courses. *2130 South Kihei Road, Kihei. 866-224-4159; 808-879-3066; e-mail: thescubagod@hotmail.com; www.scuba gods.com.*

Scuba Shack Certified divers as well as new divers will enjoy the services of Scuba Shack. Dive sites include locations around Maui and Molokini. Dive instruction available up to Dive Master, and specialty courses are offered as well as referral programs. Their 40-foot dive boat will accommodate 12 divers split into two groups. Snorkel enthusiasts are invited as well so that divers and non-divers can enjoy the experience together. Scuba Shack also offers programs especially for kids 5 and up. Underwater photographers welcome. Scuba Shack has been highly ranked in recent years in Reader's Choice polls in *Scuba Diving Magazine.* 2349 South Kihei Road, Kihei. *877-213-4488; 808-879-DIVE; e-mail: wetanku@maui.net; www.scubashack.com.*

Trilogy With an impressive fleet of catamarans, Trilogy offers snorkel and scuba excursions to Lana'i, Molokini and sites off West and South Maui. Caters to certified divers and offers introductory dives for the beginner. Beach dives are also provided. Open-water and advanced open-water instruction is also available. A good company for the family interested in learning to dive. They have lots of experience with introductory divers. Introductory scuba $59, certified one-tank scuba dive $49, two-tank Lana'i dive $139. *Excursions depart Lahaina and Ma'alaea harbors. 888-628-4800; 808-874-5649; e-mail: info@sailtrilogy.com; www.sailtrilogy.com.*

Tropical Divers Caters primarily to beginning and novice divers with introductory dives and certification instruction. More experienced divers will benefit as well with charter boats to the back wall of Molokini and Lana'i. Specialty instruction is also available such as night diving, multilevel diving, underwater photography, nitrox and others. *800-994-6284; 808-667-5309; 808-669-6284; e-mail: getwet@scubamaui.com; www.scubamaui.com.*

SEA EXCURSIONS, SAILING (*See also* Cruises; Snorkeling)

Maui offers a bounty of choices for those desiring to spend some time in and on the ocean. Boats available for sea expeditions range from spacious trimarans and large motor yachts to a submarine or the zodiac-type rafts for the more adventurous. Or, if you prefer, there are small boat rentals (Hobie Cats) available at many of the beachside cabanas at major resorts. Excursion boats seem to have a way of sailing off into the sunset. The number of new ones is as startling as the number of operations that have disappeared since the last edition of this book.

You can choose a large-group trip or a more pampered small-group excursion with a maximum of six people. Two of the most popular snorkeling excursions are to Molokini and Lana'i. Competition to Molokini has become fierce; 20 to 30 boats a day now arrive to snorkel in this area. Many more boats now take trips to Lana'i as well. Most sailboats motor to these islands and, depending on wind conditions, sail at least part of the return trip. All provide snorkel equipment. One of the nicest amenities on a number of boats is the option of a freshwater shower. Some of them even solar-heat their water, which provides a refreshing rinse-off after your saltwater snorkel/swim. Food and beverage service varies and is reflected in the price. Many sailboats are available for hourly, full-day or longer private charters. *Note:* Due to weather conditions, your trip to Molokini may, at the last minute, be altered to another location, usually along the southern shore of Maui.

Most of the major companies offer seasonal whale-watching tours (December through April), and some are now promoting dolphin-watching trips as well.

In the following list, phone numbers of the excursion companies are included; however, most activity desks can also book your reservation. Unless you have a lot of extra time, avoid the timeshare offers; you may get a discount on an activity, but you'll end up spending at least a portion of a day hearing their sales pitch. The best deal with an activity operator is **Tom Barefoot's Cashback Tours**, who can book most boats (as well as other island activities) and offers a 10 percent refund (with no timeshare involvement). *Located in Lahaina at 834 Front Street and in Kihei at 2395 South Kihei Road. 888-222-3601; 808-661-8889; www.maui.net/~barefoot.*

America II This unique sailing vessel was built to compete in the 1987 America's Cup races in Fremantle, Australia; *America II* was skippered by John Kollius but lost to Dennis Connor of the *Stars & Stripes.* Enjoy a snorkeling and sailing experience on this 65-foot

(12-meter) class yacht. Morning and afternoon sails as well as sunset sails are $40 for adults, children (12 and under) half-price. Two-hour seasonal whale watching, too. Excursions include soda, juice, water and snacks. Private charter is also available at $500 for the first two hours, $100 for each additional half-hour. *Departs Lahaina Harbor. 888-667-2133; 808-667-2195; www.galaxymall.com/stores/americaII.*

Atlantis (Submarine) The *Atlantis* submarine tours the underwater world beyond Lahaina Harbor. The total excursion time is 1 hour 50 minutes, with the underwater submarine portion lasting about 45 minutes. Child rates apply to kids 12 and younger, but they must be at least 36 inches tall to ride aboard *Atlantis*. The *Atlantis* adventure includes an ocean cruise out to the dive site (with whale watching in season) and complimentary beverages. The dive descends to a depth of 120 feet. The fully submersible submarine is an 80-ton, 65-foot touring vessel that accommodates 48 passengers.

MOLOKINI

Molokini is a distinctive landmark off the South Maui coastline and one of the most popular sea excursion destinations. It is located 8 miles off the Ma'alaea Harbor and most of the tours depart from that port. Most trips are taken in the morning. There are some afternoon trips, but expect rougher ocean conditions. On occasion even the morning trips are forced to snorkel at an alternative site, usually La Perouse or another spot off the South Maui coastline.

The remnant of a 10,000-year-old dormant volcano reveals only one crescent-shaped portion of the crater rim and serves as a sanctuary for marine and bird life. The inside of the crater offers a water depth of 10 to 50 feet; a 76-degree temperature and visibility sometimes as much as 150 feet on the outer perimeter creates a fish bowl effect. According to legend, the atoll of Molokini was created as the result of a jealous rage. Pele had a dream lover, Lohiau, who lived in Ma'alaea, located north of Makena. Lohiau married a *mo'o* (lizard) and Pele was so angry she bisected the lizard. The head became Molokini islet and the tail became Pu'u Ola'i, the rounded hill at the end of Makena.

Molokini has had some turbulent years. Long before tourist boats frequented this sight, it was used by the Navy as a bombing target. Obviously, the aquatic life and the reef system were decimated. The many tour boats dropping anchors further damaged and destroyed the reef. Fortunately, concerned boat operators were granted semi-permanent concrete mooring anchors, thereby preventing further reef damage. Today, Molokini is a marine sanctuary and one of the most popular and beautiful snorkeling sites in the state of Hawai'i.

They operate six dives daily, beginning at 9 a.m. from Lahaina Harbor. There is a short boat ride to reach the submarine, and it's fun to watch it suddenly emerge out of the depths of the Pacific. Then you step across from the tender and load onto the submarine. The seats are lined up on both sides in front of half a porthole. The area is a little close, but the temperature is kept cool and comfortable. There are plenty of fish, and fish cards at each station help you identify them. Rocks and coral formations create an environ that is somehow extraterrestrial. Much of what you see could also be seen snorkeling, but the submarine ride is a novelty and a great alternative for non-snorkelers. $79.99 adults, $42 children. Inquire about their combination packages that include the submarine trip combined with a helicopter tour, lu'au, Maui Tropical Plantation tour, admission to Maui Ocean Center and/or Sugar Cane Train ride. *808-667-2224; 800-548-6262; www.atlantisadventures.com.*

Blue Water Rafting These folks were among the first to initiate ocean rafting on Maui back in 1985. They operate a 6-passenger, 19' *Norvuania* and two 24-passenger high-powered rigid-hulled inflatables. This is for those die-hard snorkelers who enjoy an early-bird arrival to the crater to explore up to three different sites. It isn't always a gentle trip, so definitely for the adventurer. Trip includes a lunch and beverages. Snorkel Molokini or the Kanaio Coast, where you can explore caves and lava arches. Snorkeling tours range from $45 to $110 for adults and $39 to $95 for children. Two-and-a-half-hour seasonal whale watching is also offered. Also inquire about private charters. *Trips depart Kihei Boat Ramp. 808-879-7238; www.bluewaterrafting.com.*

Captain Steve's Take a trip aboard their rigid-hull raft to do some snorkeling and see whales and dolphins. One of the last owner-operated companies, Captain Steve really is your captain. He's been doing it for nearly 20 years and offers a variety of snorkel outings including a 6-hour winter and summer snorkel trip to Lana'i; $150 adults, $95 children 12 and under. Two-hour seasonal whale watching is also offered at $45 adults, $35 kids 12 and under. Online discounts are available. Maximum 20 passengers aboard his 32-foot, high-tech raft. *Departs Mala Wharf. 808-667-5565; www.captainsteves.com.*

Dive Maui Visit Lana'i or Molokini and enjoy a snorkel or scuba excursion with the folks of Dive Maui. Dive Maui primarily caters to scuba divers and offers snorkel adventures along the way. Dive Maui can also arrange packages such as whale watching, snorkeling and lu'au or dinner cruises. *866-821-7450; 808-667-2080; www.divemauiscuba.com.*

Expeditions Ferry service from Lahaina to Lana'i five times daily (currently 6:45 a.m., 9:15 a.m., 12:45 p.m., 3:15 p.m., 5:45

p.m.) and equal returns from Manele Bay (8 a.m., 10:30 a.m., 2 p.m., 4:30 p.m., 6:45 p.m.); $50 round-trip adult, $40 child. If you'd like to explore Lana'i on your own, you can take the early-morning ferryboat over and return on the late-afternoon trip. From the dock it is a moderate but easy walk to Manele Bay and the adjacent Manele Bay Resort. Once you arrive on Lana'i there is a shuttle that runs between the dock and the two resorts that charges $15 round-trip to Manele Bay and $25 round-trip to the Lodge at Koele. Expeditions can combine your boat trip with golf, a round of play at Lana'i Pines (a sporting clay course), or a night at Manele Bay Hotel or Lodge at Koele. *800-695-2624; 808-661-3756; www.go-lanai.com.*

Friendly Charters Friendly Charters has been operating on Maui since 1983. Your trip will be aboard the *Lani Kai*, a 53-foot double-deck catamaran that was launched in 1997. Two heads, two freshwater showers, water slide, snorkel staircase and trampoline. Protected cabin area. Continental breakfast and deli lunch. Morning and afternoon Snorkel Molokini tours starting at $40. Underwater cameras and Snuba are optional. Book online and save 20 percent. *888-983-8080; 808-244-1979; www.mauisnorkeling.com.*

Frogman Charters Frogman has been in operation since 1986 and offers snorkel and scuba adventures plus seasonal whale watching on their 55-foot sailing catamaran, *Frogman*. They depart Ma'alaea Harbor each morning at 6:30 a.m. Frogman morning Molokini/Turtle Town snorkel cruise is $79.95 adults/$49.95 kids (ages 4 to 12). Online discounts are available. *Six locations around the island. 888-700-3764; 808-662-0075; www.bossfrog.com.*

Gemini Charters The *Gemini* is a 64-foot catamaran with glass-bottom view ports that departs daily from Ka'anapali Beach in front of the Westin Maui. Year-round picnic snorkel sails (4 ½ hours) provide snorkel equipment including prescription masks, flotation devices, snorkel instruction, a freshwater shower and a hot buffet lunch. The picnic/snorkel cruise is $90 for adults, $70 teens (13 to 19) and $50 children 2 to 12. Enjoy the two-hour Champagne Sunset Sail with champagne, beer, wine, mai tais and non-alcoholic beverages; $55 adults, $45 teens and $35 kids 2 to 12. Seasonal morning and afternoon whale watching with a marine naturalist on board and an underwater hydrophone to listen to the whales singing. Private charters are available for groups, weddings or special occasions. *800-820-7245; 808-669-0508; www.geminicharters.com.*

Hawaii Ocean Rafting This family-owned and -operated business takes 14 passengers aboard their raft for half-day snorkeling adventures ($69.95 adults, $49.95 children) or a full-day Lana'i trip ($109.95 adults, $79.95 children). Online discounts available. Full-day trip includes continental breakfast and deli lunch. Half-day tour visits three snorkel sites and includes continental breakfast. Private whale watching charters are also available. *808-661-7238; www.hawaiioceanrafting.com.*

Action Adventure Tours (previously known as Hawaiian Rafting Adventures) In their RAIV (Rigid Aluminum Inflatable Vessels) you can enjoy a five-hour raft/snorkel adventure, including a continental breakfast and lunch; $85. Whale-watching excursions are offered in season, as well as other rafting, ocean kayaking, and scuba outings. Check out their website for the latest tours and special online booking discounts. Departs from Lahaina. *808-874-8883; 866-529-2544; www.hawaiianrafting.com.*

Island Marine Institute Depart from Lahaina Harbor, slip #3, aboard the *Lahaina Princess* for Molokini and Turtle Reef snorkel excursions; $79 for adults; one child (12 and under) is free when accompanied by an adult. $49 for additional children. The 65-foot touring yacht takes up to 149 passengers. Includes continental breakfast, buffet deli lunch with barbecue chicken. This is the only vessel that has a 15-foot "water trampoline" that deploys on the water for you to jump on, jump from or just lie around on. The *Maui Princess*, a 150-passenger 118-foot touring yacht, offers fine-dining cruises with stunning views of the island sunsets. The menu includes roasted chicken or prime rib, salads, vegetable *du jour,* breads, desserts and beverages of your choice. Departs at 5:30 p.m. and returns at 8 p.m.; $79 for adults and $59 for kids 12 and under. The *Moloka'i Princess* offers one-day package excursions to the island of Moloka'i as well as one-way ferry passage to the island, seven days a week. The 100-foot interisland yacht is state-of-the-art and will take you there in style. Look for whales along the way. Call or check the website for departure times and current rates. These vessels are also available for private charters. Seasonal whale watching is available on all their vessels as well. Save by booking online; AAA members receive a 15 percent discount. *800-275-6969; 808-667-6165; www.mauiprincess.com.*

Island Star Offers custom charters only. Choose from a variety of tours ranging from a two-hour sunset sail to a week of sailing around the islands aboard the 57-foot *Island Star.* Master stateroom with deluxe king bed, forward cabin with four berths and a private port cabin. Two heads, plus hot and cold water pressure are amenities. Your crew includes a scuba instructor, marine naturalist and chef. USCG certified for 28 passengers but will comfortably sleep 10. Ask about snorkeling and whale-watching tours on their ocean-going rafts or private sightseeing on a sleek, high-speed Scarab. *888-677-7238; 808-669-7827; www.islandstarsailing.com.*

Kapalua Kai Their 53-foot wing-mast, 49-passenger catamaran offers plenty of shaded area in their open-air salon embellished in teak and state-of-the-art sound system. Four-hour picnic/snorkel trip includes equipment and a buffet lunch. Departs 10 a.m. Adults $90, children 2 to 12 $60. The Sunset Sail offers finger sandwiches, veggie platter and fresh fruit platter with sails hoisted through the sunset. $55 adults, $40 children. Departure times vary depending upon the time of year, between 4 and 5 p.m. Both tours have a premium bar and the food is about the best you'll find. Private charters are also available upon request with a two-hour minimum. *They operate out of Whalers Village in Ka'anapali. 808-665-0344; 808-667-5980; www.sailingmaui.com.*

Kiele V A 55-foot catamaran that departs from the beach at the Hyatt Regency, Ka'anapali. Snorkel excursions daily, 10 a.m. to 2 p.m., $85 for adults, $70 for teens and $50 for children under 12. Seasonal whale watching is offered from 3:30 p.m. to 5:30 p.m., $55 for adults, $45 for teens and $35 for children under 12. *808-667-4727.*

Lahaina Honu This is certainly one of the most unusual "vessels" on the island. The bright yellow amphibious vehicle takes passengers on a land tour, then drives into the ocean for a sea tour. Tours depart daily from Lahaina Harbor. About 90 minutes long. Adults $30; $15 children under 16. *808-662-4668; www.lahainahonu.com.*

***Lahaina Princess**—See* Island Marine Institute.

Makena Boat Partners *Kai Kanani*, 46-foot catamaran, departs from the beach fronting the Maui Prince Hotel. Early morning Sunrise Express trip (2 hours) starts at $44. Four-hour Molokini picnic/snorkel cruise is also offered, as well as seasonal whale watching. Children 14 and under are half-price; one per paying adult. *808-879-7218; www.kaikanani.com.*

Maui Classic Charters The *Four Winds* departs daily from Ma'alaea to Molokini with a maximum of 112 passengers. *Four Winds II* is a 55-foot glass-bottom catamaran that offers a morning half-day snorkel sail, $84 for adults, $49 for children 3 to 12. Breakfast is a varied selection of fresh bagels and cream cheese with jellies and fresh pineapple and orange slices and barbecue lunch. An afternoon snorkel cruise, departing at 1:30 p.m., is offered at $42 for adults and $29.95 for children. Beer, wine and soda included as well. Freshwater showers and an on-board waterslide add to the day's fun. There are two decks, one covered and one uncovered, and those of you who prefer to stay dry can sample the scenic underwater delights through their submarine-style glass-bottom hull. An optional activity is Snuba ($45 extra), which takes six people at a time with air tanks carried on rafts that float at the surface, as well as underwater video and cameras. Snorkel excursions are also available on the 54' catamaran, *Maui Magic*, departing at 7 a.m. Seasonal whale watching is also offered, starting at $44 for adults, discounts for children. Online advance booking discounts are available. *800-736-5740; 808-879-8188; www.mauicharters.com.*

Maui Dive Shop Besides selling scuba and snorkel gear, they also offer boating activities and combination packages (snorkeling with other island activities). Three-hour Molokini/Turtle Town snorkel tour is $44 per person, $39 for children 4 to 12. Many other snorkel and scuba tours are offered. Combination tours include "Fire & Water"—Lu'au and Molokini snorkel cruise, $99; "Sun to Sea"—Bike downhill and a Molokini snorkel cruise, $139; "Inside & Out"—Snorkel Molokini and visit the Maui Ocean Center, $54; "Above & Below"—A Molokini snorkel trip and a 45-minute helicopter trip, $194; "Night & Day"—A Molokini snorkel and dinner and dancing on the Maui Princess, $109. Stop by and pick up a copy of their free dive guide. *They have a number of shops around the island: 800-542-3483 e-mail: info@mauidiveshop.com; www.mauidiveshop.com.*

Maui-Moloka'i Sea Cruises The *Prince Kuhio* is a 92-foot motor yacht. Whale watching, private charters, and a half-day snorkel tour to Molokini/Turtle Town, departs Ma'alaea at 7 a.m.. This boat has the benefits of a larger vessel with more comforts, but with a bigger capacity there are a lot more people. Molokini snorkel rates are $85.99 for adults, $65 for teens (13 to 18) and $52 for children 12 and under. Children under 5 sail free. Their snorkel trips include continental breakfast, deli lunch and beverages. You and your family can also enjoy Snuba with this company. Seasonal whale watching departs daily with a field naturalist onboard. *800-468-1287; 808-242-8777; www.mvprince.com.*

Maui Princess—*See* Island Marine.

Moloka'i Princess—*See* Island Marine.

Ocean Activities Center Departures from Ma'alaea aboard the 37-foot Tolleycraft *No Ka Oi III* for deep-sea sport fishing. Sail aboard the 65-foot catamaran *Wailea Kai* or power cat *Maka Kai* for Molokini picnic snorkel (sportfishing also available on the *Maka Kai*) or a sunset cruise. *808-879-4485; 800-798-0652; www.mauioceanactivities.com.*

Ocean Riders "Adventure rafting" on one of their rigid-hull, 28' inflatable rafts with a maximum capacity of 18. They feature unusual full-day snorkel and dive destinations (depending on daily weather conditions). Reefs of Kaho'olawe, Moloka'i's cliffs or Lana'i. Seasonal whale watching. Continental breakfast included and snacks throughout the day. Check in at 6:30 a.m. *Departs Mala Wharf in Lahaina. 800-221-3586; 808-661-3586; e-mail: oriders@maui.net; www.maui.net/~oriders.*

Pacific Whale Foundation Cruises A variety of adventures await you aboard their 54-foot power catamaran *Ocean Explorer* or their graceful 50-foot sailing catamaran *Manute'a*, both departing out of Lahaina Harbor. Its fleet at Ma'alaea Harbor includes the *Ocean Odyssey*, a state-of-the-art 149-passenger power catamaran with all of the luxurious amenities, as well as the 65-foot *Ocean Spirit*, which can accommodate a manifest of 142 passengers. Whale watching December 1–May 15 with prices varying, they offer special kid and family rates. The Molokini and Turtle Arches excursion (7 a.m. to noon) departs Ma'alaea, $79.95 for adults, kids six and under free with each paying adult. Kids 7-12 are $29.95. They also offer an Oceanic Dolphin and Snorkel Eco-Adventure, 8:30 a.m. to 1 p.m. Cost is $79.95 for adults, $29.95 for kids 7 to 12, under 6 free. Their Lana'i Wild Dolphin and Snorkel Eco-Adventure aboard the *Manute'a* is $74.95 for adults, $29.95 for kids 7 to 12, kids under 6 free. Book online for a 10 percent discount. Portion of proceeds from tours benefit aquatic wildlife. *800-942-5311; 808-249-8811; www.pacificwhale.org.*

Paragon Sailing Charters They have two 47-foot catamarans, *Paragon I* and *II*, built in California with state-of-the-art rotating carbon fiber masts. The Cabin House offers shade and shelter, and trampolines offer outside lounging. Their five-hour Molokini Sail & Snorkel departs from Ma'alaea Harbor, offering a morning snorkel-sail that begins with a 7:30 a.m. departure and a continental breakfast as you head toward Molokini. Snorkel gear is provided and they have small-size gear for children. A fresh hot/cold-water shower is located on top of the swim ladder for after your swim and before a buffet lunch with refreshments. Maximum of 49 passengers. $85 for adults, children 12 and under half price. Children three and under sail free. Their afternoon 3-hour Speed Sail & Snorkel Coral Gardens trip includes snorkeling followed by a speed run back; $51 for adults, children under 12 half price. Trip includes appetizers and beverages. Depart aboard their second vessel from the Lahaina Harbor at 8:30 a.m. for an all-day Lana'i trip that includes a deluxe continental breakfast. Unloading is done at Manele Bay on Lana'i and guests are provided with snorkel gear, picnic baskets, beach mats and umbrellas for 2.5 hours of dining and ocean fun before reboarding the boat. En route back, while catching the afternoon tradewinds, they serve desserts, champagne and have an open bar. Halfway back, the captain stops for a deep-water swim before returning to the Lahaina Harbor at 4 p.m. Cost is $149 adults, $99 children. Limited to 24 passengers per trip. Their Sunset Sail trip departs Lahaina at 5 p.m. with an open bar and appetizers. The vessel is licensed for 49 passengers, but they take a maximum of 24. $51 for adults, $34 age 12 and under. Save 15 percent by booking online. *800-441-2087; 808-244-2087; fax 808-878-3933; www.sailmaui.com.*

The Pride of Maui A 65-foot Maxi catamaran featuring a spacious indoor sundeck, barbecue grills, hot showers, water slide, glass-bottom view port and handicap access. Daily departures begin at 8 a.m. from the Ma'alaea Harbor. Their morning trip includes a continental breakfast and a hot barbecue lunch with beer and mai tais. This trip includes a 5-hour cruise to Molokini and Turtle Town (Pu'u Ola'i). Depending on weather conditions, other snorkel locations may be Olowalu or Coral Gardens. The afternoon cruise offers snacks and beverages (mai tais and beer at an additional cost) and an optional lunch. This trip lasts three hours and goes to two snorkel sites (Molokini if weather permits). Whale watching offered seasonally aboard their 45-foot monohull luxury yacht, *The Leilana.* Underwater video cameras are also available for rent. The boat accommodates up to 149 passengers but the crew intentionally limits the number of passengers to ensure a quality experience. Morning snorkel $86 adults, $53 children age 3-12. Afternoon snorkel $35 adults, $27 children. (Note: The afternoon sails, on any excursion, can be a rougher and windier trip.) *877-867-7433; 808-242-0955; www.prideofmaui.com.*

Rainbow Chaser Given the name the *Honeymoon Boat*, this is for adults only or for private family charter. There is a maximum of six passengers, sharing three private staterooms, for this all-day Lana'i excursion featuring fine cuisine for breakfast, lunch and dessert. Relax, snorkel or enjoy a blue-water swim. *Departs from Lahaina. 800-667-2270; 808-667-2270; www.rainbowchasermaui.com.*

Reef Dancer For a truly unique viewing experience of Maui's mystical underwater world, board the exclusive *Reef Dancer*. Get close and personal with Hawai'i's unique marine life. This is a semi-submersible, meaning it only partially submerges, so anytime you feel a bit claustrophobic, you can go up on top for some fresh air. The glass-paneled hull allows viewing on both port and starboard sides so you don't miss any of the action. The bottom is six feet below the surface and they cruise around the ocean floor off of Puamana. *Reef Dancer* scuba divers will be in the water to bring the most interesting sea creatures right up to your window while the adventure is videotaped. Be sure to bring your camera as well; 400 ASA films works best. *Reef Dancer* departs five times daily from Lahaina Harbor and has a maximum capacity of 34. The one-hour trip runs $32.95 for adults, $18.95 for children 6 to 12 years, free for 5 and under. Their 90-minute tour includes a second turtle site, $44.95 adults, $24.95 children. If you have enjoyed snorkeling on Maui, you won't see much more through the viewing windows. But if you are unable or unwilling to get wet, this is a trip worth considering. *888-667-2133; 808-667-2133; www.galaxymall.com/stores/reefdancer.*

Scotch Mist Charters *Scotch Mist II* is a Santa Cruz 50-foot sailboat that took first place in the 1984 Victoria-Maui International. Take an afternoon "Fast is Fun" sail along the West Maui coast from May to December; $35 for adults, $17.50 for kids 5 to 12. Or enjoy a 4-hour sail and snorkel excursion to the best sites along the coast. Gear, snacks and beverage provided. Available May through December and departs 8 a.m.; adults $60, kids 5 to 12 $30. Savor a two-hour champagne and chocolate sunset sail year-round; $40 adults, $20 kids 5 to 12. Sorry, no children under five permitted on this cruise. Seasonal whale-watching excursions are offered four times daily starting at $35 for adults and $12.50 for kids. Private charters are also available. *Departs Slip #2 at Lahaina Harbor. 808-661-0386; fax 808-667-2113; www.scotchmistsailingcharters.com.*

Sea Escape Boat Rentals Rent a boat for your own excursion. They offer two 26-foot Shamrocks or a 21-foot Bayliner Trophy. Shamrock rents for $550 for up to five hours; Bayliner Trophy rents for $375 for up to four hours. Additional hours available at a reduced fee. *808-879-3721; www.maui-boat-rental.com.*

Shangri-La This sleek, high-performance, custom 65-foot catamaran offers private charters by the hour only. The vessel was custom built by owner/operators Peter Wood and Inca Robbin with a dream of yacht retirement and the South Pacific in mind. The vessel

TRILOGY: A BEST BET

The Coon family knows better than to mess with a good thing. The morning boat trip over to Lana'i still starts earlier than most would like, but once underway with warm (yes, still homemade by the Coons) cinnamon rolls and a mug (the ceramic kind, no Styrofoam here!) of hot chocolate or coffee, it seems all worth the effort. Don't forget to bring the camera. Trilogy boats now take guests Monday through Friday for snorkeling, sun and fun at Manele Bay. (On Saturdays, snorkeling is off the boat, not at the beach.) Beginning snorkelers are carefully instructed before entering the ocean. And they also have an eco-enrichment summer camp program for kids. If you would prefer, you can skip the tour of Lana'i City and snorkel even longer (but only on weekday trips). The chicken is cooked on the grill by the ship's captain and served on china-type plates, accompanied by a delicious stir-fry, fresh rolls and salad. The eating area has a series of picnic tables and is pleasantly shaded by an awning. 808-874-5649; 888-628-4800; www.sailtrilogy.com.

is tastefully decorated and spacious, with guest comfort in mind. Day charters are available for $1,000 per hour with space for 49 guests. Specialty cruises include wine-tasting dinners, candlelight dinners, weddings, eco tours and scuba diving. Price includes a USCG-certified captain and crew. Catering from the Hula Grill Restaurant, open bar, along with snorkeling and flotation equipment available. Extended charters are available for a maximum of six guests. On-board gourmet chef and meals, hostess, kayaks, snacks, fuel and bar are provided according to your desires and added to the final billing. *Depart from Lahaina. 888-855-9977; 808-665-0077; www.sailingmaui.com.*

Teralani They offer snorkel, sunset and whale-watching excursions aboard their two catamarans, *Teralani I* and *Teralani II*. The Premier Snorkel Sail & BBQ is $115 for adults, $89 for teens and $69 for children. The dinner sunset whale-watching cruise is $75 for adults, $65 for teens and $55 for children. Late morning snorkel/sail is $89 for adults, $79 for teens and $59 for children. Whale-watching excursions offered seasonally. The *Teralani I* and *II* board passengers from the beaches of the Sheraton Maui and Royal Lahaina as well as Dig Me Beach in Ka'anapali. Private charters are also available. *808-661-0365; fax 808-661-0448; www.teralani.net.*

Trilogy Trilogy's impressive fleet includes the *Trilogy I*, 64-foot cutter-rigged catamaran with maximum capacity of 55 passengers; *Trilogy II*, 55-foot sloop-rigged catamaran, maximum of 44 passengers; *Trilogy III*, 51-foot sloop-rigged with a maximum of 36 passengers; *Trilogy IV*, a 50-foot sloop-rigged with a maximum of 49; *Trilogy V* and *VI* are 54-foot. The *Manele Kai* is a 32-foot rigid aluminum, high-speed, inflatable zodiac. Children ages 3 to 15 are half-price off adult fare on all tours. There are numerous tour options.

Their Discover Lana'i excursion is offered Monday through Friday and begins at 6:15 a.m., when you'll meet a Trilogy First Mate at the Trilogy parking lot on Dickenson Street. Enjoy hot chocolate, coffee, fresh fruit and those very special homemade cinnamon rolls en route. Trilogy arrives at Manele Harbor on Lana'i by 8:30 a.m., which leaves plenty of time for a guided van tour of Lana'i City, snorkeling and scuba at Hulopo'e Bay Marine Sanctuary before a hot barbecue lunch at their private picnic area. The afternoon affords another opportunity to snorkel and swim or the option of a guided tour of Lana'i City. It is approximately 2 p.m. when you depart Manele Harbor, arriving at Lahaina Harbor between 3:30 and 4 p.m. Discover Lana'i Sail and Discover Lana'i Sunset are each $179, discounts for children. Scuba is an additional fee. Discover Lana'i with Kayaking, $239.

On Saturday their Ultimate Adventure in Paradise differs in that you snorkel from the vessel off the coast of Lana'i and enjoy a "Jeep Safari" of the island. They also offer Lana'i Overnight packages Monday through Friday with a stay at the Manele Bay Hotel or Lodge at Koele. Cost is $239. Discover Molokini Sunrise Sail is aboard *Trilogy V.* Breakfast is the same as on the Lana'i excursion; lunch consists of hot barbecue teriyaki chicken, green salad, corn on the cob and dinner rolls. Vegetarian selection also available. Price is $110 for adults.

Board on Ka'anapali Beach for a *pupu* and sunset sail. This is an outstanding opportunity to see the beautiful coastline of Maui from the ocean. Beer, wine and soft drinks are available as well as a very impressive selection of appetizers including flank steak grilled up for you by the captain. So leave the kids at the condo and enjoy a special evening. The sunset sails are a far better value than a dinner cruise and the *pupus* on this trip were hearty. Deluxe Ka'anapali Sunset Sail, $59.

The Trilogy Ka'anapali Snorkel Sail meets in front of Ka'anapali Beach Hotel for beach loading aboard the *Trilogy IV* at 8:45 a.m.—a good choice for those of you who aren't early risers. Their continental breakfast is followed by snorkeling at Honolua Bay (weather permitting) and a second site of the Captain's choice. Lunch fare is the same as above and you'll arrive back at Ka'anapali Beach at 2:30 p.m. Ka'anapali Snorkel Sail, $110.

A summer program for kids, Camp Trilogy offers an eco-enrichment opportunity for the whole family between June through August, as well as during major holidays. The program begins with a snorkel lesson with Camp Trilogy's counselors and then a guided reef tour. Organized beach games and activities teach team-building skills as well as respect for the environment. Camp Trilogy kids receive special T-shirts, eco-coloring books and their own barbecue. Cost is $152.71 ($63 per child in addition to the regular fare of $89.71). *180 Lahainaluna Road, P.O. Box 1119, Lahaina, HI 96767-1119. 888-628-4800; 808-874-5649; fax 808-667-7766; www.sailtrilogy.com.*

Ultimate Rafting Departs Lahaina Harbor, slip #17, aboard their rigid "V" hull high-speed inflatable with awning for shade and swim ladder for easy ocean entry. All tours are catered with local fruit, sweet breads, fresh vegetables and dips and a deli-style lunch. Half- and full-day trips to Lana'i (April–November) are offered with wildlife viewing (including seasonal whale watching) tours (December–April). Four-hour Lana'i snorkel trips are $99 for adults, $49 for kids 6 to 12. A two-hour sunset and seasonal whale-watching tour is $35 adults, $19

UNDERWATER PHOTOGRAPHY

You may feel the urge to rent an underwater camera to photograph some of the unusual and beautiful fish you've seen. By all means try it, but remember, underwater fish photography is a real art. The disposable underwater cameras are fun and inexpensive and available everywhere, but your resulting photos may be disappointing. There are several videotapes of Maui's marine life available at the island bookstores if you want a permanent record of the fish you've seen. Several of the sea excursions offer video camera rentals.

kids. Check their website for specials and other tours. *808-667-5678; fax 808-667-7611; www.ultimatewhalewatch.com.*

SNORKELING (*See also* Scuba Diving; Sea Excursions, Sailing)

The coastlines of Maui offer exceptionally clear waters, warm ocean temperatures and abundant sea life with safe areas (no adverse water conditions) for snorkeling. If you are a complete novice, most of the resorts and excursion boats offer snorkeling lessons. From the youngest to the oldest, everyone can enjoy this sport. It requires little experience and no diving underwater to see all the splendors of the sea. If you are unsure of your snorkeling abilities, the use of a flotation device may be of assistance. Be forewarned that the combination of tropical sun and the refreshing coolness of the ocean can deceive those snorkeling blissfully on the surface and result in a badly burned backside. Water-resistant sunscreens are available locally and are recommended.

All snorkeling boat trips provide equipment as a part of their package. Some offer prescription masks. It is convenient but expensive to rent snorkel (and any other) equipment at the beachside activity booths. You can get gear at a dive shop for a week or pay the same for a one-day beachside rental. Rental prices at the shops are very competitive, running about $2.50 per day and as little as $10 a week. Children's equipment is less at $1.49. Prescription masks will be slightly higher. If you plan on doing a lot of snorkeling, the purchase of your own equipment should be considered. Good quality gear is available at all the dive shops. Less expensive sets can be purchased at Longs or Costco. Most major dive shops can fit you with a prescription mask, as long as your vision impairment is not too severe. As a contact wearer with a strong prescription, I wear my soft lenses and have no problem with a good-fitting mask. Most dive shops rent snorkel equipment. Here are a just a few options.

Mask-Fins-Snorkel Rentals

Auntie Snorkel in Kihei (Rainbow Mall); 808-879-6263

Maui Dive Shop at Kamaole Shopping Center, Lahaina Cannery Mall, Honokowai Market Place, Whalers Village and Harbor Shops at Ma'alaea; 808-661-5388 is their Lahaina shop

Snorkel Bob's in Kihei 808-875-6188 and 808-879-7449; Lahaina 808-661-4421, Napili 808-669-9603; www.snorkelbob.com

Snorkel's -n- More in Lahaina 808-665-0804

Snorkeling Spots

Good snorkeling spots, if not right in front of your hotel or condo, are only a few minutes' drive away. Generally, the best snorkeling at all locations is in the morning until about 1 p.m., before the wind picks up. For more information on each area and other locations, see Chapter 5. The following are my favorites, each for a special reason.

'Ahihi-Kina'u Natural Reserve Approximately five miles past Wailea. No facilities. This is not a very crowded spot and you may feel a little alone here, but the snorkeling is great with lots of coral and a good variety of fish.

Black Rock Fronting the Sheraton Maui Resort in the Ka'anapali Resort area. Pay for parking at Whalers Village and walk down the beach. Clear water and a variety of tame fish that expect handouts. My niece was lucky enough to see manta rays when she was snorkeling here.

Honolua Bay No facilities, park alongside the road and walk a .25 mile to the bay. A Marine Life Conservation area, this is possibly the best snorkeling on Maui, anytime but winter.

Kapalua Bay Off-street parking, restrooms and showers. A well-protected bay and beautiful beach fronting the grounds of the Kapalua Bay Hotel. Limited coral and some large coral heads, fair for fish watching. Arrive early as parking is very limited. Best snorkeling is at the south end of the beach (toward Lahaina). You can often see turtles in this bay.

Malu'aka Beach Located in Makena, no facilities and roadside parking. Good coral formations and a fair amount of fish at the left end of the beach.

Molokini Crater This volcanic remnant affords excellent snorkeling. See "Scuba Diving" above for additional information.

Namalu Bay Park at Kapalua Bay, walk over from Kapalua Bay to the bay that fronts the grounds of the resort. Difficult entry, very good on calm days.

Olowalu At mile-marker 14, about 5 miles south of Lahaina. Generally calm and warmer waters with ample parking along the roadside. Very good snorkeling. If you find a pearl earring, let me know, I *still* have the match.

A good way to become acquainted with Maui's sea life is a guided snorkeling adventure with Ann Fielding, marine biologist and author of Hawaiian Reefs and Tidepools and Underwater Guide to Hawai'i. She takes small groups (minimum 2, maximum 6) to the best location, generally Honolua Bay in summer and 'Ahihi Kina'u Reserve in winter. These excursions begin with an introductory discussion on Hawaiian marine life, identification and ecology, followed by snorkeling. Flotation devices, snorkel gear and lunch are included. A great educational experience for the kids and parents. 7:30 a.m.-12:30 p.m.; adults $90; children 15 and under $80. 808-572-8437; e-mail: annf@maui.net; www.maui.net/~annf.

Ulua-Mokapu Beach Well-marked public beach park in Wailea with restrooms and showers. Good snorkeling on the Ulua side of the rocky point separating these two picturesque and beautiful beaches.

SNORKELING TOURS

Maui Snorkel Tours with Suzzy Robinson, A Shoreline Eco-Adventure Suzzy Robinson and her associates share their love of the ocean with beginning, intermediate or advanced snorkelers. They promise there is something for everyone. A pre-snorkel briefing is followed by snorkel instruction and a narrative tour. $90 adults and children. *808-268-9840; www.mauiscuba.com/snorkel.*

SNUBA (*See also* Scuba Diving; Sea Excursions, Sailing)

One of the newer water recreations available is Snuba, a combination of snorkeling and scuba diving. It allows the freedom of underwater exploration without the heavy equipment of scuba diving. In brief, the Snuba diver has a mask and an air hose that is connected to the surface. Some of those currently offering Snuba in addition to cruises are *The Pride of Maui*, Maui-Molokai Sea Cruises (*Prince Kuhio*), Boss Frog's and Maui Classic Charters (*Four Winds*). (Fee in addition to cruise approximately $40 to $50). Also Aqua Adventure Charters offers a three-hour Snuba and snorkel cruise. Adults $134; children (3 to 12) $109. Must be 8 years or older to Snuba. Aqua Adventure, *866-472-2782; 808-573-2104; www.mauisnorkelsnuba.com.*

SPAS/FITNESS CENTERS/HEALTH RETREATS

Many of Maui's resorts have fitness centers. Some resorts charge resort guests a usage fee, others give complimentary guest privileges.

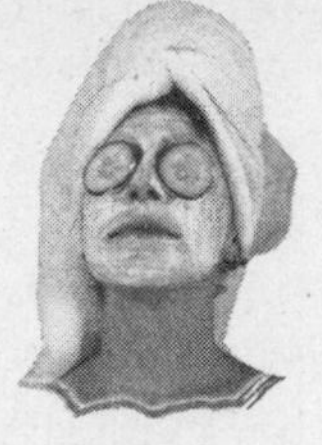

A number of them allow non-resort guests for a day-use fee. If you are interested in keeping in shape and you have no fitness center at your resort, here are a few fitness clubs that welcome drop-in guests.

Gold's Gym *Ka'anapali, 808-667-7474; Wailuku Industrial Park, 808-242-6851; Lipoa Shopping Center, Kihei,808-874-2844; 871 Kolu Street, Wailuku, 808-242-5773.*

Sports Club Kahana These folks have a lot of extras with Kahana Care (for kids), a boxing ring, a climbing wall and massage therapy. *At the Valley Isle Resort. 4327 Lower Honoapi'ilani Road. 808-669-3539; www.sportsclubkahana.*

24-Hour Fitness *150 Hana Highway, Kahului. 808-877-7474.*

Maui's spas offer something for everyone. Luxurious treatments for the ladies. A tension-releasing massage for the guys after a golf game. And a spa visit is a great way for moms and daughters to enjoy a day of pampering together. Teenage girls may love getting a facial, and it is great for their complexions as well. There are many spas and massage centers on Maui, large and small, with expansive facilities and exotic services or simple treatment rooms. There are also a number of companies that offer outcall services—therapists will come to your home, condo or hotel room to provide professional treatments. Following is a list of some of the spa services available:

Aloha Spa The massage comes to you. Aloha Spa offers island-wide outcall services to homes, hotels, condos or wherever you might be staying. A variety of massage techniques are offered by professional therapists. I have experienced their service in my own home, and it was wonderful. No hassle—they bring everything they need. You just relax and enjoy. *808-573-2323; www.alohaspamaui.com.*

★ **Hotel Hana-Maui Honua Spa** This beautiful new spa, opened in 2004, has the loveliest natural setting of any spa I've seen in Hawai'i. The 7,650-square-foot facility is situated on one acre of landscaped grounds overlooking Hana Bay and Ka'uki Hill. The ambiance here is all about nature, tranquility and glowing good health. The men's and women's locker rooms are beautifully appointed with mahogany lockers and bamboo floors. The locker room area includes steam room, cold plunge pool, whirlpool spa and outdoor lava rock showers. Iced cucumber or lemon water, chilled cloths and herbal teas are provided. In the relaxation room, where you wait for your therapist or rest between treatments, there is also a basket of fresh fruit, and you can choose to sit indoors or outdoors where you'll enjoy the soft breezes and ocean view. During my recent visit, I experienced the Honua Rainforest Mist Facial, a signature treatment of the spa. My therapist greeted me with a cup of warm chamomile mint tea before beginning my treatment, a soothing facial combined with hand and foot massage using a unique blend of native fruits and nut oils ($130 for 60 minutes; $190 for 90 minutes, including full body massage). The Honua Spa offers a wide selection of treatments—massage therapies, body treatments, facials and packages—ranging from $65 (30-minute treatments) to the $560 Couples Retreat, providing couples' spa treatments in the privacy of a specially designed suite for two. The Honua Spa also features a unique tandem Watsu pool, used for therapeutic water massages. The good news about this new spa? It is absolutely exquisite in every way. The bad news? This is an exclusive spa, open only to guests of Hotel Hana-Maui and Hana residents (guests of Hana residents are allowed if accompanied by the resident. Proof of Hana address must be shown.) If you are staying at Hotel Hana-Maui, don't miss this wonderful spa experience. Check in advance to see if any special spa packages are being offered by the hotel. 808-270-5290; www.hotelhanamaui.com.

Makai Massage & Bodywork A friendly little boutique spa located at Napili Kai Beach Resort in West Maui. They don't have a big, fancy facility, but they offer an amazing variety of massage techniques ($50 for 25 minutes; $85 for 55 minutes; $125 for 85 minutes), body treatments, facials and other delightful treatments (such as a rosemary/peppermint oil scalp massage or a honey almond hand and foot scrub). They also offer island-wide outcall services, so let them come to you. *808-662-0887; www.makaimassage.com.*

★ ***Maui School of Therapeutic Massage*** Whether venturing to Haleakala for an early-morning sunrise or visiting the Tedeschi Wineries, be sure to include a stop in Makawao at the Maui School of Therapeutic Massage. This is one of the best deals on the island. Appointments are required. The cost for a one-hour massage is an unbelievable $25. Current clinic hours are Monday, Wednesday and Friday 1 p.m. to 9 p.m., Tuesday and Thursday 9 a.m. to 5 p.m. and Sunday 5 to 9 p.m. There are other massage schools on Maui but I haven't tried them all; check the phone book for other listings. *1043 Makawao Avenue (upstairs). 808-572-2277; www.massagemaui.com.*

The Ritz-Carlton, Kapalua Spa services and a fitness center. The fitness center is complimentary for hotel guests, visiting guests are $25 per day, but the fee is waived if you purchase a 60-minute spa service. Personal training, body composition analysis, sports massage, *lomi lomi*, reflexology, oceanside massage or even in-room massage are available. The boutique spa facility was renovated in 2004 and includes 10 treatment rooms. *808-669-6200.*

★ ***Spa Grande*** The Grand Wailea Resort Hotel & Spa is the largest spa facility in the state of Hawai'i. Designed with Italian marble, original artwork, Venetian chandeliers, mahogany millwork and inlaid gold, this 50,000-square-foot facility offers two full floors of invigorating fitness, rich luxury, soothing relaxation and stimulating rejuvenation. Whether you need your rusty joints oiled and massaged, your body reshaped and freshened with a honey steam wrap, or you just want to come out with your mane washed and conditioned with the essence of Maui Mist, Spa Grande is the place to point your ruby slippers for the ultimate in luxurious pampering. This magical "Oz" takes you around the globe with a blend of European, Indian, Oriental and American spa philosophies and treatments, but it's the Hawaiian Regional regime that makes this spa unique. Cleanse with the Hawaiian Salt Glo Scrub, relax with the healing lomi lomi massage or Hawaiian Limu Rejuvenator body masque and soak in a soothing bath of seaweed or fragrant tropical enzymes. Then sit under an indoor waterfall to massage and relieve tired back muscles or refresh under an "ordinary" shower with extraordinary Honey Mango Bath Gel. The fitness center offers daily fitness classes, weight room, cardiovascular equipment and personalized instruction; there's also an aerobics studio and racquetball and squash court (the only ones on Maui). The facilities, services and amenities at this spa are too numerous to name, so visit the hotel's website for more details. Believe me, the moment you enter this incredible place, you'll know you're not in Kansas anymore. *808-875-1234; e-mail spa@grandwailea.com, www.grandwailea.com.*

Spa Kea Lani The spa facility at Fairmont Kea Lani Hotel in Wailea. Experience a variety of massage techniques with their Massage Combo or try a synchronized "double massage"—the ultimate in relaxing massage therapy. Refreshing body treatments, rejuvenating wraps, facials and waxing services are available individually ($70-$195) or as part of a treatment package (couples package up to $500).The hot-rock massage is simply too divine for words. The technique apparently began in the Midwest, but here on Maui they use palm-size warmed beach rocks to massage the body. They also offer a special facial for teens at the spa ($125). Or focus on fitness with a personal training session in their workout facilities. *808-875-2229.*

★ ***Spa Moana*** The newly-expanded 15,000-square-foot, oceanfront spa at the Hyatt Regency in Ka'anapali offers a 5,000-square-foot fitness center with ocean view, 15 treatment rooms, a full-service beauty salon, a relaxation lounge, sauna and steam rooms, and two luxury spa suites for couples. Spa guests also have the option of massages, manicures and pedicures in oceanfront cabanas.

One signature treatment of Spa Moana is its Moana Scrub and Body Wrap, featuring a delicious-smelling tropical scrub of nuts and citrus to exfoliate and nourish the skin. Other treatments inspired by Hawaiian traditions include lomi lomi or hot stone massages and seaweed body wraps. In addition, the spa menu offers traditional favorites like shiatsu, deep-tissue massage, Swedish massage, a variety of facial treatments, enzyme facial peels and even couples' massage lessons. Wet treatment services include vichy showers and mud wraps. The spa's lovely beachfront relaxation room offers a serene area to rest while refreshing yourself with fresh fruit, chilled lemon-orange water or passionfruit tea. Spa Moana offers a number of treatments for couples (or friends who would enjoy having treatments in the same room), as well as teens age 12 to 17. Mom and daughter can make a day of it at the spa with the Keiki and Teen Adventure treatments, including a Teen Lokahi Foot Massage ($25) or the ultimate You Glow, Girl package featuring a customized facial, salt glow scrub, pedicure and manicure ($200). Services are also available for younger girls (age 6 to 12), including a keiki foot massage, manicure or Glitter Princess Makeup application. Men's and women's locker rooms are equipped with steam rooms, dry saunas and whirlpool baths. Also take a few minutes to browse in the spa's shop. They carry several lines of skin and spa products, as well as some unique items like lavender dog shampoo, chocolate mac nut Ka'anapali coffee scrub, sensual couples' products (like chocolate body frosting), robes, candles and other gift items. The spa's signature Lokahi aromatherapy and body care products are also featured in the shop. Non-hotel guests may use the fitness/spa facilities for $25 a day; treatments from $80-$350. Reservations required. 808-667-4725; www.maui.hyatt.com.

★ ***Westin Maui Resort & Spa*** The Spa at The Westin Maui is the newest major spa facility in West Maui. The 14,000-square-foot spa, salon and fitness center opened in 2004 and features a full menu of services, including a number of Westin's signature "Heavenly" treatments. The facility includes 16 treatment rooms, men's and women's locker rooms with steam room, sauna, whirlpool spa and Westin's famed two-headed Heavenly Showers. Included are two rooms equipped with Vichy shower and a hydrotherapy tub with 98 jets. The large workout facility offers state-of-the-art equipment and a view of the hotel's tropical pool area and ocean, as well as an open-air yoga and fitness studio. The delightful thing about this spa is their emphasis on lavender for their signature products (who doesn't love lavender?). The spa has partnered with a lavender farm in

Upcountry Maui to create unique organic treatments, body products and refreshments—the oceanview relaxation room offers chilled pitchers of ice-cold lavender lemonade along with hot lavender herbal teas. I am partial to the 80-minute Island Lavender Body Butter Treatment ($175), which starts with an exfoliating scrub consisting of island sugar, lavender and passionfruit. After showering off the fragrant scrub, your skin is lathered with a rich blend of warm cocoa butter, shea butter, coconut and mango, then you are wrapped in a warm cocoon to "baste" while your therapist gives you a soothing scalp massage. This treatment is, to use Westin's term, "heavenly." I have experienced a gazillion spa treatments over the years and this is the most moisturizing treatment ever. Plus the cocoa butter makes you smell like a fresh chocolate-chip cookie. Do check out this new spa. Even if you're not a lavender fan, they offer a wide range of other treatments and scents (like seaweed masks, mud wraps and bamboo scrubs), for men, women, couples and keiki (there is a special spa menu for children 12 and under). *808-661-2525; www.westinmaui.com.*

SPELUNKING

★ ***Maui Cave Adventures*** All that is missing is Willie Wonka and the Oompa-Loompas on this cave adventure. The Scenic Walking Tour takes you to a wondrous world of lava, with oozing brown formations that look like rich, dark chocolate. The name of this region in Hana is Ka'eleku, or "standing in a dark hollow cavity." Obviously, the early Hawaiians felt that this cave was a prominent landmark in the area. Interestingly enough, however, the early history of these caves is unclear. Chuck Thorne has traversed miles of the underground passages and has yet to find any evidence of petroglyphs. He believes that during times of war the women and children may have been kept safely underground in these caverns while the men fought off attacks from neighboring island chiefs. It was also a safe haven in modern times. Chuck's backyard caves were identified as a bomb shelter during the Cold War. There is room for 14 folks, so that'll be Chuck and 13 explorers. The caves are unique and exciting. The scenic walking tour is very easy and necessitates ducking slightly in only one area. With plenty of fresh air and large caverns there isn't even a claustrophobic feeling to the tour. (The Wild Adventure Tour, however, takes you to more small caverns.) Chuck explains his quest to reach the end of the lava tube. He's explored the shore from the ocean (he's also an experienced scuba diver with a book on the subject) and has yet to find an entrance. Judging by the air flow, the caves definitely go somewhere. He's managed, a rock at a time, to open up new sections of the lava tube and there is still a lifetime's worth to be explored. Chuck points out interesting lava phenomena and if you have any interest in geology you'll find it fascinating. This is the only Hawaiian cave open to such a tour. The 1- to 1.25-hour Scenic Walking Tour is $29 for kids or adults, minimum age 6; the 2- to 2.5-hour Wild Adventure Tour is $79 and requires a little more agility. The minimum age is 15 years. Closed-toe shoes, long pants and T-shirts are suggested. Gloves, flashlights and hardhats are provided for both tours; hip packs with water and snacks are provided on their Wild tour. Scheduled tours are offered Monday through Saturday; call about Sunday tours. Reservations highly recommended. Call 8 a.m. to 8 p.m. *P.O. Box 40, Hana, HI 96713; 808-248-7308; e-mail: info@mauicave.com; www.mauicave.com.*

SURFING (*See also* Body Surfing)

Honolua Bay is one of the best surfing spots in Hawai'i, and undoubtedly the best on Maui, with waves up to 15 feet on a good winter day and perfect tubes. A spectacular vantage point is on the cliffs above the bay. In the summer this bay is calm and, since it is a marine reserve, offers excellent snorkeling. Also in this area is Punalau Beach (just past Honolua) and Honokeana Bay off Ka'eleki'i Point (just north of the Alaeloa residential area). In the Lahaina area there are breaks north and south of the harbor and periodically good waves at Awalua Beach (mile-marker 16). On the north shore, Ho'okipa Beach Park, Kanaha Beach and Baldwin all have good surfing at times. In the Hana area there is Hamoa Beach. There are a couple of good spots in Ma'alaea Bay and at Kalama Beach Park. Conditions change daily—even from morning to afternoon—around the island. Check with local board rental outlets for current daily conditions.

★ ***Goofy Foot Surf School*** Ever see the old Disney cartoon where Goofy is surfing? Well, standard surfing position is left foot forward, but Goofy has his right forward. (Guess the artists weren't surfers.) The resulting term "Goofy Foot" applies to those folks who surf Goofy-style. Tim Sherer, "Board Director," guarantees you'll stand in your first two-hour lesson or the experience is on Goofy Foot. Class sizes are kept small, not more than five students to an instructor. Tim and associates begin your 2-hour introduction to surfing at the beach in front of 505 Front Street, Lahaina. The boards are marked with lines to help you position your feet. The first 30 minutes or so are spent learning the different body and foot positions for surfing and the transitions between. After that, it's out to the harbor, where the waves break small but are long and consistent. My teenage nieces loved their experience at Goofy Foot and both were able to stand on their surfboard by the end of the 2-hour class. The instructors are very patient and, with five or less to a group, pay personal attention to each student. Two-hour beginner lessons (daily at 8 a.m., 11 a.m. or 2 p.m.) are $55 per person. Two-hour private lessons are $125. The six-hour Beginner Surfing Camps are like "instructional beach parties" that include an extended three-hour introductory surfing lesson, lunch, discussions about surfing and its history, with additional tips, advice and instruction to take you to the next level. From $250 per person to $700 for groups of five. This company is a great choice for kids and all beginning surfers. Office and surf shop: 505 Front Street #123, Lahaina. *808-244-9283; www.goofyfootsurfschool.com.*

Hawaiian Island Surf and Sport This company has teamed up with the professional certified instructors from Action Sports Maui to provide surf instruction for first-timers to advanced. Their Baby Steps program is for kids only, from age 6 up, $79 for two hours. Just Do It is for beginners of any age, $79 for two hours. Intermediate, advanced and tow-in surfing (for seasoned surfers) are available also. *415 Dairy Road, Kahului, HI, 96732. 800-231-6958; 808-871-4981; e-mail: lessons@hawaiianisland.com; www.hawaiianisland.com.*

Nancy Emerson School of Surfing "Learn to Surf in One Lesson." By the age of 14, owner Nancy Emerson had won three international surfing contests and was ranked #2 in women's amateur surfing. She and her staff offer group, private and semiprivate lessons from $75 for a two-hour clinic to $265 for the group Day Camp (breakfast and lunch included). *808-244-7873; e-mail: nancy@surfclinics.com; www.surfclinics.com.*

Outrageous Adventures "Learn from the Locals" with their team of instructors. Three classes daily (8 a.m., 11 a.m. and 2 p.m.) with free hotel pickups available. You'll surf off the beach in Lahaina. *545 G Front Street, Lahaina; 877-339-1400; 808-669-1400; www.youcansurf.com.*

Surf Dog Maui Private and small groups learn surfing from their mobile surf clinic. Lessons based on wherever surf and weather conditions are the best. Lessons by appointment. Board rentals available. *Lessons at Puamana Park. 808-250-7873; e-mail: surfdog@maui.net; www.surfdogmaui.com.*

SWIMMING

Kihei Aquatic Center The Kihei Aquatic Center is located just below the highway at 303 East Lipoa Street. This is a community center with free use of all facilities. Open 9 a.m. to 4:30 p.m. Monday, Tuesday, Thursday, Friday and Saturday. On Wednesday they are open 10 a.m. to 4:30 p.m. and Sunday from noon to 4:30 p.m. *808-879-4364.*

Lahaina Aquatic Center On the Westside there is the Lahaina Aquatic Center at the corner of Honoapi'ilani Highway and Shaw Street. No charge for use of the facility or services including water aerobics and swimming lessons. Open daily 9 a.m. to 4:30 p.m. Monday, Wednesday, Saturday; 9:30 a.m. to 4:30 p.m. Tuesday and Friday; 10 a.m. to 4:30 p.m. Thursday; 12 to 4:30 p.m. Sunday. *808-661-4685.*

TENNIS

Tennis facilities abound on Maui. Many condos and major hotels offer tennis facilities. Also, there are quite a few very well-kept public courts. They are, of course, most popular during the cooler early morning and early evening hours.

Public Courts

Hali'imaile One court by the baseball park.

Hana Hana Ball Park, one double lighted court.

Kahului Maui Community College (Ka'ahumanu and Wakea Avenue) has four unlighted courts. Kahului Community Center (Onehe'e and Uhu Street) has four lighted courts. The Kahului War Memorial Complex has four lighted courts plus a practice area, located at Ka'ahumanu and Kanaloa Avenue. *808-270-7389.*

Wailuku Wells Park has six courts; five are lighted. South Market Street and Wells Street. *808-270-7389.*

Kihei Kalama Park has four lighted courts. Six unlighted courts in park fronting Maui Sunset condos. *808-879-4364.*

Lahaina Lahaina Civic Center has five lighted courts. There are four lighted courts at Malu-ulu-olele Park. *808-661-4685.*

Makawao Eddie Tam Memorial Center has two lighted courts. *808-572-8122.*

Pukalani Pukalani Community Center has two lighted courts, located across from the Pukalani Shopping Center. *808-572-8122.*

Kula There are two lighted courts at Kula Community Center. *808-572-8122.*

Private Courts

These private courts have facilities open to the public.

Hyatt Regency, Ka'anapali Six unlighted courts. 7 a.m. to dusk. Guest and non-guest rates. *808-661-1234 ext. 3174.*

Kapalua Resort, Kapalua Resort guest and non-guest rates. The Tennis Garden has 10 courts, 4 are lighted. Tennis attire required at all times. *808-669-5677.* The Village Tennis Center also has 10 courts, 4 lighted. *808-665-0112. www.kapaluamaui.com*

Makena Tennis Club Two lighted courts. Guest and non-guest rates. 5415 Makena Alanui, Makena Resort. *808-879-8777.*

Maui Marriott Beach & Tennis Club Pro shop, fitness center and tennis courts open daily from 7 a.m. to 8 p.m. Racquets and tennis shoes available for rent. Lessons available. Marriott tennis passes can also be used at the Royal Lahaina and Sheraton Maui. *808-661-6200.*

Royal Lahaina Tennis Ranch, Ka'anapali The largest facility in West Maui with 11 courts, 5 lighted including 1 stadium court. Pro shop and snack bar open 8 a.m. to noon and 2 to 7 p.m. Courts available until 8:30 p.m. (See also "Maui Marriott Beach & Tennis Club" listing above.) *808-667-5200 or 808-661-3611 ext. 2296.*

Sheraton Maui Tennis Club, Ka'anapali Three lighted courts and pro shop open daily from 8 a.m. to noon and 2 to 8 p.m. (See also "Maui Marriott Beach & Tennis Club" listing above.) *808-667-9200 or 808-661-0031 ext. 8208.*

Wailea Tennis Club, Wailea Has 11 plexipave courts, 3 lighted. 7 a.m. to 7 p.m. Court fee $12/hour. (Your first hour is guaranteed with your reservation, then you can continue to play anytime during the rest of the day that the courts are free.) Juniors (under age 12) are free with two paid players. *808-879-1958 for court reservations; 800-332-1614 for general information; www.waileatennis.com.*

Resort Courts for Guests Only

Hale Kamaole, Hotel Hana-Maui, Ka'anapali Alii, Ka'anapali Plantation, Ka'anapali Royal, Ka'anapali Shores, Kahana Villa, Kamaole Sands, Kihei Akahi, Kihei Alii Kai, Kihei Bay Surf, Kuleana, Ma'alaea Surf, Mahana, Makena Surf, Maui Hill, Maui Islander Hotel, Maui Lu Resort, Maui Vista, Papakea, Puamana, Royal Kahana, Sands of Kahana, Shores of Maui, The Whaler.

THEATER, MOVIES AND THE ARTS

There is a Consolidated Theatres six-plex cinema at the Ka'ahumanu Center and a four-plex in Kihei's Kukui Mall. In Lahaina, there is a Wallace Theaters tri-cinema at The Wharf Cinema Shopping Center and another set of four theaters at the Lahaina Center off Front Street. The Maui Mall Megaplex in Kahului offers their twelve theaters with stadium seating.

The Wallace theaters (Wharf Cinema, Front Street Theaters and Maui Mall Megaplex) offer senior and child discounts, matinee discounts and "Thrifty Tuesdays," when select movies are offered at $6.00. The Consolidated theaters (Ka'ahumanu Center Theaters and

Kukui Theaters) offer senior and child discounts, as well as $6 bargain matinee shows.

Film buffs will enjoy the **Maui Film Festival**, a series of award-winning, critically acclaimed films shown weekly in the state-of-the-art Castle Theater at Maui Arts & Cultural Center. Admission is $10, or purchase a passport for $40 good for five films. The festival expands to Wailea in June, offering two weeks of premiere films and entertainment under the stars during the "Celestial Cinema." In December, the premiere series becomes "First Light" and runs for two weeks over the holidays at the Maui Arts & Cultural Center. And for films particular to the Pacific/Asian culture, don't miss the **Hawaii International Film Festival** at MACC in November. *808-572-3456; www.mauifilmfestival.com.*

The Maui Arts & Cultural Center offers everything from local community events to concert performances by internationally known performers. Entertainers as diverse as Tony Bennett, Pearl Jam, Tibetan monks, the Lakota Sioux Indian Dance Theatre, Harry Belafonte, the Doobie Brothers, Santana and the Vienna Boys Choir have performed at the center. It has also featured the ballet, symphony, multicultural music and dance presentations, and art gallery exhibits. *808-242-7469; www.mauiarts.org.*

Maui On Stage produces a full season of professional-quality plays and musicals, performed almost every weekend from October through June. Comedies, musicals and dramas are balanced with classic and contemporary theater. In existence since the 1920s when two theater groups (the Maui Players and Little Theatre of Maui) joined forces, they have continued in varying forms and locations (interrupted only by World War II in the '40s and a fire in the '80s) until settling into their present home at the renovated Historic Iao Theatre on Market Street in Wailuku. *808-242-6969; www.mauionstage.com.*

The Maui Academy of Performing Arts clearly has it all when it comes to entertainment. An educational and performing arts organization for kids and adults, the Academy is located at the old National Dollar Store on Main Street in Wailuku. They offer community theater performances, special events, ongoing dance and drama classes, and special drama and dance workshops for kids and adults. Visitors welcome. Larger productions are currently held at the Maui Arts & Cultural Center. *808-244-8760; www.mauiacademy.org.*

★ The Maui Theatre presents *'Ulalena* (which means "Wind from the North"), one of the most amazing and innovative theatrical presentations in the state of Hawai'i. Picture a Hawaiian hologram, shadow poetry, a waterfall of illusion, virtual rain showers created from pure imagination, and a liquid stage that goes from the drama of hot lava to the lilt of cool ocean waves. This is just part of the experience that is *'Ulalena*. I recommend this for the discerning visitor who appreciates a more sophisticated show that combines provocative thought and educational culture along with sheer entertainment. They provide you with a flyer upon entrance, and I highly recommend you read it before the show starts—you'll understand the experience far better. The theater is state-of-the-art, costumes and sets colorful and creative, and the choreography and presentation is at times astounding, other times breathtaking. An excellent show for the whole family. Shows are Tuesday through Saturday at 6:30 p.m. Ticket prices are $48; premium seats $58; and $68 for the backstage package. ($28/$38/$45 for children age 12 and under.) It's a bit pricey, but you won't see anything else like it in Hawai'i. Refreshments are available for purchase. *Old Lahaina Center, 878 Front Street, Lahaina; 877-688-4800; 808-661-9913; www.mauitheatre.com.*

The dinner theater **Tony 'n Tina's Wedding** takes place three nights a week at the Hyatt Regency Maui. See "Lu'aus and Dinner Shows" in Chapter 4 for more information.

Warren & Annabelle entertain each evening with an intimate magic club show. See "Magic Shows" in this chapter for more information.

★ The **Masters of Hawaiian Slack Key Guitar Concert Series** takes place weekly at the Ritz-Carlton, Kapalua. Slack key is a traditional Hawaiian guitar style, and at these weekly concerts you will have the privilege of hearing Hawai'i's finest slack key artists in an intimate theater setting (120 seats only). The concerts, featuring a different guest artist each week, take place Tuesday evenings at 6 p.m. and 8:30 p.m. Tickets are $40. *888-669-3858; 808-669-3858; www.slackkey.com.*

WATERSKIING

Maui Ocean Activities This company offers waterskiing in the Ka'anapali area, along with a variety of other water activities. Also available is the aqua sled (banana boat), along with private coastal tours and seasonal whale watching. *808-667-1964; e-mail: beaches @maui.net; www.maui.net/~beaches.*

WHALE WATCHING (*See also* Cruises; Sea Excursions)

Every year beginning mid-December and continuing through mid-April (official whale season—but peak sightings are January through March), the humpback whales arrive in the warm waters off the Hawaiian islands for breeding and their own sort of vacation. The sighting of a whale can be an awesome and memorable experience with the humpbacks (small as whales go) measuring some 40 to 50

WHALE RULES

Humpback whales are an endangered species and are protected by Federal law. It is illegal to: (1) operate an aircraft within 1,000 feet of a humpback whale; (2) approach (by any means, whether it be swimming or by boat) closer than 100 yards of a humpback whale or within 300 yards of a humpback mother and calf; (3) disrupt the normal activity or behavior of a humpback whale. This is considered harassment. Enjoy the beauty of these magnificent and gentle creatures, but do not approach them.

feet and weighing in at some 40 tons. The panoramic vistas as you drive over the Pali and down the beachfront road to Lahaina afford some excellent opportunities to catch sight of one of these splendid marine mammals. (Yes, whales are mammals, not fish. They are warm-blooded, breathe air, bear live young and nurse them with milk.) However, please carefully pull off the road to enjoy the view. Many accidents are caused by distracted drivers during whale season.

For an even closer view, there are plenty of boat trips—from large vessels to rigid-haul rafts and kayaks. Almost every boat operator does whale-watching tours in season. Many of the tour boats have a marine biologist onboard to offer insight during your whale-watching excursion. Whale-watching cruises are an exciting and memorable way to view whales, but be aware that all reputable boat captains will respect the whales and adhere to Federal law by not approaching closer than 100 yards.

WINDSURFING

Windsurfing is a sport that is increasing astronomically in popularity. Ho'okipa Beach Park on Maui is one of the best windsurfing sites in the world. This is due to the consistently ideal wind and surf conditions; however, Ho'okipa is definitely *not* the spot for beginners. For the novice, boardsailing beginner group lessons run around $80 and generally involve instruction on a dry-land simulator before you get wet with easy-to-use beginners equipment. Some resorts offer their guests free clinics. Rental by the hour can get expensive so inquire about full-day rental rates. Equipment and/or lessons are available from the following:

Alan Cadiz' Hawaiian Sailboarding Techniques Alan Cadiz and his staff of professional instructors offer a full range of small group and private lessons for beginner or expert, including Kid's Camps and lessons. They specialize in one-on-one instruction tailored to each person's ability, travel schedule, budget and goals. 425

Koloa Street, Kahului. 808-871-5423; 800-968-5423; fax 808-871-6943; www.hstwindsurfing.com.

Aloha Windsurf Vans Call them for rental of vehicles that can accommodate windsurfing equipment. 22 *Hana Highway; 877-645-1505; 808-893-2111; www.alohawindsurfvans.com.*

Al West's Maui Windsurfing Vans and Lesson Center They offer vans with racks and hangers for boards and equipment, as well as windsurfing instruction. *180 East Wakea, Kahului. 808-877-0090 (for vans), 808-871-8733 (for lessons); 800-870-4084; e-mail: mauivan@mauivans.com; www.mauivans.com.*

Hawaiian Island Surf and Sport Sales, service, rentals, instruction and travel (condo and car packages). Three-hour windsurfing group (up to 3 students), beginner lessons or advanced start at $79. They offer surfing lessons, too. *415 Dairy Road, Kahului. 800-231-6958; 808-871-4981; fax 808-871-4624; e-mail: lessons@hawaiianisland.com; www.hawaiianisland.com.*

Maui Sports Unlimited Windsurfing classes $75 for 2 hours. Three-day Kid's Windsurfing Camps ($150) offered June to August. *111 Hana Highway, Kahului. 808-877-7778; e-mail: stottie@maui.net; www.mauisportsunlimited.com.*

Maui Windsurfari Vacation rental agency offering private homes, cottages and condos. Many of their vacation rentals are unusual due to close proximity to windsurfing locations. Packages include accommodations, rental car, windsurfing equipment and excursions. *808-871-7766; 800-736-6284; e-mail: info@windsurfari.com; www.windsurfari.com.*

Second Wind Pro shop rentals, as well as used and new sales and lessons. Also surfing and kite boarding. During summer months, there is a weekly kids' windsurf camp. Their travel desk can also assist with accommodation and car rental arrangements. *808-877-7467; 800-936-7787; e-mail: secwind@maui.net; www.secondwindmaui.com.*

ZIPLINE

Skyline Eco-Adventures Maui's newest activity and a true adventure! The experience begins with a half-mile stroll through the woods to the first of several launch platforms on the slopes of Haleakala. There, you are harnessed and hooked to an overhead line. Stepping to the edge of the platform, the thrill begins as you are launched by gravity and momentum power, "zipping" along the line across canyons and soaring over trees until you are stopped by a "catcher" at the other end. The site was designed to do minimal damage to the environment, with lines hooked to sturdy trees. The zipline experience requires you to be at least 10 years old and weigh 80 to 280 pounds. $79. *808-878-8400; e-mail: info@skylinehawaii.com; www.skylinehawaii.com.*

CHAPTER 7

Lana‘i

A visit to Lana‘i is truly an excursion into Hawai‘i's past. Still largely undeveloped (except for the island's two spectacular luxury resorts), Lana‘i has no stoplights, no traffic jams, no shopping malls, Starbucks or Burger Kings. It has one tiny town, Lana‘i City, and a great deal of charm. Lana‘i is a peaceful place, a place to relax and appreciate the island's unique beauty.

Lana‘i Best Bets

- A round of golf on either of Lana‘i's acclaimed courses: The Experience at Koele or the Challenge at Manele
- A scuba dive to Cathedrals with Trilogy
- An evening just sitting by the fire in the Great Hall of the Lodge at Koele
- An afternoon browse through Dole Park in Lana‘i City
- A meal at the Lodge at Koele's Formal Dining Room
- Getting a Jeep and heading off to explore the island
- Take your walking stick out of the closet (there is one in every room at the Lodge) and stroll the nearby trails
- Snorkeling at Manele Bay
- A kayak/snorkel trip with Adventure Lana‘i EcoCentre
- Mountain biking
- A leisurely stroll through the gardens and grounds at Manele Bay Hotel to the beach

The Pineapple Isle

The meaning of the name Lana‘i seems to be steeped in mystery, at least this was our experience. Several guidebooks report that it means "swelling" or "hump." In discussions with local residents I was told it meant the obvious interpretation of "porch" or "balcony," perhaps because Lana'i, in a rather nebulous fashion, is the balcony of Maui. So, with no definitive answer I continue the search, but in the meantime, come enjoy this piece of paradise.

Just before and immediately following the turn of the 20th century, Lana'i was a bustling sheep-and-cattle ranch. Beginning in the 1920s, Dole transformed Lana'i into the largest single pineapple plantation in the world. The 1990s brought Lana'i into the visitor industry with the opening of two elegant and classy resorts, the country-style Lodge at Koele in Lana'i City and the seashore resort at Manele Bay. Under the helm of David Murdock, the metamorphosis was a positive one, with young people returning to the island to work in the tourism industry. Pineapple fields are now a memory, and cattle again dot the landscape as the silver-blue fields of pineapple have faded into extinction.

While each isle has its own nickname, it appears that Lana'i has outgrown hers. "The Pineapple Isle" no longer bears much symbolism for an island that has been transformed from an agricultural setting to "an oasis within an oasis" for the lucky tourist. In the past it had been a wonderful retreat, and happily much of what was good about Lana'i has not changed. The slow pace of the isle has not been as significantly altered by the arrival of the mega-resort as one might imagine. What new term of endearment will be vested upon the isle? The Isle of Relaxation? Pine Isle? The Island Less Traveled? The Isle of Enchantment? Hawai'i's Most Secluded Island? Time will tell, or perhaps the tourist bureau will. Recently, promotions for Lana'i have referred to it as "Hawai'i's Most Enticing Island," and that may very well be. It certainly is seductive, in its own simple way. Lana'i offers a unique blend of ultra-luxury and quaint charm. You'll see what I mean when you visit.

With the continuing construction of luxury homes in the Koele district on 68 acres, and plans for 350 homes at Manele, the rich and famous will very shortly (if not already) be anteing up to purchase a vacation home on Lana'i. The price for a stay at the two major resorts may be steep, but if you want to indulge and experience this lovely island, read on. A luxurious and relaxing island getaway that is only eight miles (but in many ways, 30 years removed) from Maui, Lana'i will simply enchant you. If you'd like a glimpse of Lana'i via cyberspace, visit www.islandoflanai.com or www.visitlanai.net.

History of Lana'i

The historical tales of the island of Lana'i are intriguing, filled with darkness and evil. As legend has it, in ancient times the island of Lana'i was uninhabited except for evil spirits. It is said that in the olden days, those who went to Lana'i never returned and that the island was *kapu* (taboo). Hawaiians banished wrongdoers to Lana'i as punishment for their crimes. The story continues that around the 16th century on West Maui there was a chief named Kaka'alanaeo. He had a son named Kaulula'au who was willful and spoiled. The people became furious with his many misdeeds and finally rebelled and demanded that Kaulula'au be put on trial by the ancient laws. The verdict was guilty and, according to the ancient laws, his punishment was death. His father begged for his life and it was agreed that Kaulula'au would be banished to the island of Lana'i. He was set ashore near the Maunalei Gulch, the only source of potable water on the island. His father promised him that if he could banish the evil spirits from Lana'i, he could then set a bonfire as a signal and his father and the warriors would return for him. And, as luck would have it, Kaulula'au managed to trick the evil spirits and send them over to Kaho'olawe. He signaled his father and returned to Maui, heralded as a hero.

During the 16th and 17th centuries, Maui was reaching its population zenith and Hawaiians relocated to Lana'i with settlements near Keomuku and inland as well. The first archaeological studies of Lana'i were done in 1921 by Kenneth Emory from the anthropology department of the Bishop Museum. He published his work in 1923. Emory found many ancient villages and artifacts that had been, for the most part, undisturbed for hundreds of years. He found the area of Kaunolu to be Lana'i's richest archaeological region, filled with house sites and remnants of a successful fishing village. Ashes from old fires at the village sites were analyzed. The findings showed that the ashes dated from 900 A.D., much later than the other islands, which were inhabited as early as 40 or 50 B.C. He also ventured to the eastern coastline and explored Naha and Keomuku. He noted 11 *heiau*, found relics including old stone game boards, and discovered a network of trails and petroglyphs. One of the earliest *heiau*, the Halulu Heiau, is in the Kaunolu area, and it is thought that this region may have been one of the earliest Hawaiian settlements.

While the Hawaiian population increased throughout the archipelago, Lana'i was left largely uninhabited until the 1500s. In the late 1700s, two of Captain Cook's ships, the *Discovery* and the *Resolution*, reported a visit to Lana'i. They found the Hawaiians friendly along the windward coastal area where they replenished their supplies of food and water. In talking with the islanders, they estimated that the population was approximately 10,000. They observed and noted that the island was a dry dustbowl and that the people fished and grew some taro. It was about at this same time chiefs of Maui became worried that the people on Lana'i might become too powerful. So they divided Lana'i into 13 *ohana* (*ohana* means family, but this refers more to regions) and put a *konahiki* in charge of each. This insured that no one chief would be too powerful. These district names are still used today: Kaa, Paomai, Mahana, Maunalei, Kamoku, Kaunolu, Kalulu, Kealiakapu, Kealiaaupuni, Palawai, Kamao, Pawili and Kaohai.

Six months after the island was visited by Cook's vessels, a tragic event occurred that would change life on Lana'i forever. Inter-island battles among the island chiefs were not uncommon, but until this time Lana'i had remained unaffected. In 1778 Kalaniopu'u, the chief on the Big Island, launched an unsuccessful attack on Lahaina, Maui. He retreated, then turned and attacked central Maui. Here again his warriors were overcome. As they returned to the Big Island in great anger he passed the island of Kaho'olawe, which was loyal to the Maui chieftains. In retaliation, Kalaniopu'u's warriors massacred the entire population on Kaho'olawe. Bolstered by his victory, Kalaniopu'u turned once again to assault Lahaina and again was defeated. Now enraged, Kalaniopu'u and his warriors chose to strike the leeward coastal villages of Lana'i. Lana'i's warriors were unprepared and retreated to the Ho'okia Ridge, a better location from which to launch their counterattack. However, without access to

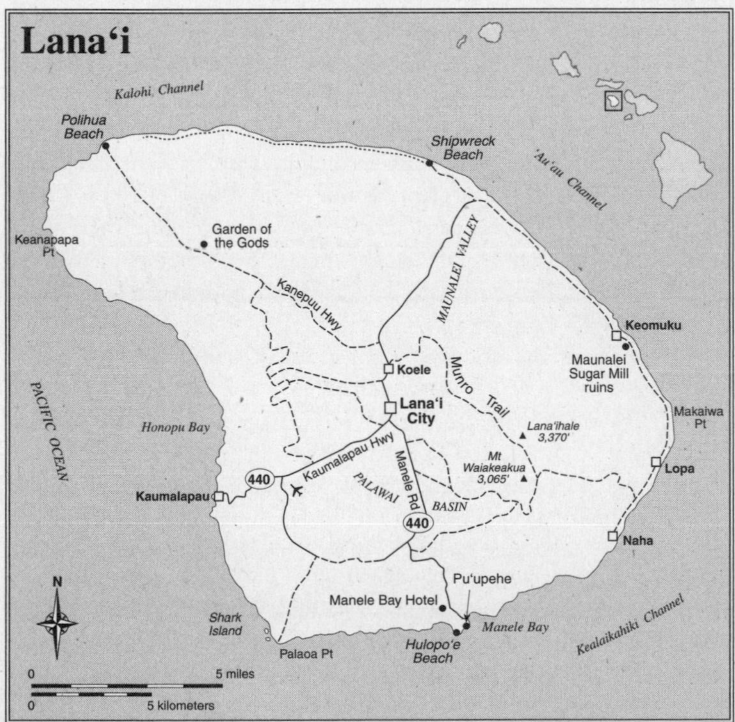

FACTS & FIGURES

A few brief island facts and figures:

- Lana'i has a population of approximately 3,000 and its major industry is tourism.
- Dole Park in Lana'i City forms the center of the town and the other Lana'i park is Hulopo'e Beach Park.
- The island plays host to three golf courses.
- The highest peak is Lana'ihale at 3,370 feet.
- The most popular visitor attractions are Keahikawelo (Garden of the Gods), Hulopo'e Bay (Marine Sanctuary), Pu'upehe (Sweetheart Rock), Lana'ihale and Kaiolohia Bay (Shipwreck Beach).
- There are three hotels with a total of 363 rooms, a few bed-and-breakfast accommodations and no vacation condominiums.
- Lana'i has four beaches (with only one accessible via paved road), and 47 miles of shoreline that surround the 141-square-mile island.

food and water, the Lana'i warriors soon weakened and Kalanaiopu'u moved quickly to crush them. The Big Island warriors continued their path of destruction around Lana'i and systematically destroyed all the villages. Kalaniopu'u returned to the Big Island of Hawai'i and there, seven months later, died. His lieutenant, Kamehameha, came to rule.

During the rule of Kamehameha the population of Lana'i once again increased. King Kamehameha and his warriors visited Kaunolu Bay on Lana'i's southwestern coastline. Here Kahekili, a brave warrior, is said to have leapt from a cliff above the sea into the Pacific waters, proving his loyalty to the king. Other warriors were then challenged to follow his example. (The area continues to be referred to as Kahekili's Leap.)

The elders from the Church of Jesus Christ of Latter-day Saints acquired land on Lana'i from one of the chiefs in 1855. In 1860 Walter Murray Gibson came to Lana'i with the intent of establishing a Mormon colony called the City of Joseph in the Palawai basin. Gibson had been instrumental in assisting Kamehameha. He served on his cabinet and was among the advisors for the construction of the Iolani Palace. He purchased 20,000 acres of land on Lana'i and obtained leases on more. By 1863 there were about 600 Mormons living on Lana'i. In 1864, when the church elders arrived to visit they discovered that Walter had purchased additional lands with church money, but had listed ownership under his own name, and he wasn't willing to release them. He was quickly expelled from the church and the Mormons went on to develop their church on O'ahu.

As owner of 26,000 acres, Gibson first established the Lana'i Sheep Ranch, which later became the Lana'i Ranch. In 1867 the population was 394 people (the 600 Mormons had departed earlier), 18,000 goats and 10,000 sheep. In 1870 Gibson attempted a cooperative farm, but this operation soon proved unsuccessful. By 1875 Gibson controlled 90 percent of the island for ranching or farming operations. In 1874, Gibson's daughter, Talula, married Frederick Harrison Hayselden, formerly of England and Australia, and by the early 1880s Hayselden was managing the ranch. Walter Gibson passed away in San Francisco in 1888 and ownership of the land transferred to his daughter and son-in-law.

In 1894 the Lana'i Ranch ran 40,000 sheep, 200 horses and 600 head of cattle in addition to large herds of goats, hogs and wild turkeys. By 1898 the ranch was in debt, but the sugar industry looked promising. The Hayseldens established the Maunalei Sugar Company on the island's windward coast. They began by building three wells and a wharf at Kahalepalaoa for shipment of the cane to Olowalu on Maui for grinding. A railroad was also built between the wharf and Keomuku, along with a two-story building, a store, a boarding house, camp houses and barracks.

In 1802, a Chinese entrepreneur spent one season attempting sugar cultivation in Naha from wild sugar cane. The Maunalei Sugar Company in nearby Keomuku did little better, lasting only a little more than two years. The Hayseldens constructed a six-mile train track for transporting their sugar cane. However, they failed to respect the local culture and custom. Stones from an ancient *heiau* were used to build part of the railroad bed and then the disasters began. Their Japanese workers fell sick and many died. The ever-important supply of drinking water went brackish and rain did not fall. Company records show the closure was due to lack of labor and water. The local population knew otherwise. Fred and Talula Hayselden soon left Lana'i.

In 1902 Charles Gay (a member of the Robinson family from Ni'ihau) and George Munro visited the island and Gay acquired the island at public auction for $108,000. He enlarged his holdings further through various land leases. Gay began making major improvements and brought cattle from Kaua'i and Ni'ihau to his new ranch on Lana'i. In 1903 Gay purchased the remaining holdings from the Hayseldens and through land leases and other avenues became the sole owner of the entire island. By 1909 financial difficulties forced Charles Gay to lose all but 600 acres of his farmland. On the remaining acres he planted pineapples and operated a piggery while moving his family from Koele to Keomuku. In 1909 a group of businessmen that included Robert Shingle, Cecil Brown and Frank Thompson purchased most of the island from Charles Gay for $375,000 and formed the Lana'i Ranch Company. At that time there were 22,500 sheep, 250 head of cattle and 150 horses. They changed the emphasis from sheep to cattle and spent $200,000 on ranch improvements. However, because the large herds were allowed to graze the entire island, destroying what vegetation was available, the cattle industry soon floundered. The island population had dwindled to only 102 at the turn of the 20th century, with 50 people living in Koele (which, by the way, means "farming") and the rest residing along the windward coastline in Keomuku. There were only 13 men to work the entire cattle ranch, an insufficient number to manage the 40,000 head of beef on land that was overgrazed by the cattle, pigs and goats that roamed freely.

George Munro, a New Zealander by birth who had visited the island in 1902, was asked to return to Lana'i by the new owners to manage the ranch. Soon after arrival he began instituting much-needed changes. He ordered sections of the range fenced and restricted the cattle to certain areas, allowing other areas to regrow. He also ordered the wild pigs and goats to be rounded up and destroyed. In 1911 a large three-million-gallon stormwater reservoir—now a beautiful reflecting pond—was built. In 1912 an effort to destroy the goat population began in earnest. The first year 5,000 goats were killed and an additional 3,300 more were destroyed by 1916. (It wasn't until the 1940s, however, that the last pigs and goats were captured.) In addition, sheep dogs were introduced to assist the cowboys.

The Norfolk pine tree planted in 1875 by Frederick Hayselden is the same one that stood outside Munro's home and has become a noted Lana'i landmark. It remains a stately sight right outside the Lodge at Koele.

Water continued to be a major concern. An amateur naturalist, Munro noted that the Norfolk pine tree outside his home seemed to capture the mist that traveled past the island. From that pine an idea was born, and Munro ordered the *paniolo* to carry a bag of Cook Island Pine seeds with them. They poked a small hole in the sack and, as they traveled the island on horseback, left a trail of seeds. The result is an island of more pines than palms. In 1914 the automobile age arrived on Lana'i in the form of a single 1910 Model T owned by George Munro. By 1917 there were 4,000 head of cattle and 2,600 sheep, but profits were slim and the Lana'i Ranch Company sold its land to the Baldwin family for $588,000. George Munro remained as foreman and the ranch slowly became more profitable. In 1920, axis deer were introduced on Lana'i from Moloka'i and a pipeline was constructed from Maunalei Gulch to provide fresh water.

James Dole came to Lana'i, liked what he saw and purchased the island in 1922 for $1.1 million from Alexander & Baldwin. George Munro was retained as manager. The Kaumalapua Harbor was dredged and a breakwater constructed in preparation for shipment of pineapple to O'ahu for processing. Lana'i developed into the single largest pineapple plantation in the world, which produced 90 percent of the United States' total pineapples. The company was called Hawaiian Pineapple Company until 1960, when the name was changed to the Dole Corporation. (Today it is called the Dole Company Foods.) Castle & Cooke acquired one-third ownership in the Hawaiian Pineapple Company soon after its purchase by Dole.

The community of Lana'i City also began in the 1920s. The houses were very small because families were discouraged. The workers arrived from Japan, Korea and the Philippines. The last residents left the Palawai and moved to Lana'i City between 1917 and 1929. The population of Lana'i soared to 3,000 by 1930. In 1923 Dole realized the need to provide a center for entertaining island guests and had "The Clubhouse" constructed. (Today it is known as Hotel Lana'i.) The dining room provided meals for guests as well as for the nurses and patients from the plantation hospital. Also constructed in the center of town was Dole Park. In the 1950s larger homes, located below Fraser Avenue, were built to accommodate the workers and their families, and employees were given the option of purchasing their homes fee simple. Today less than 100 Lana'ians are part- or full-blooded Hawaiian.

Geography and Climate

Lana'i is the sixth largest of the eight major Hawaiian islands. It is situated eight miles west of Maui and seven miles south of Moloka'i. It is likely that millions of years ago (when the glaciers were larger and the seas much lower), Maui, Lana'i, Moloka'i and Kaho'olawe comprised one enormous island. This is further substantiated by the fact that the channels between the islands are shallower and the slopes of the islands visibly more gradual than on the outer coastlines of the islands.

The island of Lana'i was formed by a single shield volcano. A ridge runs along the eastern half of the island and forms its most notable feature. This large, raised hump is dotted with majestic

MANELE BREAKWATER

The word *manele* means "soap berry plant" or is the word used for a hand-carried chair, a "sedan." The Manele boat harbor was once a small black-sand beach, and a fishing shrine found here indicates it was used by the early Hawaiians. You can spot the old *pepe* (cattle) ramp that Charles Gay used for loading his steers onto freighters.

In the 1970s E. E. Black was contracted to build the breakwater. It is traditional for any new project in Hawai'i to be blessed at the onset, but E. E. Black chose to forego the blessing. After only 20 feet of breakwater were constructed, the huge crane fell into the ocean and the people then refused to work. After great effort, another crane was brought over to lift the first from the ocean, but by the time it was recovered, the saltwater had taken its toll and it was worthless. Before resuming construction, E. E. Black held a blessing ceremony, the people returned to work, and the breakwater was completed without further incident.

Cook Island pines. The summit of the island is Lana'ihale, located at an elevation of 3,370 feet. A rather strenuous hike along the Munro Trail provides access to this summit, where you will be treated to the only location in Hawai'i where you can view (on a clear day) five other Hawaiian islands.

Maunalei and Hauola are Lana'i's two deepest gulches. Today the Maunalei Gulch continues to supply the island with its water. The center of the island, once a caldera, is the Palawai basin, which has been used as both farm and ranch land. Lana'i has one city, cleverly dubbed Lana'i City. Located at an elevation of about 1,700 feet, it can be much cooler—and wetter—than the coastline. It is the hub of the island, or what hub there is, and visitors soon learn that all roads lead to Lana'i City, where almost everyone resides. The houses are generally small, many roofed with tin, and the yards are abloom with fruits and flowers.

Rainfall along the coastline is limited to only 4 or 5 inches a year. The heart of the island and Lana'i City, however, may have rainfall of 20 inches or more, and the higher slopes receive 45 to 60 inches annually. The weather in Lana'i City might range from 80-degree days in September (with lows in the mid-60s) to cooler low-70s temperatures in January, dropping an additional 10 degrees at night. The coastline can be warmer by 10 degrees or more.

Pineapples and pines, not palms, were the predominant vegetation on the island. At its peak in the 1970s, there were 15,000 acres of pineapple in cultivation. Castle & Cook made the decision in the

1980s to diversify the island and enter the tourist industry in a big way. The pineapple fields have been reduced to only about 120 acres, just enough for local consumption. The production of hay and alfalfa is underway, and some fields are spotted with Black Angus cattle. Other acreage has been converted to an organic garden for use by the Manele and Koele restaurants.

The island flower, the kaunaoa, is an unusual vine. There are two varieties—one grows in the uplands and the other near the ocean. The ocean species has a softer vine with more vivid hues of yellow and orange than its mountainous counterpart. Strands of the vine are twisted and adorned with local greens and flowers to make beautiful and unusual leis. The mountain vines make a stiffer lei and, I was told, are used as leis for decorating animals. One of the best places to spot this plant is along the drive down to Keomuku and Shipwreck Beach or along the shoreline.

You will note that Lana'i is a very arid island. Water supply has always been a problem and most of the greenery is supplied by the Cook Island pines that dot the landscape.

Island Ecology

You'll notice very quickly that there are many birds on Lana'i, a far greater number than on Maui. Fortunately for the birds, Lana'i does not have the mongoose as a predator. Wild turkeys, the last non-native animal to be introduced to Lana'i, are abundant. The easiest place to spot them is down near the Manele boat harbor, where a group of turkeys and a pack of wild cats together enjoy the leftovers from the *Trilogy* boat's daily picnics.

Pheasant are also abundant and are hunted seasonally. Wild goats were rounded up and captured years ago. The only island pigs are in the piggery, where they are raised for island consumption. Pronghorn antelope, introduced in 1959, have now been hunted to extinction. Twelve axis deer were introduced by George Munro and have adapted well to Lana'i. It is estimated that there are some 3,000 to 6,000 animals and, given the fact that they produce offspring twice yearly, the number is ever-growing. In fact, deer far outnumber Lana'i's human population. The deer run a mere 110 to 160 pounds and are hunted almost year-round. It is easiest to spot these lean, quick deer in the early mornings or late evenings bounding across fields; during the day they seek sheltered, shaded areas. There are still a few remaining mouflon sheep, which have distinctive and beautiful curved horns. You'll note many of the houses in Lana'i City are decorated with arrays of horns and antlers across their porch or on a garage wall.

Traveling with Children

Kids of any age will love Lana'i. There are plenty of activities from beach-going to horseback riding. Older kids can take a sea kayak trip, hike, golf, or try their hand at archery or shooting at the sporting clay facility.

The Manele Bay Hotel and the Lodge at Koele offer the **Pilialoha Keiki Camp** for children 5 to 12 years. (*Pilialoha* means close friendship and beloved companionship.) The program adheres to a multi-age approach where older and younger children share, interact and have fun. Group sizes are small, allowing close attention to the interest of each child. They require a minimum of two children to operate the day and night programs and require 24-hour advance reservations. In the event your child must arrive earlier or depart later than the session, a fee of $10 per child per half-hour will be charged. The daily half-day, full-day or evening (Tuesday and Friday only) programs are full of great adventures: full-day program (9 a.m.-3 p.m.) $60, morning session (9 a.m.-12:30 p.m.) $40, afternoon session (11:30 a.m.-3 p.m.) $40, evening session (5 p.m.-10 p.m.) $55. Daily activities vary, but might include a chance to explore tide pools, play tennis, trek through the Manele Bay Gardens in search of koi fish ponds, creeping crawlers and waterfalls, or build a volcano at Hulopo'e Beach. The Pilialoha program is for registered guests only.

Babysitting is available for $15 per hour with each additional child at $3 per hour and a three-hour minimum. Also available for parents are baby joggers, umbrella strollers, cribs, childproofing of guest rooms, car seats and playpens.

FUN FOR KIDS

There are many activities your child can enjoy on Lana'i. Activities appropriate for young people include tennis lessons, half- or full-hour for youths 12 and younger; golf lessons at the Challenge at Manele (private or semi-private). Children 5 and up can enjoy a pony ride ($10), children 9 and up are invited on the one-hour Plantation horseback excursion ($35), and youth 12 and up can have private horseback riding lessons or take the two-hour Paniolo ride. A five-hour excursion on *Trilogy* is offered for $42.50 (ages 11 and younger), $85 (12 and older). Scuba and snorkeling lessons at the Manele Bay Hotel pool for those 8 years and up. Hiking, biking and sporting clay activities also available.

Weddings & Honeymoons

With its quiet, secluded nature, Lana'i may well be one of the most romantic places on earth. (Just ask Bill Gates who—famously—rented out the entire island for his wedding a few years back.) A Lana'i wedding can be arranged through the resorts. The various wedding packages include a garden setting at Manele Bay Hotel or a gazebo at the Lodge at Koele, minister, bouquet, bridal leis and much more. Or you can choose your special wedding day arrangements à la carte. Contact Castle & Cooke Resorts Wedding Services. 808-565-2426.

Getting There

To reach Lana'i you may travel by air or sea. The Lana'i Airport is serviced by **Island Air** (see "Transportation" in Chapter 1). Airfare is currently running approximately $85 from Oahu and $125 from Maui one-way to Lana'i.

From Maui, you can travel a cool and comfortable 45 minutes by boat from the Lahaina harbor aboard **Expeditions**. For a $25 one-way ticket (children $20), you can have a scenic tour spotting dolphins, flying fish and whales during the winter season. It is a pleasant way to travel, and much more affordable for a family than air transportation. The boat travels round-trip five times daily to Manele Small Boat Harbor, where a shuttle van will pick you up for transport to the Manele Bay Hotel and from there up to the Lodge at Koele. Reservations are advised, as space is limited. They can also arrange a leisurely overnight stay, golf, jeep or guided-tour package. Overnight parking is provided in Lahaina. *800-695-2624; 808-661-3756; www.go-lanai.com.*

On your return, you'll be happy to know that Lana'i Airport has a Federal agricultural inspection station so you can check your luggage directly through to the mainland.

Getting Around

For guests of the resorts or those who have golf reservations, you can take the complimentary shuttle every half-hour between Manele Bay Hotel and the Lodge at Koele. The shuttle also stops at Hotel Lana'i along the way.

For independent exploration of the island, check with **Dollar Rent-A-Car**. Compact $59.99, full-size $79.99, mini-van $129, or Jeep Wrangler $129. (The Jeep Wrangler is the only vehicle permitted to go off the paved roads.) Rented on a 24-hour basis. (Major car repairs require that the unit be transferred by barge to Honolulu, hence the inflated rates.) The rental car company notes that given the unique terrain of the island, they are not able to obtain (and therefore cannot provide) insurance of any kind on rental vehicles. Renters take full responsibility for the vehicle, whether it is damaged by the renter or a second or third party. Dollar provides complimentary shuttle service for renters to and from Expeditions (at the small boat harbor) or the airport. *800-533-7808; 808-565-7227.*

Rabaca's Limousine Service offers hourly charter rates as well as airport transfers. Neal Rabaca provides 24-hour limousine service in his seven-passenger Mercury Grand Marquis. Call for hourly rates. Island tours are also available. *P.O. Box 304, Lana'i City, HI 96763. 808-565-6670; fax 808-565-6670; e-mail: rabaca@aloha.net.*

Adventure Lana'i EcoCentre rents on- and off-road vehicles. All come with "fat" offroad mud tires, roof rack, towels, masks, fins, snorkel, ice chest and island map. Contact them for rates. *808-565-7373; e-mail: treklanai@maui.net; www.adventurelanai.com.*

What to See, Where to Shop

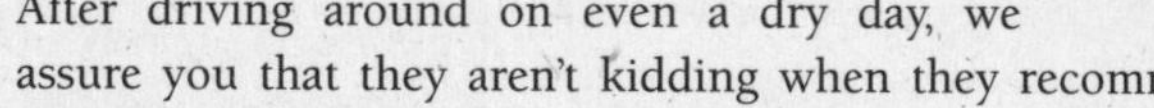

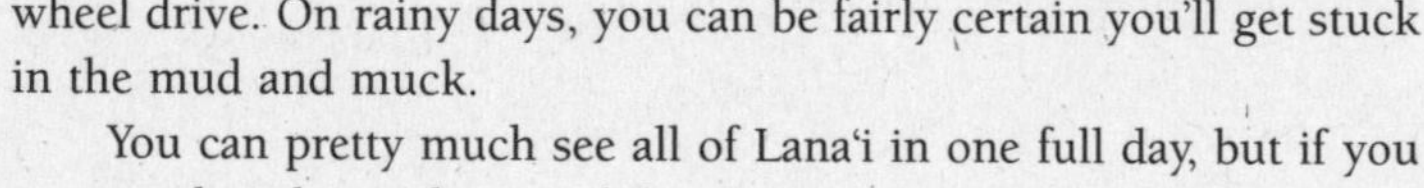

There are only three paved roads on Lana'i outside of Lana'i City, no stoplights and very few street signs once you leave town. After driving around on even a dry day, we assure you that they aren't kidding when they recommend a four-wheel drive. On rainy days, you can be fairly certain you'll get stuck in the mud and muck.

You can pretty much see all of Lana'i in one full day, but if you want to slow down, do some hiking or simply sit in the sun on a quiet beach, there is plenty to occupy you for days. Either of the resorts can provide you with a map and advice.

If you rent a car, you'll be limited to the paved roads on the island. A four-wheel-drive vehicle will get you out to more sights, as long as the roads are open. Be sure to bring along a picnic, and definitely some water. The car rental company will close roads that are impassable. You can check out the Dollar "accident" book and see why you need a four-wheel drive. The roads are a little better marked now than they were the first time I toured the island. The first part of the road to the Garden of the Gods was through pastures, and rains had left it seriously rutted. A second road next to the first was only slightly less bumpy. (Kidney buster is what they called it at the car rental agency, and for good reason.) A lovely stand of ironwoods with pale green needles covering the ground almost looked like a recent snowfall. It now takes less than 30 minutes to travel east and reach the Garden of the Gods. Just before you reach the Garden you'll note a pullout to your right. This **self-guided trail** was installed by the Nature Conservancy. The five-minute walk takes you on a visual exploration of the plants that have been introduced over the past centuries that are threatening the native species. They hope to expand the trail to include an area with more native plants.

The **Garden of the Gods** (Keahikawelo), which was named in 1935, is perhaps viewed best in the early morning or late evening when the shadows cast bizarre light on this lunar-like and rather mystical place. In the early morning, on a clear day, you can see the faint outline of Honolulu's skyscrapers and a sharp eye can observe axis deer out foraging. The rays of the sun in the early evening cast strange shadows on the amber-baked earth and huge monolithic rocks and your imagination can do the rest as the wind whistles over the landscape and you hear the distant call of a bird. Interestingly enough here, in what seems to be the middle of nowhere, are street signs. One indicates Awalua Road, which is a very rugged and steep dirt path down to the ocean. Most of these roads are used by the local residents for fishing or hunting. Be advised, if you attempt to start down, there may be no place to turn around should you change your mind. Follow Polihua Road and you'll arrive at a stretch of white sandy beach with rolling sand dunes.

According to Lawrence Kainoahou Gay, in his account entitled "True Stories of the Island of Lana'i," *Polihua* means *poli* (cover or bay) and *hua* (eggs). He reported that in this area turtles would visit to lay their eggs above the high water mark. He had seen turtles, in days gone by, that were large enough to carry three people! This beach is not recommended for swimming or other water activities.

The Kaena Road winds down to a very isolated area called **Kaena Iki Point**, which is the site of one of Lana'i's largest *heiau*.

Shipwreck Beach, or Kaiolohia, on Lana'i's northeast coast, is about a half-hour drive along a paved road from the Lodge at Koele. The road is lined with scrub brush, and as you begin the descent to the shoreline you catch a glimpse of the World War II liberty ship. Be sure to keep an eye out for pheasant, deer, turkeys and small Franklin partridges.

At the bottom of the road you can choose to go left to Shipwreck Beach or continue straight and follow the coastline on the unpaved, dusty and very rugged **Awalua Road** to the now defunct Club Lana'i.

Club Lana'i was a day resort that shuttled visitors from Lahaina, Maui, to the leeward shores of Lana'i for a day of relaxation and recreation—sort of a Hawaiian version of Gilligan's Island. It's a bit of a drive and slow-going getting there; four-wheel-drive vehicles are advised. It is about five miles down the road to **Keomuku**, where there are still remnants of the failed Maunalei Sugar Company, and a Japanese cemetery, also a memento of the failed sugar company. The old **Kalanakila Church** (aka Malamalama Church), located near Keomuku, is in the process of being renovated.

The beaches along this coastline are wonderful for sunbathing or picnicking, but not advisable for swimming. If you keep driving south, you'll run into **Lopa** and **Naha**, two uninhabited old villages. There are also some ancient Hawaiian trails at Naha. The road ends at Naha and you'll have to drive back along the same route.

If you're headed for Shipwreck Beach, drive northwest. This is **Lapahiki Road**, and while ordinarily dry and bumpy it could be impassable even in a four-wheel-drive vehicle during heavy rains. If you have a regular rental car, you can park here and walk down the road to the beach, but it is a bit of a trek. The dirt road is lined by *kiawe* trees and deserted shacks. This is a getaway spot for the local residents, although there is no fresh water. The reef along **Kaiolohia Beach** is very wide, but the surf can be high and treacherous.

There is a remnant of an old lighthouse and also some old petroglyph sites near Shipwreck Beach. The concierge desk can give you a list of petroglyphs around the island. Please respect these ancient

SHIPWRECKS AND GROUNDINGS

During a storm, waves come crashing down over the liberty ship that sits beached on the reef. This was one of three Navy L.C.M. ships that were not shipwrecked but purposely grounded here in 1941 and 1942. The other two have disappeared after losing their battle with the ocean. Barges are also towed here, anchored and left to rot. The channel between here and Moloka'i is called *Kolohi,* which means mischievous and unpredictable. The channel between Lana'i and Maui is the *'Au'au* ("to bathe") channel. There were several other ships that were wrecked here or on other parts of the island. In the 1820s the British ship *Alderman Wood* went aground and in 1826 the American ship *London* was wrecked off Lana'i. In 1931, George A. Crozier's *Charlotte C.* foundered somewhere along the beach. A 34-foot yawl called *Tradewind* was wrecked off the mouth of the Maunalei Valley on August 6, 1834, while cruising from Honolulu to Lahaina.

sites. The beach is unsafe for swimming, but you might see some people shore fishing. Sometimes after storms, interesting shells, old bottles and assorted artifacts are washed up along the shoreline.

Pohaku 'O, which roughly translates to mean "rock," is located in the Mahana region on Lana'i's leeward side. The rocks here resemble tombstones and were avoided by the early Hawaiians as a place of evil. If the breezes are favorable, the wind blowing by the rock creates an "O" sound that changes with the wind, which is the reason this rock received its evil connotations.

For another adventure, leave Lana'i City and follow Kaumalapau Highway past the small airport and continue on another five minutes toward **Kaumalapau Harbor**. It's paved all the way. The harbor isn't much to see, but the drive down to the water shows the dramatically different landscape of Lana'i's windward coastline. Here you can see the sharply cut rocky shoreline that drops steeply into the ocean, in some places more than 1,500 feet.

Kaunolu Bay can be accessed from the Kaumalapau Highway along a very rugged road. Follow the road just a bit farther and you'll reach Kaumalapau Harbor.

Hulopo'e Beach, along a crescent of white sandy beach, is a splendid marine reserve. It is in front of the Manele resort and is Lana'i's best swimming beach. As with all beaches, be aware of surf conditions. There are attendants at the beach kiosk who can provide beach safety information. Although netting and spearfishing are not allowed, shore fishing is permitted. The best snorkeling is in the morning before the surf picks up. Across the bay from the Manele Bay Hotel are a series of tidal pools. When the tide drifts down, sea creatures emerge, making this a great spot for exploration.

The Lodge at Koele and Manele Bay Hotel offer a handy *Tide Pool Guide*, prepared by Kathleen Kapalka. It notes that the Hulopo'e Bay and tidepool areas are both part of a marine-life conservation district that was set up in 1976. Also included in the conservation district are Manele Bay and Pu'upehe Cove, and as such, all animals and plants (dead or alive) are protected from collection or harm. The color brochure is an easy-to-follow guide to these wonderful tidal areas. Mollusks, arthropods, marine vertebrates, annelids, echinoderms, marine invertebrates and marine plants are described and illustrated. Safety and conservation tips include the fact that suntanning oils are detrimental and should be cleansed from the hands before reaching into the pools. This is an excellent brochure, which will make your tidal pool adventure a valuable learning experience. *Note*: Reef shoes are available at the hotel's beach kiosk for resort guests, a recommended protection when prowling around the rocky shoreline.

Climb up the bluff above the beach and you will be rewarded with a great view of Maui and Kaho'olawe. A large monolithic rock sits off the bluff. This is **Pu'upehe** (often referred to as Sweetheart Rock), which carries a poignant local legend. As with most oral history, legends tend to take on the special character of the storyteller. Such is the story of Pu'upehe. We asked people about the legend and heard different versions. One made the hero into a jealous lover, the other a thoughtful one. So here is our interpretation. There was a strong handsome young Hawaiian man whose true love was a beautiful Hawaiian woman. They made a sea cave near Pu'upehe rock their lover's retreat. One day the man journeyed inland to replenish their supplies, leaving his love in the sea cave. He had gone some distance when he sensed an impending storm. He hurriedly returned to the sea cave, but the storm preceded him and his love had drowned in the cave. He was devastated. Using superhuman strength he carried her to the top of the monolithic rock called Pu'upehe and buried her there before jumping to his death. Whether there is truth to this legend is uncertain, but some years back a scientist did scale the top of the peak, which was no easy task, to investigate. No bones or other evidence were found. However, we were told that in ancient times, the bones were removed and hidden away. And so ends this sad tale of lost love.

Manele Bay is a quaint boat port that offers excellent snorkeling just beyond the breakwater. When the surf at Hulopo'e is too strong, Lana'i tour boats often anchor here for snorkeling.

Other than the shops at the two large resorts, the only shopping area on Lana'i is at the Lana'i City Commercial Square (more commonly referred to as Dole Park, since the park is at its center)—a very large name for a very small area. Located in the heart of Lana'i City, it is an old-fashioned rectangular town square offering virtually all of the island's local restaurants, shops and grocery stores. Nearly everything (including restaurants and grocery stores) in this Dole Park area is closed on Sunday, so plan your Lana'i City shopping and dining excursion for some other day of the week or you'll be sorely disappointed.

Starting your walk from the Lana'i Playhouse and continuing down Seventh Street, you'll come to the **Mike Carroll Gallery**. Surely, this is the gem of the Dole Park shopping area. Opened in December 2002, this beautifully renovated gallery features the works of Lana'i and Maui artists, including jewelry, paintings, woodcraft, fine-art photography and antique furnishings. Open Monday through Saturday, 10ish a.m. to 5:30 p.m.; Sunday by chance or appointment. *808-565-7122; e-mail: mike@mikecarrollgallery.com; www.mikecarrollgallery.com.*

As you wander along Seventh Street note the clever street signs: "Coffee Works 1 block; Nome, Alaska 3,000 miles." You'll find restaurants Canoes Lanai and Blue Ginger Cafe (see Dining section for more information on restaurants). Just a short walk up Ilima Street is Coffee Works, if you're in the need of a snack or a pick-me-up drink.

At the corner of Ilima and Seventh Street is **Gifts with Aloha**, owned and operated by Kim and Phoenix Dupree. This store offers jewelry, *koa* products, quilts, candles and books as well as clothing and footwear. They feature raku pieces, ceramic ornaments, fusible glass, handmade beads and island wood creations made by Lana'i artists and craftspeople. Open Monday through Saturday, 9:30 a.m. to 6 p.m. *808-565-6589; www.giftswithaloha.com.*

The **Local Gentry** (owned by Jenna Gentry) is located behind Gifts with Aloha. A clothing boutique, this store offers some great clothes for men, women and children, as well as swimsuits and shoes. Open Monday through Friday, 10 a.m. to 6 p.m.; Saturday 10 a.m. to 5 p.m. *808-565-9130.*

The **Lana'i Art Center** provides arts and cultural experiences for residents and visitors through classes, workshops, studio access and their gallery and exhibitions. The gallery features works from over 20 Lana'i artists. Open Monday through Saturday, noon to 4 p.m. *808-565-7503; www.lanaiart.org.*

At Fraser Avenue, walk over to Eighth Street. You'll pass the courthouse and the wooden Lana'i Jail. Pele's Other Garden, a deli and bistro, is located here, then you'll come to **Pine Isle Market**, one of Lana'i's three grocery and general stores. Cafe 565 is next, then **Dis 'N Dat**, a delightful little store, greets you with hundreds of mobiles, glistening crystals and wind chimes dangling from the store's ceiling. Open Monday through Saturday, 10:30ish to 5:30ish (you'll notice hours are flexible on easy-going Lana'i). *808-565-9107; www.disndatlanai.com.*

Richard's Shopping Center (dating back to 1946) is next, offering another grocery/general store for residents and visitors. And that completes the Dole Park excursion. Back on Lana'i Avenue, turn onto Queens Street and look for the **Heart of Lana'i Gallery** (it's the bright yellow house behind Hotel Lana'i). The gallery is open Tuesday through Saturday (hours vary), with tea served from 2:30 to 4:30

The building in the middle of Dole Park was once a bowling alley, pool hall and restaurant until the late 1970s, when it was made into a meeting hall. As a part of the development of Lana'i, David Murdock had a large new community center built, complete with swimming pool. It's located a block away from the park.

p.m. (Owner Denise Hennig serves home-baked tea cakes and pastries at these afternoon affairs.) *808-565-7815.*

Where to Stay

There are currently three choices for hotel accommodations: Lana'i's original Hotel Lana'i, and two luxury hotels, Manele Bay Hotel and the Lodge at Koele.

CAMPING ON LANA'I

Tent camping is available at **Hulopo'e Bay Beach Park**, which has six sites. Restrooms, outdoor showers, grills, picnic tables, and drinking water. The cost is $5 for the permit and $5 per day per person, with a maximum stay of three nights. Reservations are required. Permits are issued by the administrative office of the Castle & Cooke Resorts company. They can be reached at *P.O. Box 630310, Lana'i City, HI 96763; 808-565-3982.*

Camping equipment is available for rent from **Adventure Lana'i EcoCentre**, *808-565-7373; e-mail: treklanai@maui.net; www.adventurelanai.com.*

PRIVATE HOMES

Kay Okamoto of **Okamoto Realty** offers single family homes in Lana'i City for short-term vacation rentals. 808-565-7519.

BED AND BREAKFASTS

Lana'i Plantation Home

1168 Lana'i Avenue. 800-566-6961; 808-565-6961; www.dreamscometruelanai.com.

Michael and Susan Hunter operate this B&B, also known as "Dreams Come True." The Plantation Home offers four rooms, each with a private bathroom embellished in fine Italian marble, with whirlpool tubs and ventilation skylights. Three of the bedrooms have queen beds and the other consists of two single beds. All come with hardwood floors, a built-in chest of drawers, reading lights and other amenities. A full kitchen and laundry room is also available. Primarily a B&B, the entire house can be rented and weekly rates are available. It will sleep up to ten people with two additional couch beds in the living room. B&B rates per night are $98.50 plus 11.4 percent tax and includes an island breakfast for two. Call for rate information if you're interested in renting the entire house. Also ask Susan or Michael about Lana'i adventure packages.

Hotel Lana'i

828 Lana'i Avenue (P.O. Box 630520, Lana'i City, HI 96763). 808-565-7211; 877-665-2624; fax 808-565-6450 from 7 a.m. to 8 p.m Hawaiian time; www.hotellanai.com; e-mail: hotellanai@wave.hicv.net.

Hotel Lana'i was built in 1923 by James D. Dole as a retreat for Dole Company executives and other important guests. Before the opening of the luxury resorts, this eleven-room hotel had the only accommodations on the island. You'll still find it quiet and comfortable, with rooms located in two wings of the original building and connected by a glass-enclosed veranda. All rooms have private tiled bathroom facilities, with pedestal sinks, hardwood floors, ceiling fans, country quilts and original pictures of Lana'i's old plantation days. The hotel and restaurant are owned and operated by the Richardson family. Rooms range from twins to kings, and don't plan on watching TV because there isn't any. Ask for a room on the back side if you want to go to bed early. The original caretakers' cottage is also available for rent.

There are three standard rooms: two double beds, two twin beds or one double bed ($105); three king rooms ($115); four Lana'i rooms with queen bed and view of Dole Square ($135); cottage with queen four-poster bed, TV, tub and private entrance ($175). Children under 9 are free in a room with parents, and others are an additional $10 per night. Hotel Lana'i offers a complimentary shuttle between Manele Bay Hotel and the Lodge at Koele. Transportation to and from the Manele Boat Harbor and the Lana'i Airport are provided for an extra charge. You'll want to book as far in advance as possible.

The Hotel Lana'i staff can arrange a variety of island activities, often with discounted rates. (The hotel works closely with Dollar Rental and Adventure Lana'i EcoCentre.)

★ ***Manele Bay Hotel***

Castle & Cooke Resorts, P.O. Box 630310, Lana'i City, HI 96763. 800-321-4666; 808-565-7700; fax 808-565-3868; www.manelebayhotel.com or www.islandoflanai.com.

The opulent Manele Bay Hotel is spread across the cliffside of Hulopo'e Beach like an enormous Mediterranean villa. It is a strikingly beautiful hotel with a pale green–tile roof. There are four buildings in the east wing and five in the west wing; each is slightly different. The rooms line sprawling walkways that meander through five lush courtyard gardens, each with a unique theme. The gardens include the Hawaiian, the Bromeliad, the

Chinese, the Japanese and the Kama'aina Gardens. The original resort plan called for a 450-room hotel directly on the beach, but was revised to the current structure with 250 rooms on the cliff alongside the beach. Behind the resort is the 18-hole golf course, the Challenge at Manele, which encompasses 138 acres along the ocean.

In many of the public areas the ceilings have been given special attention. In the main dining room are huge floral paintings; in the Hale AheAhe lounge you'll see fish and starfish. The resort took advantage of the talent of island residents, and much of the artwork is done by locals.

We enjoyed the proximity to the beachfront. The pool water is slightly warm, yet wonderfully refreshing. Attendants from the adjoining restaurant circulate, taking drink and sandwich orders. The poolside restaurant was a little pricey, but the portions were large. They provide a more economical children's menu here, as well as in their main dining rooms.

Be sure you take time to view the beautiful, large murals on either side of the entrance at the Manele Bay Hotel. One depicts Kaulula'au, the fallen son being taken by canoe to Lana'i. The other shows Kaulula'au, head held high in victory, standing over his signal bonfire.

If you're thinking that too much lying in the sun and fine food will affect your waistline, the fitness studio is open from 6 a.m. to 8 p.m. There is plenty of equipment for working out, then treat yourself to the steam room or a spa treatment.

This place is truly an island getaway, and many celebrities have found Lana'i to be a convenient, private and luxurious retreat. Don't be surprised if you find yourself rubbing shoulders with the rich and famous at this hotel. The Manele Bay Hotel has ranked in the top ten in *Condé Nast Traveler's* Readers' Choice Awards for a number of years. The rooms are spacious, a bit larger than the standard rooms at the Lodge. The bathroom amenities thoughtfully include suntan lotion and moisturizer in a little net bag to take along to the pool or beach. Some suites have private butler service (a fabulous amenity for families who can afford the splurge) and all have mini-bars and mini-refrigerators.

Garden Room $400, Partial Ocean View $525, Ocean View $650, Ocean Front $725, Deluxe Ocean Front $800, Mauka Mini-Suite $795, Mauka Suite $795, Ocean Mini Suite $1,200, Ocean Front Suite $1,500, Mauka Corner Suite $1,500, Makai Suite $2,000, Center Makai Suite $2,000, Makai Corner Suite $2,500, Presidential Suite $3,500.

A third person age 18 or older is charged an additional $75 per night. Maximum occupancy is three adults or four persons, including children.

Note: Change is in the works, as Four Seasons prepares to take over management at this resort and at the Lodge at Koele.

★ Lodge at Koele

Castle & Cooke Resorts. P.O. Box 630310, Lana'i City, HI 96763. 800-321-4666; 808-565-7300; fax 808-565-3868; www.lodgeatkoele.com or www.islandoflanai.com.

The serene and intimate Lodge at Koele is not what a visitor might expect to find in Hawai'i. This is not a beach resort. Instead, guests arrive via a stately drive lined with Cook Island pines to this Victorian/Plantation–era resort that typifies turn-of-the-20th-century elegance. The inscription on the ceiling of the entry was painted by artist John Wullbrandt and translates: *In the center of the Pacific is Hawai'i. In the center of Hawai'i is Lana'i. In the heart of Lana'i is Koele and it may quickly find its way into your heart as well.*

The Lodge at Koele continues to receive top accolades in *Condé Nast Traveler*'s "Gold List of World's Best Places to Stay." This award is voted upon by some 26,000 subscribers. It has always been one of my favorite island getaways, so completely different from anything else you will find in Hawai'i. You feel as if you have been transported out of the tropics to a sprawling English manor with cool, crisp mountain air.

When the Lodge at Koele was built in 1989, 35 local artists from the island of Lana'i were hired to contribute to the aesthetic design of the property. The island's unique art program was intended to introduce and integrate the small, closely knit and very talented community on Lana'i with the Lodge. The results were more extraordinary than anyone had imagined.

The 102 guest rooms at the Lodge are artistically decorated in three different fresh, bright color schemes. The artwork that lines the corridors was done by Lana'i residents and each floor has a different theme. The beds feature a pineapple motif and were custom-made in Italy, then handpainted by Lana'i artisans. The floral pictures on each door were painted by the postmaster's wife.

The rug in the entry is circa 1880, made of Tibetan wool. The Great Hall features enormous natural stone fireplaces that hint at the cooler evening temperatures here in upcountry Lana'i. The twin fireplaces on either side of the lobby are the largest in the state of Hawai'i and the Lodge itself sets the record for being Hawai'i's biggest wooden structure. The high-beamed ceilings give the room a spacious character, yet the atmosphere is welcoming and the comfortable furnishings invite you to sit and linger. Designer Joszi Meskan of San Francisco spent more than two years securing the many beautiful artifacts from around the world. A descriptive list is available from the concierge. The Great Hall's rug was handmade in Thailand for the resort and utilizes 75 different colors. Some of the furniture pieces are replicas, but many are antiques, including the huge altar desk where steaming morning coffee awaits the guests. Be sure to notice the two exotic chandeliers, with playful carved monkeys amid the leaves, designed by Joszi Meskan. The large portrait on one end of the Great Hall is of Madame Yerken, painted by Belgian artist Jan Van Born in 1852. An intricately stenciled border with antelope, deer and wild turkeys runs around the perimeter of the ceiling. Another more subtle stenciling is done around the floors. The skylights are beautiful etched glass. The furnishings are covered in lush brocade tapestries and suede upholstery in hues of burgundy, blue and green. The room is accented with fresh flowers, many of them orchids grown in the greenhouse located beyond the reflecting pool. The woodwork is finely carved, with pineapples often featured.

At the end of an exhausting day of vacationing, there is nothing like curling up in the big overstuffed armchair next to a crackling fire with an after-dinner drink to enjoy the evening entertainment (well-known Hawai'i pianist and singer Kimo Garner), play a game of checkers or visit with local women as they demonstrate Hawaiian quilting. The bellman, concierge and front desk staff are all crisply attired in pine green suits.

Several public rooms surround the Great Hall. The library overlooks spacious lawns and offers newspapers from around the world as well as books, backgammon and chess. The Trophy Room also has an assortment of board games and an interesting, but very uncomfortable, English horn chair. Both of these rooms have fireplaces that can be lit at the request of the guest. A grounds tour is offered daily. Each afternoon there is a traditional tea service offered in the Music Room, featuring a high caliber of loose-leaf and rare teas: Jasmine Dragon Phoenix Pearls, Single-estate Darjeeling and Yinzhen Silver Needles, to name a few. An assortment of tea sandwiches, warm English scones with Devonshire cream, tropical butter and fruit preserves along with cakes and pastries complement the service.

Surrounding the main building is a wonderful veranda with comfortable rattan furniture accented by Hawaiian quilted pillows. Huge trees hug the building and the view of the horses and fields beyond has a tranquilizing effect. The setting is truly picture perfect. Adjoining the Great Hall is the Terrace Dining Room, open for breakfast, lunch and dinner. The food is excellent and the service outstanding.

The hotel is located on the site of the farming community known as Koele. The pine-lined driveway was planted in the 1920s and led to the 20 or 30 homes in this area. Only two remain on the property and are owned by the Richardson family, descendants of the early Lana'i *paniolo*. The church was moved to the front grounds of the Lodge and a small schoolhouse is being restored and converted into a museum. The grounds of this country manor are sprawling and exquisitely landscaped. More than a mile of lush garden pathways and an orchid house can be enjoyed while strolling the grounds. The large reflecting pond was once the reservoir for the town of Koele.

There are plenty of activities to be enjoyed—from strolling the grounds, enjoying the putting course, swimming or just relaxing in the jacuzzi. In fact, it is so relaxing and so lovely that you won't even miss the beach. But if you're hankering for some sand and sun, it is only a 20-minute shuttle trip to the shore.

Guest bathrooms have Italian tile floors and vivid blue marble countertops. Room amenities are thoughtfully packaged and include an array of fine toiletries. There are in-room televisions with video recorders and a couple of beautifully carved walking sticks (as well as an umbrella for those upcountry showers) in the closet to tempt you to enjoy a leisurely walk around the grounds or along the Munro Trail (accessible from the Lodge). The workout facility by the pool provides free weights and aerobic machines, and the small spa facility provides a variety of massage therapies.

Garden Koele Room ($400), Koele Deluxe Room ($575), Norfolk Suite ($725), Terrace Suite ($725), Banyan Suite ($900), Koele Suite ($1,200), Fireplace Entrance Suite ($1,500), Fireplace Garden Suite ($2,200). The Koele Suites have a wraparound lanai and a separate living and sleeping area with a Murphy bed in the living room. The Garden Koele Room and Koele Deluxe Room can be combined into one large living area. The Norfolk, Terrace, Banyan or Fireplace Garden suites provide separate living room and sleeping areas, and an oversized lanai. Located along the balcony above the Great Hall, these are the only guest rooms that are air conditioned. The Fireplace suites are slightly larger than the standard rooms and just as beautifully decorated.

As much as we enjoy the Manele Bay Hotel, we find something very appealing about the Lodge in upcountry. Perhaps it is because the service is so superb, perhaps it is because the air is so fresh, perhaps it is the comfortable and homey quality of the Great Hall, or perhaps it is because we truly are in the heart of Lana'i. This resort has a special quality, and both the kids and adults in your party will be enchanted. Given the many awards and accolades they have received, we're not alone in our impressions.

Note: Change is in the works, as Four Seasons prepares to take over management at this resort and at the Manele Bay Hotel.

Where to Dine

If you want to purchase your own groceries, there are three grocery stores to choose from: **Richard's**, which has the honor of being on Lana'i since 1946, the small **Pine Isle Market**, and **International Food & Clothing**. Since everything must be brought in by barge, prices are steep. Don't be surprised if they are closed for noontime siesta, closed on Sunday and closed for the day by 6 p.m. (or earlier). Lana'i pineapples are available for sale at all three groceries. We suggest you purchase one and sample the difference between the mainland version of this fruit and the field-ripened variety.

Other than the resort restaurants, none of Lana'i's dining experiences are "fancy." They are very low-key, informal, local-style places. So don't expect great ambiance, but do expect good eats.

Hint: If you intend to dine in one of the resort restaurants on the first night you arrive, make your dinner reservation in advance. We arrived late in the afternoon at the Lodge and were unable to get a dinner reservation at the hotel until late (too late for us) in the evening. (We went to Dole Park for dinner instead.) So plan ahead for your first night's dining.

★ ***Blue Ginger Cafe***

409 7th Street (Dole Park), Lana'i City. 808-565-6363.

Hours: 6 a.m.-8 p.m. daily (until 9 p.m. on Friday and Saturday). Presently, Blue Ginger is the only Dole Park restaurant that is open for dinner on Sunday. *Comments:* Next door to Tanigawa's is the Blue Ginger Cafe, which serves up some of the best freshly made pastries in town, including their own fresh-baked bread. Start your day with omelets, breakfast burrito, banana pancakes or a "Patty Burger" (sausage, eggs and cheese). The French toast is divine. (Breakfasts $2-$8.) Lunches include sandwiches, local-style plate lunches and saimin; dinners include steak, seafood and pizza. All meals are under $15. I had the sauteed mahi with capers, mushrooms and onions and it was moist and flavorful ($13.95). My husband had the prime rib special, which included prime rib, corn chowder, a warm, buttery homemade dinner roll, and banana *lumpia* à la mode for dessert. All that for $14.95. Again, there is no fancy ambiance here, but they serve up good food and lots of it. Great T-shirts for sale, too. No credit cards accepted.

Café 565

408 8th Street (Dole Park), Lana'i City. 808-565-6622.

Hours: Monday through Friday 10 a.m.-3 p.m. and 5-8 p.m.; closed Saturday and Sunday. Café 565 features a blend of local and ethnic cuisines with daily specials. There are hot and cold sub sandwiches ($3.95-$5.25 junior size and $6.95-$9.65 full size). Specialty pizzas include tomato basil, wild garden, Greek or spicy chicken ($15.95-$19.95). Try a wild garden, Caesar, oriental chicken or tuna salad ($5.75-$8.95) and check out their daily soup and plate lunch specials (with two scoops of rice).

Challenge at Manele Clubhouse

Manele Bay Hotel. 800-321-4666; 808-565-7700; www.manelebay hotel.com.

Hours: Lunch daily 10:30 a.m.-3:30 p.m.; dinner 5:30-9 p.m. (except Tuesday and Wednesday). *Comments:* On the midday meal menu you'll find sandwiches ($13-$16), salads, appetizers, soups ($6-$22) or island favorites such as battered fish with fries or plate lunch specials ($14-$19). The evening menu offers a good selection of starters, soups and salads ($10-$18) followed by entrees such as miso-marinated salmon, Palawai chicken, Keahole lobster and oven-braised lamb shank ($26-$39). Lovely golf course and ocean views. Children's menu available.

Clubhouse Bar & Grill

Experience at Koele golf clubhouse, Lodge at Koele. 800-321-4666; 808-565-7300; www.lodgeatkoele.com.

Hours: 10:30 a.m.-4:30 p.m. *Comments:* This casual alternative offers a lunch menu with plenty of sandwich selections, from shaved roast beef with roasted peppers, onions and jack cheese to a smoked turkey club, shredded barbecue chicken or Mediterranean-style fresh grilled catch ($8-$14.50). Soup and fresh fish change daily. Indoor or outdoor lanai seating. Overlooks the Experience golf course and a scenic lake. Children's menu available.

Coffee Works

604 Ilima Street (just off Dole Park area). 808-565-6962; www.coffee workshawaii.com.

Hours: 6 a.m.-4 p.m.; closed Sunday. *Comments:* Lana'i's answer to Starbucks. Cute little coffee house in a green plantation-style cottage. Large outdoor deck seating area, shaded by umbrellas. Variety of refreshing hot or chilled coffee drinks, ice cream and pastries. Offers a wide selection of gourmet coffees by the pound.

Formal Dining Room

Lodge at Koele. 800-321-4666; 808-565-7300; www.lodgeatkoele.com.

Hours: Dinner 6-9:30 p.m. *Comments:* The menu makes excellent use of their five-acre organic farm to ensure the freshest ingredients in the meal preparations. For starters try the confit of salmon, roasted quail or pan-seared foie gras ($16-$19). Soups and salads include tomato bisque with ham and white truffle oil or Hirabara mixed greens with lemon vinaigrette and fresh clipped herbs ($13-$14). Entrees might include crispy-seared Hawaiian *moi*, roasted stuffed pheasant breast, roasted wild boar tenderloin or seared shrimp and scallops ($41-$46). For dessert, warm banana and bittersweet chocolate tart, hot apple crisp with pecan crunch and other delicacies ($11-$17). Lovely intimate setting with a fireplace. Jackets are required for men and you will need reservations. Children's menu available.

Harbor Cafe

Manele Small Boat Harbor.

Hours: 7 a.m.-2 p.m. *Comments:* They serve breakfast pastries, sandwiches, wraps, salads, box and plate lunches and assorted beverages ($1-$7). It's a cool place to rest and enjoy a light meal or shave ice while you wait for the interisland ferry.

★ *Henry Clay's Rotisserie*

Hotel Lana'i. 828 Lana'i Avenue, Lana'i City. 808-565-4700; www.hotellanai.com.

Hours: Restaurant and bar open nightly at 5:30 p.m. *Comments:* Henry Clay's Rotisserie features the Cajun-influenced island cuisine of its talented chef, Henry Clay Richardson, who held executive chef positions at some of Maui's most prestigious hotels and restaurants before he and his family moved to Lana'i. A popular hang-out for local island residents, this place was the island's first "signature" restaurant and a definite must-do on your Lana'i dining schedule. With a cozy "country inn" ambiance, complete with fireplaces, the restaurant offers indoor or outdoor lanai seating and a display kitchen where you can see the rotisseries. Servings are very generous, and we found the service to be friendly and efficient. Chef Richardson is a native of New Orleans and his heritage is reflected in his menu selections. Starter selections include Henry Clay's homemade pâté, Pacific oyster shooters, Maui onion soup au gratin (deliciously laced with Madeira), and a wonderful wild mushroom rustic pie ($6.75-$12.95). Entrees are diverse, with a toasted butternut squash ravioli with tomato fondue, an eggplant Creole with angel hair pasta, free-range Lana'i axis deer and "almost grandma's" seafood gumbo among the choices, along with the barbecue pork ribs and rotisserie chicken ($19.95-$32.95). Good food and a delightful ambiance. The pecan pie ($5.75) and grilled banana Foster ($6.50) desserts are both fabulous.

Hulopo'e Court

Manele Bay Hotel. 800-321-4666; 808-565-7700; www.manelebay hotel.com.

Hours: 7-11 a.m. breakfast; 6-9:30 p.m. dinner. *Comments:* The Hulopo'e Court in the Manele Bay Hotel is the more casual of two dining rooms at the resort and serves breakfast and dinner, with a children's menu available. Breakfast buffets $18 or $24. Breakfast à la carte entrees include brioche French toast with tropical *lilikoi* butter and cracked macadamia nuts, Hawaiian coconut and tapioca waffle with roasted island bananas, roasted vegetable frittata with island herbs and shaved parmesan, or a "Feast of Island Inspired Hash" that includes Hawaiian seafood with sweet peppers and sun-dried tomatoes and *imu*-roasted pork with Maui onions and Finnish potatoes ($10-$16). Side orders are also available as well as a bounty of fresh fruit juices, cereals and bakery items. The dinner menu is tropical American cuisine, using ingredients and flavors "from sun-drenched regions around the world." Cilantro hummus or guava-glazed baby back ribs might warm those tastebuds up for an entree of chilled lobster, prawn and scallop salad, spice-rubbed chicken, Hawaiian *moi* in a lemongrass ginger broth, "boneless" Dungeness crab or seared pork tenderloin with a cashew coconut crust ($17-$29). Children's menu available.

Ihilani

Manele Bay Hotel. 800-321-4666; 808-565-7700; www.manelebay hotel.com.

Hours: 7-11 a.m. breakfast (buffet or à la carte); 6-9:30 p.m. dinner. *Comments:* Ihilani is the Manele Bay Hotel's elegant formal dining room. The dinner menu is contemporary Mediterranean cuisine, including French and Italian specialties. A sample dinner might be ahi carpaccio ($14) or marinated beet salad ($13) followed by rosemary-roasted baby chicken, baked *onaga* in a sea salt crust, clam and scallop linguine, or *kiawe*-smoked New Zealand lamb rack ($23-$44). Evening resort attire. Children's menu available.

Pele's Other Garden

8th and Houston Street (Dole Park), Lana'i City. 808-565-9628.

Hours: Monday through Saturday 10 a.m.-2:30 p.m. and 5-8 p.m. Closed Sunday. *Comments:* A clean, cute little deli and bistro, with a black and white checkerboard floor. Pele's Other Garden is operated by Mark Zigmond, who offers wonderful New York–style deli (hot and cold) sandwiches featuring a variety of lunch meats and cheeses.

You'll also find pizzas, salads and quesadillas, too ($4.50-$7.99). Picnic lunches for two available. The dinner bistro menu includes such appetizers as shrimp cocktail, garlic bread and teri ribs ($3.50-$9). Entrees ($13-$20) range from butterfly pasta in creamy pesto with prosciutto and garlic shrimp to teriyaki ribs and rice, cheese ravioli with marinara, or beef and vegetable stew ($10-$17). Pizzas (8" $6-$8; 16" $12-$19) are also available for dinner. Dinner reservations and pre-orders recommended.

Pool Grille

Manele Bay Hotel. 800-321-4666; 808-565-7700; www.manelebay hotel.com.

Hours: Daily 11 a.m. until 5 p.m. lunch; 6-9:30 p.m. dinner (except Sunday and Monday evenings). *Comments:* Lunch offers light fare and local favorites including a smoked turkey club sandwich, lobster and shrimp club, hamburger or a vegetable and portobello panini ($10-$18). Dinner offers grilled steaks and fresh seafood in a casual setting. All dinners include soup or salad. (Dinner entrees $32-$44.) Children's menu available.

Tanigawa's/Canoes Lana'i

419 7th Street (Dole Park), Lana'i City. 808-565-6537.

Hours: Breakfast and lunch 6:30 a.m.-1 p.m.; closed Wednesday. *Comments:* A small local-style restaurant. You can select from plate lunches, sandwiches or burgers $3-$10, and breakfasts (omelets, pancakes) $5-$8. The fare is filling and the atmosphere charmingly local.

The Terrace

Lodge at Koele. 800-321-4666; 808-565-7300; www.lodgeatkoele.com.

Hours: Daily continental breakfast 6-7 a.m.; full breakfast 7-11 a.m.; lunch 11 a.m.-2 p.m.; dinner 6-9:30 p.m. *Comments:* Breakfast features poached eggs on blue crab cakes with orange hollandaise, forest mushroom omelet, or brioche French toast with vanilla bean sauce ($7.50-$19). Lunch offers a creative selection of salads and sandwiches such as mini lobster sandwiches, Lana'i venison pastrami sandwich or a burger with sharp cheddar and applewood-smoked bacon ($11-$22). Dinner features an equally tantalizing but less expensive menu than the Lodge's Formal Dining Room. Starters include grilled sea scallops, *il carnaroli* risotto, fresh salmon and crab salad or shrimp cocktail with hearts of palm ($11-$16). Entrees offer chef's seafood selection of the day, fresh fettuccine and braised clams, barbecue smoked boneless pork ribs, baked stuffed *walu* or oven roasted veal chop ($24-$37). Dinner reservations are recommended and evening resort attire is requested. Children's menu available.

Beaches

Along Lana'i's northern shore is **Polihua**. There is an interesting stretch of long sand dunes. This coast is often very windy, and some days the blowing sand is intense. The surf conditions are dangerous and swimming should never be attempted. Also along the northern shore is the area from **Awalua to Naha**. The beaches are narrow and the offshore waters are shallow with a wide reef. However, the water is often murky. Swimming and snorkeling are not recommended. **Lopa**, on the eastern shore, is a narrow white-sand beach that can be enjoyed for picnicking and sunbathing. Surf conditions, however, can be dangerous.

Along the western coastline is **Kaunola**, a rocky shore with no sandy beach and no safe entry or exit. Conditions can be dangerous. Swimming is not advised at any time. Also on the western shore is **Kaumalapau Harbor**, the deep-water harbor used for shipping. Water activities are not recommended at any time.

The southern coastline affords the safest ocean conditions. Manele Bay is the small boat harbor, but water activity is not recommended due to heavy boat traffic. **Hulopo'e Bay** is the island's best and most beautiful white-sand beach. It is located in front of the Manele Bay Hotel. It is popular for swimming, surfing, boogie boarding and snorkeling. The tide pools make for fun exploration and, although a marine preserve, shore fishing is permitted. On summer weekends the camping area is often filled with local residents. However, large swells and high surf conditions can exist. During times of high surf, undertows become very strong. During these times it is not safe to stand or play even in the shore break, as severe injury can occur. Be aware of water safety signs. There are no lifeguards on duty; however, there are attendants at the resort's beach kiosk who might be able to answer questions you have. Never swim alone and always exercise good water safety judgment.

Where to Play

Lana'i offers a wealth of interesting activities for adults and children of all ages. There are short as well as ambitious hikes, and plenty of fun can be enjoyed off-roading to beaches and geological formations in a Jeep. You can spot axis deer, wild turkeys and perhaps even a mouflon sheep. Ocean activities include kayaking, scuba diving and snorkeling.

If exploring the island's beauty is not enough, kids might like trying their hand at the Lana'i Pine Sporting Clays (adjacent to the Lodge at Koele), where they provide youth-level target shooting. The pools at the Lodge at Koele and Manele Bay Resort both offer cool diversion, and those kids who hope to be a future Tiger Woods might enjoy the recreational putting course behind the Lodge at Koele. Feel like a *paniolo*? Then sign up for a horseback trail ride; kiddie rides are also available. Or grab a mountain bike and take off on the roads and trails. Read on to select your perfect Lana'i activities.

If you would like some company on your island tour, contact *Adventure Lana'i EcoCentre*, which offers guide services. They also offer guided group hikes, ocean activities and other tours. *808-565-7373; e-mail: treklanai@maui.net; www.adventurelanai.com.*

ARCHERY

Lana'i offers a modern archery range at the **Lana'i Pine Sporting Clays** complex. The 12-station range is set up for 5, 10, 15 and 20 yards, for the novice, intermediate or advanced archer. Recurve, compound and youth bows are available for rent at the pro shop. Private and group lessons are offered. The range is located on the north side on the plains of Mahana. There is complimentary transportation from the Lodge at Koele. Hours are 9:15 a.m. to 2:30 p.m. daily. Introductory lessons are $45 per hour (including equipment). Maximum of six per group. Range use for experienced archers is $35 per hour, including equipment, or $25 if you bring your own equipment (crossbows are not allowed). Arrangements can be made through the concierge at all Lana'i resorts.

ART & CULTURE

Lana'i Art Program If you're a resident or a visitor and interested in pursuing your artistic talents, you can register for the Lana'i Art Program. Classes are taught by local and visiting artists and might include a variety of paint medias or craft classes. *Raku* (Japanese pottery), silk screening, herbal wreaths, *gyotaku* (Japanese art using real fish to imprint a design on T-shirts). It is also a great place to purchase artwork done by local artists. The shop is open whenever they have volunteers. *339 7th Street, Lana'i City. 808-565-7503.*

Lana'i Visiting Artist Program Lana'i is abloom with artistic opportunities. The island's Lana'i Visiting Artist Program was initiated in 1992 to provide the Lana'i community and visitors an opportunity to interact with distinguished artisans from varying fields. Chefs, authors and artists are among the guests to visit the island each year. Check the website for the island and you will be directed to upcoming Artists in Residence events; www.lanai-resorts.com. All events (except dinners) are free of charge. For further information about the Visiting Artist Program, contact Castle & Cooke Resorts at 800-321-4666.

Lana'i Conference Center For history buffs, there is a permanent exhibit of Lana'i artifacts on display at the Lana'i Conference Center, the meeting and convention facility perched on a seaside knoll just above the Manele Bay Hotel. These items were returned "home" after their initial discovery and display at Honolulu's Bishop Museum.

BIKING

Lodge at Koele Mountain bikes can be obtained at the Lodge at Koele Activity Desk. Rates are $8 per hour or $40 for a full day (8 hours). A backpack lunch will be provided for an additional charge. You can enjoy Lana'i's scenic pathways or tour around town at your own pace.

Adventure Lana'i EcoCentre This company offers mountain bike rentals—24-speed aluminum-frame bikes. Beginning bicyclists can enjoy a van-supported downhill tour. You bike down the Keamoku switchbacks and then head down to the beach road to Federation Camp for refreshments, some short hikes to the petroglyphs and time for hunting shells and spotting humpback whales (seasonally). Contact them for rates. *808-565-7373; e-mail: treklanai@maui.net; www.adventurelanai.com.*

FISHING

Deep-sea fishing excursions are available. Check with the concierge at any of the resorts or hotels. The **Kila Kila**, a 53-foot luxury sportfishing boat, offers sportfishing charters and seasonal whale-watching tours. Half-day charter for a maximum of six people (4 hours) is $825; full day (8 hours) is $1,200. *Contact the Lana'i resorts or 808-565-6613.*

GOLF

There are a number of options for the golfer on Lana'i. There are two award-winning courses: The Experience at Koele and the Challenge at Manele. In addition, there is an older 9-hole community course (Cavendish), and a fun executive putting course adjacent to the Lodge.

Putting Course Golfers and non-golfers of all ages will delight in the executive putting course at Koele, a beautifully manicured course with assorted sand traps and pools lined with tropical flowers and sculptures. No charge for resort guests.

Challenge at Manele The Challenge at Manele, designed by Jack Nicklaus, opened on December 25, 1993. Built on several hundred acres of lava out-croppings among natural *kiawe* and *ilima* trees, this links-style golf course features three holes constructed on the cliffs of Hulopo'e Bay, using the Pacific Ocean as a dramatic water hazard. The five-tee concept challenges even the best golfers, requiring precise tee shots over natural gorges and ravines, while the average golfer will enjoy the beautiful vistas and play that isn't too punishing. 7,039 yards from the black tees. Par 72. *808-565-2222.*

The Experience at Koele This 18-hole course was designed by Greg Norman and Ted Robinson. The beauty of the course, with its lush natural terrain marked by thick stands of Cook Island pines and panoramic views, make concentrating on the game difficult for even the most expert golfer. The signature 17th hole plays from a 250-foot elevated tee to a fairway bordered by a lake on the right and trees and dense shrubs on the left. The course is laid out on a multi-tiered plan. The upper seven holes meet the lower eleven at the beautiful eighth tee. From the top of the bluff at the eighth tee is a view so stunning that our first thought was that this could be right out of Shangri-La. The mist floats by this enchanted valley filled with lush vegetation, and there's a lovely lagoon. The lagoon at one time had served as a back-up reservoir for the old cattle ranch. 7,014 yards from the tournament tees. *808-565-4653.*

Course rates for the 18-hole Challenge at Manele or The Experience at Koele is $225 for non-guests and $185 for hotel guests. Reservations for either course can be made from the mainland via their toll-free number 800-321-4666. www.lanairesorts.com.

Cavendish Golf Course The Cavendish, a 9-hole, 36-par, 3,071-yard course, runs along the front of the Lodge at Koele and was the island's first golf course. It is a community course and there is no phone, no clubhouse and no charge. (Donations are suggested to help with upkeep.) The first hole is a bit difficult to find. Drive up Fifth Street (toward the mountains) and turn left on Nani Street. It will lead you to the old clubhouse (often there is no one there, but local golf groups sometimes use it). No fee, no check-in, no starting time. Just grab your clubs and walk on the course.

HIKING

Walking sticks are provided in all the rooms at the Lodge at Koele for guest usage. It's almost impossible to resist strolling around the pastoral grounds. Near the Lodge at Koele are two small houses.

These were originally located where the orchid house is now. The Richardson families live here and their ancestors were among the early Lana'i *paniolos*. You can stroll around the front grounds to view the enormous Norfolk pine or watch guests try their hand at lawn bowling, croquet or the golf putting course. Walk down to the horse stables or peek inside the old church. The stables are new, but the church was relocated due to the construction of the Lodge. A small school was also moved and it is currently being restored and perhaps will one day house Lana'i's first museum.

The **Munro Trail** is a nine-mile arc trek along the ridge of Lana'i. The view from the 3,370-foot summit of Lana'ihale can be spectacular on a clear day. (This route can also be tackled by four-wheel-drive vehicles, but only during very dry conditions.) For the adventurous, there is also the **High Pasture Loop**, the **Old Cowboy Trail**, **Eucalyptus Ladder** or **Beyond the Blue Screen**. A light-to moderate-weight raincoat might be a good idea to take along if you're planning on hiking. The concierge can provide you with a map showing the various routes. Picnics can be provided by the hotel.

The Lodge offers a daily guided five-mile hike up to the **Koloiki Ridge**. The hike includes snacks and drinks and departs at 11 a.m., returning at 1:30 p.m. This is arranged through the hotel concierge. The fee is $20 per person; $65 per person, including backpack lunch. The Manele Bay Hotel offers a 90-minute guided nature hike on Tuesday and Friday mornings at 9 a.m. that goes up to **Sweetheart Rock**. This is an easy to moderate hike. Fee $15 per person. Private hikes can also be arranged through your resort concierge.

If you'd like to learn more about the flora of Hawai'i and the plight of the native species, contact The Nature Conservancy. Guided hikes can be arranged or you can enjoy a self-guided walk in the preserve. *730 Lana'i Avenue. 808-565-7430.*

Adventure Lana'i EcoCentre also offers some guided day hikes. Contact them for rates. *808-565-7373; e-mail: treklanai@maui.net; www.adventurelanai.com.*

HORSEBACK RIDING

The Lodge at Koele The Stables at Koele feature an impressive selection of rides, from a ten-minute children's pony ride to one- to three-hour group treks through the plantation along wooded trails (trail availability changes from year to year). More experienced riders can enjoy private rides and longer trips with a stop for lunch. Riding lessons (a two-rider limit

per lesson) are also available. Riders must wear long pants and sports shoes and children must be at least nine years of age and four feet, six inches in height to ride. Maximum weight of riders is 200 pounds. Safety helmets are provided for all riders. Prices begin at $10 for the children's introductory experience and $65 per person for the one-hour group ride on the Ko'ele trail. Private trail rides start at $90 per person for the first hour, $150 for two hours. Riding lessons start at $60 per hour. *Reservations can be made through the concierge at all of the hotels or 808-565-4424.*

HUNTING

Axis deer (*chital*) hunting is available year-round on the island of Lana'i and is managed by Castle & Cooke Game Management. Guided one-day hunting excursions $750 per person, plus a $105 fee for a non-resident license. This includes services of a guide with a 4-wheel-drive vehicle, light breakfast and lunch on the day of the hunt, complete caping, salting of hide or cape, and cleaning, loan of equipment (canteens, pack boards, knives, day packs), and assistance in packing out meat. *Contact Game Management, P.O. Box 630310, Lana'i City, HI 96763. 808-565-3981.*

Should you bring your own firearm, gun lockers are available at both the Lodge at Koele and the Manele Bay Resort. Be aware that any firearm brought into the state of Hawai'i for longer than three days must be registered with the State. Also, considering the prohibitions against transporting firearms by aircraft (even in checked luggage), it's best to leave yours at home.

Lana'i Pines Sporting Clays An unusual recreational option is the target range on the hillside just behind the Lodge at Koele. There is a free shuttle from the lodge. The 14-station solar-powered traps are designed to entice beginners and challenge experts. Choose packages with 50 ($85) or 100 ($145) targets. Packages include gun and cartridges, vest, eye protection and foam ear protection. After 100 targets the charge is $.80 per target and $8 per box of shells. À la carte pricing for cartridges and targets is available, as are gun rentals. Introductory instruction starts at $75 per person; private lessons are offered upon request. The complex also has six air rifle stations for novices and youngsters. Price is $36.75 for 204 shots. The range is open from 9:15 a.m. to 2:30 p.m. *808-559-4600.*

Lawn bowling and both English and American croquet fields surround the Lodge at Koele.

KAYAKING

Adventure Lana'i EcoCentre They offer kayak rentals that include towels, snorkel gear, paddles, life jackets and dry bags. They also offer a half-day snorkel/kayak adventure; full-day and overnight excursions can be arranged. Contact them for rates. *808-565-7373; e-mail: treklanai@maui.net; www.adventurelanai.com.*

Trilogy Lana'i Ocean Sports Trilogy offers a guided ocean kayaking excursion, Monday through Saturday mornings. All trips include hotel pickup, both single and double kayaks, snorkel gear and accessories, lunch, sodas and snacks. $125 per person. *Contact Trilogy through the resort concierge or call Trilogy direct at 888-628-4800; www.visitlanai.com or www.sailtrilogy.com.*

LAND TOURS

Adventure Lana'i EcoCentre Try their 4x4 adventure trek, which is a four-hour beginning-level jeep excursion available in the morning or afternoon. They stop at Lana'i's Cook Island pine forest on the Munro Trail and explore ridges and gorges, viewing ferns and tropical plants. On to the Garden of the Gods and a stop at Shipwreck Beach. Contact them for rates. *808-565-7373; e-mail: treklanai@maui.net; www.adventurelanai.com.*

OFF ROADING

See "Getting Around" above for information on Jeep rentals.

SCUBA DIVING/SNORKELING

Diving the waters of Lana'i is guaranteed to instill awe in both the beginning and advanced diver. The island's volcanic origin has created spectacular lava arches, tubes and pinnacles, with **Cathedrals** being the most popular dive site. But it doesn't stop there. Lana'i offers an impressive array of dive sites along the eastern shore, down around the southern shore, and up the west coast of the island. In typical Hawaiian fashion, you won't be disappointed with the myriad colorful varieties of marine life. Many of the dive sites are open to blue water, which means that if you keep a sharp eye out you may encounter whales, whale sharks, sharks and manta rays. To learn more about Lana'i dive sites, you can browse the web pages of Maui dive operators. We have found Maui Scuba Dive's web page to be very detailed and informative: www.scubadivemaui.com.

Trilogy Lana'i Ocean Sports Most scuba diving and snorkel excursions originate from Maui but if you are enjoying a pleasant stay on Lana'i, Trilogy Ocean Sports on Lana'i offers snorkel and scuba boat trips from Manele Harbor or beach dives in Hulopo'e Bay. One of the most exciting dives offered by Trilogy is the Cathedral Sunrise

RESORT TOURS

Both Manele and Koele offer daily complimentary tours of their resorts. Just sign up at the concierge desk. The tour of Koele is especially informative and discusses the many unique pieces of art gracing the lobby, making it a worthwhile 30 minutes.

Guests and non-guests can rent a mountain bike at the Lodge at Koele ($8/hour, $40/day) and ride into town or around the resort paths. In the early morning or early evening, they are allowed to ride along the golf course paths. One evening we followed one of the garden paths behind the putting green that led to a very steep golf cart track from the lower nine holes to the upper nine. It was so steep, in fact, that it proved quite a challenge to just walk the bikes up. After the journey up, we were delighted to find an ample supply of water and cups that reappeared every couple of holes on the golf course. Once on top, we biked around a few holes of the golf course that were fairly level. We were pleasantly surprised to find ourselves at the tee off for the eighth hole of the golf course and, as previously described, it was an inspirational location. We then attempted to ride down from the tee to the green. The path down was so steep that it required our brakes on full force to go slow enough to maintain control. Beyond is another picturesque lagoon and more golf cart trails to follow on flat ground. The walk into town takes about 15 minutes at a fairly brisk pace, but only about 5 minutes by bike. Biking is a good option for seeing Lana'i City or if you just want to sample some of Lana'i's local eateries.

Both resorts have wonderful swimming pools. The Koele pool, flanked by two bubbling jacuzzis, was seldom busy during

Special. This dive location is reportedly one of the premier dive sites in the Pacific. The majority of Cathedrals stand 80 feet below the surface, but one can still manage to see it at 50 to 60 feet. The main entrance is approximately 60 feet under and the back entrance lies at approximately 90 feet. Usually there is very little current and visibility is excellent, with at least 120 feet distance. Upon descending with your Trilogy guide, the Cathedral arches emerge from the blue—these arches mark the main entrance and are large enough to drive a bus through! The entire channel is riddled with old lava tubes that create an early-Gothic ambience. Cathedrals is actually one big lava tube with many small openings that allow for beams of light. This one-tank certification dive meets at Manele Harbor at 6:30 a.m. and returns by 8 a.m., leaving the rest of the day open for golf, horseback riding or the spa. The Cathedral Sunrise Special is $95 plus tax and only for certified divers. You can combine this dive

our stay. The Manele pool is slightly larger and, at a lower elevation than Koele, became quite hot during the afternoon. The adjacent poolside restaurant provided refreshing drinks and light fare. Guests at the resorts have pool privileges at both facilities.

Scuba diving, fishing expeditions, kayaking and other ocean excursions can be arranged through the concierge at either resort. At both resorts, a sheet describing the activities for the next day is left in the room with the evening maid service.

Lodge at Koele Complimentary coffee and tea are available in the lobby and each of the accommodation wings each morning. The Music Room has an array of interesting musical instruments lining the walls, and the grand piano may be used by guests. This is also where you'll find a delightful afternoon tea. In the Trophy Room are board games, or sit back and relax with a book in The Library. Complimentary videotapes are available at the concierge for guests to view in their rooms. A grounds tour is offered daily and at night there is entertainment by pianist Kimo Garner in the Great Hall. The twin fireplaces are ablaze and the overstuffed chairs invite you to slow down and relax. The fireplaces are lit, upon request, in the Library, Music or Trophy rooms. This may be as close to heaven on earth as you can get.

Manele Bay Hotel Manele also has varied daily activities. A tour of the resort is available and in the evening there is entertainment and complimentary *pupus* (5 to 6 p.m.) at Hale AheAhe. Complimentary videotapes are available for guest use in their rooms and complimentary morning coffee is a pleasurable experience in the Orchid Lounge or Coral Lounge.

with Trilogy's Lana'i Adventure Scuba and save $30, for a total of $195. Trilogy also offers a morning Snorkel Sail for $110 per person. A Sunset Sail is available as well. *Contact Trilogy through the resort concierge or call Trilogy direct at 888-628-4800; www.visitlanai.com or www.sailtrilogy.com.*

Adventure Lana'i EcoCentre This company offers private scuba dives, snorkel tours and rents equipment. Contact them for rates. *808-565-7373; e-mail: treklanai@maui.net; www.adventurelanai.com.*

SPAS & FITNESS CENTERS

The Lodge at Koele A small fitness center and spa, complimentary for resort guests, is located at the Lodge at Koele and is open from 6 a.m. to 7 p.m. Massages and specialty treatments are available between 10 a.m. and 5 p.m. and include facials, body scrubs and a variety of massage styles. Private and small group yoga sessions are also offered.

Manele Bay Hotel The Spa at Manele is a full-service spa with an elegant yet simple tone, a place where guests will be pampered but not overwhelmed by a grandiose facility. Features include men's and women's locker rooms, his-and-hers red cedar sauna and granite steam rooms. Treatments include hot stone massage and hot stone facials. There are six indoor private massage rooms and four outdoor garden and oceanview private massage areas, as well as facial rooms, manicure stations, pedicure thrones and a salon. *808-565-2088.*

SURFING

Adventure Lana'i EcoCentre Surfboards and boogie boards are available at Adventure Lana'i EcoCentre. Or try out their novice surf safaris for *keiki* or Big Kahunas. Local surf instructors demonstrate techniques, etiquette and all basic skills on lightweight wooden longboards. Safari includes snacks and sodas. Contact them for rates. *808-565-7373; e-mail: treklanai@maui.net; www.adventurelanai.com.*

TENNIS

There are plexi-pave tennis courts available at both the Lodge and the Manele Bay Hotel. Court fees are $15 per hour. Instructional clinics and tournaments take place on a regular basis. Private lessons are available as well.

There is also a public court at Lana'i School in Lana'i City. Free play; lighted court. 9 a.m. to 9 p.m. daily.

THEATER

The refurbished **Lana'i Playhouse** has been Lana'i's movie theater since 1993. There is one screen for movies. Adults (13-59) $7; seniors (60+) $4.50; children (4-12) $4.50. Matinees $4.50 for all.

SWEET MAUI MOON

Now after the sun goes to sleep,
My Sweet Maui Moon will whisper to me
'cause now that you've gone and said "goodbye,"
My Sweet Maui Moon sings a lullaby

And finding her way to the sea,
She never fails to look down on me
'cause now that you've gone and said "goodbye,"
My Sweet Maui Moon sings a lullaby

CHORUS
And it doesn't matter what mood I am in
Or whether I'm feeling down
'cause sometimes I'm losin' and sometimes I win
And She never lets me down

And rising up into the sky,
My Sweet Maui Moon will kiss me goodnight
'cause now that you've gone and said "goodbye,"
My Sweet Maui Moon sings a lullaby

And it doesn't matter what mood I am in
Or whether I'm feeling down
'cause sometimes I'm losin' and sometimes I win
And She never lets me down
Now that you've gone and said "goodbye,"
My Sweet Maui Moon sings a lullaby....

Our thanks to Keola Beamer for permission to reprint these lyrics.

Recommended Reading

Allen, Gwenfread. *Hawaiian Monarchy Kings and Queens*. Pacific Monograph. 1999.

Barnes, Phil. *A Concise History of the Hawaiian Islands*. Hilo, Hawai'i: Petrogylph Press. 1999.

Bartholomew, Gail and Bren Bailey. *Maui Remembers*. Mutual Publishing. 1994.

Beamer, Nona. *Na Mele Hula*. Honolulu: University of Hawaii Press. 1998.

Bird, Isabella. *Six Months in the Sandwich Islands*. Honolulu: Booklines. 1998.

Chisholm, Craig. *Hawaiian Hiking Trails*. Lake Oswego, Oregon: Fernglen Press. 1994.

Clark, John. *Beaches of Maui County*. Honolulu: University Press of Hawaii. 1989.

Cook, James, et al. *The Explorations of Captain James Cook in the Pacific, as told by his own Journals*. Dover Publishing. 1971.

Daws, Gavan. *Shoal of Time*. Honolulu: University of Hawaii Press. 1989.

Fielding, Ann. *Hawaiian Reefs and Tidepools*. Honolulu: Island Explorations. 1998.

Grant, Glen. *Glen Grant's Chicken Skin Tales*. Honolulu: Mutual Publishing. 1998.

Kane, Herb Kauainui. *Ancient Hawaii*. Kawainui Press. 1998.

Kepler, Angela. *Maui's Hana Highway*. Honolulu: Mutual Publishing. 1995.

Kyselka, Will and Ray Lanterman. *Maui, How It Came to Be*. Honolulu: The University Press of Hawaii. 1980.

Malinowski, Mel. *Snorkel Maui and Lanai*. Indigo Publications. 2000.

Malo, David. *Hawaiian Antiquities*. Honolulu: Bishop Museum Press. 1903/1951/1987.

Palancy, Tom. *So You Want to Live in Hawaii*. Maui: Barefoot Publications. 1999.

Pukui, Mary K., et al. *The New Pocket Hawaiian Dictionary*. Honolulu: The University of Hawaii Press. 1998.

Reece, Kim Taylor. *Hula Kahiko: Images of Hawaii's Ancient Hula*. Gecko Stufs. 1999.

Smith, Robert. *Hiking Maui*. Maui: Hawaiian Outdoor Adventure. 1999.

Sterling, Elspeth. *Sites of Maui*. Honolulu: Bishop Museum Press. 1998.

Stevenson, Robert Louis. *Travels in Hawaii*. Honolulu: University of Hawaii Press. 1991.

Titcomb, M. *Native Use of Fish in Hawaii*. Honolulu: University of Hawaii Press. 1982.

Twain, Mark. *Letters from Mark Twain*. Honolulu: University of Hawaii Press. 1989.

Westervelt, H. *Myths and Legends of Hawaii*. Honolulu: Mutual Publishing. 1989.

Whitman, John. *An Account of the Sandwich Islands*. Salem, Oregon: Topgallant Publishing. 1979.

One cannot determine in advance to love a particular woman,
nor can one so determine to love Hawaii.
One sees, and one loves or does not love.
With Hawaii it seems always to be love at first sight.
Those for whom the islands were made,
or who were made for the islands,
are swept off their feet in the first moments of meeting embrace
and are embraced.

Jack London

Index

Lodging Index

Hostels

Rental Agents

Dining Index

Dining Index by Cuisine

Paradise Family Guides

Ideal for families traveling with kids of any age—toddlers to teenagers—Paradise Family Guides offer a blend of travel information unlike any other guides to the Hawaiian islands. With vacation ideas and tropical adventures that are sure to satisfy both action-hungry youngsters and relaxation-seeking parents, these guides meet the specific needs of each and every family member.

Hidden Guides

Adventure travel or a relaxing vacation?—"Hidden" guidebooks are the only travel books in the business to provide detailed information on both. Aimed at environmentally aware travelers, our motto is "Where Vacations Meet Adventures." These books combine details on unique hotels, restaurants and sightseeing with information on camping, sports and hiking for the outdoor enthusiast.

Ulysses Press books are available at bookstores everywhere. If any of the following titles are unavailable at your local bookstore, ask the bookseller to order them.

You can also order books directly from Ulysses Press
P.O. Box 3440, Berkeley, CA 94703
800-377-2542 or 510-601-8301
fax: 510-601-8307
www.ulyssespress.com
e-mail: ulysses@ulyssespress.com

PARADISE FAMILY GUIDES

____ Paradise Family Guides: Kaua'i, $16.95
____ Paradise Family Guides: Maui, $16.95
____ Paradise Family Guides: Big Island of Hawai'i, $16.95

HIDDEN GUIDEBOOKS

____ Hidden Arizona, $16.95
____ Hidden Bahamas, $14.95
____ Hidden Baja, $14.95
____ Hidden Belize, $15.95
____ Hidden Big Island of Hawaii, $13.95
____ Hidden Boston & Cape Cod, $14.95
____ Hidden British Columbia, $18.95
____ Hidden Cancún & the Yucatán, $16.95
____ Hidden Carolinas, $17.95
____ Hidden Coast of California, $18.95
____ Hidden Colorado, $15.95
____ Hidden Disneyland, $13.95
____ Hidden Florida, $18.95
____ Hidden Florida Keys & Everglades, $12.95
____ Hidden Georgia, $16.95
____ Hidden Guatemala, $16.95
____ Hidden Hawaii, $18.95
____ Hidden Idaho, $14.95
____ Hidden Kauai, $13.95
____ Hidden Maui, $13.95
____ Hidden Montana, $15.95
____ Hidden New England, $18.95
____ Hidden New Mexico, $15.95
____ Hidden Oahu, $13.95
____ Hidden Oregon, $15.95
____ Hidden Pacific Northwest, $18.95
____ Hidden Salt Lake City, $14.95
____ Hidden San Francisco & Northern California, $18.95
____ Hidden Southern California, $18.95
____ Hidden Southwest, $19.95
____ Hidden Tahiti, $17.95
____ Hidden Tennessee, $16.95
____ Hidden Utah, $16.95
____ Hidden Walt Disney World, $13.95
____ Hidden Washington, $15.95
____ Hidden Wine Country, $13.95
____ Hidden Wyoming, $15.95

Mark the book(s) you're ordering and enter the total cost here ⇨ [ ]

California residents add 8.25% sales tax here ⇨ [ ]

Shipping, check box for preferred method and enter cost here ⇨ [ ]

❑ Book Rate (free) ❑ Priority Mail/UPS Ground (call for rates)
❑ UPS Overnight or 2-Day Air (call for rates)

Billing, enter total amt. due here and check payment method ⇨ [ ]

❑ CHECK ❑ MONEY ORDER
❑ VISA/MASTERCARD________________________ EXP. DATE __________

NAME ________________________ PHONE __________

ADDRESS ____

CITY ________________________ STATE ______ ZIP ________

MONEY-BACK GUARANTEE ON DIRECT ORDERS PLACED THROUGH ULYSSES PRESS.

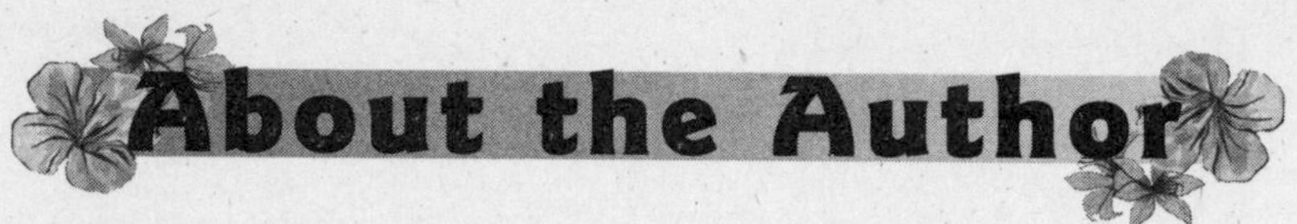

About the Author

CANDY ADAIR ALULI grew up in California, but moved to the Hawaiian Islands in 1983 and never looked back. She fell in love, married a "local boy" and now resides happily on the island of Maui with her husband, Nane, and a houseful of seriously pampered pets. In addition to her role as author for this guidebook, Candy owns a public relations agency and represents a variety of clients across the state.